Bulloch Genealogy (continued)

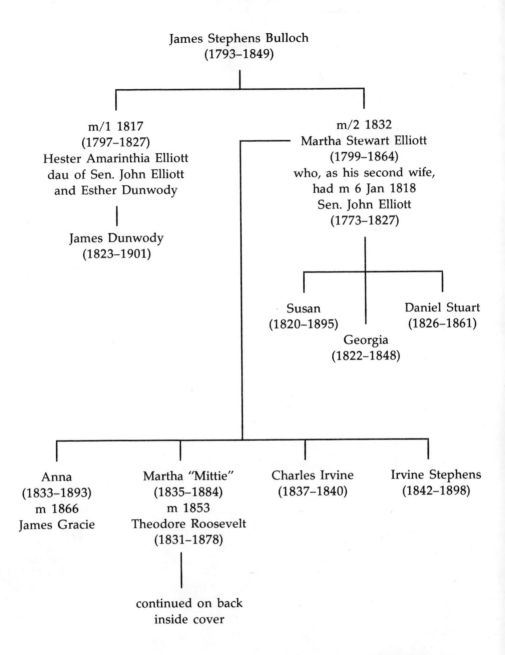

James Stephens Bulloch
(1793–1849)

m/1 1817
(1797–1827)
Hester Amarinthia Elliott
dau of Sen. John Elliott
and Esther Dunwody

James Dunwody
(1823–1901)

m/2 1832
Martha Stewart Elliott
(1799–1864)
who, as his second wife,
had m 6 Jan 1818
Sen. John Elliott
(1773–1827)

Susan
(1820–1895)

Georgia
(1822–1848)

Daniel Stuart
(1826–1861)

Anna
(1833–1893)
m 1866
James Gracie

Martha "Mittie"
(1835–1884)
m 1853
Theodore Roosevelt
(1831–1878)

Charles Irvine
(1837–1840)

Irvine Stephens
(1842–1898)

continued on back
inside cover

Bulloch Genealogy courtesy of Clarece Martin

Theodore Roosevelt

Many-Sided American

Papers presented at Conference on
"Theodore Roosevelt and the Birth of Modern America,"
Hempstead, Long Island, New York, April 19–21, 1990,
sponsored by
Hofstra University's Long Island Studies Institute
and the Hofstra Cultural Center

Publication of this book was made possible,
in part, by support from the
Roosevelt Savings Bank
Garden City, New York

Theodore Roosevelt
Many-Sided American

Edited by

Natalie A. Naylor
Douglas Brinkley
John Allen Gable

**Prepared under the auspices of
Hofstra University**

Heart of the Lakes Publishing
Interlaken, New York
1992

Permission to use extended quotations from copyrighted works has
been given as follows: From *All in the Family*, by Theodore Roosevelt,
copyright 1929 by Theodore Roosevelt, reprinted by permission of the
publishers, The Putnam Publishing Group; from *The Roosevelt Family of
Sagamore Hill*, by Hermann Hagedorn, copyright 1954 by Hermann
Hagedorn, reprinted by permission of the Theodore Roosevelt
Association which now owns the copyright.

Library of Congress Cataloging-in-Publication Data

Theodore Roosevelt—many-sided American / edited by Natalie A. Naylor,
Douglas Brinkley, John Allen Gable.
    p.   cm.
Papers presented at "Theodore Roosevelt and the birth of modern
America," Hempstead, Long Island, New York, April 19–21, 1990,
sponsored by the Long Island Studies Institute and the Hofstra Cultural
Center, Hofstra University.
Includes bibliographical references and index.
ISBN: 1–55787–085–3 (acid-free paper)
1. Roosevelt, Theodore, 1858–1919—Congresses.   2. Roosevelt
    family—Congresses.   3. United States—Politics and govern-
    ment—1901–1909—Congresses.   4. United States—Politics and
    government—1909–1913—Congresses.   I. Naylor, Natalie A.
    II. Brinkley, Douglas.   III. Gable, John A.
E757.T385   1992
973.91'1'092—dc20
[B]   92–22029
                                                              CIP

A *quality* publication of
Heart of the Lakes Publishing
Interlaken, New York 14847

Contents

The Strenuous Life: Early Life and Career

The Presidency: The Square Deal

The Presidency: "Speak Softly and Carry a Big Stick"

The Bull Moose: The Post-Presidential Years

TR: The Image and the Memory

Epilogue

Illustrations

The drawing approved by the Roosevelt Family and by the Roosevelt Memorial Association
Drawing Copyright by Hubbell Reed McBride, from photographs from life copyright by and with permission of Underwood & Underwood, International News Reel Corp., Pach Bros., Brown Brothers, Rockwood Studio, Wm Van der Weyde (from Bust by James Earl Fraser), The Independent (from photograph by T.W.Ingersoll), Post Intelligencer . . . . Also from photographs by permission of the Roosevelt Memorial Association, C.Le Gendre, R.N.Chandler, Beatrice Hall.
Copley Print reproductions copyright by Curtis and Cameron, Incorporated ∞∞ Publishers ∞∞ Boston

"AND ONE MAN IN HIS TIME PLAYS MANY PARTS ∞∞"

Courtesy Theodore Roosevelt Collection, Harvard College Library

"And One Man in his Time Plays Many Parts." A composite drawing (c. 1922) by Hubbell Reed McBride from photographs.

Introduction

Nature writer John Burroughs said of his friend Theodore Roosevelt: "Roosevelt was a many-sided man and every side was like an electric battery. Such versatility, such vitality, such copiousness, have rarely been united in one man."[1] Edmund Morris, in his keynote address at the Hofstra University conference, "Theodore Roosevelt, The Polygon," observes that, "Theodore Roosevelt was the most superabundant President in our history." Morris notes that TR's polygonal quality or many-sidedness has become "the leitmotif of Rooseveltian scholarship." That leitmotif is evident in this collection of essays. "Theodore Roosevelt fits into no foursquare format," Morris states. "No matter how large the confines of study, he always requires extra space, added dimensions." A second theme running through this volume is the judgment that TR is important, that he looms large in U.S. and world history. A third theme that emerges is that, even though much remains to be studied and debated, the time has come when we have sufficient perspective and evidence to render a verdict on the question of whether or not Theodore Roosevelt was a great, as well as an important, political leader and president.

TR's many-sidedness has earned him the appellations of "American Renaissance Man" and "the most interesting American." Indeed, only Benjamin Franklin and Thomas Jefferson seem obvious rivals to the multiplicity of Roosevelt's roles, interests, talents, and accomplishments. TR was naturalist, Phi Beta Kappa graduate of Harvard, rancher in the "wild West," prolific author on diverse subjects, hunter, conservationist, historian, colonel of the Rough Riders, winner of the Nobel Peace Prize, politician, intellectual, public official, explorer, and statesman. He was a deputy sheriff in the Dakota Territory and police commissioner of New York City. He was one of the first fifteen people elected to the American Academy of Arts and Letters, president of the American Historical Association, and founder of the National Collegiate Athletic Association. He led scientific expeditions to Africa and South America, and in Brazil he put a river on the map, the "Rio Roosevelt." He was elected to the New York State Assembly in 1881 at the age of twenty-three, and for nearly four decades was a leading figure in American politics and government. In 1901, at the age of forty-two, he became the youngest president in history. As president, TR "busted" trusts, built the Panama Canal, launched a broad and multifaceted conservation program, led the United States onto the stage of world leadership, regulated big business, and fathered the modern presidency and the modern Navy. He preached the "strenuous life," the "Square Deal," the "New Nationalism," and "speak softly and carry a big stick." The "Teddy Bear" was named after him, and he was called the "Rough Rider" and the "Bull Moose."

Theodore Roosevelt's importance seems as obvious as his visage on Mount Rushmore. And as time passes, it seems clear that sculptor Gutzon Borglum made a sound choice after all when he decided, not long after TR's death, to include the twenty-sixth president in that group of the American great on the mountain in South Dakota.

Given Theodore Roosevelt's polygonal quality, a collection of essays on different facets of TR's life, career, and world seems much in order as an introduction not only to the twenty-sixth president, but also to the state of Roosevelt scholarship in the final years of the century, sometimes called the "American century," that began in what his daughter Ethel Roosevelt Derby described as "the brave, bright morning" of TR's presidency.

Hofstra University, with its distinguished history of organizing presidential conferences, decided that a reevaluation of the life and times of Long Island's only U.S. president was long overdue. Hofstra's Long Island Studies Institute scheduled a conference on "Theodore Roosevelt and the Birth of Modern America" for April 19–

21, 1990. In cooperation with the Theodore Roosevelt Association (TRA), Hofstra issued a call for papers. The response in the scholarly community was encouraging and overwhelmingly favorable, confirming our expectation of great interest in Theodore Roosevelt and his era.

In testament to the importance of the conference, the TRA used the Hofstra conference as a forum to bestow its highest award, the Theodore Roosevelt Distinguished Service Medal, to: former secretary of the Navy and arms control expert, Paul H. Nitze; author and social critic, Tom Wolfe; and former New York

Congressman and Bull Mooser, Hamilton Fish, Sr.

Featuring Edmund Morris's keynote address, fifty scholarly papers and special addresses, an exhibit on "Theodore Roosevelt of Sagamore Hill" in Hofstra's Filderman Gallery, a tour of Sagamore Hill and reception at the Old Orchard Museum, a showing of James Whitmore's performance of *Bully* and other TR films, and a presentation of *Tintypes* by Hofstra's Drama Department, the conference was a memorable event.[2] The Hofstra Cultural Center handled conference arrangements under the able direction of Laura J. Labenberg, conference coordinator. This edited volume of essays, comprised of many of the best papers presented, is a permanent record of the conference.[3] Divided into sections arranged topically and chronologically, beginning with Edmund Morris's thematic "Theodore Roosevelt, The Polygon," and concluding with John Allen Gable's overview, "The Man in the Arena of History: The Historiography of Theodore Roosevelt," the book represents the latest word in virtually all aspects of TR scholarship, beginning with his ancestral roots. (Roosevelt and Bulloch genealogies are on the endpapers.) Dr. Gable has added a chronology of Roosevelt's life and an annotated bibliography for reference purposes.

The Roosevelt family has been in the public eye for about a century, and as a subject seem to provide evidence for the saying that Roosevelts are never boring. This testimony can be seen in the first group of essays by Clarece Martin, Robert B. MacKay, Richard W. Turk, Sylvia Jukes Morris, Richard P. Harmond, Richard J. Loosbrock, Charles W. Snyder, and David M. Esposito, as well as in essays in later sections by Stacy Rozek Cordery, on Alice Roosevelt's contributions to her father's diplomacy, and James L. Golden, on TR's influence on Franklin D. Roosevelt. The title of the section, "He Who Has Planted Will Preserve," is a translation of the Roosevelt family motto, *Qui plantavit curabit*, which is carved over the west entrance doorway of Sagamore Hill, TR's Long Island home in Oyster Bay. Martin shows that TR had a vital Southern heritage as well as Knickerbocker roots, and MacKay examines the Oyster Bay environment of the Roosevelts. Neglected but important figures in the Roosevelt family are given attention in Turk's study of TR and his brother Elliott Roosevelt, Harmond's essay on TR's cousin the financier W. Emlen Roosevelt, and Esposito's biographical sketch of TR's son

Archibald B. Roosevelt. Sylvia Jukes Morris, who has written the only biography of Edith Kermit Carow Roosevelt, TR's First Lady, presents a concise and informative biographical profile of Mrs. Roosevelt. And Loosbrock and Snyder portray Theodore Roosevelt, Jr., as an interesting personality with a remarkable and important career.

Theodore Roosevelt's early life and career before the presidency has received much attention in recent years, most notably in the award-winning biographies by Edmund Morris and David McCullough. The period before 1901 continues to attract historians and writers, as shown in essays by Robert B. Charles, Edward L. Schapsmeier and Frederick H. Schapsmeier, James F. Vivian, Lawrence H. Budner, and Jay Stuart Berman. Charles, working from recently discovered papers, presents what is the first detailed study of TR's time as a law student at Columbia University and how that experience affected his thinking. Budner, Vivian, and the Schapsmeiers show the enduring interest in TR's encounters with the "wild West," and indicate the important influence of the West on Roosevelt. Berman, author of *Police Administration and Progressive Reform: Theodore Roosevelt As Police Commissioner of New York* (1987), goes beyond the colorful anecdotes to give in his concise essay a much-needed look at TR's police period from the perspectives of the social sciences and the history of police work.

The essays on Theodore Roosevelt's presidency have been divided into two sections. The first, "The Square Deal," covers domestic policies and the institution of the presidency, while the second, "Speak Softly and Carry a Big Stick," deals with TR's naval and foreign policies.

Different facets of TR's domestic policies and of Roosevelt's role in the history of the presidency as an institution are chronicled in essays by William Lemke, Arthur M. Schaefer, Paul Schullery, Char Miller, Edward S. Lewis and William D. Pederson, and Willie Pigg. Pigg examines TR's administration by using the model of presidential power developed by the noted political scientist Richard E. Neustadt, and concludes that Neustadt's theories provide a useful tool for analysis of Roosevelt's leadership. Lewis and Pederson, in part building on the much discussed theories of "presidential character" advanced by the political scientist James David Barber, argue that TR's concept of the "strenuous life" is in line with recent ideas about physical and mental health, and maintain that TR was among the eleven most mentally healthy presidents. Miller's essay examines the important and productive relationship between TR and his chief forester, Gifford Pinchot. Schullery, a prolific writer on nature and the history of conservation, focuses on the problem that many people today have in reconciling TR's love of hunting with his role as a conservationist. Schaefer places Roosevelt's intervention in the anthracite coal strike of 1902 in its full historical context. Lemke shows TR as presidential politician in action on a tour of New England.

Important facets of TR's foreign and naval policies as president are examined in essays by Richard H. Collin, Robert W. Love, Jr., Aaron P. Forsberg, George W. Collins, Stacy Rozek Cordery, Stefan H. Rinke, James R. Reckner, and Frederick W. Marks III. Love gives an overview of the U.S. Navy during the Roosevelt administration, while George W. Collins discusses the Navy and the Moroccan hostage crisis of 1904. Reckner, whose book *Teddy Roosevelt's Great White Fleet* (1988) won the Theodore and Franklin D. Roosevelt Naval History Prize of the New York Council of the Navy League in 1989, presents new interpretations of the complex history of the famous voyage of the "Great White Fleet" around the world in 1907–1909. The essays by Cordery, Forsberg, and Rinke examine in detail specific aspects of TR's foreign policies. All three essays examine Roosevelt's personal approach to diplomacy, respectively through his use of his daughter "Princess Alice" Roosevelt as a goodwill emissary, and the significance of his close friendships with the French ambassador, J. J. Jusserand, and the German ambassador, Speck von Sternburg. But Cordery, Forsberg, and Rinke show that hard-headed calculations based on *realpolitik* rather than personal considerations or prejudices governed TR's conduct of foreign policy.

Richard H. Collin, author of *Theodore Roosevelt, Culture, Diplomacy, and Expansion* (1985) and *Theodore Roosevelt's Caribbean* (1990), two highly original studies, and Frederick W. Marks III, author of *Velvet on Iron: The Diplomacy of Theodore Roosevelt* (1979), one of the most incisive monographs ever written on Roosevelt, are in the forefront of the recent revisionist work being done on the subject of Theodore Roosevelt and foreign policy; and their essays in this collection express their controversial views on TR's conduct of foreign affairs. Both historians defend Roosevelt's dealings with Colombia, Panama, and other Caribbean and Latin American nations, and maintain that TR was a highly sophisticated, successful, and prescient practitioner of *realpolitik*. Collin emphasizes the cultural context of foreign policy, and Marks takes a comparative approach to claim "true greatness" for TR as a statesman.

Theodore Roosevelt's post-presidential years, studied in essays by Tweed Roosevelt, Fred Greenbaum, Richard J. Donagher, John W. Furlow, Jr., Maceo Crenshaw Dailey, Jr., Matthew J. Glover, and John Milton Cooper, Jr., are the least understood phase of TR's career, and these papers give new insights and information on the challenges and difficulties faced by TR in the autumn of his strenuous life. Tweed Roosevelt gives a colorful account and new look at his great-grandfather's famous African expedition. Greenbaum looks at the 1912 presidential contest from what may be called the Robert M. La Follette perspective, while Donagher examines the nuts and bolts that produced victory for TR in Pennsylvania in 1912. Furlow studies the lives and ideas of two prominent members of the Progressive party in Pennsylvania, former Chief Forester Gifford Pinchot, who was twice elected governor of the state, and his dynamic wife, Cornelia Bryce Pinchot. Dailey traces over a period of nearly two decades the relationship of TR and the black leader Emmett Jay Scott, an associate of Booker T. Washington. Glover examines TR's probable candidacy for the presidency in 1920, and what Roosevelt's platform might have been. John Milton Cooper, Jr., author of *The Warrior and the Priest: Woodrow Wilson and Theodore Roosevelt* (1983), *Pivotal Decades: The United States, 1900-1920* (1990), and other books on the progressive period, gives a trenchant, provocative, and fascinating overview and interpretation of TR's last years, emphasizing Roosevelt's continuing and considerable influence on U.S. and world history in that period. In what is one of the most important essays written on Roosevelt in the last thirty years, Cooper concludes that "in the last analysis, the significance of his last decade became the man."

The image, cultural uses, memorialization, and legacies of Theodore Roosevelt are examined in essays by John R. Lancos, David H. Wallace, Monica T. Albala, Kathleen M. Dalton, James L. Golden, and John Robert Greene. Lancos and Wallace, both with the National Park Service, U. S. Department of the Interior, look at two TR National Historic Sites: the Theodore Roosevelt Birthplace in New York City and Sagamore Hill in Oyster Bay, Long Island. Lancos traces the history of the reconstruction and operation of the Theodore Roosevelt Birthplace by the Woman's Roosevelt Memorial Association and the Roosevelt Memorial Association, organizations that eventually merged to form the present Theodore Roosevelt Association. Wallace gives an account of the history of, and some of the changes in, the interior of TR's Sagamore Hill home. Albala catalogs many of the uses of TR's image in popular culture, while Dalton, noting that TR is a "multivocal" cultural symbol with many meanings for Americans, focuses on the strong "spiritual" tradition associated with Roosevelt's image. Dalton says that over the years TR's most ardent admirers have employed the former president's image to perpetuate and promote patriotic, ethical, cultural, and religious values. Golden examines what he views as Theodore Roosevelt's considerable influence on his fifth cousin, Franklin D. Roosevelt. Greene looks at the uses TR's successors in the White House have made of his image.

While not all the facets of the many-sided Theodore Roosevelt, nor all the major events of his long career, are presented in the essays in this volume, the breadth and depth of these essays as a collection provide a formidable introduction to the life, times, ideas, and career of the president who remains arguably "the most interesting American."

Natalie A. Naylor
Douglas Brinkley
John Allen Gable

NOTES

1. "Letter from John Burroughs," in *Theodore Roosevelt: Memorial Addresses Delivered Before the Century Association, February 9, 1919* (New York: The Century Association, 1919), pp. 55-60.

2. The Roosevelt Savings Bank of Long Island provided important financial support for the conference. The substantial assistance and cooperation of the Theodore Roosevelt Association in the conference is reflected also in the extensive report on the conference in the *Theodore Roosevelt Association Journal* 16 (Fall 1990): 3-9. The names of the many other individuals and groups who contributed to the success of the conference are included in the conference program.

Conference sessions were recorded and audiotapes of all the sessions, as well as the conference program, exhibit catalog, and papers not included in this volume are on deposit in the Long Island Studies Institute collections at Hofstra University. These manuscripts include: Robert E. Clark, "Roosevelt and Genteel Traditions: Learning, Imperialism, Reform, Reputation"; James J. Kolb, "The Birth of Musical Comedy in the Progressive Era"; Todd Kroening, "Theodore Roosevelt, Big Business, and the Ford Franchise Tax"; J. Lance Mallamo, "Meadowcroft and the Sayville Roosevelts"; Ron Marmarelli, "Muckraking and Progressive Journalism"; Christopher Merritt, "National Park Service Preservation and Programs at Sagamore Hill"; Gil Troy, "The Traditionalist as Subversive: President Theodore Roosevelt Campaigns"; and Richard A. Winsche, "Finley Peter Dunne, Mr. Dooley, and Tiddy Rosenfelt."

3. In preparing this volume for publication, we have had the able assistance of Irene McQuillan, secretary for the Long Island Studies Institute, in typing many of the papers, and Lisa MacLeman in copyediting the manuscript and indexing the book.

Courtesy of National Park Service,
U.S. Department of the Interior
Gutzon Borglum's face of Theodore Roosevelt carved on Mount Rushmore. Mount Rushmore National Memorial is located near Rapid City, South Dakota.

Theodore Roosevelt: Chronology

John Allen Gable

October 27, 1858	Theodore Roosevelt was born at 28 East Twentieth Street, New York City, son of Martha Bulloch Roosevelt and Theodore Roosevelt, Senior.
1876–1880	Attended Harvard College.
June 30, 1880	Graduated from Harvard, *magna cum laude*, member Phi Beta Kappa.
1880–1882	Entered Columbia Law School in October 1880; discontinued study of law in 1882 without taking a degree or becoming a lawyer.
October 27, 1880	Married to Alice Hathaway Lee.
November 8, 1881	Elected to New York State Assembly from New York City; reelected 1882, 1883; Minority Leader 1883.
1882–1884	Served in New York State Assembly.
1882	*The Naval War of 1812*, first book by TR published.
1883–1884	Established two cattle ranches, Maltese Cross and Elkhorn, near Medora, Dakota Territory (in region now part of North Dakota).
February 12, 1884	Daughter Alice Lee Roosevelt was born.
February 14, 1884	Double tragedy: TR's wife Alice Hathaway Lee Roosevelt and mother Martha Bulloch Roosevelt died in the same house, on the same day, New York City.
1884–1886	Cattle rancher in Dakota.
1885	Sagamore Hill, TR's Oyster Bay, Long Island, New York home, completed.
November 2, 1886	Defeated as Republican candidate for mayor of New York City.

December 2, 1886	Married to Edith Kermit Carow in London.
1887	TR and Edith Roosevelt took up residence at Sagamore Hill. They have five children: Theodore (1887), Kermit (1889), Ethel Carow (1891), Archibald Bulloch (1894), Quentin (1897).
1889–1896	*The Winning of the West*, his four-volume history of the frontier is published.
May 7, 1889–May 5, 1895	U.S. Civil Service Commissioner, Washington.
May 6, 1895–April 19, 1897	President of the Board of Police Commissioners, New York City.
April 19, 1897–May 6, 1898	Assistant Secretary of the Navy.
May 15–Sept. 16, 1898	Served with First U.S. Volunteer Cavalry Regiment, the "Rough Riders," during Spanish-American War. TR commissioned Lieutenant Colonel, promoted to Colonel of regiment.
July 1, 1898	Rough Riders fought in Battle of San Juan Hill, Cuba.
November 8, 1898	Elected governor of New York.
Dec. 31, 1898–Dec. 31, 1900	Governor of New York.
November 6, 1900	Elected vice president on Republican ticket with President William McKinley.
March 4–Sept. 14, 1901	Vice President of the United States.
September 14, 1901	Took oath of office as president in Buffalo, New York, after death of President McKinley.
Sept. 14, 1901–Mar. 4, 1909	Twenty-sixth President of the United States.
February 19, 1902	Ordered antitrust suit under Sherman Act to dissolve Northern Securities Company, first of 45 antitrust suits.

May 22, 1902	Crater Lake National Park, Oregon established. Other National Parks established by TR are Wind Cave National Park, South Dakota (1903); Sullys Hill, North Dakota (1904); Platt National Park, Oklahoma (1906); Mesa Verde National Park, Colorado (1906).
June 17, 1902	Newlands Reclamation Act signed, leading to first 21 federal irrigation projects, including Theodore Roosevelt Dam, Arizona.
October 1902	Settled Anthracite Coal Strike.
February 14, 1903	Department of Commerce and Labor established.
February 20, 1903	Elkins Antirebate Act for railroads signed.
March 14, 1903	Proclaimed Pelican Island, Florida as first federal bird reservation; total of 51 bird reservations established by Roosevelt administration.
November 18, 1903	Treaty signed with Panama for building of Panama Canal, which was completed in 1914.
November 8, 1904	Reelected president over Democrat Alton B. Parker.
December 6, 1904	Issued "Roosevelt Corollary" to Monroe Doctrine in annual message.
June 2, 1905	Wichita Forest, Oklahoma made first federal game preserve. Other federal game preserves established by TR are Grand Canyon (1908); Fire Island, Alaska (1909); and National Bison Range, Montana (1909).
February 1, 1905	National Forest Service established.
March 4, 1905	Inaugurated for second term.
September 5, 1905	Portsmouth Treaty signed ending Russo-Japanese War after mediation by TR.

January 1906	Algeciras Conference opened as TR mediated dispute between France and Germany over Morocco.
June 8, 1906	Antiquities or National Monuments Act signed, by which TR established first 18 "National Monuments," including Devils Tower (1906), Muir Woods (1908), Grand Canyon (1908), and Mount Olympus (1909).
June 29, 1906	Signed Hepburn Act giving Interstate Commerce Commission power to regulate railroad rates.
June 30, 1906	Signed both Pure Food and Drug Act and federal meat inspection law.
November 8–26, 1906	President and Mrs. Roosevelt went to Panama to inspect building of the canal, the first time a president leaves U.S. while in office.
December 10, 1906	Awarded Nobel Peace Prize for ending Russo-Japanese War in 1905; first American to win Nobel Prize in any field. (TR received award while in Europe in 1910.)
Dec. 16, 1907– Feb. 22, 1909	Voyage of the Great White Fleet around the world.
May 13-15, 1908	First Conference of Governors met at the White House to consider problems of conservation.
June 8, 1908	Appointed a National Conservation Commission to prepare first inventory of natural resources.
February 18, 1909	North American Conservation Conference convened at White House.
March 4, 1909	TR's administration ended and succcessor William Howard Taft inaugurated.
March 1909– June 1910	Led expedition to Africa for Smithsonian Institution, then toured Europe.
August 31, 1910	Delivered "New Nationalism" address,

Osawatomie, Kansas.

February 21, 1912	Announced candidacy for Republican nomination against President Taft, declaring "my hat is in the ring."
June 18–22, 1912	Republic National Convention met in Chicago; Taft renominated; Roosevelt supporters bolted, charging "theft" of nomination.
August 5–7, 1912	Convention of new National Progressive party (nicknamed "Bull Moose" party) held in Chicago, adopted reform platform, and nominated TR for president and Governor Hiram W. Johnson of California for vice president.
October 14, 1912	Shot in Milwaukee in assassination attempt.
November 5, 1912	Democrat Woodrow Wilson elected president over TR, who came in second, and Republican Taft.
May 26–31, 1913	Trial of *Roosevelt vs. Newett*: TR's successful libel suit against Michigan editor who called him a drunk.
October 4, 1913	Sailed for South America for lecture tour and jungle expedition.
Feb. 27– April 27, 1914	Roosevelt-Rondon Expedition, sponsored by American Museum of Natural History and Brazilian government, explored Brazil's "River of Doubt," now named "Rio Roosevelt."
April 19– May 22, 1915	Trial of *Barnes vs. Roosevelt*: TR won libel suit launched by Republican leader William Barnes, Jr.
June 7–10, 1916	Republican and Progressive national conventions met in Chicago, at same time in different halls, in effort at joint nomination.
June 10, 1916	TR nominated by Progressives; Charles Evans Hughes nominated by Republicans; TR declined Progressive nomination and eventually backed Hughes.

May 19, 1917	President Wilson refused Roosevelt's offer to raise and lead volunteer division in World War I.
July 14, 1918	Quentin Roosevelt, TR's youngest son, killed as fighter pilot in France.
January 6, 1919	Died in his sleep at Sagamore Hill of coronary embolism at age 60.

TR and the naturalist John Muir riding out of the Valley of Yosemite

Prologue

Courtesy of Theodore Roosevelt Collection, Harvard College Library,
Wallace Finley Dailey, Curator

President Theodore Roosevelt at the White House

1

Theodore Roosevelt, The Polygon

Edmund Morris

"There was so much of him," Edward Wagenknecht wrote in 1958. This sentiment, this half-weary, half-worshipful admission that Theodore Roosevelt was the most superabundant President in our history, this apology for the fact that no writer has ever been able to capture the half of him, has become such a leitmotif of Rooseveltian scholarship that it should be chiseled in marble somewhere on the grounds of Sagamore Hill.

One might almost say there was *too* much of him. The historical Theodore Roosevelt fits into no foursquare format. No matter how large the confines of study, he always requires extra space, added dimensions. Perhaps the new mathematics of superstrings, which postulates a variety of dimensions beyond the laws of geometry, will help future scholars figure him out. In the meantime, we have to fall back on the metaphors that writers have traditionally used to disguise their basic incomprehension of Theodore Roosevelt.

These images are often torrential, like Lord Morley's famous equation of the President with Niagara Falls. (If his lordship had ever seen the Zambesi in flood at Victoria Falls, I think he would have upgraded his simile!) There are the radioactive comparisons: for example, Edith Wharton saying every encounter with Theodore Roosevelt was like a morsel of radium glowing permanently in the memory, and Owen Wister describing him as a conflagration that cast light without shade. Then there's the steam-power group, such as Henry Adams's likening of his career to the trajectory of the Chicago Express, or Joseph Foraker's phrase, "a steam engine in trousers," or this rather grudging tribute, written in 1905 by Henry James: "Verily, a wonderful little machine: destined to be overstrained perhaps, but not as yet, truly, betraying the least creak."

I have myself tried to compare him to a cyclone, in that he tended to become unstable at times of low pressure. "The slightest rise in the barometer outside, and his turbulence smoothed into a whir of coordinated activity, while a core of stillness developed within. Under maximum pressure Roosevelt was sunny, calm, and unnaturally clear." Literary images, however, are subjective, whereas popular curiosity is objective. The reader soon tires of cyclones and steam engines and conflagrations and cascades, and says, "Enough metaphor already, what was he *like*? Give us some facts, give us the length and breadth of him."

"Well," says the biographer, "he stood five foot nine inches in his size seven shoes, his chest measured a fairly normal forty-two inches, and he hit the scales at about 185 to 200 pounds. Yet everybody who met him agreed that Theodore Roosevelt was a giant." "Giant in what sense?" "In the sense that Lyman Gage said he was mentally and physically the equivalent of two strong men. Gifford Pinchot claimed he ate enough for three. James Amos said no, easily four. Charles J. Bonaparte estimated that his mind moved ten times faster than average, and Theodore Roosevelt himself, modestly remarked, 'I have enjoyed as much of life as any nine men I know.' "

"Those last figures," says the reader, still frustrated, "are merely figures of speech." The biographer bridles. "You want specific figures? How's this: I've been studying the man for nearly fifteen years—4,934 days to be precise—and I still can't see all of him." The reader very properly ignores this plea for sympathy. "If you don't see all of him, what *do* you see?"

One can only project the macrocosm from the microcosm. For example, here is just one facet, one fleck of quartz from the edge of one stone on one face of the pyramid that is Theodore Roosevelt. The biographer draws a card at random out of his files, headed *TR's Membership of Various Clubs and Societies.* "Now understand," he says, "the man was not particularly clubby. By-laws and bad food and big leather chairs held no charm for him. He once visited a conservative club with a Progressive friend and said afterward they felt like two Airedales wandering into a convention of tomcats. Theodore Roosevelt simply patronized organizations that appealed to his particular interests. Here's the list: American Bible Society; Authors League of New York; American Merchants Association; National Association of Audubon Societies; National Municipal League (founder-member); The Optimist Club of America (member,

Executive Committee); Playground Association of America; American Irish Historical Society; American Bison Society (Honorary President); American Historical Association; Boone and Crockett Club (founder-member); National Arts Club; American Academy of Arts and Letters; Union League Club; Union Society of the Civil War; National Institute of Arts and Letters (founder-member); Century Club; Harvard Club; Bird Club of Long Island; Cosmos Club; Metropolitan Club; and the Biological Society of Washington.

"All these," the biographer adds, "represented just a fraction of his activity. Here, if you will allow me to flick through my chronological cards, are some of his more serious accomplishments.

"Theodore Roosevelt graduated *magna cum laude* from Harvard University; he was the author of two ornithological papers, a four-volume history, *The Winning of the West,* considered definitive in his lifetime, and a history of the Naval War of 1812 which remains definitive to this day. He also wrote biographies of Thomas Hart Benton, Gouverneur Morris, and Oliver Cromwell, and some fourteen other volumes of history, natural history, literary criticism, autobiography, political philosophy, and military memoirs—not to mention countless periodical articles, and approximately seventy-five thousand letters by the time he left the White House. He spent nearly three years of his life in Europe and the Levant, and had a wide circle of intellectual correspondents on both sides of the Atlantic. He habitually read one to three books a day, on subjects ranging from architecture to zoology, averaging two or three pages a minute, effortlessly memorizing the paragraphs that interested him. He could recite poetry by the hour in English, German, and French. He married two women and fathered six children. He was a boxing championship finalist; a Fifth Avenue socialite; a New York State Assemblyman; a Dakota ranchman; a deputy sheriff; U.S. Civil Service Commissioner; Police Commissioner of New York City; Assistant Secretary of the Navy; Colonel of the Rough Riders; Governor of New York; Vice President and finally, President of the United States. He was respected by Washington's scientific community as a skilled paleontologist and taxidermist—during the White House years, specimens that confused experts at the Smithsonian were routinely sent to him for identification—and he was recognized as the world authority on the big game mammals of North America."

When we view all these facets, and the list is but partial, we begin to realize that Theodore Roosevelt was more than pyramidal, he was a polygon: a trigonometrical entity of numberless surfaces, intersections, and interstices, of translucent, unfathomable distances. There is a passage in *The Ambassadors* where Strether looks out from a high vantage point on the polygon that is Paris, and Henry James unforgettably evokes (in language that recurs to me whenever I ponder Theodore Roosevelt) "a jewel bright and hard, twinkling and trembling . . . what seemed all surface one moment seemed all depth the next."

I should mention that the attributes and achievements I've just listed refer only to TR's first fifty years. I will spare you a further list of the accomplishments he packed into his last ten, except to say that the total of books rose to thirty-eight, the total of letters to 150,000, and the catalog of careers extended to include world statesman, big-game collector for the Smithsonian, magazine and newspaper columnist, and South American explorer.

If it were possible to take a cross-section of Theodore Roosevelt's personality, as geologists say, ponder a chunk of continent, one would be presented with a picture of seismic richness and confusion. The most order I have been able to make of it is to isolate four major character seams. They may be traced back to childhood. Each seam stood out bright and clear in youth and early middle age, but they began to merge about the time he was forty. Indeed the white heat of the Presidency soon fused them all into solid metal. But so long as they were distinct, they could be identified as aggression, righteousness, pride, and militarism. Let us ponder the development of each.

The most fundamental characteristic of Theodore Roosevelt was his aggression—conquest being, to him, synonymous with growth. From the moment he first dragged breath into his asthmatic lungs, the sickly little boy fought for a larger share of the world. He could never get enough air; disease had to be destroyed; he had to fight big heavy books to gain a man's knowledge. Just as the struggle for wind made him stretch his chest, so did the difficulty of relating to his abnormally contrasted parents expand his imagination. Theodore Senior was the epitome of hard Northern manhood; Mittie Roosevelt the quintessence of soft Southern femininity. The Civil War—the first political phenomenon their young son was ever aware of—symbolically opposed one to the other. There was no question as to which side, and which parent, Teedie preferred. ("Teedie" was the family's nickname for young Theodore Roosevelt.) He prayed to God, in Mittie's presence, to "grind the Southern troops to powder," and Appomattox reinforced his belief in the superiority of strength over weakness, right over wrong, realism over romance. His observations in natural history gave him further proof of the law of natural selection, long before he fully understood Darwin and Herbert Spencer. From early on the rule of tooth and claw, sharpened by intelligence, was a persistent theme in Theodore Roosevelt's writing. Blood-sports enabled him to feel the "strong eager pleasure" of a little shrew vanquishing a larger foe. His dancing and whooping after killing large animals struck more than one observer as macabre. At college, he selected the most unobtainable mate—"See that girl? I'm going to marry her. She won't have me, but I am going to have her!"—and he ferociously pursued her.

During his first years in politics, in the New York State Assembly, he sought power through constant attack. The death of Alice Lee, coming as it did just after the birth of his first child—at the moment of fruition of his manhood—only intensified his will to fight. He went West, to where the battle for life was fiercest. The West did not welcome him; it had to be won, like everything else he lusted for. Win it he did, and in doing so he built up the splendid body that became an inspiration to the American people. By living on equal terms with the likes of Hashknife Simpson, Bat Masterson, Modesty Carter, Bronco Charlie Miller, and Hell-Roaring Bill Jones, he added another mental frontier to those he had already acquired by birth and inheritance. Theodore Roosevelt, Eastern son of a Northern father and a Southern mother, could now call himself a Westerner as well. "Had it not been for the years [I] spent in North Dakota," he said later, "I would not have been President of the United States."

Theodore Roosevelt's second governing impulse was his righteousness. As one reviewer of his books remarked, "He seems to have been born with his mind made up." No shocks disturbed that sheltered childhood in New York City. Privately educated, he suffered none of the traumas of school. Thanks to the security of his home, the strong leadership of his father, and the adoration of his brother and sisters, Teedie entered adolescence with no sexual or psychological doubts whatsoever. Or if he had any, he simply reasoned them out according to Judeo-Christian principles, reached the proper moral decision, and that was that. "Thank heaven!" he wrote in his diary after falling in love with Alice Lee, "I am perfectly pure." His three great bereavements (the death of his father in 1878, and the almost simultaneous deaths of his mother and wife in 1884, in the same house and on the same day) came too late to do him any permanent emotional damage. They served only to re-convince him that he must be strong, honest, clean-living, and industrious. "At least I can live," he wrote, "so as not to dishonor the memory of the dead," and never was a cliché more heartfelt. Experiment after experiment proved the correctness of his instincts—in defying the Harvard doctor who ordered him to live a sedentary life, in marrying successfully, in winning international acclaim as writer and politician long before he was thirty. As a rancher, he proceeded to knock down rude cowboys, pursue boat thieves in the name of the law, and preach the gospel of responsible citizenship. One of the first things he did after Benjamin Harrison appointed him Civil Service Commissioner was to call for the prosecution of a postmaster-general who just happened to be the President's best friend. "That young man," Harrison growled, "wants to put the whole world right between sunrise and sunset." Theodore Roosevelt's moralizing as Police Commissioner of New York City was so egotistical that the *Herald* published a transcript of one of his speeches with the personal pronoun "I" emphasized in heavy type. The effect, on a page of gray newsprint, was of buckshot at close range. This did not stop Theodore Roosevelt using the personal pronoun thirteen times in the first four sentences of his account of the Spanish-American War. In fact the story went around that halfway through the typesetting, Scribner's had to send out for an extra supply of capital I's.

The third characteristic of Theodore Roosevelt's personality was his sense of pride, both as an aristocrat and an American. From birth, servants and tradespeople deferred to him. Men and women of high quality came to visit his parents and treated him as one of their number. He accepted his status without question, as he did the responsibilities it entailed. At a very early age he had to accompany his father on excursions to a lodging-house for Irish newsboys and a night school for young Italians. It cannot

have escaped his attention that certain immigrant groups tended
be more primitive than others. Grand tours of Europe and the
Levant taught him that this was not due to ethnic inferiority, so
much as centuries of economic and political deprivation.
Prosperous countries, like England and Germany, were relatively
peasant-free. But in Italy, women and children scrabbled like
chickens for scraps of his food, and in Ireland, people lay down
in the road from sheer hunger. From what he read, things were
no better in the Slavic countries. Only in the United States, with
its limitless economic and personal opportunities, could these
peasants better themselves and become, free, enlightened,
all-around Americans.

Here I must emphasize that Theodore Roosevelt was not a
snob in the trivial sense. He had nothing but contempt for the
Newport crowd, and the more effete members of the Four
Hundred. When he said, at twenty-one, that he wanted to be a
member of "the governing class," he was aware that that class
was socially beneath him. At Albany, and in the Badlands, and as
Colonel of the Rough Riders, he preferred to associate with men
who were coarse but efficient, rather than those who were
polished and weak. He believed, he said, in "the aristocracy of
worth." On the other hand, John Blum has noted that President
Roosevelt never appointed impoverished, unlettered men to
responsible positions. He made political capital out of the fact that
his sons attended the village school at Oyster Bay along with the
sons of his servants, of whom at least one was black, but as soon
as the boys reached puberty, he whisked them off to Groton.
Only the very young or very old dared call him "Teddy" to his
face. Theodore Roosevelt was a patrician to the tips of his tapering
fingers, yet, he enjoyed until death an almost unnatural identity
with the masses. "Whenever I see in an audience," he wrote, "a
grim-featured old fellow with a hickory shirt and no collar or
cravat and only one gallus to keep up his trousers, there is a man
to whom I can surely appeal in the name of something loftier than
his mere material well-being." Perhaps Theodore Roosevelt best
defined his appeal when he said that in addressing such basic
Americans en masse, he "put into their hearts and minds the
thoughts they felt but could not say."

The fourth and final major trait of Theodore Roosevelt's
character was his militarism. I need not deal with it in detail
because it is a familiar aspect of him, and in any case did not

manifest itself much during his presidency. There is no doubt that in youth and again in old age, he was in love with war, yet oddly enough, of all of our great presidents he was the most peaceful (indeed, he won the Nobel Peace Prize in 1906) and the least associated with war.

He did not lack for military influences as a child; four of his Georgian ancestors had been military men, and two of his uncles served with distinction in the Confederate Navy. When little Teedie learned to read, he reveled in stories "about the soldiers of Valley Forge, and Morgan's riflemen," and confessed, "I had a great desire to be like them."

In his senior year at Harvard, he suddenly developed an interest in strategy and tactics, and began to write *The Naval War of 1812*; within eighteen months he was the world expert on that subject. As soon as he left college, he joined the National Guard and quickly became a captain, which stood him in good stead when he was called upon to lead the Rough Riders in 1898. Throughout his literary years he made a study of historic campaigns, both classical and modern, and he would wage great battles with knives and forks and spoons on the White House tablecloth. He understood that these battles were fought by thinking men, that mental courage was superior to physical bravado. Nobody thrilled to the tramp of marching boots more than he, yet he believed that men must march for honorable reasons, in obedience to the written orders of a democratically elected Commander in Chief. In that respect, at least, the pen was mightier than the sword.

Power became TR, and absolute power became him best of all. He loved being President, and was so good at his job that the American people loved him for loving it. He genuinely dreaded having to leave the White House, and let us remember that a third term was his for the asking in 1908. But his reverence for the Washingtonian principle that power must punctually revert to those whose gift it is, persuaded him to make this selfless sacrifice in his prime. For that, if for nothing else, let us remember Theodore Roosevelt the Polygon with admiration.

"He Who Has Planted Will Preserve"

The Roosevelt Family

The Roosevelt Family of Sagamore Hill in 1903. *From left to right*: Quentin Roosevelt (1897–1918), killed as a pilot in World War I; President Theodore Roosevelt (1858–1919); Theodore Roosevelt, Junior (1887–1944), author, public official, won Medal of Honor as Brigadier General in World War II; Archibald B. Roosevelt (1894–1979), hero of both world wars, conservationist; Alice Lee Roosevelt (1884–1980), daughter of TR's first wife Alice Lee (1861–1884), Washington's "Princess Alice" married Congressman Nicholas Longworth of Ohio; Kermit Roosevelt (1889–1943), explorer, writer, served in both World Wars; Edith Kermit Carow (Mrs. Theodore) Roosevelt (1861–1948); and Ethel Carow Roosevelt (1891–1977), married Dr. Richard Derby, saved Sagamore Hill as an historic site.

2

The Southern Heritage of Theodore Roosevelt

Clarece Martin

Through countless generations, the golden threads of moral strength, duty, and service are woven into the fabric of Theodore Roosevelt's Southern heritage. Each generation had its leader who chose to serve rather than to be served. The history of the Bulloch family of Georgia, Theodore Roosevelt's maternal ancestry, is a chronicle of courage and valor.

Over the mantel in the nursery of the Theodore Roosevelt Birthplace in New York City is a portrait of Anna Bulloch Gracie, young Theodore's beloved "Aunt Annie." To one side of her portrait stands a small sampler embroidered with the words, "Annie Bulloch, Roswell, 1843." In the adjoining bedroom of Theodore's parents is the portrait of his mother, Mittie Bulloch Roosevelt. A sampler Mittie embroidered like that of her sister Anna's can be seen in the Theodore Roosevelt Birthplace Museum.

In 1843 when they were embroidering their samplers in the parlor of Bulloch Hall, the family mansion in Roswell, Georgia, Anna Bulloch was ten years old. Mittie was eight. They lived on the Georgia frontier with their parents, Major and Mrs. James Stephens Bulloch, and the large and complex Bulloch family. Only five years before this time, Cherokee Indians occupied the land where they lived.

Following the removal of the Indians from the Blue Ridge foothills of north Georgia in 1838, the Bullochs joined a small group of Presbyterians on the Georgia coast and journeyed 350 rugged miles to this wilderness settlement called Roswell. These colonists sought a more healthful climate and the opportunity to acquire and develop the vast and fertile Indian lands. The early families bought stock in a cotton mill built by the town's founder, Roswell King. With slave labor they built imposing homes, a school for their children, and a Presbyterian church in which to worship. James Stephens Bulloch was not the first, nor would he be the last of the Bulloch family lineage to brave unknown lands.[1]

The first James Bulloch to leave his homeland for the American frontier was a well-educated Scottish clergyman from Glasgow who in 1729 crossed the ocean, landing in Charleston, S.C. At first he was a merchant in Charleston. Later he owned a large Carolina plantation on which it was said he entertained General James Edward Oglethorpe, founder of the Georgia colony. The year he arrived in Charleston, James Bulloch and Jean Stobo, daughter of the Reverend A. Stobo, were married.

The Reverend Stobo and his wife had sailed from Scotland in 1699 aboard the *Rising Star,* one of four ships of emigrants who expected to find a new life in the West Indies. Landing on the Isthmus of Darien, now called Panama, several were captured by the Spanish and imprisoned and many perished. The Stobos were among the small group of survivors who eventually were allowed to depart. As they turned toward Scotland a violent storm sank two of the ships and carried the other two into Charleston harbor.

While the ships were being repaired, Rev. Stobo and his wife went ashore for him to officiate at a wedding in Charleston. They remained on shore for the night, when a sudden storm sank the last two ships, drowning everyone on board. The Stobos remained in Charleston where he became pastor of the Presbyterian church. Their daughter Jean and James Bulloch were wed in 1729.[2] (See Bulloch Genealogy inside front cover.)

A son, Archibald Stobo Bulloch, was born to Jean and James Bulloch in 1730. Following his wife's death, James Bulloch moved to Savannah to claim a royal grant of 2,000 acres of Georgia coastland. His son Archibald studied law in Savannah and became an eloquent speaker and a patriot in America's fight for freedom. In 1765, his wife Mary DeVeaux, daughter of French patriot James DeVeaux, bore Archibald Bulloch a son who was christened James Bulloch.

At forty-two, Archibald Bulloch was elected speaker of the Royal Assembly and twice was elected a delegate to the Continental Congress. In 1776, he was elected president of the Executive Council and commander in chief of Georgia. Under his bold leadership the colony of Georgia was united in support of independence. At the height of his career he led a daring attack against the British on a nearby island. Though under constant fire from offshore ships, none of his men were lost in the attack.

The Honorable Archibald Bulloch was stricken and died in his home in Savannah on February 22, 1777. His thirteen-year-old son James escaped from Savannah as it lay under siege by the British and made his way to Virginia to fight with the colonists there. Within four years, he had advanced to the rank of captain.

After the war Captain James Bulloch returned to Georgia to marry Anne Irvine of Liberty County, daughter of Dr. John Irvine and his wife Ann Elizabeth Baillie. Dr. Irvine was former physician to the admiralty of London and assistant personal physician to King George III of England. Both the Irvine and Baillie families traced an unbroken lineage 400 years back to Robert II, king of Scotland. James and Anne Irvine Bulloch's second son James Stephens Bulloch, born in 1795, would become the grandfather of Theodore Roosevelt.[3]

Dr. Irvine and his family were members of Midway Congregational Church in Liberty County on the Georgia coast, forty miles south of Savannah. General Daniel Stewart, his wife Susannah Oswald Stewart, and their family also were members of the same church. Through this family connection, the Irvines' grandson James Stephens Bulloch of Savannah and the Stewarts' daughter Patsy, called Martha, became friends. Rumors persisted among the early families of Roswell that Martha and James were in love and that a misunderstanding caused a rift in the romance.

General Stewart, a Revolutionary War hero and famous Indian fighter, left home at fifteen to join the fight for freedom. Taken prisoner in Carolina and chained aboard a British ship, he managed to escape and swim to shore, where he rejoined his regiment. He achieved the rank of colonel when he was twenty-two. On returning to Liberty County after the war, he found Midway Church and most of the plantations destroyed, though his plantation, Tranquil Hill, was spared. Many years later his granddaughter Mittie Bulloch Roosevelt named the Roosevelt home at Oyster Bay on Long Island, Tranquility, for the old family plantation on the Georgia coast.[4]

General Stewart, whose wife Susannah had died when Martha was eight, was summoned to fight marauding Seminole Indians on the Georgia-Florida border. To assure Martha's proper care during his absence, he gave her hand in marriage to his trusted friend Senator John Elliott, a widower twenty-six years her senior. A highly respected gentleman of great integrity, Senator Elliott had expressed deep admiration and the desire to marry the beautiful eighteen-year-old Martha. John Elliott and Martha Stewart were wed at Midway Church on January 6, 1818. One week earlier in the same church, John Elliott's daughter Hester had married James Stephens Bulloch, Martha's rejected young suitor. Martha now became James Stephens Bulloch's stepmother-in-law.

After a six-year tenure in Washington, Senator Elliott and his wife Martha, with their three children, Susan, Georgia, and Charles returned to Georgia. The baby Charles died in infancy, and a son Daniel Stuart was born two years later in 1826. Senator Elliott died the following year, as did his daughter Hester, leaving her husband James Stephens Bulloch and their young son James Dunwody Bulloch. Five years later, in 1832, Martha Stewart Elliott and James Stephens Bulloch were wed. The staid and proper members of Savannah society considered it to be in very poor taste for Martha to marry her stepson-in-law, though they were related only by previous marriages.[5]

James Stephens Bulloch became highly successful as a cotton factor, president of the United States Branch Bank, deputy collector of the Port of Savannah, with the rank of major in the elite Chatham Battalion. He also was a director in the company that financed the *Savannah*, the first steamship to cross the Atlantic Ocean. His love for the sea and ships was a strong influence on his son James Dunwody Bulloch who chose the life of a mariner as his profession.[6]

After the birth of the Bulloch's daughter Anna in 1833, ten-year-old James Dunwody Bulloch was sent to Hartford, Connecticut to school. Two years later, though expecting another child, Martha Bulloch sailed on the long and perilous voyage to Connecticut to visit young James. Her baby daughter Martha, called Mittie, was born in Hartford on July 8, 1853.[7]

In 1839, when Charles Irvine, the Bulloch's third child, was an infant, Martha and James packed their belongings, their children, and their servants and moved to the north Georgia frontier village of Roswell. Besides James and Martha, their family consisted of Susan, Georgia, and Daniel Stuart Elliott, and Anna, Mittie, and Charles Irvine Bulloch. Sixteen-year-old James Dunwody Bulloch had joined the U.S. Navy as a midshipman that year and did not make the journey with them to Roswell.

The infant Charles Irvine Bulloch died in 1840, three months before his third birthday, and the Bulloch's last child, Irvine

Stephens Bulloch was born in 1842. Georgia Elliott died in 1848, followed five months later by the sudden death of James Stephens Bulloch, who was stricken and died on February 18, 1849, while teaching his Sunday school class at the Presbyterian church. Martha donned the black attire of mourning when Georgia died and wore only black for the remainder of her life.[8]

After Major Bulloch's death, Martha struggled with heavy debts and little income as she attempted to provide for her large family and twenty-five slaves who tended the house and fields. She was forced to sell Bulloch Hall to a friend who allowed her to remain there with her family until she was able to buy the home back from him.[9]

Courtesy of Clarece Martin

Bulloch Hall, Roswell, Georgia

Susan Elliott, Martha's eldest daughter, had married a young doctor from Philadelphia, Hilborne West, whom she met while visiting friends in Savannah. Doctor West's sister Mary was the wife of Silas Weir Roosevelt, eldest brother of Theodore Roosevelt (Sr.). The Wests' stories of the Bulloch family and their life on the Georgia frontier kindled the interest of nineteen-year-old Theodore. In the spring of the year 1850, during the Wests' annual visit with Martha Bulloch, Theodore came to Roswell and visited the Wests and the Bullochs for two weeks.

Anna Bulloch, who was seventeen, was a serious, dependable young lady, predictable, strong of character, and an indulgent protector of her adored younger sister Mittie. Like Theodore, she was independent and self-sufficient. Anna and Theodore were alike in many ways. Fifteen-year-old Mittie, however, was the opposite. Pampered and protected, she was accustomed to having her way, to being served and cared for. Beautiful, capricious, and spirited, her humorous stories and ludicrous mimicry kept everyone entertained. When Theodore returned to New York, he had Mittie's tiny gold thimble tucked inside his vest pocket.[10]

During the next two years, Mittie and Anna attended Barnhamville Academy in South Carolina. Theodore traveled abroad with his parents. After graduating in the spring of 1853, Mittie and Anna went to Philadelphia to visit Susan and Hilborne West. Theodore arrived soon afterwards. Mittie at eighteen was even more beautiful and captivating than he had remembered. When the two young ladies boarded the train for Georgia, Mittie wore an engagement ring from Theodore.[11]

They were married on December 22, 1853, at Bulloch Hall, in a wedding Roswell has never forgotten. Returning to New York City with Theodore's parents the Cornelius Van Schaack Roosevelts and his brother Cornelius, Mittie and Theodore soon moved into a tall, narrow, brownstone on East 20th Street, a wedding gift from his parents who lived close by. Their baby daughter Anna was born a year later.[12]

As the clouds of war darkened the nation, the separation of the Bulloch family at this perilous time was difficult for Mittie and unbearable for Anna and Mrs. Bulloch. In 1856, Mrs. Bulloch rented Bulloch Hall to Roswell friends and she and Anna moved to New York City to live with Mittie and Theodore, enrolling Irvine Bulloch in the University of Pennsylvania. On October 27, 1858, young Theodore was born, with his grandmother Bulloch in close attendance. Elliott was born two years later, and Corinne in 1861 as the War Between the States tore the nation apart.[13] (A Bulloch-Roosevelt Genealogy is inside the back cover.)

Anna Bulloch tutored the children with their lessons. Mrs. Bulloch gave Mittie companionship and moral support. "Grandmamma" Bulloch and Aunt "Annie" were adored by the children. Their tales of life in Roswell, the Indians and wild animals, Uncle Remus and Br'er Rabbit, and the slaves, kept them enthralled by the hour.[14] The children never realized the anguish and grief in the hearts of these three brave women as they struggled to keep love, peace, and unity within the Roosevelt family circle during those times of stress and conflict.

Irvine and James Dunwody Bulloch returned south to enter the Confederate Navy when the Civil War became imminent. With fifteen years' naval experience, James Dunwody Bulloch was given full authority and funding to acquire ships for the Confederate Navy. Irvine became a Sailing Master on ships his brother acquired for the Confederacy. As the war progressed, communications with Irvine and James Bulloch ceased, for their wartime activities were highly secret.[15]

Letters from family and friends in the South were all but nonexistent. News from the South was heart-breaking as Union soldiers marched through Georgia, destroying everything in their path. When notified that her son Daniel Stuart Elliott lay dying in Marietta from consumption contracted while in the army, Martha Bulloch was unable to obtain permission to go to him.[16] As her spirits and health steadily declined, Mittie and Anna kept the devastating war news from her. She was not told of the capture of Roswell nor of the destruction there. Only at war's end did Mittie and Anna learn that Bulloch Hall and the other large old homes in Roswell and the Presbyterian church had been spared. Mrs. Bulloch did not know that Irvine and James survived the war, for she died in 1864 before the war ended.

Theodore Roosevelt, Sr.'s wartime service as a member of the Union Allotment Committee took him away from home for long periods of time. The children's loyalty, as well as that of the other members of the Roosevelt family and their friends, was, of course, with the North. There was jubilation at the news of each Union victory, causing great distress to Mittie and Anna. At the time Mittie most needed her husband's love, support, and strength, he was not there. Her health declined under the stress of the war, of managing the large home and staff, and of the four lively children who were beyond her control.[17]

At war's end the Roosevelt household once again became more normal, though Mittie's health was fragile. In 1866, Anna Bulloch was married to James King Gracie whose family built Gracie Mansion, now the home of New York City's mayors.

Irvine Stephens Bulloch and James Dunwody Bulloch, denied
amnesty by the U.S. government, lived the remainder of their
lives in Liverpool, England.

During a number of Roosevelt family visits to the Bullochs in
Liverpool, and after listening to the reminiscences of his uncles'
wartime naval experiences, young Theodore was fired with
determination to complete the book *The Naval War of 1812*, which
he had begun writing while a student at Harvard.[18] Theodore
Sr.'s sudden death at forty-seven in 1878 left his family
devastated. Mittie died six years later at age forty-nine.

President Theodore Roosevelt visited Roswell for the first
time in 1905 and again in 1912. He knelt at the altar of the
Presbyterian church where his mother and her family had
worshiped, then toured the rooms of Bulloch Hall. Speaking to
the people of Roswell on October 26, 1905, the day before his
forty-seventh birthday, from the bandstand erected on the town
square for the occasion, he said:

> You have no idea what it means to me to come to the home
> of my mother and my mother's people, and to see the spot I
> knew so well from what my mother and aunt have told me. It has
> been exactly as if I were revisiting some old place of my
> childhood. Those stories taught me what a real home life was and
> should be. All these anecdotes, I can see now, taught me an
> enormous amount. It has been my very great good fortune to
> have the right to claim that my blood is half southern and half
> northern. I have the ancestral right to claim a proud kinship with
> those who showed their devotion to duty as they saw the duty,
> whether they wore the gray or the blue.[19]

From his Bulloch ancestors Theodore Roosevelt inherited a
spirit of courage and adventure, a love of people, of nature and
wildlife, and the exhilaration of the challenge and the chase. At
his mother's knees he learned of love, tenderness, warmth, and
loyalty. From her came his humor, his sense of drama, his ability
to spin yarns, and his fine art of mimicry. His Grandmamma
Bulloch and Aunt Annie taught him the basics and value of
knowledge and wisdom and graciousness. The rich tapestry of
his life was loomed of the warp and the woof of his Southern
heritage, the influence of both North and South, the weaknesses
and strengths, the differences and similarities. These finespun
threads wove the character of the remarkable man that he was.

NOTES

Unless otherwise indicated, Bulloch-Roosevelt correspondence cited is from Theodore Roosevelt Collection, Houghton Library, Harvard University.

1. Sarah Blackwell Gober Temple, *The First Hundred Years: A Short History of Cobb County, in Georgia* (Atlanta: Walter W. Brown Publishing Company, 1935), pp. 112–16; Clarece Martin, *A Glimpse of the Past, The History of Bulloch Hall and Roswell. Georgia* (1973; reprint, Atlanta: Historic Roswell, Inc., 1987), pp. 1–2, 9–17; Clarece Martin, *A History of the Roswell Presbyterian Church* (Dallas: Taylor Publishing Company, 1984), pp. 17–21; Herman Hagedorn, reminiscences, interviews, and notes made during visit to Roswell in early 1900s, from Theodore Roosevelt Collection, Harvard University.

2. Clarece Martin, "Georgia's Historic Link to the 'Panama Canal,'" *Atlanta Journal-Constitution Magazine*, March 19, 1978, pp. 27–28; Clarece Martin, "Theodore Roosevelt's Ancestral Link to the Panama Canal," *Theodore Roosevelt Association Journal* 3 (Summer 1981): 15-17.

3. James Stacy, *History and Published Records of the Midway Congregational Church, Liberty County, Georgia* (1894, 1903; reprint, Spartanburg, SC, 1979), pp. 283, 298; J. G. B. Bulloch, *A History and Genealogy of the Families of Bulloch and Stobo and of Irvine of Cults* (n. p., n.d., The Reprint Company [1911]), pp. 12–22, 30–39. Charles C. Jones, Jr., *Biographical Sketches of the Delegates from Georgia to The Continental Congress* (1891; reprint, Boston: Houghton, Mifflin, and Company, 1927), pp. 14–15, 27.

4. Lucian Lamar Knight, *Georgia's Landmarks, Memorials, and Legends*, 2 vols. (Atlanta: n.p., 1914), 1: 334; Mittie Bulloch Roosevelt to Cousin Laura (Mrs. Joseph L. Locke), August 29, 1877, Southern Historical Collection, Wilson Library, University of North Carolina, Chapel Hill.

5. John Elliott to Martha Stewart, October 11, 1817; James Holmes to Martha Stewart, October 11, 1817; James Holmes, "Dr. Bullie's" Notes, *Reminiscences of Early Georgia and of Philadelphia and New Haven in the 1800s*, ed. Delma Eugene Presley (1875–1880; reprint, Atlanta: Cherokee Publishing Company, 1976), p. 39; Stacy, *History and Published Records of the Midway Congregational Church*, p. 83; Anna Roosevelt Cowles Reminiscences, October 23, 1924–August 19, 1929; W. Sheffield Cowles, Jr., Private Collection, Farmington, CT.

6. Knight, *Georgia's Landmarks*, 2: 228, 837.

7. Anna Bulloch to Mittie Bulloch Roosevelt, Savannah, Georgia, April 8, 1854, "I have no recollection of the twenty-two months before you were born! . . . we were so inseparable it seemed as if nothing could divide us."; Cowles Reminiscences; Mrs. J. Bartow Wing, owner of Bulloch Hall, description of President Theodore Roosevelt's second visit in 1912, written in 1963, from Roswell Presbyterian Church History Room Collection.

8. Roswell Presbyterian Church Cemetery Records, History Room Collection.

9. Quit Claim Deed, Bulloch Hall, March 14, 1908, shows the home sold by administrator of James S. Bulloch property on

December 7, 1850, to Archibald Howell for $3,350, and sold again on
December 16, 1872, by Hilborne West of Philadelphia, executor of
Martha Bulloch estate; Temple, *First Hundred Years*, pp. 111–16, 521.

10. Interview by author on September 25, 1982, with Mr. W.
Sheffield Cowles, Jr., at his home in Farmington, CT; *Day Before
Yesterday, The Reminiscences of Mrs. Theodore Roosevelt, Jr.* (Garden City,
NY: Doubleday and Co., 1959), p. 38.

11. Interview by author on February 16, 1973, at the Presbyterian
Home in Summerville, SC, with Mrs. A. Wadley Kirkland,
granddaughter of Mary Jane Macfie of Columbia, SC, close friend and
classmate of Mittie and Anna Bulloch at Barhamville Academy near
Columbia, in the early 1850s; Mittie to Theodore, Sr., Roswell,
Georgia, June 1, 1853, "My ring has caused quite an excitement."

12. Interviews with Mrs. W. E. Baker (Evelyn King), bridesmaid
in Mittie Bulloch-Theodore Roosevelt wedding; William Jackson,
Roswell Presbyterian Church sexton and Bulloch Hall doorman at
wedding, and Maum Grace Robinson, Martha Bulloch's maid, in
Atlanta Journal, October 8, 1905, before visit by President Theodore
Roosevelt; description of Bulloch-Roosevelt wedding by Mrs. Baker
during interview by Margaret Mitchell for *Atlanta Journal Magazine*,
June 10, 1923.

13. Martha Bulloch to Susan West, October 28, 1858.

14. Theodore Roosevelt to Joel Chandler Harris, October 12, 1901,
from the White House in *Theodore Roosevelt's Letters to His Children*, ed.
Joseph Bucklin Bishop (New York: Charles Scribner's Sons, 1919), pp.
67–68.

15. Philip Van Doren Stern, Introduction to New Edition, *The
Secret Service of the Confederate States in Europe or How the Confederate
Cruisers Were Equipped* by James Dunwody Bulloch, 2 vols. (1883;
reprint, New York: Thomas Yoseloff, Sagamore Press, 1959), 1: ix.

16. Lucy Elliott, wife of Daniel Stuart Elliott, to Martha Bulloch,
June 21, 1861.

17. Mrs. A. Wadley Kirkland told the author in an interview that
on two separate occasions Mittie told Mrs. Kirkland's grandmother
(Mary Jane Macfie McMaster) that she (Mittie) waved a Confederate
flag out of the window of their home in New York as Union soldiers
marched by during the Civil War.

18. Stern Introduction to *The Secret Service of the Confederate States
in Europe*, by Bulloch, 1: xvi.

19. Speech made by President Theodore Roosevelt during visit to
Roswell on October 16, 1905, published in the *Atlanta Constitution*,
October 17, 1905.

3

Turmoil Begat "Tranquility": The Theodore Roosevelts Move to Oyster Bay

Robert B. MacKay

After several summers spent exploring watering places along the east bank of the Hudson between Tarrytown and Riverdale, Theodore Roosevelt, Sr. (1831–1878) "hired" a country house that was to become known as Tranquility.[1] David McCullough and Edmund Morris, in their biographies of the twenty-sixth president, link the senior Theodore's decision to try Long Island with his move uptown that year to a new townhouse on 57th Street and a desire to be closer to his family when they were at the shore.[2] Indeed, Theodore Sr. appears to have been considering the prospect of summering at Oyster Bay for some time. The previous summer he had written to his daughter, Bamie (Anna Roosevelt, 1855–1931), that he failed to understand how brother James Alfred "could come from there [Oyster Bay] all summer long."[3] Comparing the north shore village with the Panfield (New Jersey) resort he was then visiting, Theodore lamented:

> As I look at this lovely quiet inland place, it seems very tempting but how infinitely the water would add to its attractions. One of these days I hope to have my own little place furnished with "elegant" simplicity that I can turn the key upon when summer is over but which will give me what I have so often longed for, a spot in the country to call my own. I wonder if it will ever come, it has always been a dream of mine.[4]

Yet was Oyster Bay in 1874 really the peaceful family colony by the sea of the popular image replete with the "little places" of Theodore's dreams? Research into the origins of one of Long Island's earliest summer colonies presents a somewhat different picture. Theodore was not just joining his family by the shore, but a good portion of his Union League Club circle as well. Moreover, Oyster Bay was already such a popular resort by the decade following the Civil War that Roosevelt might have had trouble both finding and holding on to a place if there had not been a severe recession and a spectacular bankruptcy.

As early as 1833, Scottish voyager James Stuart reported in his travelogue, *Three Years in North America*, that Oyster Bay was "much resorted to as a summer retreat" and the hotel at Oyster Bay was "large and was well filled" during his visit.[5] "Charmingly picturesque" is the way Long Island historian Benjamin Thompson described the north shore village six years later, noting that it was "one of the most desirable places of residence in this part of Long Island and some gentlemen of wealth and taste have made choice of it."[6] Among those personages was no less a figure than Washington Irving, then perhaps America's most famous author, who visited his nephew Gabriel's place on Cove Road to "enjoy the salt breezes."[7] Oyster Bay was only twenty-seven miles from New York and "in the midst of country which doesn't correspond in the least" to the popular image of Long Island as a place of "dreary sandy wastes," as Theodore's Union League acquaintance Joseph Choate noted in later years.[8]

Although it could be reached by the steamboat *D. R. Martin* in three hours from Manhattan, the north shore village's resort prospects received a major boost when the Long Island Railroad extended a branch from Hicksville to Syosset in 1854, providing regularly scheduled transportation to the city more than a decade before the tracks reached Glen Cove and the south shore resorts. For the man of affairs, commuting time to Syosset before the Civil War took just two hours and fifteen minutes, almost comparable to the present time.[9] The summer colony made frequent use of this rail link as Amos Boerum's yellow stage made scheduled runs to Syosset for mail and passengers. James K. Gracie even thought it important enough to have the stationery used at his summer place Gracewood inscribed with the notation "R. R. Station, Syosset, L. I."[10] Indeed, it was from the Syosset depot that Theodore Sr. saw his son off to his freshman year at Harvard on September 27, 1876.

Besides its scenic attributes and transportation advantage, Oyster Bay owed its mid-nineteenth century popularity to the success of native sons and a new form of recreation, yachting. Members of the Townsend, Sampson, Smith, Underhill, Weekes, and Youngs families, along with the Joneses of Cold Spring Harbor, had been prominent in New York City mercantile and Episcopal church circles since the eighteenth century. The decision of some key members of these families to establish summer places in Oyster Bay in the third quarter of the last century sparked the summer movement. Several even invested in the phenomenon. Dr. Oliver L. Jones and the Hon. Solomon Townsend (1805–1880), the wealthy New York tea, spice, and liquor merchant who resided at Raynham Hall, owned area hotels.[11]

The most influential of these rusticators with ancestral roots in the vicinity was John A. Weekes (1820–1901). A principal in the New York law firm of Weekes and Foster and a popular figure in the city where he was a member of the Union League Club and chairman of its building committee, Weekes had transformed the old DeKay place east of the village into Cove Hill, an imposing French Second Empire mansion. The marriage of his sister Julia Mary (1827–1896) to another prominent Manhattan attorney, Henry G. deForest (1820–1889), had led to Nethermuir, the deForests' 1862 country seat south of Laurelton Hall near the head of Cold Spring Harbor. Edward M. Townsend, Jr. (1829–1904), another Union Leaguer, was improving a house on the road to Tranquility which he had acquired at a court auction in 1867.[12] And the heretofore mentioned Dr. Oliver Jones resided in Long Island's largest mansion, the great Greek Revival house at the top of the Cold Spring Harbor hill on the road to Syosset, which had been built by his wife's uncle, Walter Restored Jones of whaling fame. Native daughters were also playing a part in the development and popularization of the summer colony. The recently widowed Sarah Sampson Adam was summering in her ancestral home on Lexington Avenue in 1874 and was soon to spend part of the fortune her late husband John H. Adam (1822–1870) had amassed as president of the New York Gas Light Company to build one of the resort's most stylish country houses. Also known as Hillside, the 1878 Potter and Robertson-designed manse was an early example of the Shingle Style in America.

Joining these summer residents with Oyster Bay roots were many who were new to the region. To the west of the hamlet on the shore road to Bayville, James W. Beekman (1815–1871) built his picturesque villa The Cliffs in 1863–64. Designed by the ecclesiastical architect Henry G. Harrison in the Gothic Revival style, the Beekman mansion was one of the show places of the summer colony. Its romantically landscaped setting was influenced by the theories of Alexander Jackson Downing with whom Beekman had worked in the previous decade on establishing New York's Central Park. Beekman was an attorney and a civically-minded member of one of New York's most prominent families, who had served in the New York State Assembly and Senate. He knew Theodore Roosevelt, Sr., well, having been an organizer of the Union League and supporter of such causes as the creation of Central Park, election reform, free public education, and emancipation. Beekman's Civil War experience had paralleled Theodore's. He had worked for the U.S. Sanitary Commission, a precursor of the Red Cross. Beekman's neighbor to the west on the Bayville shore, New York financier and real estate magnate Col. S. Van Rensselaer Cruger, was a veteran of Sherman's march to the sea. Also active in state politics, Cruger served for some years as chairman of the Republican County Committee of New York City and in 1888 was a candidate for lieutenant governor. The Colonel joined the Union League the year James W. Beekman died and apparently owned the colony's poshest country seat which Theodore's sister-in-law, Anna Bulloch Gracie, called "handsome" in an 1887 letter.[13]

East of the hamlet on Cove Neck, Benjamin L. and Edward H. Swan had built country houses as early as the mid-1850s and were trying their hand as gentlemen farmers in 1874. Sons of a prominent Boston merchant and Manhattan landowner, the Swans were not members of the Union League, but the names of two of their younger brothers and a brother-in-law can be found on the club's rolls during this period. Benjamin's house, later rented by young Theodore before the completion of Sagamore Hill, was a relatively modest two-story affair in the vernacular Bracketed or Italianate style then popular on Long Island. Edward's manse, The Evergreens, however, was a much grander brick edifice, having been rebuilt after a fire in 1872 in the fashionable French Second Empire mode by New York architect John W. Ritch. The Roosevelt and Swan children were to become life-long friends. Young Theodore considered Edward's daughter, Emily, to be one of the prettiest girls in Oyster Bay and taught her to play the new game of lawn tennis in 1879.[14]

A final Union Leaguer, the eminent New York physician Dr.

James R. Wood, lived on the other side of Cove Neck a few hundred yards from Laurelton Hall. Among his students had been the young Oliver Jones.

Unfortunately, the names of many other habitues of the watering spot are lost to time since they never purchased property. The membership rolls of the Seawanhaka Corinthian Yacht Club, founded in 1872 by Benjamin L. Swan's son, Billy, suggest, however, that the north shore village was frequented by a much larger body of summer visitors than the assessor's records would indicate. For example, Bayard Foulke, an ardent yachtsman, hired the old Remsen farm on the shore road to Bayville in 1867 and again in 1868 to participate in the informal amateur races held at Oyster Bay each summer, as his son recalled in later years.[15] Frederic Giraud Foster leased a farm on the same road for a long period. Both men were to "crew" for Hilbourne L. "Hilly" Roosevelt and his mate Cornelius Roosevelt in July of 1874 on board the schooner *Addie*, in the first open amateur race sponsored by the new yacht club.

The names of many of the other participants in this race must have been familiar to Theodore. There were Schuylers, Vails, Weekes, and Abercrombies on board various boats, as well as salty Union League members C. B. Smith and Governeur Morris, Jr.

It's no wonder that at the height of the season, rooms were hard to find in Oyster Bay despite Townsend's Simcoe House, A. A. Reed's octagonal Acker Nassau House across the street, and various boarding houses. Oyster Bay had been "discovered" by a number of interlocking circles ranging from the yachting fraternity to the Union League membership who were engaged in a continual social ritual forever visiting or receiving their friends.

Anna Bulloch Gracie's letters to her niece, Corinne Roosevelt Robinson, chronicle the social scene at the shore. In a June 13, 1886, account of her day's activities, Anna complains to Corinne that shortly after breakfast Mr. Swan arrived with "a superb basket of roses." He paid a long visit, delaying her shopping trip to the village. "Immediately after lunch while dressing to call for Mr. Graham to go to Mrs. Cruger's, Julia Swan and Mr. Irving called, Jimmie saw them, then Nellie Beekman came" further delaying the Gracies' departure.[16] Oyster Bay in 1874 was clearly not a place to commune with nature in solitude. It was a summer extension of Knickerbocker society and particularly popular with those whose business interests in the city required periodic attention. Newport and the Jersey shore were too distant for most of these gainfully employed and civically-involved Union Leaguers.

Theodore might not have found suitable lodgings at all had it not been for the panic of 1873 which had caused the business failure of Otis D. Swan (1821–1894), the younger brother of Benjamin and Edward. Otis, a lawyer turned stockbroker, had been a founder of the Union League and served as the club's secretary during the Civil War. Unlike his brothers, who had built country houses facing the bay, Otis settled for the old Greek Revival manse on the south side of Cove Road, opposite John A. Weekes's place. This was the Tranquility of Theodore's dreams which Otis was forced to give up for rooms at Mrs. Gibson's boardinghouse in the village. Although the panic had also hurt Edith Carow's father and other prominent Knickerbockers, Wall Street was surprised by Otis's failure since the brothers Swan were thought to be wealthy, each having inherited a reported half-million dollars from their father. Moreover, Otis was "highly esteemed for his social qualities," as his friend W. H. Macy, the president of Seamen's Savings Bank, was later to note and had fine connections with the business community.[17] He was a director of the Bleecker Street Saving Institution and many charitable organizations including the New York and Lenox hospitals, the Home for the Ruptured and Crippled, and the Society Library Association. In Oyster Bay he had been on the Building Committee for the Rev. Benjamin L. Swan's new Presbyterian church and was superintendent of the Sunday School while his wife sang in the choir. A good club man, known for his aptitude at drafting resolutions, Swan also served as treasurer of the Union League's Building Fund Committee after the Civil War, whose membership included J. A. Roosevelt and J. A. Weekes. Nevertheless, this prominent figure whose very name the *New York Sun* said was "the open sesame" to the doors of fashion and influence did fail and was only able to reestablish his business after several friends reportedly invested $10,000 apiece.[18]

Theodore must have wondered at the close of each season whether Otis's financial recovery would end their summers at Tranquility. His answer came early in December 1876 when Otis

suddenly offered to sell Tranquility's furnishings which
Roosevelt agreed to acquire. Three weeks later, Otis, having said
good-bye to his Bible class in Oyster Bay, left Tranquility where
he had been spending the winter with his wife. The Swans drove
to Syosset with a large quantity of luggage, entered the parlor car
of a New York-bound train, and were not seen again. Within a
few days rumors were rife on Wall Street and on December 27,
the scandal broke in the New York papers. Otis Swan had
misappropriated several hundred thousand dollars, including
money from an estate for which he was the court-appointed
trustee, his sister's portfolio, and the building fund of the Union
League Club! The *New York Herald* reported his friends "were
astonished that such a truly good man could be guilty of such
flagrant wrong" and hoped he would return despite the reports
he had fled to his brother Robert's farm near Geneva, New York
(Rose Hill, now a historic house museum). Theodore Roosevelt,
John A. Weekes, James A. Roosevelt, and other prominent

Courtesy of Theodore Roosevelt Association

"Tranquility," in Oyster Bay, Long Island, New York, 1878. Persons
pictured are believed to be Martha Bulloch Roosevelt and Theodore
Roosevelt, Sr., the parents of President Theodore Roosevelt; seated on
the lawn are Corinne Roosevelt, sister of TR on the right, and Edith
Kermit Carow, who later became TR's second wife.

Knickerbockers who had social or business dealings with Swan awoke on December 28 to find their names listed in all the major dailies. Articles entitled "The Flying Swan," "Broken Trusts," "Ruin in Stock Gambling" ran for days in the city papers as more information became known.[19] Reporters descended on Oyster Bay, giving the watering spot more publicity than it was to see again until another member of the summer colony entered politics.

Hence, the tumultuous default of Otis D. Swan led to Tranquility remaining in the hands of the Theodore Roosevelts into the early 1880s. Little is known about the activities of Otis during these years, but Swan family legend holds that Otis's brothers eventually made good his debts and helped him make a new start in Emporia, Kansas, where he became a reporter for the local paper. By the time of his death in 1894, Otis had become a prominent citizen of the Sunflower state. He was secretary of the Emporia Land and Investment Co. and a trustee of Emporia College.

In October 1884, six years after his father's death, the future president, Theodore Roosevelt, was elected to membership in the Union League over the objection of supporters of James G. Blaine whose nomination the young New York assemblyman had opposed at the Republican Convention that June.[20] Tranquility's owner in the final decades of the nineteenth century was John A. Weekes. The venerable country house was torn down in the mid-1930s: a post-World War II split level now occupies its site.

NOTES

1. Although the Roosevelts had been frequenting Oyster Bay for some time before Theodore's arrival (his father, Cornelius Van Schaack Roosevelt, having died there in 1871), Queens County Registry of Deeds libers indicate that the first Roosevelt to own property was James Alfred who purchased the land to build Yellowbanks in 1880 (Liber 560, p. 124). Which village dwelling (or dwellings) the Roosevelts rented in those early years is not known, but a surviving lease for the 1878 season between Richard Irvin, owner, and James Alfred Roosevelt, leasee, proves that for at least that summer they resided in the East Main Street house now owned by Dr. James Trousdell (the lease dated May 1, 1878, is the possession of Mrs. Bradford G. Weekes, Oyster Bay). Irvin, who had purchased this house in 1860, called the place Hillside. It was sold out of the family in 1914 to a Mr. and Mrs. Cook of Georgia who are said to have added the portico.
2. David McCullough, *Mornings on Horseback* (New York: Simon

and Schuster, 1981,) pp. 141–42; Edmund Morris, *The Rise of Theodore Roosevelt* (New York: Coward, McCann and Geoghegan, 1979), p. 75.

3. Theodore Roosevelt to Martha Bulloch Roosevelt, June 29, 1873. Theodore Roosevelt Collection, Houghton Library, Harvard University (hereafter cited as TR Collection).

4. Ibid.

5. James Stuart, *Three Years in North America* (Edinburgh: Robert Cadell, 1833), p. 422.

6. Benjamin Thompson, *History of Long Island* (New York: E. French, 1839), p. 331.

7. This was the house later known as Tranquility. Francis Irvin, *Oyster Bay in History* (Oyster Bay: The Oyster Bay Historical Society, 1962,), p. 165.

8. McCullough, *Mornings on Horseback*, p. 142.

9. A letter in the Society for the Preservation of Long Island Antiquities' archives dated July 5, 1855, from Caleb Swan to his nephew, Edward, owner of one of Oyster Bay's first country houses, documents the rapidity of travel by rail. Caleb informs his nephew of his safe return to the city following a stay in Oyster Bay but complains that the train which left Syosset depot at 7 a.m. was slow and he had not reached his townhouse in lower Manhattan until 9:45 a.m., a half hour later than usual. When one realizes that Caleb crossed the East River by boat before boarding a horse-drawn omnibus, the achievement is even more remarkable.

10. Anna Bulloch Gracie to Corinne Roosevelt Robinson, undated letter of 1886, TR Collection.

11. Townsend's Simcoe House in Oyster Bay was the village's largest, while Jones's Laurelton Hall, a one-hundred room hotel on the west side of Cold Spring Harbor, was the region's newest, having been built between 1872–73 on the site of his father's country house.

12. Wm. Mitchell, Referee, Edward M. Townsend, Queens County Probate Liber 256'163. Later rented by the J. West Roosevelts, this house was dubbed Imbecility by the family.

13. Anna Bulloch Gracie to Corinne Roosevelt Robinson, dated Gracewood, June 12, 1887, TR Collection. Although no views of the first Cruger house survive, its site was later occupied by the Pierce-Williams mansion.

14. McCullough, *Mornings on Horseback*, p. 221.

15. W. P. Stephens, *The Seawanhaka Corinthian Yacht Club: Origins and Early History 1871–1896* (New York: Privately printed, 1963), p. 13.

16. Anna Bulloch Gracie to Corinne Roosevelt Robinson, TR Collection.

17. *New York Tribune*, December 28, 1876.

18. *New York Sun*, December 29, 1876.

19. Ibid., *New York Tribune*, December 28, 1876; *New York Herald*, December 28, 1876.

20. *A History of the Union League Club* (New York: Dodd, Mead, 1963), pp. 126–29.

Edith Kermit Carow Roosevelt in 1900. Theodore Roosevelt called this the "goddess" picture; it was his favorite photograph of his wife.

4

A Tale of Two Roosevelts

Richard W. Turk

There are two images of Elliott Roosevelt. The first is that of Theodore's brother, companion of his youth, sportsman, traveler, socialite, loving father of Eleanor—subject to mysterious seizures, fated to die at a tragically early age. The other Elliott carried within himself the seeds of his own destruction. He was unable to develop any purpose in life, ran with a fast crowd of young socialites, began to drink heavily, and in time involved himself and the family in a series of embarrassing episodes by fathering a child out of wedlock, and contesting all attempts to get him to seek help. Ultimately, he was forced to separate from his wife and children to die a hopeless alcoholic at age thirty-three. This chapter explores the origins of both images.

The point at which to begin is among those who were contemporaries of Elliott. Who better than his brother? Theodore Roosevelt's autobiography is disappointing in this respect. Although he mentioned that he had two sisters and a brother, that is as close as he came to discussing Elliott in direct fashion at all.[1] The family members he did discuss were his father Theodore ("the best man I ever knew"); his mother, Martha Bulloch Roosevelt; his maternal grandmother, Martha Stewart Elliott Bulloch; his maternal aunt, Anna Bulloch Gracie; and his maternal uncles, James Dunwoody Bulloch and Irvine Stephens Bulloch.

One can infer Elliott's presence in TR's autobiography. For instance, he referred to hunting with the Meadowbrook hounds; Elliott was a member of the Meadowbrook hunt. TR mentions his preference for rowing over sailing; Elliott was the sailor in the family, as his sister Corinne attested.[2] Could Theodore have had his brother in mind when he later noted that a "cruel, selfish, . . . licentious" individual was an "abhorrent member" of the community? He had only "scorn and contempt" for a brutal husband—a man who failed to show "full loyalty and consideration" to his spouse. "Moreover, he must work, he must do his part in the world."[3] If indeed he had Elliott in mind as these lines were penned, fifteen years after Elliott's death, it suggests that the scars had not yet healed.

Elliott's sister Corinne did mention him in her account of Theodore. Martha Bulloch was quoted at the time of the family's first trip to Europe in 1869, "Elliott is the leader of children's sports."[4] Corinne herself noted that her brother Elliott was "always the leader" in contests of running and racing and leaping, although Teedie "did his part whenever his health permitted."[5] She also devoted some space to the three younger children's sojourn in Dresden during the second European trip. At the time of her father's death in 1878, she noted how Elliott's "young strength was poured out to help his father's condition."[6] Corinne also wrote about the hunting trip Elliott and Theodore took together in September-October 1880. Then silence descended—broken only by mention of Elliott's death. "No one, not even my brother Theodore himself, was ever more loved by those with whom he came in contact than was the 'Ellie' of the early days in 20th Street." TR himself had written her then: "I know how you loved Elliott; what a gallant, generous, manly boy he was. So many memories come back to me."[7]

The first volume of *The Letters of Theodore Roosevelt* also dealt circumspectly with Elliott. There are no letters from Theodore to Elliott included. Only in letters to his sisters, Anna and Corinne, was Elliott mentioned at all during the last fifteen years of the latter's life. If Elliott's health was a matter of growing concern to the family, no mention of it occurred in the *Letters* until the summer of 1889: "poor, dear old Nell; I suppose it is useless to wish that he would put himself completely under a competent physician; I did my best to get him to."[8] One must read between the lines to learn of Anna's trip to Europe to help Elliott and his family in February 1891. There is no mention whatever of Theodore's trip to Paris to confront Elliott the following January. In a letter to Anna just before Elliott's death, TR wished that "Corinne could get a little of my hard heart about Elliott; she can do, and ought to do, nothing for him. He can't be helped, and he must simply be let go his own gait."[9] Two weeks later, he wrote: "Elliott is up and about again; and I hear is already drinking heavily; if so he must break down soon. It has been as hideous a tragedy all through as one often sees."[10] This grim assessment was all too accurate; Elliott died two days later.

It was in his daughter Eleanor's recollections that Elliott's personality began to emerge. First to appear in 1933 was *Hunting Big Game in the Eighties: The Letters of Elliott Roosevelt, Sportsman.* Eleanor acquired her father's letters from various sources, primarily from other family members. She did not believe that they possessed any historical importance, but thought their publication would have some interest to the reading public as well as among the Roosevelts. The letters began with one dated June 1, 1873, written from Dresden when Elliott was thirteen. There also were letters written during a trip Elliott made to northern Florida (February–March 1875), during his brief sojourn at St. Paul's School (September–October 1875), two trips to Texas and the Southwest (January–March 1876; winter-spring 1877), the trip to India (November 1880–spring 1882), and a sprinkling of letters from 1883 to 1889. Eleanor suggested that her father's "rather gay, sporting life" began to take a toll upon his health. She attributed it in part to "his Indian fever."[11] Elliott's letters to his daughter completed the collection. The first was dated October 9, 1892, and the last August 13, 1894.

In the initial volume of her memoirs, *This Is My Story,* published in 1937, Eleanor became more explicit about her father's illness. Although uncertain as to its cause, and claiming she herself had not realized "anything was wrong," her father, she said, began to drink, ushering in a "period of harrowing anxiety [for the family] which was to last until his death in 1894."[12]

Nonetheless, through Eleanor's eyes, Elliott's good qualities far outweighed the bad. The word "love" is dominant. In both books she referred to her father as "the one great love of my life."[13] He was described as "kind," "good looking," and possessed of a "charming personality."[14] Thus the tendency of those family members who knew and loved Elliott—his daughter Eleanor in particular—was to protect, to repress, to deny that anything was seriously wrong. Roosevelt biographers would be less charitable.

Joseph Lash was one of the first to present a reasonably complete picture of Elliott Roosevelt. The picture that emerged troubled him. The "promise" of his early years gave way to the pathos of "wasted talents," and that in turn to the "stark tragedy of an enormously attractive man bent on self destruction." What was it, he asked, that made Theodore strong and Elliott weak?[15]

Lash suggested that several factors contributed to Elliott's weakness: his father's early death; the inheritance which permitted Elliott to live in "the exciting world of society and sport"; having to live with a brother who "always thought he could do things a little better than anyone else"; and, finally, his drinking.[16] Lacking "that foolish grit of Theodore's," Elliott "was incapable of sustained effort except in sports, and followed the easier and ever more tempting path of achieving success and approval through his charm and his accomplishments as sportsman and man-about-town."[17] Lash thus set the stage for his subsequent account of Elliott's "crack-up," the breakup of his marriage, and his early death. The latter, he suggested, "made it possible for his daughter to maintain her dream-picture of him." Yet there was another image which occasionally surfaced: an image of "the father who lacked self control, who could not face responsibility, who expected to be indulged."[18] It adds up to a considerable indictment—one that other biographers have embellished but not altered.

In Edmund Morris's *The Rise of Theodore Roosevelt* and Sylvia Jukes Morris's *Edith Kermit Roosevelt,* it was Elliott's "crack-up" that received the most attention: the flight to Europe in 1890, the breakup of the family, the paternity case involving the servant girl Katy Mann, and the public squabble over Elliott's estate. In Edmund Morris's unsparing judgment, Elliott wanted it all: "to hold on to his wife and children as symbols of respectability, to drink as much as he liked, sleep with whomever he pleased, and squander his money on himself, rather than alimony and paternity suits."[19]

David McCullough's *Mornings on Horseback,* by contrast, gave a portrayal of Elliott upon his return from India in 1882. He commented upon "Elliott's effortless charm, his generosity and humor, his way of talking to people . . . [which] made him so very attractive." Elliott "had none of the self-righteousness which in his brother put some people off; and little or none of Theodore's combativeness or bombast." Perhaps he belonged, "like some of his Bulloch forebears" with "the young bloods at the Savannah Club." This was not unflattering. Yet in the book's afterword McCullough noted succinctly: "Elliott's tragic life ended in August 1894, at age thirty-four, after a tortuous battle with alcoholism."[20]

Another extended portrait of Elliott appeared in Geoffrey

Ward's *Before the Trumpet*. Ward suggested that Elliott realized "he would never be able to hold his own in the loving but relentless competition that characterized life among the Oyster Bay Roosevelts." Even more significantly, Ward observed that although Elliott "claimed never to be jealous of his brother's successes" his "tributes" to Theodore were suspect. Ward, in fact, believed Elliott had become envious of "the older brother who seemed always able to do everything better than he could."[21] The balance of Ward's account, based substantially upon Eleanor's recollections and Lash's biography, contains the familiar story of Elliott's marriage to Anna Hall and the events which followed.

Lash himself meanwhile had returned to the subject of Elliott in the opening chapter of *Love, Eleanor*. His summation goes beyond other interpretations (including his own earlier one) to probe Elliott's psyche. Recognizing the "great love and fellowship" that once had existed between the two brothers, Lash observed that "as they grew to adulthood" it was impossible for Elliott to "live up to the image of a man that society demanded and his brother epitomized." Elliott's "effeminate characteristics"—his ambivalence, his gentleness, his spontaneity—were at odds with the values of late Victorian American society, " and this may have been the root of his nervousness, the explanation of his illnesses, . . . his self destructive alcoholism and addiction to drugs."[22] Where then does all this leave us?

Part of the tragedy of Elliott Roosevelt's life lies in the fact that Theodore was his brother, and Eleanor his daughter. Their prominence ensured that his life and accomplishments would be measured against theirs; his deficiencies compared with their strengths. Despite the initial efforts of those who knew him best—Anna, Corinne, Theodore, Eleanor—to obscure certain aspects of his life (both because of the very real pain of recollection, and with an understandable desire to preserve the reputation of the family), the path initially blazed by Joseph Lash would be followed and embellished by other Roosevelt biographers.

In doing so, the biographers concentrated on the latter stages of Elliott's life at the expense of the earlier. Little detailed analysis has been made of the first two decades. Where he appears, it is as "Theodore's brother"—almost as if he had no independent personality or life of his own. A few writers mention Elliott's trip to India, but with the exception of McCullough none deal with it prominently.

When Elliott is encountered, usually about the time of his marriage to Anna Hall, he already "has begun to drink heavily," and is spending much of his leisure time with the Meadowbrook crowd. Thus there is perhaps some sadness, but little surprise, at Elliott's subsequent deterioration and collapse. The real human tragedy which is occurring takes on elements of caricature.

Elliott's problem of substance abuse needs to be placed within the context of his time—much as McCullough has done in connection with Theodore's asthma.[23] To what extent was alcoholism considered a disease; to what extent merely a character defect? How successful were attempts at control? Was there a significant degree of recidivism? When and under what circumstances did substance abuse become a problem for Elliott? How prevalent was alcoholism in American society?

Greater attention needs to be paid to Elliott's early life. There is much in the Roosevelt collection at Harvard and the FDR Library at Hyde Park that bears upon it which has been underutilized if indeed utilized at all. Not only might these materials yield answers to some of the questions already posed, but they may also help restore some balance to the portrayal of Elliott.

A significant component of this needed reappraisal lies within the extended Roosevelt family and, in particular, in the developing relationship between Elliott and Theodore. Elliott, because of his physical prowess and better health, may have been "older brother" for a time. He was a better swimmer and sailor; he could run faster; he was a superior horseman and sportsman. Yet in time, and for a multiplicity of reasons, Theodore became in fact what he was by birth—older brother and eventually head of the family.

Corinne Roosevelt, writing to her fiancé Douglas Robinson in 1881, commented how Elliott had been "such a loving tender brother" to her. "How different people are," she mused. Teddy is "devoted to me too, but if I were to do something that he thought very weak or wrong, he would never forgive me, whereas Elliott, no matter how much he might dispise [sic] the sin, would forgive the sinner."[24]

A letter to Elliott from his Aunt Ella in 1882 also is illuminating. She recounted to him a conversation with his brother "mostly about you darling":

> We gloried in you together—Teddie exclaiming "What a
> fellow that is!" Then he told me of your little hunting trip
> together [1880], & of his curiosity in the beginning to see
> what kind of sportsman you were, as he had hunted with all
> the boys & beaten them. But he said he had to frankly
> acknowledge that you were not only far the better shot—but
> had infinitely greater & better powers of endurance.
> Described to me some of the little episodes of your trip, &
> spoke of you with such intense brotherly pride. From this we
> passed on to the "other battles" & yours & his future & I was
> so glad to find that Teddie too thinks so highly of your great
> power of influence with others. He spoke of the differences
> between you in this respect, with such noble generous
> warmth & said that where he would naturally wish to
> surpass other men he could never hold in his heart a jealous
> feeling towards you.[25]

Both letters say as much about Theodore Roosevelt as they
do about Elliott. The Roosevelt boys were no strangers to sibling
rivalries. Unlike some sibling rivalries, theirs continued long after
both boys matured. His occasional disclaimers notwithstanding,
there literally was no area in which Theodore was willing to
recognize or accept his brother's superiority. Surely over time this
took its toll upon Elliott. Add to this TR's well-developed sense
of righteousness and morality and you have the likelihood that
Theodore himself was part—a large part—of Elliott's problem. If
Theodore truly grieved for his brother, the grief ought to have
been tinged by remorse.

NOTES

1. Theodore Roosevelt, *An Autobiography* (New York: Macmillan
Company, 1913), p. 6.
2. Ibid., pp. 34, 36.
3. Ibid., pp. 177–78.
4. Corinne Roosevelt Robinson, *My Brother Theodore Roosevelt*
(New York: Charles Scribner's Sons, 1921), pp. 42–43.
5. Ibid., p. 46.
6. Ibid., pp. 104–5.
7. Ibid., pp. 156–57. Corinne confused the year of Elliott's death
(1894) with that of her aunt Anna Bulloch Gracie, who died in 1893.
Corinne's older sister Anna, who was much less sympathetic toward
Elliott, hardly mentioned him at all in the collection of Theodore's
letters to her, published shortly after TR's death. See Anna Roosevelt
Cowles, ed., *Letters from Theodore Roosevelt to Anna Roosevelt Cowles,
1870–1918* (New York: Charles Scribner's Sons, 1924).

8. Theodore Roosevelt to Douglas and Corinne Robinson, July 28, 1889, in *The Letters of Theodore Roosevelt*, ed. Elting E. Morison, 8 vols. (Cambridge: Harvard University Press, 1951–54), 1: 174.

9. Theodore Roosevelt to Anna Roosevelt, July 29, 1894 in Morison, *Letters*, 1: 392.

10. Theodore Roosevelt to Anna Roosevelt, August 12, 1894, in Morison, *Letters*, 1: 393.

11. Anna Eleanor Roosevelt, ed., *Hunting Big Game in the Eighties: The Letters of Elliott Roosevelt, Sportsman* (New York: Charles Scribner's Sons, 1933), p. 166.

12. Eleanor Roosevelt, *This Is My Story* (New York: Harper and Brothers, 1937), p. 8.

13. Roosevelt, ed., *Hunting Big Game*, p. viii; Roosevelt, *This Is My Story*, p. 8.

14. Roosevelt, ed., *Hunting Big Game*, p. 181; Roosevelt, *This Is My Story*, p. 6.

15. Joseph P. Lash, *Eleanor and Franklin: The Story of Their Relationship Based on Eleanor Roosevelt's Private Papers* (New York: W. W. Norton and Co., 1971), p. 3.

16. Ibid., p. 10.

17. Ibid., p. 11.

18. Ibid., p. 57.

19. Edmund Morris, *The Rise of Theodore Roosevelt* (New York: Coward, McCann and Geoghegan, 1979), p. 440. See also Sylvia Jukes Morris, *Edith Kermit Roosevelt: Portrait of a First Lady* (New York: Coward, McCann and Geoghegan, 1980), pp. 133–36, 140–44.

20. David McCullough, *Mornings on Horseback* (New York: Simon and Schuster, 1981), pp. 246–47, 368. Carleton Putnam's biography of TR contains a good account of the trip the two brothers took to hunt in the Midwest in August and September 1880; otherwise he has little to say of Elliott. See Carleton Putnam, *Theodore Roosevelt: The Formative Years, 1858–1886* (New York: Charles Scribner's Sons, 1958), pp. 202–8.

21. Geoffrey C. Ward, *Before the Trumpet: Young Franklin Roosevelt, 1882–1905* (New York: Harper and Row, 1985), pp. 260, 262.

22. Joseph P. Lash, *Love, Eleanor: Eleanor Roosevelt and Her Friends* (Garden City, NY: Doubleday and Co., 1982), pp. 16–17.

23. McCullough, *Mornings on Horseback*, pp. 90–108.

24. Corinne Roosevelt to Douglas Robinson, March 14, 1881, Papers of Corinne Roosevelt Robinson, Roosevelt Family Papers, Houghton Library, Harvard. It is only fair to note that she recanted her observation of TR in a letter to Douglas Robinson of March 31, 1881.

25. Ella (Mrs. Irvine T.) Bulloch to Elliott Roosevelt, January 8, 1882, Papers of Elliott Roosevelt, Sr., Roosevelt Family Papers Donated by the Children, FDR Library, Hyde Park, NY. The complete letter is reproduced in *Hunting Big Game*, ed. Eleanor Roosevelt, pp. 141–44.

5

Portrait of a First Lady

Sylvia Jukes Morris

Shortly after the death of Theodore Roosevelt, the historian, W. R. Thayer, wrote to his widow, Edith. "He would have been less, but for you. We old friends always knew this and we were silently grateful to you."*

Although contemporaries recognized Edith Kermit Roosevelt's importance to the twenty-sixth president, subsequent generations have tended to overlook her. She thwarted would-be biographers by being that strange anomaly, a public figure who remained private in the glare of the spotlights. She granted no interviews, disliked being photographed, and protected her children from the overly curious. "One hates to feel that all one's life is public property." Nor was she a political activist in the manner of her niece, Eleanor Roosevelt. Only after her death, when her diaries and letters surfaced, was it possible to give her the place she deserves in the gallery of presidential wives.

Yet hers is first and foremost a love story, for from early infancy she adored Theodore Roosevelt. Much as she cared for her children, and shattered as she was by two world wars, the relationship with him was paramount.

Edith was just forty when the assassination of William McKinley had catapulted TR into the position of chief executive. Although she had already spent twelve years in public life, in the White House she visibly blossomed. The president relied on her wisdom particularly in the choice of political appointments. He said that whenever he went against her advice, he made a mistake. "We all knew," their daughter Ethel once said, "that the person who had the long head in politics was Mother." The

---

* For sources, see Sylvia Jukes Morris, *Edith Kermit Roosevelt: Portrait of a First Lady* (New York: Coward, McCann and Geoghegan, 1980, and Vintage paperback, 1990). This essay is adapted from a slide lecture Mrs. Morris presented at the Theodore Roosevelt Conference.

columnist Mark Sullivan, wrote that she was, in the opinion of many, "greater among women than her husband among men."

Edith Kermit Carow was born on August 6, 1861 in Norwich, Connecticut. Her maternal grandfather, General Daniel Tyler, in whose house she spent her early years, was an expert in artillery and the smelting of iron, and he served in the Army of the Mississippi during the Civil War. Edith inherited his stately demeanor and sapphire blue eyes, as well as a small annuity which would keep her financially independent.

Her paternal grandfather, Isaac Carow (of French Huguenot descent), was a merchant prince, whose fleet of ships transported such cargo as ivory combs, violin strings, sugar, and blackstrap molasses between England, New York, and the West Indies. He bequeathed Edith his impressive library along with a cellar of fine Madeira wines.

Edith's mother, Gertrude, was a plain woman educated in the finest schools of New York and Paris. Although her singing voice was of operatic quality, she never performed professionally. After the births of Edith and her other daughter Emily, she became increasingly melancholic and hypochondriac. The excessive gambling and drinking habits of her husband, Charles, exacerbated these traits.

Under Charles Carow's mismanagement, the shipping line collapsed. By the time Edith was six years old, the family never owned a house of their own. In summer, they stayed with the Tylers in Red Bank, New Jersey, and in winter with an aunt in New York City.

Charming and erudite when sober, Charles taught Edith Latin, horseback riding, and how to identify birds and plants. He also encouraged her love of theater, so that after his early death she had only fond memories of him.

During Edith's months in New York, she attended the Roosevelt's nursery school in their brownstone on East 20th Street. Since she was always neatly dressed and meticulous in her habits, her classmates called her "Spotless Edie." A shared love of books and nature drew her so close to "Teedie," the Roosevelt's oldest child, that he missed her badly during a European trip. "Her face," he wrote when shown a picture of Edith, "stirred up in me homesickness and longings for the past. . . ."

As adolescence approached, the two friends enrolled in Mr. Dodsworth's famous school for dancing and deportment on 26th

Street and Fifth Avenue. Here they learned to waltz and polka and how to conduct themselves in society. Edith was in demand as a partner, but Theodore usually won out. On her dance programs, his name appeared more often than any other.

For regular schooling, Edith attended Miss Comstock's, an exclusive private establishment on West 40th Street, near the New York Public Library. She continued with Latin, and became fluent in French, but her best subject was English literature. She loved Shakespeare, and knew *As You Like It* and *Macbeth* by heart. A copy of the complete plays accompanied her everywhere, and Theodore always said she was the most cultivated person he knew.

In the summer of 1878, two years after Theodore went to Harvard, he and Edith quarreled. The break came, according to him, because "both of us had tempers that were far from being of the best." Soon afterwards, Theodore fell in love with a tall, fair Bostonian named Alice Hathaway Lee. "You see that girl there," he said to a friend. "She won't have me, but I will have her."

And, after graduating, he did. At the wedding, Edith Carow reportedly "danced the soles off her shoes"—more likely in frustration than happiness. At the same time, she never doubted that some day, somehow, she would marry Theodore Roosevelt.

Before the newlyweds could move into Leeholm, their hilltop house at Oyster Bay, Alice died of Bright's Disease, having given birth to a daughter named after her. Devastated by her death, and that of his mother on the same day, Theodore went West to be a rancher. In his absence, builders completed the Long Island house with its spectacular views of the Sound. On his return, Theodore changed its name to Sagamore Hill, after an Indian chief who once lived nearby.

If Edith wondered what a widower with only one child wanted with a twenty-two room country mansion, she had scant opportunity to ask. Theodore had told his sisters, Bamie and Corinne, that during visits East he preferred not to see Miss Carow. He did not believe in second marriages, and perhaps feared the reawakening of romantic feelings.

But one day in the fall of 1885, either by chance or design, the old friends bumped into each other as Edith left Bamie's house. She was now a poised, fresh-complexioned twenty-four-year-old with chestnut hair and a gentle smile. Long-suppressed emotions surfaced, and soon after this encounter they began

meeting—clandestinely at first in the Carow's parlor on East 36th
Street. By the time they appeared together at a Sagamore Hill
Hunt Ball, they had secretly agreed to marry. Edith, meanwhile,
would go ahead with plans to live—more economically—abroad
with her mother and sister, and Theodore would return
temporarily to North Dakota.

To everyone's surprise, the *New York Times* announced the
pending nuptials. Theodore suspected a servant, who had seen
frequent envelopes addressed to Edith, of leaking the news. In a
letter of apology to Bamie, Theodore rebuked himself for his
inconstancy. "Were I sure there were a heaven, my one prayer
would be that I would never go there, lest I should meet those I
loved on earth who are dead." Nevertheless, he told his sister, it
was true that later in the year he intended to marry.

Edith wrote frequently from London, and in one of her few
letters to survive said: "You know I love you very much and
would do anything in the world to please you. You know all
about me, darling; I never could have loved anyone else. I love
you with all the passion of a girl who has never loved before."
And then she added: "And Mama says I must tell you that I am
very practical and know a great deal about money."

This was a timely boast, for Theodore was about to lose half
of his cattle, or a quarter of his patrimony, in a catastrophic
Badlands winter. It would be left to Edith to make order of his
ravaged finances.

The wedding of Theodore Roosevelt to Edith Carow took
place on December 2, 1886, in St. George's, Hanover Square,
London, during a fog. On the way to the church, Theodore's best
man, the English diplomat Cecil Spring-Rice, darted from the
carriage to buy him a pair of gloves. As Edith walked up the misty
nave, all she could see, iridescent in the gloom, was Theodore's
orange haberdashery.

During a three-month honeymoon in Europe, Edith became
pregnant. With this pending addition to the family, the question
then arose of what was to become of Baby Alice. Theodore had
cavalierly given her to the unmarried Bamie to take care of, and
he assumed this arrangement would continue. But Edith insisted
on raising the child as her own.

In the first two years of their marriage, Theodore
supplemented his income by writing articles, as well as a
substantial history, *The Winning of the West*. Being appointed Civil

Service commissioner in 1889 gave him a regular salary, and, for the winter months, he moved his family to a rented house in Washington.

Edith enjoyed the sophisticated social life of the capital and soon became a member of the cultivated group which assembled at the LaFayette Square house of Henry Adams. But motherhood rapidly became her chief preoccupation. Between 1887 and 1897, she gave birth to five children. Ted came first, followed by Kermit in 1889, Ethel in 1891, Archie in 1894, and then Quentin. (In the White House a final pregnancy ended in miscarriage.)

When Theodore became governor of New York in 1899, his money worries ceased. With a salary of $10,000 (comparable to over $100,000 now) and a large architectural folly of a house with eighteen bedrooms, which was heated at state expense by 350 tons of coal a year, Edith settled in happily with her six "bunnies." She left Albany with reluctance when Theodore was tapped for the vice presidency in 1901, and still thought fondly of those two years there even after the assassination of McKinley elevated her to the White House.

On a teenage visit to the Executive Mansion, Edith had been impressed by the splendid halls once roamed by Lincoln. Now, as its mistress, she found them gloomy with their dark frescoed ceilings and heavy Victorian furniture. More critical than the decor were the impossibly cramped second floor living quarters, and the inconvenience of having the president's office right next to the sitting room. Edith said it was worse than "living over the store."

Clearly, drastic changes were necessary, and she called in the New York architectural firm of McKim, Mead and White to draw up plans. Theodore prevailed on Congress to approve them and, in the summer of 1902, with a budget of over a half a million dollars, the work to restore the mansion as near as possible to its original classical design began.

Out went the fine Tiffany screen from the North Vestibule (never since found), and down came the large conservatory. Where the latter once stood, the architects followed a plan of Thomas Jefferson and constructed a colonnade to link a new West Wing of executive offices to the house. In the basement, in place of ducts and pipes, they carved out a series of elegant reception rooms, and Edith converted the corridor linking them into a gallery of portraits of First Ladies.

She kept in close touch with Charles McKim. "I do not like my writing desk at all," she wrote in response to one blueprint. "I think it ought to be made to match the furniture." In October, as the work neared completion, Edith ordered an inventory of all White House possessions, so that future presidents could not dispose of them at will.

One item hitherto "lost" to the White House was a lusty oil by George Watts entitled *Love and Life*, which Edith's prudish predecessors had banished to the Corcoran Gallery. She retrieved it and hung it directly opposite her own desk in the upstairs gallery at the heart of the living quarters. From here, having dispensed with the office of housekeeper, she supervised all activities, public and private, of the establishment.

The White House had not seen such an accomplished hostess since the days of Dolley Madison. To help her, she appointed a native Washingtonian, Isabelle Hagner, to be the first social secretary. To complement the cultivated Americans who graced her dinner tables (Henry James, Augustus St. Gaudens, Owen Wister, and John La Farge were among them), Edith ordered a complete set of Wedgwood china decorated with the Great Seal of the United States. This acquisition inspired her to collect at least one piece representing each previous administration. These acquisitions grew, and became the nucleus of the present Smithsonian White House china collection.

Friday evening "musicales" were a feature of the winter season under Edith's supervision. Several hundred guests assembled in the East Room to hear such artists as Ignace Jan Paderewski, Ferruccio Busoni, and the Vienna Male Voice Choir. The young Pablo Casals performed in the Roosevelt White House sixty years before he played for the John Fitzgerald Kennedys. Theodore was usually bored at these concerts: his idea of good music was a rousing Sousa march. His choice of a suitable gift for the classical musicians was a signed copy of his book, *The Rough Riders*.

Edith's day in the White House began with a family breakfast at 8:15. By 9:00, after a walk in the garden with Theodore, she was at her desk, clipping important articles from newspapers, answering letters, planning menus and guest lists, and scrutinizing the appointment schedule. Between 11:00 and 12:00 on Tuesdays she held lively discussions with cabinet members' wives. Theodore invariably brought guests to lunch at 1:30, and after that Edith received callers, or went "snooping" in search of antiques, for which she had an infallible nose.

At 4:00, mounted on her favorite horse Yagenka, she accompanied Theodore on his daily ride through Rock Creek Park. On these outings, she looked so young that people mistook her for the president's daughter. In Ethel's judgment, she was not a first-rate horsewoman because she did not hunt, but she handled her mount expertly. When she got back she read to the children, and afterwards joined Theodore and yet more guests for dinner.

Theodore enjoyed the role of chief executive as well as any president, but as the years in office took their toll, Edith noticed lines appearing on his face, and a paunch above his waistline. She might raise an eyebrow at twelve eggs for breakfast, and rich deserts with cream running over the side of the plate for lunch, but on the whole Edith believed that a man with a huge brain needed plenty of nourishment. Neither she, nor anyone except perhaps the doctor, knew that by the age of forty Theodore Roosevelt suffered from arteriosclerosis.

Early in TR's second term, attempting to lure him away from the cares of state, Edith bought a small hunting lodge on five acres of land in the foothills of the Blue Ridge Mountains 125 miles from the capital. It cost $195, and she named it "Pine Knot."

The lodge consisted of only one room on the ground floor and two bedrooms upstairs. There was a piazza with a hammock for reading, and woods for walking. Edith bought supplies of pork, ham, and codfish at a local store, and Theodore shot deer, partridge, and quail. He also prepared their two meals a day: steak and eggs for breakfast; chicken, corn bread, and wild strawberries for dinner. Edith did the washing up with water from a well. There was no electricity. After weekends here, Edith saw the lines fade and the color return to her husband's cheeks.

At the end of her seven and a half years in the White House, Edith received nothing but praise. The secretary of the Institute of Architects said that she had made the White House "a charming and refined mansion." Julia Foraker, wife of a senator hostile to TR, described her as "the loveliest and wisest of hostesses." To Henry Adams she was the best-read of companions, and Archie Butt, TR's military aide, wondered "when the White House would again have such a mistress." She was, he said, like "a luminiferous ether pervading everything and everybody."

Edith returned happily to Sagamore Hill. But the decade following was far from tranquil. World War I brought horrors beyond imagining for the Roosevelts. Archie was wounded in a leg and arm, and in the waning days of the conflict Quentin was shot down over German lines and killed. Intellectually, he was the brightest of the children, and the one most like TR. Both parents were heartbroken but showed no bitterness. "You can't bring up boys to be eagles," said Edith bravely, "and expect them to turn out sparrows." But Theodore knew she would carry the wound green to her grave.

He never recovered from Quentin's death himself, and after a series of illnesses he died of a pulmonary embolism at sixty, as he had predicted he would. His valet woke Edith to give her the news. In her diary for that day she wrote only "Theodore died at 4:00 a.m. Had had sweet, sound sleep."

"Live for the living," was Edith's motto and she spent her remaining twenty-nine years obeying it. She entertained children and grandchildren and travelled all over the world. "I have salt water around my heart," she often said. Ships were her favorite form of transport, and each winter she would sail off for the Caribbean, or Latin America or Greece. With Kermit, she took the Trans-Siberia Railroad across Russia, and she was in Japan just after the great earthquake of 1923.

In the late 1920s, Edith surprised everyone by buying a house in Brooklyn, Connecticut, once owned by her great-grandfather Tyler. Why, her family wondered, did she want to spend summers in a hot valley when she could be on the breezy shores of Long Island? "I love to see my grandchildren's little faces, but I prefer to see their backs," she joked. Perhaps, too, after some sixty years of Roosevelts, she felt a need to explore her own roots.

Resolutely private since the White House years, Edith nevertheless came out publicly in support of Herbert Hoover. She was annoyed at being mistaken for Franklin Delano Roosevelt's mother, and even his wife. In tones strongly reminiscent of British royalty, she spoke out for the Republican candidate in a Madison Square Garden broadcast. An accomplished and manipulative orator, she would ask, "Shall I make them laugh, or shall I make them cry?"

Old age brought physical ailments and World War II brought emotional traumas almost beyond endurance. All three

Edith Kermit Roosevelt
From a 1921 drawing by John S. Sargent

remaining sons enlisted. Archie was wounded in the same leg and arm as in World War I. Theodore, Jr., landed in Normandy on D-Day and soon after suffered a fatal heart attack. Kermit, in an alcoholic depression, shot himself while with the Army in Alaska. "You will know how the bottom has dropped out for me," he had written his mother on the death of TR, "for who has lost father has lost all."

One final horror disturbed Edith's last years. On August 6, 1945, her eighty-fourth birthday, the United States dropped the atom bomb on Hiroshima. Nagasaki followed three days later. For one who had lived through a Civil War and seventeen administrations of twenty-seven different presidents, seven of whom she had known personally, the nuclear holocaust was a gruesome finale.

In spite of this, and the deterioration of her heart, she continued to be interested in the world. When the famous photojournalist Stefan Lorant came to interview her, they sat before the fire at Sagamore Hill and he was enchanted by her conversation and spiritedness. "You know, Mrs. Roosevelt," he said, "if I were ten years older, I would propose to you." Quick as a whip she came back: "And if I were ten years younger, I would accept."

On September 30, 1948, Edith Kermit Roosevelt died peacefully in her sleep at the age of eighty-seven. She had always loved poetry, and one of her favorite verses, by Walter Savage Landor,* seems to sum up her life and character.

> I strove with none, for none was worth my strife;
> Nature I loved, and next to Nature, Art.
> I warmed both hands before the fire of life.
> It sinks, and I am ready to depart.

---

* "The Dying Speech of an Old Philosopher."

6

Cousins:
William Emlen Roosevelt, the Banker,
and Theodore Roosevelt, the Politician

Richard P. Harmond

Theodore Roosevelt was a remarkable man. He also belonged to a remarkable family. And it is worth emphasizing that, wholly aside from parents and siblings, members of that family, including a grandfather and several uncles and cousins, had a considerable impact on Theodore's life and career. One of these family members, William Emlen Roosevelt (1857–1930), was not only Theodore's first cousin, but also his close friend from their childhood to the end of TR's days.

Though the early years are not well-documented, there is little question that Emlen was one of Teddy's circle of youthful intimates. Soon after young Theodore founded his Roosevelt Museum of Natural History in 1867, Emlen gained admittance, and became the permanent secretary of the museum. Later, when the Roosevelts began summering at Oyster Bay, the cousins swam and sailed together and challenged each other in athletic contests. In 1878, Emlen accompanied Theodore on a hunting expedition to Maine and in 1879 he again joined Theodore on a trip to that state.[1]

The following year, Theodore took a different sort of trip—down the aisle to marry Alice Lee. And cousin Emlen was among the ushers at the celebration.[2]

In the meantime, Emlen had embarked on his career. With his education by private tutors completed, he joined his father, James Alfred (1825–1898), and uncle, Theodore Sr., in the family banking business, Roosevelt & Son. He began as a bookkeeper about 1875, but with the death of Theodore Sr. in 1878, was made a full partner. Emlen had found his niche as an investment banker. At his father's death in 1898, Emlen became the head of Roosevelt & Son, and at the same time, this austere and cautious man assumed his father's place at the head of the Oyster Bay Roosevelts.[3]

Of course, Theodore, an ebullient risk-taker, had staked out a different career course for himself. After graduating from Harvard in 1880, he studied law briefly at Columbia. He became disillusioned with—and perhaps bored by—the law, however, and gave up his studies.[4] He began attending meetings at Morton Hall, the District Republican Association on East 59th Street in Manhattan. Initially, Emlen and some other family members were none too happy about TR's entrance into politics. But they relented. And to encourage him, wrote Emlen many years later,

> I went with him into Morton Hall—and joined the ranks of the political workers. I dropped out after a year because I could not give the time to it and I did not relish the personnel of that organization. But Theodore stuck to it. He had the personality and the spirit and he was able to impress these people.[5]

He impressed other people as well, for in 1881 TR was elected for the first of three terms to the New York Assembly. Various appointed and elected governmental positions followed culminating in the presidency. Needless to say, Theodore had found his niche.

Despite their dissimilar callings, the cousins remained firm friends. Although Emlen had about as much use for politicians as Theodore had for financiers, the cousins corresponded, met when their schedules permitted, and, with their families, summered together at Oyster Bay where they had adjoining estates. Since they were in such different fields of endeavor, they were able to avoid the risk of being competitors. These two highly intelligent and strong-willed men complemented rather than competed with each other, as a family member has observed of their relationship.[6]

Their relationship was complementary in an additional sense. While Theodore was pursuing his career, Emlen was looking after his finances. By overseeing Theodore's trust account, Emlen, a shrewd and careful investor, freed TR of that burden (and doubtless did a better job of it than Theodore would have done). Moreover, Emlen offered his cousin personal advice on his finances (for instance, on budgeting his income and on the preparation of his will);[7] and provided kindred services such as paying TR's local taxes, covering an overdrawn checking account, and preparing his cousin's income tax returns.[8]

If Emlen was Theodore's personal banker, he found other roles to fill when his cousin became president, including that of cheerleader. In truth, Emlen took immense pride in Theodore's rise to the presidency. He wrote to TR shortly after had taken the oath of office in September 1901:

> I have bothered my head ever since you took the oath of office to know how to help but have not seen how. Perhaps the best thing I can do is not to give you all the advice I would like to. Perhaps I can only help in a minor way by taking some of the small worries off your shoulders. I do not know when your salary begins and can see your expenses begin at once. If you wish any ready money you had better let me furnish it than be under any pressure in the matter. Of course your family all feel a personal responsibility about your administration and for the honor of the name must be allowed to help.[9]

And help he did.

In the first place, Emlen was a generous campaign contributor. In 1903, when TR was anxious to secure the election to the New York Assembly of W. W. Cocks, a Nassau County Republican, who was short of campaign funds, Emlen contributed $600 for that gentleman's "election expenses."[10] The following year, with Theodore's election at stake, Emlen asked his cousin how much he wanted from him. And he did not protest when TR (who wrote that he hesitated "to take advantage" of Emlen's "kindness") suggested the sum of $3,000. Later in the year, Emlen gave another $500 "for the work in Nassau County."[11]

While these amounts may not seem large, they probably represented something of a strain on Emlen's resources. As he explained to TR in 1908, "During the past ten years I have so reduced my outside business to attend to family affairs and charities that I have not much business and must now set it going again."[12]

Another way Emlen sought to assist TR was with advice, particularly, though not exclusively, on economic matters. Once he even became involved in a well-intentioned, but potentially harmful diplomatic gesture.

In February 1906, Emlen alerted Theodore to a resolution adopted by the trustees of the Seawanhaka Corinthian Yacht Club (of which Emlen was an officer) to hold a race commemorating the anniversary of the meeting of the Russian and Japanese envoys at Oyster Bay (from whence a year earlier they had sailed to Portsmouth, New Hampshire). As Emlen explained the thinking of the trustees:

> The Seawanhaka Yacht Club wanted to hold this race and thought possibly they could get the Ambassadors of Russia or Japan, perhaps both, to take an interest. It seems popular with crowned heads to give cups for yacht races at present. While you are not personally mentioned in the matter, still we thought it right to consult with you before going on with the offer, and see if you had any objections. . . . Also, if you take sufficient interest, I would like to know if it would be proper for us to show your answer to this letter to the Ambasadors, that they might understand that, while not officially connected with the matter, it had your sympathy.[13]

"My advice," responded the president with some alarm, "would be very strongly not to try to get the Ambassadors or Russia and Japan to that race." Theodore continued:

> You could not do it unless I tendered them an invitation and that would make the whole matter official, and some very disagreeable incidents might occur, while in any event the precedent set would be unfortunate. . . . It is not a peace to which the Russians will look back with any satisfaction, simply because it is not a war to which they will look back with any satisfaction; while I have very strong reasons for disapproving of the proposition because everyone would inevitably attribute the whole move to me and say it was done to glorify myself.[14]

Thereupon the trustees abandoned their scheme for a "peace yacht race."

Emlen avoided further diplomatic ventures, and, save for occasional recommendations on officeholders, he kept clear of politics, too. He focused his advice on economic policy. The president, of course, had his own agenda, as well as other counsellors. Nonetheless, TR valued his cousin's opinions, and, at times, found them persuasive.[15]

Shortly after becoming president, for example, the *New York Times* reported TR as being in favor of a government-owned cable company between mainland United States and the newly acquired possessions of Hawaii and the Philippine Islands. Emlen read the report and, not unexpectedly, urged upon TR the advantages of a privately owned cable company. He wrote the president that neither the army or navy, both of which "wish the honor and glory of laying the cable," possessed the necessary expertise to carry out such a challenging task. He believed, too, that after being linked by cable with the Philippines, it was in "our commercial interest in the East," to be connected with Japan and China, "and, of course, no foreign government could permit for one moment the landing on their shores of a Government cable." However, he opined, "A private corporation, which would be subject to local law is entirely a different matter." He also pointed out tellingly that a government-owned cable company would be met "by the strongest opposition by some of the largest financial interests in the country," which, in turn, "will very much increase the difficulties of getting any part of the measure through Congress." Finally, Emlen asserted his belief "that in the hands of an American company the Government will be perfectly protected as to the speed and economy in sending of its messages and the mercantile community will get quicker and cheaper service."[16]

TR thanked Emlen "heartily" for his letter. "For various reasons," he wrote to his cousin, "including those you mention I do not believe that a Government owned cable is at the moment desirable. I may change my mind, but this is my present belief." Theodore did not change his mind, and in 1902 he granted a contract to lay a Pacific cable to Clarence Mackay's company.[17]

The year 1902 was notable for the other decisions by the Roosevelt administration. In February, the government announced that it would file a suit under the Sherman Antitrust Act to dissolve the Northern Securities Company—a giant holding company that aspired to create a transportation monopoly in the Northwest. And in October, TR settled the famous Anthracite Coal Strike. Both events, but especially the latter, were on Emlen's mind when, in November 1902, he wrote to TR:

> You are right in dealing with the trusts, but the greatest trust is the labor trust, and to a large extent the thinking community believe that it . . . is a more serious danger to the prosperity of the country; and is at present entirely uncontrolled, and that your attitude on the subject will have much to do with the lines along which the control will be exercised.[18]

TR replied:

> It is a little difficult to know how to phrase what you want phrased about labor because there is absolutely no way by which under our present Constitution Congress can reach

> what you desire. [Elihu] Root will be in this evening and I am
> going to see if I could at least express the needed truths, albeit
> in some general fashion.

Theodore might have added that it would have also been
politically difficult to do what Emlen wished. Still, in his
December 1902 message the president expressed the "needed
truths" by appealing to corporations and unions to

> refrain from arbitrary and tyrannous interference with the
> rights of others. Organized capital and organized labor alike
> should remember that in the long run the interest of each
> much be brought into harmony with the interest of the
> general public; and the conduct of each must conform to the
> fundamental rules of obedience to the law, of individual
> freedom, and of justice and fair dealing toward all.[19]

Not surprisingly, Emlen a banker, was prepared to offer his
advice to Theodore on the country's money and banking
problem. And as with his suggestions on a Pacific cable company
and labor unions, that advice was on the conservative side.
Eventually, a bolder policy was adopted than Emlen approved
of, or, in fact, than TR had at first contemplated.

There was wide agreement early in this century that among
the major problems facing the banking system was its lack of
"elasticity." The issuance of bank notes was at the time based on
the value of federal government bonds held by national banks.
More notes could only be obtained by acquiring additional
bonds, which meant that the amount of bank notes in circulation
was dependent on the federal debt, rather than on the currency
needs of business.[20]

How did the business community believe this difficulty
should be handled? In 1906 a currency committee of the
formidable New York Chamber of Commerce released a report
offering its solution to the "elasticity" problem. The committee's
plan, which was representative of current Wall Street thinking,
had two parts. The first, admittedly "radical" in character, dealt
with the possible establishment of a central bank under
government control. The second, more conservative, and by the
committee's reasoning more feasible part of the plan, proposed
that national banks, in times of stringency, be permitted to issue
supplemental currency based on a percentage of their general
assets. The additional note issue was to be taxed so that once the
days of credit stringency were passed, the supplemental currency
would be redeemed.[21]

Possible solutions to the currency problem were not confined to the Wall Street establishment. In October 1906, Charles H. Treat, an officer in the Treasury Department, submitted a memorandum to TR suggesting the use of clearinghouse banks as one possible answer. The memorandum offered another plan "by which banks, holding a specified proportion of their capital in bond secured circulation, should, under a graduated tax, be permitted to issue unsecured notes, the tax being high enough to retire the notes from circulation when no longer required."[22]

The president circulated Treat's memorandum among a small group of businessmen-advisers. One of them was Emlen, who, having gone over the document with a few "intimate friends," wrote Theodore in late October that in his opinion,

> to deal through Clearing House banks is not practicable. . . . The other plan of using unsecured but taxed currency, seems the most practicable one; but . . . it should not be issued for the purpose of giving banks additional profits, but to meet times of stringency; in reality it is an emergency currency.[23]

Some weeks later, in his December 1906 message to Congress, the president acknowledged the need for a more elastic currency, and drawing on the Treat memorandum, and the advice he had received from Emlen and others, presented to Congress a plan whereby,

> national banks should be permitted to issue a specified proportion of their capital in notes of a given kind, the issue to be taxed at so high a rate as to drive the notes back when not wanted in legitimate trade. This plan would not permit the issue of currency to give banks additional profits, but to meet the emergency presented by times of stringency.[24]

Before another year had passed, events overtook TR's proposal for an emergency currency. The panic of October 1907 demonstrated the defects in the banking system and rapidly created something of a consensus in the banking community favorable to extensive changes in that system.[25]

Emlen, however, was not convinced. On November 8, he informed his cousin that,

> My attitude toward currency reforms remains unchanged . . . we are better off without any at the present time, and difficult as the situation is, it should be worked out under present laws. It is the result of a financial debauch, and any of the measures I have heard proposed mean possible inflation, but, if the pressure is so strong that some emergency currency

must be provided, I have already indicated the only line along which I think it may even be reasonable possible to attempt it.[26]

TR concurred. "I feel as you feel," he wrote to his cousin on November 9,

that our present situation is the result of financial debauch, that is the result of extravagance and reckless speculation intensified by the effect of a few striking instances of dishonesty in high places. I do not think any currency law could guarantee us against a recurrence of these conditions; but as I am not an expert in finance, it is a matter of a good deal of difficulty for me to explain to those who claim to be, why I do not intend to back up these proposals.[27]

To which Emlen responded a few days later,

In regard to the currency matter . . . all this asset currency means inflation and while the conservative banks would not have it outstanding most of the time, the speculators would be inclined to always have some of it. And in an emergency . . . all the weak banks would have their emergency circulation out, and when the acute pinch came they would have no free assets which they could offer as security to the better banks who might wish to come to their rescue.[28]

Reflecting this viewpoint in his December 1907 Message to Congress, TR called for an "emergency currency" based on "adequate securities" and "issued under a heavy tax." This, of course, was the proposal found in the Treat memorandum, and in Theodore's Message to Congress a year earlier.[29]

The president soon changed his mind, however, as he was overtaken by congressional action. In January 1908, the powerful senator from Rhode Island, Nelson W. Aldrich, having conferred with New York's "distinguished financiers," introduced a bill which provided that any national bank could apply to the comptroller for the right to issue emergency currency secured by the deposit of state, municipal, or railroad bonds. Opposition, in considerable measure of a sectional nature, emerged against the Aldrich bill in the Senate, as well as in the House. Because of the dispute, the situation became increasingly complicated, and by April Emlen confessed to TR that, "I understand very little of what is going on in Washington."[30]

Meanwhile, the president, who was receiving conflicting advice from various quarters on the money issue, entered the fray.[31] He met frequently in April with Aldrich, House Speaker

Joseph Cannon, and George W. Perkins of J. P. Morgan and Company, and together they worked out a compromise. As a result, in May 1908, Congress passed the Aldrich-Vreeland Act. Intended as a temporary expedient, this piece of legislature: provided for an emergency currency (limited to $500 million) based on *any* securities held by a bank, whether state, city, town or county bonds, or commercial paper (these short-term notes were the chief stock in trade of Western banks); set up clearinghouse associations which each bank was required to join before receiving the right to issue such currency; and authorized the appointment of a National Monetary Commission to reform the U.S. banking system.[32]

Emlen probably was not all that pleased with the Aldrich-Vreeland Act.[33] As a banker he feared the measure's inflationary potential. And as a conservative he disliked change. All of which raises an obvious question: How did Emlen react to the Square Deal, and to his cousin's increasing progressive utterances during the last two years of his presidency?

Suprisingly, there was much in the Square Deal that Emlen supported. Thus, he declared himself "delighted" with most of TR's Message to Congress in December 1906, wherein the president recommended: an eight-hour day for American wage workers; an improved employer's liability law; a "drastic and thoro-going child labor law for the District of Columbia and the Territories"; the compulsory investigation of labor disputes; strengthening of the Pure Food Act; and enlargement of the powers of the ICC. The cousins agreed too on the desirability of the federal incorporation of the country's railroads.[34]

On the other hand, they did have their differences. Emlen took exception to Theodore's advocacy of a graduated inheritance and income tax. "As you know, I do not believe in graduated taxes," he wrote to TR once. "It is not the possession of wealth," he claimed, "but the use of it, that we should legislate about."[35] Again, in the spring of 1906, Emlen complained of what he thought was the efforts of soft-coal miners to establish the closed shop and he urged TR to make a statement in favor of the open shop. TR quickly rejected that idea, informing Emlen that "I do not think it would be wise to make such a statement—in fact I think it would be foolish." Emlen, deferring to his cousin's judgment, wrote that he agreed "it would not be wise" for the president to make such a declaration.[36] Unlike his cousin, Emlen never seems to have conceded a place for unions and big labor in U.S. industrial society.[37]

During the last year-and-a-half or so of Theodore's presidency, occasionally a certain edge crept into their exchanges. In May 1907, for example, Emlen lectured his cousin that,

> Legislation even the wisest and best where it necessitates a change in the methods that we use in the conduct of business is very disturbing, and much of the recent legislation in many parts of the country has been most unwise. Much of what you wish to accomplish has been done by establishment of higher standards of morality in business matters and except along the line of greater publicity in corporate conduct, I do not believe much can be wisely accomplished. The present moment does not seem opportune for new changes.[38]

TR thought otherwise. "To trust to the slow growth of high public spirit in Harriman and Company," he informed Emlen,

> is a little bit like the attitude of those men who cater to the labor vote in politics, who always state that we must trust to the growth of the spirit of order in mobs and try to quell them by the use of an efficient police force. It is no more possible to substitute the growth of morality for the interference of the Government in one case than in the other.[39]

Emlen returned to the same theme later in the year. Writing in October, during the gloomy days of the 1907 panic, he hoped

> there may be no unnecessary irritation of the situation, and for the next sixty days, I hope it will not be necessary for you to make many speeches. . . . Much as I sympathize with what you are trying to accomplish, I do not feel much can be done in the way of new legislation at the present time. We have gotten, to my mind, entirely beyond that, and must try to get people's minds quieted down, and financial matters running on a more tranquil basis.[40]

Nor was Emlen finished. In late October, he again stressed to his cousin the need for "as little uncertainty as possible as to the conditions under which business can be done, in other words, as little agitation for new laws and methods as possible." "I feel you have a responsibility for the future," he wrote pointedly to TR. "Now that evils are laid bare and the people have taken fright at what they see I think a change in your attitude should take place," Emlen insisted.[41]

Theodore acknowledged receipt of these messages, politely

asserted that he agreed "substantially" with what Emlen had
written, and expressed the hope that he would soon see his
cousin at Oyster Bay.[42] Of course, TR, as we well know, did not
change his attitude. And as far as we can tell, there were no
further epistolary lectures from Emlen during the remainder of
Theodore's presidency.

Clearly, neither man wished a quarrel. The bonds of family,
a long friendship, and mutual respect overrode the cousins'
philosophical differences. Moreover, while Emlen was
admonishing Theodore for his actions in Washington, D. C., he
was shielding his cousin's reputation from attacks in New York
City. Rumors on Wall Street that TR was "partially insane
through excessive drinking," roused Emlen to TR's defense. As
Theodore reported to Henry Cabot Lodge, in September 1907,

> You will be amused to learn that the attacks upon me have
> made dear, good Emlen and Christine [Emlen's wife] rabid
> advocates of me. Hitherto they have been earnest friends, but
> with an effort, because they did not approve of some of my
> public acts; but when they found their capitalist friends
> charging me with drunkenness and insanity, they began
> seriously to revise their estimate of these same capitalists.[43]

That fundamental loyalty was on display again when TR
resumed his political career in 1912. Whatever Emlen may have
thought of his cousin's political ideology—and one can easily
imagine at least a few items in TR's platform that Emlen
disapproved of—he liberally supported him in 1912. Emlen gave
$50,000 to the Bull Moose cause, ranking him among the seven
major contributors to TR's campaign.[44]

As it turned out, there were no further political campaigns for
Emlen to subsidize. Theodore did not again run for office after
the Bull Moose campaign.

No one can have an important political career without the
backing of family and friends. Theodore Roosevelt was fortunate
on both counts. Among these friends was his cousin, William
Emlen, who served TR in several significant ways. In the first
place, Emlen carefully managed Theodore's finances, relieving
him of that distracting, time-consuming, and sometimes
worrisome responsibility. Second, he acted as an informed and
trusted—if rather conservative—adviser to TR, on financial and
economic policy. Third, he contributed generously to Theodore's
campaigns. And last, Emlen, an admiring booster of his cousin,
lent TR the support and loyalty that one old friend always prizes

from another.

Be it said, too, that TR knew the value of the relationship. Now "my dear fellow," he once wrote to Emlen, "I wish you to understand that I appreciate the staunch and loving friendship you and yours have shown us during these years."[45]

As a memorial to that friendship, Emlen, after purchasing the property, set up a bird sanctuary in 1923 adjacent to Youngs Cemetery in Oyster Bay where Theodore was buried. It was a memorial, as the *New York Times* observed, that Theodore "would have liked," and that was "in every way fitting."[46]

Theodore Roosevelt's bookplate, showing the Roosevelt family coat of arms. The name Roosevelt means "field of roses" in Dutch and a field with roses is shown in the coat of arms. The family motto, *Qui Plantavit Curabit*, may be translated as "He Who Has Planted Will Preserve."

NOTES

1. Paul Russell Cutright, *Theodore Roosevelt: The Making of a Conservationist* (Urbana: University of Illinois, 1985), pp. 8, 74–76, 110–14, 122–23; *Theodore Roosevelt's Diaries of Boyhood and Youth* (New York: Charles Scribner's Sons, 1928), pp. 355, 361.

2. Nicholas Roosevelt, *Theodore Roosevelt: The Man As I Knew Him* (New York: Dodd, Mead, 1967), p. 21.

3. *New York Herald Tribune,* May 16, 1930; *New York World,* May 16, 1930.

4. David McCullough, *Mornings on Horseback* (New York: Simon and Shuster, 1981), pp. 279–80.

5. W. Emlen Roosevelt, "Early Recollections: Bankers" (typescript copy at the Theodore Roosevelt Association, Oyster Bay), p. 4.

6. Interview with Mr. P. James Roosevelt, Emlen's grandson.

7. William Emlen Roosevelt to Theodore Roosevelt (hereafter cited as WER to TR), June 24, 1918, Theodore Roosevelt MSS (Library of Congress: Microfilm edition). All subsequent correspondence, unless otherwise attributed, is from this source.

8. For example, WER to TR, Feb. 9; May 26, 1915; December 3, 1917; and April 17, 1918. John Gable informed me that at one point when TR was financially hard-pressed, Emlen came to his assistance by purchasing some Sagamore Hill acreage.

9. WER to TR, Sept. 26, 1901.

10. TR to WER, October 2, 1903, WER to George W. Davison, October 7, 1903.

11. WER to TR, May 16, 18, 1904; TR to WER, May 17, 1904; WER to TR, September 26, 1904.

12. WER to TR, April 15, 1908.

13. WER to TR, February 21, 1906.

14. TR to WER, February 22, 1906.

15. Nicholas Roosevelt, *Theodore Roosevelt,* p. 47.

16. *New York Times,* September 17, 1901; WER to TR, September 26, 1901, Roosevelt MSS.

17. TR to WER, September 27, 1901; Elting E. Morison, ed. *The Letters of Theodore Roosevelt,* 8 vols. (Cambridge: Harvard University Press, 1954), 3: 153.

18. WER to TR, November 25, 1902.

19. TR to WER, November 6, 1902; *Compilations of the Messages and Papers of the Presidents,* 20 vols. (New York: Bureau of National Literature, 1917), 15: 6,716.

20. See, Milton Friedman and Anna Jacobson Schwartz, *A Monetary History of the United States, 1867–1960* (Princeton: Princeton University Press, 1963), pp. 168–69.

21. *The Currency: Report by the Special Committee of the Chamber of Commerce of the State of New York* (New York, 1906), pp. 22–25, for the committee's summary.

22. Charles H. Treat ("Currency Reform") to TR, October 18, 1906. Whether Treat had read the Chamber of Commerce plan is unknown but clearly parts of his proposal were similar to the chamber's plan.

23. WER to TR, October 23, 1906. Emlen, who clearly deplored the fact, felt that "a certain amount of inflation" was all but inevitable with the issuance of an emergency currency (WER to TR, December 7, 1906).

24. *Compilations of Messages,* 16: 7,050.

25. James Livingston, *Origins of the Federal Reserve System: Money, Class, and Corporate Capitalism, 1890–1913* (Ithaca, NY: Cornell University Press, 1986), pp. 173–74.

26. WER to TR, November 8, 1907. At least in part, the president was correct in tracing the panic to "extravagance and reckless speculation" (Morison, *Letters of Theodore Roosevelt,* 5: 747).

27. TR to WER, November 9, 1907.

28. WER to TR, November 11, 1907.

29. Compilations of Messages, 16: 7,082.

30. Livingston, *Origins of the Federal Reserve System,* pp. 181–85; WER to TR, April 15, 1908.

31. Morison, *Letters of Theodore Roosevelt,* 6: 1,046.

32. Livingston, *Origins of the Federal Reserve System,* pp. 186–87.

33. There is no explicit correspondence on the issue but see Morison, *Letters of Theodore Roosevelt,* 6: 908. Actually, the Act headed off a more radical proposal that called for *replacement* of bond-secured with an asset currency.

34. *Compilations of Messages,* 16, 7,035–43; WER to TR, Dec. 7, 1906, March 28, 1907, and TR to WER, March 29, 1907, Roosevelt MSS.

35. WER to TR, December 7, 1906. TR eventually developed certain reservations about the income tax. Morison, *Letters of Theodore Roosevelt,* 8: 884.

36. WER to TR, April 3, 23, 1906, and TR to WER, April 20, 1906.

37. For Theodore's views of labor, consult, George F. Mowry, *The Era of Theodore Roosevelt,* (New York: Harper and Row, 1958), pp. 141–42.

38. WER to TR, May 24, 1907.

39. TR to WER, May 27, 1907.

40. WER to TR, October 22, 1907.

41. WER to TR, October 29, 1907.

42. TR to WER, October 24, 30, 1907.

43. Morison, *Letters of Theodore Roosevelt,* 5: 803. Several years later, TR took a Michigan editor to court for circulating a rumor that he got drunk "and that not infrequently, and all of his intimate friends knew about it" (Morison, 7: 671). Emlen, "greatly incensed" by this attack on his cousin, was among those who testified on TR's behalf. Since the editor could not produce a single witness to substantiate his charge, TR won his case. And at his request the court assessed the offending editor damages of *six cents.* As Theodore was unable to do so, Emlen paid to have the trial testimony printed in order "to have a complete copy of the official record which contradicts the libel." See, *Roosevelt vs. Newett: A Transcript of the Testimony taken and depositions read at Marquette, Michigan* (Privately printed, 1914).

44. John Gable, *The Bull Moose Years: Theodore Roosevelt and the Progressive Party* (Port Washington, NY: Kennikat Press, 1978), p. 181.

45. TR to WER, November 8, 1904.

46. *New York Times,* October 31, 1923.

7

Worthy Son of a Worthy Sire—The Early Years of Theodore Roosevelt, Jr.

Richard J. Loosbrock

In 1931 *Fortune* magazine described the Roosevelts as follows:

There is, of course, no laying down a specific description that will precisely fit every member of so large a clan. Yet one can describe "a Roosevelt" and be fairly sure that three out of four epithets hit the mark. In the first place a Roosevelt is likeable; the people who have to do with him become his friends and become warmly attached to him. He has a great deal of energy and vitality—there is not a Roosevelt whose biography isn't full of things that he has done and places he has been. He is . . . an extrovert. You will seldom find him occupied over matters of pure intellect: he has practical concerns. He is probably a merchant (in more recent times an engineer) or a banker, possibly a politician. His avidity for knowledge is really an avidity for experience—you will not find him in one of the learned professions. . . . The same qualities which determine his profession determine his amusements: he likes the out of doors, he likes the spice of danger, he likes to hunt game, and he is almost certainly skipper of a sailboat. What is more, he is well-to-do because his family has a high average of business competence.[1]

Although the writer probably had Theodore or Franklin in mind, the description also fitted Ted Roosevelt, eldest son of the former Republican president. He made his mark as a businessman, author, soldier, and explorer, as well as an administrator. He was as close to a Renaissance man as any of us are likely to meet in the twentieth century. Likeable (the number of people who considered him to be "my best friend" was considerable), energetic, practical, daring, poetical (his wife commented that he knew more poetry by heart than any person that she had ever known),[2] brave, and above all, an American, with American virtues and American values, Ted's early years foreshadowed a solid and distinguished career.

Theodore Roosevelt, Jr., was born on September 13, 1887, at

the family home at Oyster Bay. Until his father became more prominent, most of his time was spent there. An early letter, to his mother, possibly a school assignment, described a fight that he had with another small boy, whom he described as a "tuf," on the way home from dancing class.[3] His sister Alice described how Ted, during the 1896 presidential campaign, lectured the hired men and the maids at Sagamore Hill on the evils of William Jennings Bryan's concept of free silver, using money and a loaf of bread as props.[4] A year later his father described his eldest son as "more like me as I am now than as I was when I was his age. He is almost as fond of books, in fact quite as fond, but he is a tougher, hardier little fellow, more at home among other boys, and fonder of outdoor sports."[5] Despite this analysis, the father continued to impress his own style upon his son.

His father's role in the Spanish-American War undoubtedly had an effect upon the future military interests of the eldest son. One of Ted's early works of art was a colored drawing of his impression of the charge up San Juan Hill. On July 15, 1898, his father, in a letter headed "outside Santiago," described how well the Rough Riders had performed. Theodore Roosevelt also promised to give Ted his revolver and Kermit his sword ("unless I should have to carry them in another war"), while bemoaning the fact that he had nothing similar to give to Archie and Quentin at that time.[6]

Later, when Ted was strongly considering making application to either West Point or Annapolis, his father attempted to dissuade him. If he really wanted a military career, he should proceed. However,

> In the Army and the Navy the chance for a man to show great ability and rise above his fellows does not occur on the average more than once in a generation. When I was down at Santiago it was melancholy for me to see how fossilized and lacking in ambition, and generally useless, were most of the men of my age and over, who had served their lives in the Army.[7]

Apparently this helped to convince young Ted, who would follow his father's example through a keen interest in military affairs, but would serve on active duty only in times of national emergency. Throughout much of his youth, Ted Roosevelt was besieged by all sorts of illnesses, including boils, tonsillitis, and double pneumonia, to mention only a few. Perhaps the most serious was a succession of headaches which afflicted him while the family was living in Washington when his father was serving as President McKinley's assistant secretary of the Navy. After examining the boy, Dr. Alexander Lambert, who was a friend of Theodore, advised him that Ted was facing a nervous breakdown. The doctor warned the elder Roosevelt that he was pushing his son too hard, and received in return a promise that he would cease and desist. Theodore Roosevelt admitted that he had been tempted to push his son because he "has bidden fair to be all the things I would like to have been and wasn't."[8] This was an early recognition of what would be a constant theme in the relationship between this father and his eldest son: the father trying to make the son into the sort of youth that he wished that he had been, and the son attempting to emulate his father's life and accomplishments. Ironically, the son would ultimately outshine his father in military matters, receiving the same Medal of Honor that the elder desperately wanted, but failing in politics, a field in which the father excelled, but which the elder felt was a poor substitute for military glory.

After finally surviving all of his childhood diseases, Ted Roosevelt graduated from Harvard in 1908, and began working at the mill of a carpet factory in Thompsonville, Connecticut. Refusing an allowance from his family, he began at the bottom, earning seven dollars a week while demonstrating a real aptitude as a wool sorter, an ability that his wife later summed up as "totally useless in later life!"[9]

His courtship largely coincided with his days at the carpet factory. In 1910, a week after his father's triumphant return from his African hunting trip and European tour, Ted Roosevelt married Eleanor B. Alexander of New York City. The newspaper accounts of the wedding stressed the role of the groom's father and mentioned the hundreds of former Rough Riders who had come to greet their old leader and had stayed for the nuptials. An indication that the bride would fit into the Roosevelt family quite well was the mention that her entire trousseau was of American manufacture and labor.[10]

It was to be a long and happy marriage. It is a cliche of modern times, but Ted and Eleanor really were "best friends," and revelled in each other's company. Many of his letters contained the sentence, "I love you more than tongue can tell." Particularly in later years, she was frequently referred to as the "other Eleanor Roosevelt," but Ted's wife could and did take comfort in the fact that Herbert Hoover referred to her as "Eleanor the Good," in contrast to another Eleanor Roosevelt.[11]

The first years of their married life were spent in California, where Ted was assigned to the Hartford Carpet Company's San Francisco office. Not long after Woodrow Wilson became president, U.S. relations with Japan became tense over various bills designed to curb the holding of land by Japanese considered by the California legislature. Eleanor and Ted were on a visit to Sagamore Hill during this crisis. Although Theodore Roosevelt was quietly using his influence with his Japanese contacts and California Governor Hiram Johnson, his Progressive party running-mate, to quiet the waters, Eleanor was appalled to find that her father-in-law and husband were eagerly discussing the possibility of a war in which they both could participate. The father would raise and command the division, and the son would be a member of it. It was a precursor of similar events in 1917 and 1918.[12]

There seemed to be little future in the carpet business, so in 1912 Ted and Eleanor returned to New York, where he became a bond salesman and investment banker with Bertron Griscom and Company. This was only the means to the end. Ted had always hoped to go into public service of some sort, preferably elected office. Since he had no professional training, he threw himself into his work, in hopes that he would make enough money to provide for his family while he engaged in what he considered to be his patriotic duty.[13]

That patriotism was soon to be tested. With the outbreak of the war in Europe in 1914, the interest of some business and professional men turned to thoughts of some type of military training. The sinking of the *Lusitania*, in May 1915, brought their concerns to a head. Law partners Grenville Clark and Elihu Root, Jr. joined with Ted Roosevelt to consider plans for an uncertain future. Roosevelt's was the first of fifteen signatures to a telegram sent to President Wilson seeking assurances that similar future actions on the part of Germany would not be permitted. The Committee of 100 was formed, consisting largely of second-generation social and political gentlemen, mostly Harvard graduates under the age of 35. A military camp for college students was being held at Plattsburg Barracks that summer of 1915, and young Roosevelt took the lead in getting General Leonard Wood, his father's former commanding officer, to agree to a Business Men's Camp there also. Here young to middle-aged, reasonably well-to-do, socially prominent businessmen would pay their own expenses to learn the rudiments of military training to be ready for their country's call if and when it came.[14]

When the United Stated entered the war in April 1917, Ted Roosevelt was 29 years old, a successful banker, and a major in the Officer's Reserve Corps, having achieved this through successful completion of the 1915 and 1916 Plattsburg Camps. He was ordered to active duty at Plattsburg for another summer's training. Ted, for probably the only time in his life, asked his father to intercede and use his influence. Theodore Roosevelt wrote to General John J. Pershing, congratulating him on his selection as head of the American Expeditionary Force, and asking if Ted and his brother Archie could serve with Pershing's men in France as enlisted men, if reserve officers would not soon be going "over there."

Approval soon came. On June 20, 1917, Ted Roosevelt and his brother sailed for France to serve as officers in the American Expeditionary Force.[15] On July 4 he was in Paris. His brother's battalion participated in the famous "Lafayette, we are here" ceremony in Paris that day. Ted Roosevelt was concerned that the morale of the French was "in a bad way," and felt that the arrival of the Americans would help immensely. He also complained that the French "seem to regard a bath as unnecessary and all the world as a water closet."[16]

By August 1917, all of the four Roosevelt boys were in France. There was a female Roosevelt there as well. Eleanor Roosevelt, Ted's wife, was determined to be near her husband. Leaving their three children in her mother's care, she had volunteered to serve with the Y.M.C.A., the organization in charge of recreation for American soldiers in France, as a full-time volunteer.[17] In an exchange of messages in July, Ted had cabled, "Do not come until I cable." Eleanor came anyway, and was rewarded by a telegram from her husband welcoming her to France, saying "Simply delighted you are here. Felt sure you would come all along. You are to stay until the war is over."[18] Once again the couple's strong feelings for each other had been demonstrated.

Ted Roosevelt's war record was outstanding. He commanded the 1st Battalion, 26th Infantry, and later the entire regiment. His entire service was with the First Division, whose claim was that it was "First to Fight." He was gassed at Cantigny and received a machine-gun bullet through the leg at Soissons. Typically Ted managed to evade the usual medical evacuation system by catching a ride on an artillery limber, then in a motorcycle sidecar, and ultimately by borrowing an auto and driver from a high-ranking friend. He finally was carried into Eleanor's Paris apartment where he demanded a bath and food, rather than medical attention. Fortunately Richard Derby, his sister's husband who was a division surgeon, stopped by and ordered Ted to get proper medical attention.[19]

Ted Roosevelt received the Distinguished Service Cross, the Distinguished Service Medal, and the Purple Heart with Oak Leaf Cluster. But perhaps two other tributes pleased him even more than the official ones. His fifth cousin, Franklin D. Roosevelt, who now had his father's old job as assistant secretary of the Navy, came to France on an inspection tour, talked to both Ted and Archie, and later said that he envied them their uniforms, and added, "They both have really splendid records."[20] After the war he received a letter from the future General George C. Marshall, which stated that "your record as a fighting man [was] one of the most remarkable in the A.E.F.... among the finest examples of leadership, courage and fortitude that came to my attention during the war."[21]

With the war successfully concluded, young Roosevelt could now turn his attention to another matter that interested him, that of organizing an association of service veterans. As he wrote to his wife:

> We were talking over the affairs of the A.E.F. and the necessity for forming an association which would contain all those in the U.S. Army during this war, a sort of G.A.R., which should be in the proper hands and used for good things. I am going to start to work right away, but it is a terrific job and one that is pockmarked with difficulties.[22]

A morale conference in Paris was an opportunity for Colonel Roosevelt and about twenty other officers to issue a call for a caucus to be held there, March 15–17, 1919. This was the genesis of what was to become the American Legion.[23]

Ted Roosevelt returned to the U.S. in time to attend the domestic Caucus of the American Legion, held at St. Louis on May 8–10, 1919. He served as temporary chairman of the meeting, and could undoubtedly have been elected the first permanent chairman had he not withdrawn from the race, fearing that his name might inject a partisan political coloring to the proceedings. He did this in spite of an impassioned nominating speech by Sergeant Jack Sullivan of the state of Washington, who ended his oration with the ringing words, "I deem it an honor and a privilege . . . to place the worthy son of a worthy sire in nomination—Theodore Roosevelt, Junior."[24]

As soon as the American Legion seemed to be able to stand on its own two feet, Ted Roosevelt ceased to play a major role, although he had a continuing interest in the organization. He was now able to concentrate on what he believed would be the chief focus of his future career, that of public service, especially in the field of elective politics. The period of preparation was over. He was now ready to proceed with his effort to be truly "the worthy son of a worthy sire," in a career that would culminate on June 6, 1944 at wind-swept Utah Beach, when he won the Medal of Honor that his father had coveted.

NOTES

1. Quoted in Cleveland Amory, *Who Killed Society?* (New York: Harper and Brothers, 1960), p. 323.

2. Mrs. Theodore Roosevelt, Jr., *Day Before Yesterday, The Reminiscences of Mrs. Theodore Roosevelt, Jr.* (Garden City, NY: Doubleday and Company, 1959), p. 41.

3. Theodore Roosevelt, Jr., to Edith Kermit Roosevelt, n.d., Box 61, Theodore Roosevelt, Jr., Papers, Manuscript Division, Library of Congress, Washington, DC.

4. Alice Roosevelt Longworth, *Crowded Hours* (New York: Charles Scribner's Sons, 1933), p. 13.

5. Theodore Roosevelt to Mrs. Ellen L. Gray, March 31, 1897, Box 77, Theodore Roosevelt, Jr., Papers.

6. Theodore Roosevelt to Theodore Roosevelt, Jr., July 15, 1898, Box 61, Theodore Roosevelt, Jr., Papers.

7. Joseph B. Bishop, ed., *Theodore Roosevelt's Letters to His Children* (New York: Charles Scribner's Sons, 1929), pp. 85–86.

8. Hermann Hagedorn, *The Roosevelt Family of Sagamore Hill* (New York: Macmillan Company, 1954), p. 50.

9. Roosevelt, *Day Before Yesterday*, p. 45.

10. Various newspaper clippings, Box 63, Theodore Roosevelt, Jr., Papers.

11. Various letters from Eleanor Alexander Roosevelt to Herbert Hoover, File no. 3666, Herbert Hoover Presidential Library, West Branch, Iowa.

12. Hagedorn, *The Roosevelt Family*, p. 334.

13. Roosevelt, *Day Before Yesterday*, pp. 58, 60.

14. John P. Finnegan, *Against the Spector of a Dragon; The Campaign for Military Preparedness, 1914–1917*, Contributions in Military History,

No. 7 (Westport, CT: Greenwood Press, 1974), pp. 65–67; John G. Clifford, *The Citizen Soldiers: The Plattsburg Training Camp Movement, 1913-1920* (Lexington: University Press of Kentucky, 1972), pp. 54–57.

15. Frank E. Vandiver, *Black Jack; The Life and Times of John J. Pershing*, 2 vols. (College Station: Texas A. & M. University Press, 1977), 2: 692.

16. Theodore Roosevelt Jr., to Eleanor Alexander Roosevelt, July 4, 1917, Box 61, Theodore Roosevelt, Jr., Papers.

17. Roosevelt, *Day Before Yesterday*, pp. 76-77.

18. Theodore Roosevelt, Jr., to Eleanor Alexander Roosevelt, July 3 and July 20, 1917, Box 61, Theodore Roosevelt, Jr., Papers.

19. Roosevelt, *Day Before Yesterday*, pp. 100–102.

20. Frank Freidel, *Franklin D. Roosevelt: The Apprenticeship* (Boston: Little Brown and Company, 1952), p. 358.

21. George C. Marshall to Theodore Roosevelt, Jr., undated [probably in 1920], Box 61, Theodore Roosevelt, Jr., Papers.

22. Theodore Roosevelt, Jr., to Eleanor Alexander Roosevelt, January 21, 1919, Box 61, Theodore Roosevelt, Jr., Papers.

23. Richard J. Loosbrock, *The History of the Kansas Department of The American Legion* (Topeka: Kansas Department of The American Legion, 1968), pp. 8–13.

24. Proceedings and Committees, Caucus of The American Legion, St. Louis Mo. (n.p., n.d.), p. 39.

Courtesy of National Park Service
Sagamore Hill National Historic Site

Theodore Roosevelt, Jr. (1887–1944), son of President and Mrs. Theodore Roosevelt. His house, "Old Orchard," is now a museum and part of the Sagamore Hill National Historic Site.

8

An American Original: Theodore Roosevelt, Jr.

Charles W. Snyder

To many people, Ted Roosevelt[1] was a man who never quite lived up to expectations. "For years," Ted's wife Eleanor[2] wrote in her memoirs, "people anxious to find fault would declare that Ted would never be the man his father was."[3] Constantly measured against one of the giants of American history, whose name he bore, Ted could only too quickly be found wanting. Few would accept him as a man who made his own mark.

For his part, Ted had no wish to escape his father's legacy. The main reason for the "intensity of effort which lasted throughout his life" was, Eleanor wrote, "a strong feeling that he must prove worthy of his father."[4] At the same time, he knew that he must carve out his own identity. When invited to join an organization of descendants of presidents, Ted declined on the grounds that:

> I don't believe in "descendants of." I have somehow the feeling that this does not check with my conception of a democracy. Though I have been in politics most of my life, I do not quote my Father in my speeches, and I do not speak at celebrations in honor of his memory. This is not because I do not agree with what he advocated, and did, for I most emphatically do. He represents in my opinion the very soundest approach towards American politics and life. On the other hand, I feel that I should be accepted and treated by the American people as merely an American who has himself done thus and so.[5]

As TR's eldest son, Ted learned early that having a famous father was a mixed blessing. His father's expectations for him subjected him to such pressure that, at the age of ten, he "was diagnosed as suffering 'nervous prostration.'" Promising to ease up thereafter, TR explained that Ted had "bidden fair to be all the things I would like to have been and wasn't, and it has been a great temptation to push him."[6]

Determined to be more than just TR's son, Ted asserted his independence as soon as possible. "When I was young and in Harvard," he recalled, "I crammed my work into three years, as I was anxious to get out and test my ability to stand up on my own feet in the real world."[7] Soon afterward, he married Eleanor Alexander, with whom Ted would enjoy a family life that was the centerpiece of his existence.[8] In her early married life, however, Eleanor's greatest challenge was adapting to the frenetic Roosevelt way of life. In the course of one summer, she lost twenty-six pounds and never regained them.[9]

Ted's first job in the "real world" was as a mill hand in a carpet factory. Eventually, he went on to investment banking in New York, and by 1915 he was earning $150,000 a year. The young couple lived within a strict budget, hoping to accumulate a nest egg that would give Ted the independence needed for a political career.[10]

Ted's plans were sidetracked by the First World War. When the United States entered the war, Ted served with the rank of a major. He compiled an exceptional combat record, fighting at St. Mihiel; at the Meuse-Argonne; at Mouzon on the Meuse and Sedan, where he won the Silver Star; and at Cantigny, where he won the Distinguished Service Cross for exposing himself to enemy fire in order to rescue a wounded member of his raiding party.[11] Ted's efforts did not go unnoticed at headquarters. George C. Marshall, then an aide to General John J. Pershing, later wrote to Ted:

> With no idea of flattery and with absolute honesty, I tell you that my observation of most of the fighting in France led me to consider your record as a fighting man one of the most remarkable in the entire A.E.F. Based on personal knowledge of conditions, I consider your conduct as a battalion commander in Picardy during the last week of May and the first week of June 1918, as among the finest examples of leadership, courage and fortitude that came to my attention during the war. [12]

Since Marshall was not known for flattery, this tribute is all the more impressive.

At the end of the war, Ted joined like-minded soldiers in founding the American Legion, in the hope that the camaraderie of wartime might be preserved to help make a better world in time of peace.[13] Ted confidently believed that the shared experiences of the war would unite, as never before, Americans of different classes, races, religions, and sectional backgrounds. Such hopes would be largely disappointed in the 1920s.

In 1919, however, Ted had more immediate concerns. His father died on January 6 that year. Ted decided to carry the family banner into politics and, like his father thirty-eight years earlier, was elected to the New York State Assembly. His term is best remembered for his voting (in a small minority) against the expulsion of five Socialists who had been elected to the Assembly.[14]

The following year, Ted campaigned for Republican presidential candidate Warren G. Harding. The Democrats, meanwhile, nominated Franklin D. Roosevelt, Ted's distant cousin, for vice president. Perturbed that voters assumed FDR was TR's son, Republican managers sent Ted on a Western campaign tour, during which he said of FDR: "He is a maverick. He does not have the brand of our family."[15] The long feud between the Oyster Bay and the Hyde Park Roosevelts had begun.

Harding won the election easily, and appointed Ted assistant secretary of the Navy, a job his father and FDR had held before him. They had helped to build up the Navy, but Ted had the less dramatic duty of assisting Secretary of State Charles Evans Hughes negotiate the Naval Limitation Treaty of 1922 that substantially reduced the world's battle fleets. But Ted also worked to defeat efforts in Congress to make further, unilateral cuts. "I wish there was some way that the people could know," Richard Byrd wrote Ted after the proposed cuts were voted down, "how you have . . . saved the Navy from disaster."[16]

Ted's service to the navy was unfortunately overshadowed by the infamous Teapot Dome scandal. In 1922, Secretary of the Navy Edwin Denby consented to the lease of the naval oil reserve near Teapot Dome, Wyoming, to an oil company headed by Harry Sinclair. Ted had formerly been a director and stockholder of the Sinclair Oil Company, and his younger brother Archie Roosevelt had worked there since 1919. In 1924, Ted learned from Archie that Sinclair may have bribed Secretary of the Interior Albert Fall to obtain the lease. Ted notified the Senate Committee on Public Lands, breaking what would prove one of the worst scandals in U.S. history. Although Ted's only role in Teapot Dome was helping to expose the scandal (the Senate Committee's final report fully vindicated him), his former connection with Sinclair made it only too easy for political opponents to "smear him with oil."[17]

Their chance to do so came in 1924, when Ted left the Navy Department to run for governor of New York against the incumbent, Al Smith. A victory would bring him a giant step further along the trail his father had blazed, but circumstances were not auspicious. As Ted remembered it,

> a large section of the [Republican] organization in New York State never has liked me and never will like me. They only nominated me against Al Smith because at the eleventh hour the candidate that they had picked on, Eddie [H. Edmund] Machold, the Speaker of the Assembly, refused to run because he was sure he would be beaten badly. I was supposed to be a beaten man from the start.[18]

With characteristic energy and optimism, the challenger stumped the state, making 200 speeches in eighteen days. His steps were dogged by his first cousin, Mrs. Franklin D. (Eleanor) Roosevelt, who campaigned for Smith in a car topped with a mock-up of a giant tea kettle that spouted steam, suggesting that Ted had been implicated in Teapot Dome. The future First Lady later confessed that this was a "rough stunt," adding that "I never blamed my cousin when he retaliated in later campaigns against my husband." For his part, Ted attacked Smith's policies on taxation and government reorganization, but too often repeated tenuous charges prepared for him by the party organization that Smith could easily refute. In the end, Ted lost the election by 108,000 votes.[19]

The defeated candidate consoled himself with what he called "an involuntary holiday." It speaks volumes about Ted that his idea of a "holiday" was to undertake, along with his brother Kermit, a six-month long expedition to Central Asia, sponsored by the Field Museum of Natural History. The purpose of the expedition was to obtain specimens of large mammals of the region, especially the *Ovis poli*, a great wild sheep first described by Marco Polo. The brothers succeeded in bagging eight *Ovis poli*, along with many other specimens. This success led three years later to an expedition to Southeast Asia that featured the collection of a giant panda.[20]

In May 1929, while Ted was still in Asia, President Herbert Hoover appointed him governor of Puerto Rico. Although weak from a fever that had caused him to lose forty pounds from his already lean frame, Ted used the voyage home to begin studying Spanish. He delivered his Inaugural Address in that language, an effort that gratified his audience. The new governor envisaged Puerto Rico as a crossroads for the cultures of the United States and Latin America, a role the island could best fulfill as a self-governing commonwealth. This vision would be realized in 1952.[21]

The most pressing problems Governor Roosevelt faced, however, were economic. He began a campaign to publicize the privation he found on the island and stimulate charitable contributions. He also worked on long-term solutions, such as land reform, education, and industrialization. A $500,000 bond issue financed the purchase of land from large sugar plantations. Former tenant farmers could lease, and eventually buy, their own plots, to produce badly needed food. As for education, Ted tripled the number of rural high schools, stressing vocational training. He established a Board of Commerce and Industries that undertook the effort to attract manufacturers to Puerto Rico. Eleanor provided a good example of what could be accomplished by starting a small needlework factory, whose products were soon in demand in fashionable New York department stores.[22] In June 1932, President Hoover appointed Ted governor general of the Philippines. There too he began land reform and education programs. During the 1932 presidential election between Hoover and FDR, Ted made a live broadcast from Manila advocating the beleaguered president's reelection. The speech, heard on nationwide radio from across the Pacific, ended whatever chance there was that FDR would keep his Republican cousin in charge of the Philippines. Much as he would have liked to continue with the job that he had only just begun, Ted knew the political facts of life. When FDR won the election, Ted was asked by reporters how he was related to the new president. "Fifth cousin, *about to be* removed," was his apt reply.[23]

Soon back in the United States, Ted sought a career in the private sector. Eventually he went into publishing as vice president of Doubleday, Doran and Co. in nearby Garden City, Long Island. "It is intensely interesting work," he wrote friends, "the only work I have really ever enjoyed outside of politics."[24]

But the publisher had not abandoned politics. He regularly toured the country campaigning for opponents of FDR's New Deal. His views, the New Dealers retorted, differed profoundly from his father's. Indeed, Ted's clashes with FDR frequently sounded like a contest of prospective heirs to TR's political estate.

"I know it to be a fact," Ted wrote, "that Franklin Roosevelt always opposed my father politically. I don't object to that, but I do object to him now . . . trying to pretend otherwise."[25] Ted believed that the New Deal had little in common with TR's Square Deal. Personal freedom was endangered, Ted believed, by the New Deal's centralization of authority, a concern that intensified in 1939 with the outbreak of war in Europe. "I don't believe our democracy could stand the effect of another great struggle," Ted warned, remembering how the executive had mushroomed during the First World War. "During wartime, there would be a dictatorship. An economic crisis would follow and give excuse for continuation of a dictatorship."[26] Such was the danger Ted saw in the New Deal.

Despite many bitter setbacks in the long battle against the New Deal, the prewar years were generally happy ones for Ted and Eleanor. They finally built a home of their own, which they called Old Orchard because it was "in the center of the old apple orchard, which, come spring, will be a dream of loveliness." The new homeowners liked nothing better than to invite friends for the weekend. Guests might find themselves sharing their visit with anyone from Alexander Woollcott to Charles Lindbergh. Friends would remember Ted's exuberant personality, his "great irresistible grin . . . and his roar of laughter [that] would fill a room or send birds flying startled from their tree-tops."[27]

These peaceful years were all the more precious because the peace was so fragile. During the eighteen months following the outbreak of war in Europe, Ted worked hard to keep the United States out of the war. His "isolationism" grew from disillusionment with the fruits of victory in World War I. As he put it in 1940:

> Twenty-three years ago, with hundreds of thousands of other young Americans I went to a war in France. We were told that we were fighting "a war to end war," "a war to make the world safe for democracy." Theoretically we won that war. One look at the world today is sufficient commentary on the value of our victory.

Based on experience, Ted believed that "nobody wins a war. . . . The best that can be said for war is that sometimes one loses less by fighting than by refusing to fight."[28]

If America had to fight, Ted wanted her to be ready. He broke ranks with most other isolationists by backing FDR's trading of obsolete destroyers to Britain in exchange for a series of bases.[29] In the same spirit, he supported the draft law passed in 1940.

Ted believed in preparedness, not only for the nation, but for himself. A colonel in the Reserves, he went on active duty for four weeks of training in the summer of 1940. Afterward, he wrote to a critic of isolationism:

> I believe wholeheartedly in building our defense. I have given proof of my belief through my own actions. . . . Oddly enough, this is just what the largest number of vocalized interventionists have not done. Most of the vocal interventionists did not fight in the last war, and will not fight in this, and have done little if anything to prepare themselves personally for the battle into which they would thrust us.[30]

By the spring of 1941, Ted's belief in preparedness was setting him apart from many other isolationists, some of whom were saying they would not fight if war came. Ted did not want to be "yoked up" with those whose views he did not share. After all, as he wrote to his son that spring, it was inevitable that we would go to war by the autumn of 1941.[31]

Ted believed the time had come for Americans to close ranks. On March 19, he spoke at a "Wake Up, America" rally in New York, calling for national unity and declaring himself a wholehearted supporter of the president's national defense policy.[32] This support went beyond talk. He applied for active duty, and, in April 1941, was given command of his old regiment, the Twenty-sixth Infantry, First Division, at Fort Devens, Massachusetts.

A week after Pearl Harbor, Ted was promoted to the rank of brigadier general. On December 22, he paid a well-publicized visit to his cousin in the White House. Ted told reporters afterwards that "this is our country, our war, and our president."[33] Considering their many years of political conflict, the meeting of the two Roosevelts aptly symbolized national unity.

Ted went overseas in June 1942 as second in command of the First Division under Major General Terry Allen. Ted made a great record as a fighting general. In November, he took part in the invasion of Algeria, where the First Division got its baptism of fire against Vichy French forces at Oran. His troops admired his courage, and enjoyed his disregard for spit and polish. On the other hand, Generals George S. Patton and Omar Bradley, who commanded the Second Corps, of which the First Division was a part, were becoming dissatisfied with both Ted and General Allen. Bradley later wrote of them: "Both men were exceptional leaders revered by their men, but both had the same weakness: utter disregard of discipline, everywhere evident in their cocky division." When Allen botched an assault on Troina in Sicily in 1943, Bradley relieved both Allen and Roosevelt.[34]

Ted's next assignment took him to Sardinia, where, on the heels of Italy's surrender in September 1943, an Italian paratroop division was uncertain for which side they were now to fight. Ted inspected these troops, accompanied by only a single O.S.S. officer, who later recalled that Ted,

> By the sheer force and charm of his personality and an exhibition of the coolest gallantry . . . won the wavering troops to a wild personal ovation. . . . [After the war, one of the paratroopers] told me that he and five others had been designated to kill us when we came to review the division. . . . When Ted and I arrived they were so impressed by his manner and the fact that we were alone and unarmed that they were delighted to become our Allies.[35]

After Sardinia, Ted served in the Italian campaign as chief liaison officer between General Mark Clark and Free French Forces under General Juin, service for which he received the medal of Officer of the Legion of Honor.[36]

Ted was determined to take part in the upcoming Allied invasion of Western Europe. After a number of requests, he was assigned to the Fourth Division, then training in England, as deputy commander under Major General Raymond O. Barton. After recovering from a severe case of pneumonia in March 1944, he underwent amphibious training for the upcoming invasion.[37]

Not content with being part of the invasion force, Ted wanted to lead the first troops to hit the beach. His initial requests for such hazardous duty were denied. After all, Ted was fifty-six years old, needed a cane because of an arthritic hip, and had recently recovered from a serious illness. Undeterred, he wrote to General Barton to request the assignment, concluding that "I know personally both officers and men of these advance units and I believe it will steady them to know I am with them." General Bradley put it more strongly when he wrote years later that he granted Ted's request, "believing that his presence with the assaulting forces would be an inspiration."[38]

Thus it was that on June 6, 1944, Ted Roosevelt, nearly forty years older than the men he led, came ashore in the first of the assault boats to land on Utah Beach. He immediately realized that they had touched down some distance from the planned landing point. Improvising, he led the troops off the beach, over a sea wall, and inland, where they established secure positions. He knew that, as more waves of troops landed, they would have to come the same way.[39] Time and again he returned to the beach.

> He repeatedly led groups over the sea wall and established them inland. . . . Although the enemy had the beach under constant direct fire, Brigadier General Roosevelt moved from one locality to another, rallying men around him, directed and personally led them against the enemy. Under his seasoned, precise, calm, and unfaltering leadership, assault troops reduced beach strong points and rapidly moved inland with minimum casualties. He thus contributed substantially to the successful establishment of the beachhead in France.

Thus read the citation accompanying the Congressional Medal of Honor which was awarded to Ted for his actions on D-Day; actions that General Bradley called the bravest he had ever known.[40]

In the weeks that followed the invasion, Ted took part in the advance into Normandy, using as his headquarters a truck that had been captured from the Germans. General Eisenhower said that Ted "had absolutely vitalized the Fourth Division," and decided to appoint him commander of the Ninetieth Division on July 12. But the order was never signed. On the night of July 11, 1944, Ted died in his truck of a heart attack.[41]

On July 14, Ted was buried in the U.S. military cemetery in Normandy. Generals Patton and Bradley were among the pallbearers. Toward the end of the funeral service, nearby anti-aircraft guns fired at some German planes, unknowingly giving Ted a final salute. Patton recorded in his diary that Ted "was one of the bravest men I ever knew."[42]

Ted had fought the war with energy and zest; he gave it everything he had. But all the while, his thoughts, like those of his comrades, were of home, of his family, and of the house called Old Orchard, where he had expected to spend the long evening of his life, but in which he lived only three years. At Christmas 1943, the last Christmas of his life, he wrote to his wife Eleanor:

> Christmas is coming and that gives a touch of pathos—soldiers do so want to be home. Not only soldiers

but generals. I know an old bald-headed general who keeps thinking of Christmases at Oyster Bay, the carols, the stockings, the wind sighing around the eaves—and the family. But let's forget about him. He's old anyhow and has always liked to pretend he's tough.[43]

Ted Roosevelt *was* tough. He was tough enough to enjoy life to the fullest, and face up to death; tough enough to love peace, and meet the challenge of war; and tough enough to inherit one of the greatest names in U.S. history, and add to its luster.

NOTES

1. Theodore Roosevelt, Jr., (1887–1944) was the son of President Theodore Roosevelt (1858–1919). Unless otherwise clear from the context: Theodore Roosevelt, Jr., will be referred to as Ted; his father as TR; and his distant cousin, Franklin D. Roosevelt, as FDR.

2. Ted's wife, Eleanor Alexander Roosevelt, will be referred to as "Eleanor." She should not be confused with Ted's first cousin, also named Eleanor Roosevelt, who was married to Franklin D. Roosevelt.

3. Mrs. Theodore Roosevelt Jr., *Day Before Yesterday* (Garden City, NY: Doubleday and Co., 1959), p. 126.

4. Ibid., p. 60.

5. Theodore Roosevelt, Jr., (hereafter cited as TR Jr.) to G. A. Cleveland, November 12, 1937, Library of Congress, Manuscripts Division, The Papers of Theodore Roosevelt, Jr., (hereafter cited as Papers), Box 22.

6. Quoted by Hermann Hagedorn, *The Roosevelt Family of Sagamore Hill* (New York: Macmillan Co., 1954), p. 50.

7. TR Jr. to Karl T. Compton, December 6, 1937, Papers, Box 22.

8. Ted and Eleanor were married in 1920. They had three sons, Theodore III, Cornelius, and Quentin and a daughter, Grace. On the pleasure Ted derived from his family life, see Theodore Roosevelt, *All in the Family* (New York: G. P. Putnam's Sons, 1929).

9. Roosevelt, *Day Before Yesterday*, p. 61.

10. Ibid., pp. 44–45, 58, 66. It has been argued that Ted's business career made him a more conventional Republican than his father had been. Lawrence H. Madaras, "The Public Career of Theodore Roosevelt, Jr." (Ph.D. diss., New York University, 1964), pp. 246–47.

11. *New York Times*, April 22, 1941, clipping in Papers, Box 68; Roosevelt, *Day Before Yesterday*, pp. 97–118.

12. George C. Marshall to TR Jr., n.d. [1920], Papers, Box 29.

13. Roosevelt, *Day Before Yesterday*, pp. 119–23.

14. Ibid., pp. 123–25.

15. Quoted by Kenneth S. Davis, *FDR: The Beckoning of Destiny 1882–1928* (New York: G. P. Putnam's Sons, 1975), p. 621.

16. Richard Byrd to TR Jr., December 1, 1923, Papers, Box 27.

17. Roosevelt, *Day Before Yesterday*, pp. 152–59; Madaras, "The

Public Career of TR, Jr.," pp. 214–18.

18. TR Jr. to Frank W. Buxton, March 10, 1938, Papers, Box 39.

20. Theodore Roosevelt [Jr.] and Kermit Roosevelt, *East of the Sun and West of the Moon* (New York: Blue Ribbon Books, 1926), p. 1; Roosevelt, *Day Before Yesterday*, pp. 167–69, 207–9, 217–18. The first Field expedition was described in Roosevelt and Roosevelt, *East of the Moon*. The second expedition was described in Theodore Roosevelt [Jr.] and Kermit Roosevelt, *Trailing the Giant Panda* (New York: Charles Scribner's Sons, 1929); and Theodore Roosevelt [Jr.] and Harold Coolidge, *The Three Kingdoms of Indo-China* (New York: Thomas Y. Crowell Co., 1933).

21. Roosevelt, *Day Before Yesterday*, pp. 216, 225, 250–351.

22. Ibid, pp. 231–40; Madaras, "The Public Career of TR, Jr." pp. 255-69.

23. Roosevelt, *Day Before Yesterday*, p. 304. Ted was FDR's fifth cousin once removed.

24. TR Jr. to Mr. and Mrs. Henry Beston, September 25, 1935, Papers, Box 26.

25. TR Jr. to H. T. Holcomb, January 17, 1938, Papers, Box 23.

26. TR Jr. Speech at Topeka, Kansas, quoted in *New York Times*, January 30, 1940, clipping in Papers, Box 68.

27. TR Jr. to Mr. and Mrs. Henry Beston, February 13, 1938, Papers, Box 26; Sir John Wheeler-Bennett, *Special Relationships* (New York: St. Martin's Press, 1976), pp. 44–46.

28. TR Jr. Address before the Republican Convention, Nebraska, May 2, 1940, manuscript in Papers, Box 46.

29. TR Jr. to Cornelius Roosevelt, September 9, 1940, Papers, Box 6.

30. TR Jr. to Henry S. Woodbridge, February 7, 1941, Papers, Box 6; TR Jr. to Cornelius Roosevelt, March 21, 1941, ibid.

31. TR Jr. to Archie Roosevelt, Jr., April 9, 1941, Papers, Box 6; TR Jr. to Cornelius Roosevelt, March 21, 1941, ibid.

32. *New York Times*, March 20, 1941, p. 15.

33. Ibid., December 23, 1941, p. 11.

34. Maxwell Hamilton, "Junior in Name Only," *The Retired Officer* 37 (June 1981): 28; Omar N. Bradley and Clay Blair, *A General's Life, An Autobiography* (New York: Simon and Schuster, 1983), pp. 136, 195.

35. Serge Obolensky, quoted in Roosevelt, *Day Before Yesterday*, pp. 446–47.

36. Roosevelt, ibid., pp. 447–49.

37. Ibid., pp. 450–51.

38. TR Jr. to Barton, May 26, 1944, quoted in John Francis Neylan, *Theodore Roosevelt, Jr., Brigadier General, United States Army, Beyond the Call of Duty,* (San Francisco: privately printed, 1947), pages not numbered; Bradley and Blair, *A General's Life*, p. 224.

39. Roosevelt, *Day Before Yesterday*, pp. 454–55.

40. Quoted in Howard Teichmann, *The Life and Times of Alice Roosevelt Longworth* (Englewood Cliffs, NJ: Prentice Hall, 1979), p. 187; Roosevelt, *Day Before Yesterday*, p. 455.

41. Ibid., pp. 456–57; Harry C. Butcher, *My Three Years with*

Eisenhower (New York: Simon and Schuster, 1946), p. 612.

42. Martin Blumenson, *The Patton Papers 1940–1945* (Boston: Houghton Mifflin Co., 1974), pp. 480–81.

43. TR Jr. to Eleanor Roosevelt, December 23, 1943, Papers, Box 6.

The Roosevelt family at the White House in 1909. *From left to right*: Ethel Carow Roosevelt, Kermit Roosevelt, Quentin Roosevelt, Edith Kermit Carow (Mrs. Theodore) Roosevelt, Theodore Roosevelt, Jr., President Theodore Roosevelt, Archibald Bulloch Roosevelt, Alice Roosevelt Longworth, and her husband, Congressman Nicholas Longworth.

9

Refulgent Thunderer:
Archibald Bulloch Roosevelt, 1894-1979

David M. Esposito

In October 1979, many people were surprised to hear that Archibald Roosevelt, son of former President Theodore Roosevelt, had passed away. Not that most Americans knew he was alive, but the idea of one of TR's boys having lived so long into the century provoked public interest. Archibald was eighty-five and had outlived all of his brothers by at least thirty years. Although he had been very outspoken in the 1950s and 1960s, he disappeared from the public eye in the 1970s. He lived a full life, but unlike his brothers, succeeded in avoiding most of the pitfalls that endanger the children of famous men.

Of all Theodore Roosevelt's sons, it seems that Archie tried most to separate himself from his father's legacy. He loved his father dearly, but worked to establish his own independent personality. Indeed, he was as different from Theodore as he was from his own brothers. Archie hunted, as they all did, but was not able to safari to strange and dangerous places. Although he was an outdoorsman, he was not an explorer; no river bears his name, nor did he bring back any previously unheard of creatures from far away lands. He was active in Republican politics, but never ran for elective office nor held any government post. Out of financial necessity, he rejected his father's anti-materialism and spent most of his life working as a municipal bond salesman on Wall Street. Above all, he was a Victorian gentleman whose personality and outlook ceased developing at the moment of his father's death.[1] In time, he became the most outspokenly conservative Roosevelt.

Archibald Bulloch Roosevelt was born in 1894 to Theodore and Edith Kermit (Carow) Roosevelt in Washington, D.C., while Theodore was a U.S. Civil Service commissioner. He was their third child, and the fourth of five children. He had an older half-sister, Alice.[2]

Little Archibald really began to come into his own after an anarchist's bullet made his father president of the United States in 1901. Like his siblings, Archie seemed to regard the White House as a public playground where no manner of youthful exuberance was forbidden. Archie distinguished himself by sliding down the banister into one diplomatic reception and arriving at another on stilts. Later, when he fell ill, his brother Quentin brought Archie's favorite pony up the White House elevator to his room.[3] In addition, the lads had the best playmate any child could ask for in their father. He reacted to their shenanigans with characteristic grace, and joined in at opportune moments.

In time, Archie reluctantly followed family tradition by going to Groton, but had to return home due to a bout with diphtheria. While recovering at Evans' desert school in Mesa, Arizona, Archie precluded his return to Groton by sending a classmate a postcard asking, "How is the old Christ Factory?" His card fell into the clutches of the humorless Rev. Endicott Peabody, who told the embarrassed former president of the United States to find another school for his son.[4]

Archie entered Andover Academy and found it to his liking. He graduated in 1913 and entered Harvard that fall. Because he was the son of the popular former president, things he did that were not otherwise newsworthy found their way into print. A prime example of this unwarranted media attention occurred when he nearly got expelled from Harvard over a disagreement regarding a lab fee.[5] It was no doubt an interesting piece of family trivia, but not worth the attention of the nation's leading newspapers.

Believing that citizens should learn military drill in case the nation should soon be forced to defend itself, Archie and his brothers followed their father's lead regarding the preparedness movement. With relations between the U.S. and Imperial Germany deteriorating, he attended the summer civilian training camp at Plattsburg, in 1915 and 1916. He took the civilian soldiering quite seriously, to the point of ordering his brother Quentin punished for mishandling a gun. He even tried to organize a preparedness drill team at Harvard over the objections of college President A. Lawrence Lowell. He finished his education a year early and followed brother Ted to work for the same Connecticut carpet manufacturer.[6]

When war came in April 1917, the Roosevelt boys were ready. There was one last important item for Archie to take care of before he could go overseas to help make the world safe for democracy. A week after Congress declared war, and two days after receiving his commission, Archibald married Grace Lockwood in Boston. Although they had dated for years, theirs was a whirlwind courtship—they were engaged for all of seven days. In addition, the wedding demonstrated Archie's perseverance. He had to get a court order to allow him to get married because of the national emergency and his freshly minted lieutenant's bars. The wedding was an important ceremony for the Roosevelt family, since all assembled knew that the boys (with some help from their father) would soon be serving abroad. Although a joyous occasion, it was the last time that they would all be together in this world. A little more than a month later Archie and Theodore, Jr. sailed to join General John Pershing and the fledgling American Expeditionary Force (AEF) in France.[7]

Archie rose to the rank of captain in early 1918, becoming the youngest company commander in the AEF. Father Theodore was initially concerned because this appointment put Archie under brother Ted's direct command (Ted was battalion commander), but the brothers worked together with exemplary efficiency. Three days after his promotion in France, his son Archibald Bulloch Roosevelt, Jr., was born to Grace in Boston.[8]

In March 1918, Archie was badly wounded leading his troops in combat. He was gassed, took shrapnel in the arm and leg, and lay unattended 14 hours, insisting that surgeons see to his men first. Initially doctors thought they would have to amputate his leg, but managed to save it. For his courage, Marshal Joseph Joffre awarded him the Croix de Guerre before he was off the operating table. Writing to Grace, Teddy Jr. misrepresented the gravity of Archie's wounds. Ted averred, "he is not seriously hurt and will recover absolutely."[9] In fact, Archie never fully recuperated. In July, while recovering from surgery to reattach a severed nerve in his arm, the young captain received a double dose of bad news—his brother Quentin was killed in aerial combat and Ted was wounded at Soissons.[10]

In September 1918, Archie returned home still suffering from his wounds. He enjoyed his first glimpse of his son Archie Jr., and his last moments with his beloved father. He was the only son present when the armistice came in November 1918, and when his father passed away early the next year. It was a poignant moment when he wired his brothers in Germany the bad news, "The old lion is dead."[11]

It would seem that Archibald Roosevelt was instinctively courageous both in and out of uniform. Unlike most men, and to his own personal detriment, Archie was drawn to the sound of gunfire. It was his way. In February 1919, while still recovering from his war wounds, he came upon a policeman chasing a pair of armed robbers down a city street in a running gun battle. Naturally, Archie gave chase, and when the officer wounded one criminal, the young veteran collared the miscreant in order to allow the policeman to pursue the other.[12]

With the war over and a family to support, Archie needed a job and turned to his brother Ted for help. Theodore Jr. asked oil man Harry Sinclair to hire the young veteran. Earlier, Ted had been a director at Sinclair, but had severed his business ties during the war. Unfortunately for both Roosevelts, Sinclair complied.[13]

Archie was happy with Sinclair and arranged several important foreign deals for the company. At the same time, Theodore became assistant secretary of the Navy in the Harding administration. In 1922, the U.S. Senate began to look into irregularities surrounding the lease to Sinclair of naval oil reserve lands at Teapot Dome, Wyoming. At first, neither young Roosevelt could believe that the oil baron was involved in truly nefarious practices. As Archie wrote wryly in his memoirs, he thought Sinclair hired him because he "was such a brilliant & intelligent young man." In fact, Sinclair merely wished to exploit the Roosevelt name.[14] In 1924, Archie uncovered evidence that Sinclair had bribed the secretary of the interior in order to obtain the concession. Archie immediately resigned and testified before the Senate investigating committee. It did little good for either Roosevelt, even though they were not involved in any illegal activity. Sinclair was not harmed by Archie's testimony, and Ted's reputation (and political career) never fully recovered.[15]

Archie refused to quit the business world and quickly joined Roosevelt & Son. The financial firm had been founded by relatives years before, and was now managed by his cousin W. Emlen Roosevelt. Although he knew nothing about the business, and had few business contacts and no capital, Archie thrived. He soon mastered the tax-exempt bond market; it became his life's work and his passion. He earned a partnership in just two years. He was good at his job and enjoyed it, even in the dark years following the stock market crash. His playful nature showed itself on business calls, where he would literally throw his hat into a client's office. If it came sailing back out, he knew he did not have a sale. In 1934, conforming to the Banking Reform Act of 1933, Roosevelt & Son divided into component parts. Archie and several partners took the municipal bond element and formed the firm of Roosevelt & Weigold.[16]

As the financial catastrophe ground through the national economy, Archie found it necessary to supplement the family income. He opened a small private school on his property with his wife Gracie serving as headmistress. Although he hired professional educators to provide instruction in certain subjects, Archie returned at nights to read poetry to his exhausted charges. His favorites included Kipling which he recited entirely from memory.[17]

Archie's impishness did not entirely dissipate with maturity. He stopped by the White House in 1929 with his children in tow and asked to see "Mr. Hoover." When guards at the gate replied that the president was currently out of town, Archie explained that he had not brought his family to see President Herbert Hoover. They were there to visit "Ike" Hoover, an old family friend and chief usher at the White House.[18]

Convinced that the nation had to control fiscal outlays during the Great Depression, the bond salesman helped found the National Economy League (NEL) in 1932. Both President Herbert Hoover and his Democratic opponent, Franklin D. Roosevelt (a distant cousin), claimed to subscribe to the NEL's fiscal conservatism. As executive secretary of the NEL, Archie spoke frequently to congressional committees and denounced plans to pay a bonus to veterans of the AEF. As a spokesman for conservative finance during the Depression, Archie became a lightning rod for liberal critics. Rep. Wright Patman (D-Texas) levelled a series of spurious charges against Roosevelt, suggesting that he had received a $750,000 "gift" from the United States by profiting from government mail contracts to the Roosevelt Steamship Company. In a public statement, Archie dismissed Patman's fantasies: he was not a part owner of the company, he did not even own any stock in the steamship line. He had served briefly as a director, but not for pay. The reason Patman wished to smear his good name was the bonus that Archie still opposed. He predicted that government payments to healthy veterans would create "a privileged class of voters, subsidized at the expense of the entire nation."[19]

Roosevelt's conservatism was not strictly partisan, nor was sensible finance a Republican issue. Nevertheless, Archie was one of very few of the Republican Roosevelts to vote for cousin Franklin in the November 1932 election. He even attended FDR's inauguration in March 1933, with Archibald Jr. in tow. This moment of political nonpartisanship was quite brief. FDR soon threw financial orthodoxy to the winds with his New Deal alphabet soup agencies. Feeling betrayed, Archie never voted for FDR again.[20]

Archie's life was not without a measure of tragedy. His brother Kermit was an alcoholic who refused treatment. Kermit, seeking the adventure civilian life denied him, sailed for England the moment Germany invaded Poland in September 1939. Sadly, Kermit was so debilitated that the English had to send him home after a short period of service. From there, Kermit's life careened downhill until Archie was forced to incarcerate his brother in an alcohol rehabilitation program in Connecticut. To make matters worse, Kermit sued Archie to try to win his release.[21] Archie managed to keep the whole sad story out of the papers and avoid public scandal. Kermit recovered sufficiently to join the U.S. army, but killed himself in Alaska during World War II.

Although he favored a strong national defense, Archibald opposed U.S. involvement in World War II until the moment Japanese bombs rained on Pearl Harbor.[22] With the debate over U.S. foreign policy ended, Archie returned to active service as a lieutenant colonel—the oldest battalion commander in the Pacific theater. Like all Roosevelt men, he marched toward the sound of guns, and distinguished himself in combat repeatedly. He even had a ridge on New Guinea named after him. On Biak Island in 1944, he was wounded in the same arm and leg injured in 1918. In addition, he was suffering from pneumonia and malaria. He was sent home to recuperate and received his second Purple Heart and a Silver Star with Oak Leaf Cluster.[23]

In July 1945, the old soldier insisted that he either be allowed to return to combat or retired. General George Marshall, Army chief of staff and the highest ranking military officer in the U.S., reviewed Archie's case personally. He supported the doctors who found Archibald unfit for combat. Despite the ruling of General Marshall, Theodore Roosevelt's son appealed again, and the army held a hearing on his case at the hospital where he was recovering. The doctors did not doubt his courage; they merely observed that after being wounded in both world wars, gassed in the first, and suffering chronic malaria in the second, it was time for fifty-one year old Archie to let younger men carry on the war. Reflecting on the situation later in life, Archie admitted that the doctors were probably right. He left the service in August 1945. Archibald emerged from the war as the sole survivor of Theodore Roosevelt's four sons. Both Kermit and Theodore Jr. perished in the service of their country during World War II.[24]

Archie had removed his capital from the firm of Roosevelt & Weigold in 1942, due to personality conflicts with his partner. After coming home from the war, he had to create a new company if he wished to remain in his chosen profession. With another partner, Archie formed Roosevelt & Cross, and, under his direction, it quickly became one of the most respected tax-exempt bond firms in the field. He gave his firm leadership and poise, but not an accountant's skills. He was not an expert in finance, and honestly had no idea what was on the books. Archibald served as chairman of the new firm until, at age 75, he went into semi-retirement.[25]

As the years passed, Archie became increasingly conservative and outspoken. Asked why he supported Dewey in 1948, the Republican stalwart claimed President Harry Truman "encourages and protects the Communists and fellow travellers high in our government."[26] Although an avowed agnostic, he testified repeatedly before the House Un-American Activities Committee (HUAC) and called its members not to shrink from their duty of exposing the "small but effective percentage" of Communists in America's clergy. He formed an organization called The Alliance to supply HUAC with documentary evidence of Communist infiltration. He professed "that there was a deep laid plot" by the "Reds" to enslave American religion. He also recommended an investigation of the New York entertainment industry.[27]

His continued demands for investigations after 1952 caused acute embarrassment to the new Eisenhower administration.

Now that a Republican was president, the Communists in government issue worked against the party. Nevertheless, Archie continued to align himself with the radical conservatives. When Senator Joe McCarthy's notorious aide Roy Cohn was forced to resign, Roosevelt organized a 2,000 seat dinner at the Astor Hotel in his honor. At the testimonial, Archie attacked the *New York Times* and *Herald Tribune,* arguing that they had marked leading anti-Communist figures for elimination by smear tactics. His audience booed the papers' names loudly.[28]

Archibald elaborated on his concerns in a series of letters to a young friend in 1954. "When you compare our government to that of the Communists and infiltrationists and internationalists of this country . . . we are about forty years behind them." He associated "subversive organizations" with "big tax-exempt foundations [which] have plenty of money & are able to help their comrades." According to Roosevelt, patriotic Americans needed to organize like the enemy and "establish 'cells'" of their own.[29] Despite his momentary rhetorical excess, Archibald never actually tried to put this idea into practice.

Archie also opposed the Eisenhower administration's attempt to liberalize the McCarran-Walter Immigration Act. He told HUAC that the law should be made more, not less, restrictive and that the move for revision was the work of "hard core" Communists and "a few bleeding heart" Americans. Archie quoted his father as saying that the United States should not become "a polyglot boardinghouse" for immigrants.[30] Consistent in his conservative principles, Archie opposed Supreme Court activism and U.S. participation in the United Nations and the World Court. He also kept an eye on "security risks." When Harvard University offered the controversial nuclear scientist Dr. Robert Oppenheimer a temporary appointment as a lecturer (after his government security clearance had been revoked unfairly), Roosevelt swung into action. He organized fellow alumni into the "Veritas" committee (Latin for truth, and Harvard's motto) to rescind the appointment, citing the scientist's "highly questionable moral background."[31]

In 1966, at the urging of William Loeb, outspoken conservative editor of the Manchester (N. H.) *Union Leader,* the bond salesman began to write his memoirs. He never finished them, and perhaps it is just as well. His work is a lengthy diatribe against what he perceived as the growing socialization of

America. For example, on page two he identified the *New York Times,* for those who did not already know, as "the leading Socialistic newspaper in the U.S." Other controversial aspects included his recommendation to militarize public education, and his assertion that American colleges and universities were using anthropology "as a socialist political vehicle to prove preconceived ideas on the non-existence of race."[32]

Archibald objected to any suggestion, even when voiced by friends and family, that his conservative political opinions might have offended his cosmopolitan father. A little primary research on his part proved to Archie that he had been right all along, and that Dad was more conservative than presently portrayed. In 1968, he cobbled together some of his father's speeches into a little volume he edited and titled *Theodore Roosevelt on Race, Riots, Reds, Crime.* Acting as if nothing important had happened to the United States since 1900, the bond merchant resuscitated and portrayed as relevant his father's version of turn-of-the-century conventional wisdom. Though professing not to editorialize, Archie misrepresented some of his father's statements with misleading captions. "The Tyranny of Minorities" was not, as the editor implied, the threat from racial minorities, but rather the danger of the U.S. being dominated by a financial elite. Archie's ties to Wall Street probably rendered his father's original meaning unpalatable. In addition, it seems doubtful that President Roosevelt actually "Warned against Policies Which Bred 'Beatniks.'"[33]

Although it seemed at times as if there were no position too reactionary for him to embrace, his conservatism was tempered by a life-long appreciation of the environment and a commitment to public service. He was an ethical hunter, and helped revitalize the Boone & Crockett Club that his father founded. In 1963, he was elected club president for life in reward for his many services. He was a founding member of the Municipal Bond Club of New York. He served as a trustee of the New York Zoological Association, as a member of the World Wildlife Federation, and treasurer of the Long Island Nature Conservancy. He opposed New York State's spraying the pesticide DDT and led a petition drive to stop the practice in the late 1950s.[34]

In addition to being a raconteur of legendary proportions and writing numerous passages of doggerel verse, Archibald was, as one friend observed, "a good Scotch drinker." Yet boldly recognizing his family's history of trouble with alcohol, Archie became a non-alcoholic member of Alcoholics Anonymous and served as national treasurer from 1953 to 1966. Although reportedly "not strong on finance," his greatest contribution was his prominent commitment to the fellowship which helped legitimize the organization to the public.[35]

As the 1960s came to a close, Archie began to wind down his public campaigning. Perhaps he saw that the nation had changed greatly from that of his youth, and things had developed in ways that neither he nor his father could have predicted all those years ago on the White House lawn. He could not have held the principles he espoused and been happy with America in the 1960s. Perhaps he stopped talking publicly when he realized that no one was listening.

The final measure of tragedy occurred in 1971, when Archie's wife of fifty-four years died in a car crash. His beloved Grace had given him four children, one son and three daughters. Now she was dead, and part of Archie died too. Although he survived the accident, he retired from active life and moved to Florida. He kept his hand in business, directing a bank for a number of years, but no one who knew him could believe that his heart was in it. As Archie's cousin P. James Roosevelt observed, "it was Gracie's death . . . that set Archie down the trail to retirement, retreat, and, at the end, his own death."[36]

In 1979, Archibald Roosevelt died. But time had stopped for Archie long before he passed away. His America, turn-of-the-century Long Island certainties and Victorian morality, was no more. He was a man of deep personal integrity who could not cut his conscience to fit twentieth-century fashions. He refused to accept modern America the way he found it, and spent most of his adult life fighting to restore and preserve older values. He did not win, nor does it seem that he actually expected to. Archibald Roosevelt was a refulgent thunderer; he merely demanded—and seized—the opportunity to fight for those things in which he believed.

NOTES

1. Telephone interview with Archibald Bulloch Roosevelt, Jr., October 17, 1989.

2. Sylvia J. Morris, *Edith Kermit Roosevelt* (New York: Coward, McCann and Geohegan, 1980), p. 150.

3. P. James Roosevelt, "'The Old Fighting Man Home From the Wars,' Archibald B. Roosevelt, A Biographical Tribute," *Theodore Roosevelt Association Journal* 6 (Winter 1980): 2.

4. Archie Roosevelt, *For Lust of Knowing* (Boston: Little, Brown, 1988), p. 24.

5. *New York Times* (hereafter *NYT*), April 3, 1916.

6. *NYT*, July 19, 1916. Archibald Bulloch Roosevelt, "Memoirs," pp. 49-50, 74-75, manuscript at the Archibald Bulloch Roosevelt Collection in the Theodore Roosevelt Collection, Houghton Library Archives, Harvard University (hereafter cited as ABRC).

7. Morris, *Edith*, pp. 412-13. *NYT*, April 7 and 14, 1917.

8. Mrs. Theodore Roosevelt, Jr., *Day Before Yesterday* (New York: Doubleday, 1959), p. 89; *NYT*, February 16 and 19, 1918.

9. Theodore Roosevelt, Jr., to Grace Roosevelt, March 1918, ABRC.

10. Roosevelt, *Day Before Yesterday*, pp. 95, 100; *NYT*, March 14, 1918, April 1, 1918, and July 23, 1918.

11. Morris, *Edith*, p. 434.

12. *NYT*, February 1, 1919.

13. Roosevelt, *Day Before Yesterday*. p. 148.

14. Archibald Roosevelt, "Memoirs," p. 79.

15. J. Leonard Bates, *The Origins of Teapot Dome* (Urbana: University of Illinois Press, 1963), pp. 211–13. Lawrence Madaras, "The Public Career of Theodore Roosevelt, Jr." (Ph.D. diss., New York University, 1964), pp. 210, 213-19.

16. P. James Roosevelt, "Old Fighting Man," p. 3; October 17, 1989 interview with Archibald B. Roosevelt, Jr.

17. According to Archibald Jr., father "spoke French with a German accent" (Archibald Roosevelt interview); Morris, *Edith*. p. 94.

18. *NYT*, May 5, 1929.

19. *NYT*, June 24, July 18, July 27, and September 17, 1932.

20. Archie Roosevelt, *Lust*, p. 33.

21. Morris, *Edith*, pp. 503–5.

22. Although he supported U.S. intervention after the attack, he later repented—just as he did after the Great War. In his memoirs he wrote that getting involved in World War I was a mistake, and "we certainly made a much bigger error getting into World War II" (Archibald Roosevelt, "Memoirs," p. 94).

23. Archie Roosevelt, *Lust* pp. 99, 131; *NYT*, September 17, 1943, July 14, 1944.

24. Lt. Col. B. W. Davenport to Roosevelt, July 7, 1945; "Hearing at Oliver Hospital, Augusta, Georgia, July 24, 1945," ABRC.

25. Bill Fippinger to P. James Roosevelt, November 13, 1979, ABRC; telephone interview with John Dighton, current president of Roosevelt & Cross, March 26, 1990.

26. *NYT*, October 24, 1948.

27. Archie Roosevelt, *Lust*. p. 11; *NYT*. July 8, 1953, September 13, 1953, August 13, 1955.

28. *NYT*, July 29, 1954.

29. Archibald Roosevelt to Edward Horan, December 11, 1954, January 7 and 8, 1955, ABRC.

30. *NYT*, November 13, 1956.

31. *NYT*. March 25, 1957, December 9, 1961.

32. Archibald Roosevelt, "Memoirs," pp. 2, 46, 68.

33. Archibald Roosevelt, ed., *Theodore Roosevelt on Race, Riots, Reds, Crime* (West Sayville, NY: Probe Research, 1968). More disturbing to TR enthusiasts may be the numerous quotes that are *not* misrepresented.

34. His hunting accomplishments were modest. On his Boone & Crockett Club data sheet he wrote: "No trophies in record books. Trips, when compared to other members of the club, are lame. I have done all the padding possible, in order not to look too inactive compared to other club members." Boone & Crockett Personal Data Sheet (1966), ABRC; *NYT*, October 11, 1944 and May 30, 1957.

35. Frank Mauser, archivist of Alcoholics Anonymous to author, January 3 and 30, 1990; telephone interview with Dennis Manders, former controller of A.A., January 26, 1990.

36. P. James Roosevelt, "Old Fighting Man," p. 3.

Courtesy of Theodore Roosevelt Association

On November 8, 1954, the 50th anniversary of TR's reelection in 1904, his daughter Alice Roosevelt Longworth unveiled a portrait of the 26th president at the National War College, Washington, D.C. Assisting were President Dwight D. Eisenhower, Lt. General H. A. Craig, U.S. Air Force Commandant, and Oscar S. Straus II, president of the Theodore Roosevelt Association.

The Strenuous Life:

Early Life and Career

Courtesy of Theodore Roosevelt Collection, Harvard College Library

Thomas Nast in 1889 pictured Theodore Roosevelt the cowboy as U.S. Civil Service Commissioner, a post he held 1889–1895. On "Uncle Sam's Ranch," TR is breaking a bronco labeled "civil service reform for spoilsman." After his years as a rancher in North Dakota, Theodore Roosevelt (the only president born in New York City) was often pictured in cartoons as a cowboy.

10

Theodore Roosevelt, The Lawyer

Robert B. Charles

*Far better it is to dare mighty things, to win glorious triumphs,
even though checkered by failure, than to take rank with those
poor spirits who neither enjoy much nor suffer much, because
they live in the gray twilight that knows not victory or defeat.*

Theodore Roosevelt[1]

Until recently, there was scant evidence that Theodore
Roosevelt was a serious student of the law. He never graduated
from law school, never gained admission to a state bar, and
seldom mentioned his legal training. Even admiring biographers
have routinely relegated his law study to a few disparaging
paragraphs or an elliptic footnote. Now comes evidence that
between October 1880 and September 1882 TR was sincerely
dedicated to becoming a trained lawyer.

Two dust-covered boxes, retrieved from the cellar of the
Columbia Law School, have yielded seven volumes, or 1,189
pages, of TR's handwritten Law School Notes (hereafter referred
to as the "Notes").

For this chapter, the Notes have been cross-referenced to TR's
Columbia Law School records, private diaries, personal
correspondence, and secondary accounts of TR at law school.
This chapter cuts a narrow swath—TR's legal education.

Five questions guide our discussion. First, what is the
prevailing view of TR's legal training? Second, what do TR's
Columbia Law School Notes tell us about the depth and breadth
of his legal training? Third, what evidence corroborates the view
that TR was a serious student of law? Fourth, how does one
explain TR's sudden decision to eschew both graduation and
private practice after two years of study? Fifth, how did TR's legal
training influence his later life?

The Prevailing View

Among TR scholars, the prevailing view is that TR's legal education was little more than a short-lived lark. Accordingly, while TR has been acknowledged as an expert in a variety of fields,[2] he has never been credited with being a lawyer.

Edmund Morris, TR's Pulitzer Prize-winning biographer, devotes only two of 741 pages to TR's study of law.[3] In a spartan footnote, Morris concludes that TR did no more than "pay lip service to the law" after October 1881.[4]

Similarly, Carleton Putnam devotes only eight pages of his masterful biography to TR's legal studies.[5] To Putnam, the study of law was a mere distraction from early activities which defined TR—outdoor adventure, politics, family life, Harvard, cattle ranching.

Galloping the same worn trail, Lewis Einstein offers a pithy and typical assessment: TR "took up law and dropped it. . . . [He] was studying law and writing, a 'History of the Naval War of 1812.' . . . His interest in the law had always been feeble."[6] For Einstein, as for Morris and Putnam, TR's other interests precluded any serious devotion to the law.

William Roscoe Thayer, relying almost exclusively on TR's *Autobiography*, allows two paragraphs on the subject—and one surprisingly hyperbolic conclusion. Says Thayer: "[TR's] law studies seem to have absorbed him less than anything else that he undertook during his life."[7]

Paul Cutright marches single-mindedly past the whole question. Cutright overlooks Columbia Law School, explaining simply, TR "studied law under his uncle, Robert Barnhill Roosevelt."[8]

In sum, TR's biographers accord this unglamorous topic—his legal education—the cursory treatment that his otherwise daring life would appear to warrant.

Joseph Bucklin Bishop, alone among TR's biographers, senses something deeper in TR's uncharted, but not wholly unknown, formal exposure to the law. Bishop's treatment of TR's legal training is short, but not dismissive. Bishop pauses for two observations before advancing to flashier topics. First, TR "had at the time [while in the New York Assembly, in January 1882] no intention or expectation of abandoning the profession of law for a political career."[9]

Second, TR's early exposure to corporation law "made an impression upon young Roosevelt's mind which was never wholly effaced, but which deepened and strengthened as time went on and found expression later in his action as President in the direction of regulating and controlling the conduct of great corporations."[10] Why have so few TR scholars made this connection?

Bishop declines to credit TR with broad or systematic knowledge of the law. Still, he dares to attribute TR's strong anticorporation sentiments to *law school*. Moreover, that attribution is made in 1920, when the strongest evidence for its truth remained with TR's old law school classmate, Walter Trimble.

Since Bishop's daring conjectures, hardly an historian has bothered to give this unlikely topic a second viewing. Now, a rare discovery warrants reopening this long-forgotten trail.

TR's Columbia Law School Notes

TR's Columbia Law School Notes have, rather unexpectedly, come to light. They tell us volumes—seven, to be exact—about what topics TR studied and how intensively he studied them. A total of 1,189 handwritten pages are now held at the Columbia University Law School Library in New York City.[11]

These Notes have never been quoted, never cited, never referred to, never mentioned by *any* of TR's biographers. Crumbling and fading, but well-organized (by TR himself), the Notes detail his formal training in the law. TR scholars will rightly pose two questions: Where did the Notes come from? What, precisely, do they say?

Where the Notes Came From

The Notes were acquired by Columbia University in 1976 from Mary R. Pease (née Trimble). Mysteriously, this acquisition was only announced in a limited-circulation alumni publication, and then only in 1981.[12]

A one-page announcement explained: Mary R. Pease (Trimble) "acquired the books from her parents who had in turn received them from her father's brother, Walter Trimble, Roosevelt's Harvard College roommate. They [TR and Walter Trimble] came to Columbia Law School together and though Trimble graduated, Roosevelt did not." The announcement concluded: These notebooks "give some insight into . . . the mind of the man who would become the nation's 26th President."[13]

A more recent conversation with Mrs. Pease, now in her eighties, confirmed the story. While sorting through papers that had belonged to her father, Mrs. Pease apparently "just came across the notebooks in [her] attic." Her father was Richard Trimble, a member of the Harvard Class of 1880. Walter Trimble was her father's brother, a member of the Harvard Class of 1879. In Trimble family lore, the brothers were close friends of TR's. Mrs. Pease noted proudly, for example, that Walter had been a member of Harvard's Porcelain Club with TR, while Richard had later joined TR "out west, as a cattleman."[14]

Description of the Notes

In short, the Notes indicate that TR studied law with vigor. More specifically, they lay a foundation for the belief that TR's study, contrary to the prevailing view, was broad, systematic, regular, intended to prepare him for private practice, and periodically interrupted by inspired doodling.

Broad. Based on the fully dated entries in TR's signed notebooks, reticent historians will be hard-pressed to deny that TR studied a variety of legal subjects. The five fully dated notebooks (i.e., month, date, and year) fall into three groups: Municipal Law (three notebooks); Real Estate Lectures (one notebook); and Law (one notebook). These five are accompanied by two volumes bearing incomplete dates. Of the undated volumes, one is inscribed "Theodore Roosevelt" and includes a lengthy discourse on Criminal Law. The other is plainly not in TR's hand.[15]

In the period 1880 to 1881, municipal law was a fanning, ubiquitous subject. Among the topics subsumed were domestic relations, contracts, copyright, inheritance (i.e., wills), employer-employee relations (i.e., labor law), civil procedure, naturalization of aliens (i.e., immigration law), trusts, evidence, patents, negotiable bills (i.e., commercial paper), insurance, corporation law, and even selected torts, including libel and slander.[16] Each topic appears in TR's municipal law notebooks.[17]

The legal topics appearing in TR's notebook entitled "Law" range from jurisprudence and moral law to international and constitutional law. Also in this volume is a substantial body of writing entitled "Method of Preparing Case for Argument."

By far the thickest volume is "Real Estate Lectures." Dated 1881, signed by TR and inscribed "Columbia Coll. Law School," the exclusive focus of this volume is real property.

The sheer volume of TR's signed, fully dated Notes is impressive—no fewer than 738 pages. On average, TR wrote eight pages of notes per day, including dictations.

Systematic. TR's handwriting is, in all subjects, steady. Flowing across brown and crumbling pages, it betrays no weariness, no gaps in logic, no breaks in transcription, and no weakness in TR's resolve to follow his respective mentor's legal reasoning.

In the real estate notebook, all major areas of prevailing common law are methodically set forward. TR writes boldly then faintly, as the ink in his fountain pen rises and falls. Occasionally, he switches to pencil. Now and again, he uses a straight edge to organize legal authorities into charts and tables.

Elsewhere, unpleasant topics are dutifully discussed. On January 25, 1881, for example, TR confronts the unseemly topic of criminal seduction.

> Seduction accompanied with breach of promise of marriage is sometimes a crime. Thus by law of Congress when [a female] passenger is seduced by a [male] master of [a seafaring] vessel or other employee it is a crime. N.Y. statute refers solely to cases of breach of promise where [a female] is of chaste character. Conviction can not be had solely on testimony of [the female] seduced[,] and the subsequent intermarriage of parties is a bar to conviction.[18]

On January 26, 1881, TR explores the "rights of a bastard child." On January 27, 1881, he discusses the rights of "inheritance" upon death.[19]

Nor do scholarly or eccentric case references escape his attention. Discussing criminal defenses, for example, TR concludes a subsection entitled "Want of Mental Capacity" with this addendum: "For an interesting case on monomania where a person was in the habit of stealing ladies shoes. [See] 2 Parker 43."[20]

Beyond cases and statutes, TR allows time for a few principles. On law school itself, he observes: "We are concerned with [the] question of what law is, not what it ought to be."[21] Such a stunted inquiry was no doubt disappointing to young TR.

More broadly, TR's attention came to rest on the institutions of democracy and the sources of their legitimacy. On October 8,

1881, TR wrote: "[I]n [the] U.S. supreme power is in [the] people, and some of it is parcelled out to Congress, some to States, and the residuary still remains with the people, in the shape of the Constitution."[22] The American presidency had yet to be imbued with the level of influence it possesses today; ascendancy of that institution awaited a leader capable of recognizing and effectively employing the "bully pulpit" for "the people," the leadership eventually provided by Theodore Roosevelt.

The Notes also confirm TR's early and exceptional attentiveness to the rights and concerns of women, particularly in the legal relations of marriage and divorce.

Finally, TR excelled at getting the pithy best down on paper; he was an accomplished practitioner of creative abbreviation. *Which* became *wh*, *for* simply 4, *and* an ampersand; *equals* became =, and *male* and *female* devolved into respective signs (i e., ♂ and ♀).

Regular. While some Notes are either unsigned or undated, 738 pages are both signed and fully dated. That set breaks into eighty-two daily entries. These entries illuminate only short periods. Still, they imply high, regular attendance. TR's signed, dated Notes suggest an average attendance of three to five class days per week; each class lasted one-and-a-half hours.[23]

Figure 1 shows the number of Notes dated and undated, signed and unsigned, and the totals for each category. Figure 2 shows TR's attendance, based on signed, fully dated Notes.

Figure 1
Total Pages Signed/Dated

	Signed	Unsigned	Total
Total Pages Dated	738	53	791
Total Pages Undated	224	174	398
Total	962	227	1189

TR's private diaries, personal correspondence, and other documents (discussed below) indicate that he was going to "the law school"[24] during periods for which we, unfortunately, do not have signed or dated Notes.[25]

Preparation for private practice. TR's Notes strongly suggest that he viewed law school as preparation for private practice. Indeed, TR appears to have anticipated becoming a litigator.

Figure 2
Theodore Roosevelt's Attendance
(from signed, dated notes)

Year	Month	Signed and Dated Entries	Comments	Average Days Per Recorded Week
1880	November	—	Dated but not signed	—
	December	9	Notes only after 12/9/1880	3.0
1881	January	16		4.0
	February	15		3.7
	March	20		5.0
	April	—	Dated notes missing	—
	May	—	Dated notes missing	—
	June - September	—	Summer Vacation	—
	October	11		5.2
	November	7		3.5
	December	4		4.0
1882	January - September	—	Dated notes missing	—

At one point, he devotes a full twenty-three pages to the "Method of Preparing [a] case for argument."[26]

In TR's hand, the Notes remind an aspiring litigator of how to ply his trade: "1st thing to be done is to master leading principles applying to case. . . ." Next consult legal "digests"; several pages follow on how to use them. TR continues:

> After the reports have thus been considered a suggestion of importance should be made, that a lawyer should not only study his own case but should examine all the authorities that can be cited by his opponent. He may thus be prepared to discredit his adversary's cases by showing that they have been overruled or if not that they conflict with well established principles.[27]

There follows a full discussion of litigation tactics. The prospective litigator is then equipped with his essential trail-markers. TR records: "The next pt [sic] to be considered is the mode of preparing one's material for presentation to the court. . . . The power to make points well must depend upon the power to reason correctly which can be learned, however, from study of good examples."[28]

TR meticulously observes the mechanics of putting a case before a judge:

> At head of first page appears name of the court in full then the names of the parties in brackets then the word points. If there is also a Statement of facts made these words should appear before the word pts. The paper used should be legal cap [sic] & all the papers referring to same should be fastened together. The document should then be signed by counsel & folded in 4 = folds. On back should be written Name of Court; 2d Names of parties in brackets[;] 3d the word points[;] & 4th the name of the counsel.

Surely, this is not the stuff of which exams are made; these are the practical minutiae of private practice. If TR had not harbored an inclination to apply these pointers, would he have meticulously recorded them? These and other references invite the inference that TR treated law school, at least occasionally, as preparation for private practice.

Interrupted by doodling. TR's penmanship is almost unbroken—almost. An attentive reader will stumble over choice doodles. Any reader familiar with parallel events in TR's life will find these doodles intriguing.

On October 20, 1881, for example, TR's attention appears to slip in Municipal Law; the topics under discussion are life insurance and negotiable bills.[29] Across the page run ten intricate arrowheads, each artfully drawn and boasting a spearlike shaft.[30] Could these arrowheads have drifted back to TR from his 1878 and 1879 adventures in the Indian territories of Maine?[31]

Another day, TR appears to be daydreaming about his 1881 summer vacation in Europe. A classic British battle axe is neatly sketched. From his private diary, we learn that TR visited the medieval Castle Blarney on May 22, 1881, and the Tower of London on June 2, 1881. At the Tower, TR found "the crown jewels and armour . . . very interesting." Elsewhere, with uncanny accuracy, TR scrawls two silhouette maps of France.[32]

Perhaps most foreseeable, yet most electrifying, are the boat-shaped figures which appear on the inside rear cover of the third Notebook of "Municipal Law 1881." TR scholars will recognize these figures; they are the famous "little ships" of which TR became so fond during 1880 and 1881.[33] Here, the "little ships" are engaged in a heavy cross fire. These figures assist in corroborating TR's 1881 work on *The Naval War of 1812*—a definitive analysis of naval ballistic and ship movements during the War of 1812. TR's *Naval War* was completed in December 1881.[34]

The Corroborating Evidence

TR's two-year regimen of law study is corroborated by Columbia University records, his private diaries, personal correspondence, and secondhand accounts.

TR's Columbia University Records

The Records Division at Columbia University holds "The Junior Law Register 1880–81" and "The Senior Law Register 1881–82." Both volumes recite TR's name, address (6 West 57th Street), and registration for academic years 1880–81 and 1881–82.[35] "The Columbia University Alumni Register 1754–1931"[36] indicates that TR was a nongraduate of the Law Class of 1882. While one law professor, John W. Burgess, recalled TR as "very accurate in examination,"[37] the Records Division seems not to possess TR's course grades.[38]

TR's Private Diaries

TR's private diaries 1878–85 are preserved in the Theodore Roosevelt Collection, Harvard College Library, Cambridge, Massachusetts.

The diaries chronicle TR's study of law from November 1880 through October 1881. The entries are short but insightful. Over the intervening 111 years, diaries for the period February 15, 1882, to January 1, 1883, appear to have been lost. Nevertheless, what remains is illustrative.

TR travelled from Chestnut Hill, Massachusetts, to New York City on October 3, 1880 to matriculate at Columbia Law School. (His marriage to Alice Lee would be on October 27, 1880.)[39]

On Wednesday, November 17, 1880, TR recorded for the first time going "to the law school." On November 24, 1880, he was already writing that "the law work is very interesting." By Saturday, December 4, 1880, he had concluded: "I like the law school work very much."[40]

Returning from his 1880-81 Christmas vacation, TR wrote on January 4, 1881: "Began work at Law School." He added: "Always walk up and down to & from Law School." In fact, each class day, TR was walking from his home at 6 West 57th Street to the Law School at 8 Great Jones Street and back—a hike of "about 6 miles."[41] Those who doubt TR's dedication to law might ponder this question: How many of today's law students would trek six miles a day to attend classes?

On January 6, 1881, TR happily records: "Every moment of my time occupied." On January 21, 1881, came another cheerful entry: "Argued case in moot court; successful."[42]

Under first-year pressures, TR assured himself on February 24, 1881: "Am still working hard at the law school." Five weeks later, on March 30, 1881, he wrote: "Am studying very hard at the law school."[43]

Then, on April 13, 1881, TR got an opportunity to see legal theory in action. He confided to his diary: "Came back to N.Y. Succeeded in arresting a swindler, had quite a struggle with him." On April 19, 1881, just six days later, TR's prosecutorial determination produced results: "Had the swindler indicted by the Grand Jury." TR adds nonchalantly: "The weather is superb for driving."[44]

On April 23, 1881, as TR grew closer to his long-planned summer vacation with Alice, he noted: "Am working tolerably hard at my law." One week later: "Had the swindler put in the penitentiary for six months."[45]

As the 1881 spring semester wound down, TR wrote: "Besides working pretty well at the law, I spend most of my *spare* time in the Astor Library, on my 'Naval History.'" Just prior to the official end of term, TR appears relieved. "My law school work is over," he wrote on May 11, 1881.[46] He and Alice were off to Europe!

Returning from a summer abroad, TR dove into the law again. On October 6, 1881, he observed: "Began at the Law." TR also acknowledged personal pressures specific to the month of October, 1881. TR was conducting a campaign for the New York Assembly and facing a December publishing deadline for his *Naval History.* He confided: "Am working fairly, at my law, hard at politics, and hardest of all at my book ('Naval History'), which I expect to publish this winter."[47]

TR's Personal Correspondence

Beyond his Notes, Columbia records, and diaries, TR's personal correspondence between October 1880 and September 1882 corroborates devotion to the law. In a letter to Alice dated March 29, 1881, TR writes: "I have been studying hard all day." This reference can only be to law. Similarly, in an October 14, 1881, letter to Alice, TR explains the several pressures under which he is laboring—work on his book, work on his political campaign, and work at the law. He notes: "and the law is pretty hard."[48]

A further indication that politics did not quickly subvert TR's resolve to become a practicing lawyer appears in a letter dated November 10, 1881, to Harvard classmate Charles Grenfill Washburn. In the letter, written after TR had already won a seat in the New York Assembly, TR proclaims: "Finding it would not interfere much with my law I accepted the nomination to the assembly, and was elected. . . . But do'nt [sic] think I am going to go into politics after this year, for I am not."[49]

While TR reconsidered, there is little reason to doubt his sincerity at the time; his priority was law. If it appears a precarious leap from these indicia to the conclusion that TR studied law through late 1882, consider two further letters. In mid-September 1882, TR wrote a letter to his sister Anna. There he identified his pursuit of law as a leading reason for not settling outside New York City. Even at this late date, TR did not indicate that politics had taken priority over law. He wrote:

> The only, or at least the chief drawback [to buying a farm in the country] is the distance from New York [City]. Still, if I were perfectly certain that I would go on in politics and literature I should buy the farm without hesitation; but *I consider the chances to be strongly favorable to my getting out of both—and if I intend to follow law or business I ought to stay in New York [City].*[50]

The most powerful corroboration of TR's conscientious pursuit of law through late 1882, however, is a letter to his mother dated July 5, 1882. In the letter, he emphasizes his 1882 commitment to law. "I have decided to study law . . . during three or four days a week for the rest of the summer," he writes. If TR studied "three or four days a week for the rest of the summer," he concluded his law studies near the date on which he wrote to

Anna, on September 15, 1882. On that date at least, TR remained convinced that he should "follow law or business."[51]

Secondhand Accounts of TR at Law School

TR was taught by Professors Theodore W. Dwight (Municipal Law), John W. Burgess (International and Constitutional Law), George Chase (Criminal Law), and probably John F. Dillon (Real Estate).[52] Dwight, Burgess, and Chase were esteemed tutors of law. Columbia was, at the time, reputed to be among the best law schools in the Western world.[53]

Burgess recalled TR precisely: "He entered our School of Law as a member of the class which would graduate in the summer of 1882. He registered however for all the courses in political history, public law, and political science and appeared to be more interested in these than in the topics of municipal law. . . . He was very quick in comprehension, very articulate in examination, and the most rapid and voluminous reader of references in the school."[54]

Burgess's general recollections shed additional light on TR's approach to law school. "As my subjects in the law curriculum were optional, . . . and the only incentive to take them was the acquisition of the knowledge they represented, I had in my Law School class generally and almost exclusively the most intelligent and best prepared men coming from the best colleges in the land . . . my class consisted of about fifty out of the five hundred students of the Law School, and I could rely upon every one of them to prepare himself to recite each day on the lecture of the day before and on the references given."[55] Separately, we know that TR's law texts were inspirational and demanding.[56]

By contrast, Professor Dillon's influence on TR may have been quite negative. TR's lifetime discomfiture with the perceived absence of scruples among "many of the big corporation lawyers" may have originated with Dillon, who moonlighted as corporate counsel while teaching.[57]

Finally, a few accounts from TR's classmates survive. For example, young TR is said to have arrived one day in class covered with a generous coating of mud. Somehow, while walking to school, he had managed a spectacular fall on Broadway Avenue. Classmate George Thompson recalled TR's resolve: "His face had a look of determination. . . . The students applauded his entrance, but he sat down at once on the little platform at Professor Dwight's feet and commenced to pay strict attention to business."[58]

The Decision Not to Graduate or Practice

The assembled pieces of evidence—TR's newly discovered law Notes, his Columbia University records, his private diaries, his personal correspondence, and secondhand accounts of TR at law school—strongly suggest that TR's legal training was sustained and conscientious. Why, then, did he choose not to graduate or to enter private practice? This knotty question is both more complex and less elusive, than most scholars have thus far surmised.

Biographers who have mentioned TR's law study have been content to assume that TR's interest in politics or his boredom with law made politics an inevitable choice. The choice was not, in fact, inevitable.

TR had always wanted a private career. As late as 1901, he was still "ask[ing] Associate Justice [of the U.S. Supreme Court] Edward D. White for advice on resuming his long-abandoned legal studies."[59] Nor was young TR as wealthy as some assume.[60] Moreover, TR did not immediately pursue a political career; instead he headed West to cattle ranch. Of course, TR's abiding interest in the public good must have gnawed at him, but so did law. TR confessed to finding "the law work . . . very interesting" and, while he condemned corporate lawyers,[61] had intended to be a litigator.[62]

The best answer is probably neither boredom nor the ineluctability of politics. Rather, it is circumstance. During late 1882, the requirements for graduating Columbia Law School and entering private practice in New York changed. Just as TR was preparing for his "comprehensive examination," traditionally administered on completion of a student's second and final year of law study, Columbia announced a third year requirement.[63] To make matters worse, the New York State legislature in 1882, revoked Columbia's long-standing "diploma privilege." All Columbia graduates were suddenly required to pass a separate, state-administered bar examination prior to entering private practice.[64]

Even if young TR had believed himself adequately prepared for a state bar examination, he is unlikely to have concluded that a third year of law school was worth the additional costs: time away from political involvement, time away from Alice and his mother, time away from outdoor adventures, and one more year's tuition fees.

The Influence of Law Study

TR seldom drew attention to his formal legal training. The reasons for this, while cloaked, are not beyond deduction.[65] Nevertheless, historians will wonder: What influence did TR's formal legal training have upon his later life? The influences are subtle and worthy of deeper study.[66] Some are apparent. TR relied heavily on legal principles in his political decision making. He was well aware of the ways in which the law was deficient and susceptible to misapplication.[67] He was acutely aware of the limits and possibilities of international law.[68] Politically and legally, he pursued, regulated, and disdained "great law-defying corporations of immense wealth." Assiduously, he championed constitutional reforms, such as equal protection of the laws for women in the workplace, women's suffrage, and labor protection.[69]

Perhaps most significantly, TR spoke and understood the language of the law. This permitted him, for example, to pursue orderly cross-examination of his critics.[70] He also conducted sophisticated investigations of the bar, judiciary, and police-trial systems, as well as highly effective negotiations.[71]

Conclusion

Between October 1880 and September 1882, Theodore Roosevelt was a devoted student of law. Evidence for this proposition, including TR's Columbia records, private diaries, personal correspondence, and secondhand accounts of TR at law school, has long been available. Nevertheless, the available evidence may not have been sufficient to support the conclusion that TR was a trained lawyer. The discovery of more than 1,100 pages of TR's handwritten law Notes now makes that conjecture highly tenable.

NOTES

1. Address to the Hamilton Club, Chicago, April 10, 1899.
2. Edmund Morris has nimbly synthesized TR's intellectual reach: He was "equally comfortable with experts in naval strategy, forestry, Greek drama, cow punching, metaphysics, protective

coloration, and football techniques." Edmund Morris, *The Rise of Theodore Roosevelt* (New York: Ballantine, 1979), p. 23.

3. Morris, *The Rise of Theodore Roosevelt*, pp. 139–41.

4. Ibid., pp. 772-73, n. 68.

5. Carleton Putnam, *Theodore Roosevelt*, vol. 1: *The Formative Years, 1858–1886* (New York: Scribner's, 1958), pp. 216–22, 227-28.

6. Lewis Einstein, *Roosevelt: His Mind In Action* (Boston: Houghton Mifflin, 1930), p. 141.

7. William Roscoe Thayer, *Theodore Roosevelt: An Intimate Biography* (Boston: Houghton Mifflin, 1919), p. 32.

8. Paul Russell Cutright, *Theodore Roosevelt, the Naturalist* (New York: Harper, 1956), p. 33.

9. Joseph Bucklin Bishop, *Theodore Roosevelt and His Time* (New York: Scribner's, 1920), pp. 6-7.

10. Ibid.

11. Since 1976, the Notes have been stored in two boxes in the cellar of the Columbia University Law School; they are presently preserved in the Special Collections Division of the Columbia Law School Library.

12. See *Columbia Law Alumni Observer* (Nov.-Dec. 1981): 10.

13. Ibid.

14. Conversation with Mrs. Mary R. Pease (New York, NY), July 1990. The Harvard University Archives confirms that Walter and Richard Trimble graduated from Harvard in 1879 and 1880, respectively, and that both TR and Walter Trimble were members of the Porcelain Club. Moreover, the Records Division at Columbia University confirms that Walter Trimble matriculated at Columbia Law School in October 1880, the same month and year in which TR matriculated.

15. The seven appear to have been purchased at "Joseph Laurier, Stationer, No. 1 Great Jones St., New York." (See inside front covers.)

16. See, Julius Goebel, Jr., and the Foundation for Research in Legal History, *A History of the School of Law: Columbia University* (New York: Columbia University Press, 1955), p. 80. See also Putnam, *Theodore Roosevelt*, 1: 218.

17. See the Notes, Municipal Law Notebooks numbers 2, 3, and 4.

18. The Notes, Law Notebook, January 25, 1881.

19. Ibid., January 26, 1881; and January 27, 1881.

20. The Notes, undated volume.

21. The Notes, Law Notebook, October 7, 1881; see also, for example, Theodore Roosevelt, *Theodore Roosevelt: An Autobiography* (New York: Macmillan, 1913), p. 478.

22. The Notes, Law Notebook, October 8, 1881.

23. See Goebel, *History of School of Law*, p. 61.

24. Theodore Roosevelt, November 17, 1880, Private Diaries, 1878-1885. TR's private diaries are preserved in the Theodore Roosevelt Collection, Harvard College Library.

25. See, TR, Private Diaries, April 13, 1881; April 19, 1881; April 23, 1881; April 30, 1881; May 2, 1881; May 11, 1881. See also notes 35 and 36 below and accompanying text.

26. See Municipal Law Notebooks numbered 2 and 3.

27. Ibid.

28. Ibid.

29. See Municipal Law Notebook number 3, October 20, 1881.

30. Ibid. More arrowheads appear on the inside cover of Municipal Law Notebook number 2.

31. Curious, too, are the cleverly drawn slingshot and feathered arrow on the inside cover of Municipal Law Notebook number 3. In 1878 and 1879, TR trekked extensively "in the wilds of Aroostook County, in northern Maine," as well as up Mount Katahdin, and along the Munsungen Lakes. Morris, *The Rise of Theodore Roosevlt*, pp. 98, 117, 118.

32. Municipal Law Notebook number 3; TR, Private Diaries, May 22, 1881; June 2, 1881, Municipal Law Notebook number 3.

33. Putnam writes: "One can, with the help of Owen Wister, visualize him standing on one leg in front of a bookcase at 57th Street, the other leg crossed behind, toe touching floor, while he scribbles on a slide drawn out from the shelves, and Alice hurries in exclaiming, 'We're dining out in twenty minutes, and Teddy's drawing little ships.'" Putnam, *Theodore Roosevelt*, 1: 221.

In a previously unpublished letter to Alice Lee dated March 29, 1881, TR wrote: "Darling Baby, I have been studying hard all day—only drawing a few 'little boats'—and did not go out driving" (Roosevelt to Alice Lee, March 29, 1881, by permission of the Roosevelt Collection, Harvard College Library, Cambridge, MA).

34. See Morris, *The Rise of Theodore Roosevelt*, pp. 153-54.

35. See "The Junior Law Register 1880-1881" and "The Senior Law Register 1881-1882," preserved at Columbia University Archives, New York, NY

36. See "The Columbia University Alumni Register 1754–1931" (New York: Columbia University Press, 1932), preserved at Columbia University Archives, New York, NY. Incidentally, TR did receive an honorary LL.D. (law degree) from Columbia in 1899.

37. See John W. Burgess, *Reminiscences of an American Scholar* (New York: Columbia University Press, 1934), pp. 212–14.

38. Courses and grades for many of the Columbia Law School students registered between the years of 1881 and 1883 are not available.

39. See, for example, Michael Teague, "Theodore Roosevelt and Alice Hathaway Lee: A New Perspective," *Harvard Library Bulletin* (Summer 1985): 230.

40. TR, Diaries, November 17, 1880; November 24, 1880; December 4, 1880.

41. TR, Diaries, January 4, 1881; February 23, 1881.

42. TR, Diaries, January 6, 1881; January 21, 1881. Moot (or mock) court competitions were optional. See Goebel, *History of School of Law*, pp. 80, 81, 94. They were, however, "strongly recommended to students" as "direct training for regular work in the profession" (Goebel, pp. 418–19 n.95, quoting Columbia Law School *Announcement, 1878–79).*

43. TR, Diaries, February 24, 1881; March 30, 1881.
44. TR, Diaries, April 13, 1881; April 9, 1881.
45. TR, Diaries, April 23, 1881; April 30, 1881.
46. TR, Diaries, May 2, 1881 (emphasis added), May 11, 1881. Note, "the Term commence[d] on the first Wednesday of October, and continue[d] until May 17th. The course of study embraced two years." Goebel, *History of School of Law*, p. 61.
47. TR, Diaries, October 6, 1881.
48. Morris, *The Rise of Theodore Roosevelt*, pp. 153-54; unpublished letter to Alice Lee (October 14, 1881), by permission of the Roosevelt Collection, Harvard College Library, Cambridge, Mass.
49. Letter to Charles Grenfill Washburn (November 10, 1881), quoted in Elting E. Morison, and John Blum, eds., *The Letters of Theodore Roosevelt*, 8 vols. (Cambridge: Harvard University Press, 1951–1954), 1: 55.
50. Letter to Anna (September 15, 1882), quoted in ibid., p. 56 (emphasis added).
51. Letter to TR's Mother (July 5, 1882), quoted in ibid., p. 56.
52. Since Dwight taught Municipal Law in 1880 and 1881, and three of TR's four Municipal Law notebooks are dated 1881, we may assume Dwight was one of his instructors. Burgess has specifically recorded his impressions of TR. Chase is referred to in a set of TR's "criminal law" notes. Dillon was appointed Professor of Real Estate (and Equity Jurisprudence) in 1879. See Goebel, *History of School of Law*, pp. 35–39, 84, 94.
53. Dwight was Columbia's leading intellectual. As one Englishman declared: "[Columbia] possesses the best law school in the United States, and one quite unlike any institution existing in England. At this school there are constant classes filled with pupils who are taught the elements of English law by one of the ablest professors that any school of law ever possessed . . . a man of genius who knows how to teach what his pupils need to learn. Professor Dwight . . . has a reputation . . . as the greatest living American teacher of law. . . ." (Goebel, *History of School of Law*, p. 63). Burgess taught Constitutional History, International Law, Constitutional Law, and Political Science. Additionally, in 1881, he started "a School designed to prepare young men for the duties of Public Life [and] . . . entitled a School of Political Science" at Columbia. Goebel, *History of School of Law*, p. 89. Chase was professor of Criminal Law, Torts, and Procedure. Goebel, *History of School of Law*, pp. 79, 83. For Dillon, see text above.
54. Burgess, *Reminiscences of an American Scholar*, pp. 212–14.
55. Ibid. See also, Putnam, *Theodore Roosevelt*, 1: 85-87. Burgess was "not happy unless he had around him a circle of devoted and enthusiastic disciples" (Goebel, *History of School of Law*, p. 87).
56. TR's texts included the unrivalled *Blackstone's Commentaries*, *Parsons on Contracts*, *Greenleaf on Evidence*, and the *New York Code of Civil Procedure*. See Putnam, *Theodore Roosevelt*, 1: 218; Goebel, *History of School of Law*, p. 80.

57. "Judge" John F. Dillon taught real estate law at Columbia from fall 1879 to spring 1881. TR's signed Real Estate Lectures bear the date 1881. We cannot, therefore, be certain that Dillon instructed TR. See TR, *Autobiography*, p. 55, for his view of corporation lawyers. While teaching, Dillon served as general counsel to Union Pacific Railroad. Dillon's Columbia salary was apparently twice that of a non-Columbia professor; yet he flatly stated that his reason for leaving Columbia was that this salary "was much less than he could make in [private] practice" (Goebel, *History of School of Law*, p. 94). Dillon's preoccupation with economic gain is not likely to have inspired lessons in public-spiritedness, professional morality, or corporate scruples; as Bishop conjectured, it may have seeded TR's profound distaste for corporate law and the behavior of big corporations. See, Bishop, *Theodore Roosevelt and His Time*, pp. 6-7.

58. Putnam, *Theodore Roosevelt*, 1: 219, quoting George Thompson.

59. Morris, *The Rise of Theodore Roosevelt*, p. 737.

60. See TR, *Autobiography*, p. 56.

61. TR, Diaries, November 24, 1880; TR, *Autobiography*, p. 55.

62. See above section on "Preparation for Private Practice," text accompanying notes 30-34. Even Putnam has acknowledged that "[TR's] position . . . was not precisely one of spurning the legal profession because of moral scruples" (*Theodore Roosevelt*, 1: 220).

63. The third year, not previously required for graduation from Columbia Law School, would be spent in the classroom or "as a clerk in a law office" (Goebel, *History of School of Law*, pp. 104, 433, n.144). Notably, Professor Dwight opposed the third year requirement throughout the 1870s because "he still doubted that young men would stay that long in a law school that required three years' study for a bachelor's degree" (Goebel p. 74).

64. As Goebel explained, "The class that was graduated in 1881 was the last group to be admitted to the New York Bar merely upon presentation of a diploma from the Columbia College Law School" (ibid, p. 104; see also pp. 53, 426, n.68).

65. TR's silence permitted him to remain untainted by association to the law, while strenuously reviling unscrupulous private practitioners. See, for example, Theodore Roosevelt, *Presidential Addresses and State Papers of Theodore Roosevelt* (P. F. Collier, 1905; reprint New York: Kraus Reprint Company, 1970), pp. 419–20, 539, 541–43. TR was also loathe to begin an undertaking without completing it; he may have felt perpetual unease at not having graduated or gained admission to any bar. Further, TR habitually underemphasized his intellect. See, for example, Einstein, *Roosevelt: His Mind In Action*, p. 14; Cutright, *Theodore Roosevelt the Naturalist*, p. 31. Finally, since TR's legal training began in November 1880 and concluded in late 1882, it overlapped the major portion of his marriage to Alice Lee. When his young wife died in early 1884, he was hurtled into one task above all else. Wrote Edmund Morris, "Nostalgia . . . if painful . . . must be suppressed, until the memory [of anything connected to Alice] is too dead to throb" (*The Rise of Theodore Roosevelt*, p. 243). Returning to memories of his law school period may

have invariably summoned up other memories, about which TR would not let himself think.

66. For a preliminary assessment, see Robert B. Charles, "Legal Education in the Late Nineteenth Century, Through the Eyes of Theodore Roosevelt," unpublished manuscript, held at the Theodore Roosevelt Collection, Harvard College Library, Cambridge, MA; Long Island Studies Institute, Hofstra University, Hempstead, NY; and Columbia University Law School Library, New York, NY. This 82–page manuscript provides a more detailed discussion of TR's legal training and the influence of that training on his life.

67. See e.g., TR, *Autobiography*, pp. 132, 137, 172, 196, 314, 316–17, 389–90, 448; see also, TR, *Presidential Addresses*, p. 540.

68. As president, TR consciously acted in accord with international law, for example, by persuading Mexico to bring "the first case ever . . . before the [International Court of Justice, or] Hague Court" (TR, *Autobiography*, p. 554). He also "substitut[ed] friendly and judicial for violent methods" in negotiating peace between warring Russia and Japan (TR, *Autobiography*, pp. 559, 547-74). When international law failed to achieve a moral imperative, TR departed from it, but with an acute awareness that he was doing so. In 1903, TR intervened on behalf of Panamanian revolutionaries in their civil war. He dispatched an American warship to the region. That action facilitated Panama's independence from Colombia and thus the start of work on the Panama Canal, an international waterway. TR defended this bloodless intervention not by recourse to international law, but by citing "international morality" (see TR, *Autobiography*, pp. 548, 561).

69. See TR, *Autobiography*, pp. 165, 437, 466. Among TR's achievements in the realm of labor were seminal child labor statutes, workmen's compensation, regulation of hours required of workers in highly concentrated industries (e.g., railroads), and minimum national health and safety regulations (TR, *Autobiography*, pp. 477–78).

70. TR's skills as a cross-examiner stood him in good stead as Civil Service commissioner. Accused of investigating corruption like an old English "Star Chamber" with "leading questions," TR shot back like a trained litigator: "Of course I used leading questions! I have always used them in examinations of this kind and always shall use them . . . to get at the truth" (Morris, *The Rise of Theodore Roosevelt*, p. 449, quoting TR). See also TR, *Autobiography*, pp. 140-42.

71. TR, *Autobiography*, pp. 469, 473; see also, Morris, *The Rise of Theodore Roosevelt*, pp. 521, 561; for example, giving rise to receipt of the 1906 Nobel Peace Prize for successfully ending the Russo-Japanese war.

Courtesy of Theodore Roosevelt Collection, Harvard College Library

Theodore Roosevelt on the round-up
in the Dakota Territory in 1885.

11

Theodore Roosevelt's Cowboy Years*

Edward Schapsmeier and Frederick H. Schapsmeier

Stepping down from the train one day late in the summer of 1883 a twenty-five-year-old, genteel-looking New Yorker gazed at the small and forlorn town of Little Missouri. The eastern "dude," with flashing teeth and conspicuous spectacles, had penetrated deeply into Dakota Territory seeking entry into a remnant of the Old West. Before Frederick Jackson Turner "nailed up his thesis on the doors of history,"[1] Theodore Roosevelt had discovered the West. The subsequent five years of his life transformed a weak tenderfoot into a robust man. These were to be the cowboy years.

No longer did the shrill cry of the Sioux warriors break the stillness of the present nor did the thundering hoofs of gigantic herds of bison echo across the vast stretches of the Dakota Badlands. What remained was a sparse population, consisting mostly of ranchers and a docile remnant of the once proud Sioux nation. The vast plains, ravaged by nature, stood as a challenge to civilization with its clay buttes resembling primitive altars, seemingly awaiting some strange offering to redeem it from its past.

Cursed by a climate of extremes, frequent droughts transformed the grass-laden prairies into parched deserts while in winter cattle-killing freezes often brought disaster to the hardy inhabitants who battled the elements in this harsh environment. A U.S. cavalry general aptly described it as "Hell with the fire gone out."[2] A less harsh appraisal by a fellow rancher of Teddy Roosevelt described the Badlands as "a wild romantic rock

---

*This piece is largely based upon our article "Theodore Roosevelt's Cowboy Years," which originally appeared in the *Journal of the West* 2 (July 1966): 398-408, copyrighted by the *Journal of the West* and used with permission.

garden of the gods where in peace and security the wild and untamed revelled in the exalted atmosphere with which nature had surrounded them."[3]

Roosevelt's father had advised his frail son, "You have the mind, but not the body ... Theodore, you must *make* your body."[4] Afflicted with asthma, endowed with poor eyesight, and chronically ill (possibly with psychosomatic overtones), the future of the sickly lad seemed dismal. Teddy's own estimation of his physique was succinctly summarized by Henry Pringle who said: "When he was old enough, the boy detested his puny body."[5]

The senior Roosevelt strongly encouraged Teddy to study wild life and took him on camping trips. He even built a gymnasium in their fashionable Manhattan home to more or less pressure Teddy to take up a regular regimen of exercise. As a student at Harvard, where he graduated *magna cum laude*, TR defied his doctor's orders to live a sedentary life by continuing his hiking and taking up boxing as well. But it was not until the years spent in the Wild West setting of the Dakotas, however, that his quest for physical health and prowess was successfully achieved.

Already imbued intellectually with the Social Darwinist credo of the survival of the fittest, TR deliberately pitted his developing body against the rugged frontier environment. His first foray into the Badlands was for the thrill of hunting in a wild and untamed region: the authentic environment that had produced self-reliant individualistic Americans. He was immediately captivated by the awesome scenery and austere atmosphere. It was the Wild West of the cowboy and TR was enthralled with its unrefined splendor. Reminiscing years later, he described the initial allurement, "It was a land of vast silent spaces, of lovely rivers, and of plains where the wild game stared at the passing horseman. It was a land of scattered ranches, of herds of longhorned cattle, and of reckless riders who unmoved looked into the eyes of life or death."[6]

The young patrician who had gone West seeking excitement convinced two experienced ranchers to enter into a business partnership with him. Sylvane Ferris and Frank Merrifield, albeit with some doubts, joined forces with the Eastern greenhorn in a ranching enterprise. A $14,000 investment by Roosevelt helped to allay any lingering fears. In reply to Merrifield's inquiry as to whether Roosevelt desired a receipt for his check, Teddy breezily answered (in the best fashion of the code of the West), "Oh, that's all right, if I didn't trust you men, I wouldn't go into business with you."[7]

Theodore Roosevelt returned to his Manhattan home on West Forty-fifth Street after a brief sojourn in the Dakotas in 1883. But a series of sad events was to drive him back within a very short period. Tragedy struck with vengeance on February 13-14, 1884. Within a twelve-hour span, death claimed both his mother and beloved wife Alice. The death of his father from cancer in 1878 had been a traumatic shock to TR, but now his grief was inconsolable. Consequently, it was a disconsolate and melancholy mourner who returned to his Dakota ranch in the spring of 1884. Seeking solace and merciful distraction from his personal bereavement, TR increased his investment and buried his sorrow in a frenzy of activity. He plunged into the everyday work performed by experienced cowhands with the ferocity of a zealot, sometimes tempting fate beyond its prudent limit. "Black care rarely sits behind a rider whose pace is fast enough"[8] was TR's formula for forgetting his intense sorrow.

Learning to be a cowboy, Roosevelt recalled many years later, "implies the endurance of rough fare, hard living, dirt, exposure of every kind, [and] no little toil."[9] It was the kind of action that purged from his memory the painful thoughts of the past and by doing so it rejuvenated within him a new zest for life. Its effect upon him was dramatic. Parallel to his psychological recovery was the development of a new physical robustness. To his sister Anna, Teddy wrote (with an element of pride and joy): "Well, I have just been having a glorious time here, and well hardened now (I have just come from spending *thirteen* hours in the saddle)."[10] The cathartic effect of cowboy life was becoming apparent as he later wrote Anna, "The country is growing on me, more and more. . . ."[11] After purchasing a fancy cowboy outfit, TR wrote his old friend Henry Cabot Lodge in August 1884, "You would be amused to see me in my broad sombrero hat, fringed and beaded buckskin skirt, horse hide chaparajos or riding trousers, and cowboy boots, with braided bridle and silver spurs."[12]

Displaying a raw courage rather than finesse, TR as the neophyte cowboy took his turn at breaking wild broncos. "Some horses are almost incurable vicious,"[13] he exclaimed. An eyewitness account of one of Teddy's rides related that his "hat, glasses, six shooter, everything unanchored about him, took [the] count! But there was no breaking his grip."[14] On another occasion it was observed that "four times the [wild] beast threw him, but on the fifth time . . . [it] made Roosevelt a winner. . . ."[15]

The crusty and weatherbeaten cowhands soon accepted Roosevelt. They admired his good-natured tenacity and graciously overlooked what they considered eccentric habits—such as shaving and brushing his teeth daily. One cowboy expressed amazement how Teddy could communicate effectively with his ranch hands in his strange Harvard accent without using profanity: "Beats hell, now, the way he kin handle his tongue: Never knowed 'twas possible, nohow, to punctooate feelin's proper, 'thout shootin' irons, or leastwise, cuss words. . . ."[16]

The Western experience of ranching and hunting was literally transforming the blue-blooded, effete easterner into a full-fledged, red-blooded western cowboy. Roosevelt penned this recollection many years later: "We knew the toil of hardships and hunger and thirst, but we felt the beat of the hardy life in our veins, and ours was the glory and joy of living."[17] He also wrote: "The hunter is the archetype of freedom. His well-being rests in no man's hands save his own."[18] He envisaged hunting as symbolizing humanity's confrontation with nature. In the Darwinian world of tooth and claw, the fittest survived and the weak fell prey. Therefore the shooting of game animals was simply part of the natural scheme of things—not a wanton destruction of wildlife. The western spirit, which had no "fear neither man, brute, nor element,"[19] was to him worthy of respect and preservation. He subsequently founded the Boone and Crockett Club for hunters to preserve the heritage "of the wilderness . . . with its bold, wild freedom."[20] The same club also fostered "preservation of wild game"[21] for the future, particularly big game such as bears and big-horn sheep—the "noblest of game animals."[22] The code of the West once again mesmerized TR as cartoonist Clifford K. Berryman's publicity testified to his refusal to shoot a roped defenseless bear (thus immortalizing the "Teddy Bear").[23]

The Darwinian concept of natural selection became the manner in which Roosevelt interpreted history. The American pioneer was truly a "conqueror" and this enabled the vanguard settler to subject the wilderness. Inherent in Theodore Roosevelt's finest historical work, *The Winning of the West*,[24] was the implicit idea of conquest. Also implied was the suggestion that "Anglo-Americans enjoyed a biological as well as cultural supremacy."[25] The fittest survived and thus the Indians were swept away and their domain claimed by the victors. Roosevelt thought like a true westerner when he wrote: "In our history we have had more trouble from Indian tribes which we pampered and petted than from those we wronged. . . ."[26]

The value derived from his ranch life was of far greater significance to Roosevelt than the considerable monetary loss which was incurred.[27] William Sewall, who had taken Roosevelt on camping trips in New England, believed the years TR spent in the Dakotas produced a startling metamorphosis. Sewall maintained: "He went to Dakota a frail young man suffering from asthma and stomach trouble. When he got back into the world again he was as husky as almost any man I have ever seen who wasn't dependent on his arms for a livelihood."[28]

William Roscoe Thayer, an early biographer of Roosevelt, likewise concluded that "Roosevelt's experience established in him that physical courage which his soul had aspired to in boyhood. . . . To have gained solid health, to have gained mastery of himself, and to have put his social nature to the severest test and found it flawless, were the valid results of his life on the Elkhorn Ranch."[29]

Refreshed in spirit and strong in body, Theodore Roosevelt reentered politics in 1886 as a candidate for mayor of New York City. Undaunted by defeat, he accepted an appointment to the Civil Service Commission in 1887 so that he could remain active in public life. That same year Roosevelt re-married, taking for his wife the vivacious Edith Kermit Carow. He no longer needed the Dakotas as a refuge. TR liquidated his ranch holdings and established his permanent residency at Sagamore Hill, at Oyster Bay on Long Island. An appointment as the assistant secretary of the Navy in the McKinley administration gave TR the opportunity to prepare the United States for its "splendid little war" with Spain. After rounding up some Dakota cowboys and calling them "Rough Riders," Colonel Roosevelt led his volunteer cavalry to a moment of glory at the Battle of San Juan by fearlessly capturing Kettle Hill.

Increasingly, reality appeared to be a part of a Darwinian

natural order of things to TR and the defeat of Spain in 1898 was a simple demonstration to him of the survival of the fittest. The victory attained in the Spanish-American War was representative to Roosevelt of U.S. superiority over the decadent Spanish. TR desired to see the United States become a world power on the international scene and was worried lest national indolence undermine its will to attain and maintain its newly won status. In 1899, Theodore Roosevelt spoke to the Hamilton Club and warned: "A life of slothful ease, a life of that peace which springs merely from lack of either desire of power to strive after great things, is as little worthy of a nation as of an individual."[30]

As a war hero, Theodore Roosevelt was elected governor of New York in 1898. The political boss, Mark Hanna, was glad to have TR elevated to the vice presidency in 1900 to get rid of him. But Hanna was shocked when, in his words, that "damn cowboy" was thrust into the White House following the assassination of President McKinley in 1901. While president, Theodore Roosevelt constantly preached and practiced the active life. He never tired of admonishing the American people to remain strong and repeatedly urged the nation to accept its international responsibilities. "In a democracy like ours," President Roosevelt told an audience in Milwaukee, "we cannot expect the stream to rise higher than its source."[31] The United States, he remonstrated, could be a powerful nation only if the people were energetic and willing to assume individual responsibilities. With that in mind, President Roosevelt was not above exhorting parents to "bring up your children not so they will shirk difficulties, but so that they will overcome them. . . ."[32]

Theodore Roosevelt abhorred weakness and despised the unctuous do-gooder. Whereas he believed that all people should have a "square deal," TR did not favor coddling anyone. He did come to accept the Reform Darwinism of the progressive movement that acknowledged adverse social conditions as a factor in creating underprivileged groups. Roosevelt opposed Woodrow Wilson's domestic goal of breaking industry into small units, since this would negate the "New Nationalism" and stifle the growth and competitive strength of the U.S. economy. When President Wilson spoke of being too proud to fight and failed to prepare the nation for defending its rights, TR felt only disdain for what he regarded as Wilson's naive idealism and mawkish sentimentality.

Roosevelt's realism dictated the necessity of accepting national self-interest as the vital criteria for formulating a foreign policy. Thus TR believed it was salutary for the United States to reap the rewards of empire in the Pacific at the expense of Spain and to virtually take the Panama Canal. The United States was to assume the role of policeman in Latin America and should intervene on the world scene whenever national interest so demanded. TR considered Japan and Germany to be rivals that needed to be held in check. The survival of the fittest applied to the international picture and TR counselled the wise use of military preparedness to maintain a balance for power that was favorable to the United States. While favoring the use of military force when necessary, Roosevelt was not a wanton warmonger. His intervention at the Algeciras Conference in 1906 prevented an outbreak of war between Germany and France, and his role as mediator in the Russo-Japanese War in 1905 won him a Nobel Peace Prize.

President Theodore Roosevelt did more for conservation than any of his predecessors. As chief executive, Roosevelt set aside land for wildlife refuges, enlarged forest reserves, gave impetus to the development of national parks, and urged reclamation (he saw at firsthand the arid Dakota plains).[33] Future generations, he was convinced, must be allowed to come into contact with nature in the wild, because that was the one remaining link between the modern generation and its pioneer heritage. National growth and greatness were also dependent upon adequate protection of the nation's natural resources. Roosevelt admitted that his assignment had been difficult: "It has been no slight task to bring before ninety million people a great conception like that of conservation, and convince them that it is right."[34]

One of Theodore Roosevelt's biographers posed the question as to whether "Roosevelt's great physical force had not developed too harsh an intolerance as a by-product."[35] TR's relentless assault upon his former cohort William Howard Taft and his strong attacks upon Wilson were at times exaggerated and filled with rhetorical overkill. When deprived of the Republican presidential nomination in 1912, Roosevelt wrote to his friend of the Dakotas: "But I either had to fight or to lie down . . . and I do not like to lie down."[36] Fighting like a symbolic bull moose, TR waged political combat against all those who threatened him. Jack Willis, who had accompanied Roosevelt on many of his cowboy exploits, noted the tendency of TR to adopt the code of the West:

> The men of the Old West were simple and direct in their ways and strong in their likes and dislikes. . . . One of their rules of conduct was the old maxim which they often quoted: "My friends can do no wrong and my enemies can do no right." Roosevelt adopted that principle as his own and adhered to it as religiously as though he had been born with the words in his mouth.[37]

One might also assert that the diplomatic "Big Stick" was born in the Badlands, since on the frontier one did not need to bluff with verbal bravado with six-guns very much in sight.

In appraising the career of Theodore Roosevelt, critic Gerald Johnson claimed, "He was a sham as a cattleman and a sham as a Westerner, but that is far from proof that he was a sham as a man."[38] It was true that many of Roosevelt's deeds seemed melodramatic and in retrospect he appears as a character drawn from one of Owen Wister's western novels. (Wister was TR's close friend and also went West for his health.) Despite the legendary embellishments that soon enveloped his western adventures, TR derived his credo of life from his Dakota experience. His adventurous existence on the frontier reinforced the dictums of Charles Darwin and Herbert Spencer. He was, perhaps, one of the few intellectuals of his time to see a theory confirmed in real life. In the primitive Dakotas, Roosevelt learned from experience that frontier conditions and nature in the raw tolerated neither weakness nor timidity. By subjecting himself to the ordeal of pioneer existence, TR was not playing cowboy—he was a cowboy. "The West seemed to complete Roosevelt's self-transformation,"[39] concluded biographer John Milton Cooper, Jr. This came to be his way of life. It was manifested in his political philosophy and public life.

Theodore Roosevelt placed a great premium upon the educative value of his rugged training in the Dakotas. He told a Sioux Falls audience, after the city was a part of the state of South Dakota: "I regard my experience during these years when I lived and worked with my fellow ranchmen on what was then the frontier as the most important educational asset of all my life."[40] In his autobiography, TR explained that contact with men who worked with their hands "enabled me to get into the mind and soul of the average American."[41]

The cowboy years occupied a significant part of the formative years of Theodore Roosevelt. In existential terms, TR chose to be an authentic westerner as the true American prototype and then became one. He lived life to the hilt and used his presidency as a

Courtesy of Theodore Roosevelt Association

"The Long Trail," J. N. "Ding" Darling's tribute to TR, was published in the *Des Moines Register* at the time of Roosevelt's death in 1919.

bully pulpit to preach the virtues of the strenuous life (which he also practiced).

When Theodore Roosevelt died in 1919, at age sixty-six, the famous cartoonist J. N. "Ding" Darling drew a likeness of TR as an obituary. Owen Wister penned a descriptive, epitaph-like statement that epitomized the departed Roosevelt. It read: "In cowboy dress, on his horse headed for the Great Divide: but he is turning back for a last look at us, smiling, waving his hat. On his horse: the figure from other days; the Apparition; the crusader, bidding us farewell."[42]

Even though Theodore Roosevelt is gone, his giant face carved in granite still watches over his beloved Badlands from its high perch on Mount Rushmore. When we look up to view this gigantic monument, our eyes are facing upward toward the vast, limitless sky. TR would have liked that.

NOTES

1. Julian Ernest Choate, Jr., and Joe B. Frantz, *The American Cowboy* (Norman: University of Oklahoma Press, 1955), p. 13.

2. William Wingate Sewall, *Bill Sewall's Story of T.R.* (New York: Harper and Brothers, 1919), pp. 15–16.

3. Lincoln A. Lang, *Ranching with Roosevelt* (Philadelphia: J. B. Lippincott Company, 1926), p. 46.

4. Bert McDowell, "Theodore Roosevelt," *National Geographic Magazine* 114 (October 1958): 572. TR recalled that his father "refused to coddle me, and made me feel that I must force myself to hold my own with other boys and prepare to do the rough work of the world." Letter, TR to his sister Corinne, in Corinne Roosevelt Robinson, *My Brother Theodore Roosevelt* (New York: Charles Scribner's Sons, 1921), p. 50.

5. Henry F. Pringle, *Theodore Roosevelt: A Biography* (New York: Harcourt, Brace and Company, 1931), p. 4.

6. Theodore Roosevelt, *An Autobiography* (New York: Charles Scribner's Sons, 1922), p. 93.

7. Hermann Hagedorn, *Roosevelt in the Bad Lands* (Boston: Houghton Mifflin Company, 1921), p. 43.

8. Theodore Roosevelt, *The Works of Theodore Roosevelt, National Edition*, ed. Hermann Hagedorn, 20 vols. (New York: Charles Scribner's Sons, 1926), 1: 329 (hereafter cited as *Works*).

9. Theodore Roosevelt, *Ranch Life and the Hunting Trail* (New York: G. P. Putnam's Sons, 1907), p. 10.

10. Elting E. Morison et al., eds., *The Letters of Theodore Roosevelt, The Years of Preparation, 1868–1898*, 8 vols. (Cambridge: Harvard University Press, 1951), 1: 73.

11. Ibid., 1: 73–74.

12. Ibid., 1: 77.

13. Roosevelt, *Ranch Life*, p. 33.

14. Lang, *Ranching with Roosevelt*, p. 184.

15. Hagedorn, *Roosevelt in the Bad Lands*, p. 274.

16. Lang, *Ranching with Roosevelt*, p. 260.

17. Roosevelt, *Autobiography*, pp. 93–94.

18. Roosevelt, *Ranch Life*, p. 83.

19. Ibid., p. 82

20. Theodore Roosevelt, *The Winning of the West*, 3 vols. (New York: G. P. Putnam's Sons, 1889), 1: 137.

21. Theodore Roosevelt joined with George Bird Grinnell, the editor of *Forest and Stream* magazine, to found the Boone and Crockett Club in 1887. This hunting club combined the promotion of the "manly sport" of hunting with the study of wild life. The club also sought to promote legislation for the preservation of wild game and encouraged scientific exploration. See George Bird Grinnell, ed. *American Big Game in Its Haunts* (New York: Forest and Stream Publishing, 1904), p. 485.

22. Roosevelt, *Ranch Life*, p. 61.

23. For additional information on the bear incident, see pp. 552–53 in Monica T. Albala's chapter 38 below, "Theodore Roosevelt: The Man and the Image in Popular Culture."

24. Theodore Roosevelt, *Thomas Hart Benton*, vol. 7 of *Works*, p. 12. Henry Steele Commager contends that *The Winning of the West* and the *Naval War of 1812* are the only serious works of history written by Theodore Roosevelt that have stood the test of time. Since Roosevelt wrote hastily and often while engaged in several activities, his promise as a historian was never fully developed. See Henry Steele Commager, *The American Mind: An Interpretation of American Thought and Character Since the 1880s* (New Haven: Yale University Press, 1950), p. 347.

25. John Morton Blum, *The Republican Roosevelt* (Cambridge: Harvard University Press, 1954), p. 28.

26. Theodore Roosevelt, *The Strenuous Life*, (New York: P. F. Collier and Son, 1900), p. 29.

27. During the winter of 1886-1887, the cattle on TR's ranch froze to death at an appalling rate due to the endless sub-zero weather and frigid blasts of wind from Canada. He wrote his sister Anna, "I am bluer than indigo about the cattle; it is even worse than I feared. I wish I was sure I would lose no more than half the money I invested out here." See Morison, *The Letters of Theodore Roosevelt*, 1: 126–27.

28. Sewall, *Bill Sewall's Story of T.R.*, p. 41.

29. William Roscoe Thayer, *Theodore Roosevelt, An Intimate Biography* (Boston and New York: Houghton Mifflin Company, 1919), p. 68.

30. Roosevelt, *Works*, 2: 3.

31. Theodore Roosevelt, *The New Nationalism* (New York: The Outlook Company, 1910), p. 194.

32. Ibid., p. 124.

33. Roosevelt, *Autobiography*, p. 393.

34. Roosevelt, *New Nationalism*, p. 100.

35. Carleton Putnam, *Theodore Roosevelt, The Formative Years, 1858–1886* (New York: Charles Scribner's Sons, 1958), p. 548.

36. Jack Willis to Horace Smith, *Roosevelt in the Rough* (New York: Ives Washburn, 1931), p. 548.

37. Ibid., p. 99.

38. Gerald W. Johnson, *American Heroes and Hero Worship* (New York: Harper and Brothers, 1943), p. 218.

39. John Milton Cooper, Jr., *The Warrior and the Priest: Woodrow Wilson and Theodore Roosevelt* (Cambridge: Harvard University Press, 1983), p. 30.

40. Roosevelt, *New Nationalism*, p. 106.

41. Roosevelt, *Autobiography*, p. 120.

42. Owen Wister, *Roosevelt: The Story of a Friendship* (New York: Macmillan Company, 1930), p. 8. For more on Wister's friendship with TR, see G. Edward White, *The Eastern Establishment and the Western Experience: The West of Frederic Remington, Theodore Roosevelt, and Owen Wister* (New Haven: Yale University Press, 1968).

Theodore Roosevelt's Elkhorn Ranch cabin located on land now part of the Theodore Roosevelt National Park, Medora, North Dakota. (The cabin is no longer standing.)

12

Badlands Bricolage: Forgotten Fragments Culled from the Local Press

James F. Vivian

Theodore Roosevelt's last visit to the American West occurred in October 1918. Montana's state Republican committee had pressed him just after Labor Day to do something about the Nonpartisan League (NPL), a renegade faction that threatened to divide the party in the northwest on the eve of congressional elections. Roosevelt agreed, and the result was a hurried trip to Billings where, in the course of a two-hour speech, he heaped scorn and complaint on the movement and accused its leadership of harboring less than patriotic motives. His friends, including quite a few veterans of the open range who had come to town for the occasion, generally sided with him. "Everyone of my old ranchmen and cowboys, without an exception, have told me that the . . . League represents the very worst type of Bolshevist movements in their state," Roosevelt wrote. All across North Dakota, the NPL's home base, and into the Twin Cities, he continued the attack, delivering no fewer than five speeches in one day upon reaching Minneapolis on the homeward run to New York.[1]

Meanwhile, several of these old-timers had conceived the idea of a grand reunion, which they tentatively planned for the coming spring in the Badlands. Although reluctant and probably just a little dubious, Roosevelt evidently succumbed to their insistent appeals, promising to block out a week or more of his schedule at an appropriate point. It was not to be. The reunion, modified in both form and duration, went forward nonetheless, at the instigation of a half-dozen of Roosevelt's ranching partners and cohorts who still resided in the area and who increasingly painted a romanticized image of the old days.[2]

Hermann Hagedorn, recognizing the opportunity thus created, substituted for Roosevelt at the reunion. A local newspaper avidly watched his extended stay and tour of the Badlands and the side trip to the Black Hills.[3] Hagedorn's working visit yielded two notable dividends: the book, *Roosevelt in the Badlands*, and a film, which had a premier showing at the "Bijou" in Dickinson in 1920. Bucolic scenes clipped from the film helped carry the story in *The Indomitable Teddy Roosevelt*, a 1983 film shown in a two-hour television special aired in June 1986.

Recently the Theodore Roosevelt Nature & History Association of Medora, North Dakota reissued the book. It remains a singular production that, except for Hagedorn's timely and dogged efforts, could not have been composed in the same manner by a different means. Already much of Medora and the Badlands had gone into rapid and irreversible decline, several persons had died, and at least as many others had departed for distant locations. Hagedorn himself alluded to difficulties in gathering print materials (he offered five dollars per issue for missing editions of the *Bad Lands Cow Boy*); and quite a few interviews depended literally on his going the extra mile to obtain them.

Yet, through the years, widely varied entries, especially of reminiscences and recollections, have found their way into the local press. I became aware of their scope two years ago while poring over unindexed newspaper files for the circumstances of Roosevelt's later visits to North Dakota. These trips totalled six instances between the vice presidential campaign swing in 1900 and the attack on the NPL in 1918. My book, published under the auspices of the Theodore Roosevelt Medora Foundation in honor of the state's centennial observance, attempted to capture Roosevelt's application of his Badlands experience in his career and in his speeches.[4]

All of the following fragments share two characteristics in common: they relate to the Badlands frontier of Roosevelt's day, and they are the products of serendipity. None appears in Hagedorn or, for that matter, in the literature known to me, whether by Roosevelt's own rendition or the parallel biographical work on the Marquis de Mores.[5] These fragments are offered in a spirit of historical inquiry. Some of the information is frankly incidental, possibly trivial. Parts of it are suggestive. The balance may contain elements of relative importance. Additional corroboration is admittedly wanting in all cases.

One item involves a scurrilous allegation. Robert Cory, now retired, is a former Minot, North Dakota, journalist who appreciated the interplay of historical influences. In 1963, in his weekly column entitled "Tumbling Around These Prairies," Cory told of an Indian legend that featured Brown Head and Cedar Wood, two Hidatsa women whom Roosevelt supposedly met, by turns, upon employing them at his Elkhorn ranch. Cory acknowledged that his principal source on the Fort Berthold reservation was vague on dates and details and that, besides, no substantive record of any such relationship had been uncovered. Yet, the legend had survived three generations of reservation lore and, in one of its versions, even had Roosevelt married to both women. Mutual incompatibility explained the early breakup of the first relationship, whatever its nature. The second, concerning Cedar Wood, amounted to desertion when Roosevelt decided to return permanently to the East, leaving her, it was said, some household goods and a modest grant for her support.[6]

Hagedorn, who gave a public address at Minot State College in 1958, the centennial of Roosevelt's birth, refuted the charge in a two-page reply. Yes, he knew of the story, he said, without divulging a source, but he had been wholly unable to confirm that Roosevelt ever hired Indians for any purpose, much less as domestics. Roosevelt's associates, those whom Hagedorn consulted in preparing his book, scarcely hinted at the idea. Further, Hagedorn believed it significant that, given Roosevelt's often controversial career, neither his rivals nor detractors had muckraked this slander upon his reputation.[7]

Cory devoted a friendly column to Hagedorn's letter, and there the question rests in complete peace. Were it not for Cory's publicizing the story, I would not have known of it, either as rumor or by insinuation. It circulates in no part of the state today, to my knowledge.

Another item involves Orrin "Dad" Kendley, also known as "Nitch," an otherwise shadowy figure who appears briefly in Hagedorn as the protagonist in an anecdote. Actually, Kendley figured among a clutch of able wranglers, drovers, and stage drivers who found a career in the Badlands. Kate Brower interviewed him in Medora in 1922, when he had become a slightly bent and bronzed old man responsible for keeping the railroad's water tank filled. Kendley, according to Brower, escorted her to his shack a short walk away, opened the door, and pointed excitedly across the room. "Look'a there," he said proudly, "that's Teddy's own desk. He wrote some of his *Hunting Trips of a Ranchman* on it. He gave it to me when he went back East." The desk, so-called, proved to be a simple arrangement of a few planed boards cut to size, nailed into the proper shape, and painted a green-gray color.[8]

"We were overrun with dudes in those days," Kendley explained, "dudes who came out to hunt and to start ranches, some of 'em." He elaborated:

> It didn't take us long to find out Teddy wasn't that kind. He never was what you'd call an expert horseman, but he had a brass monkey's nerve. Why, I've seen him crossing that river [gesturing at the Little Missouri], crossing it horseback when it was high water and logs rolling past every few feet. When he'd make it and the boys'd bawl him out for being reckless, he'd laugh and show his teeth to beat the cars.

"I'm telling you the straight of the story," Kendley insisted, detecting a skeptical droop in the reporter's brow. "He liked to gab as much as the others, but he wasn't one to talk a lot in a crowd, like most of the city dudes. That's one reason the boys liked him. He knew a lot but he never tried to show off."

"Naturally," Kendley continued, "none of us know'd he'd ever be president. We wouldn't have treated him like so much of a human if we had. We just thought he was a bright young feller, a dead game sport, honest and real—what they call these days a regular guy."[9]

Organized religion took up but three pages in Hagedorn's book, chiefly to account for its conspicuous absence in Medora. True, the Marquis's wife built the Catholic chapel at the edge of town, which received little use, and an occasional Protestant preacher stopped by in the course of a desultory circuit. Beyond that, Hagedorn's sources spoke to the subject in bemused, if not irreverent, tones, as if embarrassed by the turn of conversation.

But what of Roosevelt himself? In 1935, when the Reverend Henry B. Schaffner died at age ninety-two, he had long since become a resident homesteader along the Knife River northwest of Bismarck. Years earlier Schaffner, a graduate of Acadia College in Nova Scotia, Canada, presided at the First Baptist Church in Fargo, starting in 1881. Later he organized the congregation in Dickinson, thirty miles east of Medora, serving as its first minister. From this base, his ministry reached into the Badlands and adjacent areas of the Dakota Territory. Schaffner afterward claimed, in language that seemed to imply more than a passing acquaintance, that Roosevelt attended his sermons.[10] When and how many, there is as yet no indication. Does a serious description lie hidden in an obscure small-town weekly? I wonder, and invite others to join the search.

Dr. Victor H. Stickney opened his practice in Dickinson the same year that Roosevelt arrived in Medora. Although many know of Stickney's generous eulogy, privately published in 1922, few have heard of his speech to the state banker's association in 1923, in which he recalled the lawlessness that prevailed in the territorial frontier. The land itself featured "magnificent proportions and a weird beauty that gripped one like a spell," he said, striving for eloquence. "From the Missouri to the Rockies lay the sweep of a province untamed; as fine a limit of earth as was ever traversed by the shadow of a cloud; clean and primal as if but yesterday it had received the sanction of God at the end of His sixth day's work. You could ride a horse through its expanse for months without striking a furrow or a fence."[11]

There, Stickney said, the individualist's creed held absolute sway. "Most contentions" between parties were settled privately, "a pair of colts and a handful of cartridges entering largely into the matter under adjudication." Few objected, certainly not vocally. "The contestants were usually undesirable gunmen, and whatever the outcome ... it was felt the welfare of the community would be advanced." The burial, quickly accomplished and devoid of ceremony, saw everyone adjourn to the nearest "depot," the accepted euphemism for a saloon, to down full jiggers of "snake bite" or "rope burn" while exchanging views of the incident. Maybe someone remembered to notify the sheriff 125 miles away, maybe not. Vigilante squads, he said, supporting Roosevelt's letters and writings, signalled the coming of a new order beginning in 1884.[12]

Yet, according to James Foley, the heyday of rampant lawlessness had to have been short-lived after the introduction of a major investment in 1881—namely, a large cattle herd whose owners demanded government protection. Previously both Indians and whites entered the Dakota Badlands only occasionally and then chiefly for hunting. Indians typically skirted the area for a combination of practical, cultural, and religious reasons, whereas whites, whether wayward drifters or hopeful settlers, knew of better prospects elsewhere.[13]

Foley hired on the Marquis's management staff in 1884. The Marquis retained him in 1886 to superintend the herd-and-rendering plant upon deciding to go chasing after other winsome rainbows. Foley not only spent the rest of his life in Medora (he died in 1917), but also had patrolled the Badlands in its frontier glory while a sergeant stationed since 1879 at the Fort Lincoln encampment near Bismarck. His reminiscences tell mostly of his military experience and the Marquis's heady plans. There are few references to Roosevelt and the other ranchers, and one of them, declaring that Roosevelt numbered among the lucky handful who recovered their losses following the disastrous winter of 1886-87, is clearly erroneous.[14]

It is doubly unfortunate that Foley failed to depict more of Badlands society and culture. Although this was his intention in perhaps two or three articles, his passion for ancient Roman history lured him into wasteful analogies. Foley is rather definite on one point, however. He reminds us that Mingusville, situated about thirty miles to the west on the dusty plain of extreme eastern Montana, was initially called Keith. Mr. and Mrs. Gressy (or Grisy), partners of Pierre Wibaux, renamed it after themselves before quitting in discouragement and returning to France. Except for its seasonal water supply, Mingusville held no particular advantage until the booming cattle industry of the mid-1880s overwhelmed the narrow valley floor at Medora. Foley thought that as many cattle may have been shipped from Mingusville as from Medora simply because the latter could not accommodate the size of some herds. Since Roosevelt described little of his business operations, we should allow for the possibility of his using both loading stations.[15]

Foley called Roosevelt the very personification of American-ism, with a capital "A"—a proposition, he said, in which everyone, regardless of preference or party, had to concur. But as a Badlands rancher, he was "modest, very modest. He was as meek as Moses," Foley wrote. Even after publication of the auto-biography, the majority of Americans knew little of Roosevelt's ties to Dakota. The Northern Pacific's action in raising a track-side billboard celebrating the fact, Foley believed, had been altogether necessary.[16]

From Foley at last we learn the true identity of "Hell Roaring" Bill Jones, the "Foul Mouth." Jones, according to Foley, was really Patrick McCue, from County Cavan, Ireland, who emigrated to

New York in the early 1870s. He joined the army, which assigned him to Fort Pembina at the junction of the Red River of the North and the Canadian border. Soon McCue deserted, changed his name, and made his way to Fargo, where he hired on either the grading crew or survey party of the Northern Pacific until the railhead reached Bismarck. He freighted the mails to Fort Stevenson for a time, where the Missouri River bends westward ninety miles to the north, but eventually went to Billings, Montana, where he claimed to have operated a saloon. Roosevelt met him in the summer of 1884 when Jones hired out as a range hand at the Chimney Butte ranch. The high point of his life had to have been his election to two terms as the first sheriff of Billings County. "Jones," said Foley, had "a very limited education," continually exposed in his adoption of a Welsh name. Jones also possessed "a fund of Irish wit," an easy sociability, and despite a gruff exterior, generous inclinations—traits which partly compensated for two utterly disgusting habits, wearing anything but clean clothes and spewing horrid obscenities.[17]

These, then, are some of the fragments that have come to light. You are welcome to your independent conclusions, of course, but you might want to withhold judgment. My hunch is that there is more to be found. I am even now following an attractive lead. He is James Foley, Jr., a talented writer, sturdy Republican, and professional journalist, who achieved greater renown in his avocation as a poet, humorist, and author of children's stories.[18] The journalism, segments of which recount the Badlands of his youth, Foley sold ad hoc to metropolitan newspapers in the Midwest and the East. The search must necessarily proceed slowly and deliberately. He appears to have left behind no record or list of these intermittent efforts. A year's work should yield reportable results.

NOTES

1. Elting E. Morison, ed., *The Letters of Theodore Roosevelt* (Cambridge: Harvard University Press, 1957), 8: 1,379–80, 1,386–87, 1,391–92; James F. Vivian, "The Last Round-up: Theodore Roosevelt Confronts the Nonpartisan League," *Montana Magazine of Western History*, 36 (Winter 1986): 36–49.

2. Hermann Hagedorn, "Conversation at Dusk Along the Little Missouri," *The Outlook* 123 (September 24, 1919): 137–43; and Hagedorn, "The Roosevelt Country," ibid., 129 (October 19, 1921): 254–59.

3. *Recorder-Post* (Dickinson, ND), June 13, June 30, and July 4,

1919, pp. 1, respectively.

4. James F. Vivian, *The Romance of My Life: Theodore Roosevelt's Speeches in North Dakota*, (Fargo, ND: Theodore Roosevelt Medora Foundation, 1989).

5. Donald Dresden, *The Marquis de Mores: Emperor of the Badlands* (Norman: University of Oklahoma Press, 1970); D. J. Tweton, *The Marquis de Mores* (Fargo, ND: Institute for Regional Studies, 1972).

6. *Minot Daily News* (ND), February 2, 1963, p. 2.

7. Ibid., July 13, 1963, p. 5.

8. *Bismarck Tribune* (ND), October 27, 1922, p. 1.

9. Ibid.

10. Hermann Hagedorn, *Roosevelt in the Badlands* (Boston: Houghton Mifflin, 1921), pp. 325-28; *Bismarck Tribune*, June 11, 1935, p. 2.

11. Victor H. Stickney, *Theodore Roosevelt, Ranchman* (Pasadena, CA: Post Printing, 1922); *Bismarck Tribune*, June 27, 1923, p. 2.

12. *Bismarck Tribune*, June 27, 1923, p. 2. Stickney's "Early Days in Western Dakota Territory," *The Commercial West* 44 (July 14, 1923): 22–24.

13. *Fargo Forum* (ND), July 1, 1915, p. 4.

14. Hagedorn, *Roosevelt in the Badlands*, p. 355; *Bismarck Tribune*, March 4, 1914, p. 5.

15. Donald H. Welsh, "Pierre Wibaux, Badlands Rancher" (Ph.D. diss., University of Missouri, 1955), chap. 4; *Bismarck Tribune*, March 4, 1914, p. 5.

16. *Bismarck Tribune*, March 4, 1914, p. 5.

17. Ibid., March 20, 1914, p. 5; Jones obituary, ibid., August 12, 1911, p. 5.

18. Cf. Kathie A. Anderson, ed., *North Dakota: Literary Heritage of a Prairie State* (Grand Forks: University of North Dakota Press, 1990), pp. 98–101.

13

Hunting, Ranching, and Writing: Did Theodore Roosevelt's Western Experiences Significantly Influence His Later Career and Political Thought?

Lawrence H. Budner

It was evening when Colonel Theodore Roosevelt arrived at the Waldorf Hotel in Fargo, North Dakota, on September 4, 1910. The next day, Labor Day, he would address an audience of more than 20,000 on the rights and duties of labor and management. Before dinner, he was persuaded to speak to a crowd that had gathered outside the hotel. From the balcony, he recalled the days he had spent as a rancher at Medora. "If it had not been for what I learned during those years . . . here in North Dakota," he declared, "I would never in the world have been president of the United States." With a politician's flair, he assured the crowd that he was happy to be "back home again."[1] The following day, at the laying of the cornerstone of the Carnegie Library of Fargo College, he added: "And whatever of value there was in my work as president depended largely upon the fact that I knew and sympathized with our people as you can only know and sympathize with those with whom you have worked and . . . lived."[2] Should these statements be taken literally, or would it be more realistic to discount them as merely the hyperbole of a successful politician? Roosevelt, after all, has been accused of leaving self-serving "posterity letters."[3] What do his private correspondence and other writings reveal? What are the remembrances of those who knew him? How did TR's life in the West influence his political career and progressive political philosophies? Was it a democratizing experience? Did it lead to his strong interest in conservation and reclamation?

Living Life to the Fullest

In 1883, Roosevelt made his first trip to Medora, on the banks of the Little Missouri. He hoped to shoot his first buffalo while it was still possible. After two arduous weeks, he finally made his kill. His guide, Joe Ferris, remembered, "I never saw anyone so enthused in my life." It was on this trip that arrangements were made for Roosevelt to go into the cattle business.[4]

TR bunked during the buffalo hunt with Gregor Lang and his son Lincoln who recalled that both took "an instant liking to Roosevelt." After each evening meal in the Lang's crude cabin, Roosevelt and the elder Lang talked late into the night. Lincoln felt that although they differed on some points, they agreed on the basic issues because "the true spirit of democracy was theirs."[5]

It was not unusual in those days for wealthy young easterners to vacation in the West, but usually they enjoyed most of the luxuries they were accustomed to in the East. Since the Civil War, according to G. Edward White in *The Eastern Establishment and the Western Experience*, "a class of 'Protestant Patricians' led the nation and dominated its traditions." The easterners of this type who came West were usually from Ivy League universities, the same clubs, and the social register.[6] They viewed the cowboy as a semi-barbaric laborer. In 1881, President Chester Arthur's first message to Congress referred to "a band of armed desperadoes known as cowboys."[7] But, if the cowboy had a bad image, the westward movement was nonetheless having a profound influence upon the American imagination. The West seemed limitless in scope and socially less confining. Its spirit of adventure captured the imagination of many affluent easterners.[8] It became fashionable to own or to invest in a ranch in the West.

While sharing some of his social peers' reasons for going West, Roosevelt's motivations were more complex. The resulting experiences were immeasurably more lasting than he had anticipated. Initially, he was drawn to the Badlands by the desire to obtain a buffalo head trophy, as well as by a love of nature and a spirit of adventure. Then came a desire to become a ranch owner in anticipation of financial rewards. With the death of his wife, he sought escape. Later he learned that the West was an attractive and highly marketable subject to write about. As he explained in a letter to his sister Corinne, dated May 12, 1886, "I really enjoy this life. I have managed to combine an outdoors life, possessing much variety, and excitement and now and then a little adventure with a literary life also."[9]

Between 1883 and 1886, TR made eight trips to the Dakotas. Cumulatively, he resided there approximately 426 days, but he had lived life to the fullest, running two cattle ranches, the Chimney Butte and the Elkhorn. He remembered, "It was still the Wild West in those days, the Far West, the West of Owen Wister's stories and Frederic Remington's drawings, the West of the Indian and the buffalo hunter, the soldier and cow-puncher. That land of the West has gone now. . . . In that land we led a free and hardy life, with horse and with rifle."[10]

Perhaps the highlight of TR's two trips to the Badlands in 1885 was spring roundup. He spent thirty-two days working side by side with ordinary cowboys and following the instructions of the captain of the roundup. TR wrote: "A ranchman is kept busy most of the time, but his hardest work comes during . . . roundups . . . it is also the pleasantest part of a cowboy's existence." It was difficult and dangerous work, requiring long hours in the saddle with little sleep. Once he worked for thirty-six consecutive hours. He remembered, "When the work is over . . . the men gather round the fire . . . to sing songs, talk, smoke, and tell stories."[11]

The Results of the Experience

Democratizing influences. A clean living man of inexhaustive energy, a hard worker who respected other hard working men and women, a lover of nature, an avid hunter, a man of limitless courage, this proponent of the strenuous life truly loved his days in the West. Roosevelt gained physical strength and improved his health and self-confidence, but most of all he learned much about "ordinary working men and women." In a speech at Sioux Falls on September 9, 1910, he referred to his years in the territory of Dakota and said, "I regard my experiences during those years . . . as the most educational asset of all my life."[12] His books and letters are filled with expressions of friendship, admiration, and respect for the men and women he knew in the Badlands. He was continually surprised at the intellect of the people with whom he worked and lived. It would be difficult to share a blanket with a man and not have egalitarian thoughts. TR later wrote: "No guests were ever more welcome at the White House than these old friends of the cattle ranches and the cow camps."[13]

From an analysis of available evidence some conclusions

emerge. TR's character was shaped by multitudinous influences. Prior to Harvard, he had been privately tutored. His brothers, sisters, and cousins were his childhood playmates. He had twice travelled abroad and at Harvard he was, by all accounts, a snob. Edward Wagenknecht wrote, "Roosevelt had a social background and he took it for granted even when he disparaged it."[14]

There had also been the moderating influence of his father and three visits to New York tenements. Yet, it was in the West that TR first had daily contact with working men and women on a basis of virtual equality. He learned to respect and admire, even to emulate, their many good qualities. As he shared their hardships and adventures, he developed a new appreciation for the men and women of the West.

This opinion is supported by the writings of many historians. Frederick Jackson Turner, in a review of *The Winning of the West*, observed that "Mr. Roosevelt's appreciative sympathy with frontiersmen, due to part to his own Western experiences, has enabled him to depict the movement as probably no other man of his time could have done."[15] Hermann Hagedorn, a keen and admiring observer of Theodore Roosevelt, wrote that "he plunged into the life of the Bad Lands seeking to comprehend the emotions and the mental processes, the personalities and the social conditions that made it what it was."[16] Henry Pringle, a highly critical biographer, conceded that "Roosevelt established himself with the cowboys, whose riding, recklessness, and exhibitionism he admired extravagantly. That Roosevelt, wearing eyeglasses and christened 'Four-Eyes,' was able to win their respect is no small tribute to his character."[17] Carleton Putnam concluded that his hunting trips gave TR "a sense of kinship with the life and character of the wilderness" and the roundups instilled in him "communion with the personality of the cowboy."[18] William Henry Harbaugh believed that the West "had encouraged his growing tendency to judge men on their merits rather than their social backgrounds. They had developed his natural qualities of leadership."[19]

According to Edmund Morris, after the boat chase and capture of Redhead Finnegan and his men, Roosevelt "had become a minor folk hero." Cowboys now regarded him as "one of our crowd . . . a fearless bugger."[20] In referring to *Ranch Life and the Hunting Trail*, David McCullough believed that Roosevelt "wrote of the cowboy with an appreciation not to be found in the work of previous writers. He wrote of their courage, their phenomenal physical endurance. He liked their humor, admired the unwritten code that ruled the cow camp."[21]

It is also true that TR's writings, especially on an intellectual level, occasionally displayed a condescending attitude toward his western friends. Perhaps there was a touch of *noblesse oblige* in "Mr." Roosevelt's relationships with the cowboys and ranchers. Lewis Einstein wrote that "the cowboys liked him, but no cowboy ever mistook him for one of their own." He believed that Roosevelt was "in the West but not of the West."[22] He expected all of the cowboys and most of his fellow ranchers to address him as "Mr." Roosevelt. Nonetheless, the preponderance of evidence offers compelling proof that his western associations tempered his views. It had been a series of democratizing experiences that shaped a now more mature Theodore Roosevelt.

This is not to say that he had become, or ever truly became, a democrat; like many of his generation he was influenced by Herbert Spencer's "social Darwinism." However, as John Morton Blum pointed out, in time "Roosevelt . . . rejected the attitude toward poverty of the Malthusians and social Darwinists. In politics, at roundups, in battle, he worked and fought with all types of men and won their admiration. . . . He felt that they deserved better housing, shorter hours of labor, increased opportunities to reach a higher level of existence."[23]

In *Woodrow Wilson and the Progressive Era*, Arthur Link wrote of Roosevelt's contribution to the Progressive Era: "there is no doubt that the service he rendered the reform movement was substantial."[24] Roosevelt's "Confession of Faith" at the Progressive party convention in 1912 was "a statement of social and economic principles that was a classic synthesis of the most advanced thought of the time."[25]

Even if, as Blum has said, Roosevelt "was never a Jeffersonian,"[26] the West had a continuing influence on TR's career and political thought. It helped him to develop a sincere concern for the needs and desires of the "average" American and contributed to his becoming a leading spokesman for progressivism in the first two decades of this century. His interest in conservation and reclamation was, at least in part, an expression of his desire to help the people of the West whom he had grown to admire and it was also a concomitant of what he learned in the West.

Conservation and reclamation. This view is substantiated by how quickly after leaving the West TR became a leading proponent of conservation and reclamation. Lincoln Lang, in describing the rugged beauty of the Badlands said, "Among the few who recognized it as something like its true valuation was . . . Theodore Roosevelt."[27] According to Paul Russell Cutright, the conservationist author, "Roosevelt had indeed fallen in love with the Badlands. . . . Uppermost in his thoughts now and then were . . . the scarcity of the buffalo and other large game animals in the valley of the Little Missouri . . . he knew that this reduction in numbers had been due to the indiscriminate slaughter by the guns of 'Man the destroyer.'"[28]

Soon after TR left the West and as a result of numerous long discussions, begun in early 1887 between Roosevelt and George Bird Grinnell, editor of *Forest and Stream*, the Boone and Crockett Club was formed. In time it became a powerful force in advancing the cause of preservation of America's natural resources. After becoming its first president in early 1888, TR appointed a Committee on Parks "to promote useful and proper legislation towards the enlargement and better government of the Yellowstone National Park." In April 1890, Grinnell wrote the *New York Tribune* saying that Theodore Roosevelt "could now be counted among the [forest] reserve's most enthusiastic defenders." Thanks to their efforts, Congress in 1894 passed the Park Protection Act.[29] That same year, mentioning his position as president of the Boone and Crockett Club, TR wrote Secretary of the Interior Hoke Smith: "It will be an outrage if this government does not keep the big Sequoia Park, the Yosemite, and such like places."[30] As governor of New York, he wrote the National Irrigation Congress:

> I believe in the vital necessity of storing the floods and preserving the forests, especially throughout the plains and Rocky Mountain regions. The problem of the development of the greater West is in a large part a problem of irrigation. Any man who has ever dwelt on the great plains knows what a serious matter not only the water supply, but the wood supply is to the farmer.[31]

Roosevelt was without question America's most effective conservationist. As governor of New York, he became the first major political figure publicly to express his views on the subject. Cutright wrote that "the existing population of the United States should be forever grateful that in 1901 a man came to Washington as chief executive who, by instinct, training, and practical knowledge was a conservationist."[32] Shortly after becoming president, on December 19, 1901, he urged Congress to create a national forest reserve. According to Harbaugh, TR "had then plunged headlong into the seven year struggle" for conservation and reclamation. He threw his support behind a Democratic sponsored irrigation and reclamation measure, the Newlands bill.[33] On June 13, 1902, TR wrote Speaker of the House Joseph Cannon concerning the legislation, "This is something of which I have made careful study . . . from my acquaintance with the far West . . . I believe in it with all my heart."[34]

TR's achievements in this field, indeed, were remarkable. While president, he added more than 150 million acres of timberland to reserves, doubled the number of national parks, and created fifty-five wildlife refuges. Cutright suggested that "to be sure Roosevelt's youthful background in natural history was later supplemented by knowledge gained in the Dakota Badlands and other parts of the West."[35]

Reclamation (as distinct from conservation) was Roosevelt's first priority. In his first message to Congress on December 3, 1901, he said, "It is right for the National Government to make the streams and rivers of the arid region useful by engineering works for water storage. . . . The government should construct and maintain these reservoirs."[36] TR later wrote: "The impatience of the Western people to see immediate results from the Reclamation Act was so great that . . . the work was pushed forward at a rate previously unknown in Government affairs."[37] Cutright stated that Roosevelt's "years in the West had given him abundant opportunity to observe . . . the crying need for reclamation of land through irrigation and reforestation."[38]

On May 13, 1908, President Roosevelt opened the Governor's Conference on the Conservation of Natural Resources—attended by thirty-eight governors, justices of the Supreme Court of the United States, leaders of finance and labor, scientists, and publicists. "The President's address was a testament of faith and a statement of hope," said Harbaugh. "The monumental significance of the Governor's Conference can only be suggested." Three years later, Dr. Charles Van Hise, pioneer conservationist and president of the University of Wisconsin wrote about TR's efforts on behalf of conservation and reclamation, "What he did to forward this moment . . . will place him . . . [as] one of the greatest statesmen of any nation of any time."[39]

Conclusion

TR was a complex person. Undoubtedly he and his subsequent achievements were influenced by differing motivations. Perhaps, he was not truly a democrat as he described himself, but he was the leading spokesman of progressivism in the first decade and a half of this century. Even a patrician snob can be, and in this instance was, influenced by 426 days in the West—hunting, ranching, and writing.

Theodore Roosevelt may have best described what he believed to be his true thoughts in a letter to Secretary of State John Hay in 1903. He tells of a trip in the West. TR spoke in numerous small cities and towns, and usually the audience consisted of farmers, their hired hands, and their wives. Then TR added: "For all the superficial differences between us . . . these men and I think a good deal alike or at least have the same ideals."[40] Would or could he have said that before he lived in the Badlands? It is highly unlikely.

NOTES

1. James F. Vivian, "Meet Me in Medora," *Horizons Magazine* 17, no. 2 (Spring 1987): 29.
2. Theodore Roosevelt, "Address at Laying of Corner-Stone of Carnegie Library, Fargo College, September 5, 1910," *Fargo College Bulletin* 7, no. 3 (November 1910): 5.
3. Jacques Barzan and Henry F. Graff, *The Modern Researcher*, 4th ed. (San Diego: Harcourt Brace Jovanovich, 1985), p. 164.
4. Hermann Hagedorn, *Roosevelt in the Bad Lands* (Boston and New York: Houghton Mifflin Company, 1921), pp. 21–45.
5. Lincoln Lang, *Ranching with Roosevelt* (Philadelphia and London: J. B. Lippincott Company, 1926), pp. 103–6.
6. G. Edward White, *The Eastern Establishment and the Western Experience: The West of Frederic Remington, Theodore Roosevelt, and Owen Wister* (New Haven: Yale University Press, 1968), pp. 1–5.
7. Ibid., p. 49
8. Ibid, p. 31.
9. Elting E. Morrison, ed., *The Letters of Theodore Roosevelt* (Cambridge: Harvard University Press, 1951), 1: 99.
10. Theodore Roosevelt, *An Autobiography* (New York: Macmillan, 1913), p. 103.
11. Theodore Roosevelt, *Hunting Trips of a Ranchman* (New York:

G. P. Putnam's Sons, 1885), pp. 15–18.

12. Hagedorn, *Roosevelt in the Bad Lands*, p. 2.

13. Roosevelt, *An Autobiography*, p. 132.

14. Edward Wagenknecht, *The Seven Worlds of Theodore Roosevelt* (New York: Longmans, Green and Co., 1958), p. iii.

15. Frederick Jackson Turner, a review of Theodore Roosevelt's *The Winning of the West* (vol. 4) in *The American Historical Review* 2 (October 1896): 171–76.

16. Hagedorn, *Roosevelt in the Bad Lands*, p. 109.

17. Henry F. Pringle, *Theodore Roosevelt: A Biography* (New York: Harcourt, Brace and Company, 1931), p. 97.

18. Carleton Putnam, *Theodore Roosevelt: The Formative Years 1858-1886* (New York: Charles Scribner's Sons, 1958), pp. 528, 529.

19. William Henry Harbaugh, *Power and Responsibility: The Life and Times of Theodore Roosevelt* (New York: Farrar, Straus and Cudahy, 1961), p. 62.

20. Edmund Morris, *The Rise of Theodore Roosevelt* (New York: Coward, McCann and Geoghegan, 1979), p. 330.

21. David McCullough, *Mornings on Horseback* (New York: Simon and Schuster, 1981), p. 340.

22. Lewis Einstein, *Roosevelt: His Mind in Action* (Boston and New York: Houghton Mifflin Company, 1930), p. 38.

23. John Morton Blum, *The Republican Roosevelt* (Cambridge: Harvard University Press, 1954), p. 29.

24. Arthur S. Link, *Woodrow Wilson and the Progressive Era, 1910-1917* (New York: Harper and Row, 1954), p. 2.

25. Ibid., p. 16

26. Blum, *The Republican Roosevelt*, p. 5.

27. Lang, *Ranching*, p. 33.

28. Paul Russell Cutright, *Theodore Roosevelt, The Making of a Conservationist* (Chicago: University of Illinois Press, 1985), pp. 148, 149.

29. Ibid., pp. 173, 174.

30. Morison, *The Letters*, 1: 371.

31. Morison, *The Letters*, 2: 142.

32. Cutright, *The Making of a Conservationist*, pp. 205, 212.

33. Harbaugh, *Power and Responsibility*, pp. 320, 321.

34. Morison, *The Letters*, 2: 272, 273.

35. Cutright, *The Making of a Conservationist*, p. xi.

36. Theodore Roosevelt, "Message of the President of the United States to the Two Houses of Congress," December 3, 1901 (Washington, DC: Government Printing Office), pp. 20, 21.

37. Roosevelt, *An Autobiography*, p. 431.

38. Cutright, *Theodore Roosevelt the Naturalist* (New York: Harper and Brothers, 1956), p. 165.

39. Harbaugh, *Power and Responsibility*, pp. 334, 336.

40. Theodore Roosevelt, *Cowboys and Kings: Three Great Letters by Theodore Roosevelt* (Cambridge: Harvard University Press, 1954), p. 2.

Courtesy of Theodore Roosevelt Collection, Harvard College Library

Theodore Roosevelt in his office as President of the Board of Police Commissioners of New York City, a post he held 1895–1897.

14

Theodore Roosevelt as Police Commissioner of New York: The Birth of Modern American Police Administration

Jay S. Berman

The professional model of police administration was in its earliest stages of development in 1895.[1] The outgrowth of the progressive drive for efficiency in law enforcement, this approach to reform would dominate the theory and practice of American policing in the coming twentieth century. Beginning as indignant condemnation from the pulpit, press, and podium, the professional model was born from the reformers' recognition of the need for a coherent theory of policing and a practical agenda for change. They sought an alternative to the conventional assumptions that the police force was essentially a component of city politics and that its function, structure, and personnel should be viewed accordingly. The reformers held that police should be seen as a disinterested, nonpartisan agency of government, responsible for the most efficient delivery of services by the most qualified personnel available. Rather than viewing the police officer as an unskilled, obligated servant of the political machine, the reformers envisioned a competent individual with a commitment to public service.

Although Theodore Roosevelt and his contemporaries in the early police reform movement were not specifically cognizant of a "model" per se, they embraced a philosophy and approach to law enforcement which would later come to be known as "police professionalization." Wayne K. Hobson notes that "the emphasis on expertise, the distrust of politics, the use of administrative structures and the values of efficiency, all of which many historians have come to identify with the major segments of the progressive impulse, were interrelated and closely associated with professionalism."[2] As Samuel Walker has observed, at the end of the nineteenth century, police reform ideas coalesced around the concept of professionalization and the professional model became the dominant rationale for a wide variety of strategies for change.[3]

Progressive police reform efforts in cities across the United States commonly began with agitation for official investigations of police misconduct. The revelations of these inquiries, often shocking and sensational, ignited public outrage and generated campaigns for change. The archetypical example of these movements was the anti-Tammany crusade conducted in New York between 1892 and 1894, the resulting Lexow Committee investigation of the New York Police Department, and the subsequent election of a reform administration led by Mayor William Strong in November 1894.

Strong's election as mayor and his subsequent appointment of Theodore Roosevelt to the office of president of the Police Board, presented reformers with access to seats of power and an invaluable opportunity to put their prescription for efficient law enforcement into practice. In Theodore Roosevelt, the reformers found the perfect candidate to confront the awesome challenge of bringing the professional model to the New York Police Department. Roosevelt had already demonstrated in his previous government experience a belief in and a capability to effect change by adopting, managing, and administering. He believed that "ideals should be high, and yet they should be capable of achievement in practical fashion."[4] As John Morton Blum has noted of Roosevelt: "He did not, like many of his liberal contemporaries, expect new laws or theories in themselves to provide good government. To that end he relied upon his own strength of character, upon the agencies of administration he valued, and upon the able men he sought for appointments."[5]

The central focus of the present study is the premise that Roosevelt's administration of the New York Police Department followed the professional model. The essential elements composing the model had emerged in progressive proposals for police reform and included the following:

1. *The military analogy*—the utilization of military terminology, procedures, accoutrements, and discipline as means of improving the efficiency, image, and professional identity of the police.

2. *Strong, centralized executive control*—the consolidation of departmental authority, direction, and operations in central headquarters for purposes of introducing

businesslike order to the police organization and reducing autonomy of the ward-based precincts.

3. *Recruitment of qualified personnel*—the introduction of high entrance standards, rigorous screening procedures, and civil service testing in the selection process in order to infuse the police with a cadre of capable public servants.

4. *Police training*—the institution of mandated training to instill specialized skills, technical competence, and improved performance.

5. *Application of technology*—the application of modern scientific techniques, instrumentation, and equipment to enhance operational effectiveness.

The following discussion will examine the conceptual basis and Roosevelt's application of each element of the professional model in his effort to reform the New York Police Department.

The Military Analogy

The military analogy was in vogue among progressive police reformers of this period. Viewing the police in terms of military structure and function was seen as a means of promoting efficiency, order, and discipline. The armed forces were rigidly authoritarian and strictly hierarchical, a suitable example for the ideal police department the progressives were attempting to achieve. Adaptation of the military analogy to civilian policing facilitated implementation of other elements of the professional model, the practical and successful application of which could be observed in the armed forces.

Roosevelt enthusiastically embraced the military ideal and applied it in his approach to police administration. He called the police force "a half-military organization" and stated that "many of the principles upon which it is governed are analogous to those which obtain in the army or navy."[6] Roosevelt often employed military terminology in his work. He spoke of "warring against crime," of the "war against corruption," and of the "resolute warfare against every type of criminal."[7] He argued for improving "the fighting efficiency of the police."[8] Roosevelt's administration was marked by extensive utilization of military trappings in the New York Police Department, particularly the awarding of medals, citations, and honors.[9] Great emphasis was placed on recognition of gallantry and of "specially meritorious conduct."[10] Roosevelt repeatedly applied the qualities of a soldier to police officers—courage, bravery, discipline, and valor—"qualities upon which we insisted and which we rewarded."[11] During Roosevelt's term as president, the Police Board implemented several new policies which were based on military analogy. In an effort to enhance the appearance of police officers, new regulation uniforms were adopted which incorporated the double-breasted British army box coat and regulation U.S. army leggings.[12] The "School of the Soldier" was incorporated as number 371 of Departmental Rules and Regulations and specified detailed march and drill procedures that were developed for regular exercises and special occasions, such as the annual police parade.[13]

Roosevelt's infatuation with the military analogy was evident in his ideas concerning police promotion. Taking the position that "the best soldiers are those who win promotion by some feat of gallantry on the field of battle," the Police Board president considered deeds of heroism as the most important criteria for advancement within the department.[14] Roosevelt's explanation of the promotion policy clearly stated this view:

> In making promotions we took into account not only the man's general record, his faithfulness, industry and vigilance, but also his personal prowess as shown in any special feat of daring, whether in the arresting of criminals or in the saving of life—for the police service is military in character, and we wished to encourage the military virtues.[15]

A fundamental and highly visible problem that plagued U.S. police departments in the nineteenth century was the lack of discipline among police officers. Inspired by the military analogy, the reformers sought to instill a sense of discipline and martial spirit in the rank and file. The professional model would be successfully implemented only if the strong police leadership it advocated was provided with the means to exercise administrative control over police officers on the street. Various approaches to this end were developed, including appointment of drill masters, required military deportment, disciplinary proceedings modeled on court-martial, and increased use of fines and suspensions.[16]

Within days of assuming office, the Strong-appointed Police Board began to confront the problem of discipline that had been endemic in the New York Police Department. The board issued a series of orders intended to communicate its position on discipline. All members of the force were informed of the board's insistence upon "the rigid enforcement henceforth of every rule and regulation of the Department."[17] All officers were instructed to exhibit "gentlemanly deportment . . . whether in the station house or in the street . . . to every man, woman, or child, rich or poor alike."[18] All sworn personnel were forbidden to join or contribute to any political organization and warned that any political allegiances would be regarded as a violation of law with serious consequences.[19]

Roosevelt attempted to deliver a strong message to the ranks that the prevailing casual attitude toward discipline and proper conduct would no longer be tolerated. The New York Police Department witnessed an unprecedented number of fines and dismissals during the Roosevelt administration, May 1895 to April 1897. A yearly comparison of disciplinary actions in the department demonstrates the extent of the change:[20]

	1893	1894	1895	1896	1897
Total complaints brought against officers	4,209	3,890	3,757	5,439	6,134
Total monetary fines imposed	$15,664	$14,871	$23,139	$29,768	$35,759
Total days fined without pay	4,759	4,248	6,064	8,269	10,217
Total officers dismissed from force	11	41	88	81	98

Strong, Centralized Executive Control

The concept of strong, centralized executive control was entirely consistent with Roosevelt's administrative philosophy. During his term of office, he was able to effect several significant policy and operational changes which served to strengthen and expand the role of central headquarters in the New York Police Department while curtailing the autonomy of the precincts. Taking a direction advocated by contemporary police reformers, the department adopted a more businesslike approach to management under Roosevelt. The support staff at headquarters was increased with hiring of additional clerks, secretaries, and stenographers. A review of Police Board budget activity during 1895 and 1896 reveals frequent transfers within the Salary Fund, from the uniformed to the clerical force, as well as a noticeable expansion of the clerical lines.[21]

A more intensive effort to closely monitor the financial affairs of the scandal-ridden police department was also undertaken. Tighter controls were quickly instituted over disbursements from the department's $6 million budget.[22] Purchases of equipment and supplies, long used as a means of political patronage, were now required to undergo a formal contract process. Sealed bids, accompanied by a presentation of working samples before an open meeting of the Police Board, were demanded of all vendors wishing to conduct business with the department.[23] Stringent fiscal controls also extended to routine operational expenditures. The board required that all disbursements of departmental funds be authorized in writing, only upon formal requisition, and that all expenses incurred at the precinct level be carefully examined and audited.[24]

The police department's policy manual had not been updated for several years when Roosevelt was appointed to the Police Board. The manual was an essential source of department-wide direction and coordination. Roosevelt appointed a committee of ranking officers to conduct an extensive review of written policy. The committee collected all orders, rules, and regulations in effect and formulated them into a revised and condensed manual.

The board further authorized the printing of 7,500 copies of the *Manual of Rules and Regulations* for distribution to all officers.[25] Such a move was noteworthy in view of the fact that promulgation of formal written rules and regulations, and their distribution to personnel in the form of a manual, did not become common practice in U.S. law enforcement until the 1970s.

In a significant move to extend the influence of the departmental administration, Roosevelt sought to strengthen the Central Detective Bureau located at headquarters. This was a basic strategy of the period reformers to reduce the power of the precincts.[26] A new commander was assigned to the bureau, the staff was increased, twenty-four-hour coverage was instituted, and a telephone was installed.[27] The role of the Central Detective Bureau was redefined to encompass a more aggressive pursuit of criminal activity, particularly in areas of vice and excise law enforcement. Roosevelt missed no opportunity to contrast his performance with that of "the old regime," noting that Detective

Bureau arrests in his first year of office were double the previous year (2,527 to 1,384) with significant increases in convictions, years sentenced, and fines imposed.[28]

Roosevelt's efforts to strengthen the central executive control of the police department included closer direction of precinct operations. A complete inspection of all precinct station houses was undertaken, with many found to be in poor repair and "some of them in a positively unsanitary condition."[29] As a result of the survey, extensive repairs, including the installation of new fire escapes, were made on all precinct stations.

Roosevelt initiated the expansion of the department's inspectional apparatus as a means of effecting greater disciplinary control. Pursuing his policy of strengthening the role of central headquarters, the Police Board president increased the number of inspection districts from three to six, reducing the number of precincts overseen by each inspector and thus improving the capability of departmental administration to monitor compliance in the precincts.

Recruitment of Qualified Personnel

Civil service and recruitment were Roosevelt's special interests as a police commissioner. He was determined to bring his ideas and experience as a member of the United States Civil Service Commission to bear upon the problem of personnel in the New York Police Department. A special committee appointed by Mayor Strong to investigate appointment procedures in the department confirmed that police positions were generally secured through political influence or by outright purchase, while civil service rules "did not interfere seriously with either practice."[30] Roosevelt's argument for higher admissions standards for police officers was a quintessential progressive statement for police professionalization:

> It may be well, at the outset, to state that patrolmen receive ultimately $1,400 a year and that from their ranks are developed a chief, a deputy chief, five inspectors, thirty-seven captains, nearly 200 sergeants and nearly 200 roundsmen, with salaries ranging from $6,000 to $1,500. The highest among these men occupy positions of trust as important as there are in the city, and even the ordinary patrolman is an exceptionally well-paid public official in a position of exceptional responsibility. To many of our poorer fellow citizens, he is the embodiment of government itself, and it is

> to him that they must look for law and justice. Such an officer, therefore, should not only be brave, honest, and physically powerful, but also possessed of intelligence distinctly above the average.[31]

In his first week in office as Police Board president, Roosevelt set into motion the machinery for upgrading the police department's selection process. On May 15, 1895, he announced that the first examination for patrolmen under the new administration would be conducted to fill 300 vacant positions. An unprecedented campaign was launched to publicize the upcoming examinations. Roosevelt directed the preparation and distribution of a printed announcement to be sent to all interested individuals, informing them of the new formalized testing procedures. In order to obtain the largest possible pool of qualified applicants, Roosevelt expanded recruitment efforts to include all areas of New York State, resulting in large numbers of applicants from small rural upstate communities. The ambitious campaign and the publicity it generated resulted in a record 18,000 requests for applications.[32]

The admissions standards for patrolmen were reviewed and revised by the Police Board. The minimum height requirement was raised from 5 feet 7 inches to 5 feet 8 inches, weight from 133 pounds to 140 pounds, and chest measurement from 33 inches to 34-1/2 inches.[33] The age range for an appointment was set at twenty-one to thirty years of age, marking the first time an upper age limit was established by the department. These new admissions standards were highly significant in view of the fact that minimum height, weight, and age limits were not universally adopted by police departments in the United States until the 1940s.[34]

Roosevelt initiated the adoption of a complete set of new regulations governing the personnel selection and testing process. All entry-level positions in the department were made subject to competitive examination, including uniformed patrolmen, matrons, surgeons, and clerical personnel. Perhaps Roosevelt's most significant contribution as police commissioner was the construction of a rational, systematic testing procedure that became the model for police personnel selection methodology in the United States. Roosevelt designed the format of medical, written, and physical agility examinations supplemented by background investigations of all applicants.

The results of the recruitment and selection effort undertaken during Roosevelt's term as police commissioner were impressive. Due to existing vacancies, yearly increases in positions, and a special authorization by the New York State Legislature creating 800 new police officer positions, the Roosevelt board was given a unique opportunity to substantially alter the complexion of the New York Police Department. A total of twenty-four examinations for patrolmen were conducted between July 15, 1895 and January 1, 1897, yielding three times as many appointments as had ever been made in a comparable period in the department's history. More new police officers were appointed during this eighteen month span than in the previous six years combined.[35] The following statistics reveal the scope of this effort:[36]

Patrolman Positions July 15, 1895-January 1, 1897

Requests for applications	18,000
Applications issued	17,750
Applications returned	9,889
Rejected for minimum requirements (height, weight, age)	445
Notified for medical examination	8,099
Rejected for medical reasons	3,624
Failed written examination	4,455
Notified for athletic examination	1,517
Failed athletic examination	58
Recorded on eligible list	1,517
Selected and appointed	1,467

Such numbers are remarkable in view of the fact that prior to 1896, the number of new appointments to the department had averaged only seventy per year![37] Roosevelt was particularly gratified by the large number of persons requesting applications. This he interpreted as newfound public confidence in the fairness and integrity of the selection process. He also noted, with pride, that, while all graded examination papers were open to inspection and appeal, not one protest of the final results or ratings was registered with the Police Board.[38]

During Roosevelt's term as commissioner, there was a noteworthy increase in the presence of women in the New York

Police Department. Roosevelt created a sensation when he named Minnie Gertrude Kelly to the $1,700 per year position of clerk to the president of the Police Board, marking the first time a woman was appointed to an administrative position in the department's history. This action was hailed by the *New York Recorder* as "another illustration of the onward march of women . . . who are gallantly storming and carrying the batteries of prejudice and conservatism."[39] Roosevelt vastly expanded the number and role of police matrons. In 1896, thirty-two women were appointed to new matron positions, the largest number ever in a single year.[40] The duties of the matrons were broadened to initiate twenty-four hour coverage of most precinct houses. Their responsibilities included searching female suspects; processing, escorting, and supervising female inmates in precinct detention facilities; and caring for lost children. The Police Board devised specific new rules and regulations governing the matrons and specified a dress code which called for "a neat dark blue or black dress, with skirts two inches from the ground."[41] Despite the emerging recognition of female criminality and of the vital role of women in policing, the New York Police Department did not open its ranks to women as fully sworn officers until 1921.

Police Training

One of the most notable developments to occur during Roosevelt's term as Police Board president was the opening, on December 30, 1895, of the New York Police Department School of Pistol Practice. A series of firearms-related accidents and failures by officers to shoot properly at critical moments had prompted the board to examine firearms proficiency among patrolmen. Their findings revealed that the majority of officers were poor marksmen, and that most had never received any training in the care and use of their weapons.[42] The result was the establishment of the School of Pistol Practice, marking the first organized, mandated training in the history of the police department. The school was authorized by resolution of the Police Board "with a view of increasing the efficiency of the Police force, and of establishing systematic instruction."[43]

The school was located at the Eighth Regiment Armory at 94th Street and Park Avenue in Manhattan and had a full-time staff of five instructors. Instruction and practice were held every weekday afternoon between the hours of one and five o'clock.

Every officer in the department was required to attend at least two days per year, with the opportunity for additional voluntary instruction while off-duty. Platoons from each precinct were scheduled for one-hour sessions and marched as a group from their station houses to the armory.[44]

Although this training effort was modest by modern standards and was limited strictly to firearms instruction, its significance may be demonstrated by the fact that, with the exception of the Cincinnati Police Department's School of Instruction, it was the only formal police training program in the United States at this time. The New York School of Pistol Practice would eventually evolve into the establishment of the New York City Police Academy in 1909.

Application of Technology

Upon becoming police commissioner, Roosevelt endeavored to introduce several new technological advances into the archaic operations of the New York Police Department. In February 1896, the Police Board had received a recommendation from the Medico-Legal Society of New York urging the adoption of the Bertillion system of identification.[45] After studying the method, the board approved its implementation. The Bertillion system had four components: precise physical measurements of eleven key parts of the body, utilizing standardized instruments and recording procedures; exact notations on the location of distinguishing features, such as scars and deformities; front and side view photographs; and imprints of finger marks.[46] Prior to the adoption of the Bertillion method, the department had relied entirely upon available photographs and newspaper descriptions for identifying criminals.[47] In conjunction with the establishment of the new system, a photographic studio and developing facility were constructed at police headquarters. In the past, prisoners had to be marched through the city streets from headquarters to private commercial photographers to have their pictures taken. A "rogue's gallery" was also set up at the Mulberry Street offices for the display of suspect photographs.

Communications had long been a problem hampering the daily operations of the New York Police Department. When Roosevelt assumed the presidency of the Police Board, the ancient telegraph system, installed in the 1850s, was still the basic communications link between police headquarters and the various precincts. The Police Board resolved to overhaul the existing telegraph network. Police lines had been strung along the poles of various private telegraph companies across the city, making them susceptible to interference from overhead lines and vulnerable to destruction during civil disturbances. The board authorized the placement of conductors, connecting central headquarters to the precincts, to be placed underground and underwater across rivers, enabling the department to maintain exclusive control over its lines.[48] The board also ordered the installation of an experimental telephone system. In July 1895, 100 telephone sets and a fifty-drop switchboard were ordered from the Metropolitan Telephone and Telegraph System for a six-month trial term costing $500.[49] However, as no funding from the state for the project was forthcoming, the full system was not implemented.

Roosevelt and his fellow police commissioners had more success in the area of transportation. Patrol wagons had been in use in other cities since the 1880s, but none had yet been acquired in New York when Roosevelt took office. Sixteen new horse-drawn patrol wagons were purchased by 1896 and were used to answer over 30,000 calls in their first year in service, including transporting prisoners and conveying large numbers of officers to fire and accident scenes.[50]

New York's many waterways required the police department to maintain a harbor patrol. The vessels used by the patrol were old rowboats, dating back to the 1860s, which Roosevelt called "practically useless."[51] A survey of various types of power-driven launches was conducted and after investigating the alternatives, the board purchased lightweight naphtha-powered launches that required no special operating knowledge and could be fueled for thirteen cents an hour.[52]

The most publicized improvement in the mobility of the force during Roosevelt's administration was the formation of the police department's Bicycle Squad. The Bicycle Squad was started with four officers chosen from sixty applicants. In addition to traffic duty, the cyclists soon proved their worth by arresting drunken, reckless, and speeding horsemen and drivers, by stopping runaway teams of horses, and by pursuing and apprehending thieves and pickpockets. Roosevelt authorized the transfer of monies from other departmental accounts to increase the squad's personnel and to purchase additional bicycles.[53] In its first year of operation, the squad was expanded to twenty-nine officers and was responsible for 1,366 arrests.[54] Eventually the bicycle squad grew into an elite corps of 100 members, occupying its own station house and given special uniforms. The squad was widely publicized and became the model for similar units in other cities.

Another noteworthy application of technology was the adoption of new standard weapons by the police department. Soon after taking office, Roosevelt ordered a study of service revolvers in use by members of the force. Heretofore, the Smith and Wesson revolver had been the department's prescribed standard weapon. Investigation revealed, however, that the uniform weapon requirement had never been enforced by previous administrations.

After a series of accidental discharges and other firearms-related accidents which caused death or injury to several police officers and civilians, Roosevelt decided to remedy the problem. A committee of police officers and outside firearms experts was appointed to examine the various revolvers in use and to select a standard firearm best suited for police use. Manufacturers and dealers were invited to submit samples for test and consideration. After extensive technical evaluation and ballistic testing, the committee recommended and the Police Board approved the newly developed Colt .32 double-action police revolver with four-inch barrel.[55] All officers who did not possess the former standard Smith and Wesson in good condition (a number amounting to over half the force) and all new recruits were required to purchase the new Colt. The Colt .32 was eventually acquired by all officers in New York and became the most popular police revolver in the United States.

Conclusion

Roosevelt's efforts to reorganize the New York Police Department clearly constituted an application of the professional model of police administration. His employment of military procedures and discipline, his consolidation of administrative control in central headquarters, his extensive overhaul and upgrading of recruitment processes and standards, his initiation of firearms training, and the introduction of new technology demonstrated the feasibility of the concepts of reform in the largest police department in the United States. This translation of the theory of the professional model into actual practices and policies was Roosevelt's most significant contribution to the birth of modern American police administration.

NOTES

This essay is drawn from material previously published as part of Jay S. Berman, *Police Administration and Progressive Reform: Theodore Roosevelt as Police Commissioner of New York* (Westport, CT: Greenwood Press, 1987).

1. Ernest S. Griffith, *A History of American City Government, The Conspicous Failure, 1870-1900* (New York: Praeger Publishers, 1974), p. 273.

2. Wayne K. Hobson, "Professionals, Progressives, and Bureaucratization," *The Historian* 39 (1977): 640.

3. Samuel Walker, *A Critical History of Police Reform* (Lexington: Lexington Books, 1977), p. ix.

4. Theodore Roosevelt, *Works of Theodore Roosevelt*, Memorial Edition (New York: Charles Scribner's Sons, 1923), 18: 92.

5. John Morton Blum, *The Republican Roosevelt* (New York: Atheneum, 1966), p. 22.

6. Theodore Roosevelt, "Taking the Police Out of Politics," *Cosmopolitan* 20 (November 1895): 45.

7. Theodore Roosevelt, "Administering the New York Police Force," *American Ideals* (New York: The Review of Reviews Company, 1900), pp. 215-29.

8. Theodore Roosevelt, *Autobiography* (New York: Macmillan Company, 1913), p. 194.

9. New York Police Department, *Annual Report-1896*, p. 17.

10. TR, *Autobiography*, p. 193.

11. Ibid., pp. 195, 209.

12. New York Police Board, Minutes, February 4, 1896, p. 539, typescript at Theodore Roosevelt Birthplace National Historic Site, New York, NY.

13. Ibid., p. 592.

14. TR, "Taking the Police Out of Politics," p. 45.

15. TR, "Administering the New York Police Force," p. 226.

16. Robert Fogelson, *Big City Police* (Cambridge: Harvard University Press, 1977), p. 81.

17. Police Board, Minutes, May 17, 1895, p. 28.

18. Avery Andrews, "Citizen in Action: The Story of T.R. as Police Commissioner" (unpublished manuscript, Theodore Roosevelt Collection, Harvard University Library, Cambridge), p. 44.

19. Police Board, Minutes, May 22, 1895, p. 39.

20. Police Department, *Annual Report–1896*, p. 7.

21. New York Police Board, Minutes, 1895, p. 82.

22. New York Police Department, *Annual Report–1896*, p. 74.

23. New York Police Board, Minutes, 1895, pp. 299-319.

24. Ibid., p. 592.
25. Ibid., p. 956.
26. Fogelson, *Big City Police*, p. 58.
27. Police Board, Minutes, November 19, 1895, p. 410.
28. Police Department, *Annual Report–1896*, p. 17.
29. Ibid., p. 16.
30. Martin J. Schiesl, *The Politics of Efficiency* (Berkeley: University of California Press, 1977), p. 208.
31. *New York Sun*, February 6, 1897, p. 1.
32. Police Department, *Annual Report–1896*, p. 86.
33. Police Board, Minutes, May 15, 1895, p. 23, also *New York Sun*, May 16, 1895, p. 1.
34. National Commission on Law Observance and Enforcement, *Report on the Police* (1931, reprint; Montclair, NJ: Patterson Smith, 1968), pp. 62–63.
35. TR, "Report to the Mayor by the President of the Police Board," 1896, Municipal Archives, New York City, pp. 8–11.
36. Police Department, *Annual Report—1896*, pp. 86–87.
37. Ibid.
38. Ibid., p. 85.
39. Henry Pringle, *Theodore Roosevelt* (New York: Harcourt, Brace and Company, 1931), p. 137.
40. Police Board, Minutes, September 4, 1895, pp. 286–87.
41. Ibid., p. 288.
42. Avery Andrews, "Citizen in Action," p. 44.
43. Police Board, Minutes, October 4, 1895, p. 336.
44. Ibid., p. 337.
45. Ibid., p. 568.
46. David Johnson, *American Law Enforcement: A History* (St. Louis: Forum Press, 1981), p. 109.
47. Police Department, *Annual Report–1896*.
48. Ibid., p. 49.
49. Police Board, Minutes, July 10, 1895, p. 162.
50. TR, "Report to the Mayor," p. 9.
51. Ibid., p. 10.
52. Ibid.
53. Police Board, Minutes, March 13, 1895, p. 603.
54. Police Department, *Annual Report–1896*, p. 24.
55. Police Board, Minutes, June 3, 1896.

Theodore Roosevelt in his office as Assistant Secretary
of the Navy, a post he held 1897–1898.

The Presidency:
The Square Deal

LAYING THE FOUNDATIONS

Courtesy of Theodore Roosevelt Collection, Harvard College Library

"Square Deal" cartoon by Robert Carter from the 1912 campaign: Theodore Roosevelt began using the "square deal" slogan in 1903. At Syracuse, New York, on September 7, 1903, TR said: "We must act upon the motto of all for each and each for all. . . . We must treat each man on his worth and merits as a man. We must see that each is given a square deal, because he is entitled to no more and should receive no less."

15

Teddy Downeast:
The 1902 New England Tour and the Style
and Substance of Roosevelt's Leadership

William Lemke

On the morning of August 22, 1902, having made the passage across sparkling Long Island Sound from Oyster Bay, a typically jaunty Theodore Roosevelt stepped ashore in Connecticut. The first modern American president thus began a thirteen-day speaking tour the length and breadth of the nation's oldest region. The New England tour demonstrated his great popularity, and afforded Roosevelt his first sustained opportunity to delineate his positions on the trust issue and the Monroe Doctrine. It also showcased TR's adept manipulation of symbols, notably his ability to associate his leadership with a wide range of personalities—from war heroes and public figures to backwoodsmen. Finally, incidents of Roosevelt's communion with the masses, particularly at Pittsfield, Massachusetts, reminded everyone of the fragile basis for the new leadership. The tour was more than just another presidential road show. It was a defining episode of Theodore Roosevelt's presidency.

The New England trip, the most extensive speaking tour since TR assumed office, was the first of three tours planned for the president before the fall elections. The itinerary maximized Roosevelt's exposure, with stops in each of the region's six states, starting in Connecticut on August 22 and ending there on September 3. In addition to speeches in the larger cities, the president's special five-car train stopped at a number of small villages where the chief executive made brief remarks. Most of the journey was by rail, but there were several short carriage excursions. Roosevelt even rode in an automobile in Hartford (a purple-lined Columbia Electric Victoria), another presidential first for a president who set many. Whenever possible, drives around the towns and cities were substituted for indoor receptions. Speechmaking was limited to the president, and no handshaking was permitted. The restrictions were partly to prevent delays in Roosevelt's minutely planned schedule, but they were for security reasons as well. Nobody could forget the fatal result of President McKinley's close proximity to the public almost exactly a year earlier. While the president was to be seen and heard by as many people as possible, an effort was made to limit his actual physical contact with them.

"Whatever may be the real object of this roundabout tour," commented the *Portland Eastern Argus,* "there is no partisanship involved in a presidential journey through the United States, for it has now become in the eyes of the people the right and proper thing for every chief executive to do."[1] Roosevelt's predecessors, notably Benjamin Harrison and William McKinley, had made lengthy speaking tours. They were not, in themselves, novel by 1902. However, the conclusion of the *Eastern Argus* (interestingly enough, a pro-Democratic paper) is at least open to modification. The tour coincided with the beginning of the campaign season in most states; the exception was Maine, where it came right before the early September state elections. Granted, the GOP held clear majorities in Congress, led on the state level, and hardly faced a vigorous threat in New England. "The average New England Democrat doesn't expect his reward in this life," one newsman wrote.[2] Still, there was the tendency of the party in power to sustain losses in a nonpresidential election. Roosevelt's appearances could be helpful to Republicans. Certainly they were useful to an "accidental president" eager to build his political capital for nomination and election in his own right in 1904.

Correspondence between TR and Henry Cabot Lodge, a key promoter of the tour, indicates that the Massachusetts senator had partisan concerns. "I do not want to go to Boston at all," Roosevelt complained to Lodge, pointing out that he had recently spoken at Harvard's commencement. "If I do go couldn't I speak before the Social Settlement people? . . . I hail the chance on these trips to talk to some special subject, for it is a terrific strain to have to meet the same kind of an audience and to make the same kind of speech again and again." Lodge replied that Boston had already been scheduled, adding, "I know what a strain the conventional wayside speech is but you need not talk more than five minutes. . . . It is really to show yourself, no more." Lodge and Massachusetts Governor Winthrop Murray Crane did not consider the settlement visit a good idea since "we have tried for obvious reasons to make everything [seem] purely official." But, Lodge adroitly concluded, if TR was *determined* to see the settlement folk, "I approve because I want you elected in case I should be defeated for the Senate. So that I may have the cabinet to fall back upon—State Department preferred."[3] Lodge, like Roosevelt, had his eye on the political future.

Roosevelt intended to emphasize two issues. "I should like to keep this anti-imperialist issue to the fore in the congressional campaign," he told Lodge, "for if it is made the main issue we can certainly beat the Democrats out of their boots."[4] The other issue, much more sensitive, was the trusts. Roosevelt had given some indication of his feelings in his December message to Congress, but these were so hedged that even the most conservative Republicans could easily applaud the message. The antitrust persecution of Northern Securities, initiated in May 1902, reflected a less than passive attitude toward corporate power, but it required further explanation. Roosevelt preferred to position himself on this issue rather than tackle that of tariff revision, at least in New England, where the subject of a reciprocity treaty with Canadians was a volatile issue within GOP ranks. In the background loomed the growing crisis posed by the anthracite coal strike.[5] Economic danger clouds were forming on the political horizon. Roosevelt felt he had to say something or risk losing the appearance of confronting them.

On a personal level the tour proved a smashing success. Large and enthusiastic crowds greeted Roosevelt. He had already emerged as a distinctive political "character," and he lived up to expectations. Adulatory press coverage and the mass response to TR, in supposedly staid New England, bordered on frenzy.[6]

Hermann Hagedorn described Roosevelt addresses as "actually a single address, delivered in parts, one in one city, another in another—presenting the trust problem as he saw it." His first major speech on trusts was in Providence, Rhode Island, on August 23. TR accepted the inevitability and necessity of corporations, but conceded there had been abuses of corporate power. "The great corporations . . . are the creatures of the State," he argued, "and the State not only has the right to control them, but it is in duty bound to control them wherever the need of such control is shown." Claiming the states were inadequate regulators, and evincing concern about court favoritism to corporations, Roosevelt said, "The nation must assume the power of control by legislation; if necessary by constitutional amendment." In just two important sentences, TR had used the word "control" four times. Roosevelt's message, according to the *New York Times,* "was listened to with unusual interest."[7]

Still tantalizingly vague as to specifics, the president foreshadowed the later Roosevelt in his August 25 speech in Boston when he said, "We must probably experiment somewhat. . . . I want laws that will enable us to deal with any evil no matter what shape it takes." TR hastened to add that he wanted a national corporate law comparable to that of Massachusetts (apparently not one of the states he had in mind in Providence), saying, "So you can see, gentlemen, I am not advocating anything very revolutionary." Roosevelt spent much of the rest of his New England swing modifying the impact of his trust statements. In Fitchburg, Massachusetts, on September 2, he charged that anybody who advocated a *general* assault on corporate power was "at least a quack, and at worst an enemy to the Republic." An improvement of "these great industrial problems, of which this so-called problem of the trusts is but one" could be accomplished by "getting power somewhere" and using that power "fearlessly, but with moderation."[8] TR was ready to be fearlessly moderate! He had carefully staked out maneuvering room in the greatest possible middle ground.

Contrary to Hagedorn's analysis, Roosevelt spoke about other topics than the trusts. Indeed, his first major speech, appropriately enough at Hartford's Coliseum on August 22, was a vigorous defense of the New Imperialism. He trumpeted the successful administration of empire in the Caribbean and Philippines, and boasted that the soon-to-be-built Isthmian canal would be "the greatest engineering feat of the twentieth century." He dismissed whatever atrocities that the army committed in the War of the Philippine Insurrection as mere aberrations that should not undermine support for imperialism. Roosevelt used the occasion of his appearance at the home of Navy Secretary William Moody in Haverhill, Massachusetts, on August 26 to stress that the "good work of building up the navy must go on without ceasing." Naval power was crucial to America's defense. Simultaneous with the president's tour, naval war games were being conducted off the New England coast. So dramatic and realistic were headlines depicting the progress of the "cruel war" offshore that casual readers might have confused the games with the real thing. Our fleet prevailed.[9]

Although Roosevelt stressed the U.S. Navy's defensive role in Haverhill, he indicated the next evening in Augusta, Maine, that there was an area where the fleet's role might be more offensive. Speaking in the illuminated shadow of James G. Blaine's mansion, TR said:

> Our interest in the Monroe Doctrine is more complicated than ever before. The Monroe Doctrine is simply a statement of our very firm belief that on this continent the nations now existing here must be left to work out their own destinies among themselves and that the continent is no longer to be regarded as colonizing ground for any European power. The one power on the continent that can make that doctrine effective is, of course, ourselves for in the world as it is, gentlemen, the nation which advances a given doctrine likely to interfere in any way with other nations must possess power to back it up if she wishes the doctrine to be respected. We stand firmly on the Monroe Doctrine.[10]

The significance of these words was not lost upon London, Berlin, and other foreign capitals far beyond the capital of Maine. Such statements, on economic and foreign policy issues, positioned Roosevelt for future actions. Their ambiguity was partly political, and partly reflected the incomplete formulation of specific policies.

The tour was also an extended illustration of the Rooseveltian style. Less oratorical than conversational, TR's "stump" speaking could be most effective. This was particularly so in brief appearances where the president had limited opportunity to establish rapport. A representative example occurred during a stop at Old Orchard, Maine. As he often did, Roosevelt drew attention to the Civil War veterans in the crowd:

> Now you, over there. [Pointing.] He was in the great war. Yes. When you went to war and moved into battle you took an immense interest in what the man on your right hand and your left hand did, but you did not care in the least whether they were bankers or lumbermen or farmers or what, if they staid put. [Cries of "That is right."] That is what you wanted. [Cheer and cries of "God bless you."]
>
> What you wanted was to know that the man had the right stuff in him. [A voice: "That is it."] And if he had, you were for him. [A voice: "Yes, Sir."] And if he did not, you were not for him. You have got to have the same principle in citizenship. . . .

The State can do something for all of us, but not as much as we can do for the State. [A voice: "Amen."] And not as much as each man can and must do for himself. That is what is going to count in the long run. [A voice: "That's business."][11]

Having foreshadowed phrases associated with the journalist Tom Wolfe and John F. Kennedy in another era, Roosevelt moved on to Portland. There he deftly associated himself with two Maine figures of national fame.

TR addressed over half of his speech to the living legend who shared the platform, Joshua Chamberlain. A Bowdoin professor, authentic war hero, and one of Maine's most popular (and controversial) governors, the old soldier was the living personification of the "Scholar in War and Politics" that Roosevelt idealized. The president noted how pleased he was to be "greeted here . . . by you, general, to whom it was given at the supreme moment of the war to win the supreme award of a soldier of honor to a man, and may we keep ourselves from envying him because to him fell the supreme good fortune of winning the Medal of Honor for mighty deeds done in the mightiest battle that the nineteenth century saw, Gettysburg." Roosevelt clearly *did* envy Chamberlain, and confided, "Now, general, I was a very little time in *my war,* you were a long time in *yours,* and I did not see much fighting, but I saw a lot of human nature. . . ."[12]

Having established a public bond with the old hero, the former Rough Rider also used the occasion to praise Thomas Brackett Reed. Once a political intimate of the rising Theodore, Reed was TR's choice for the 1896 Republican presidential nomination. A man of wide cultural interests, literary ability, and caustic wit, Reed once said, "Theodore, I commend you for your original discovery of the Ten Commandments"—and got away with it. In Portland, Reed's hometown, Roosevelt praised the onetime "czar" as his ideal of a responsible and effective political leader. Left unsaid was the fact that the former Speaker of the House of Representatives, a Civil War veteran and product of an earlier patrician-politician school, had resigned from Congress in bitter disagreement with the New Imperialism TR so ardently espoused. When the two men met in Portland, more than a generational passing of the torch was symbolized.[13]

Later, in Augusta, the president paid homage to the memory of James G. Blaine. The young TR had been distinctly uncomfortable with the scandal-tainted "Plumed Knight's" 1884 presidential bid. But he nevertheless supported the "Continental Liar from the State of Maine." Now he carefully centered upon Blaine's later role as secretary of state, and managed to associate Blaine's Pan-Americanism with his own more aggressive hemispheric stance.[14]

If there was disingenuousness in Roosevelt's public associations with the dead Blaine and the soon-to-die Reed, there was little regarding his affection for William (Bill) Wingate Sewall of Island Falls, Maine. The bewhiskered old guide had taken the youthful TR on hikes through the Aroostook woods. With cousin Wilmont Dow, Sewall managed Roosevelt's Elkhorn Ranch in the Dakotas. If anybody was a surrogate father to Theodore Roosevelt, it was Bill Sewall. From the moment he reached Maine, the president repeatedly expressed his desire to see Sewall. He played town crier from the balcony of the Bangor House on August 27, entreating somebody in the crowd to find Sewall and "say for me that I expect him to dine with me in the hotel." At this point the guide, who had been waiting to be publicly called forth by the president, emerged.

"I am glad to see you, Bill," said Theodore Roosevelt.

"You ain't no gladder than I be," replied the woodsman.[15]

The president then regaled his audience with reminiscences of his hunting days with Sewall, noting that the last meal he had in Maine had been muskrat stew. After partaking of presumably different fare at the hotel, Sewall accompanied TR for the rest of the day, making droll remarks that the national press contingent eagerly transcribed. It made good copy.[16]

A natural friendship, it was also one that humanized the patrician Roosevelt's image. TR often used his relationship with Sewall and similar types to symbolize his closeness with the Common Man. Edmund Morris has noted that, while Roosevelt idealized such "coarse, efficient men," he did not appoint them to positions of power. He did make Bill Sewall postmaster of Island Falls, a position of some power in Aroostook County, Maine! Roosevelt stayed up "until a late hour talking over old times" with Sewall and, as his train headed through the night for New Hampshire, the president slept aboard it for the first time on his journey.[17]

TR needed the rest to prepare him for what turned out to be a frenzied reception. At the Weirs on August 28, local authorities lost all semblance of control, and in Concord troops had to use rifle butts to restrain the crowd. Such scenes highlighted the dangers inherent in the exposure of a highly popular figure like Roosevelt to the masses. Early in the tour there had been similar disturbances in Massachusetts. Although the Maine crowds were more orderly, the two-man Secret Service contingent had its anxious moments. In Portland an enthusiastic female admirer threw a bouquet, "a regular hot-liner," right at the president's head. Roosevelt did not dodge the floral missile but, removing his hat with his left hand, caught it neatly with his right hand in "a muscular sweep of his arm which brought cheers from the crowd and an answering laugh from him."[18] It turned out to be a winning moment, but what if somebody had thrown something more lethal than a bouquet?

There were more such moments. When a reporter in Portland reached for a note pad in his trousers, William Craig, a jumpy Secret Service agent, thought the man was "drawing" a gun. In Augusta, some excited soul actually fired a revolver when the president arrived. In Waterville, a local politician ran after the departing TR and shoved "something" wrapped in chamois-skin into Roosevelt's hand. The Secret Service men "looked nervous," but the mysterious object turned out to be only an axe specially made for the president. In New Hampshire, Roosevelt and Senator Redfield Proctor of Vermont disappeared from sight for hours while hunting boar in the Corbin Preserve. Later, when the novelist-politico Winston Churchill took the reins of TR's carriage to drive him across the border to Windsor, Vermont, Senator Proctor was not the only person nervous about Churchill's strenuous driving style.[19]

During most of the journey the president traveled in his special railroad car, the *Mayflower,* but at various points there were carriage excursions between railheads (such as that with Churchill). On September 3, the last day of his tour, Roosevelt was proceeding by carriage through the Berkshire region of Massachusetts when a freak accident almost took his life. As the president's landau turned across trolley tracks on the outskirts of Pittsfield, it was hit by a speeding trolley car. Agent Craig was killed, Roosevelt's driver was badly injured, a horse died, and the carriage was demolished. The president, Governor Crane, and Secretary George Cortelyou were thrown about forty feet. Luckily, they landed on soft earth. The Massachusetts governor emerged unscathed; Roosevelt and Cortelyou were bruised but apparently not in shock. The president, immediately on his feet, ascertained that Craig was dead, and approached the motorman of the car, one Euclid Madden. Shaking his fist, Roosevelt cried, "This is the most damnable outrage I ever knew." When TR asked why the trolley car had not slowed upon its approach, the motorman replied that he had the right of way.[20]

It was an incredibly close brush. Almost exactly a year after McKinley's assassination, the accident might have made Secretary of State John Hay president of the United States. Roosevelt, his face discolored by a bruise, continued his tour, stopping at a few more towns. He was back at Sagamore Hill that evening. A scheduled visit by the Russian Archduke Boris the next day was not canceled. The president soon undertook the second planned speaking tour, this time to the South. Deeply upset by the death of Craig, a favorite with his children, he described his own escape from death as "providential." Yet Roosevelt also tried to downplay the accident. Replying to a solicitous telegram from King Edward VII, he said, "My hurts were trivial."[21]

They were not. An injury sustained by his left leg forced the president to abruptly terminate his third tour, of the West, in late September. He submitted to an emergency operation to drain the abscessed wound in Indianapolis and returned to Washington, where a second operation was performed. For some time, during the crucial coal strike negotiations that ensued, the president was confined to a wheelchair or crutches. Eventually the leg healed, but not completely. It would be a recurring source of pain for the rest of his life.[22]

Some commentators thought the leg operation was *politically* providential, since it kept the president from travelling further west where he would eventually have to address the tariff issue. Roosevelt wondered how "to handle it as not to cause great damage. There are a good many worse things than the possibility of trolley car accidents in these trips!" he joked to Secretary Hay. He told Senator Orville Platt of his relief that "before the accident came I was able to make my speeches on the trusts. . . ." Lodge, who had left Roosevelt's party before the Pittsfield visit due to illness, had not initially realized the seriousness of Roosevelt's injuries. On September 25 he wrote, "I know I urged the tours . . . and yet I have been miserably anxious all the time you were on the road.... You have helped the campaign wonderfully and are stronger than ever in the real affection of the people." Roosevelt confessed to his friend, "My leg was attended to just in time." Nevertheless, Lodge continued to press the injured TR to take action in the coal strike to avert "political disaster." "[T]he appearance of trying to do something will help wonderfully," he wrote. The campaign continued. Roosevelt did do something about the strike. The 1902 elections were highly favorable to the Republican party.[23]

The New England tour was an important part of the campaign—and a crucial point in Roosevelt's young presidency. He had, however sketchily, discussed major issues in a manner that projected leadership while allowing him considerable latitude for future action. His unique personal style and rapport with the masses was demonstrated. Theodore Roosevelt's mastery of the American political scene was apparent.

NOTES

1. *Portland Eastern Argus*, August 25, 1902, p. 6.
2. John A. Garraty, *Henry Cabot Lodge: A Biography* (New York: Knopf, 1953), p. 232. Lodge, one of the chief promoters of the tour, was apparently more interested in maintaining his dominance in the Massachusetts GOP against free-trade Republican rivals. In addition to Garraty, chap. 13, see Karl Schriftgiesser, *The Gentleman from Massachusetts: Henry Cabot Lodge* (Boston: Little, Brown, 1944), pp. 206–8. Lodge was also concerned at this point about son-in-law "Gussie" Gardner's campaign for a congressional nomination.
3. TR to Lodge, August 11, 1902; Lodge to TR, August 17, 1902; and Lodge to TR, August 20, 1902, in *Selections from the Correspondence of Theodore Roosevelt and Henry Cabot Lodge, 1884–1918*, ed. Henry Cabot Lodge (New York: Scribner's, 1925), 1: 525–27.
4. Ibid., TR to Lodge, July 30,1902, 1: 421.
5. TR began to privately address the strike issue just before embarking on his tour, asking Philander Knox, "What is the reason we cannot proceed against the coal operators as being engaged in a trust?" The strike continued to be on his mind throughout the tour. TR, in Augusta, Maine, wrote Nelson W. Aldrich that "the labor situation caused by the anthracite coal business is bad—politically as well as otherwise." TR to Knox, August 21, 1902, and TR to Aldrich, August 26, 1902, *The Letters of Theodore Roosevelt*, ed. Elting E. Morison (Cambridge: Harvard University Press, 1954) 3: 323.
6. For example, Maine newspapers referred to TR as "a typical specimen of perfect manhood," *Portland Evening Express*, August 8, 1902, p. 1, and "The Ideal of the People," *Lewiston Evening Journal*, August 26, 1902; and described his speeches as "Strong and Manly

Utterances by a Strong and Manly Man," *Kennebec Journal*, August 27, 1902, p. 2.

7. TR, *Presidential Addresses and State Papers* (New York: Review of Reviews, 1920), 1: 98–108; *New York Times*, August 24, 1902, p. 1. After chastising the rich who abused their power, TR proceeded to Newport to act as godfather in a christening at the villa of his friend Winthrop Chanler (*New York Times*, August 25, 1902, p. 1).

8. *Addresses*, 1: 108–18, and 137–44.

9. Ibid., 1: 85–98, and 118–22.

10. *Kennebec Journal*, August 27, 1902, p. 2. TR stressed the point elsewhere, notably in a speech at Proctor, Vermont, on September 1, when he said "the Monroe Doctrine will be respected as long as we have a first-class efficient navy and not very much longer" (*New York Times*, September 2, 1902).

11. *New York Times*, August 27, 1902, p. 2.

12. Ibid. Emphasis added.

13. Reed quoted in William A. Robinson, *Thomas B. Reed: Parliamentarian* (New York: Dodd, Mead, 1930), p. 147. Roosevelt felt Reed failed to win the 1896 nomination because he was not sufficiently aggressive on the monetary issue (Robinson, p. 320), and later found Reed's anti-imperialism "painful and disappointing to me beyond words" (p. 370). Just prior to his death, Reed was in the Capitol. "The President's message was just being read in the House, and one of the members coming from the floor repeated a highly colored phrase about the result of our Philippine policy. Reed's eyes flashed and he said with his old fire, 'I suppose he put that there for the same reason that they put tails on coats—for the benefit of the lackeys.'" Samuel W. McCall, *The Life of Thomas Brackett Reed* (Boston: Houghton Mifflin, 1914), p. 275.

14. *Kennebec Journal*, August 27, 1902, pp. 1–2. In fact, Blaine, like Reed, represented the Old Guard and, had he lived, probably would have opposed the New Imperialism.

15. William Wingate Sewall, *Bill Sewall's Story of TR* (New York: Harper, 1919), pp. 107–8; *Bangor Daily News*, August 28, 1902, p. 2.

16. *Portland Evening Express*, August 28, 1902. For more information on the Sewall-TR relationship, in addition to Sewall's book, see Paul Russell Cutright, *Theodore Roosevelt: The Making of a Conservationist* (Urbana: University of Illinois Press, 1985); Hermann Hagedorn, *Roosevelt in the Bad Lands* (Boston: Houghton Mifflin, 1921); and Michael T. Kinnicutt, "We hitched well . . . from the first" (*Down East*, October 1982, pp. 48–52).

17. Morris, "Theodore Roosevelt, the Polygon," chap. 1, supra; *New York Times*, August 28, 1902. An example of TR's use of his relationship with Sewall is his explanation of his early lack of support for the effort to achieve social and economic justice: "The good citizens I then knew best, even when themselves men of limited means . . . were no more awake than I was to the changing needs the changing times were bringing" (TR, *An Autobiography* [New York: Macmillan, 1913], pp. 86–87). Reading Sewall, it is clear how attuned he was to TR. "Some folks said that he was headstrong and

aggressive," Sewall wrote of TR, "but I never found him so except when necessary; and I've always thought being headstrong and aggressive, on occasion, was a pretty good thing. . ." (*Sewall's Story*, p. 4).

18. *Portland Eastern Argus*, August 29, 1902; *Portland Advertiser*, August 27, 1902.

19. *Portland Eastern Argus*, August 27, 1902, p. 1; *Portland Advertiser*, August 28, 1902, p. 1; *Kennebec Journal*, August 28, 1902, p. 1; *New York Times*, August 30, 1902, p. 1; Robert W. Schneider, *Novelist to a Generation: The Life and Thought of Winston Churchill* (Bowling Green, OH: Bowling Green University Popular Press, 1976), p. 60. Churchill was running for a seat in the New Hampshire legislature. He won. For more on his relationship with TR, see Warren I. Titus, *Winston Churchill* (New York: Twayne, 1963).

20. *New York Times*, September 4, 1902, pp. 1–2. *Kennebec Journal*, September 10, 1902, p. 7. A number of observers believed that the driver of the president's carriage was partly responsible for the mishap. An inquest and trial were held, and Madden was found guilty of manslaughter. He was fined $500 and sentenced to six months in jail, but released after four months and payment of his fine by the Pittsfield Electric Street Railway Company. Several historians refer to Roosevelt's "automobile" accident, e.g., Noel Busch, *T. R.: The Story of Theodore Roosevelt and His Influence on Our Times* (New York: Reynal, 1965), p. 177, and William H. Harbaugh, *Power and Responsibility: The Life and Times of Theodore Roosevelt* (New York: Farrar, Straus, 1961), p. 172, but the only time on this trip Roosevelt was *apparently* in an automobile was on August 22, in Hartford. Despite lengthy debate over the adequacy of presidential protection, from December 1901 through early 1903, Congress refused to extend it. See Richard B. Sherman, "The President and the People: Presidential Protection Procedures, 1901–1933," *Prologue* 18, no. 4 (Winter 1986): 222–39.

21. *New York Times*, September 6, 1902; TR to Edward VII, September 6, 1902, *Letters*, 3: 325. According to legislation passed in 1886, if the president and vice president were killed or disabled the secretary of state would succeed to the presidency. Provision was made for Congress to call a special election.

22. *New York Times*, September 24, 1902, p. 1; *New York Times*, September 29, 1902, pp. 1–2.

23. TR to Hay, September 18, 1902; TR to Platt, October 2, 1902, *Letters*, 3: 327 and 335, Lodge to TR, September 25, 1902, Lodge to TR, September 27, 1902, *Correspondence* 1: 529–31. Governor Crane, TR's fellow accident victim, was one of the president's key advisers in the coal strike, and recommended that TR convene a White House meeting of union leaders and mine operators. Crane had, earlier in the year, successfully mediated the Boston teamsters' strike. See Carolyn W. Johnson, *Winthrop Murray Crane: A Study in Republican Leadership 1892–1920* (Northampton: Smith College, 1967).

16

Theodore Roosevelt's Contribution to the Concept of Presidential Intervention in Labor Disputes: Antecedents and the 1902 Coal Strike

Arthur M. Schaefer

Antecedents and Status of Presidential Intervention at the Turn of the Twentieth Century

By the turn of the twentieth century the long period of labor experimentation with alternative philosophies, organizational forms, and strategies had largely come to an end. The meteoric rise and decline of the Knights of Labor saw the last of the important movements based on class consciousness, political action, and visionary schemes designed to escape the wage system. With the founding of the American Federation of Labor in 1886, the basic structure of the modern American labor movement began to emerge with its underlying philosophy of accepting rather than escaping the wage system.

With it came a vision of the labor movement as an integral part of the market system. Primary reliance was to be placed on organization coterminous with the trade or industry, job rather than class consciousness and the use of collective bargaining backed by the economic power of the strike in achieving goals limited to wages and working conditions. The terms and conditions of labor were to be decided by the exercise of countervailing private economic power sufficient to induce the contestants to reach a meeting of minds.[1] But the dawn of the era of large and powerful corporations faced by large, powerful, and militant labor organizations ushered in with it the possibility that the contestants, in exercising their private economic power, might bring greater pressure to bear on the public through the widespread interruption of essential production or services, than they brought on each other. Large-scale strikes in the last two decades of the nineteenth century had alerted the public to the existence in its midst of a power capable of much mischief. As Herbert Croly expressed it,

> it is obvious that the development in this country of two such powerful and unscrupulous and well-organized special interests has created a condition which the founders of the Republic never anticipated, and which demands as a counterpoise a more effective body of national opinion, and a more powerful organization of the national interest.[2]

When Roosevelt encountered the anthracite coal strike early in his presidency, he had little useful precedent to guide him. There had been previous instances of presidential intervention in labor disputes: Jackson's, in a canal strike in 1834, the first known instance of presidential intervention; Lincoln's intervention in a longshoremen's strike in New York in 1863; Harrison's intervention in a western metal mining strike in 1892; McKinley's intervention in the same industry in 1899; and, the two best known, Hayes's intervention in the rail strike in 1877 and Cleveland's intervention in the Pullman strike in 1894. Though limited, this experience, in particular the strikes of 1877 and 1894, established the federal government as the only political unit capable of dealing with a problem that had become national in character, and established the president as the only officer of the federal government capable of mobilizing, as Croly said, "a more powerful organization of the national interest." These events also underscored the inadequacy of law and operative ideals bearing upon the responsibilities of the government vis-à-vis the exercise of private economic power. The federal government was poorly equipped to deal with the problem, especially in a just and equitable manner. The two principal questions raised by these strikes were: (1) under what conditions may or should the president intervene and (2) given intervention, how should that intervention be conducted?

Many strikes of that era were violent affairs often characterized by open warfare between the contestants. Spontaneous strikes, lack of union organizational structure and discipline sufficient to cope with large-scale strikes, employers' refusal to recognize unions as legitimate organizations and the perception of unions as a threat to private property, inexperience with orderly processes of collective bargaining, and frequent use of strikebreakers all contributed to less than peaceful confrontations. Presidential intervention at the invitation of state officials to restore law and order in such cases epitomized the pursuit of a clearly defined and thoroughly constitutional presidential function. Such was the case in the Maryland canal strike in 1834, in the western metal mining strikes and, to a certain extent, in the rail strike of 1877. Most of these strikes were not what would later come to be called "national emergency disputes." They created no public hardship outside of the localities in which they occurred. Lincoln's intervention, undertaken as a wartime measure, lay clearly within the orbit of accepted presidential powers. But the rail strike of 1877 was a different matter. For the first time in the nation's history, a peacetime strike was perceived by a large segment of the public as a clear and present danger, not because of the violence which accompanied it, but because the railroads had become the arteries of commerce in an increasingly interdependent national economy. Despite that, President Hayes scrupulously refrained from intervening, unless requested to do so by state officials, which effectively deprived him of any presidential initiative and proved to be a major impediment in his efforts to deal with the strike and its consequences.[3]

President Cleveland pursued a much bolder course in his intervention in the rail strike of 1894.[4] The president intervened without awaiting a request from the state governors and sometimes contrary to their wishes, though he and his attorney general, Richard Olney, were hard-pressed to come up with suitable justifications during the strike.[5] His boldness embroiled him in heated disputes with several governors, particularly Altgeld of Illinois,[6] and he ultimately paid a high political price for it. Nevertheless, the Supreme Court decision in the Debs case[7] firmly established the legitimacy of such intervention, though the Court's decision made in clear that it applied only to railroads. Other industries, including coal mining, were, as yet, beyond the reach of the commerce clause of the Constitution.

Prior to the coal strike of 1902, the presidents dealt with strikes much as they might have dealt with insurrections or unruly mobs. The use of federal marshalls backed by troops where necessary—preceded often by presidential proclamations, declarations of martial law when deemed expedient, injunctions and criminal prosecutions for those who persisted—was the standard format. Yet, to resort to coercive measures, by depriving the workers of the only means they had to bring pressure to bear upon the employers, amounted in most cases to strike breaking. The government made no effort to bring the parties together, to induce them to modify extreme positions, to offer alternative solutions, or to treat with them in the even-handed fashion of an honest broker concerned only with the public interest. Both Hayes and Cleveland were aware that a fundamental difference existed between a labor dispute and civil strife,[8] but neither intervened in a manner that would have reflected this: Hayes could not, given the character of the strike and the means to which he had access, and Cleveland chose not to. But it was clear, to some at least, that a mode of intervention which failed to recognize the aspirations of working men concerned with the conditions under which they should labor for the profit of others and which also ran the risk of converting private disputes into conflicts between the government and its citizens was a dangerous one unsuited to a free society.

Background of the Coal Dispute

While the conditions under which the miners labored in the anthracite and bituminous coal fields were similar, the economic structures of those industries were quite different. Bituminous coal mining was spread over a wide area, the industry composed, by and large, of a substantial number of highly competitive firms, and the product was basically an industrial product. Anthracite mining was limited to a small region of Pennsylvania, the mines mostly owned and controlled by the coal-carrying railroads,[9] and the product, at that time, was a major consumer product. Because of the isolated character of coal mining, the degree of control exercised by the companies over coal-mining communities, the existence of sharp religious and ethnic factionalism among miners, and the simultaneous organizing efforts of competing labor organizations, unionization of the coal fields had always been a difficult task, especially in the anthracite fields. Unlike the bituminous coal operators who viewed unionization as a stabilizing force in a fiercely competitive industry, the coal-carrying railroads neither needed nor welcomed an organization that they regarded at best as a disruptive threat to their management prerogatives and at worst as a radical challenge to private ownership of the means of production. Not until 1890—when the competing organizations merged to form the United Mine Workers of America—were the workers able to effectively challenge the operators in the bituminous branch of the industry. Only by the end of the decade had organization in the anthracite segment processed far enough to contest the power of the coal-carrying railroads. In 1898, John Mitchell, a young official who had much to do with the success of the new union, ascended to the presidency of the United Mine Workers and in 1900 it was felt that the union was in a position to make demands on the anthracite operators and, if need be, back them with a strike.

In many respects, Mitchell was a peerless labor leader. He thoroughly understood the principles of trade unionism and gained the respect and support of the labor movement as a whole, including that of Samuel Gompers, rather than alienating them as Debs had done in the rail strike of 1894.[10] Like Debs, Mitchell realized that violence inevitably led to defeat but, in contrast with Debs, he knew that to control it, responsible local leadership was essential and he had taken great pains to develop that necessary ingredient.[11] He knew how to gain the unwavering devotion of his men, weld them into a powerful striking force, and articulate their case before the public. Mitchell was also aware that a strike called at the right time and under the right conditions could gain influential support from outside the labor movement and he knew how to enlist that support.

It was, therefore, not chance that dictated the calling of the strike in September 1900 in the midst of McKinley's campaign for reelection against William Jennings Bryan—at a time when the weather might be expected to turn suddenly cool. Nor was chance relied on to determine the reaction. Senator Mark Hanna, chairman of the Republican National Committee, was a power among industrialists and a known quantity to the leaders of coal unionism.[12] He had been the first bituminous coal operator to recognize the union and he had done so voluntarily. He was one of the first industrialists ever to sign a collective agreement, and was known for his fairness to his employees and for his good faith in dealing with the union. Moreover, McKinley and Hanna were political friends of Michael Ratchford, Mitchell's predecessor who had resigned the presidency of the union to accept a political appointment.[13] Finally, if needed, there was a further safeguard on which Mitchell could rely to protect the strike from unfavorable intervention. Bryan and Governor Altgeld had practically read Cleveland out of the Democratic Party at the convention of 1896, partly on the basis of his intervention in the Pullman strike, and they had inserted a plank in the party's platform condemning presidential intervention in labor disputes of the sort that Cleveland had used.[14]

Insofar as possible presidential intervention was concerned, Mitchell was in a comfortably strong position. He had only to hold his men solid and wait for the approaching election, mixed hopefully with a sufficiently persuasive fear of coming cool weather. Should the president feel compelled to intervene, it was fairly certain that neither by personal inclination nor political position, vis-à-vis Bryan, could McKinley's manner smack of strike breaking without incurring grave risks of disrupting sensitive political alliances within his own party or providing Bryan with a telling issue on which to attack him, especially in the important states of Ohio, Illinois, Indiana, and Pennsylvania where the union was strongly organized.

The course of events in the dispute followed rather closely the scenario that Mitchell had anticipated. Hardly had the strike begun when administration leaders perceived the probable effects it could have on the election and took steps to get it settled.[15] Hanna first tried to reason with the presidents of the coal-carrying railroads but, when he found them adamant, he went over their heads to J. P. Morgan, playing heavily no doubt on the fear of a victory for the "radical" Bryan and his ardent supporter, the "anarchist" Altgeld. A meeting between Mitchell and Morgan was arranged, compromise terms worked out,[16] the railroad presidents received their orders and the strike was over in the short period of six weeks. Mitchell had shown for the first time in American labor history, that a union could organize and conduct a large-scale strike in such a way as to gain public approval and favorable government intervention.

The 1902 Anthracite Strike

Even though the operators had been thoroughly outgeneralled and defeated in the strike of 1900, as Mitchell observed, "It was felt by both sides that the struggle was not conclusive."[17] The union had not been recognized by the anthracite operators. Rather than meet with representatives of the workers to negotiate a collective agreement, the operators merely posted new terms of employment on breakers and towers and immediately set about making preparations to destroy the union.[18] When the "agreement" expired as scheduled in April 1901, the union request for negotiations to draw up a new agreement was countered by posted employer notices extending the current terms to April 1902. Senator Hanna's intervention on behalf of the National Civic Federation[19] failed to temper the operators' intransigence, and the union decided to await a more favorable opportunity. The following spring, when the anthracite operators again refused to discuss the union's demands, a strike vote was taken and the strike commenced on May 12, 1902, with an estimated 147,000 miners responding to the strike call.[20]

At the time of the coal strike, Roosevelt had been in office only eight months. His initial reaction to the strike was one of interest, but not alarm. On June 8, he asked Commissioner of Labor Carroll D. Wright to investigate the dispute and, if possible, to obtain an agreement to arbitrate. But the operators refused to accept arbitration, as they had on previous occasions, and Wright's report,[21] submitted some two weeks later with proposed recommendations for a settlement, was not made public until August. There was little public concern over a shortage of coal at that time of year. Few people believed that the strike would last long enough to become critical and hence there would have been little, if any, support for intervention even had Roosevelt been so inclined. Nevertheless, for the first time, a president had shown an interest in an objective, dispassionate consideration of the merits of the issues in a labor dispute and had at least signalled that his office stood ready, if need be, to assist the parties, in an even-handed fashion, in reaching a meeting of minds on the issues.

Throughout the summer the workers held fast, their loyalty to Mitchell unshaken.[22] The operators remained adamant and the strike dragged on into September. By that time the stockpiles accumulated by the operators for the purpose of defeating the strike began to disappear, and acute shortages of coal developed. The public became apprehensive lest a sudden change in the weather catch them without the means to heat their homes. The price of coal, when coal was obtainable, soared to such heights that many could no longer afford it. Schools began closing for lack of fuel and the fall congressional elections were approaching. Because Senator Henry Cabot Lodge, Roosevelt's close personal and political friend, feared "an overturn" in the coming elections he urged the president to bring pressure on the operators—*"not in public* of course," for that was "out of the question."[23]

Mitchell had again engineered the circumstances of the strike in a manner calculated to maximize the power of the strikers. His careful organization and personal charisma held the men together, minimized violence, and brought the strike to the point where it was perceived as a threat to the continued supply of a good deemed essential to the public welfare.[24] He stood persistently against any action, especially sympathetic strikes, that would have undermined public confidence in the union.[25] Above all, he appealed, as one contemporary observer phrased it, "to the Anglo-Saxon sense of justice" by arguing the miners' case firmly and resolutely before the public without invective or recrimination and tempered always by a readiness to compromise or arbitrate.[26]

Theodore Roosevelt was as much at a loss in dealing with the coal strike as his predecessors had been in similar situations. He was, as he remarked in his reply to Lodge, at his "wits' end how to proceed."[27] There was, he wrote, "literally nothing, as far as I have yet been able to find out, which the national government has any power to do in the matter."[28] There is no doubt that he considered the intervention by Hayes and Cleveland in the railroad strikes as a perfectly valid exercise of presidential authority and thoroughly approved of the methods they employed.[29] But nothing in those instances provided Roosevelt with acceptable criteria justifying presidential intervention in the coal dispute. Mitchell's conduct of the strike was exemplary. The prevailing opinion and legal precedents of the times held the coal industry to fall outside the protection of the commerce clause of the Constitution, and there was no interference with a federally protected activity such as carriage of the mails nor had the miners infringed any federal law.

If the methods employed by Cleveland and Hayes were not open to Roosevelt, neither was McKinley's. The latter's method depended upon a particular set of circumstances; the position the president had taken on policy questions of vital interest to the business community, and on previous usage. Mark Hanna had been seeking a solution to the crisis almost from the very beginning, and had at one point even succeeded in getting an agreement between Mitchell and Morgan, only to have it turned down by George Baer, the president of the Philadelphia and Reading Railroad and leader of the coal-carrying railroad presidents.[30] As Roosevelt explained to Lodge, the operators were determined that there would not be a repetition of the events of 1900, that the men would not be given a triumph over them for political purposes, and, he continued, it was out of the question for the president who thundered against the "malefactors of great wealth" to expect any favors from those who bore the brunt of his attacks.[31] Nor, indeed, could he expect any favors from the labor side for he had no close ties with the labor movement.

Despite the apparent bars to action, Roosevelt knew that if he did not act, "the public at large" would "tend to visit upon our heads responsibility for the shortage in coal. . . ."[32] He was moreover an energetic, action-oriented individual who would have found it impossible, as president, to remain immobile in the face of a national crisis. Lacking precedent, he set about developing his own and, in the process, established principles that would form the basis for more equitable presidential intervention in future labor disputes.

Basically, Theodore Roosevelt started from the premise that organized groups possessing considerable economic power were a fact of life in the modern world. Though he was known as the "trust buster," he was in fact not the trust buster that legend would have him be. If there was any president of that era who deserved the name of trust buster, it was William Howard Taft, not Theodore Roosevelt. During Taft's four years in office almost twice as many antitrust cases were initiated as during Roosevelt's almost eight years in office. But Roosevelt was too perceptive and too prescient to be misled by the assumption contained in the Sherman Anti-Trust Act that the exercise of monopoly power could be controlled solely by the simple expedient of dismemberment and divestiture. He was aware that economies of scale might dictate the existence of large-scale firms capable of exercising considerable economic power and that, in such cases, the preferable alternative would be to control the exercise of that economic power rather than sacrifice the benefits of large scale production.

For Roosevelt, the policy of repressing concentrations of economic power was not only a failure because it went counter to the dominant economic trend, it was also mischievous because in such concentration there was positive good. It was good in business because it resulted in greater efficiency, and it was good in labor organization because it represented an offset, or what Galbraith would later call a "countervailing power" to the already existing concentration in business and thereby guarantee justice to the worker. Yet, while such private concentrations of power represented potential good, they also represented potential evil. Hence, rising above these private concentrations of power, in Roosevelt's scheme, was the national government, policing the use of that power and dispensing ultimate justice. As Roosevelt expressed it with respect to labor unions:

> I wish to see labor organizations powerful; and the minute that any organization becomes powerful it becomes powerful for evil as well as for good; and when organized labor becomes sufficiently powerful the State will have to regulate the collective use of labor just as it must regulate the collective use of capital.[33]

Roosevelt was, therefore, neither pro- nor anti- bigness or smallness and neither pro- nor anti- business or labor. He was aware that concentrated economic power was a fact of twentieth-century economic life, and he was opposed to the unbridled exercise of excessive economic power from whatever source it derived and whatever the circumstances of its use. Whenever and wherever it manifested itself, Roosevelt felt that it was incumbent upon the modern state to intervene and control it in order to prevent the evil of which it was inherently capable. From that derived his well-known stewardship theory, enunciated in connection with the actions he took in the coal strike, the precepts of which were, first and primarily:

> Occasionally great national crises arise which call for immediate and vigorous executive action, and that in such cases it is the duty of the President to act upon the theory that he is the steward of the people, and that the proper attitude for him to take is that he is bound to assume that he has the legal right to do whatever the needs of the people demand, unless the Constitution or the laws explicitly forbid him to do it.[34]

> [Second, that the president should avoid intervention as long as he possibly can,[35] but third that] No man and no group of men may so exercise their rights as to deprive the nation of the things which are necessary and vital to the common life.[36]

> [Fourth] It is to the interest of everybody that law and order shall prevail. . . because the question of rights and wrongs of

the controversy cannot be settled. . . . until there is order. . . . There can be no justice without law and order.[37]

[But fifth,] law and order are well-nigh valueless unless used as a foundation upon which justice is built up as a superstructure.[38]

[Sixth, for the president,] it is never well to take drastic action if the result can be achieved with equal efficiency in less drastic fashion.[39]

Finally, there was a seventh precept which Roosevelt never stated explicitly but one he often alluded to and of which he was keenly aware, particularly in his actions during the coal strike, to wit: the president must intervene in such a manner as to gain and hold or enhance public confidence in and support for the action taken.

It is apparent that Roosevelt, in effect, reversed the concepts which had guided presidential intervention up to that time. Where previously, some specific grant of authority had been sought, Roosevelt, faced with a public crisis, unable to seek favors from either of the parties, and not able to find his authority spelled out, adopted a view which swept away restrictions that had troubled his predecessors. According to the theory, the ultimate determinations of the existence of a public emergency dispute rested with the president. The extent and limitations of his powers in this respect were determined, barring applicable legislation, by the conditions and circumstances of the dispute, and only the president could determine when and where these circumstances and conditions reached the point at which the dispute threatened the public interest. It was a bold and sweeping concept which gave recognition to the fact that in a modern and constantly changing economy an ever widening circle of industries might be brought within the presidential orbit, as they subsequently were—one that focused attention on the president as the primary agent of that process. A "steward of the people" cannot lightly abdicate that responsibility, and must be ever alert to see that the nation is not deprived "of the things which are necessary and vital to the common welfare," whatever those "things" might currently be.

Having determined that a labor dispute or strike was one vitally invested with the public interest, the next question raised by Roosevelt's theory was what should the president do in that event? Again, in this respect, it contrasted sharply with the guiding principles governing the interventions of Hayes, Cleveland, and, for that matter, any other instance of presidential intervention up to that time. In a very real sense, these were all-or-nothing responses. Either the government threw its full power into the dispute, or it did not act at all. Either the strike was crushed or it was allowed to go on. But Roosevelt neither wished to crush the strike not did he wish to let it go on. He evolved, therefore, the concept of a continuum of presidential intervention. While the president "is bound to assume that he has the legal right to do whatever the needs of the people demand," nevertheless, he should never take a "drastic action" when a "less drastic action will suffice." This opens up the full range of possibilities reaching from no action through intervening stages to bringing the full power of the state into play. Roosevelt was aware that, in addition to the powers vested in the president as the commander in chief of the nation's military forces which was what presidents had for the most part relied on heretofore in their interventions in labor disputes—there exists first, the power, dependent on his prestige, that accrues to the president as interpreter of the national well being and spokesman for the nation, and second, the power deriving from the authority vested in the president to recommend legislation to Congress. Before he himself was president, Woodrow Wilson was to write, clearly with Roosevelt in mind, that the president is

> the only national voice in affairs. Let him once win the admiration and confidence of the country, and no other single force can withstand him, no combination of forces will easily overpower him. . . . If he rightly interpret the national thought and boldly insist upon it, he is irresistible.[40]

Roosevelt utilized that power with great care and skill during the coal strike, knowing full well that, while "irresistible" under the right circumstances, it was a capricious power easily dissipated by misuse.[41] When Carroll D. Wright failed in his mission in June, as previously noted, the president abandoned further efforts until September. It was clear that in June he had no genuine public support for intervention, whereas in September he did have that support. The question at the later date was how best to utilize existing public opinion in making his initial move. That opinion was strongly against a continuation of the strike and it was favorable to the miners for the reasons already set forth. On the other hand, the behavior of the railroad presidents, particularly that of George F. Baer, could not have been better calculated to alienate the public. Not only had they peremptorily refused to negotiate or arbitrate, they had publicly assumed an attitude of pompous arrogance toward the union and all who offered their good offices in an effort to bring the strike to an end. The most imprudent aspect of their behavior was the impression they gave of being recklessly indifferent to public anxiety regarding coal shortages.[42]

Nevertheless, it is doubtful even at that stage that the president could have taken any action which would have so transgressed the perceived rights of the operators as to shock the public. But the president could invite the parties to a White House conference which would serve to impress the public with the urgency of the dispute, send a clear signal that the president regarded the dispute and strike as a major national problem, and use the prestige of the presidency as a lever to induce the parties to either reach a settlement or arbitrate the dispute.[43] While a White House conference had never been tried before and was thus a new precedent, it was not a "drastic action" and it could only gain for the president increased public confidence and support. Knowing also that the operators were in a vulnerable position publicly, Roosevelt intended to threaten them with his powers as chief legislator by warning them that he would "advise action along the line I have explained in my speeches but of a much more radical type in reference to their business unless they wake up."[44]

Mitchell strengthened his public position by conducting himself in his usual statesmanlike manner, both during and after the stormy session. The operators, by viciously attacking Mitchell and Roosevelt during and after the meeting, succeeded only in divesting themselves of the last shred of public support they might have counted on.[45] Roosevelt could now safely disregard the operators. His next move was to place the burden on Mitchell, which he did by publicly requesting Mitchell to order an immediate resumption of work. In return for that, the president promised to appoint a commission to investigate the dispute and make recommendations which he (the president) would "do all within his power" to effectuate.[46] It was a more drastic step, but Roosevelt clearly had public support for it. Nevertheless, Mitchell turned the president's request down as being too vague. In doing so he strengthened the president's public position, vis-a-vis the adversaries in the coal dispute, and opened the way for Roosevelt's third step—his contemplated seizure of the coal mines.

Presidential seizure of a firm or industry because of a labor dispute in that day and age would have been a vast and drastic innovation totally beyond anything in American experience or tradition. Roosevelt, aware that to take such a step oblivious to its impact on public sentiment would invite defeat, sought to fit his contemplated seizure into the pattern of American experience by secretly arranging to have the governor of Pennsylvania request federal aid on a prearranged signal from the president. At that point, Roosevelt planned to send in the army, seize the mines, order a resumption of production, and appoint a panel to make recommendations regarding the terms of a fair and equitable settlement which the president would then implement.[47] Ever mindful of the impact of his actions on public opinion, Roosevelt intended to recall from retirement Major General J. M. Schofield, former commanding general of the U.S. Army and perhaps the most distinguished American military man then living, and instruct him to "act in a purely military capacity under me as commander-in-chief, paying no heed to any authority, judicial or otherwise, except mine."[48] To investigate the dispute and decide on the terms of settlement, Roosevelt sought to appoint a commission ". . . which would command such public confidence as to enable me without too much difficulty, to enforce its terms upon both parties."[49] Still true to his precept of never taking a drastic action where a less drastic one would, with equal efficiency, suffice, Roosevelt sought to avoid compulsory arbitration by dispatching Secretary of War Elihu Root to New York City to lay the plan before Morgan, in order to pry out of the operators an agreement to arbitrate the dispute before a presidentially appointed commission.[50] Root was successful in that endeavor, the parties agreeing to submit the dispute to the president's commission. The strike ended without the necessity of seizure.

Roosevelt's handling of the coal dispute marked a major turning point in presidential intervention in labor disputes. Above all, it was based on full acceptance of the labor movement as an integral part of the modern market economy. It recognized the fact that twentieth-century market structures were likely to be characterized by large concentrations of economic power on both sides of the market. At the same time, it posited the notion that when those concentrations of economic power came into conflict in such a way as to threaten injury to the public, then self-interest must give way to a higher common good which could only be achieved by means of common national action operating through the agency of the state. It was, moreover, marked by a determination to introduce fairness and equity into the process in a way that had never been attempted before. Finally, it is clear that Roosevelt worked on the basis of a continuum extending from no intervention to the contemplation of a plan that involved the use of the full force of the power of the state to seize the industry and impose terms of settlement. In that process, each separate presidential move possessed four characteristics: (1) it offered a possible solution; (2) it served to bring a little more pressure on the parties to come to terms than had the previous move; (3) if it failed, it left the president in a stronger position than he had been in before and opened the way to more drastic action; and (4) each presidential move, even the most drastic, was so structured that it came within prevailing experience and tradition. Taken as a whole, it was a masterful display of presidential ingenuity which recognized, for the first time, the nature of the twentieth-century economy and set the stage for future presidential interventions in labor disputes while safeguarding the principles of a free and democratic society.

NOTES

1. See Selig Perlman, *A Theory of the Labor Movement* (New York: Macmillan, 1928); Sidney and Beatrice Webb, *Industrial Democracy* (London: Longmans, Green, 1897); Marc Karson, *American Labor Unions and Politics, 1900–1918* (Carbondale: Southern Illinois University Press, 1958); Gerald N. Grob, "Origins of the Political Philosophy of the A.F. of L., 1866–1896," *The Review of Politics*, 22, no. 4 (October 1960): 496–518.

2. Herbert Croly, *The Promise of American Life* (New York: Macmillan, 1914), pp. 130–31.

3. Federal troops were used in nine of the fourteen states affected by the strike. Hayes intervened on two grounds other than an invitation from state officials. One was the case in which a railroad was in federal receivership and the other was to protect federal property. Both were minor in terms of their impact on the strike. Throughout the strike, Hayes exhibited a high degree of uncertainty regarding the role that he should play and the powers that were available to him. He seriously considered declaring martial law for a while, then abandoned the idea. Also he was uncertain as to who

should command federal troops when they were used. Initially he placed them under the command of state governors but later placed them under the command of the army. In some cases he dispatched troops at the request of the state governors and then restricted them to the protection of federal property. However, he was new in office and the political circumstances surrounding his election no doubt led him to exercise great caution. For the circumstances surrounding the strike and the president's intervention, see Joseph A. Dacus, *Annals of the Great Strikes* (St. Louis: Scammel and Company, 1877); Charles Richard Williams, ed., *Diary and Letters of Rutherford Birchard Hayes* (Columbus: Ohio State Archaeological and Historical Society, 1924); "Hayes's Notes of Four Cabinet Meetings" *American Historical Review*, 37, no. 2 (January 1932): 286–89; Robert V. Bruce, *1877: Year of Violence* (Indianapolis: Bobbs-Merrill Co., 1959).

4. Circumstances surrounding the rail strike of 1894 may be found in United States Strike Commission, *Report on the Chicago Strike of June–July, 1894* (Washington, DC: U.S. Government Printing Office, 1895); Almont Lindsey, *The Pullman Strike: The Story of a Unique Experiment and of a Great Labor Upheaval* (Chicago: The University of Chicago Press, 1942); Ray Ginger, *The Bending Cross: A Biography of Eugene Victor Debs* (New Brunswick: Rutgers University Press, 1949).

5. See Grover Cleveland, *Presidential Problems* (New York: Century Co., 1904); Henry James, *Richard Olney and his Public Service* (New York: Houghton Mifflin Co., 1923).

6. Cleveland's communications to Altgeld may be found in Albert Ellery Bergh, ed., *Grover Cleveland, Addresses, State Papers and Letters* (New York: Sun Dial Classics Co., 1909). The texts of the messages from Altgeld to Cleveland are given in Harry Barnard, *"Eagle Forgotten": The Life of John Peter Altgeld* (Indianapolis: Bobbs-Merrill Co., 1938), chap. 29. In addition to Altgeld, the governors of Colorado, Kansas, Missouri, Oregon, Idaho, and Texas strenuously objected to Cleveland's intervention in their states.

7. Ex parte "In the Matter of Eugene V. Debs et al.," *Records and Briefs of the U.S. Supreme Court*, vol. 158.

8. See Hayes diary entry of August 5, after the strike was over, in *Diary and Letters of Rutherford Birchard Hayes*, 3:440. Cleveland had long recognized this as well as the need for some type of governmental machinery which would enable the government to intervene in such disputes on a fair and equitable basis. See his letter accepting the nomination for the governorship of New York dated October, 7, 1882; his letter accepting the nomination for president dated August 18, 1884; and his "Special Message to Congress Recommending Legislation Providing for the Arbitrament of Disputes Between Laboring Men and Employers' of April 22, 1886, among others in Bergh, *Grover Cleveland, Addresses, State Papers and Letters*.

9. These were: The Erie; The New York, Ontario & Western; The Philadelphia & Reading; The Delaware & Hudson; The Delaware, Lackawana & Western; The Lehigh Valley.

10. See Elsie Glück, *John Mitchell, Miner: Labor's Bargain with the Gilded Age* (New York: John Day Co., 1929). In Gompers's view, the

American Railway Union was the "first attempt to displace the principles of the trade union" and "Eugene V. Debs loomed on the horizon as a leader of irregular movements and lost causes." The United Mine Workers union was a full fledged affiliate of the A. F. of L. See Samuel Gompers, *Seventy Years of Life and Labor: An Autobiography* (New York: E. P. Dutton and Co., 1925) especially 1: 403.

11. Mitchell's own account is to be found in his *Organized Labor, Its Problems, Purposes and Ideals and the Present and Future of American Wage Earners* (Philadelphia: American Book and Bible House, 1903).

12. See Herbert Croly, *Marcus Alonzo Hanna, His Life and Work* (New York: Macmillan, 1912). For an account of Hanna's work in industrial relations, see especially chaps. 9 and 25.

13. Glück, *John Mitchell*, pp. 39–40.

14. Altgeld's role is described in Barnard, *"Eagle Forgotten."* Chap. 34. For Bryan's own account of it, see his *The First Battle: A Story of the Campaign of 1896* (London: Sampson Low, Marston and Co. n.d.), chap. 28. The nonintervention plank is given on p. 408.

15. For example, Secretary of State John Hay in a letter to Henry Adams dated September 25 wrote, "Hanna has been crying wolf all summer, and he has been much derided for his fears, but now everybody shares them. Bryan comes out a frank anarchist again in his letter of acceptance; and Mitchell with his coal strike has thrown at least a hundred thousand votes to him." Quoted in James Ford Rhodes, *The McKinley and Roosevelt Administrations, 1897–1909* (New York: Macmillan Co., 1922), pp. 139–40.

16. The terms of the settlement are quoted in Glück, *John Mitchell*, pp. 82–83.

17. Mitchell, *Organized Labor*, p. 368.

18. Ibid., p. 369.

19. The National Civic Federation, formed in Chicago in 1893, was originally intended as a forum for the discussion of vital questions of public policy. Early on it became interested in the labor problem and gradually became active in the field of industrial mediation and conciliation. By 1902, its Mediation and Conciliation Department included some of the most prominent political, labor, and religious leaders in the nation. Both Mitchell and Hanna were active in the work of the Federation, Hanna having been one of its organizers and its first president. See Marguerite Green, *The National Civic Federation and the American Labor Movement* (Washington, DC: Catholic University of America Press, 1956).

20. Details concerning the strike and the issues in dispute may be found in Anthracite Coal Strike Commission, *Report to the President on the Anthracite Coal Strike of May-October 1902* (Washington, DC: U.S. Government Printing Office, 1903); and in Robert J. Cornell, *The Anthracite Coal Strike of 1902* (Washington, DC.: The Catholic University Press, 1957).

21. Carroll D. Wright, "Report to the President on the Anthracite Coal Strike," *Bulletin of the Department of Labor* 43 (November 1902).

22. So great was the devotion of the miners to Mitchell that the governor of Pennsylvania reputedly said, "the miners would not

return to work if a soldier were strapped to the back of each one of them." Quoted in Peter Roberts, "The Anthracite Coal Strike in its Social Aspects," *The Economic Journal*, 13 (March 1903): 24

23. Letter from Lodge to Roosevelt dated September 22, 1902, in *Selections from the Correspondence of Theodore Roosevelt and Henry Cabot Lodge*, ed. Henry Cabot Lodge (New York: Charles Scribner's Son's, 1925), 1: 529 (emphasis Lodge's). On September 25, Senator Lodge again urged upon the president the necessity of some action, admitting, however, that he had no solution to offer. He suggested that Attorney General Philander C. Knox, might use his personal influence with the operators since he "knows all those men and I know no one keener or bolder than he." See pp. 530, 532.

24. See Mitchell, *Organized Labor*, especially chap. 36 entitled "The Proper Conduct of a Strike." There was some violence but not sufficient to warrant public intervention. See Anthracite Coal Strike Commission, *Report to the President*, pp. 72–79, 137–40; Glück, *John Mitchell*, pp. 111, 114–15.

25. Mitchell thwarted a strong effort within the union to call the bituminous miners out in a sympathetic strike in violation of their contracts with the bituminous operators. See Glück, *John Mitchell*, pp. 103, 107–10. For this he drew a glowing public tribute from Senator Hanna and he gained the respect and sympathy of the bituminous operators. See the excerpt of a speech delivered by Senator Hanna on August 9, 1902, quoted in Croly, *Marcus Alonzo Hanna*, pp. 396–97.

26. Roberts, "Anthracite Coal Strike," p. 23.

27. Roosevelt to Lodge dated September 27, *Selections*, 1: 534.

28. Ibid., p. 533.

29. In his fourth annual message to Congress on December 6, 1904, Theodore Roosevelt said, in reference to "capital and labor": "if there is resistance to the Federal courts, interference with the mails, or interstate commerce, or molestation of Federal property, or if the State authorities in some crisis which they are unable to face call for help, then the Federal Government may interfere." Cited in Hermann Hagedorn, ed., *The Works of Theodore Roosevelt, Memorial Edition* (New York: Charles Scribner's Sons, 1925), 17: 251–52. Moreover, while Theodore Roosevelt realized that there were abuses in the use of the injunction in private labor disputes, he did not believe the courts should be shorn of their right to issue injunctions in those cases and he certainly believed that the injunction, when wielded by the national government in a labor dispute, was a perfectly proper and necessary device (ibid., p. 332). For his violent reaction to Debs and Altgeld see ibid., 16: 363–65.

30. Letter from Hanna to Roosevelt dated September 28, 1902, in Joseph Bucklin Bishop, *Theodore Roosevelt and His Time Shown in His Own Letters* (New York: Charles Scribner's Sons, 1920), 1: 201. See also Croly, *Marcus Alonzo Hanna*, p. 398.

31. Roosevelt to Lodge, September 27, 1902, *Selections*, p. 534.

32. Roosevelt to Hanna, September 27, 1902, quoted in Bishop, *Theodore Roosevelt and his Time*, 1: 201.

33. Theodore Roosevelt, *An Autobiography* (New York: Charles Scribner's Sons, 1913), p. 109. This point of view was not even remotely acceptable to the trade union movement. According to accepted trade union philosophy, the economic destiny of the membership rested exclusively in their own economic power and there was no superior authority, governmental or otherwise, which could dictate its use or set limits to its achievement. See especially W. Milne-Bailey, *Trade Unions and the State* (London: George Allen and Unwin, 1934). After the strike of 1902, Roosevelt and Mitchell developed a close friendship but the relationship between other figures in the labor movement, especially Gompers and Roosevelt, was one of strong mutual distrust. See Gompers, *Seventy Years*, 1: 526–36 and 2: 264; and Karson, *American Labor Unions*, chap. 3.

34. Roosevelt, *Autobiography*, p. 464.

35. Ibid., p. 446.

36. Ibid., p. 473.

37. Speech at Columbus, Ohio, September 10, 1910, in Hagedorn, *The Works of Theodore Roosevelt*, 18: 216–18.

38. Roosevelt, *Autobiography*, p. 473.

39. Ibid., p. 476.

40. Woodrow Wilson, *Constitutional Government in the United States* (New York: Columbia University Press, 1921), p. 68.

41. See his address before the national convention of the Progressive party in Chicago, August 6, 1912, in Hagedorn, *The Works of Theodore Roosevelt*, 19: 409–10.

42. Examples of this attitude, among numerous others, are to be found in a letter from Baer to Mitchell quoted in *Anthracite Coal Strike Commission, Report to the President*, p. 35, and in the odious "Divine Right of Capital" letter written by Baer to a Mr. Clark quoted in Henry F. Pringle, *Theodore Roosevelt, a Biography* (New York: Harcourt, Brace and Co., 1931), p. 268.

43. The idea of a White House conference was suggested to Roosevelt by Governor W. Murray Crane of Massachusetts. See Pringle, *Theodore Roosevelt*, p. 270. The meeting actually took place at the temporary executive mansion located at 22 Lafayette Place as the White House was being renovated.

44. Roosevelt to Lodge dated September 30, 1902, *Selections*, 1: 535.

45. Examples of statements the operators made to the press following the conference may be found in Pringle, *Theodore Roosevelt*, p. 272.

46. Telegram from Theodore Roosevelt to Lodge dated October 7, 1902, *Selections*, 1: 538.

47. Roosevelt, *Autobiography*, pp. 474–76.

48. Ibid., pp. 474–75.

49. Ibid., p. 474.

50. For the issues with which the commission dealt and its recommendations, see Anthracite Coal Strike Commission, *Report to the President*, especially pp. 42–87. See also John Graham Brooks, "The Public and the Anthracite Coal Strike," *The Economic Journal* 13

(September 1903): 364–72; and E. Dana Durand, "The Anthracite Coal Strike and its Settlement, *The Political Science Quarterly* 18, no. 3 (September 1903): 385–414. For his arbitration commission, Roosevelt planned to use former President Grover Cleveland, Carroll D. Wright, and Judge George D. Gray of Delaware, ". . . a Democrat whose standing in the country was second only to that of Grover Gleveland." See Roosevelt, *Autobiography*, p. 476.

Courtesy of Theodore Roosevelt Collection, Harvard College Library
President Theodore Roosevelt at
Brattleboro, Vermont, September 1, 1902

17

Theodore Roosevelt: The Scandal of the Hunter as Nature Lover

Paul Schullery

Last year I served on a board of consultants for a large midwestern museum. Our assignment was to advise and assist the museum staff in preparation of a major traveling exhibit about bears and humans. We were a diverse group: several leading bear ecologists, a folklorist or two, an American Indian specialist, some wildlife managers, and myself, a historian of conservation and sporting culture.

One area of special interest and importance to us was the American Indians' relationship with bears. Many tribes have rich traditions and spiritual associations with bears, and have left a spectacular legacy of objects, rituals, beliefs, and lore that lends itself to interpretation in the exhibits we envisioned. This is truly wonderful material, and we were all excited about the prospect of employing it to suggest some of the fascinating complexities of bear-human interactions.

Later in our deliberations, we turned to the subject of modern American bear hunting. Most of the group, including several of the biologists and wildlife managers, more or less dismissed the topic because of their personal experiences with bear hunters whom they found to be shallow and insensitive.

Only a few of us saw a peculiar inconsistency: when a band of Indian braves from Vancouver Island a couple hundred years ago hunted and killed a bear, it is anthropology; when a group of white guys from Detroit go out today and kill a bear, it is just that—a group of white guys killing a bear.

Much is lost in that simplistic view. In all aspects of their hunting behavior, both the Indians and the white men were the product of centuries of social evolution, as well as being the product of their own natural environments. Perhaps the average Indian would have been better able to express the heart of his beliefs about hunting than the average hunter from Detroit; perhaps not. That should not matter to the scholar, who should be more broadly concerned with what cultural and environmental processes went into the makeup of the individual.

Even the casual observer of sport must notice the parallels that follow the sport of hunting from culture to culture: the desire and even reverence for the trophy, the celebrated "communing with nature," the respect for the quarry, the complex and even ritual behaviors that attach themselves to the sport and its equipment, the passages of manhood so often associated with the hunting of big game, the society of hunters as they pursue the game, and other universally common aspects of the hunting experience.[1]

But it must be said that all this cultural richness may be lost when all *your* culture is showing you at the moment is a beery, inarticulate slob hunter who just shot a twenty-five-pound bear cub and is proud of it. The immediacy of one's own culture's product—with all its warts and embarrassments—may make it harder to admire than the products of another culture, safely viewed through the filters of time and historical nostalgia.

But we who pretend to take a more dispassionate, professionally distant view cannot afford the luxury of focusing exclusively on the individual product of any culture. We know that the individual may express some of the culture's tendencies without truly representing the culture's best hopes. We must draw back, and to the extent we are permitted to pass judgment at all, we must be prepared to pass judgment on the entire culture.

Largely because of its intense emotional context in today's world, many people, including scholarly people who should know better, have a great deal of trouble standing back far enough to recognize hunting for what it is, a complex product of many centuries of cultural, political, and ecological processes, most of which the hunter may be no more aware of than are his critics. The first step in coming to terms with Theodore Roosevelt's lifelong enthusiasm for hunting is recognizing that, as scholars, we must be careful to understand our own cultural context well enough to examine his. Therefore, some cautionary examples in the historiography of the hunting issue as it has focused on Roosevelt are in order.

This is not an exercise designed to convert any anti-hunters to hunting. Nor is it an attempt to make hunters think a little harder about their place in the modern world, although I wouldn't mind affecting the thinking of both groups. My goal is simply to elevate the scholarly discussion of hunting—especially as it applies to Theodore Roosevelt—to a level similar to what we accord any other legitimate historical subject. Hunting, I fear, has not received the sort of disciplined attention we require of ourselves in dealing with, say, Roosevelt's international diplomacy or his views on race.

I will use examples to suggest three types of errors that creep into our thinking. I'm sure there are others, but these capture most of the major problems I have encountered.

First, there is the error of simple factual distortion. I can only guess at the causes, but it appears most likely that a writer's view may be so colored by his or her own view of hunting, or by raw emotion, that facts are only an obstacle. One of the most grievous such errors I have encountered on this subject was committed by Emily Hahn, writing in *American Heritage*. In an article on Roosevelt's friendship with the legendary African hunter Frederick Courteney Selous, Hahn referred to Selous and his colleagues as slaughterers of game, and displayed no understanding of their role in the study of wildlife or the development of a legitimate and ultimately conservationist form of African big game hunting. More to the point, she characterized Roosevelt as, "the last person in the world to feel squeamish about bloodletting,"[2] and described his famous African hunt as follows: "Roosevelt continued his triumphant way, shooting practically everything that moved and collecting so much that the museum respectfully but firmly refused to put it all on view."[3]

This sort of emotional messiness all too much characterizes modern writing about the sportsmen of other eras. Hahn, obviously distraught over the "slaughter" of wildlife, seems not to have looked beyond her own indignation. If she had, she might have found numbers that confounded her simplistic, if ever more fashionable, view.

Roosevelt and his son, Kermit, killed 512 animals on this long ten-month hunt in 1909-1910, including many small mammals and birds.[4] Many of these were used as food to supply the large staff of the safari. They kept, as Roosevelt said, "about a dozen" as trophies.[5] The rest were gladly received by the Smithsonian, the museum that helped fund the expedition.

During my five years as a museum director, I discovered that very few people realize that museums maintain what are called "study collections" of far greater size than could ever be exhibited. There have often been good reasons for this. For example, in a zoological collection, one may seek to document intraspecies variation, something that in Roosevelt's day could only be done through collection of multiple specimens. Thus, for every mouse on exhibit, there may be scores or even hundreds of mouse skins in storage for use by mouse researchers. Such practices explain why, contrary to Hahn's view, Roosevelt's expedition made such a monumental contribution to the Smithsonian collection.

Some evidence of this is provided by the total kill of the expedition. As it turned out, the animals killed by the Roosevelts amounted to about five percent of the total of the expedition. The team of Smithsonian naturalists who accompanied his expedition collected another 10,000 animals. According to Paul Cutright, writing in *Theodore Roosevelt, the Naturalist*, "the Smithsonian-African Expedition enriched the National Museum to the extent of 5,013 mammals, 4,453 birds, 2,322 reptiles and amphibians, not to mention thousands of fish, insects, plants, and a quantity of anthropological material."[6] Whatever differences Roosevelt may have had with the museum over how many items would be exhibited, his twelve trophies seem quite modest next to that total.

This is not to say that we would approve of such a take today. The science of wildlife ecology—and the practice of museum exhibitry and collection—have come a long way. Advances in many fields, including photography and sound recording, have convinced most modern researchers that intensive specimen collection is unnecessary, and in some cases even harmful to rare species. But Roosevelt did not make his trip nor did the Smithsonian endorse and sponsor it in 1990.

One can only do so much about this sort of distortion; its sources are deep and subjective, and it probably cannot be prevented. Hahn plainly disapproved of hunting in principle. That was her right, a right her audience must respect. But it was hardly her right to so completely distort historical reality. At least in scholarly circles, we can learn to apply the normal conventions of evidence, and forewarn our readers if we approach the topic with certain convictions or value judgments they may not share.

Another kind of error, one I find much easier to tolerate, is the result not of indignant moralizing but of simple lack of knowledge of Roosevelt's world, or of the world of outdoor life. In Edmund Morris's superb book *The Rise of Theodore Roosevelt*, there was an account of an 1884 hunting trip in which TR killed "170 items in just forty-seven days."[7] Morris was clearly troubled by this number of deaths. It does sound like an alarming total, at first glance. But it must be evaluated for its contents, and its purpose.

First, fifty of the 170 "items" were trout. A good many more were grouse, doves, ducks, and rabbits.[8] Those of you who have spent any time in the woods hiking with a heavy pack may already have learned that a trout will not fuel you for very many miles. Roosevelt was not only trophy hunting; as on the African hunt, he was feeding his party, in this case a guide and himself. Two men, riding, climbing, hiking, and performing all the other tasks associated with a long wilderness trip burn up a lot of calories in forty-seven days.

I want to make it clear, however, that there was probably some meat that was left behind or went uneaten. If Roosevelt happened to shoot an elk or bear, almost certainly the hunters only took the choice portions; they couldn't carry more, or keep it from spoiling, without a lot of work. In their day, however, and under those circumstances, this was not seen as a significant waste; after all, Roosevelt hunted big game more for the experience and the trophies than for the meat.

The third type of error is the least susceptible to simple analysis, and the type that in the long run probably has done the most harm to Roosevelt's historical image. In Edward Wagenknecht's enduring book, *The Seven Worlds of Theodore Roosevelt*, the author struggled nobly to maintain objectivity about Roosevelt's passion for hunting, and offered some penetrating observations on the subject. He displayed considerable sympathy for his complex subject, but finally had to admit that he just could not understand "how a man who loved animals as much as Roosevelt did could still *enjoy* killing them."[9]

People who hold this view are rarely as kind as Wagenkecht. Too often Roosevelt is seen as some sort of twisted butcher who killed for the sick thrill of it, who collected trophies to prove his manhood.[10] Ironically, some of the same people who abhor Roosevelt's behavior will fawn (with embarrassing condescension) over American Indian cultures that displayed similarly complex relationships with animals, such as tribes who called bears their brothers but prized the bear's various parts—claws, teeth, hides, and so on—for food, ornaments, trophies, or clothing. Human culture is not simple, but we often find it convenient to view it simplistically.

On the other hand, the traditional defenses of Roosevelt as a hunter only go part way in providing sufficient historical context to deal with this dilemma of Wagenknecht's. Roosevelt, we are told, saved millions of animals—through enactment of conservation legislation, and through his writings—for everyone he may have killed. He created vast reserves of public domain. He was, without question, one of the greatest observers and writers about big game in his day; he never killed just to kill, usually writing later about the habits of the animal, often on the basis of what he learned by examining the carcass. He lived an honored and respected code, within which the kills he made were moderate. He was, in fact, a major force in developing and promoting the sporting code that still guides the conscientious sportsman (remember that it was sportsmen, not their critics, who gave us terms like "slob hunter" and "game hog").[11]

But however persuasive these defenses may be in convincing us that Roosevelt is deservedly a hero of sportsmen, they don't really answer Wagenknecht's question. All right, so he was a great conservationist and a leader of high sporting principles and all that; the question remains—How could he enjoy killing things?

To understand, we must be prepared to explore more than the statistical realities of his kills, or the physical necessities of getting meat in the wilderness. We must examine the philosophical core of the sporting tradition, and beware of the potential limitations of our own preconceptions about that tradition.

We might start by recognizing that it is not safe to directly equate sport with fun. Sport, like music, painting, or any other similarly ancient human pursuit, may at times be fun in a simple sense, or it may evoke in us many other feelings. Some of Roosevelt's best-remembered hunts would hardly sound like fun, for all of the trudging through mud, freezing in wet tents and other suffering. Sport is not a simple idea, and reducing the moment of the kill to so simple an emotion as fun (or, to use Wagenecht's term, enjoyment) hardly does justice to what has led up to or follows that moment.

Therefore, we had best recognize that killing is not sport. Sport is an involved process of which killing is a part. Roosevelt provided excellent, if perhaps nontypical, examples of this.

Consider his African hunt. Though it lasted only months, it was something he dreamed of for most of his adult life. That dream involved TR in encyclopedic reading, in lengthy correspondences with many people, and in no end of formal preparations—shopping for equipment, planning, and so on. These activities, over the course of twenty or thirty years, are all easily recognizable by serious sportsmen as part of the sporting life.

Then there was the hunt, each twenty-four hours a tapestry of stunning dawns, new acquaintances, new sights and knowledge, adventures, old friendships, firelit evenings, and the stirring nightsounds everyone who has visited Africa remembers. In between, there was the kill, or each kill. Some of those kills were probably quite routine, others were frightening almost beyond belief. Each was unique.

Then there is the memory of the experience, not just of the kill but of all the moments that stick in one's mind from such a great adventure. In Roosevelt's case, of course, remembrance was complemented by journalism and essay, as he preserved, celebrated, and further explored the experience in his writings. That too is part of sport, a part that always absorbed Roosevelt, both as writer and reader. Not only was he one of the foremost writers on hunting in American history, he was a fervent bibliophile, with what may have been the finest big game library in the United States at the time.[12]

And so it is that in order to come to terms with Roosevelt's hunting, we must come to terms with a great deal more than how he might have felt at the moment that he shot something. We must understand that his feelings at that moment were a small part of the hunting experience, which, in temporal terms, is ninety-nine percent getting ready and remembering, and one percent pulling the trigger. Whatever position our own moral code may hand us about hunting, we had best be sure we

Courtesy of Theodore Roosevelt Collection, Harvard College Library

President Theodore Roosevelt
at Newcastle, Wyoming, May 30, 1903.

understand the ninety-nine percent before we speak too judgmentally about the one percent.

Hunters, at least those articulate enough to scrutinize and write about the experience, have expressed a wide variety of views on the moment of the kill. For some, it is said, the hunter kills in order to have hunted; killing is part of the greater process. For some, it is even seen as a necessary evil. For others, the kill is the most important instant in the process, and a hunt without a kill is a complete disappointment.[13] But I think it safe to say that, whatever view an individual hunter may take, he or she is doing a great deal more in the woods than looking for something to kill, and that hunting is a great deal more than the moment of the kill.

At its best, as Roosevelt attempted to exemplify it, it is a way of life, a means of appreciating the natural world.

No self-respecting historical scholar would dream of commenting offhandedly about Roosevelt's views on naval strategy. First, there is research to be done, not only in the general history of naval strategy but also in the origins of Roosevelt's own highly formed and widely published views of the subject. And yet quite a few scholars—and a host of popular writers who profess objectivity—have not hesitated to speak offhandedly about Roosevelt's sporting activities without any effort to examine the foundations and evolution of the sporting traditions that shaped that aspect of his life.

Hunting is under attack in modern America.[14] More people (both pro and con) than ever before seem reluctant to let their neighbors make their own choices about this issue; it is increasingly politicized, and increasingly newsworthy. Theodore Roosevelt, as perhaps the most famous sport hunter in American history, is tossed around by all parties as an example of whatever each party wishes to prove. He is a symbol of many things in this debate, many of which are not fair to him or to history. However the issue is eventually resolved, it will be a credit to the historical profession if Roosevelt and his beliefs are treated with scholarly respect, and if the real Roosevelt, rather than some caricature, emerges as the one most recognized by the public.

NOTES

1. There is surprisingly little in the way of scholarly literature about the evolution of hunting practices from so-called primitive peoples to today's societies. An eloquent and milestone overview of the philosophy of hunting that contains considerable material on the consistencies of the hunting impulse across cultures is Jose Ortega y Gasset, *Meditations on Hunting*, trans. Paul Shepard (New York: Charles Scribner's Sons, 1985). Perhaps one reason that scholars occasionally have difficulty developing a scholarly perspective on the history of hunting is that so few have taken the subject on as a field of study. Like some other recreational pursuits, hunting seems to have been viewed not as an element of culture but as a vacation from it, a sort of analysis-exempt aspect of daily life. This view trivializes something of great significance.

2. Emily Hahn, "My Dear Selous," *American Heritage*, April 1963, p. 41.

3. Ibid., p. 96.

4. Theodore Roosevelt, *African Game Trails* (New York: Charles Scribner, 1910), p. 533.

5. Ibid., p. 534.

6. Paul Cutright, *Theodore Roosevelt, the Naturalist* (New York: Harper and Brothers, 1956), p. 209.

7. Edmund Morris, *The Rise of Theodore Roosevelt* (New York: Random House, 1979), p. 286.

8. This issue of the amount of game killed is not a simple one. In Roosevelt's day, for example, some types of animals, such as jackrabbits and coots, were deemed suitable for target practice. Roosevelt participated in these "varmint hunts," and some animals are still treated more or less this way today. Values change, and sporting ethics are always evolving. The point is not that Roosevelt killed only what he needed; he killed game only within the constraints of the highest sporting standards of his day. We do not have to approve of those standards in order to recognize that he was a product of his time, rather than of ours.

9. Edward Wagenknecht, *The Seven Worlds of Theodore Roosevelt* (New York: Longmans, Green, 1958), p. 20.

10. Thomas Altherr, "'The Best of All Breathing': Hunting as a Mode of Environmental Perception in American Literature and Thought from James Fenimore Cooper to Norman Mailer" (Ph.D. diss., Ohio State University, 1976), p. 215. Altherr's dissertation is a rare and largely successful attempt to analyze an element of the hunting culture—its literary expressions—over an extended period of time. His chapter on Roosevelt "and the emergence of the American hunter-naturalist ideal" is an interesting introduction to some of the central issues that faced hunters in Roosevelt's time. He cites writers who have taken the view that Roosevelt enjoyed killing because he was mentally deranged.

11. A useful overview of the rise of the sportsman-conservationist in America is John Reiger, *American Sportsmen and the Origins of Conservation* (New York: Winchester Press, 1975).

12. Frederick Goff, "T.R.'s Big Game Library," *Quarterly Journal of the Library of Congress* 21, no. 3 (1964): 166–72.

13. One of the most careful analyses I have seen of hunters' views on the kill is Ann Causey, "On the Morality of Hunting," *Environmental Ethics*, Winter 1989, pp. 327–43.

14. Michael Satchell, "The American Hunter Under Fire," *U.S. News & World Report*, February 5, 1990, pp. 30–36.

18

Keeper of His Conscience?
Pinchot, Roosevelt, and the Politics of
Conservation

Char Miller

Gifford Pinchot and Theodore Roosevelt loved to play games, especially those in which they could flash their youthful vigor or test their manly prowess. They discovered their mutual delight in such things when, in February 1899, Pinchot first visited the then-governor of New York in Albany. "We arrived just as the Executive Mansion was under ferocious attack from a band of invisible Indians," Pinchot fondly recalled in his autobiography, "and the Governor of the Empire State was helping a handful of children escape by lowering them out of a second story window on a rope." That night Pinchot and Roosevelt indulged in a few games of their own. The taller Pinchot used his long reach to good effect in a round of boxing: "I had the honor of knocking the future President of the United States off his very solid pins," he would boast. Bragging rights were not his alone. The smaller, albeit more powerfully built Roosevelt came back to overwhelm his lanky guest in a wrestling match. By such physical contact was their friendship sealed.[1]

Their sweaty embrace was more than simply an example of male bonding, however. It reflected, even as it helped initiate, an intellectual closeness that henceforth would characterize their personal relationship and public careers. But just how far did this merger of body and soul go? Apparently it went no little distance. Their friendship only deepened during Roosevelt's years as president, when Pinchot served first as chief of the Forestry Division of the Department of Agriculture and later as chief of the new U.S. Forest Service. More than a kept bureaucrat, Pinchot became a significant figure in the president's so-called Tennis Cabinet—not for these hale fellows the domestic, feminine, and interior implications of a "Kitchen Cabinet." The context for their evolving relationship continued to be the great outdoors. Together they would chop wood for exercise, set off on extended tramps through Washington's Rock Creek Park, ride horses, and swim the Potomac River in late fall. These interactions were important for Roosevelt who, just before he left the White House in 1909, wrote Pinchot that "for seven and a half years we have worked together, and now and then played together—and have been altogether better able to work because we have played." It was no less important for Pinchot; it was by sharing in this strenuous life that he had become one of the president's "faithful bodyguard."[2]

Gifford Pinchot (1865–1946) headed the Division of Forestry in the Department of Agriculture, 1898–1905, and was named first chief of the new Forest Service by President Theodore Roosevelt in 1905. Pinchot was later elected governor of Pennsylvania in 1922 and 1930.

Pinchot was one of the faithful in another sense. He and the president seemed of like minds, especially on matters of federal conservation policy. They were, like many of their generation, appalled by the destruction of nature, a destruction everywhere visible in early twentieth-century America. The solution, they believed, lay in federal regulation and scientific management of natural resources; only this approach, guided by the appropriate experts, would insure the nation's survival. So parallel ran their thoughts that Roosevelt reportedly confided to Robert Underwood Johnson, an editor of *The Century* and strong supporter of the conservation movement, that on questions of conservation the chief forester was in truth the keeper of his conscience.[3]

What Roosevelt meant by his declaration is not altogether clear, however, at least not to those scholars who have sought to interpret it. Many of the president's biographers, for instance, have taken it at face value, and like Henry Pringle have suggested that Pinchot was therefore the "dominant influence" in shaping Roosevelt's conservation policies. A sense of dominance lies at the heart of historian Stephen Fox's evaluation, too: "Theodore Roosevelt explicitly, all but uncritically, put Pinchot in charge of his conservation interests." This vision of Pinchot's flawed conscience has not surfaced in biographical assessments of the forester's career, for obvious reasons. Instead, Pinchot scholars have employed Roosevelt's assertion to show how close the two men's relationship in fact was, thereby illuminating his significance in the development of a national conservation policy during the Progressive Era.[4]

Each of these perspectives is a tad self-serving, of course. Indeed, what none of these scholars has asked is why the president spoke to Johnson in the way that he did (if he did), and what this might have meant in terms of the formulation of public policy. How much leeway did Pinchot have to craft the federal conservation agenda during the Roosevelt years? Were the decisions he reached his own or were they rather reflections of an administrative consensus, one that Roosevelt determined?

Some of the answers to these questions are most fully revealed in these two men's reactions to one of the most important conservation issues to emerge during Roosevelt's tenure in the White House—the decision to dam the Hetch Hetchy Valley. An analysis of their response to the proposed dam in California's Yosemite National Park helps deepen our understanding of the internal workings of the Roosevelt administration as it grappled with a matter of great national concern. Revealed, too, is the special role Pinchot played in these administrative debates, a role that does not quite square with the long-held belief that he was the master architect of, and guiding force behind, the federal government's conservation agenda during the first decade of the Progressive Era.

The Battle for Hetch Hetchy

Throughout the late nineteenth and early twentieth centuries, engineers for the city of San Francisco sought to alleviate the city's chronic water shortages, concluding that the best option lay in capturing the clear waters of the Toulumne River some 200 miles to the east. The only catch was that the Hetch Hetchy Valley, which they hoped to use as a reservoir, lay within the confines of Yosemite National Park. It was for this reason that in 1903, 1905, and again in 1906, San Francisco petitioned the federal government for permission to build a dam on this public land. Each petition managed to spark an ever-larger amount of controversy. The outcry became so vigorous that Hetch Hetchy still stands as one of the seminal moments in the history of the conservation movement in the United States.[5]

This debate had pitted two old friends against one another—John Muir, president of the Sierra Club, and Gifford Pinchot. The former argued strenuously that Hetch Hetchy, whose beauty he had so lovingly evoked in many books and articles, should remain forever wild. Pinchot no less strenuously asserted that the valley's stunning natural beauty should not stand in the way of development for the public good. At such opposite poles were they, and so rancorous was the debate that swirled around them, that Muir and Pinchot assume center stage whenever the battle for Hetch Hetchy is recounted. They eclipse all other actors, including the president Pinchot served, overshadowing even the valley itself as the prime object of attention.

The historical narrative of this struggle would seem to support their centrality. It was after all to Pinchot that the secretary of interior, Ethan Hitchcock, turned for advice concerning the advisability of granting San Francisco's petition.

Pinchot's response was blunt. A dam in Hetch Hetchy "would not injure the national park or detract from its beauties or natural grandeur," a declaration that mystified Muir. As he put it in a letter to Johnson, "I cannot believe Pinchot, if he really knows the valley, has made any such statements, for it would be just the same thing as saying that flooding Yosemite would do it no harm."[6]

Actually Pinchot's position was more complex than his public statements would suggest. In a confidential letter to William Colby, secretary of the Sierra Club and a close friend of Muir's, he indicated that the Roosevelt administration believed that San Francisco should first use Lake Eleanor as a reservoir; its capacity should supply the city for at least fifty years, "and perhaps twice as long," sparing Hetch Hetchy for several generations.[7]

That political compromise aside, Pinchot and Muir still disagreed in principle as to the proper balance that was to be struck in this case, indeed in any case. For Pinchot, the preservation of the natural landscape must be set against possible material benefits; for Muir, the very notion that a "balance" might even exist was itself weighted in the favor of developmental interests. In this environment, future compromises by definition would be difficult to arrange.[8]

They became even more so when, in the next year, the Great Earthquake devastated San Francisco. In its wake the city reapplied for a permit to build the dam; Hitchcock had rejected the city's initial petition, and thus Pinchot's report, indicating that it violated the legal status of the national park system, an argument that Muir had advanced successfully. But the catastrophe changed the grounds of discussion, at least for Pinchot. He now abandoned the Lake Eleanor option, and in a letter to the city's engineer, Marsden Manson, held out the hope that "in the regeneration of San Francisco its people may be able to make provision for a water supply from the Yosemite National Park." He would, he assured Manson, "stand by to render any assistance which lies in my power."[9]

Once again, Muir's power matched that of the chief forester. He stepped up his public campaign to challenge Pinchot's posture, to sound the alarm throughout the United States. Over the next couple of years, he spun out a series of provocative essays on Hetch Hetchy that built broad public support for the valley's preservation. So effective was this campaign, which gained strong public and media support, that Congress, despite the administration's support for the Hetch Hetchy Dam bill, constantly delayed action on the legislation. Moreover, the fight went so far that Pinchot's reputation as a conservationist was itself called into question. His misguided actions in the Hetch Hetchy affair, *The Independent* editorialized in 1910, have "put a severe strain upon the confidence of his supporters." Hetch Hetchy, it concluded, was "nothing less than conservation staked to the ground."[10]

Much *was* at stake, as the final legislative hearings in 1913 demonstrated. Although Pinchot was no longer head of the Forest Service, he nonetheless testified on behalf of San Francisco, testimony that proved crucial in determining the final vote in the city's favor. Muir himself stoked public opinion, writing essay after essay, letter after letter, hoping to cancel the effectiveness of Pinchot's testimony. Bitter allegations and personal attacks filled each man's public statements—Pinchot sneered at the sentimentalists' fond regard for land that was but a swamp, and Muir lashed out at the "temple destroyers" for whom the almighty dollar was the new god—charged rhetoric that only further polarized the debate.[11]

The controversy, then, seemingly ended as it had begun. Muir and Pinchot apparently determined its tempo and impulse, beginning with their private correspondence and personal negotiations in the first years of the century, escalating later in the public confrontations and verbal sparing during the early 'teens. As the title of the most recent documentary about Hetch Hetchy—*The Wilderness Idea: John Muir, Gifford Pinchot and the First Great Battle for Wilderness* (1989)—indicates, this was a two-man show.[12]

These two combatants' certitude and mutual animosity were not solely responsible for the timing and character of the debate, however. Indeed, without ignoring the influence of the thousands who also were directly engaged with this national discussion, there was one other major figure who had as much to do with shaping its contours as did Muir and Pinchot—President Theodore Roosevelt.

His contributions to the debate are of a different order than theirs, one key being that his philosophy of conservation neatly balanced the beliefs of Muir and Pinchot; he drew upon the preservationist and utilitarian ideals of conservation for which they were the leading exponents, but was not doctrinaire in his application of their principles. This did not make his decision concerning Hetch Hetchy any easier; in fact, it made it all the more tension-filled. Unlike Muir and Pinchot, Roosevelt could see both sides, could be of two minds. His ability to accept such ambiguity, even to foster it, was not only crucial to the evolution of the whole affair, but reflected something else. He was his own man.[13]

He demonstrated this independence throughout the Hetch Hetchy controversy. In 1903, just as the debate was heating up, Roosevelt went camping with Muir throughout Yosemite. In asking Muir to serve as his guide for the trip, the president had promised "to drop politics absolutely for four days and just be out in the open with you." He kept part of that promise, at least. The president remembered those four days with great delight, remembering especially the valley's extraordinary natural landscape, including "the solemn temple of the giant sequoias" where they first camped and their final site "fronting the stupendous rocky mass of El Capitan, with the falls thundering in the distance on either hand."[14]

Theirs was not just a sightseeing tour, however; neither man was about to forego politics. Instead they engaged in extended discussions of the political future of the conservation movement generally, and more specifically over ways in which to protect Muir's beloved Sierras, discourse that bore fruit. Shortly after leaving Yosemite, Roosevelt urged the secretary of the interior to make the northern Sierras a part of the National Forest Reserves. It is no wonder that later Muir would gush that "I never before had met so interesting, hearty, and manly a companion. I fairly fell in love with him."[15]

That love, and influence, only went so far. When two years later a question arose as to how much federal control would be exerted in Yosemite, a question linked to San Francisco's petition to build the dam in Hetch Hetchy, Muir tried to exploit his earlier visit with Roosevelt. He wrote the president suggesting that he had made a promise to protect the national park from commercial development. Roosevelt brushed aside Muir's claim, dismissing also his and the Sierra Club's denunciation of the proposed dam as "too vague." On these and other matters, the president wrote Muir's close friend Robert Underwood Johnson, that caution was essential: "My own belief is that California will resent anything like interference on my part." Roosevelt, in short, was not about to be stampeded into sharing Muir's perspective.[16]

His chief forester could not buffalo him either. In the summer of 1907, for instance, as Pinchot and the new interior secretary, James R. Garfield, were preparing to release yet another report in favor of a reservoir in Hetch Hetchy, Roosevelt suggested that they think again about alternate sites. Pinchot was delegated to visit Muir in California to solicit his views. Muir argued pointedly that Hetch Hetchy must be saved from destruction, and followed this verbal report with a lengthy written one to Garfield. In the end, Muir's brief persuaded neither Garfield nor Pinchot, and they informed the president that Hetch Hetchy remained the best site for a reservoir. In forcing his staff to reexamine their beliefs, however, Roosevelt had helped shape his own. It was only after this reevaluation that he decided to accept their recommendation; with Roosevelt, policymaking was an intense event designed to build strong consensus.[17]

TR deliberately made the process all the more intense when in September of that year he wrote a letter to Muir that laid out his assessment of the political situation surrounding Hetch Hetchy and suggested ways Muir could challenge the very findings embedded within Roosevelt's subordinates' report.

The president admitted that "Pinchot and Garfield are rather favorable to the Hetch Hetchy plan, but not definitely so"—an indefiniteness that would have surprised them. Roosevelt then asserted that he would do everything in his power "to protect not only Yosemite . . . but other similar great beauties of this country"—an assertion that must have been music to Muir's ears. But Roosevelt was acutely aware of the dilemma in which he thereby found himself, noting that if the preservation of these lands were "used so as to interfere with the permanent material development of the State . . . the result will be bad." This economic constraint reinforced a political one. "You must remember," he wrote, "that it is out of the question permanently to protect [these beauties] unless we have a certain degree of friendliness toward them on the part of the people of the State in which they are situated." Such support had not yet been manifest in the case of Yosemite; rather the reverse was true. Everyone seemed in favor of the project, said TR, "and I have been in the disagreeable position of seeming to interfere with the development of the State for the sake of keeping a valley, which apparently hardly anyone wanted to have kept. . . ." Roosevelt was not about to flaunt public opinion.[18]

He was not shy, however, about encouraging others to act as he could not. He made it quite plain that the key to preserving Hetch Hetchy lay in the development of a groundswell of popular support, something it presently did not have. Were this political liability overcome, the administration's position might well change to meet new political conditions. As Roosevelt declared, "I would not have any difficulty at all [in supporting your position] if, as you say, nine-tenths of the citizens took ground against the Hetch Hetchy project." It was all a matter of politics.[19]

Muir took full advantage of the president's insights. It was only after receiving this letter, for instance, that Muir, along with the Sierra Club and its allies, swung into action, sparking intense publicity and increasingly favorable press for their cause. This close scrutiny could not materialize until after the report of Garfield and Pinchot circulated within the administration, a report that conceded Hetch Hetchy's beauty but concluded that the need for the reservoir was too pressing to ignore; it emerged too only after the secretary of the interior granted San Francisco's application. But the pressure Muir and others would generate in 1908 and 1909 would only be effective in the realm of electoral politics in any event. There it proved quite successful, too, as Congress, confronted with enormous public opposition, refused to act on the measure. Hetch Hetchy, for the time being, was safe; it would not be inundated during Roosevelt's watch.[20]

Muir's success at this stage of the debate was not without its share of irony for Roosevelt must be given partial credit for defeating his own administration's proposal. This suggests again how independent and complicated his conservation beliefs truly were, an independence and complexity he gave clear voice to in his final message to Congress in December 1908. Here he touted the pressing need to preserve wilderness for its own sake, most notably the Yellowstone and Yosemite National Parks: "In both, all wild things should be protected and the scenery kept wholly unmarred," the president declared, a declaration that historian Roderick Nash believes repudiated Pinchot's stance on Hetch Hetchy. A more careful reading of Roosevelt's message reveals, however, that his support for preservation was—as always—coupled with an equally vigorous championing of the utilitarian conservation Pinchot especially espoused. The president argued, for instance, that those national parks adjacent to national forests, including Yellowstone and Yosemite, should "be placed under the control of the forest service of the Agriculture Department, instead of leaving them as they are now, under the Interior Department and policed by the army." A transfer of authority of this kind would have seriously challenged the preservationist agenda. In this particular balance between the utility and preservation of wilderness, Roosevelt once again demonstrated that his conscience was his own.[21]

The Lightning Rod Man

If this was so, why then suggest otherwise, as Roosevelt reportedly did in a conversation with Johnson at the height of the Hetch Hetchy debate? In part Roosevelt did so because Pinchot was an important influence on Roosevelt's conservation politics and policies. The chief forester's insistence upon the advantages of utilitarian conservation, his emphasis on the economic benefits and political equality that such conservation could produce, had a pronounced impact on Roosevelt. Pinchot, for instance, helped draft many of Roosevelt's speeches relating to forestry and conservation while he was governor of New York, and then later when TR was president. These contributions, among others, earned Roosevelt's deep appreciation and high praise: "Gifford Pinchot is the man to whom the nation owes most for what was accomplished as regards the preservation of the natural resources of our country," he asserted in his autobiography. "He led, and indeed during its most vital period embodied, the fight for preservation through use of our forests." Among many talented public servants, Roosevelt affirmed, Pinchot "stood first."[22]

That this translated into administrative influence, is beyond doubt. Not so obvious is the role this influence gave him within the administration. A clue to his function emerged in one of the rationales Roosevelt offered for allowing San Francisco to build a dam in Hetch Hetchy that appeared in a letter he wrote to Johnson. In it the president commented rather offhandedly that as "for the Hetch Hetchy matter, it was just one of those cases where I was extremely doubtful." But he finally set those doubts aside, and "came to the conclusion that I ought to stand by Garfield and Pinchot's judgement in the matter." To judge from this text, his subordinates' certitude had won out over presidential ambivalence.[23]

There is more to Roosevelt's description than that. His words also reveal an important dimension in the political relationship between the president and his chief forester. In establishing Pinchot (and Garfield) as the dam's chief advocates within the administration, in indicating that he ought to "stand by" them despite his own doubts, Roosevelt underscored the manner in which Pinchot especially served as the administration's point man, as Roosevelt's lightning rod. Pinchot's job was not simply to articulate governmental policy but to act as if it were his policy, thereby catching the thunderbolts subsequently hurled by those opposed to that particular policy. In this he would spare his superior no little heat.

One of those so deflected was John Muir. In the final stages of the debate over Hetch Hetchy, for instance, Muir was furious with Pinchot's forceful advocacy of the dam, an advocacy that Muir believed Roosevelt would have preempted had he been president in 1913. After all, it "was Roosevelt who [in 1905] tried to save the valley, at least for a generation or two, by compelling San Francisco to first develop the Lake Eleanor and Cherry River to the utmost," a memory that conveniently neglected Pinchot's role in the development of this idea. He too had supported this proposition, and had even served as the administration's spokesman for it in 1905. That Muir forgot about his arch rival's role in these discussions testifies to how effectively Pinchot had fulfilled his job to shield Roosevelt from criticism, protection that enabled the president's reputation to remain intact, if not to flourish.[24]

Clear political gains flowed from this symbiotic relationship, but its design depended as well on both men's willingness to invest in it. There is no question that Pinchot's investment was as personal as it was political. Like many of the other younger men drawn to work for Roosevelt, he was in awe of the chief executive, and he displayed his fierce adoration by hurling himself into his work for each of the more than seven years Roosevelt held office. All this struck Pinchot's parents as excessive, and they blamed Roosevelt for so abusing their son. One of their friends, for example, reported to them of "the way you are sacrificing youself" for a president who apparently "did not care for anyone's health or comfort." This friend had advised too "that you were being exhausted by [Roosevelt] and his ways," an observation that, James Pinchot advised his son, "tallies with what I think and your mother thinks."[25]

Most of all they thought his career was in jeopardy. You will "soon be a used up man—old and worn out," a forty-two-year-old without a future, his father predicted in 1907. "If you are to have [one] of any kind you must begin to prepare for it," something he was incapable of as long as he remained in his present state of adoration. "The time has come when you should take a stand and save yourself while you can," no easy task, the Pinchots understood, for Roosevelt was a "vampire."[26]

Certainly Roosevelt made shrewd use of the younger man's energy and devotion. He revealed how he had handled Pinchot in a 1910 letter to Henry Cabot Lodge, his close friend and adviser. Roosevelt, then on an expedition in Africa, had just learned that his successor, President William Howard Taft, had fired Pinchot for insubordination during the Ballinger-Pinchot furor. The former president confided that he was "very sorry about Pinchot. He was one of our most valuable public servants," valuable particularly for his enthusiasms: "He loved to spend his whole strength, with lavish indifference to any effect on himself, in battling for a high ideal." His zealous personality, then, perfectly qualified him to serve as Roosevelt's lightning rod man, and in that capacity to do much good.[27]

But for Pinchot to be effective, Roosevelt observed, his energies had to be carefully harnessed, something apparently Taft had not understood: "Not to keep him thus employed rendered it possible that his great energy would expend itself in fighting the men who seemed to him not to be going far enough forward." Like the land itself, Pinchot needed to be managed.[28]

That management did not include giving Pinchot free rein over the president's conscience. On the contrary, Roosevelt's letter to Lodge reminds us exactly whose administration it in fact had been, and who by extension bore ultimate responsibility for decisions that were made concerning the environment. Always there was an important and precise distinction between Roosevelt's and Pinchot's duties and roles, between those of the chief forester and the chief executive, a distinction between superior and subordinate that perforce shaped the conception, articulation and, ultimately, course of the conservation movement in the Progressive Era.

NOTES

1. Gifford Pinchot, Diary, February 4–5, 1899, Pinchot Papers, Library of Congress (hereafter cited as GP); Gifford Pinchot, *Breaking New Ground* (New York: Harcourt, Brace, 1947), p. 145; Kathleen Dalton, "Why America Loved Teddy Roosevelt: Or, Charisma is in the Eyes of the Beholders," in *Our Selves/Our Past: Psychological Approaches to American History*, ed. Robert J. Brugger (Baltimore: Johns Hopkins University Press, 1981), p. 269–91.

2. Roosevelt to Pinchot, March 2, 1909, *The Letters of Theodore Roosevelt*, ed. Elting Morrison, 8 vols. (Cambridge: Harvard University Press, 1954), 6: 1,541 (hereafter cited as *Letters*); Roosevelt to Kermit Roosevelt, February 10, 1904, in *Letters*, 4: 724; McGeary, *Pinchot*, pp. 65–67; Dalton, "Why America Loved Teddy Roosevelt."

3. M. Nelson McGeary, *Gifford Pinchot: Forester-Politician* (Princeton: Princeton University Press, 1960); Pinchot, *Breaking New Ground*; Robert Underwood Johnson, *Remembered Yesterdays* (Boston: Little, Brown, 1923), p. 310; Samuel P. Hayes, *Conservation and the Gospel of Efficiency: The Progressive Conservation Movement, 1890–1920* (Cambridge: Harvard University Press, 1959); and Clayton R. Koppes, "Efficiency, Equity, Esthetics: Shifting Themes in American Conservation," in *The Ends of the Earth: Perspectives on Modern Environmental History*, ed. Donald Worster (New York: Oxford University Press, 1988), pp. 230–51.

4. Henry F. Pringle, *Theodore Roosevelt: A Biography* (New York: Harcourt, Brace, 1984), p. 303; Roosevelt, *Autobiography* (New York: Charles Scribner's Sons, 1913), pp. 313, 428 address the question of Pinchot's influence on the president's policies as does Johnson, *Remembered Yesterdays*; Stephen Fox, *The American Conservation Movement: John Muir and His Legacy* (Madison: University of Wisconsin Press, 1985), p. 130; Michael Cohen, *The Pathless Way: John Muir and American Wilderness* (Madison: University of Wisconsin Press, 1984), pp. 296–97, 323–29; Linnie Marsh Wolfe, *Son of the Wilderness: The Life of John Muir* (Boston: Houghton Mifflin, 1945), pp. 275–76, 311–14; McGeary, *Pinchot*, pp. 56–57, 65–67, 109; Harold Pinkett, *Gifford Pinchot: Private and Public Forester* (Urbana: University of Illinois Press, 1970), pp. 53–55; Harold K. Steen, *The U.S. Forest Service: A History* (Seattle: University of Washington Press, 1976), pp. 69–100.

5. Roderick Nash, *Wilderness and the American Mind* (New Haven: Yale University Press, 1982), pp. 180–81.

6. Muir to Johnson, March 23, 1905, Robert Underwood Johnson Papers, Bancroft Library, University of California, Berkeley (hereafter cited as RUJ).

7. Pinchot to William Colby, February 17, 1905, GP; Muir to Johnson, September 11, 1913, RUJ.

8. Michael Smith, *Pacific Visions: California Scientists and the Environment, 1850–1915* (New Haven: Yale University Press, 1987), pp. 159–66; Muir to Johnson, March 23, 1905, RUJ; Pinchot to William Colby, February 17, 1905, GP.

9. Pinchot to Marsden Manson, May 28, 1906, published in *The Independent*, August 8, 1908, pp. 375–76.

10. See Muir's essays in *Our National Parks* (Boston: Houghton Mifflin, 1909) and *The Yosemite* (New York: Century, 1912); "Pinchot and Hetch Hetchy," *The Independent*, August 8, 1910, pp. 375–76; "A High Price to Pay for Water," *The Century*, August 1908, pp. 632–34.

11. *New York Times*, December 4, 1913, pp. 3, 8; Pinchot to Frederick Noble Perry, September 18, 1903, RUJ; Nash, *Wilderness and the American Mind*, pp. 164–72.

12. One exception to this trend is Kendrick A. Clemens, "Politics and the Park: San Francisco's Fight for Hetch Hetchy, 1908–1913," *Pacific Historical Review* 48 (May 1979): 185–215.

13. Nash, *Wilderness and the American Mind*, pp. 162–64; Paul R. Cutright, *Theodore Roosevelt: The Making of a Conservationist* (Urbana: University of Illinois Press, 1985).

14. Roosevelt to Muir quoted in Cutright, *Roosevelt*, p. 247.

15. Muir quoted in Fox, *Muir*, p. 126.

16. Roosevelt to Johnson, January 17, 1905, *Letters*, 4: 1,104.

17. Pinchot to Roosevelt, October 11, 1907 quoted in Nash, *Wilderness and the American Mind*, p. 164. On Pinchot-Muir meeting in 1907, see Char Miller, "Before the Divide: Gifford Pinchot, John Muir and the Early American Conservation Movement," (Washington, DC: Society of American Foresters, forthcoming).

18. Roosevelt to Muir, September 16, 1907, *Letters*, 5: 793.

19. Ibid.

20. Nash, *Wilderness and the American Mind*, pp. 164–70.

21. Theodore Roosevelt, *Works* (New York: Charles Scribner's Sons, 1926), 17: 618-19; Nash, *Wilderness and the American Mind*, p. 168.

22. Roosevelt, *Autobiography*, p. 429.

23. Roosevelt to Johnson, December 17, 1908, in *Letters*, 6: 1,428.

24. Muir to Johnson, September 11, 1913, RUJ. Pinchot continues to play this role in the historiographical accounts of conservation in the Progressive Era. Every commentary that depicts Pinchot as a pernicious influence on the president, as his dark side—and there are many—unconsciously reinforces the symbiotic relationship the two men fashioned in the first years of this century. See in particular Paul Cutright, *Roosevelt*, pp. 234–35; Fox, *Muir*; Cohen, *The Pathless Way*. Cohen so inflates Pinchot's reputation that he promotes him beyond his station, calling him the secretary of agriculture, a job Pinchot may have wanted but never obtained (p. 325).

25. James Pinchot to Gifford Pinchot, April 9, 1907, GP.

26. Ibid.

27. Roosevelt to Henry Cabot Lodge, March 1, 1910, in *Selections from the Correspondence of Theodore Roosevelt and Henry Cabot Lodge, 1884–1918* (New York: Charles Scribner's Sons, 1925), 2: 361; James Penick, Jr., *Progressive Politics and Conservation*, (Chicago: University of Chicago Press, 1968).

28. Ibid; McGeary, *Pinchot*, p. 56.

19

Theodore Roosevelt as a Model of Mental and Physical Fitness

Edward S. Lewis and William D. Pederson

Men of ordinary physique and discretion cannot be President and live, if the strain be not somehow relieved. We shall be obliged always to be picking our chief magistrates from among wise and prudent athletes—a small class.[1]

Athletics are good; study is even better; and best of all is the development of the type of character for the lack of which, in an individual as in a nation, no amount of brilliancy of mind or strength of body will atone.[2]

One of the ironies during the birth of modern America is that although Woodrow Wilson sometimes doubted Theodore Roosevelt's sanity, recent scholarship suggests that Wilson was in much worse shape, both mentally and physically, than Roosevelt. Both presidents' records raise the question of the correlation between mental and physical health. And while some scholars view the presidential occupation as a soft one because of the numerous perks attached to the office, most see it as a stressful, killing job. The case of Theodore Roosevelt offers the opportunity to examine the relationship between stress and satisfaction in the presidency.

Although the general story of Roosevelt's transformation from a sickly and weak youngster into a healthy, robust adult is generally known, this chapter extends the analysis to include his whole life, emphasizing his presidential years. Moreover, an effort is made to put Roosevelt's experience in the perspective of the other forty American presidents. He overcame his physical limitations as Abraham Lincoln overcame his educational deficiencies. In the process Theodore Roosevelt established the modern model of mental and physical fitness in the White House. He learned how to deal with stress in the presidency and thereby produced one of its five greatest performances.

For purposes of analysis and discussion, the chapter is

divided into four parts. First, the familiar story of Roosevelt's physical transformation is recounted. Overcoming illness and frailness, he became modern America's first great exponent of physical fitness in the White House. He established the presidential role in physical fitness for Americans which has become increasingly important since World War II. Second, Roosevelt's mental health is examined to determine if it is possible to empirically measure a president psychologically. An effort is made to define mental health and then use a comparative framework based on nearly 600 American historians who ranked presidents using measures that may assess psychological health. The research suggests that Theodore Roosevelt is one of our eleven most mentally healthy presidents.

Next, Roosevelt's physical exercise in the White House is compared to other presidents like him mentally and to those who are classified differently. The record suggests that the presidents like Roosevelt mentally also practiced various forms of "the rugged life." They made vigorous physical exercise a part of their daily lives. When the Roosevelt-like presidents, in terms of mental and physical fitness, are compared empirically, in terms of life expectancy and years served, a pattern is revealed. Although the presidency is commonly described as a killing job, the Roosevelt-like presidents served almost twice as long as the other presidents and they are the only presidents who lived longer than the typical white male of their age group. Vigorous physical exercise seems to be the key. When Roosevelt left the presidency, his exercise diminished and his most extreme behavior occurred.

Finally, a set of conclusions is presented to summarize Roosevelt's contribution to the model of the mentally and physically fit modern president. Presidents who psychologically fulfill themselves through the arena of politics are what Abraham Maslow classified as self-actualizers, or healthy individuals. The research presented in this chapter is consistent with earlier findings that suggest these presidents tend to be the most decent or magnanimous, the most open, and the most political. They are politicians with democratic values. Theodore Roosevelt in many ways emerges as the model president during the early twentieth century.

The Physical Transformation

"Theodore . . . you have the mind but you have not the body, and without the help of the body the mind cannot go as far as it should. You must *make* your body. It is hard drudgery to make one's body, but I know you can do it." The boy's reaction was the half-grin, half-snarl which became world famous. Jerking his head back, he replied through clenched teeth: "I'll make my body."[3]

On the basis of a physician's recommendation after examining twelve-year-old Theodore, his father challenged his son to develop a body equal to his growth in mind and spirit. Theodore immediately followed the advice of the major hero in his life after his father equipped the second-floor of their home as a gym and later built a complete gymnasium on the top floor of their second home.[4] Indeed, exercise machines became a part of his routine for the rest of his life. He had a gym built in the White House and even had one set up on the ship he took to Africa after he left the presidency. Although his level of exercise would vary over the years, it became a key part of his thinking. When he did not get enough exercise in his official positions in public service, Roosevelt always noted it. He needed vigorous exercise to lead a balanced life.

His interest grew from using weights to participating in a wide variety of sports and other kinds of outdoor recreation. He took up boxing after losing a fight with several teenagers. He soon developed interests in mountain climbing, wrestling, hiking, hunting, swimming, tennis, bowling, and dancing. His period of teenage athletics was capped by a runner-up award in lightweight boxing at Harvard University. Nonetheless, after a complete medical examination in 1880, Theodore learned that the combination of asthma and exercise had strained his heart. A physician warned him that he would need to select a sedentary occupation and refrain from strenuous exercise. Yet, Roosevelt rejected this advice and kept it secret.[5]

Instead, Theodore continued to follow the advice of his father. As if necessary to prove to others that he was physically equal, the once sick and frail child became, in 1881, one of the first unskilled climbers to conquer the Matterhorn. A year later his activities included playing ninety-one games of tennis in a single day.[6] Exercise became play for him.

In addition to its playful function, exercise served as a release from stress during the first years of his political career. When he served in the New York legislature, he would begin the morning with sessions of boxing and long walks as a way to deal with fourteen-hour work days.[7] His vigorous exercise became an important asset in dealing with stress, particularly after the deaths of his first wife and mother.

The twenty-five-year-old widower used physical exercise out West to overcome the greatest depression of his life, which he refused to discuss. His rugged exercise finally peaked in 1885, while in North Dakota:

> Some extraordinary physical and spiritual transformation occurred during this arduous period. It was as if his adolescent battle for health, and his more recent but equally intense battle against despair, were crowned with sudden victory. The anemic, high-pitched youth who had left New York only five weeks before was now able to return.[8]

Although this level of physical fitness fluctuated during the next twenty-five years, Roosevelt seldom stopped exercising for long. He continued to add new sports and recreation to his physical regimen.

After his second marriage, he soon picked up a habit of eating too much and gaining weight. Despite hikes along Rock Creek in Washington, D.C., when he served as a civil service commissioner for six years, he suffered his longest illness (eight days) since childhood. His bronchitis recurred for a week three years later. Yet, although he ate more and did not exercise as much as he had in earlier years, he still continued to add new sports. He even taught himself to downhill ski.[9]

Roosevelt waged a conscientious fight to maintain his level of physical fitness. After he returned to Washington in 1897 as the assistant secretary of the Navy, he insisted others also stay fit. He soon fired Navy Department employees who rated below par on their physical fitness tests. To maintain his own physical fitness, he continued to go on major hikes in Rock Creek Park. Even during the Spanish-American War, Roosevelt continued to practice what he preached by refusing to ride while his troops walked.[10] Despite his compulsive eating, his concern over physical fitness continued during his White House years as he purposely strove to stay fit.

Roosevelt's Mental Health

No Chief Executive, certainly, has ever had so much fun. One of Roosevelt's favorite expressions is "dee-lighted"—he uses it so often, and with such grinning emphasis, that nobody doubts his sincerity. He indeed delights in every aspect of his job.[11]

Before comparing Roosevelt's record of physical fitness to other presidents, attention needs to be directed to his mental health. As the author of thirty-eight books, including several classics, no one doubted his brilliance, but Roosevelt's sanity was at times questioned by Henry Adams, Mark Twain, Woodrow Wilson, and others. Fortunately, the work of psychologists, political scientists, and historians now makes it possible to measure and define psychological health.

One political scientist asserts that our mentally healthiest presidents are the most active in office at the same time they enjoy their work.[12] There's no question that Theodore Roosevelt was an active president and an active person his entire life; if anything he was, possibly, hyperactive. Although his major living biographer views Roosevelt as having more fun in office than any other president, it is very difficult to measure the level of enjoyment that presidents experience. Rather than trying to measure enjoyment, it might be easier to make comparisons in terms of a president's flexibility or inflexibility in office. In other words, in addition to activeness that allows for healthy human beings to enjoy their work, flexibility may be another dimension of mental health. In fact, one psychologist defines psychological health as

flexibility, the freedom to learn through experience, the freedom to change with changing internal and external circumstances, to be influenced by reasonable argument, admonitions, exhortation, and the appeal to emotions; the freedom to respond appropriately to the stimulus of reward and punishment, and especially the freedom to cease when sated. The essence of normality is flexibility in all of these vital ways. The essence of illness is the freezing of behavior into unalterable and insatiable patterns.[13]

After identifying activity and flexibility as keys to mental health, it becomes possible to measure presidents in relation to each other on these two dimensions. When the poll results of nearly 600 American historians are adapted to determine our

Table 1
Presidential Classifications

Barber[a]		Pederson Extension[b]	
Active-Positive		**Active-Flexible**	
Jefferson	+2.01	F. Roosevelt	+1.31
F. Roosevelt	+1.61	T. Roosevelt	+0.19
Truman	+1.25	Truman	+0.31
Kennedy	+1.06	Kennedy	+1.61
Ford	+0.93	Lincoln	+1.50
Carter	+0.91	Jefferson	+1.35
Bush	+0.44	Washington	+0.57
	+0.03	Madison	+0.58
Active-Negative		**Active-Inflexible**	
J. Adams	+1.51	Jackson	−1.40
A. Johnson	+1.39	L. Johnson	−0.47
Wilson	+1.05	Wilson	−2.23
Hoover	+0.59	Polk	−0.19
L. Johnson	+0.34	J. Adams	−0.85
Nixon	+0.20	Cleveland	−0.88
	+0.12	A. Johnson	−2.18
	+0.01	J.Q. Adams	−1.15
Passive-Positive		**Passive-Flexible**	
Madison	−0.06	Monroe	+1.03
Taft	−0.16	Taft	+0.01
Harding	−0.24	Van Buren	+0.19
	−0.34	McKinley	+0.49
	−0.59	Eisenhower	+1.21
	−0.69	Arthur	+0.18
	−0.74	Hayes	+0.14
	−0.95	Harrison	+0.186
	−1.22	Fillmore	+0.27
	−1.26	Buchanan	+0.01
	−1.29	Pierce	+0.16
	−1.37	Grant	+0.59
	−1.66	Harding	+1.17
Passive-Negative		**Passive-Inflexible**	
Washington	−0.14	Hoover	−1.01
Coolidge	−0.56	Tyler	−1.09
Eisenhower	−0.86	Taylor	−0.76
	−1.30	Coolidge	−0.83

most active and flexible presidents, Theodore Roosevelt ends up as one of eleven presidents in this category (see Table 1). He is the second most active president in office—only Franklin Roosevelt ranks as a more active chief executive. On the other hand, TR is the least flexible among the presidents who are rated as mentally healthy presidents.

In short, Theodore Roosevelt was not only brilliant but also psychologically fit. Despite his overcompensation for early ill health through physical exercise, he showed more restraint than he is generally credited. Although he often sounded militant with aggressive rhetoric and super-patriotism, this resulted primarily from the mixed loyalties of his parents during the Civil War. He remained mentally stable in office, with a sound view of recreation and sports. In 1906, Roosevelt became the first president to win the Nobel Prize.

Exercise as an Oval Office Stress Reducer

Theodore Roosevelt used physical exercise for several purposes. As indicated earlier, he used it to transform his frail body into a firm one; he used it to counter stress in office, as well as to control his weight; and he used it as a basis for promoting the rugged life as an ideal for the American public. The classical

Sources and Notes for Table 1:
    a. James David Barber, *The Presidential Character*, 3rd ed. (Englewood Cliffs, NJ: Prentice-Hall, 1985); James David Barber, "Adult Identity and Presidential Style," *Daedalus* 97 (1968): 938-68; and James David Barber, "George Bush: In Search of a Mission," *New York Times*, January 19, 1989, p. 31.
    b. William D. Pederson, "Amnesty and Presidential Behavior," *Presidential Studies Quarterly*, 7 (1977): 178, reprinted in William D. Pederson and Ann M. McLaurin, eds., *The Rating Game in American Politics* (New York: Irvington Publishers, 1987) p. 75; William D. Pederson, ed., *The "Barberian" Presidency* (New York: Peter Lang, 1989) p. 116. The extension is adapted from Gary M. Maranell, "The Evaluation of Presidents," *Journal of American History* 57 (1970): 109-10. Maranell's poll was conducted during March 1968. Two presidents, William Henry Harrison and James A. Garfield, were excluded since each served less than a year in office.
    The numbers to the left of each name indicate degree of activeness: a high positive score is active, a high negative score is passive. The numbers to the right of each name indicate the degree of flexibility: a high positive score is flexible, a high negative score is inflexible.

ideal of a sound mind in a sound body not only fits Theodore Roosevelt, but he felt the American character depended on it.

His rigorous exercise in the White House is legendary. He set up the first gymnasium there. At the 1905 Portsmouth Conference he stunned his associates when he dove off a ship for a short swim in the bay.[14] He went on marathon walks and rides, including one in 1909 to prove to the military that he could beat the standards he set for them. Although he was forced to discontinue boxing in 1904 after he lost sight in one eye, he merely switched to jujitsu and soon set up the first White House tennis court so he could play. He also rowed, sailed, and played polo during his presidential years. His behavior was so contagious that it motivated his top secretarial aide, William Loeb, Jr., to get into physical shape.[15]

Though he viewed these years as merely a "busy sedentary life" compared to his earlier years, through executive action he found time to make football a safer game to play. One of his presidential conferences led to the formation of the American Rules Committee for football in 1906. He established the model for modern presidents to take an active interest in the country's recreational activities and physical fitness.[16]

The pattern of physical vigor that Theodore Roosevelt set in the White House has been followed by our other most active and flexible presidents. The comparative record suggests that the "active-flexible" presidents tend to participate in the most recreational activities, spend more time engaged in physical exercise in the White House, and participate in the most strenuous kinds of exercise. In comparison to the other presidents, the Theodore Roosevelt-type of president leads a vigorous mental and physical routine which tends to promote enjoyment of the office.

For example, Franklin Roosevelt was a constant golfer and excelled in sailing. When polio struck him, he adapted to a new routine of regular swimming. He had a pool built at the White House in 1933 and became an avid swimmer. Although Harry Truman was not athletic, he used the White House pool and developed a reputation for his long, strenuous morning walks. In a sense, John Kennedy recaptured the robust image of a "wise and prudent athlete" due to his youth when assuming the presidency. Kennedy was a sports lover who continued FDR's daily swims and enjoyed sailing. Yet, he also enjoyed touch football, fishing, and golfing in the White House. Even though he had to give up golf after reinjuring his back, his avid interest in sports continued. In 1963, again in the TR mode, he set up the President's Council on Physical Fitness and Sports, and initiated the President's Physical Fitness Award for middle and high school students.

Our three most recent mentally healthy presidents have likewise followed the model that Theodore Roosevelt began. Gerald Ford was our most gifted athlete president, despite his media image.[17] He was an avid skier and golfer during his White House years and was an All-America offensive lineman at the University of Michigan. Jimmy Carter played softball and tennis, as well as regularly swimming, hiking, bowling, skiing, and jogging. Although not recognized as an athlete, he admitted that jogging was the "high point of his day," and that he maintained a "strenuous exercise program" all his life.[18] In 1980, he convened the White House Symposium on Fitness and Sports Medicine for Family Physicians. In terms of violent physical exercise for extended periods, George Bush is perhaps the best example of a much older president who acts and looks much younger through his remarkable interest in sports, recreation, and physical exercise. A former college baseball player, he plays tennis, softball, and horseshoes; fishes, hunts, sails, golfs, and jogs.[19] He also admires and identifies with TR.[20]

In contrast to the most active and flexible presidents, the other presidents took a much milder approach to physical exercise. Woodrow Wilson took up golf in the White House only after his physician advised him on the need for exercise. Lyndon Johnson's exercise in the White House was limited to use of the swimming pool, and Richard Nixon's main physical exercise was bowling. The more passive presidents tended to have similar records, practicing mild forms of physical exercise in the White House—even for those who had once been athletes. Taft's exercise was mainly limited to golf, as was Eisenhower's. Ike only took up swimming in the White House under his physician's orders. Unlike the active and flexible presidents, he did not enjoy it.

The result of vigorous exercise among presidents, or the lack of it, is revealed in a comparison of their mortality records. Despite serving almost as long as the others, the most active and flexible presidents lived the longest after serving in the Oval

Office. In fact, these presidents are the only ones to live longer than the average white male of their time (see Tables 2 and 3). Vigorous exercise seems to be a key to the reduction in the stress experienced during the presidency. Although the presidency is commonly regarded as a killing job, those who maintain a balanced mental and physical fitness record tend to avoid curtailed life expectancy.[21]

Table 2
Years in Office and Age at Death*

President	Years in Office	Age at Death	President	Years in Office	Age at Death
Active-Positive			**Active-Negative**		
F. Roosevelt	12.107	63.197	Jackson	8.000	78.233
T. Roosevelt	7.468	60.195	L. Johnson	5.162	65.595
Truman	7.775	88.63	Wilson	8.000	67.101
Jefferson	8.000	83.225	Polk	4.000	53.616
Washington	7.844	67.808	J. Adams	4.000	90.677
Madison	8.000	85.285	Cleveland	8.000	71.268
Average:	8.532	74.724	A. Johnson	3.882	66.586
			J. Q. Adams	4.000	80.612
			Average	5.631	71.711
Passive-Positive			**Passive-Negative**		
Monroe	8.000	73.184	Hoover	4.000	90.195
Taft	4.000	72.477	Tyler	3.910	71.808
Van Buren	4.000	79.633	Taylor	1.351	65.622
Eisenhower	8.000	79.548	Coolidge	5.584	60.507
Arthur	3.455	56.121	**Average:**	3.711	72.033
Hayes	4.000	70.288			
B. Harrison	4.000	67.562			
Fillmore	2.647	74.164			
Buchanan	4.000	77.107			
Pierce	4.000	64.874			
Grant	8.000	63.238			
Harding	2.414	57.748			
Average:	4.710	69.662			

*Assassinated presidents are omitted.

Table 3
Presidential Life Expectancy

President	Age at First Inaug-ural	Years of Life after First Inaugural		Years Above (+) or Below (-) Expected Life
		Expected	Actual	
Active-Positive				
F. Roosevelt	51	21.8	12.1	− 9.7	− 9.6
T. Roosevelt	42	26.2	17.3	− 8.9	− 8.8
Truman	60	15.3	27.7	+12.4	+12.7
Jefferson	57	16.4	25.3	+ 8.9	+ 8.9
Washington	57	17.1	10.6	− 6.5	− 6.5
Madison	57	16.3	27.3	+11.0	+11.0
Average:	54	18.9	20.1	+ 0.85	+ 1.3
Active-Negative				
Jackson	61	13.5	16.3	+ 2.8	
L. Johnson	55	19.6	9.2	−10.4	
Wilson	56	17.1	10.9	− 6.2	
Polk	49	21.5	4.3	−17.2	
J. Adams	61	14.4	29.3	+14.9	
Cleveland	47	22.1	23.3	+ 1.2	
A. Johnson	56	17.2	10.3	− 6.7	
J. Q. Adams	57	16.3	23.0	+ 6.7	
Average:	55	17.7	15.8	− 1.9	
Passive-Positive				
Monroe	58	15.6	14.3	− 1.3	− 1.3
Taft	51	20.3	21.0	+ 0.7	+ 0.8
Van Buren	54	17.2	25.4	+ 8.2	+ 8.2
Eisenhower	62	14.6	16.2	+ 1.6	+ 1.7
Arthur	50	20.2	5.2	−15.0	−15.0
Hayes	54	18.0	15.9	− 2.1	− 2.1
B. Harrison	55	17.2	12.0	− 5.4	− 5.4
Fillmore	50	20.7	23.7	+ 3.0	+ 2.1
Buchanan	65	11.9	11.3	− 0.6	− 0.6
Pierce	48	22.0	16.6	− 5.4	− 5.4
Grant	46	22.8	16.4	− 6.4	− 6.4
Harding	55	18.0	2.4	−15.6	−15.6
Average:	54	18.2	15.0	− 3.2	− 3.2

Table 3 (continued)

President	Age at First Inaug- ural	Years of Life after First Inaugural		Years Above (+) or Below (-) Expected Life	
		Expected	Actual		
		Passive-Negative			
Hoover	54	18.9	35.6	+ 16.7	
Tyler	51	19.2	20.8	+ 1.6	
Taylor	64	12.8	1.3	–11.5	
Coolidge	51	21.4	9.4	–12.0	
Average:	55	18.1	16.8	– 1.3	

Sources and Notes for Table 3:

Adapted from data of the Metropolitan Life Insurance Company and the U.S. Department of Health and Human Services in *U.S. News and World Report*, Nov. 24, 1980, p. 26. Life expectancy based on white males born in the same years as presidents. Slightly different figures in extreme right column for expected years of life are adopted from data in Bill McAllister, "The Precarious Role of the President's Physician," *Washington Post Health*, Feb. 9, 1988, p. 13.

It is interesting to note that two presidents not among the most active and flexible group lived the most years beyond their normal life expectancy. Yet they too engaged in physical exercise. For example, Herbert Hoover lived nearly seventeen years more than the average life expectancy. Although not a natural athlete, he exercised as a child and played football at Stanford University. As one of the most skillful fisherman among the presidents, he wrote a book on the subject. More important, perhaps, is the fact that for six days a week in the presidency, he played medicine ball—throwing an eight-pound ball over a ten-foot net.[22] John Adams was a walker and rode horseback for many years after he left the White House.[23] He lived nearly fifteen years more than the average life expectancy.

In contrast, Theodore Roosevelt's exercise tended to dip sharply as he became older—particularly after he left the White House. His weight increased as his exercise decreased, although he seemingly had good intentions of following the vigorous physical routine of his earlier years.[24] He proudly set up a gym on the ship which took him to Africa. Nevertheless, soon after his arrival, the natives called the ex-president "the man with the big paunch." Although he was still in good shape for the 1912 presidential campaign and had recovered from being shot, the 1913–1914 expedition to Brazil marked his final decline. By 1917 he had to go to a camp to try to lose weight.[25]

Conclusions

In summary, Theodore Roosevelt established the model for the modern presidency in terms of mental and physical health. Although the conventional wisdom is that the presidency is a killing job, the evidence suggests that those presidents who are the most active and flexible use physical exercise to cope with the stress that is indigenous to the Oval Office. The active and flexible presidents fulfill themselves through the presidency.[26] They make work enjoyable through their physical and mental fitness. Roosevelt's emphasis on leading the strenuous life corresponds to a modern medical notion that "exercise can retard as much as 50 percent the decline that aging causes across the whole range of physiologic function."[27] Moreover, his experience in overcoming physical deficiencies remains a model for those who choose to improve themselves.

This research is also consistent with previous findings that suggest the most active and flexible presidents tend to be the most decent or magnanimous, the most open, and the most political.[28] They are individuals with democratic values who maintain their balance in life through vigorous physical activity.[29] Theodore Roosevelt is the model of mental and physical fitness in the modern presidency.

NOTES

Our appreciation to Kenneth G. Kuriger, Jr., with *The Shreveport Times*; Dr. John Allen Gable, executive director of the Theodore Roosevelt Association; Mary L. Bowman and Ann M. King, the Noel Library, Louisiana State University in Shreveport.

1. Woodrow Wilson, *Constitutional Government in the United States* (New York: Columbia University Press, 1908), pp. 79–80.

2. Theodore Roosevelt, "Athletes, Scholarship, and the Public Service," Address at the Harvard Union, Cambridge, February 23, 1907, in *The Works of Theodore Roosevelt* (New York: Charles Scribner's Sons, 1926), 13: 560.

3. Edmund Morris, *The Rise of Theodore Roosevelt* (New York: Ballantine Books, 1979), p. 60.

4. Ibid., p. 75.

5. Ibid., pp. 63, 129.

6. Ibid., pp. 148, 181.

7. Ibid., p. 231.

8. Ibid, p. 303.

9. Ibid., pp. 368, 445, 475, 477.

10. Ibid., pp. 581, 583, 588, 639.

11. Ibid., p. 17.

12. James David Barber, *The Presidential Character*, 3d ed. (Englewood Cliffs, NJ: Prentice Hall, 1985).

13. Lawrence S. Kubie, *Neurotic Distortion of the Creative Process*, (Lawrence, KS: University of Kansas Press, 1958), p. 20.

14. Joseph L. Gardner, *Departing Glory* (New York: Charles Scribner's Sons, 1973), p. 75.

15. William D. Pederson, "The President and the White House Staff," in *The Rating Game in American Politics*, ed. William D. Pederson and Ann McLaurin (New York: Irvington Publishers, 1987), p. 95.

16. John Durnat, *The Sports of Our Presidents* (New York: Hastings House Publishers, 1964), p. 84.

17. Gerald Ford, "Skiing at Vail/Beaver Creek," *Vis a Vis*, November 1988, pp. 133-39.

18. "Carter Calls Jogging High Point," *St. Louis Post-Dispatch*, February 3, 1980, p. 7C.

19. Burt Soloman, "Want Clues to Bush's Character?" *National Journal*, May 13, 1989, pp. 1,196–97.

20. *New York Times*, March 22, 1989, p. 11.

21. Robert E. Gilbert, "Personality, Stress and Achievement: Keys to Presidential Longevity," *Presidential Studies Quarterly*, 15 (1985): 33-50.

22. Herbert Hoover, *The Memoirs* (New York: Macmillan Company, 1952), p. 327.

23. Homer F. Cunningham, *The Presidents' Last Years* (Jefferson, NC: McFarland and Company, 1989), p. 10.

24. Robert C. Kimberly, "The Health of Theodore Roosevelt," *Theodore Roosevelt Association Journal* 5 (1979): 7–11.

25. Gardner, *Departing Glory*, pp. 120, 383.

26. James C. Davies, *Human Nature in Politics* (New York: John Wiley, 1963).

27. James C. Conniff, "Medicine Catches Up With The Sports Boom," *New York Times Magazine*, October 5, 1980, p. 54.

28. William D. Pederson, ed., *The "Barberian" Presidency* (New York: Peter Lang, 1989); and William D. Pederson, "Ford's Pardon of Nixon: Machiavellian or Magnanimous Leadership" (Paper delivered at the Gerald R. Ford Conference, Hofstra University, April 8, 1989).

29. Gerald F. Roberts, "The Strenuous Life: The Cult of Manliness in the Era of Theodore Roosevelt," (Ph.D. diss., Michigan State University, 1970), p. 92.

20

The Neustadian Model of Presidential Power and the Presidency of Theodore Roosevelt: An Empirical Test

Willie Pigg

The study of presidential power has long been one of the dominant interests of scholars concerned with the workings of the American political system. Edward S. Corwin's *The President: Office and Powers* was once generally accepted as the definitive statement within this area of research.[1] According to Corwin, presidential power is found within the office itself. This legalistic view of presidential power, derived from Corwin's analysis of the Constitution, Supreme Court decisions, congressional statutes, and customary practices, dominated scholarly thought in political science for many years.[2] Richard E. Neustadt's *Presidential Power: The Politics of Leadership*, originally published in 1960 and most recently updated in 1980, presents a significantly different view of presidential power. Published at the height of the behavioral revolution in political science, Neustadt (who has had considerable practical experience working within the Bureau of the Budget and the White House Office) contends that presidential power cannot be understood in purely legal or constitutional terms. Maintaining that the formal institutional powers of office do not provide a secure enough base for a president to exert firm decisive leadership, Neustadt is concerned less with the office than with the qualities that a president must display while in office if he is to be a leader in fact as well as in theory.

Indicating that his theme is "personal power and its politics: what it is, how to get it, how to keep it, how to use it," Neustadt says his purpose is "to explore the power problem of the man inside the White House."[3] In his calculus of presidential power, Neustadt seems to contend that presidential powers of command are generally unworkable. At least such powers are severely limited. Therefore, to Neustadt: "Presidential power is the power to persuade."[4] The success of any president rests with his ability to convince other political actors (members of the bureaucracy, cabinet members, congressmen, and party leaders) that "what he wants of them is what their own appraisal of their own responsibilities require them to do in their own interest, not his."[5] Even though the authority and status of a president gives him built-in advantages in dealing with those persons he must persuade, a president's chances of success will be enhanced if he protects his own public standing by making choices that will maximize his prestige before those actors in the governmental process with whom he must negotiate.

Furthermore, Neustadt contends that the man in the White House should always look to extend his power in order to use the presidency as a force to overcome the fragmentation of the American political system. To Neustadt, strong executive leadership is not only eminently desirable but absolutely necessary to surmount the inertia of Congress and the federal bureaucracy in order to produce enlightened programs in social welfare, civil rights, and international relations. Neustadt's work, while often being characterized as Machiavellian,[6] was almost universally hailed as a brilliant and pioneering contribution to the literature on the American presidency. Indeed, *Presidential Power* is often ranked as a true classic of modern political science.

While acknowledging the significance of Neustadt's contribution to our understanding of presidential power, it should be pointed out that Neustadt has not been without his critics. Harry A. Bailey has classified the works of Neustadt's critics into three basic bodies of literature.[7] One body of post-Neustadt research on the presidency says that Neustadt was basically correct in his analysis but his system is not complete because he fails to distinguish between the president's need to acquire power and the purposes for which that power should be used. Furthermore, Neustadt is criticized for an over reliance on persuasion and bargaining at the expense of command as tools which the president may employ to insure that his desires are carried out. Scholars whose work fall within this body of research are Thomas Cronin,[8] John Hart,[9] Peter Sperlich[10] and George Edwards.[11]

A second body of post-Neustadt writing on presidential power returns to the tradition established by Corwin. This body of literature indicates that presidential power can best be understood by an analysis of the prerogatives that a president receives from the Constitution. This return to Corwin's public law approach is best represented by the work of Richard Pious.[12] Finally, a third body of recent literature on the presidency indicates that power in this area of study can best be understood by combining Neustadt's model of presidential power with the public law approach of Corwin and Pious. As Bailey points out, writers within this body of literature view Neustadt's "persuasion-as-power model" and the Corwin-Pious "prerogatives-of-office-as-power models" as "opposite sides of the same (power) coin."[13] Most representative of research expressing this approach to the study of the chief executive's power is the work of Raymond Tatalovich and Byron Daynes.[14]

Even after an examination of criticisms which have been directed at Neustadt's work, we are still left with the fact that his observations constitute the closest thing to a workable theory of presidential power ever developed. Yet, as Peter W. Sperlich and Norman C. Thomas have pointed out, there have been few serious attempts to empirically test the conception of presidential power which Neustadt devised.[15] Neustadt's analysis in his original work was based on observations of modern presidents—Franklin Roosevelt, Truman, and Eisenhower. In later editions of his work, Neustadt added additional commentaries on Kennedy, Johnson, Nixon, and to a much lesser extent, Ford and Carter. One possible area for the empirical testing of the Neustadian model lies in the vast quantities of historical data which exists on earlier American presidents.[16]

Such an empirical test can be made by applying Neustadt's model of presidential power to the presidency of Theodore Roosevelt. Scholars are virtually united in their recognition of Roosevelt as an innovator in the utilization of presidential power.[17] After almost a century of congressional dominance at the national level, Roosevelt emerged as a forerunner of the modern, activist president. As one biographer has remarked, Theodore Roosevelt can be considered "the first great President-reformer of the modern industrial era."[18] In virtually every aspect of government in which the president has any role to play, Roosevelt extended the breadth of presidential influence. Unlike many of his predecessors, Roosevelt wanted to exercise great power.

Scorning presidents such as James Buchanan for failing to take needed action "unless the Constitution explicitly commands the action,"[19] Roosevelt revealed his views on presidential power in his well-known elaboration of the Stewardship Theory of the presidency. Writing in his *Autobiography*, Roosevelt contended "that the executive power was limited only by specific restrictions and prohibitions appearing in the Constitution or imposed by the Congress under its Constitutional powers. My view was that every executive officer, and above all every executive officer in high position, was a steward of the people." Furthermore, Roosevelt added, ". . . I did and caused to be done many things not previously done by the President and the heads of the Departments. I did not usurp power, but I did greatly broaden the use of executive power. In other words, I acted for the public welfare . . . whenever and in whatever manner was necessary. . . ."[20] Such remarks (written after TR had left the presidency) have done much to generate a popular image of Theodore Roosevelt as a dynamic, forceful president who aggressively extended the influence of executive authority beyond levels reached by his predecessors. I fully accept the idea of Roosevelt as an innovator, whose imaginative use of the executive office served as a model for modern twentieth-century activist presidents. I also believe that many of the restraints on presidential power which Neustadt observed restricting the action of presidents during the post-World War II era also affected TR during his tenure as chief executive. To test Neustadt's power model, the successes and failures of the Roosevelt administration in acquiring and exercising power must be examined in order to see if Neustadt's propositions effectively explain the events of the Roosevelt years. In short, the appropriateness of Neustadt's model must be examined as an analytic tool for better understanding Roosevelt's contributions to the presidency.

The Neustadian Model of Presidential Power

Before beginning any specific application of Neustadt's propositions to the behavior of Theodore Roosevelt as president, it is necessary to examine more fully the Neustadian model. A condensed version of the full Neustadt schema appears here in Figure 1. As this figure reveals, Neustadt offers a prescription for how a president can be a powerful leader. Presidential

Figure 1
Condensed Version of the Neustadian Model of Presidential Power

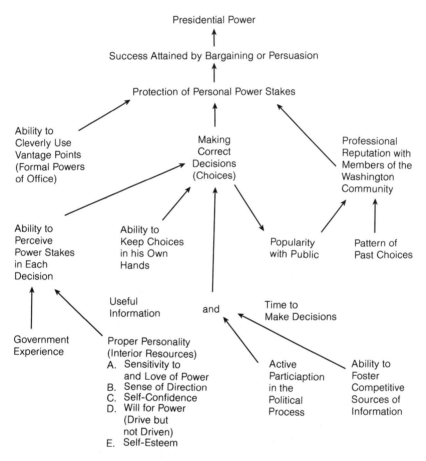

Presidential Power

↑

Success Attained by Bargaining or Persuasion

↑

Protection of Personal Power Stakes

Ability to Cleverly Use Vantage Points (Formal Powers of Office)

Making Correct Decisions (Choices)

Professional Reputation with Members of the Washington Community

Ability to Perceive Power Stakes in Each Decision

Ability to Keep Choices in his Own Hands

Popularity with Public

Pattern of Past Choices

Government Experience

Useful Information

and

Time to Make Decisions

Proper Personality (Interior Resources)
A. Sensitivity to and Love of Power
B. Sense of Direction
C. Self-Confidence
D. Will for Power (Drive but not Driven)
E. Self-Esteem

Active Participation in the Political Process

Ability to Foster Competitive Sources of Information

Sources: Richard E. Neustadt, *Presidential Power: The Politics of Leadership* (New York: John Wiley and Sons, 1980); Peter W. Sperlich, "Bargaining and Overload: An Essay on Presidential Power," in *Perspectives on the Presidency*, ed. Aaron Wildavsky (Boston: Little, Brown and Company, 1975), pp. 406-30; Thomas E. Cronin, *The State of the Presidency* (Boston: Little, Brown and Company, 1980), chap. 4.

leadership to Neustadt is measured not so much by actions taken by the individual within the White House as by what effect his actions have upon others. The central question, therefore, in evaluating presidential performance is how successful a president is in achieving and maintaining his influence with those with whom he must bargain. Formal constitutional and statutory powers are no guarantee of success. Despite his formal grants of power, a president "does not get action without argument."[21] The successful president must combine these formal grants of power with a faculty for successful bargaining if he wishes to have his say in the policy-making process.

At the core of Neustadt's model is his maximization-of-power hypothesis. According to this dictum, the successful president must seek to maximize his personal power. To be successful, he must jealously guard his power prospects for the future. A president must constantly make choices—decisions to act or not to act in specific situations. The general overall pattern of these choices, how successful or unsuccessful they are, will determine how competent a president is in guarding his own power prospects. In order for a president to make the right decisions (choices), he must have access to the best available information, time to make decisions, and he must concentrate as much decision-making power as possible in his own hands. Finally, he must possess the necessary temperament and political experience that produces self-confidence and an ultimate sense of direction.

The members of "the Washington community,"[22] whom the president must persuade, constantly examine the choices he makes. From this scrutiny, a pattern emerges that enables a president to build a professional reputation which in turn affects either favorably or unfavorably his power stakes. A president's popularity with the American people also affects a president's influence. The greater his favor with the people in general, the more unlikely it is that the "Washingtonians"[23] will resist him. The president's personality is important in determining his popular prestige to a certain extent, but ultimately his popular support is determined by the public reaction to how he is performing the overall functions of his job. Finally, the Neustadian analysis is concerned with power in a general sense: how the president improves his chances for control of the policy process at any time, not just in specific situations.

Theodore Roosevelt and Domestic Politics:
A Replication of the Neustadt Model

What follows is basically an effort to see if the Neustadian maximization-of-power model is an appropriate lens for examining and explaining the behavior of Theodore Roosevelt as president. I believe that it is an effective tool for performing this purpose—especially in domestic policy matters. Just as Neustadt used brief case studies and historical examples selected from empirical evidence drawn from the administrations of presidents from Franklin Roosevelt to Jimmy Carter, a similar approach can show that Neustadt's propositions are well illustrated by the evidence of TR's presidency. While the examples presented in this study are generally supportive of Neustadt's ideas, the model will not be accepted without reservation. In the realms of international relations and defense policy, the historical evidence of the Roosevelt years will indicate that his power to command was of considerably greater importance than the Neustadian model indicates. Finally, data drawn from the Roosevelt years will show that some of the modifications of the Neustadt schema proposed by Neustadt's critics have considerable validity.

Of all Neustadt's maxims, the following is the most central to his model: A president must genuinely desire to maximize his power. If he does not have a will for power, he cannot be effective as a leader. Theodore Roosevelt certainly possessed such a will for power. Like Franklin Roosevelt, Neustadt's model of the ideal president, TR's desire for power was based upon a belief that strong executive leadership was needed for the very survival of American society. This belief gave Roosevelt a sense of direction which always guided his actions as president. A sense of direction or a sense of purpose such as TR possessed is a key component of the inner resources which Neustadt believed any successful president must have. Roosevelt believed in social order. Throughout his presidency, he displayed a fear of any movement that could disrupt that order. At one extreme, he distrusted what he considered radical mass movements led by such reformers as William Jennings Bryan and the socialist Eugene Debs. At the opposite end of the political spectrum, he feared those whom he referred to as "malefactors of great wealth." These leaders of the nation's great corporations, who were unwilling to adjust themselves to new social forces and changing times, were just as dangerous to American society as were the radical reformers.

Either extreme, if it gained total control, could destroy the social fabric of America and precipitate the nation into national disorder. As president, Roosevelt thought of himself as representing a mid-point between the two extremes. As Richard Hofstadter has written, "he despised the rich, but he feared the mob."[24] Only by acting to expand his power as president could he lead the national government into a role in which the forces of extremism in American society could be balanced.

Courtesy of Theodore Roosevelt Collection, Harvard College Library
Theodore Roosevelt in his study at Sagamore Hill in 1905

Theodore Roosevelt's will for power was also a product of his own personality. TR needed power. He delighted in its exertions. Roosevelt's drive for power has often been explained as a result of his efforts to compensate for his own physical inferiorities, with which he struggled as a child.[25] In a sense his whole life was an effort to compensate.[26] He developed his asthma-ridden body in a home-based gymnasium; he associated with work-hardened cowboys; he engaged in a brawl in a western bar and sparred with professional boxers in the White House; he joined the army and led a calvary charge against the Spaniards; finally, he entered politics where his drive for success was channelled ultimately into maximizing his power as president.

Neustadt certainly favors presidents who have a drive for power. In later editions of his book, he tells us that there is a difference between one who has a drive for power and one who is excessively driven to power. Drive is necessary but "driveness" may prove destructive for the officeholder and the system. Speaking of Johnson and Nixon after events of the Vietnam war and Watergate had only recently passed into history, Neustadt says, "Each was a driving man and driven, tending to excess, compulsive in seeking control, taking frustration hard."[27] Roosevelt was not excessively driven to power. The worst behavior of his public career came in the years after he was divorced from power: his prejudiced attacks against German-Americans during World War I; his calls for mass deportation of radicals; his hatred and envy of Woodrow Wilson; his advocacy of the benefits of compulsory peacetime industrial service for American youth; his condemnation of all conscientious objectors; and his wholesale glorification of war.[28]

Neustadt also favors presidents who possess the right temperament for utilization of power once it is achieved. Neustadt does not spell out exactly what the right temperament for a president is. He does indicate that the successful president must have self-confidence as well as the ability to avoid taking himself too seriously. Certainly Roosevelt possessed great self-confidence,[29] reflected in the surety with which he acted throughout his term in office.

Roosevelt also possessed the kind of experience that Neustadt favored in presidents. A much-quoted Neustadt maxim states: "The Presidency is no place for amateurs."[30] When Vice President Theodore Roosevelt was elevated to the presidency with the death of McKinley, he certainly was no amateur. He brought to the office vast experience in government as a member of the New York state legislature, as a U.S. Civil Service Commissioner, as president of the Police Board of New York City, as assistant secretary of the Navy, and finally as governor of New

York. His political training in the Governor's Mansion at Albany certainly helped to prepare him for his battles with Congress.

Theodore Roosevelt's personality and governmental experience constitute two of the components of what Neustadt refers to as the power base of any president. The third component of such a power base is what Neustadt designates as vantage points of the office, that is, the formal powers of the office plus opportunities to perform needed services that the office provides its holder. All components of Roosevelt's power base were brought to bear in his leadership of Congress. These include the vantage point of his office, his governmental experience, and his personality. Roosevelt did not hold office during a time when he could count on his side a great upsurge of popular opinion in his confrontations with Congress. Economic conditions were generally good during TR's presidency. The progressive movement in America was in its infancy when Roosevelt took office. Widespread discontent among the public was generally lacking. For Roosevelt to obtain liberal reformist legislation from what was essentially a conservative institution whose members were concerned mainly with their own reelection prospects, he had to persuade Congress to follow his initiatives. If there is any one theme that permeates *Presidential Power*, it is the theme that presidential power is the power to persuade and that this persuasion comes only with bargaining.[31] The Neustadian propositions concerning bargaining are well illustrated by Roosevelt's relationship with Congress. Throughout his administration, TR practiced the art of the possible with the national lawmaking body. He showed great skill in knowing how to work with individual legislators and, at the same time, bring pressure against them. Roosevelt knew who wielded real power in Congress. When TR became president in 1901, power in Congress was heavily concentrated in the hands of a few.[32] The Senate was dominated by a controlling group which consisted of the "powerful four": John C. Spooner of Wisconsin; William B. Allison of Iowa; Orville H. Platt of Connecticut; and the "Boss of the Senate," Nelson W. Aldrich of Rhode Island. Other key Senate leaders were Mark Hanna of Ohio, who also held the post of chairman of the Republican National Committee, Henry Cabot Lodge of Massachusetts, and Tom Platt of New York. The House of Representatives during TR's administration was under the leadership, if not the dominance, of its Speaker, Joseph G.

Cannon. Before having his powers restricted by the revolt in 1910 of his colleagues, the autocratic Czar Cannon exerted control over the House to a greater degree than any Speaker before or since.

Despite the dissimilarity of viewpoints that existed between the progressive TR and the arch-conservative Cannon, Roosevelt saw the Speaker as a medium through which he could exercise power over the House if not the entire Congress as a whole, since Speaker Cannon had considerable influence even in the upper house itself.[33] Roosevelt invited Speaker Cannon to the White House for conferences two or three times per week and sometimes daily when Congress was in session. The two did not like each other personally, yet they got along well with each other without a complete break until near the end of Roosevelt's second term. Roosevelt had great respect for Cannon's judgment on political matters. He constantly solicited his advice as to the feasibility of passing particular pieces of legislation. Since the chairmen of all major committees within the House regularly conferred with the Speaker, his office became a clearinghouse of opinions to be relayed to the president. On the relationships that existed between the administration and the Speaker, Cannon stated:

> I think Roosevelt talked over with me virtually every serious recommendation to Congress before he made it, and he requested me to sound out the leaders in the house, for he did not want to recommend legislation simply to write messages. He wanted results, and he wanted to know how to secure results with the least friction. He was a good sportsman and accepted what he could get so long as the legislation conformed even in part to his recommendations.[34]

Acting through Cannon and other more ideologically compatible leaders in Congress, Roosevelt was able to carefully scrutinize the progress of the legislation he favored. He carefully communicated his ideas (often in forceful or threatening terms) about pending bills directly to all involved parties on the Hill. He constantly sought the advice of congressional leaders in drafting proposed pieces of legislation[35] as well as for his own annual messages to Congress.[36] Having read extensively in American political history, TR understood the intricacies of America's pluralistic system. He realized that congressmen had their own constituencies to appeal to; he also realized that he could appeal to their own personal natures. He respected "senatorial courtesy" and carefully fulfilled his obligations when making appointments. Despite his reputation for aggressive and sometimes even arrogant behavior, he was always courteous in formal or private meetings designed to persuade individual congressmen. He was not above the use of flattery as a tactical weapon. When he needed the cooperation of Senator Eugene Hale, chairman of the Naval Affairs Committee, he indicated in a personal letter to Hale—a man he personally disliked—that he considered him the most influential man in the Senate.

As previously noted, Neustadt points out that members of the Washington establishment, including congressmen, examine carefully the pattern of choices that a president makes. A president's reputation emerges from this outline of his past actions. According to Neustadt, the successful president should minimize the uncertainties of reward for his supporters and maximize the surety of retaliation for those who oppose him.[37] A classic case of Roosevelt's use of the subtle and ultimately the not so subtle threat of retaliation against his opposition involves TR's effort in 1906 to obtain a bill for federal inspection and control of the meat-packing industry. Roosevelt's efforts to obtain legislation in this area brought him to conflict with James Wadsworth, a New York gentleman-farmer who chaired the House Committee on Agriculture and consistently served as protector of the interests of the meat-packing industry. For years Wadsworth effectively used his power to bottle up any sort of legislation that provided for federal inspection of the industry.

Roosevelt, after reading Upton Sinclair's *The Jungle*, a book which awakened public opinion to the unsanitary conditions prevalent in the meat-packing industry, ordered a Department of Agriculture investigation of the meat-packing industry. TR wrote Wadsworth, threatening to release results of his investigation to the public. However, he indicated he would keep the information secret if Wadsworth would cooperate in releasing the bill from committee. "I should not make the report public," Roosevelt threatened, "with the idea of damaging the packers. I should do it only if it were necessary to secure the remedy."[38] When Wadsworth allowed the bill through but added amendments that gutted the legislation, Roosevelt sent a report to Congress in which he released the first part of his own investigative report which was labelled "Preliminary." He indicated privately that he would release more devastating parts of the report if Wadsworth continued his opposition. The publication of even the preliminary report had a considerable effect on meat sales as the public reacted to the horrid conditions that threatened public health. Ultimately, supporters of the packing industry, including Wadsworth, realized the president would continue to arouse public opinion against the industry in such a manner as to affect sales. Finally, because Roosevelt's opponents to the meat-packing bill realized what he would do, a compromise bill containing essentially the provisions that TR advocated was enacted into law.[39]

Theodore Roosevelt's style of bargaining with congressional leaders, of rallying public opinion behind his proposals, of threatening those who opposed him, of retreating or compromising as necessity demanded it, of flexibility in cooperating with members of the opposition party—all techniques of presidential leadership advocated by Neustadt—is amply illustrated by his efforts to secure passage of the Hepburn Act of 1906. As early as 1904, Roosevelt asked for legislation which would empower the Interstate Commerce Commission not only to publicly denounce what it considered to be unfair rates imposed by railroads, but also to put into effect what the commission considered to be reasonable rates for the industry. Essentially, TR's plan called for federal regulation of the workings of all railroads engaged in interstate commerce.

Roosevelt began his fight for this very controversial piece of legislation by raising the phony issue of tariff revision against conservative congressmen.[40] Roosevelt's letters of this period indicate that he did not want tariff revision. Indeed, he assigned this politically dangerous issue a low priority on his list of reform measures.[41] By using the sham tariff issue as a lever, Roosevelt apparently concluded a secret bargain with Speaker Cannon (possibly with Senator Aldrich's knowledge) in which Cannon would let Roosevelt's railroad legislation pass in the House if TR would not push his tariff program. Even though Cannon allowed the bill to pass in the House, it was deliberately delayed until the Senate was unable to have any time to act before it adjourned.

Roosevelt now used his vantage points—the formal constitutional powers of his office—to obtain his objective. He again raised the issue of the tariff by ordering top officials of the Panama Canal Commission to announce with much fanfare a new policy of buying materials from the cheapest suppliers whether American or not. The Republican "Old Guard" was also reminded that the president was still concerned with tariff revision through a series of newspaper reports based on "leaks" from the White House that indicated Roosevelt wished to call an extra session of Congress to deal specifically with tariff issues. Finally, the president also gave orders to his attorney general to speed up proceedings against several railroads for giving illegal rebates.

At this point in the struggle, Senator Aldrich, as leader of the opposition, attempted to block progress of the bill by the use of two strategies. First, he attempted to emasculate the power of the Interstate Commerce Commission in regard to regulation by adding amendments to the bill that would have subjected virtually any of the actions taken by the commission to broad judicial review. Second, Aldrich used his influence in the Senate to place floor leadership of the bill under "Pitchfork Ben" Tillman of South Carolina, a racist demagogue whom Roosevelt regarded with great personal animosity. President Roosevelt, without letting his antagonism toward Tillman affect his desire for a legislative victory, supported the proposals backed by Tillman and the progressive wings of both parties even though their bill called for substantially stronger regulation than the measures that TR had originally favored or the previously passed House version of the bill.

The radical Tillman proposal failed by a narrow margin in the Senate. Roosevelt, always willing to compromise, switched back to his original position and, working with an alliance of moderate Republicans, won enough Democratic and progressive support to obtain a bill that contained the basic provisions that he had originally requested. The final Hepburn bill allowed provisions in regard to the scope of judicial review that the courts would have over commission decisions to remain in the legislation which TR personally opposed. Also, the final bill was a broad, general piece of legislation. Technical difficulties, including problems with the calculation of freight differentials, soon showed that the bill was far less workable than the president believed at the time of its passage. Even so, the Hepburn bill, whose passage owed much to the fact that TR operated in much the same manner as Neustadt advocates, was a landmark piece of legislation in the development of federal control over private business.[42]

Throughout Roosevelt's presidency, the most effective persuasive weapon that he was able to employ against Congress was his ability to influence public opinion, not only to maintain his own popular prestige, but also to build support for policies he wished Congress to enact. A basic Neustadian proposition is that a president's chances for successful bargaining will be enhanced if "the Washingtonians" believe that his popular prestige is at a high level. Events and circumstances (unpleasant economic times, unpopular wars, scandals within the administration, and so forth) influence a president's prestige as much as his ability to actually lead public opinion. Neustadt certainly recognizes the value of public opinion leadership. In the most recent edition of *Presidential Power*, he presents an idea for building public support for a president by suggesting that we need a man in power who can master the medium of television (much as FDR was able to do with radio) and mobilize suburbanites and public-interest groups throughout the nation in support of his policies.[43] To Neustadt, Kennedy was a precursor of this kind of president, though the circumstances of the early 1960s were not right for the kind of successes envisioned by the author. I would suggest that the potentialities for modern leadership envisioned by Neustadt were also foreshadowed by Roosevelt's use of the print media of his era.[44]

Roosevelt's presidency coincided with the development of mass circulation newspapers and popular magazines which enabled him to take full advantage of the "bully pulpit" his position offered. TR was the first president to recognize the value of his own power of using the press as a means of communication with his vast constituency throughout the United States. He was able to use his unique ability to create controversy to provide reporters with a seemingless endless supply of exciting copy. As James David Barber observed: "Roosevelt put the story of politics as war on the front page."[45] Before his administration, newspaper correspondents had to obtain their White House stories by standing outside the front door and interviewing often impatient White House visitors on their way to and from seeing the president. Roosevelt ordered a small antechamber set aside for reporters' use. Later a fully equipped press room was added to the White House, mainly because TR wished to take advantage of close personal contacts with members of the press.

Operating in an era before the institutionalization of formal press secretaries, Roosevelt served as his own press secretary. He often handed out news stories himself and always insisted that any news item given out by the White House be submitted for his personal approval. While formal press conferences on fixed days and hours were not held in TR's administration,[46] Roosevelt did begin the practice of having reporters present for informal sessions while he met with his barber each afternoon. These sessions gave TR an opportunity to talk on a regular basis with working newspapermen, give them stories to print when other news was scarce and generally establish a rapport with the press, which he could ultimately use to his own advantage. These sessions also gave Roosevelt ample opportunity to leak stories to the press which he could utilize as threats with Congress or as trial balloons to test public opinion on particular initiatives.

On at least one occasion, Roosevelt, operating in true Machiavellian fashion, leaked a story that he knew to be pure falsification. This occurred when TR was pressing Congress for the creation of a Bureau of Corporations (an agency empowered to investigate and report on the activities of business) within his proposed Department of Commerce and Labor. The Old Guard in Congress, fearful of anything that threatened government regulation of business, used delaying tactics against him. TR responded by planting a story with newspapermen in which he indicated (without the source of the story being attributed to the White House) that John D. Rockefeller had been sending telegrams to several senators urging that they vote against the legislation. It was true that a small number of telegrams had been sent by John Archbold, an employee of Standard Oil and therefore Rockefeller, but the president realized Rockefeller was not involved directly. He had deliberately substituted a name synonymous with the evils of business monopoly in order to dramatize the struggle over the legislation and to provoke a greater public reaction in support of his program.[47] The public outcry in support of the Bureau of Corporations was so great that this legislation, which at least provided a framework for the regulation of business abuses, was enacted.[48]

The release of the Rockefeller telegram was a bold, dramatic gesture designed to mobilize public opinion. Throughout his presidency, TR always displayed a flair for the dramatic. TR's tendency for choosing theatrical gestures is well illustrated by his decision to prosecute the Northern Securities Company under the Sherman Antitrust Act. On February 19, 1902, Roosevelt startled the nation by having Attorney General Philander C. Knox announce that a suit had been brought against this giant holding company. The selection of the Northern Securities Company and the timing of the announcement were bold strokes of genius. The proposed prosecution had been kept totally secret from the media. Only TR and his attorney general knew what was coming. The Northern Securities Company, a railroad monopoly created by J. P. Morgan, James Hill, and E. H. Harriman, which threatened shippers in the Midwest with monopoly rates, was a perfect target. It was a recently assembled paper creation and therefore easily dissolved. It was extremely vulnerable to legal prosecution and extremely unpopular with the public.

In the following seven years of Roosevelt's administration, he followed this prosecution up by starting forty-four similar actions against several of the nation's largest corporations.[49] TR followed a simple criteria in selecting his targets. The combines chosen for court action were virtually all unpopular with the public, extremely visible, and generally engaging in such practices that made the government reasonably sure of winning. Roosevelt wished to secure dramatic victories often at the .expense of substantive, long-range correctives in how the economic system operated. Through these prosecutions, he generated a great deal of publicity that helped enable him to maintain his prestige, especially with middle-class Americans.

Roosevelt's action in sending the U.S. naval fleet on an around-the-world cruise despite the opposition of Congress is another classic instance of his ability to perform dramatic acts in order to publicize himself and his policies. This unprecedented action was effective in educating the American public to the value of a powerful navy. It also demonstrated to the Japanese, more than any number of speeches or messages originating in the White House, that the United States was physically prepared to face up to any sort of rivalry that might develop in the Far East. Roosevelt was also the first president to use the presidential trip or "junket" as a calculated publicity device. In 1907, TR made a highly visible trip down the Mississippi River with members of the Inland Waterways Commission mainly to build support for his programs designed to conserve natural resources.[50] Reporters went along on this trip—as they did on other speaking tours that the president organized, such as those he used during his eighteen-month fight for the Hepburn bill. As TR sought to focus public opinion against Congress to secure the passage of this act, he spoke in a variety of locations—in Chicago, before the Texas state legislature, at Chautauqua, throughout the Midwest and Southwest as he travelled to a Rough Riders reunion in Texas—always with the intention of generating favorable publicity for his program.

Thus Roosevelt's efforts to mobilize public opinion suggest that Neustadt's advice for presidents in this area is indeed valid. Neustadt also suggests that a president will be best able to protect his power stakes if he serves as his own intelligence officer. In Neustadt's terms, ". . . when it comes to power, nobody is expert but the President. . . ."[51] Certainly a president needs meaningful information in order to make decisions. He should attempt to establish multiple information channels in order to receive, Neustadt notes, ". . . every scrap of fact, opinion, gossip, bearing on his interests and relationships as President."[52] He cannot rely simply on his advisers for information. Instead, he must actively involve himself in the process by which facts come to him.

Roosevelt's efforts to reach out and collect information on which to base his decisions once again illustrate Neustadt's ideas. TR sought information from an incredible variety of sources. He rarely relied on a formal advisory process to furnish him with what he needed. Throughout his presidency, he kept up a large correspondence with people both inside and outside government.[53] He often bypassed members of his Cabinet and heads of agencies to correspond directly with lower echelon personnel. He even asked private citizens, especially journalists, to report to him on the effectiveness of governmental programs and employees. The federal bureaucracy of TR's day was infinitely smaller than the bureaucracy that latter-day presidents had to deal with. Even so, the information flow coming to TR could have led to his becoming so overloaded with detail that his presidency could have become paralyzed had it not been for his intellect and the fact that he simply sampled from the vast amount of data he collected rather than becoming immersed in its detail.

The number of formal advisers available to TR was significantly less than the number available to modern presidents.[54] Most of the help that Roosevelt received of a formal nature during his presidency came from the office of secretary to the president. Two men, George B. Cortelyou and William Loeb, Jr., served in this position during TR's administration and both were extraordinarily helpful and influential to the president. Both men helped TR in drafting his speeches, organized his travel "junkets," scheduled his time, managed the small White House clerical staff of that era, and gave the president political advice on myriad subjects. Loeb especially was important for inspiring investigations which uncovered frauds committed by the American Sugar Trust at the New York Customs House and for his effective handling of patronage. Both men were tireless workers who performed functions later done by dozens of White House assistants and both were completely loyal to TR.[55]

Roosevelt also received advice, information and considerable criticism from a group of personal friends and political sympathizers known as the "Tennis Cabinet." This rather cosmopolitan group of about thirty men consisted of such members as Senator Elihu Root, Robert Bacon of the State Department, Archie Butt, the president's military aide, and conservationist Gifford Pinchot. This small circle of informal advisers also included foreign diplomats. In matters relating to international affairs, TR often took the extraordinary step of seeking the trusted judgments of Ambassador Cecil Spring-Rice of Great Britain, Hermann Speck von Sternburg of Germany, and Jean Jusserand of France. He often consulted with these representatives of foreign governments rather than going through the regular channels of his own State Department.

The vast network that TR utilized to collect information during his administrations aided him in making the right kind of choices for maximizing his power and therefore his effectiveness as a policy leader of the type proposed by Neustadt. Roosevelt's methods of involving himself in the political process and of seeking facts from a multitude of sources enabled him to concentrate important choices from the standpoint of his own power stakes in his own hands. With this in mind, it is worth examining the most disastrous choice, from the perspective of protecting his own power reserve, that TR made during his entire tenure as chief executive. TR became president upon the assassination of McKinley. In 1904, he was re-elected in his own right. On the night of his landslide reelection, he issued a statement indicating his belief that the three and a half years he had already served constituted his first term and since he found the two-term tradition a wise restriction on the abuse of personal power, he would "Under no circumstances be a candidate for or accept another nomination."[56]

The timing of TR's announcement—that he would not seek reelection was a colossal mistake. For someone who displayed the sensitivity to power, the desire for power and the understanding of power previously discussed, it is incredible that he made himself a "lame-duck" officeholder so early in his term. He would have been only fifty years of age in 1908. He was in good physical health. He loved the exercise of power and the responsibility of decision-making, and he did not look forward to a return to life as a private citizen. Even if he had a strong desire to vacate the presidency, he should have postponed his announcement until a few months before the 1908 election. Whatever power he could have preserved because of the Washingtonians' concerns about whether he would seek reelection for another term, he lost by this one extremely ill-chosen decision. It strongly eroded his bargaining power with Congress and must be considered one of the prime reasons for his failures with that institution during his last years in office. This single decision, which was clearly in his own hands, did more to weaken his power than any other single choice he made while president or any action taken by his opponents during his administrations.

Theodore Roosevelt and Foreign Affairs: Suggested Modifications of the Neustadt Model

Evidence thus far has served to replicate Neustadt's findings. Certainly I have found Neustadt's ideas to be a useful analytic tool for understanding Roosevelt's presidency. Roosevelt's behavior as a power-maximizing president serves to illustrate the propositions and maxims that Neustadt offered. I do not accept the Neustadian model in its totality without criticism or modification. The events of the Roosevelt presidency suggest that Neustadt's model needs some revision. In foreign affairs, Roosevelt showed a fundamentally different style of behavior than in the domestic policy arena. In domestic political affairs, as the aforementioned analysis indicates, TR tended to negotiate and persuade. He used his rather effective methods of influencing public opinion to educate the public and pressure Congress in order to obtain what were usually compromises of what he initially proposed.

In foreign affairs and defense policy, Roosevelt tended to bypass Congress without hesitation and operate in a much less restrained manner. His style for obtaining objectives in these areas was to act quickly (often through the use of executive orders) and forcefully. His methods were sometimes ignoble if not unconstitutional. The results attained by TR in the foreign and defense policy arenas were also much closer to his desired outcomes in these areas than on the domestic front. The idea of presidents having greater success in dominating the nation's defense and foreign policies than in controlling its domestic policies has been well argued by Aaron Wildavsky in "The Two Presidencies."[57] While Wildavsky based his observations on data collected from the 1930s until the mid-1960s, I find that TR also had much greater freedom in the foreign policy field than the domestic one. A number of references to the events of TR's presidency will serve to illustrate this point.

Roosevelt was far in advance of the thinking of the vast majority of Americans regarding the role the United States should play in world affairs. TR believed that isolationism was a policy the United States could no longer afford. Realizing that the United States was part of an interdependent world, he was determined that the country he led should play an active part in all world events and the decisions arising out of them that could affect the national interests of his nation. In order for the United States to play this role, Roosevelt wished to build up U.S. military and naval power in order that his country could exert its will by force if necessary. He also sought to use America's rising strength to maintain a balance of power in the world in order to foster world stability and international peace. In his conduct of world relations, TR used the "big stick" with aggressiveness that sometimes amounted to jingoism. He believed in colonialism almost as an obligation of the civilized races. He favored colonies as an essential aid for the development of a strong navy. And he was willing to practice whatever power politics were necessary in order to exert control over the Western Hemisphere and especially the Caribbean—the control of which he considered absolutely necessary for America's self-interest.[58]

Roosevelt's concern with the Caribbean led to his enunciation of the well-known Roosevelt Corollary to the Monroe Doctrine, which was first contained in a letter to his secretary of state, Elihu Root, and later incorporated into his annual message to Congress in 1904. This statement announced that the United States would act as an international peace power and intervene whenever necessary to maintain stability on behalf of the debt-ridden, unstable governments of Latin America. The Roosevelt Corollary was first formally invoked when TR, acting on the basis of his constitutional powers, forced Santo Domingo to sign an agreement in which the United States would send an American to serve as collector of Dominican customs and director of national finance. When this agreement was first submitted to the Senate for ratification, the Senate tried to amend the treaty out of recognition and then failed to approve it. Roosevelt immediately implemented the arrangement by executive agreement alone. The Dominican arrangement then remained in effect for two years before the Senate formally ratified it with only minor amendments.[59] Roosevelt had little regard for the treaty-making powers of the Senate. Writing about the Senate's failure to approve his negotiated agreement, TR was frank: "The Senate ought to feel that its actions on the treaty-making power should be much like that of the President's veto; it should be rarely used."[60] It is difficult to find instances of Roosevelt bargaining with or persuading members of the Washington community throughout this affair. TR did proceed with caution before taking official action. Throughout the months that preceded the implementation of the agreement, he tested public sentiment for his revolutionary extension of the Monroe Doctrine. When he found the American public receptive to his initiatives, he acted with apparently little regard for the views of Congress.

This same pattern of independent executive action in foreign affairs is present in the events associated with the construction of the Panama Canal. Roosevelt's overwhelming passion to make the United States a formidable world power caused him to consider the construction of the canal, which would allow the U.S. Navy to move with considerably heightened speed from one ocean to the other, as one of his greatest priorities. To relate the many details of the construction of the canal would deviate from the subject. This long drama of bribery, corruption, and intrigue has been amply related before.[61] Instead, it is worth considering the style of executive leadership TR displayed in acquiring the rights to construct the canal and the unfettered, secretive manner with which he acted throughout the affair. Panama was not an independent country when Roosevelt attempted to negotiate a treaty giving the United States the right to build and defend a canal. It was a part of Colombia which was under the control of a dictator, José Manuel Marroquin. John Hay, TR's secretary of state, negotiated and signed a treaty in early January 1903 in which the United States agreed to pay the New Panama Canal Company (an organization made up of stockholders who had financed the unsuccessful De Lesseps's canal project which had collapsed in 1889) $40 million and the Colombian government $10 million plus an annual subsidy of $250,000 per year for the right to construct, administer, and defend the proposed canal. The Colombian government, probably concerned more about increasing its monetary compensation than incursions on its sovereignty, repudiated the treaty.

Roosevelt, acting without consultation with Congress, his secretary of state, or lower echelon State Department officials, engaged in an action that could have cost many American, Colombian, and Panamanian lives. An influential Republican lawyer, William Nelson Cromwell, and a French adventurer named Philippe Jean Bunau-Varilla, who had been acting as agents for the New Panama Canal Company, now undertook to organize a revolution that would engineer the secession of Panama from Colombia. Although TR did not have a direct hand in planning this revolution, he did know what Cromwell and Bunau-Varilla had planned. The revolution did occur. It was successful because TR dispatched warships with U.S. Marines to Panama (without consultation with Hay or Secretary of War Root) in order to prevent violence and "maintain free and uninterrupted transit" of the isthmus. According to Sidney Warren, the planned date of the uprising had to be delayed one day to allow time for the U.S.S. *Nashville* to reach Panama.[62] Within an hour and a half of Panama's declaration of independence, the United States formally recognized it as a nation and within eleven days a new canal treaty was negotiated between representatives of the U.S. State Department and Bunau-Varilla—the first Panamanian minister to the United States. Panama received $10 million plus the annual subsidy originally promised to Colombia, which received nothing.

Roosevelt's fait accompli of attaining the canal was eventually ratified by Congress—though his actions did receive considerable criticism within that body. While Congress debated approval of the canal treaty, TR asked Congress to give him certain grants of power regarding the actual construction of the canal. Specifically, TR wished to concentrate all authority for the canal's construction and administration in the hands of its chief engineer, George W. Goethals. When Congress refused his requests, the President took the actions he wanted by executive order. In response to criticisms of his behavior in regard to obtaining the canal, TR spoke with unshakable confidence of the correctness of his actions: "My feeling is that, if anything, I did not go far enough."[63] Addressing an audience at the University of California in 1911, TR indiscreetly boasted, "I took the canal zone and let Congress debate, and while the debate goes on the canal does also."[64]

Actions taken by Roosevelt in the Panama Canal affair showed a basic insensitivity to the sovereign rights of weaker nations. These actions, completed with little if any of the persuasive type of bargaining advocated by Neustadt, could have led to violent confrontations between U.S. armed forces and foreign nations. In other instances, Roosevelt also resorted to secret agreements that could have committed the United States to military action in other parts of the world. Convinced that the interests of America called for stability in the Far East, Roosevelt, acting through his special representative in London, Senator Lodge, and his special representative in Tokyo, Secretary of War Taft, made an unofficial gentleman's agreement in which the United States pledged, in the event of a crisis in the Far East, that it would act as a formal party to the Anglo-Japanese Alliance originally signed in 1902. This agreement, which flouted the treaty-making powers of the Senate, was kept secret until nearly twenty years later—when the historian Tyler Dennett discovered it in the Roosevelt papers while doing research for his *Roosevelt and the Russo-Japanese War*, published in 1925.

Acting in the same style of personal diplomacy, TR authorized Taft to negotiate the so-called Taft-Katsura agreement,[65] in which the United States joined Britain in recognizing Japan's "suzerainty" over Korea in return for a Japanese disavowal of any designs on the Philippines. As Arthur Schlesinger has pointed out, "Roosevelt even made personal démarches of a drastic sort to foreign governments."[66] Concerned with European intervention in the Russo-Japanese War of 1904-1905, Roosevelt responded by sending notes in which he warned ". . . Germany and France in the most polite and discreet fashion that, in the event of a combination against Japan to try to do what Russia, Germany, and France did to her in 1894, I should promptly side with Japan . . . to whatever length was necessary on her behalf."[67]

Earlier TR may have delivered an even more volatile ultimatum to Germany during a conflict between the two countries over the failure of Venezuela to meet obligations owed to citizens of Germany. When Germany threatened intervention, TR exerted pressure to have the matter settled by arbitration at The Hague. Writing years after the crisis, Roosevelt maintained that he had told the German ambassador that unless Germany submitted to arbitration, he would order the U.S. fleet under Admiral Dewey sent to Venezuela. Perhaps TR exaggerated the magnitude of the conflict. H. F. Pringle concluded that his account of the incident was "romantic to the point of absurdity."[68] At any rate, TR did order the fleet's mobilization in the Caribbean, and would have apparently taken stronger action if necessary, even to the point of involving his country in hostilities without congressional authorization.

Concerning his actions in foreign relations and defense matters, TR was basically able to attain what he wanted in these areas. He acted on his constitutional vantage points and, if necessary, was willing to engage in confrontation politics, literally daring the other branches of government to stop him, in order to get what he wanted. John Hart has criticized Neustadt for restricting his analysis of the methods by which presidents acquire power to presidents who "operate within a framework of consensus politics where influence, persuasion and bargaining" are always "central to his task."[69] The events of the Roosevelt years indicate that Hart's criticisms in this area are valid. Time and again in matters relating to foreign affairs and defense policy, TR engaged in confrontation politics with Congress. When Congress responded by trying to reassert itself, it ultimately made little difference in the outcome of policy matters. For example, Congress reacted to what it felt was TR's excessive, if not unconstitutional, use of executive orders by passing a resolution requesting that he file copies of these orders along with exact citations of the statutes or grants of power under which they were issued. Congress also suggested the creation of a panel of distinguished jurists to examine and rule on the constitutionality of these executive acts. Roosevelt totally ignored these resolutions and Congress did nothing.[70]

The previously mentioned world cruise of the U.S. fleet was another example of confrontation politics. In spite of the considerable danger involved in deploying sixteen destroyers and several lesser vessels on a 46,000-mile expedition, TR did not consult Congress nor any of its influential members, including many congressmen from eastern states who feared that America's major population centers would be left unprotected. The chairman of the Naval Affairs Committee was so angry that he threatened to withhold funding for the trip. Roosevelt replied that he had enough funds already to get the fleet to the Pacific and it would stay in that part of the world if more money were not appropriated. Congress capitulated and full funding was approved.

Neustadt has been faulted by Peter W. Sperlich for his failure to recognize the value of command as a way of acquiring and using power.[71] An analysis of TR's role in foreign and defense policies indicates that this is a facet of Neustadt's model that also deserves modification. In Roosevelt's efforts at personal diplomacy, at mobilizing U.S. military forces to back up his diplomatic moves and throughout his general conduct of policy within these areas, one finds members of the diplomatic corps, military personnel, and other employees within the executive branch of government complying with his orders as a matter of course simply because, as president, TR had the prerogative to issue them.

Even in the domestic policy arena, an area in which I have seen many examples of TR working to bargain and persuade in the manner prescribed by Neustadt, Roosevelt was able to achieve results of major importance by issuing orders or by threatening to issue them. A good illustration is Roosevelt's threat to send federal troops into the anthracite coal fields to seize the mines and have the Army operate them until the mine owners and the United Mine Workers union could agree on a settlement of their differences.[72] This threat came after weeks of unsuccessful bargaining with the two principals in the dispute. How much Roosevelt's threatened action actually helped in negotiations is impossible to prove, but his indication that he would take this unprecedented action probably had profound consequences in attaining an ultimate settlement.

TR's efforts to promote conservation is a second major illustration of how a president can profoundly affect policy outcomes within the domestic arena through the use of his power to command. In 1907, Senator C. W. Fulton of Oregon, an ardent opponent of federal conservation measures, attached an amendment to the Agricultural Appropriations bill which outlawed the creation of any new forest reserves in six western states. The amendment easily passed. TR was faced with the prospect of either vetoing the entire bill and leaving the Department of Agriculture (including the Forest Service) without funds, or of signing it and barring himself from establishing in the future any additional forest reserves in these states. During the ten days Roosevelt had in which to sign or veto the bill, he acted on the basis of his power to command. At Chief of the Forest Service Gifford Pinchot's request, presidential proclamations setting aside twenty-one new National Forests embracing sixteen million acres in the six states affected by Fulton's amendment were signed by the president just before he signed the Agricultural Appropriations bill into law.[73]

Another major criticism of the Neustadian model, which has been raised by Sperlich, is that Neustadt does not consider the possibility that persons the president wishes to influence may eventually come to identify with him and therefore respond in an affirmative manner to requests he makes of them.[74] According to Sperlich, a president "should select his associates on the basis of personal loyalty and identification, and he should attempt to create feelings of subjective identification in those in whose selection he had no voice."[75] Roosevelt's actions as a power-maximizing president suggest that Sperlich's criticism of Neustadt and his advice in this area also have considerable validity. In domestic politics, Roosevelt saw the social and economic problems created by the cultural, demographic, and financial forces of the Industrial Revolution. He determined that the national government must deal with these problems. In foreign affairs, Roosevelt was determined that the United States should utilize her resources, power, and influence in order to take her place among the leading nations of the world. In both domestic and foreign affairs, TR's vision was in step with the times. Because of this, he was able to foster loyalty and support from a vast number of associates within and outside of government. His vision of the role of government—coupled with his tactical skills in politics, his flair for the dramatic, his great self-confidence, his ability to generate controversy, and his overwhelming energy and enthusiasm—enabled him to inspire support through the ideological climate he was able to create. Members of the executive branch, congressmen, and others, often went along with his proposals simply because they believed in him and what he proposed. His ability to obtain this form of identification, based on shared values and goals (which Neustadt overlooked in his prescriptions), served as a significant component of the power base TR employed during his presidency.

Conclusion

The major intention of this study has been to conduct an empirical investigation of the appropriateness of the model of presidential power proposed by Richard Neustadt as an analytical tool for understanding the presidency of Theodore Roosevelt. Does the Neustadt model help us to understand the behavior of TR as president? The answer to this question is an unqualified yes. This work has shown that Theodore Roosevelt was a power-maximizing president of the type advocated by Neustadt. It has also shown that TR's successful extensions of presidential power, at least in the domestic political sphere, were achieved by his bargaining with other actors in the governmental process in the same manner as Neustadt advocated.

This study has not been completely supportive of Neustadt's work. The historical evidence of the Roosevelt years indicates that much of the success attained by TR in foreign and defense policy matters was achieved not so much by using the persuasion-bargaining approach described by Neustadt as through the use of the formal prerogatives of his office. Criticisms of the Neustadt model developed by Peter W. Sperlich and John Hart were shown to have considerable justification. Theodore Roosevelt was shown to use his powers of command to obtain basically what he wanted in the foreign and defense policy areas even if it meant engaging in confrontation politics with members of Congress or other actors within the political process. The work of Aaron Wildavsky in his "The Two Presidencies" was shown to have substantial merit for explaining TR's presidency in regard to these areas of executive leadership. The data drawn from Roosevelt's actions in foreign affairs and defense related matters also indicates that the public law approach of Edward S. Corwin in *The President: Office and Powers* and Richard Pious in *The American Presidency*, which emphasizes the formal constitutional grants of power a president has and thus his power to command, deserves more emphasis in the calculation of presidential power than Neustadt indicates. Even though Neustadt's work deserves some minor alterations, *Presidential Power* remains the closest thing to a comprehensive theory that has yet been produced within this area of research.

NOTES

1. Edwin S. Corwin, *The President: Office and Powers, 1787–1957* (New York: New York University Press, 1957).

2. For examples of this approach, see Herman Finer, *The Presidency: Crises and Regeneration* (Chicago: University of Chicago Press, 1960); and Clinton Rossiter, *The American Presidency* (New York: Harcourt, Brace and Jovanovich, 1956).

3. Richard E. Neustadt, *Presidential Power: The Politics of Leadership* (New York: John Wiley and Sons, 1980), p. v.

4. Ibid., p. 10.

5. Ibid., p. 35.

6. In a novel and very interesting approach, William T. Bluhm has made a comparative study of the political science of Machiavelli and Neustadt. See his *Theories of the Political System: Classics of Political Thought and Modern Political Analysis* (Englewood Cliffs, NJ: Prentice Hall, 1965), chap. 7.

7. Harry A. Bailey, "Neustadt's Thesis Revisited: Toward the Two Faces of Presidential Power" (Paper presented at the annual meeting of the Midwest Political Science Asociation, Chicago, April 1980).

8. Thomas E. Cronin, *The State of the Presidency* (Boston: Little, Brown and Company, 1980), chap. 4. This chapter was originally published as "Presidential Power Revised and Reappraised," in *Western Political Quarterly* 32 (December 1979): 381–95.

9. John Hart, "Presidential Power Revisited," *Political Studies* 25 (March 1977): 48–61.

10. Peter W. Sperlich, "Bargaining and Overload: An Essay on Presidential Power," in *Perspectives on the Presidency*, ed. Aaron Wildavsky (Boston: Little, Brown and Company, 1975), pp. 406-30.

11. George Edwards, *Presidential Influence in Congress* (San Francisco: W. H. Freeman and Company, 1980), pp. 131–35.

12. Richard M. Pious, *The American Presidency* (New York: Basic Books, 1979).

13. Bailey, "Neustadt's Thesis Revisited," p. 2.

14. Raymond Tatalovich and Byron W. Daynes, "Toward a Paradigm to Explain Presidential Power," *Presidential Studies Quarterly* 9 (Fall 1979): 428–41.

15. Sperlich, "Bargaining and Overload," p. 415; Norman C. Thomas, "Studying the Presidency: Where and How Do We Go From Here," *Presidential Studies Quarterly* 7 (Fall 1977): 170.

16. To my knowledge, the only attempt to systematically apply Neustadt's theory of presidential power to an earlier presidency has been made by Robert M. Johnstone in his *Jefferson and the Presidency: Leadership in the Young Republic* (Ithaca: Cornell University Press, 1978).

17. See for examples, William M. Goldsmith, *The Growth of Presidential Power: A Documented History*, vol. 2, *Decline and Resurgence* (New York: Chelsea House Publishers, 1974), pp. 1279–81; and James MacGregor Burns, *Presidential Government: The Crucible of Leadership* (Boston: Houghton Mifflin Company, 1965), pp. 57–66.

18. William H. Harbaugh, *The Life and Times of Theodore Roosevelt* (New York: Oxford University Press, 1975), p. 492.

19. Theodore Roosevelt, *An Autobiography* (New York: Macmillan Company, 1921), p. 395.

20. Ibid., pp. 388–89.

21. Neustadt, *Presidential Power*, p. 10.

22. Ibid., p. 44.

23. This term is defined by Neustadt as "Members of Congress and of [the President's] Administration, governors of states, military commanders in the field, leading politicians in both parties, representatives of private organizations, newsmen of assorted types and sizes, foreign diplomats [and principals abroad] . . ." Ibid.

24. Richard Hofstadter, *The American Political Tradition and the Men Who Made It* (New York: Vintage Books, 1974), p. 269.

25. Ibid., p. 270.

26. Thomas A. Bailey, *Presidential Greatness: The Image and the Man from George Washington to the Present* (New York: Appleton-Century, 1966), p. 72.

27. Neustadt, *Presidential Power*, p. 180.

28. See John M. Blum, *The Republican Roosevelt* (Cambridge: Harvard University Press, 1967), pp. 154, 157–59; and Harbaugh, *Life and Times of TR*, pp. 469–79.

29. A case may be made that TR possessed too much of this particular attribute. As president he had a tendency to act in an arbitrary manner while displaying a dogmatic certitude about the correctness and indeed the righteousness of his conduct. The Brownsville affair is a classic example of how Roosevelt's impetuous nature caused him to embark on a course which led him toward weakening his power by damaging his support among black voters. The Brownsville incident involved a group of black soldiers near Brownsville, Texas, who allegedly took part in a raid on that town in which a number of white citizens were killed. No proof was ever presented showing that any of the black soldiers had actually participated in the altercation. Roosevelt arbitrarily ordered all members of three companies (167 men) discharged without honor

from the service for refusing to divulge the identify of any alleged participants. Despite an unfavorable response by Congress and the American public to his arbitrary action, TR never admitted the slightest mistake on his part in this action which is sometimes considered the greatest black mark on his presidency, nor did he make any mention of it in his *Autobiography*. For a complete account of this episode, see John D. Weaver, *The Brownsville Raid: The Story of America's Black Dreyfus Affair* (New York: W. W. Norton and Company, 1970). See also George E. Mowry, *The Era of Theodore Roosevelt and the Birth of Modern America, 1900-1912* (New York: Harper Torchbooks, 1958), pp. 212–14; and Henry F. Pringle, *Theodore Roosevelt: A Biography* (New York: Harcourt, Brace and Company, 1931), pp. 458–64.

30. Neustadt, *Presidential Power*, p. 132.

31. Ibid., pp. 28–30. To Neustadt, bargaining is basically the trading of advantages between the president and persons of influence (congressmen, party leaders, members of the bureaucracy, etc.) whom he seeks to persuade. As Peter W. Sperlich and other Neustadian scholars have pointed out, this use of the word "bargaining" is close to the definition given by Robert A. Dahl and Charles E. Lindblom in *Politics, Economics and Welfare* (New York: Harper Torchbooks, 1963), p. 324.

32. For a brief description of the major leaders within the Congress of TR's era, see Alvin M. Josephy, Jr., *The American Heritage History of the Congress of the United States* (New York: American Heritage Publishing Company, 1975), pp. 302–3.

33. The notion of a close linkage of the powers of the president to those of the House Speaker, of the type which actually existed between TR and Cannon, has been endorsed by Neustadt as a prescription for providing effective government. See Neustadt, *Presidential Power*, p. 207.

34. Quoted in L. White Busbey, *Uncle Joe Cannon: The Story of a Pioneer American* (New York: Henry Holt and Company, 1927), p. 219. For a complete account of the relationship that existed between Roosevelt and Speaker Cannon, one should also consult Blair Bolles, *Tyrant from Illinois: Uncle Joe Cannon's Experiment with Personal Power* (New York: W.W. Norton and Company, 1951).

35. TR is generally given credit for being the first president to supplement his messages to Congress with written drafts of proposed bills.

36. These messages to Congress were lengthy, cumbersome affairs running to as much as 40,000 words in length. TR mixed his substantive legislative proposals with suggestions for laws in a multitude of fields. The vast majority of his proposals were politically impossible and years ahead of their time. As Lawrence Chamberlain has pointed out, "The messages were interesting illustrations of the range of Roosevelt's interests and the virtuosity of his mind, but they were not always of great value to Congress as solid substance from which essential legislation could be fabricated." See Lawrence H. Chamberlain, *The President, Congress and Legislation* (New York:

Columbia University Press, 1946), p. 16. In Neustadian terms, Roosevelt's failure to focus on attainable goals within his annual messages was a mistake on his part for he failed to utilize to its fullest a persuasive device in the arsenal of weapons that he could direct against Congress.

37. Neustadt, *Presidential Power*, p. 48.

38. *The Letters of Theodore Roosevelt*, ed. Elting E. Morison, (Cambridge: Harvard University Press, 1952), 5: 283, letter no. 3,922.

39. For complete accounts of the fight to obtain this bill for the regulation of the meat packing industry, see Harbaugh, *Life and Times of TR*, pp. 247–51 and Mowry, *Era of TR*, pp. 207–8. See also James Ford Rhodes, *The McKinley and Roosevelt Administrations, 1897-1909* (New York: Macmillan Company, 1923), pp. 334–36.

40. This is the conclusion reached by Roosevelt's most perceptive biographers. See Blum, *The Republican Roosevelt*, pp. 75–79 and 84–85; Mowry, *Era of TR*, p. 200; Harbaugh, *Life and Times of TR*, pp. 230–32.

41. Lewis L. Gould believes that Roosevelt's handling of the tariff question, far from showing "a shrewd and subtle design" for obtaining railroad legislation, instead indicated a failure on the president's part in dealing with an extremely complex and important issue. See Lewis L. Gould, *Reform and Regulation: American Politics, 1900-1916* (New York: John Wiley and Sons, 1978), pp. 52–64. William H. Harbaugh also sees TR's unwillingness to deal with the issue of tariff revision as ". . . one of the major failures of his presidency." Harbaugh, *Life and Times of TR*, p. 232.

42. This constitutes only the basic outlines of Roosevelt's efforts to negotiate with and persuade Congress in the passage of this bill. Complete accounts of TR's efforts in guiding the Hepburn bill through the labyrinth paths of Congress can be found in Mowry, *Era of TR*, pp. 197–206; Harbaugh, *Life and Times of TR*, chap. 14; Gould, *Reform and Regulation*, pp. 54–64; Blum, *The Republican Roosevelt*, chap. 6. One should also consult two short essays by Blum which appear as appendices in *The Letters of Theodore Roosevelt*. See John M. Blum, "Theodore Roosevelt and the Legislative Process: Tariff Revision and Railroad Regulation, 1904–1906," in *Letters of Theodore Roosevelt*, ed. Morison, 4: 1,333–42, and his "Theodore Roosevelt and the Hepburn Act: Toward an Orderly System of Control," in *Letters of Theodore Roosevelt*, ed. Morison, 6: 1,558-71.

43. Neustadt, *Presidential Power*, p. 205.

44. For scholarly accounts of TR's efforts in this area, see James E. Pollard, *The Presidents and the Press* (New York: Macmillan Company, 1947), pp. 569–600; and Elmer E. Cornwell, Jr., *Presidential Leadership of Public Opinion* (Bloomington: Indiana University Press, 1965), pp. 13–26.

45. James David Barber, *The Pulse of Politics: Electing Presidents in the Media Age* (New York: W. W. Norton and Company, 1980), p. 46.

46. This was an invention of his successor, Woodrow Wilson.

47. Presumably, the House of TR's day was more apt to respond to public opinion than the Senate whose membership was still chosen

at this time by state legislatures which were generally under the control of local political leaders.

48. Complete accounts of the process by which this legislation was passed can be found in Harbaugh, *Life and Times of TR*, chap. 9; Mowry, *Era of TR*, pp. 123–24; Pringle, *TR: A Biography*, pp. 340–42.

49. Blum, *The Republican Roosevelt*, pp. 56–68 and 119–20; Mowry, *Era of TR*, pp. 130–34; Harbaugh, *Life and Times of TR*, pp. 157-64.

50. The conservation issue also prompted Roosevelt to call for the convening of the first White House Conference of Governors. At this conference, TR used his techniques of persuasion to ultimately obtain the issuance of a Declaration of Governors calling on each state to create its own conservation commission for the preservation of natural resources. This conference not only publicized TR's national program in this area, but it also served to develop founding principles on which most states have based their own conservation programs.

51. Neustadt, *Presidential Power*, p. 109.

52. Ibid., p. 113.

53. During his public career, TR wrote an estimated 150,000 letters to political leaders, heads of state, historians, authors, scientists, and so on. This vast correspondence represented a massive effort not only to keep himself informed of changing political conditions, but also to persuade opinion leaders throughout the nation to his views about political issues.

54. See Edward H. Hobbs, "An Historical Review of Plans for Presidential Staffing," *Law and Contemporary Problems* 21 (Autumn 1956): 663–88.

55. See Louis K. Koenig, *The Invisible Presidency* (New York: Holt, Rinehart and Winston, 1960), pp. 31–32 and 136–89. One should also consult Michael Medved, *The Shadow Presidents—The Secret History of the Chief Executives and Their Top Aides* (New York: Times Books, 1979), pp. 96-122.

56. Quoted in Mowry, *Era of TR*, p. 180.

57. Aaron Wildavsky, "The Two Presidencies," in *Perspectives on the Presidency*, ed. Aaron Wildavsky (Boston: Little, Brown and Company, 1975), pp. 448–61.

58. For fuller treatments of Roosevelt's objectives in foreign affairs, see Howard K. Beale, *Theodore Roosevelt and the Rise of America to World Power* (New York: Collier Books, 1956), especially chap. 1 and pp. 225–26. See also Mowry, *Era of TR*, chaps. 9 and 10, and Blum, *The Republican Roosevelt*, especially chap. 8.

59. Mowry, *Era of TR*, pp. 158–61; Harbaugh, *Life and Times of TR*, pp. 189-92; Rhodes, *McKinley and Roosevelt*, pp. 318–19.

60. *The Letters of Theodore Roosevelt*, ed. Morison, 4: 1,145, letter no. 3,495.

61. The sources I have drawn most heavily from are Beale, *TR and the Rise of America*, pp. 103-8; Mowry, *Era of TR*, pp. 146 and 149-55; and Harbaugh, *Life and Times of TR*, chap. 12. See also the short essay by Alfred D. Chandler, Jr., "Theodore Roosevelt and the Panama Canal: A Study in Administration," in *Letters of Theodore Roosevelt*, ed. Morison, 6: 1,547-57.

62. Sidney Warren, *The President as World Leader* (New York: J. B. Lippincott Company, 1964), pp. 32–33.

63. *The Letters of Theodore Roosevelt*, ed. Morison, 3: 688, letter no. 2,916.

64. Quoted in Harbaugh, *Life and Times of TR*, p. 204.

65. Other important executive agreements entered into by TR included the Root-Takahiri Agreement of 1908 which upheld the Open Door policy in China and the Gentlemen's Agreement of 1907 which restricted Japanese immigration to the United States.

66. Arthur M. Schlesinger, Jr., *The Imperial Presidency* (Boston: Houghton Mifflin Company, 1973), p. 88.

67. Quoted in ibid.

68. Pringle, *TR: A Biography*, p. 300.

69. Hart, "Presidential Power Revisited," p. 55.

70. C. Perry Patterson, *Presidential Government in the United States: The Unwritten Constitution* (Chapel Hill: University of North Carolina Press, 1947), p. 133.

71. Sperlich, "Bargaining and Overload," pp. 419–20.

72. Harbaugh, *Life and Times of TR*, chap. 10; Mowry, *Era of TR*, pp. 134-40.

73. Harbough, *Life and Times of TR*, pp. 311–13; Mowry, *Era of TR*, pp. 214-16.

74. Sperlich, "Bargaining and Overload," p. 419.

75. Ibid.

Mount Rushmore in South Dakota

The Presidency:

"Speak Softly and Carry a Big Stick"

294

NO MOLLY-CODDLING HERE

Theodore Roosevelt's "big stick" image was applied to both domestic and foreign affairs. In this cartoon, TR wields the big stick against the trusts, Ambassador Bellamy Storer with whom he quarreled over Vatican politics, and "everything in general." The bit stick, TR explained, came from an African proverb, which he quoted as saying, "Speak softly and carry a big stick; you will go far."

21

The Big Stick as Weltpolitik: Europe and Latin America in Theodore Roosevelt's Foreign Policy

Richard H. Collin

When Theodore Roosevelt assumed the presidency on September 14, 1901, the United States was already a major world power. The United States had won a small world war with Spain in 1898—a war decided by naval victories continents apart at Manila Bay and Santiago, Cuba.[1] As an articulate American expansionist, President William McKinley's assistant secretary of the Navy, and hero of the Rough Riders, Roosevelt played a vital role in the Spanish-American War. Roosevelt prepared the Navy for war and helped win the Asiatic command for Commodore George Dewey. His legendary charge at San Juan Hill made him and Dewey America's first modern war heroes.[2] Roosevelt was a unique world leader, a writer-intellectual who became a successful soldier, an aristocrat who led a democratic people, a global visionary who deprovincialized his nation, and an international nationalist who championed world civilization and patriotic nationalism at the same time. Theodore Roosevelt was one of the most effective charismatic phrase-makers to ever capture the world's imagination.[3]

Roosevelt's colorful use of language proved to be both an asset and a liability. He made the "big stick" into a household phrase, winning public support for an expanded navy, a more efficient military bureaucracy, and an activist foreign policy.[4] But the same big stick that impressed Kaiser Wilhelm II frightened Latin Americans. American historiography has consistently stressed Latin American rather than European reaction to the big stick policy.[5] Although Latin America was the battleground in the turn-of-the-century struggle between the United States and Europe, Latin America was never Roosevelt's target. Control, not expansion, was Roosevelt's primary object. His union of power and responsibility, his intellectual commitment to the idea of civilization, and his personal indifference to the economic side of capitalism tempered the big stick.[6]

U.S. willingness to accept responsibility in Roosevelt's Corollary to the Monroe Doctrine of 1905 made Roosevelt's policy acceptable to Europe.[7] What pleased Europe displeased Latin America. Roosevelt tried constantly to make peace with Latin America. But Latin American intellectuals were frustrated by Latin American cultural and economic dependency on Europe and their awareness of Latin American vulnerability to the emerging modernism of the twentieth-century world of which the United States was the chief symbol.[8] Latin American concern was justified. Roosevelt's success in removing Europe eliminated the effective Latin American diplomatic tactic of using divisions among competing European interests to win whatever diplomatic victories were possible to weak, pre-industrial nations. Dealing with the colossus to the north was far more difficult than playing British, Germans, or French off against one another, and, when that failed, invoking the Monroe Doctrine to prevent European military intervention.

Latin American political dependency preceded Roosevelt's time.[9] In the 1820s Simón Bolívar despaired of finding a political solution to authoritarian Iberian traditions.[10] Latin America may well have been a victim of Roosevelt's success, but it was already a victim of Spanish colonialism and European cultural dependency. The Americans who wanted Europe out, did not want themselves in. Roosevelt's graphic disclaimer, "I have about the same desire to annex it [Santo Domingo] as a gorged boa constrictor might have to swallow a porcupine wrong-end to," is an accurate statement of American feelings.[11] Germany (primarily) and Great Britain were the main focus of American fears and policies. Only after the United States established control in the Caribbean—in Roosevelt's method through the measured use of power and diplomacy—could U.S. policy attempt to deal with its Latin American relationships. Roosevelt won his battle with Europe but in so doing became the historical demon blamed for losing Latin America.[12]

Great Britain had gradually begun to come to terms with the American demand for hegemony in Central America. When Roosevelt signed the Hay-Pauncefote II Treaty on December 21, 1901—his first treaty as president—Britain finally gave in to

American ambitions to be rid of the Clayton-Bulwer Treaty of 1850 which prohibited either nation from building a canal unilaterally. When the Senate rewrote Secretary of State John Hay's first version of the treaty, it insisted that an isthmian canal be American in word as well as deed, though the British fleet remained the sovereign of the seas. Resisting any conciliatory gesture to the British, including a linkage of the Alaskan boundary dispute or Canadian fishing rights, Hay-Pauncefote II was a measured public expression of American nationalism.[13] Roosevelt fully supported the diction of the treaty even while reassuring his English friends that he conceded the British navy's control of an isthmian canal in time of war.[14] Roosevelt's concession, which was true in 1901, was no longer true in 1905 when the U.S. naval building program and Britain's more pressing interests gave the Americans actual control of the Caribbean.[15]

American concern over Germany's threat also began well before Roosevelt's presidency. When Kaiser Wilhelm II supplanted Chancellor Otto von Bismarck as chief architect of German foreign policy in 1890, Germany abandoned Bismarck's continental strategy and determined to become a world power. German attempts to match Britain's naval power were disastrous to world stability. No matter how brilliant or determined the German plans, Germany could not transcend its geographical limitations nor catch up with Britain's colonial and trade empire nor with its superior industrial capacity.[16] German timing was bad. Both Japan and the United States emerged as new world powers; eventually, Germany's challenge to Britain moved both of the new powers to align with Britain and widen the German gap.[17] German friction with the United States intensified in disputes over food tariffs and American ability to export agricultural products cheaply; likewise in naval skirmishes at Samoa in 1889 and Rio de Janiero in 1893, the German seizure of Kiaochow, China in 1897, and the constant presence of German naval forces in conflict with U.S. interests at Manila Bay and the Caribbean Sea.[18]

Germany was at the heart of the new U.S. foreign policy concerns under McKinley. The seizure of Kiaochow shocked sophisticated American export businessmen. German words at Kiaochow and German aggressiveness in Shantung province and in the Caribbean frightened American diplomats. German actions at Manila Bay made a lifetime enemy of Commodore Dewey, who, as America's first four-star admiral, became head of the new Navy General Board and co-head of the Army-Navy Joint Board in 1903. Dewey never tempered his distaste for Germany.[19] American naval planners were certain that Germany threatened to destabilize the Caribbean by acquiring one or more bases as coaling stations, and eventually to pose an economic and military threat to the U.S. mainland.[20] The German naval laws of 1898 and 1900 were as revolutionary as America's worst fears. Alfred von Tirpitz, Wilhelm's secretary of the navy and Prussian minister of state from 1898 to 1916, publicly planned a 124-battleship navy aimed at supremacy over Britain and an eventual alliance with Latin America.[21] Although the German plans were unrealistic—indeed quixotic—Germany posed a threat Britain and the United States took seriously. The Boxer Rebellion in China in 1900 was ample evidence of the difficulties German aggression could cause.[22]

Although American fear of Germany, the beginnings of the immense U.S. naval mobilization, a strategic naval board, an isthmian canal commission, and colonial responsibilities in Asia and the Caribbean all began under William McKinley's presidency, it was Theodore Roosevelt who dramatized America's new role as a world power.[23] McKinley was a reluctant statesman; Roosevelt was an exuberant world leader who welcomed the new role for the United States and the new technologies of modernism. As president, TR flew in an early airplane, dived in an early submarine, and embraced the new dreadnought-class big gun battleship.[24] Roosevelt abandoned the fortress-America mentality, fully supported Mahan's concept of offensive sea power, and welcomed the chance to make the United States not just an equal world power but an influential one. Roosevelt possessed geographical advantages the kaiser lacked. He understood that, by exploiting American isolation from European rivalries, the United States could become the center of a new balance of power, neutralizing Germany and tempering British supremacy. He played a decisive role in the Asian struggle between Russia and Japan and the European dispute over Morocco in 1905. Roosevelt's intense nationalism was tempered by his equally important belief in responsibility and a commitment to the concept of civilization. By linking civilization, responsibility, and power, Roosevelt transformed his provincial nation into one with global consciousness, able to influence events not only in the Caribbean but also in Asia and Europe.[25] McKinley was an adept American national leader. Roosevelt became the preeminent world leader of his time and America's most successful globalist, willing and able to prevent wars from becoming world wars by intervening in gesture and word before military force was necessary.[26]

The German threat the Americans feared materialized in 1902, Roosevelt's first full year as president. The Anglo-German intervention of December 1902 demonstrated how even friendly European powers little appreciated the symbolism of the Monroe Doctrine, how vulnerable the Americans were to a concert of Europe, and how foolish the Europeans were to even consider such a harebrained scheme.[27] British judgment was skewed by the deaths of Lord Julian Pauncefote, the longtime British ambassador to Washington, and Queen Victoria, followed by King Edward's unexpected illness, the end of the Boer War, Lord Lansdowne's replacement of Lord Salisbury as foreign minister, and the complications of the growing naval race with Germany.[28]

Germany's diplomatic clumsiness matched its opportunistic naval policies. The kaiser hated the Monroe Doctrine and German diplomats referred to America as the United States of North America.[29] To deflect U.S. disapproval of his Venezuelan intervention, the kaiser relied on a silly goodwill visit by his brother Prince Heinrich to Washington in April 1902. Heinrich's visit was a fiasco; the Americans remained wary, and Germany hoped to shift blame for the intervention to Britain.[30] Both European powers proceeded as if the Americans could be easily sidetracked. Lansdowne, Metternich, von Bülow, and the kaiser all ignored known American sensitivity to European interventions. Italy joined the intervention through a trade off for concessions in the African colony of Somaliland.[31] Even though Germany did not have enough vessels to effectively blockade Venezuela, let alone seriously challenge the United States, German recklessness—its willingness to proceed even with obvious naval deficiencies—validated American fear of German opportunism.[32] Even Britain had to shuffle its naval resources to provide enough armored cruisers, available only after their Newfoundland fishing duties were completed in early December.[33]

The United States most feared a confrontation with Europe

over the Monroe Doctrine. Although Germany was the main worry, Britain's willingness to become involved in a Venezuelan intervention, France's quick trigger finger in the Caribbean, Italian, Dutch, and Belgium involvement in the Dominican Republic, and Spain's continued urgings of a European alliance against the United States, presented the Americans with a risky problem.[34] Until Europe took America seriously—as a matter of habit—the temptation for intervention and accidental war remained possible with friends as well as rivals.

The American naval maneuvers scheduled in June 1902 at Culebra island, five miles north of Puerto Rico, served a triple purpose. Culebra, the only deep harbor port outside of Guantánamo (still in the process of negotiation with Cuba) which could serve as an effective Caribbean naval base, had to be used, developed, and protected. The U.S. Navy shifted its emphasis from coastal defense and its mainly ceremonial role in scattered outposts throughout the world into a fighting fleet using Alfred Mahan's theories of sea power. Culebra was ideally situated for possible Venezuelan operations. Roosevelt, a master of the symbolic use of naval power and a naval intellectual of long standing, publicized the Culebra maneuvers and put Admiral Dewey, a well-known Germanophobe in charge.[35] But the Germans and British blithely ignored the presence of an U.S. fleet that easily outnumbered the Europeans in the same way they ignored the Monroe Doctrine.

U.S. naval intelligence predicted both the Venezuelan resistance and the European overreaction.[36] Roosevelt with a large navy in strategic and logistical control—and with sufficient supplies of nearby coal—could suddenly switch the U.S. posture from passive onlooker to decisive diplomatic force.[37] The Anglo-Germans were in an untenable position. Venezuela could resist any attempted invasion with impunity. Once the United States aligned with Venezuela against European intervention, the Anglo-German undertaking was doomed.[38] Roosevelt, however, made the most of the opportunity, capitalizing on public reaction to the European show of force to establish the Monroe Doctrine, for the first time, in both principle and practice. Five days after Secretary of State John Hay demanded the end of intervention and the settlement of the dispute by international arbitration—a demand consistent with President Grover Cleveland's Venezuelan policy in 1895—Britain and Germany agreed on December 17, 1902. Prime Minister Arthur Balfour publicly conceded support of the Monroe Doctrine in a speech to Parliament on December 15.[39] The kaiser replaced his American ambassador Theodor von Holleben, with Hermann Speck von Sternburg, Roosevelt's closest German diplomatic friend.[40] The continuance of the blockade through February and the legal victory of the blockading powers in the Hague Court of Arbitration ruling in 1904, does not diminish the magnitude of Roosevelt's diplomatic victory.[41] He raised European consciousness of American resistance to New World adventurism and made Europe aware that the United States was now an effective world power.

Roosevelt knew exactly what had happened. He used the "speak softly and carry a big stick" phrase in Chicago on April 2, 1903, to describe his foreign policy of defending the Monroe Doctrine and to win more support for a larger navy.[42] Unlike Grover Cleveland, who blustered (effectively), Roosevelt allowed the Europeans to escape gracefully by agreeing to keep the ultimatums off the record and by rebuking Admirals Henry Clay Taylor and Dewey for their anti-German remarks, though he privately sympathized with them.[43]

Although most accounts of the Panama Canal controversies focus on U.S. mistreatment of Colombia, Colombian domestic politics and the changing role of Europe in Central America better explain the breakdown in U.S.-Colombian relations.[44] Carlos Martínez Silva, the first Colombian diplomat to negotiate with the United States about a Panama canal, fully understood Colombia's lost advantage when the Hay-Pauncefote II Treaty eliminated Britain and the leverage Europe provided Latin American nations in their dealings with the United States.[45] Roosevelt, Hay, and Mark Hanna, the Senate's main Panama route advocate, all realized the importance of removing the French interests before the U.S.–Colombian negotiations began.[46] The diplomatic complications between the United States and Colombia were caused by Colombian domestic conflicts between Liberals and Conservatives, culminating in the War of the Thousand Days (1899-1902), which the United States helped settle at Colombia's request on board the battleship *Wisconsin* on November 21, 1902.[47]

When Colombian President José Marroquín stymied American negotiations for a Panama canal, an opposition rooted in his own resistance to Liberal modern capitalism, Roosevelt made a two-stage change in U.S. policy.[48] Under the terms of the Bidlack-Mallarino Treaty of 1846 between Colombia (then New Granada) and the United States, the U.S. recognized Colombia's sovereignty over Panama in return for an ambiguous "right of transit" across the isthmus. The United States from 1846 to 1902 acted as Colombia's ally, keeping order in Panama and preventing its independence. In its 1902 naval intervention, the United States limited its obligation to keeping the Panama railroad open, even barring Colombian troops from using it—a new policy of neutrality rather than alliance.[49]

The Colombian Senate's 24–0 rejection of the Hay-Herrán Treaty in August 1903 was a challenge to U.S. prestige and ability, reflected in the increasing demands by American newspapers for a strong U.S. response including annexation of Panama.[50] Colombia's demands for part of the $40 million the United States agreed to pay the French Compagnie Nouvelle (for the completed work on the canal and its physical property) underscored the European complications Roosevelt struggled to eliminate. U.S. abhorrence at European involvement in Panama began with Presidents Hayes and Grant and help explain the deep American attachment to an inferior Nicaraguan canal route uncorrupted by French involvement.[51] When Panamanians became convinced in 1903 that the United States would no longer automatically support Colombian hegemony if Panama seceded and Colombia remained intransigent, the Panamanians revolted and Roosevelt shifted U.S. support to Panama.[52]

Colombia responded to Panama's independence by asking Germany to establish a European protectorate against the United States. Germany quickly declined the Colombia intervention, even though just a year before it sought desperately to find a way of controlling the Panama canal.[53] Although U.S. historians focus on Roosevelt's naval intervention in Panama in November 1903 as a questionable extension of U.S. power, Roosevelt's response was measured and effective.[54] Colombia's brinkmanship diplomacy with her only ally was irresponsible and foolhardy. Colombia's only claim to sovereignty over Panama rested in the Bidlack-Mallarino Treaty of 1846. By tradition, geography, and preference, Panama was never an integral part of Colombia. The U.S. Navy provided Panama's main police force, intervening twelve times between 1856 and 1903.[55] But Colombia in 1903 was as indifferent to U.S. wishes as Britain and Germany in 1902—with the same result. The humiliating 24–0 rejection of a treaty it had negotiated, and the constant demands for renegotiation of French and American concessions the Americans considered settled, were caused by the pressures of Colombia's chaotic domestic politics.

By openly challenging the United States when Roosevelt was trying to discourage European involvement in the Caribbean, Colombia made U.S. support of Panamanian independence an attractive option. Nicaragua was not a feasible alternative. Had Roosevelt taken the Nicaraguan alternative there would be two competing canals in Central America. A partly finished Panama canal and Colombia's unsettled politics might well have transformed the isthmus into a Central American Balkans. The Americans would have been stuck with the inferior canal route, the canal question would have remained unsettled, and Europe would have remained at the center of New World diplomacy.[56] Roosevelt's haste in settling an isthmian canal was essential to the U.S. policy of excluding Europe and eliminating potential trouble spots. Nor could Roosevelt have backed down when Colombia defied the Americans. Backing down for no real purpose (except to appease a confused Colombian leadership that used diplomacy as part of its ongoing domestic revolutions, and remained indifferent to canals, development, or Panama) would have created a fatal inconsistency in Roosevelt's policy to convince Europe that the United States was strong.[57] Historians, who insist that TR could or should have waited patiently, miss the point of U.S. policy. Europe, not Colombia or Latin America, was the reason to resolve the Panama canal issue quickly. Roosevelt originally planned to ask the Senate to approve a unilateral seizure of the canal zone under the American interpretation of the Bidlack-Mallarino Treaty and subsequently let an international arbitration court assess the cost and the question of sovereignty.[58] When he learned from his own intelligence sources that a Panamanian revolution was imminent, Roosevelt supported Philippe Bunau-Varilla's alliance with the Panamanian revolutionaries, a political error which muddied the waters and made Colombia's victimization and later Latin American displeasure the main historical question of TR's Panama policies.[59]

The rape of Panama has remained a popular theme in U.S.

and Colombian historiography, but it is time that sentimentality over Colombia's martyrdom be put to rest.[60] Colombia had no real right in Panama from the start. Colombia's subjection of Panama was always based on its obligation to encourage development of a Panama canal in alliance with the United States, the treaty protector of the Colombian-Panama relationship since 1846. When Colombia, distracted by its domestic politics, played foolish games with both the United States and Panama, Roosevelt acted to protect U.S. interests and punish Colombia.[61] His policy was supported by Europeans and Latin Americans, who wanted a canal and welcomed the American ability and willingness to build it.[62] Colombia's argument was with other Colombians. American historians, who make Roosevelt responsible, ignore the real cause of the conflict: the catastrophic disordering of Colombian society in the War of the Thousand Days.[63]

European diplomats were deeply concerned at the breakdown of law and decency in what had been one of Latin America's most civilized nations.[64] French Vice-Consul Pierre Bonhenry, present at the Colombian siege of Colón, credited the United States with preventing a blood bath in Panama, not fomenting a revolution.[65] The Europeans understood the two complementary parts of Roosevelt's Panama policy: support of Panama's independence and U.S. willingness to undertake the building of a Panama Canal, a monumental engineering challenge which eventually cost $340 million, took ten years to complete, and transformed the Latin American economy.[66]

U.S. historiography has overemphasized Latin American disaffection. Latin American problems were rooted in the traditions of Spanish and Catholic authoritarianism, compounded by nineteenth-century experiments with European positivism, caudillo localism, and constant struggles between positivist liberals and conservative Catholics.[67] By Theodore Roosevelt's time, Latin America had failed to become politically, culturally, or economically self-sufficient. Had José Martí lived to free Cuba instead of Theodore Roosevelt's Rough Riders, Martí might have become the George Washington of a new culture. Instead, Latin Americans in 1900 took up José Rodó's Arielism, arguing that the coarse industrial culture of the United States threatened to despoil Latin America's innocent soul—its preindustrial, premodern culture.[68]

But Colombia's enemy from 1899 to 1903 was Colombia itself. Its constant struggle with its Andean geography made unification difficult even in mainland Colombia and impossible in distant Panama. Colombia's failures were political—not dealing honorably with Panamanian needs for a canal or realistically with U.S. power which, until 1902, it used to control Panama. Colombia's leaders, wholly absorbed in their domestic conflicts and thoroughly provincial, could not comprehend the cheap competition that an alternate Nicaraguan canal route offered the United States.[69]

In 1903 Latin America was peripheral to U.S. policy. The United States needed to keep Germany from exploiting Latin American weakness as a springboard to regional domination and as a threat to Balkanize the Caribbean. Colombia, the Dominican Republic, Venezuela, and Cuba, were all adept at playing the European card—one power or creditor against the other with the United States as the ultimate wild card to play when the Europeans tired of the game and threatened intervention.[70] When Roosevelt took Europe out of Latin America, he did in fact disarm it by removing the only weapon that weak Latin American governments had been able to use effectively. But Roosevelt did not make Latin America dependent. Colombia, after the loss of Panama and even before the discovery of oil, was stronger than it was before, economically and politically.[71] What made Latin America weak was not the colossus to the North but its traditions of Spanish authoritarianism, its romance with French intellectual elitism in the nineteenth century, its ill-defined political borders and heterogeneous populations, and the same problems in coping with modernist thought and technology that bedevilled the industrial powers.

From 1899 to 1903 Colombia was a police state. Former Foreign Minister Carlos Martínez Silva languished in a Colombian jail and died in 1903. Genuine diplomacy with such a nation was not possible. Marroquín had both too much power and too little power. He was a shrewd obfuscator, an ideologue, and an historical anachronism who fought a twentieth-century religious war which cost his nation over 100,000 lives. There were no negotiating grounds between Roosevelt's America and Marroquín's Colombia. The two sides were reduced to parodies of their positions: Catholic greed or capitalist piety. Roosevelt could effectively be criticized for supporting Colombia's subjection of Panama, but Panama did not become disaffected until after Colombia thwarted its canal. However, Marroquín did not represent all of Latin America any more than he represented all of Colombia—a nation that recovered and even flourished in the brief Reyes Quinquenio that followed the loss of Panama and the end of Marroquín's rule.[72]

Roosevelt's "big stick" was an effective image in convincing Britain to consider the United States a friend, not a rival; Germany to look elsewhere for possible imperial adventures; and France to believe that the United States could deal efficiently with French Caribbean interests.[73] Roosevelt did try to make peace with Latin America. His friendship with Colombia's Rafael Reyes, Captain Albert C. Dillingham's diplomacy with the Dominicans (elites and revolutionaries), Elihu Root's courting of Brazil's Joachim Nabuco, the *modus vivendi* and the settlement of the Dominican debt with Europe, the *Marblehead* peace treaty of 1906, the Central American peace initiatives of 1907, and the attempts to satisfy Luis Drago's demands for Latin American unilateralism, all indicate an authentic good neighbor policy.[74]

It is time to put the devil theories to rest. Roosevelt was successful in ending European activism in Latin America. He never used or intended to use the "big stick" against Latin America. He did not need to. Latin America was too weak to require a big stick. Until the discovery of oil changed its status, there was not enough of economic consequence to tempt Europe to fight the United States for it.[75] Nor did Roosevelt lose Latin America; it was never Roosevelt's to lose. The inequities of the disparity between North American wealth and political unity and Latin American poverty and political disunity continue to frustrate Latin American intellectuals who have blamed Spain, Bolivar, Europe, and the United States for Latin America's problems. Latin American governments have proven more adept at manipulating whatever power was dominant than American historians or Latin American writers have given them credit for. TR makes a convenient Protestant devil, useful for a culture with a genius for magical realism. American historians should stop making this useful fiction into inaccurate history.[76]

NOTES

1. This is based upon a larger study, Richard H. Collin, *Theodore Roosevelt's Caribbean: The Panama Canal, The Monroe Doctrine, and the Latin American Context* (Baton Rouge: Louisiana State University Press,

1990), hereafter cited as *TR's Caribbean*. David F. Trask, *The War with Spain in 1898* (New York: Macmillan, 1981) is the best recent account.

2. For Roosevelt's role see Theodore Roosevelt (hereafter cited as TR), *The Rough Riders* (1899) in TR, *Works, National Edition*, 26 vols. (New York: Scribner's, 1926), vol. 11; Gerald F. Lindermann, *The Mirror of War: American Society and the Spanish American War* (Ann Arbor: University of Michigan Press, 1974), pp. 91–113; Edmund Morris, *The Rise of Theodore Roosevelt* (New York: Coward, McCann and Geoghegan, 1979), pp. 632–61; Ronald Spector, *Admiral of the New Empire: The Life and Career of George Dewey* (Baton Rouge: Louisiana State University Press, 1974), pp. 32–39; John A. S. Grenville, *Politics, Strategy, and American Diplomacy: Studies in Foreign Policy, 1873–1917* (New Haven: Yale University Press, 1966), pp. 269–81.

3. John M. Blum, *The Republican Roosevelt* (Cambridge: Harvard University Press, 1954); Eugene P. Trani, "Cautious Warrior: Theodore Roosevelt and the Diplomacy of Activism," in *Makers of American Diplomacy from Benjamin Franklin to Henry Kissinger*, ed. Frank J. Merli and Theodore A. Wilson (New York: Scribner's, 1974), pp. 305–31; Howard K. Beale, *Theodore Roosevelt and the Rise of America to World Power* (Baltimore: Johns Hopkins University Press, 1956), especially pp. 1–13. For Roosevelt's innovative use of language see Edmund Morris, "Theodore Roosevelt as Writer," paper delivered at the Woodrow Wilson Colloquium, May 17, 1983.

4. Roosevelt first used the big stick phrase as vice president in his address at the Minnesota State Fair, September 2, 1901, in TR, *Works*, 13: 474–75. See Richard H. Collin, *Theodore Roosevelt, Culture, Diplomacy and Expansion: A New View of American Imperialism* (Baton Rouge: Louisiana State University Press, 1985), p. 2; Albert Shaw, *A Cartoon History of Roosevelt's Career* (New York: Review of Reviews, 1910), especially pp. 86, 131–45.

5. Much of the negative historiography on TR is in passing, often in generally sympathetic accounts. See Richard H. Collin, "The Image of Theodore Roosevelt in American History and Thought, 1885–1965" (Ph.D. diss., New York University, 1966), p. 135; Frederick W. Marks III, *Velvet on Iron: The Diplomacy of Theodore Roosevelt* (Lincoln: University of Nebraska Press, 1979), pp. 89–90. For a careful, critical review of recent Roosevelt foreign policy historiography, see William Tilchin, "The Rising Star of Theodore Roosevelt's Diplomacy: Major Studies from Beale to the Present," *Theodore Roosevelt Association Journal* 15 (Summer 1989): 2–26.

6. William Harbaugh, *Power and Responsibility: The Life and Times of Theodore Roosevelt* (New York: Oxford University Press, 1961); Frank Ninkovich, "Theodore Roosevelt: Civilization as Ideology," *Diplomatic History* 10 (1985): 221–45.

7. Many historians use the December 6, 1904 message to Congress to date the Roosevelt Corollary (in TR, *Works*, 15: 256–58). I prefer to date the Roosevelt Corollary from its first application in the Dominican Republic, January 1905. Roosevelt's diction did not please Europeans or Latin Americans. But U.S. assumption of control relieved Europeans who were more concerned with big power

rivalries in Asia and Africa. See Collin, *TR's Caribbean,* chapter 14.

8. See Collin, *TR's Caribbean,* chapter 1; Mary Patricia Chapman, "Yankeephobia: An Analysis of the Anti-United States Bias of Certain Spanish South American Intellectuals (1898–1928)" (Ph.D. diss., Stanford University, 1950).

9. For recent reviews of dependency theory see Thomas F. O'Brien, "Dependency Revisited: A Review Essay," *Business History Review* 54 (1985): 663–70, and William Glade, "Latin America and the International Economy," in *Cambridge History of Latin America,* 5 vols., ed. Leslie Bethel (New York: Cambridge University Press, 1981–85), 4: 46–56.

10. See especially, Simón Bolívar, "The Jamaica Letter" (1815) in *The Liberator, Simón Bolívar: Man and Image,* ed. David Bushnell (New York: Knopf, 1970), pp. 11–21.

11. TR to Joseph B. Bishop, Feb. 23, 1904, in Elting E. Morison et al., eds., *The Letters of Theodore Roosevelt,* 8 vols., (Cambridge: Harvard University Press, 1951–54), 3: 734 (hereafter cited as *Letters*).

12. See Joseph L. Arbena, "The Image of an America Imperialist: Colombian Views of Theodore Roosevelt," *West Georgia College Studies in the Social Sciences,* 6 (June 1967): 3–20. Beale, *Theodore Roosevelt and the Rise of America,* pp. 448–62, is the most influential summary of Roosevelt's shortcomings. For my argument that TR's age was a brief transitional era and that World War I helped obliterate his future influence and contributed to his image as an historical anachronism, see Collin, *TR's Caribbean,* chap. 18.

13. Charles S. Campbell, *Anglo-American Understanding, 1898–1903* (Baltimore: Johns Hopkins University Press, 1957), pp. 272–76, 350–68.

14. TR to John Hay, February 18, 1900, Morison, *Letters,* 2: 1192; TR to Arthur Lee, April 24, 1901, Morison, *Letters,* 3: 64–65.

15. Fred T. Jane, *Jane's Fighting Ships: 1906–07* (London: Sampson Low Marston, 1906), p. 89, ranked the U.S. as the world's second naval power behind Britain. Samuel F. Wells, Jr., "British Strategic Withdrawal from the Western Hemisphere," *Canadian Historical Review* 49 (1968): 335–66. Richard D. Challener, *Admirals, Generals, and American Foreign Policy, 1898–1914* (Princeton: Princeton University Press, 1973), pp. 81–178.

16. Ernest L. Woodward, *Great Britain and the German Navy* (London: Oxford Clarendon, 1935); Arthur Marder, *The Anatomy of British Sea Power* (London: F. Cass, 1940); and Paul Kennedy, *The Rise of the Anglo-German Antagonism, 1860–1914* (London: Allen and Unwin, 1980), pp. 223–88.

17. Campbell, *Anglo-American Understanding;* George Monger, *The End of Isolation* (London: Nelson, 1963).

18. John L. Gignilliat, "Pigs, Politics, and Protection: The European Boycott of American Pork, 1879–1891," *Agricultural History* 35 (1961): 3–12; Manfred Jonas, *The United States and Germany: A Diplomatic History* (Ithaca: Cornell University Press, 1984), pp. 35–69; Holger H. Herwig, *Politics of Frustration: The United States in German Naval Planning, 1889–1941* (Boston: Little, Brown, 1976), pp. 3–92.

19. Walter LaFeber, *New Empire: An Interpretation of American*

Expansion, 1860–1898 (Ithaca: Cornell University Press, 1963), pp. 354–57; William L. Langer, *The Diplomacy of Imperialism*, 2d ed. (New York: Knopf, 1951), pp. 451–54; Thomas Bailey, "Dewey and the Germans at Manila Bay," *American Historical Review* 45 (1939): 59–81; Ronald Spector, *Admiral of the New Empire: The Life and Career of George Dewey* (Baton Rouge: Louisiana State University Press, 1974), pp. 137–53.

20. Charles D. Sigsbee, Report to the General Board, May 21, 1900, Germany versus the United States—West Indies, in General Board War Portfolios, File 425, Record Group 80, National Archives; Problem of Summer, 1901, Record Group 12, Naval War College Archives, Newport, RI; John A. S. Grenville, "Diplomacy and War Plans in the United States, 1890–1917," in *The War Plans of the Great Powers, 1880–1914*, ed. Paul M. Kennedy (Boston: Unwin, 1985), pp. 1–22.

21. Jonathan Steinberg, *Yesterday's Deterrent: Tirpitz and the Birth of the German Battle Fleet* (New York: Macmillan, 1965); Ivo Nikolai Lambi, *The Navy and German Power Politics, 1862–1914* (Boston: Unwin, 1984), pp. 226–35.

22. Chester Tan, *The Boxer Catastrophe* (New York: Columbia University Press, 1955); Richard O'Connor, *The Boxer Rebellion* (London: Robert Hall, 1974), especially pp. 8–9.

23. Walter Herrick, Jr., *The American Naval Revolution* (Baton Rouge: Louisiana University Press, 1966); Daniel J. Costello, "Planning for War: A History of the General Board of the Navy, 1900–1914" (Ph.D. diss., Fletcher School of Law and Diplomacy, Tufts University, 1959); Daniel Howard Wicks, "New Navy and New Empire: The Life and Times of John Grimes Walker" (Ph.D. diss., University of California, Berkeley, 1979), pp. 407–25; Lewis L. Gould, *The Presidency of William McKinley* (Lawrence: University Press of Kansas, 1980), especially pp. 231–53.

24. Hermann Hagedorn, *The Roosevelt Family of Sagamore Hill* (New York: Macmillan, 1954), pp. 227–29; Gordon Carpenter O'Gara, *Theodore Roosevelt and the Rise of the Modern Navy* (Princeton: Princeton University Press, 1943), pp. 64–69.

25. Raymond A. Esthus, *Theodore Roosevelt and the International Rivalries* (1970; reprint, Claremont, CA: Regina Books, 1982); Ninkovich, "Theodore Roosevelt"; William Harbaugh, *The Life and Times of Theodore Roosevelt* (New York: Collier Books, 1975), pp. 260–61; Raymond A. Esthus, *Double Eagle and Rising Sun: The Russians and Japanese at Portsmouth in 1905* (Durham, NC: Duke University Press, 1988); Peter Larsen, "Theodore Roosevelt and the Moroccan Crisis, 1904–1906" (Ph.D. diss., Princeton University Press, 1984).

26. Tyler Dennett, "Could Theodore Roosevelt Have Stopped the War?" *World's Work* 49 (February 1925): 392–99.

27. Wayne Lee Guthrie, "The Anglo-German Intervention in Venezuela, 1902–03" (Ph.D. diss., University of California, San Diego, 1983) especially pp. 46–107; Holger H. Herwig and J. León Helguera, *Alemania y el bloqueo internacional de Venezuela 1902–03* (Caracas: Editorial Arte, 1977).

28. Campbell, *Anglo-American Understanding*, p. 274.

29. Herwig, *Politics of Frustration*, pp. 72–76.

30. Henry Pringle, *Theodore Roosevelt: A Biography* (New York: Harcourt Brace, 1931), pp. 281–82; Jonas, *The United States and Germany*, pp. 69–70.

31. Lord Lansdowne to Sir R. Rodd, December 5, 1902; Lansdowne to George Buchanan, December 7 and 11, 1902, FO [Foreign Office] 420/206, Public Record Office, Kew, England; Guthrie, "Anglo-German Intervention," pp. 95–97. See Maurizio Vernassa, *Emigrazione, diplomazia e cannoniero: L'interventi italiano in Venezuela, 1902–1903* (Leghorn: Editrice Stella, 1980).

32. German thoughts on occupying Venezuelan ports are in Warren G. Kneer, *Great Britain and the Caribbean, 1901–1913: A Study in Anglo-American Relations* (East Lansing: Michigan State University Press, 1975); German interests and ambitions are in Holger H. Herwig, *Germany's Vision of Empire in Venezuela, 1871–1914* (Princeton: Princeton University Press, 1986), especially pp. 93–94, 238–39. An American assessment of German superiority is in Charles D. Sigsbee, memorandum, March 22, 1902, Reel 25, Theodore Roosevelt Papers, Library of Congress (hereafter cited as TR Papers).

33. Herwig, *Germany's Vision of Empire in Venezuela*, p. 22. For the preponderance of British North American naval interests in the Newfoundland fisheries see the detailed reports in ADM [Admiralty] 128/107, Public Record Office; Harold A. Innes, *The Cod Fisheries: The History of an International Economy* (Toronto: University of Toronto Press, 1954).

34. Kneer, *Great Britain and the Caribbean*, p. 15; Jacob Hollander, "Debt of Santo Domingo," Communications from Special Agents, Microfilm M37, Roll 21, Record Group 59, National Archives.

35. Seward Livermore, "Theodore Roosevelt, The American Navy, and the Venezuelan Crisis of 1902–03," *American Historical Review*, 51 (1946): 452–71; TR to George Dewey and TR to Thomas C. Platt, June 14 and 28, 1902, both in Morison, *Letters*, 3: 275, 283; *Annual Report of the Secretary of the Navy*, 1903, Ser. 4642, pp. 646–50; Journal of the Commander-in-Chief, Dec. 1, 1902 to Jan. 1903 in Box 2, George Dewey Papers, Library of Congress; Kenneth Bourne, *Britain and the Balance of Power in North America, 1815–1908* (Berkeley: University of California Press, 1967), pp. 346–47. Peter Karsten, "Nature of 'Influence': Roosevelt, Mahan, and the Concept of Sea Power," *American Quarterly*, 23 (1971): 585–600.

36. Henry Clay Taylor, undated memorandum reprinted in A. L. P. Dennis, *Adventures in American Diplomacy, 1896–1906* (New York: Dutton, 1928), pp. 291–92.

37. The controversy over Roosevelt's ultimatum to Germany began when Roosevelt revealed it in 1916 as part of his criticism of Wilson's German policies. See TR to William R. Thayer, August 21, 1916, in Morison, *Letters*, 8: 1,101–5. The question should be put to rest by Marks, *Velvet on Iron*, pp. 38–54, 70–73; and Edmund Morris, "'A Few Pregnant Days': Theodore Roosevelt and the Venezuelan Crisis of 1902," *Theodore Roosevelt Association Journal* 15 (Winter 1989): 2–13.

38. Paul S. Holbo, "Perilous Obscurity: Public Diplomacy and the Press in the Venezuela Crisis, 1902–1903," *Historian* 32 (1970): 428–48; Edward D. Parsons, "The German-American Crisis of 1902–1903," *Historian* 33 (1971): 436–52; William Sullivan, "The Rise of Despotism in Venezuela: Cipriano Castro, 1899–1908" (Ph.D. diss., University of New Mexico, 1974), especially pp. 316–430; D. C. M. Platt, "The Allied Coercion of Venezuela, 1902–3—A Reassessment," *Inter-American Economic Affairs* 15 (Spring 1962): 3–28.

39. Campbell, *Anglo-American Understanding*, pp. 278–81; Allan Nevins, *Henry White: Thirty Years of American Diplomacy* (New York: Harper, 1930), p. 210; Collin, *TR's Caribbean*, chapter 4.

40. Blake, "Ambassadors at the Court of Theodore Roosevelt," pp. 180–89; Herwig, "Germany's Vision of Empire," pp. 202–3; French surprise at Holleben's recall is in Chargé de Margerie to Ministère des Affaires Étrangères, January 12, 1903, in Ministère des Affaires Étrangères, *Documents Diplomatique Français, 1871–1912*, 2d Série, 14 vols. (Paris: Imprimerie Nationale, 1930–55), 3: 23–27.

41. Calvin DeArmond Davis, *The United States and the Second Hague Peace Conference* (Durham: Duke University Press, 1975), pp. 72–90.

42. TR, *Presidential Addresses and State Papers*, 8 vols. (New York: Review of Reviews, 1910), 1: 265.

43. Marks, *Velvet on Iron*, pp. 43–47; TR to Taylor; TR to Dewey, March 20, 1903 in Joseph B. Bishop, *Theodore Roosevelt and His Times*, 2 vols. (New York: Scribner's, 1920), 1: 239; Spector, *Admiral of the New Empire*, pp. 145–46.

44. See Collin, *TR's Caribbean*, chaps. 5–11.

45. Dwight Carroll Miner, *The Fight for the Panama Route* (New York: Columbia University Press, 1940), pp. 110–11; Miles DuVal, *Cadiz to Cathay* (Stanford: Stanford University Press, 1940), p. 173.

46. The Story of Panama: Hearings on the Rainey Resolution Before the Committee on Foreign Affairs of the House of Representatives (Washington, DC: Government Printing Office, 1913), p. 174; Collin, *TR's Caribbean*, chap. 7.

47. J. Leon Helguera, "The Problems of Liberalism Versus Conservatism in Colombia, 1849–85," in *Latin American History: Select Problems, Identity, Integration, and Nationhood*, ed. Frederick B. Pike (New York: Harcourt, Brace, 1969), pp. 224–58; Charles Bergquist, *Coffee and Conflict in Colombia, 1886–1910* (Durham, NC: Duke University Press, 1978); Helen Delpar, *Red Against Blue: The Liberal Party in Colombian Politics, 1863–1899* (University, AL: University of Alabama Press, 1981).

48. For Marroquín's role, see Thomas R. Favell, "The Antecedents of Panama's Separation from Colombia" (Ph.D. diss., Fletcher School of Law and Diplomacy, Tufts University, 1951); Marks, *Velvet on Iron*, pp. 99–105. For the view that Marroquín was an effective political ideologue, see Collin, *TR's Caribbean*, chaps. 7–11.

49. For the interventions of 1856, 1860, 1865, 1868, 1873 (2), 1885 (2), 1901, 1902 (2) and 1903, see Milton Offutt, *The Protection of Citizens Abroad by Armed Forces of the United States* (Baltimore: Johns Hopkins

University Press, 1928); for 1856 to 1885 and 1900–1902 see *The Use of Military Force in Colombia, Senate Documents*, 58th Cong., 2nd Sess., No. 143, Serial 4,589.

50. Alfred Charles Richard, Jr., "The Panama Canal in American National Consciousness, 1870–1922" (Ph.D. diss., Boston University, 1969), pp. 166–70.

51. Miles DuVal, *And the Mountains Will Move* (Stanford: Stanford University Press, 1947), pp. 45–66; Gerstle Mack, *The Land Divided: A History of the Panama Canal and Other Isthmian Canal Projects* (New York: Knopf, 1944), pp. 300–9; David Pletcher, *The Awkward Years: American Foreign Policy under Garfield and Arthur* (Colombia: University of Missouri Press, 1962), pp. 278–83. For the technological superiority of the Panama route, see George Abbott Morison, *George Shattuck Morison, 1842-1903* (Peterborough, NH: Peterborough Historical Society, 1940), pp. 3–14; Richard, "Panama Canal in American Consciousness," pp. 116–40; Gustave Anguizola, *Phillipe Bunau-Varilla: The Man Behind the Panama Canal* (Chicago: Nelson Hall, 1980), pp. 6, 118–33, 183–87.

52. Collin, *TR's Caribbean*, chap. 9; McCullough, *Path Between the Seas*, pp. 343–60; G. A. Mellander, *The United States in Panamanian Politics: The Intriguing Formative Years* (Danville, IL: Interstate, 1971), pp. 10–22. For the British estimate that 75 percent of Panama's population was liberal and favored a canal even if secession was necessary, see G. F. Rothwinger to Lord Lansdowne, November 11, 1903, FO 420/210, p. 72, Public Record Office, Kew.

53. *Baltimore Evening Sun*, November 9, 1903; Herwig, *Germany's Vision of Empire in Venezuela*, pp. 41–74.

54. One of the mildest reproaches is in Richard W. Leopold, *The Growth of American Foreign Policy* (New York: Knopf, 1962), p. 232; one of the strongest is George E. Mowry, *The Era of Theodore Roosevelt and the Birth of Modern America* (New York: Harper, 1958), p. 155: "For Roosevelt ethics stopped at the tidewater beyond which lay a moral jungle where power was the only rightful determinant." Besides, Collin, *TR's Caribbean*, chapters 9 to 11, about the only defense of TR's Panama policies are in Marks, *Velvet on Iron*, pp. 99–105; and Robert A. Friedlander, "A Reassessment of Roosevelt's Role in the Panamanian Revolution of 1903," *Western Political Quarterly*, 14 (1961): 535–43. There are promising signs that the perception is changing. Recent and more nuanced references to Roosevelt's Panama policy are in Robert Pastor, *Condemned to Repetition: The United States and Nicaragua* (Princeton: Princeton University Press, 1987), p. 287; and Edward M. Bennett, Review of *America Invulnerable: The Quest for Absolute Security from 1812 to Star Wars*, by James Chace and Caleb Carr, *American Historical Review*, 94 (1989): 1,201. For an analysis of why historical opinion on TR is more favorable see Tilchin, "Rising Star of Theodore Roosevelt's Diplomacy," especially pp. 16–17.

55. Arnold M. Freedman, "The Independence of Panama and Its Incorporation in Gran Colombia, 1820–1830" (Ph.D. diss., University of Florida, 1978); Alex Perez-Venero, *Before the Five Frontiers: Panama from 1821–1903* (New York: AMS, 1978); Ramon Valdes, "The

Independence of the Isthmus of Panama—Its History, Causes, and Justification," in U.S. Dept. of State, *Papers Relating to the Foreign Relations of the United States* (Washington, DC: Government Printing Office 1861–), 1903 (hereafter cited as *Foreign Relations of U.S.*), pp. 319–33. For the interventions, see note 49.

56. Assistant Secretary of State Francis Loomis used the Balkan analogy in his speech before the Quill Club in New York on December 15, 1903. See *New York Times*, December 16, 1903. For the technological superiority of the Panama route, see note 51.

57. American historians have consistently sentimentalized Colombia and Marroquín accepting Colombia's arguments as a victim of American haste or imperialism at face value. Colombia's relationship with Panama and the domestic crises of its War of a Thousand Days seldom enter into American accounts almost wholly focused on what the Americans or Roosevelt did. See especially Joseph Arbena, "The Panama Problem in Columbian History" (Ph.D. diss., University of Virginia, 1970); and Favell, "The Antecedents of Colombia's Separation from Panama." Marks, *Velvet on Iron*, pp. 101–5, summarizes criticism of Marroquín and is the first American work to treat him as an effective political force. See Collin, *TR's Caribbean*, chaps. 6-11 for an extended consideration of Marroquín's importance.

58. TR, *Autobiography* (1913) in TR, *Works*, 20: 510, 549–50. The U.S. justification is contained in the John Bassett Moore Memorandum, August 15, 1903 in Miner, *Fight for the Panama Route*, pp. 427–52.

59. For Captain Chauncey Humphrey's and Lieutenant Mallet-Prevost Murphy's detailed report to TR on October 16 at the White House see Pringle, *Theodore Roosevelt*, pp. 320–21; the surviving records are in Lt. Gen. S. B. M. Young to Elihu Root, December 24, 1903, in vol. 177, pt. 1, Elihu Root Papers, Library of Congress; and War College Division Record Cards, Microfilm M1023, Roll 1, 646, 715; Roll 2, 1190, 1301, and 1400, Record Group 165, National Archives. A confirming naval report, John Hubbard to William Moody, October 17, 1903, is in Challener, *Admirals, Generals, and U.S. Foreign Policy*, p. 154. Roosevelt began the orders for naval support after the Chauncey-Humphrey meeting. A summary of the naval orders is in DuVal, *Cadiz to Cathay*, pp. 313–14. See Collin, *TR's Caribbean*, chap. 9.

60. Lucien Napoleon-Bonaparte Wyse, *Le rapt de Panama: L'abandon de canal aux Etats-Unis* (Toulon: Imprimerie Régionale Romain Liautaud, 1904), is a protest against French approval of the U.S. intervention by the man who negotiated the first French concession with Colombia in 1878. Recent accounts include Richard L. Lael, *Arrogant Diplomacy: U.S. Policy Toward Colombia, 1903–1922* (Wilmington, DE: Scholarly Resources, 1987); Walter LaFeber, *The Panama Canal: The Crisis in Historical Perspective* (New York: Oxford University Press, 1979). Most Panama canal accounts have blindly accepted the Colombian diplomatic arguments—rejected at the time by Europe and Latin American governments, and the Democratic party's initial arguments—rejected by the Congress, almost all of the press, and by whatever public opinion could be measured. The

Democratic challenge collapsed, and Roosevelt later urged his campaign strategists to use the Panama canal issue: "we have not a stronger card" (TR to Nathan Bay Scott, October 9, 1904, in Morison, *Letters*, 4: 978). For the Democratic strategy and collapse, see John R. Lambert, *Arthur Pue Gorman* (Baton Rouge: Louisiana University Press, 1953), pp. 301-8. For an early objection to the moralistic tone of historical accounts of Panama see Friedlander, "A Reassessment of Roosevelt's Role in the Panamanian Revolution of 1903."

61. For Roosevelt's justification and defense of his Panama policies see TR, January 4, 1904, message to Congress in *Story of Panama*, pp. 579–94; TR, "How the United States Acquired the Right to Dig the Panama Canal," *Outlook* 99 (October 7, 1911): 314–18. For a Colombian view that Colombia's rejection of the Hay-Herrán Treaty was "brutal," "unrealistic," and based on a "disastrous misunderstanding of the international reality," see Eduardo Lemaitre, *Reyes* (Bogotá: Editorial Iqueima, 1952), p. 202, quoted in Arbena, "Panama Problem in Colombian History," p. 236.

62. E. Bradford Burns, "The Recognition of Panama by the Major Latin American States," *Americas* 26 (1969): 3–14; John Patterson, "Latin American Reaction to the Panama Revolution of 1903," *Hispanic American Historical Review*, 24 (1944): 342–51; Louis E. Norman, "Latin American Views of Panama and the Canal," *American Review of Reviews*, March 1904, p. 335; "South American Press on the Isthmian Coup," *Literary Digest*, December 26, 1903, p. 909. There is little evidence to support David Healy, *Drive to Hegemony: The United States in the Caribbean, 1898–1917* (Madison: University of Wisconsin Press, 1988), p. 90: "The American course had rested on bottom on bullying, and virtually all Latin America saw it that way." See Marks, *Velvet on Iron*, pp. 23–24, note 33.

63. Arbena, "Panama Problem in Colombian History." See Frank Otto Gatell, "The Canal in Retrospect," *Americas* 15 (July 1958): 23–36; Favell, "Antecedents of Colombia's Separation from Colombia"; and Bergquist, *Coffee and Conflict in Colombia*. For the frequent interruption of cable communications between Colombia and the U.S. and its effect upon negotiations, see Marks, *Velvet on Iron*, pp. 101-2.

64. George S. Welby to Lord Lansdowne, January 4, 1902, FO 55/408; Claude Chaucey Mallet to Lord Lansdowne, August 7, September 1, 4, 15, October 3, November 26, 28, December 19, 1902, FO 55/408; Welby to Lansdowne, March 17, 1902; Spenser Dickson to Lansdowne, June 5, December 10, 1902, FO 55/409, PRO; Emile Gey to Ministère des Affaires Étrangères, September 18, 23, October 17, 22, 1902, Nouvelle Serie, Colombie, 4, Archives Ministère des Affaires Étrangères, Paris.

65. Pierre Bonhenry to Ministère des Affaires Étrangères, November 7, 1903, N.S., Colombie, 5, Archives Ministère des Affaires Étrangères.

66. See British Vice-Consul Spenser S. Dickson, memorandum relative to the discussions in the Bogotá press on the proposed Panama Canal as a business concern, in Arthur M. Beaupre to John Hay, *Foreign Relations of the U.S.*, 1903, pp. 169–71. See also

Bunau-Varilla's comparative cost figures in Phillipe Bunau-Varilla, *Panama, The Creation, Destruction, and Resurrection* (London: Constable, 1913), pp. 218–25. British Chargé Claude Mallet thought the American offer of $7 million gold was attractive, Mallet to Lansdowne, August 7, 1902, FO 55/408, Public Record Office. A member of Marroquín's own canal commission and a Colombian economist recommended that Colombia not ask for any concession money from the United States. See, Favell, "Antecedents of Panama's Separation from Colombia," pp. 200–4. These dissenting Colombian canal reports are in *Libro Azul: documentos diplomáticos sobre el canal y la rebellion del Istmo de Panamá* (Bogotá: Imprenta Nacional, 1904), Appendix, pp. 3–9, 18, 34–35.

67. James Lang, *Conquest and Commerce: Spain and England in the Americas* (New York: Academic Press, 1975); E. Bradford Burns, *The Poverty of Progress: Latin America in the Nineteenth Century* (Berkeley: University of California Press, 1980); W. Rex Crawford, *A Century of Latin American Thought* (Cambridge: Harvard University Press, 1961); Ralph Lee Woodward, Jr., ed., *Positivism in Latin America, 1850–1900* (Lexington, MA: Heath, 1971); Glen Caudill Healy, *The Public Man: An Interpretation of Latin American and Other Catholic Countries* (Amherst, MA: University of Massachusetts Press, 1977).

68. José Enrique Rodó, *Ariel*, trans. F. J. Stimson (1900; reprint, Boston: Houghton Mifflin, 1921). See Clemente Pereda, *Rodo's Main Sources* (San Juan: Impr: Venezuela, 1941); Martin S. Stabb, *In Quest of Identity: Patterns in the Spanish-American Essay of Ideas* (Chapel Hill: University of North Carolina Press, 1967), pp. 10–11, 34–47; Collin, *TR's Caribbean*, chap. 1; Chapman, "Yankeephobia," especially, pp. 51–69.

69. Arbena, "The Panama Problem in Colombian History," especially, pp. 56–57; British Vice-Consul William Gordon to Tomás Herrán, April 16, 1903, in Tomás Herrán Papers, Georgetown University Library; Panamanian complaints quoted in TR, Message to Congress, January 4, 1904, in *Story of Panama*, p. 589.

70. Collin, *TR's Caribbean*, chapters 3–4, 12–15, 17. See David MacMichael, "The United States and the Dominican Republic, 18711940: A Cycle in Caribbean Diplomacy" (Ph.D. diss., University of Oregon, 1964), pp. 12–256. George Crichfield, *American Supremacy: The Rise and Progress of the Latin American Republics and Their Relations to the United States Under the Monroe Doctrine*, 2 vols. (New York: Brentano's, 1908) is exhaustive on Venezuela. Russell Fitzgibbon, *Cuba and the United States, 1900–1935* (Menosha, WI: George Banta, 1935), especially pp. 108–9.

71. Bergquist, *Coffee and Conflict in Colombia*, pp. 225–47.

72. See José Concha to José Marroquín, October 2, 1902, complaining of the U.S. naval intervention: "Between a power which thus imposes its force, and a government which cannot or will not defend the national sovereignty, treaties cannot be made" (quoted in Miner, *Fight for the Panama Route*, p. 176). Though Concha's context was different, he understood that Colombia's inability to control Panama made it impossible for Colombia to deal with the United States as an equal. See also Martínez Silva's warning to Marroquín

that "Panamanians of wealth and influence will never resign themselves" to a Nicaraguan canal and would secede. Martínez Silva compared himself to Cordelia and Marroquín to King Lear listening to the wrong daughters. Carlos Martínez Silva to Marroquín, March 11, 1902 in DuVal, *Cadiz to Cathay*, p. 177; Bergquist, *Coffee and Conflict in Colombia*, pp. 225–47.

73. For Britain and Germany see Collin, *TR's Caribbean*, chap. 4. Jean-Jules Jusserand to Ministère des Affaires Étrangères, November 9, 1903, Nouvelle Serie, Colombie, 5, Archives, Ministère des Affaires Étrangères, is a thoughtful assessment of American success. For U.S.-French cooperation see Phillip Jessup, *Elihu Root*, 2 vols. (New York: Dodd, Mead, 1938), 1: 495–97; André Tardieu, *France and the Alliances: The Struggle for the Balance of Power* (New York: Macmillan, 1908), pp. 281–99. For French difficulties in Caribbean interventions, see Captain Lemogne to Ministère de la Marine (hereafter cited as MM), April 5, 1904; Boue Lapeyrere to MM, December 20, 1904 in BB[4], 1679; Lapeyrere to MM, January 27, 1906, BB[4], 1703, Archives de la Marine; Château de Vincennes.

74. Collin, *TR's Caribbean*, chaps. 11, 16; Richard H. Collin "The 1904 Detroit Compact: American Naval Diplomacy and Dominican Revolutions," *Historian* 52 (May 1990): 432–52.

75. Herbert Feis, *Europe: The World's Banker* (New Haven: Yale University Press, 1930); D. C. M. Platt, *Latin America and British Trade, 1806–1914* (London: A. and C. Black, 1972); William Glade, "Latin America and the International Economy, 1870–1914," in *Cambridge History of Latin America*, ed. Bethel, 4: 1–56, 597–603.

76. For the complexities of questions of hegemony see Healy, *Drive to Hegemony*, especially pp. 260–74. The economic consequences of U.S. hegemony began after TR's presidency either with Taft's dollar diplomacy policy or the massive economic dislocation caused by World War I. World War I, not TR's big stick, made the United States a world superpower in politics, economics, and culture.

22

TR's Big Stick: Roosevelt and the Navy, 1901–1909

Robert William Love, Jr.

Theodore Roosevelt was fond of Alexander Hamilton. It seems safe to say that TR could have personally related to the title of John Miller's classic biography of the great Federalist, *Portrait in Paradox*. TR would no doubt have realized that Miller's title applied to himself as well. Roosevelt's beliefs constituted a marvelous conflicting body of thought, and this expressed itself in no field more than naval policy and strategy.

When he succeeded McKinley in 1901, Roosevelt was certainly more familiar with the Navy Department than any other branch of the federal government. He understood more about the Navy Department than any of his predecessors or successors—with the arguable exception of his cousin, Franklin, who may have served as assistant secretary of the Navy for eight years but appears to have learned very little. As TR once observed, he had studied the workings of the Navy as a historian and had participated in its use as a policymaker. As a young man of twenty-four, just out of Harvard, TR wrote *The Naval War of 1812*, a fine study that is still accepted by many naval historians as the definitive work on the subject. Young Roosevelt's *The Naval War of 1812*, observed naval historian E. B. Potter, demonstrated "his firm grasp of naval first principles." *Sea Power*, Potter's Naval Academy textbook, leaves little doubt as to what those Mahanian "first principles" are. Roosevelt's important service as assistant secretary of the Navy during the first year of the McKinley administration exposed him to many of the figures who would command the Navy during his own presidency, especially Admirals George Dewey and Henry Clay Taylor, and aroused his interest in naval administration, a controversial topic during the Progressive Era.[1]

The earliest scholarly synthesis of Roosevelt's naval policy—indeed perhaps the first scholarly synthesis of America's naval policy—is contained in Harold and Margaret Sprout's seminal work on *The Rise of American Naval Power, 1776-1918.* The Sprouts saw the Navy as progressing from the frigate-gunboat fleets of Jefferson and Madison, which they condemned, to the dispersed station squadrons of the antebellum and Reconstruction periods, which they also disliked, to the "new Navy," built first around cruisers and soon after around battleships, a naval policy they thoroughly admired. Agreeing wholeheartedly with Mahan's capital ship thesis—"Mahan Vindicated" was the title of their chapter on the Spanish-American War—they not surprisingly found favor with Roosevelt's naval policy and strategy. They would have supported Ernest May's thesis that the United States was already established as a great power by the turn of the century, and would have dismissed the arguments that this occurred earlier by Thomas Bailey, the dean of American diplomatic historians. McKinley's assassination, they wrote, "raised Roosevelt to the presidency, thereby giving the United States a Chief Executive equipped with the knowledge, the initiative, and the driving force which were needed to launch imperial America upon an imperial naval policy." As a result, "Mahan's philosophy of sea power entered the White House in the person of Theodore Roosevelt." Whereas "in previous years . . . foreign relations and international crises had frequently influenced naval development," under TR "naval policy now began to influence the spirit and direction of American foreign relations." Moreover, they approved of his administrative methods, asserting that "the naval policy of imperial America was, in large degree, the naval policy of Theodore Roosevelt."

More recent students of the Progressive Era agreed. "In a series of letters and memoranda, which in their breadth and perception resemble those of Winston Churchill during the Second World War, he supervised every aspect of national defense," Robert Sellen wrote in 1959. "Roosevelt regarded foreign policy and naval policy as the warp and woof of a seamless garment," argued Potter. "He had in mind clearcut diplomatic ends, and . . . endeavored to fashion his weapons with these foreign policy objectives in mind." Paolo Coletta, probably the foremost naval historian of the Progressive Era, and Potter's frequent critic, went even further. "Before Alfred T. Mahan's writings in the 1890s," he observed, "international relations had largely affected American naval development. Bringing Mahan's strategic ideas into the White House, Theodore Roosevelt would use naval policy as an ingredient in determining his foreign policies."

Richard Turk—whose essay on "Defending the New Empire" in Kenneth Hagan's *In Peace and War* is the best synthesis of naval policy during the period—did not comment on this aspect of Roosevelt's leadership, but Robert G. Albion did. Clearly taking his lead from the Sprouts, Albion wrote that "no other president has matched the whole-hearted, direct support he gave to the Navy." Whereas the Sprouts and Albion clearly thought this was good, others, most notably the late Howard Beale, argued in his provocative *Theodore Roosevelt and the Rise of American to World Power* that Roosevelt's entire diplomacy failed owing to what Seward Livermore called "the distorted values he acquired as a disciple of Kipling and Mahan." It should be noted that Turk's just-published study of *The Ambiguous Relationship: Theodore Roosevelt and Alfred Thayer Mahan* suggests that TR was less of a legatee of the Mahanian synthesis than either Beale or the Sprouts believed.[2]

The bare outlines of TR's naval policy are easy to trace. He told the Naval War College in 1897 that "the American people must either build and maintain an adequate Navy or else make up their minds definitely to accept a secondary position in international affairs, not merely in political, but in commercial matters." He entered the White House at a time when battleships were the standard of naval strength; that is, the number of first-class battleships a nation possessed in its fleet—almost regardless of their overseas obligations, interests, bases, or the number of lesser vessels it deployed such as cruisers, destroyers, torpedo boats, fleet train, tenders, colliers, or transports—reflected relative naval power when compared with the battlefleets of the other maritime powers. The result was that Roosevelt himself gauged the success of his naval policy on the strength of the battle line. In this respect, he was not alone. Few pre-World War I administrations laid out a complete, long-term naval shipbuilding program, and Roosevelt and his secretaries of the Navy more often than not simply deferred to Congress or the bureau chiefs when it came to deciding the numbers of lesser

warships and auxiliaries to be built. Enthused by the war with
Spain, Congress authorized three battleships in 1898, another
three in 1899, and two more in 1900. The following session,
however, marked the end of McKinley's naval expansion
program and the establishment of a "replacement" policy. "The
reelection of McKinley and the continued secretaryship of [John
D.] Long gave every prospect of a continued policy of drift and
compromise," Potter observed with a tinge of disapproval.

Either TR dramatically reversed this short-term, one-year
trend, or breathed new life into McKinley's earlier expansion
policy for, between 1901 and 1905, Congress authorized ten
first-class battleships and increased Navy spending from roughly
$85 million to about $120 million. After his own two-year hiatus,
during which he announced a replacement policy for capital
ships, Roosevelt once again adopted an expansionist policy. "The
1906 political crisis with Japan and the launching of the British
all-big-gun battleship, the *Dreadnaught*, led the president to call
for renewed construction" the following year, according to Turk.
Overcoming stiff congressional resistance, he won authorization
for two Dreadnaught-type battleships in 1908 and another pair
in 1909. While he left office with many of his naval policy goals
"unfulfilled," the growth of the battleship fleet-in-being—shown
off to the world during the 1907–1909 cruise of the Great White
Fleet—was clearly a major accomplishment. But was fleet
expansion under TR the result of consistent policy articulated
from the top, or a continuation of the general expansionist "drift"
of the Cleveland-McKinley years?[3]

Roosevelt entered the White House possessing a high
opinion of his own ability to cast naval policy. Albert C. Stillson,
a critic of TR's direction of naval affairs, concluded that, "on
balance, Roosevelt rated high in his competence to deal with
military policy when he focused his intellect upon it." On the
other hand, few argue that he did well in selecting his secretaries
of the navy, shuffling several men, some able but most mediocre,
into and out of the Navy Department, failing to allow any one of
them to remain at his job long enough to put his own print on
American naval policy. One result was that many of them could
neither articulate nor defend the administration's naval policy.

Roosevelt inherited John D. Long, his erstwhile boss, who
had vied with him for the Republican's 1900 vice-presidential
nomination. Long was an anti-imperialist Republican and a

member of the Peace Society who was uncomfortable with the costs of naval expansion and uneasy about the fact that the United States had inexorably become a world power. Long's management philosophy, and the source of some of his troubles with the Navy Department, are illustrated in his own diary: "I make a point not to trouble myself overmuch to acquire a thorough knowledge of the details pertaining to any branch of the service . . . leaving myself to the general direction of affairs." This lack of interest in technical questions may account for the state of "drift" in naval affairs to which many of his contemporaries alluded at a time when events seemed to overtake policy. The tension between TR and Long can be seen in Long's comment about creating a naval general staff, a step he opposed on the basis that it would be a "stimulus to a chief of staff to hereafter seek always direct communication with the president; and a president with aggressive force would easily come to deal with the official who is by law made the working head . . . of the department." The model of a "president with aggressive force" was, of course, sitting in the White House at the time.[4]

Long was replaced by an ex-congressman, William H. Moody, but Moody leaned heavily on the bureau chiefs and the newly created General Board of the Navy, a policy review panel without executive function, chaired by Dewey. Moody was the first secretary to openly support the establishment of a naval general staff, and there is some evidence that he did so in the belief that it would actually strengthen the Navy Department's standing with the White House. Opposition from the bureau chiefs, the assistant secretary of the Navy, and key congressmen killed the proposal, however. Moody became attorney general in 1904 and TR replaced him with Paul Morton, a railroad manager who spent most of his time campaigning for the Republican ticket that year. His tenure was as unremarkable as that of his successor, Charles Joseph Bonaparte. In 1906, Bonaparte went to the Department of Justice and his place was taken by Victor Metcalf, a former legislator, who supported the independence of the bureau chiefs and discouraged any disturbance of the status quo. Metcalf resigned after the elections of 1908, and TR promoted Assistant Navy Secretary Truman Newbury to the cabinet.

In spite of TR's encouragement, not one of these men exhibited a sure grasp of naval policy. Moody initiated the request that Dewey's General Board devise a long-term naval ship-building program, but he had no hand in its formulation, did not question its assumptions, and did not try to get the White House or Congress to adopt its prescriptions. When asked his opinion about the goal of building up to a fleet of forty-eight first-class battleships embodied in Admiral Dewey's 1903 General Naval Scheme, Moody told the House Naval Affairs Committee, "When I talk about my opinion it is a question of whose opinion I adopt. I cannot have an opinion that is worth very much." Bonaparte's important March 1906 testimony before the House Naval Affairs Committee on whether the United States should lay down a dreadnaught-type battleship was a virtual abdication of executive functions. Having asked for two 16,000-ton battleships, Bonaparte told the committee that he would be pleased with three—or one, if that one displaced 19,400 tons, slightly more than the HMS *Dreadnaught*. He provided no particular strategic rationale for building one, two, or three. When asked by Congress why Roosevelt wanted two battleships in 1908, Secretary Truman Newberry, a Detroit industrialist, responded that he did "not feel competent in this matter to do more than call your attention to the advisability, from merely administrative reasons, of the building of these vessels, and . . . would state . . . that the ships can be built at this time at a very low cost because of the lack of work in the shipyards."

In short, TR's secretaries of the Navy often presented Congress with a picture of confusion and uncertainty. With the exception of John D. Long, they supported naval expansion in principle, but repeatedly failed to articulate specific goals and almost uniformly lacked much interest in the technical issues related to achieving concrete objectives. Historians have asserted that TR's knowledge of the Navy and his grasp of key issues of naval policy more than made up for the dreary procession of mediocrities in the Navy Department, and such an interpretation can only account for the Sprouts' claim that "executive leadership in naval policy took on new meaning under Roosevelt." Roosevelt was of the view that there were two distinct aspects to naval administration, they pointed out. Any "fairly able man" could manage the "industrial" functions of the shore establishment, but the "systematic development of policy" and the "military efficiency of the fleet" required the "most attention" of the commander in chief himself.[5]

According to the Sprouts, Roosevelt "lost no time getting his naval program under way." In December 1901, he sent Congress a "ringing appeal" for new battleship construction, but stated his goal merely as a navy of "adequate size" to defend the nation and uphold the Monroe Doctrine. The result in early 1902 was an authorization to lay down the two 16,000-ton *Connecticut*-class battleships. The following year, in the midst of the crisis with Germany over Venezuela that would lead to the 1904 Roosevelt Corollary to the Monroe Doctrine, the Navy Department asked Congress for more battleships, although as noted in Secretary Moody's testimony, the administration was not quite certain what its goal was. Dewey's Naval Scheme laid down a specific second-power rationale that was consistent with TR's foreign policy and various other strategic circumstances. To reach the goal of a fleet of forty-eight vessels, the Navy would have to lay down three or four battleships each year until 1920.

How Dewey arrived at the figure of forty-eight was unclear, since the latest German Naval Law of 1900 authorized a fleet of thirty-eight battleships by 1920—and there is no evidence that Roosevelt asked him to clarify his thinking. Moreover, the Navy's long-standing Board of Construction and Repair had the last word on warship design and building policy and, as Thomas Hone and Norman Friedman recently observed, the 1903 Naval Scheme, "set the General Board on a collision course with the Board of Construction, and the disputes between the two were finally resolved only with the dissolution of the latter in 1909." As it was, the final General Board proposal for 1903 was for only two 16,000-ton battleships, and TR merely asked Congress for an increase in the battle fleet.

When Congress debated the bill, it was keenly aware of an unusually high federal surplus and the Venezuelan crisis was at its height, with Dewey warning all in sight that the kaiser was bent on violating the Monroe Doctrine. The result was an authorization to construct three 16,000–ton battleships named the *Kansas, Minnesota,* and *Vermont,* and two slower, smaller throwbacks, the 13,000–ton battleship *Idaho* and her sister, the *Mississippi.* "Senator [Eugene] Hale [of Maine] was responsible for this," Gordon C. O'Gara insisted, "and it was done over vigorous protests from Roosevelt, Dewey, and the General Board and even the House Naval Affairs Committee." And the following year, when relations with Germany had improved and the surplus expended, TR simply ignored the General Board's call for three battleships and asked Congress to authorize only one, the 16,000-ton *New Hampshire*. Did this constitute a rejection of Dewey's Naval Scheme or an attempt to balance out the five 1903 battleships with one the following year? There appears to be no answer. Although Phillip Y. Nicholson argued that it was "the informal blueprint for American naval expansion" and formed the "basis of subsequent reports, recommendations, and arguments," he admits that "this long-term building program was never officially approved, or even debated, by any representative or public body." Indeed, it was not until Navy Secretary Josephus Daniels got into a fight with the General Board ten years later that the plan was explained to Congress.[6]

Courtesy of Theodore Roosevelt Association

President Theodore Roosevelt in 1905

TR was momentarily less alarmed about the German Navy's plans than with congressional economy. During 1904, an election year, he announced a plan to "maintain" the fleet at existing levels. In March 1905, TR confided to General Leonard Wood that he had "now reached my mark" for the battle force, a level which "puts us a good second to France and about on a par with

Germany." A few months later he announced that he would thenceforth follow a replacement policy for the battle force which could "be obtained by adding a single battleship to our Navy each year." He told Congress early in 1905 that the authorized total of twenty-eight battleships and twenty armored cruisers was enough and asked for a "replacement" policy based on an average of one battleship that year and each year thereafter. "It does not seem necessary that the Navy should, at least in the immediate future, be increased beyond the present number of units," he announced. But Congress simply ignored this policy and authorized the construction of two more 16,000-ton battleships, the *Michigan* and *South Carolina*.[7]

One of the decisive events in the naval history of the Roosevelt administration was the appearance of HMS *Dreadnaught* and the president's decision that the Navy should install a single-caliber main battery in its first dreadnaught-type, the battleship *Delaware*. "The launching of the *Dreadnaught* came at a singularly difficult time for the U.S. Navy." There were roughly twelve first-line battleships in the fleet, another thirteen under construction or authorized. "In such circumstances," Hone and Friedman pointed out, "designs could not be based solidly on experience, even though the very rapid changes in naval technology then taking place set a premium upon the operational evaluation of designs." The *South Carolina* and *Michigan* were to be armed with single-caliber main batteries consisting of eight 12-inch guns on the centerline, but Dewey, Rear Admiral Seaton Schroeder, naval inventor Captain Bradley Fiske, and Lieutenant Commander William S. Sims, TR's naval aide, on one side, and Mahan and Rear Admiral William Lee Capps, the chief of the Bureau of Construction, on the other, were embroiled in a terrific argument over the merits of the single-versus the mixed-caliber main battery. The issue was not new. Dewey had proposed building a single-caliber battleship as early as 1902, but there were opponents aplenty. "Unless the country—and Congress—are prepared for practically unlimited expenditure, bigger ships mean fewer ships," Mahan had warned Secretary Long several years earlier. Sims countered that "for the sum that it would cost to maintain twenty small battleships we could maintain a fleet of ten large ones that would be greatly superior in tactical qualities, in effective hitting capacity, speed protection, and inherent ability to concentrate its gunfire."[8] The administration had asked

Congress for two battleships for 1906, but TR did not act on the single-caliber main battery issue until the appearance of the *Dreadnaught* forced his reluctant hand and on December 19, 1906, he informed Congressman George Foss, the chairman of the House Naval Affairs Committee, that he wanted a single-caliber main battery installed in the new battleship *Delaware.*[9]

A series of overseas developments—tension with Japan over the San Francisco School Board incident and a new German Naval Law—forced TR to reevaluate his naval policy in early 1907. According to the Sprouts, these events "galvanized the President into action" and caused him to warn Congress "that we must build dreadnoughts or relinquish our policy power and position in both oceans." He approved a request for four battleships, but after a furious battle Congress halved this number and authorized the Navy to lay down the single-caliber main battery battleship *North Dakota* and another *Delaware*-class battleship. "By demanding four, Roosevelt secured two battleships instead of one, thereby smashing the one-a-year replacement policy, which he had previously endorsed." Stillson, on the other hand, concluded that "the internal logic of American naval policy was rent asunder hopelessly." Not only was the fleet hopelessly imbalanced in favor of capital ships—something even TR recognized at last—but also the lack of any orderly expansion program was preventing the Navy from exploiting new technology in digestible increments.[10]

In 1908, after Congress had appropriated funds to build a pair of *Utah*-class battleships at the height of popular enthusiasm over the voyage of the Great White Fleet, Roosevelt sent up to Capitol Hill another message asking for a total of four new dreadnoughts. The Democrats charged that Roosevelt was stoking the fires of an international naval arms race and, to please their Irish- and German-American constituents, charged TR with siding with the British in several recent international disputes. Rather than attack the popular ship-building program directly, however, congressional Democrats attempted to restrict the fleet by limiting the displacement of the battleships *Wyoming* and *Arkansas* to 21,000 tons, but the Republican majority on the Hill defeated this amendment and enacted a measure authorizing two more dreadnoughts. Thus, TR left office on the crest of the wave of the cruise of the Great White Fleet, leaving behind a legacy for Taft of a vastly expanded battle fleet—and for historians an enduring riddle about his naval policy.

Stillson's important 1962 interpretation of TR's naval policy drew on the architecture of the 1950s feud between Eisenhower and his joint chiefs of staff over the president's New Look defense program and his strategy of Massive Retaliation. He approvingly quoted General Maxwell Taylor, who had abruptly resigned as Army chief of staff over the New Look in 1959, as saying, "Our machinery for planning the defense strategy of the United States does not do the job" owing to a lack of "clear and unambiguous guidance to the military strategists." Reviewing many of these points, Stillson charged that "the naval policy of Theodore Roosevelt's administration is open to basically the same criticisms which General Taylor directed at the Executive Branch." That perspective may be less useful in evaluating Roosevelt's naval policy than Navy Secretary John Lehman's more recent campaign for a 600-ship Navy. Aware that support for President Ronald Reagan's defense policy would not last long—indeed it really only lasted from 1981 to 1984—Lehman presented Congress with a truly ambitious program during his first two years in office and by December 1982 had effectively won authorization for most of the ships he wanted. The last two *Nimitz*-class carriers, authorized in 1986, were an unanticipated extra. Clearly the Sprouts overemphasized Roosevelt's commitment to Mahan's "principles" and his vision of an American fleet, but Stillson asked too much in expecting TR to bend to a simple, straightforward plan for fleet expansion. The slow birth of the 600-ship Navy and of TR's Great White Fleet both demonstrate that naval policy is less the product of presidential or military planning—or military guidance—than of an interplay of personalities, public opinion, partisan politics, and overseas events.[11]

NOTES

1. E. B. Potter et al., *Sea Power*, 1st ed. (Englewood Cliffs, NJ: Prentice-Hall, 1960), p. 380n.

2. Harold and Margaret Sprout, *The Rise of American Naval Power, 1776–1918* (Princeton: Princeton University Press, 1939); Ernest R. May, *Imperial Democracy: The Emergence of America as a Great Power* (Cambridge: Harvard University Press, 1961); Thomas A. Bailey, "America's Emergence as a Great Power: The Myth and the Verity," Presidential Address, Pacific Coast Historical Association, 1960 (copy in Nimitz Library, U.S. Naval Academy); Robert W. Sellen, "The Just

Man Armed—Theodore Roosevelt on War," *Military Review* 32, no. 2 (May 1959): 41; Potter, *Sea Power*, p. 380; Paolo Coletta, *A Survey of U.S. Naval Affairs, 1865–1918* (Lanham, MD: University Press of America, 1987), p. 105; Richard Turk, "Defending the New Empire, 1900–1914," *In Peace and War: Interpretations of American Naval History, 1775–1984*, ed. Kenneth J. Hagan, 2d ed. (Westport, CT: Greenwood Press, 1984), pp. 186–204; Robert G. Albion, *Makers of Naval Policy, 1798-1947* (Annapolis: Naval Institute Press, 1980), p. 212; Howard K. Beale, *Theodore Roosevelt and Rise of America to World Power* (Baltimore: Johns Hopkins Press, 1956); Seward Livermore, "Review of Beale, *Theodore Roosevelt*," *American Historical Review* 76, no. 2 (1957): 947–48; and Richard Turk, *The Ambiguous Relationship: Theodore Roosevelt and Alfred Thayer Mahan* (Westport, CT: Greenwood Press, 1989).

    3. Coletta, *Naval Affairs*, p. 105.

    4. Albert C. Stillson, "Military Policy without Political Guidance: Theodore Roosevelt's Navy," *Military Affairs* 26 (1962): 19; and John D. Long, *The New American Navy* (New York: Outlook Company, 1903) 2: 184–85.

    5. Stillson, "Military Policy," p. 21; Laurence S. Mayo, ed., *America of Yesterday as Reflected in the Journal of John D. Long* (Boston: Atlantic Monthly Press, 1923), p. 157; Sprouts, *Rise*, p. 259; and Elting E. Morison, ed., *The Letters of Theodore Roosevelt* (Cambridge: Harvard University Press, 1951–52), 4: 847–48.

    6. Sprouts, *Rise*, pp. 259-60; Stillson, "Military Policy," p. 22; and Thomas Hone and Norman Friedman, "Innovation and Administration in the Navy Department: The Case of the Nevada Design," *Military Affairs* 45, no. 2 (April 1981): 58; Gordon C. O'Gara, *Theodore Roosevelt and the Rise of the Modern Navy* (Princeton: Princeton University Press, 1943), p. 65; and Philip Y. Nicholson, "Admiral Dewey after Manila Bay," *American Neptune* 37, no. 1 (January 1977): 32.

    7. Mahan to Long, January 31, 1900, Mahan Mss., Library of Congress; O'Gara, *Roosevelt*, p. 10; and Spector, *Dewey*, pp. 152–53.

    8. Hone and Friedman, "Innovation and Administration," p. 58.

    9. Richard Hough, *Dreadnaught* (New York: Macmillan, 1964), p. 36.

    10. Sprouts, *Rise*, pp. 264–68; and Stillson, "Military Policy," p. 28.

    11. Stillson, "Military Policy," p. 19.

23

Ambassador J. J. Jusserand, Theodore Roosevelt, and Franco-American Relations, 1903-1909

Aaron P. Forsberg

Jean Jules Jusserand, French ambassador and close friend of President Theodore Roosevelt, is probably best known for being a member of the president's "Tennis Cabinet." In histories of the Roosevelt years, scholars usually mention Jusserand's friendship with the president, include an anecdote or two about their walks in Rock Creek Park, and conclude that while Ambassador Jusserand had some influence on American policy, it was at the margins rather than the core.[1] A closer examination reveals that there was more to Jusserand's career than his walks with the president, and that Roosevelt's foreign policy was more complex than the pursuit of a few essential state interests. Jusserand was keenly aware of French interests, and was able to exploit the highly personal character of Roosevelt's administration to his advantage. The ambassador thus deserves part of the credit for the remarkable Franco-American diplomatic cooperation during the Roosevelt years, and his career offers insight into President Roosevelt's approach to diplomacy.

When Jusserand presented his credentials to President Roosevelt on February 7, 1903, he had already known remarkable accomplishment in both scholarship and diplomacy. In his youth he was a talented student. And in 1876, after he had completed his studies, he entered the French Consular Service. Jusserand's professional ascent at the Foreign Ministry was rapid. By the time he came to America he had served with distinction in various capacities in London, Paris, Tunis, and Copenhagen.[2]

Throughout these years Jusserand also distinguished himself as a scholar. While serving as an apprentice in Paris, he completed a doctorate in letters. Then, in London, Jusserand turned his attention to English history, and wrote prodigiously on a variety of topics in history and literature. He became friends with numerous leading scholars and took part in scholarly activities in Paris. Two of his most popular works were *English Wayfaring Life in the Middle Ages, Fourteenth Century*, and *A Literary History of the English People*.[3]

In America, Jusserand's reputation as an accomplished scholar contributed to his success in diplomacy. President Roosevelt was always eager to meet anyone "out of the common" and he took an immediate interest in the new ambassador. At their first meeting the two men established an excellent rapport. Roosevelt was interested in countless scholarly topics, some of them obscure indeed, and Jusserand's erudition impressed him.[4]

J. J. Jusserand and Elise Richards, his American wife, spent much of their first year in the United States away from Washington, making an acquaintance with the country and the American people. Jusserand nevertheless met Roosevelt several times.[5] Each time, the president's seemingly irrepressible intellectual curiosity was the driving force behind the conversation. Roosevelt read voraciously in history and literature, and he loved to talk to others about his latest interests. Many of the president's visitors certainly dreaded the prospect of having to answer myriad questions about leading English statesmen, or the Mongols, or some other exotic topic. For Jusserand, however, Roosevelt's intellectual curiosity provided the ideal opportunity to present himself in the best possible light. Having read widely, and possessing a quick mind and ready sense of humor, he entered easily into such conversation with the president.[6] With time the two men's enthusiasm for intellectual inquiry extended beyond an occasional conversation. The ambassador and his wife became regular guests of the president. Roosevelt and Jusserand also wrote to one another about their latest intellectual interests.[7] Beginning early on, the president often consulted Jusserand in choosing his readings.

Further strengthening the bond between Roosevelt and Jusserand was their similarity in world view. Both men shared a belief in the superiority of Western civilization, a faith in progress, and a reverence for patriotism. Politically they were committed to steering a course between rule by the trust builders on the one hand, and socialist revolutionaries on the other.[8]

Roosevelt's passion for scholarship was matched only by his love of the outdoors, and after a while he invited Jusserand to go on a "walk" with him in Rock Creek Park. The president's enthusiasm for "the strenuous life" being what it was, the outing was by any standard an adventure.[9] In the following months, Roosevelt invited Jusserand on several other treks and to play tennis as well. On the tennis court Jusserand was Roosevelt's equal, and the two men played frequently.[10]

Writers and historians have made much of the excursions to Rock Creek Park, portraying them as something either much more or much less significant than they really were. That such invitations were tokens of friendship and a high honor indeed, there is no doubt. But to say that they symbolized an intimate friendship between the two men—and, by extension, their respective countries—obscures more than it clarifies.[11] There exists considerable evidence, especially in Roosevelt's letters to his son Kermit, that these hikes required more effort on Jusserand's part than is usually assumed.[12] Jusserand's walks with Roosevelt thus say as much about the lengths to which the ambassador went in order to cultivate a close relationship with the president as they do about the relationship itself.

To dismiss Roosevelt's walks with Jusserand, and for that matter their friendship in general, as entertaining, but essentially trivial, is to ignore an essential characteristic of Roosevelt's foreign policy, namely his intensely personal approach to diplomacy.[13] The president had no use for impersonal dispatches and the steady routine of the State Department. He preferred to attend to affairs of state personally.[14] He made an effort to court the representatives whom foreign governments sent to Washington. This active involvement on the part of the president gave the Roosevelt years their distinctive character. It also affected the substance of the president's foreign policy. Roosevelt was a political realist, but in this environment his personal likes and dislikes invariably influenced relations between the United States and other nations.

European governments were aware of Roosevelt's preference for personal diplomacy. In 1902 the British government had appointed Sir Michael Herbert, an old friend of the president, to the diplomatic post in Washington. Soon after, the German government also attempted to win Roosevelt's favor by naming Baron Hermann Speck von Sternburg, another of the president's friends, as ambassador to the United States. Sternburg, in particular, was a regular visitor at the White House and worked hard to court the American press.[15]

Jusserand thus took seriously his job as ambassador. Ever since his youth, France had stood in Germany's shadow. After the Franco-Prussian War, the French had resigned themselves to the territorial arrangement on the continent, but they had never ceased to believe that German power was essentially hostile to France. Beginning during the 1890s the French government attempted to bolster French security by aligning other powers on the side of France. Toward this end, French leaders concluded a treaty of alliance with Russia in 1893, and settled outstanding differences over colonial matters with Great Britain in the Entente Cordiale in 1904. Jusserand had long been affiliated with the architects of this new strategy. And, as ambassador to the United States, he regarded it as his task to cultivate American goodwill toward France while making sure that the New World power did not drift into the German camp.[16]

Rather than competing with Sternburg for publicity, Jusserand chose to negotiate with Secretary of State John Hay a treaty of arbitration, and to cultivate a personal relationship with the president. Owing to the strongly isolationist sentiment of the Senate, little came of the first endeavor. But the ambassador was successful in winning over the president.[17] He even had Roosevelt reading classics of French literature such as the *Song of Roland* in his effort to portray French history and culture as favorably as possible.

The occasion which really brought Roosevelt and Jusserand together, however, was the crisis growing out of the Russo-Japanese War. After years of jockeying for power in East Asia, Russia and Japan went to war in February of 1904.[18] Although the United States and France supported opposite sides, there was never any danger that the two powers would be drawn into the conflict. At first Roosevelt enthusiastically favored the Japanese. But come autumn the ambassador found that the president's enthusiasm had waned. Convinced that both international order and U.S. security were best served by a balance of power in East Asia, Roosevelt did not relish the prospect of a Japanese victory which would destroy the Russian presence there.[19]

Toward this end, President Roosevelt and Secretary Hay first sought to prevent the instability from spreading to China. In January 1905 Roosevelt turned to Jusserand for assurances that France had no territorial designs on China; and Hay had Horace

Porter, the American ambassador in Paris, also ask the French for a statement supporting the Open Door in China. The immediate consequence of this effort was the enlistment of French support for U.S. policy.[20]

Of equal importance was the collaboration between Roosevelt and Jusserand. By this time the president was impatient to secure peace, lest the balance of power in East Asia be tipped permanently in favor of Japan. Roosevelt was impressed by Jusserand's knowledge of public affairs and his personal integrity. On several occasions he spoke confidentially with Jusserand. The two men discussed possible outcomes of the war, potential peace settlements, and the ways of achieving them.[21] Emerging from these talks was the idea of Franco-American cooperation. On May 15, 1905, Roosevelt suggested that if France were to bring the Russians to the peace table, he would work to restrain the ambitions of Japan.[22]

At this juncture the Japanese decisively defeated the Russians in a naval battle near the island of Tsushima, whereupon they requested that Roosevelt "directly and entirely on his own motion and initiative" invite Russia and Japan to meet in order to undertake negotiations.[23] The challenge for Roosevelt was to get the Russians to accept his offer, and he turned to the French government for support.[24] In June, when Secretary Hay became ill, the president turned to Jusserand for advice on how to proceed.[25] The two men met almost every day. As Roosevelt wrote in a letter to Whitelaw Reid, then American ambassador at London: "My relations with Jusserand are such that I can always go to him freely, tell him what I have been asked to do, and then say that I will either do it or not."[26]

One of the most important of these meetings took place on June 8. The peace proposal that Roosevelt had forwarded through Count Arturo Cassini, the Russian ambassador in Washington, had failed. But one presented to the Russian government by George von Lengerke Meyer, the American ambassador to Saint Petersburg, had succeeded. The task was to draft an official appeal to both Russia and Japan. The president showed the ambassador the cable he had written and asked if he had any suggestions. Jusserand proposed a few changes, intended to better safeguard the susceptibilities of Russia, and Roosevelt accepted them.[27] Two months later, the powers met at Portsmouth to negotiate a peace treaty.

The outcome of this crisis fits into a general pattern of diplomatic cooperation between the United States and France during the Roosevelt years. That there was no fundamental conflict of interest between the two countries is undeniable. But Franco-American accord during this period was much more than an absence of conflict. Jusserand worked to build on the rapprochement which followed the Spanish-American War, and Roosevelt and his administration reciprocated. The two nations cooperated to bring the crisis in East Asia to an end, to defuse the crisis created by the Franco-German clash over Morocco, to force Venezuela to pay its debts to France in 1906, to settle the future of Morocco at the Algeciras Conference the same year, and to resolve minor disputes between them by concluding another treaty of arbitration in 1908. Franco-American relations were not without controversy—such as that over the tariff, or even some aspects of the Moroccan question—but they presented a remarkable contrast to the American relationship with Germany, or even Great Britain.[28]

This diplomatic cooperation is often regarded as a corollary to the growing antagonism between the United States and Germany. That the German ambassador, Speck von Sternburg, was unable to bridge the gap can be considered further evidence of the insignificance of individual diplomats in the face of conflicting national interests.[29]

A crucial weakness in this argument is that it fails to recognize that many of the difficulties between the United States and Germany were more the consequence of misunderstanding than an irreconcilable conflict over essential state interests. It was German adventurism in Venezuela and the kaiser's efforts to involve the United States in the European rivalries which antagonized the Americans and their government. Neither endeavor was truly vital to German security, and German-American relations would certainly have been more tranquil had the German government not gone ahead with them.[30] This is where an effective German ambassador could have served Germany well. A difference which is recognized can be controlled; a difference left unrecognized is dangerous. Despite, or perhaps because of, his friendship with Roosevelt, Sternburg was unable to recognize and communicate to his superiors that the president would not align the United States on the side of Germany. The kaiser and his ministers thus persisted in courting

Roosevelt and the United States, and created for themselves precisely the sort of backlash that they had hoped to avoid.

A second problem with the argument that Franco-American accord was a consequence of American-German antagonism is that it assumes rather than proves that cooperation with France was the necessary consequence of growing difficulties with Germany. Nations can of course drift apart despite the best efforts of politicians and diplomats, but the converse is not true. Mutual accord in the face of shared interest is not given; diplomats form the crucial link between interest and action.

The most dramatic example in this regard, during this period, is the case of Anglo-American relations. Despite the record of his administration, Roosevelt was by inclination pro-British. He believed that the English-speaking peoples came nearer to one another in ideals, morality, and government than any one of them did to non-English speaking peoples. Most important, he viewed the balance of power in Europe to be between Germany and England. As Raymond Esthus has shown, "in any Anglo-German dispute, he [Roosevelt] could be counted upon to be strongly pro-British."[31] But very little came of Roosevelt's inclinations. It usually took a crisis to bring about Anglo-American cooperation.

There was never any danger that the United States and Britain would go to war, but relations between them were marred by mutual misunderstanding and mistrust.[32] The British Foreign Office bears some of the responsibility, but one of the main reasons for this friction was the president's inability to get along with the British ambassador. Sir Michael Herbert died in 1903. His successor was Sir Mortimer Durand, who occupied the post from 1904 until December 1906. Roosevelt thought Durand had "a brain of about eight-guinea-pig-power"; and the ambassador failed the celebrated "hike test."[33] Doubtless this lackluster performance was not sufficient to drive the United States and Britain apart. But it is significant, because it meant that Durand was not with Roosevelt when he discussed important issues on such informal occasions. Durand—and his superiors at the Foreign Office—were at a disadvantage from the start. Within months Roosevelt gave up on Durand and attempted instead to communicate with English officials through a variety of other channels, none as effective as a good working relationship with the British ambassador would have been. Thus, instead of working with the British to resolve the international problems of the day—restraining Japan during the Far East crisis, for example—Roosevelt turned to Jusserand. Through the French ambassador, rather than through connections with England, President Roosevelt came to play a role in managing the international rivalries of the day.

The years 1903–1909 witnessed a high degree of diplomatic cooperation between France and the United States. A convergence of national interests provided the context within which this mutual accord flourished. But state interests do not explain all. In Jusserand, the French government had an especially capable advocate. By several strange twists of fate, Jusserand was particularly well suited to get along well with President Roosevelt. And he rose to the occasion. In their friendship and their collaboration in conducting affairs of state, the Roosevelt-Jusserand relationship is without parallel in the history of Franco-American relations. By the end of Roosevelt's presidency, France had gone farther toward winning America's favor than the other European powers. This outcome was not foreordained—it owed a great deal to the work of Ambassador Jusserand. Viewed in this light, and against the records of his foreign counterparts, one can only conclude that Jusserand was a remarkably effective ambassador.

But this story contains an element of tragedy. Jusserand's relationship with Roosevelt was not only a mark of his success, it was also the very basis of his privileged position in Washington. When Roosevelt stepped down from office, Jusserand's popularity in American circles did not diminish. But his access to the chief executive vanished overnight. And later, especially after the Democratic victory in 1912, Jusserand's close association with Roosevelt actually worked against him. Resourceful as usual, Jusserand worked to cultivate goodwill toward France among a wider public. That he was successful in this pursuit there can be no doubt. But never did the response he evoked ever match the influence he had while Roosevelt was in the White House. However ineffective, this latter strategy was not meaningless, for like Roosevelt's face-to-face diplomacy, the appeal to enlightened opinion gave the age its character, thus setting it apart from our own.

NOTES

1. Standard accounts include Howard K. Beale, *Theodore Roosevelt and the Rise of America to World Power* (Baltimore: The Johns Hopkins University Press, 1956); Nelson Manfred Blake, "Ambassadors at the Court of Theodore Roosevelt," *Mississippi Valley Historical Review* 42 (September 1955): 179–206; Raymond A. Esthus, *Theodore Roosevelt and the International Rivalries* (Waltham, MA: Ginn-Blaisdell, 1970); Marvin R. Zahniser, *Uncertain Friendship: American-French Diplomatic Relations Through the Cold War* (New York: John Wiley and Sons, 1975); and Tom T. Lewis, "Franco-American Diplomatic Relations, 1898–1907" (Ph.D. diss. University of Oklahoma, 1970).

2. The best introduction to Jusserand is his own account: J. J. Jusserand, *What Me Befell: The Reminiscences of J. J. Jusserand* (Boston and New York: Houghton Mifflin, 1934) (hereafter cited as *Befell*). In this book Jusserand includes a considerable number of journal entries and excerpts from letters written years before. The documents contained in the Jusserand papers further confirm the reliability of his testimony: Papiers Jusserand, Archives du Ministère des Affaires Étrangères, Paris, France.

3. On Jusserand's scholarship, see his own account in *Befell* (pp. 28–51 and 70–106); and see contemporary analysis such as that in Brander Matthews, "A French Ambassador on English Literature," *Putnam's Monthly* 7 (February 1910): 560–564; and G. Gregory Smith, "An Ambassador of the Republic of Letters," *Blackwood's Edinburgh Magazine* 176 (October 1904): 490–500.

4. The "out of the common" quote is taken from Jusserand, *Befell*, p. 253. For Roosevelt's account of their first meeting, see Theodore Roosevelt (hereafter cited as TR) to Kermit Roosevelt, February 8, 1903, in Elting E. Morison, ed., *Letters of Theodore Roosevelt*, 8 vols. (Cambridge: Harvard University Press, 1951–1954), 3: 422. For Jusserand's account see *Befell*, p. 221.

5. TR and Jusserand met on eight occasions in 1903 for certain: February 7 and 24; April 27 and 30; June 12, 15, and 24; and November 11. See Jusserand, *Befell*, pp. 219–60. His account is corroborated by the "Chronology" in Morison, *Letters*, 4: 1,356–64; contemporary press coverage ("At the White House" in the *Washington Star*); and Jusserand's correspondence with Roosevelt and with his own government. For Jusserand's view at the time, see his dispatch to Foreign Minister Théophile Delcassé (hereafter cited as TD), January 25, 1905, Commission pour la publication des documents relatifs aux origines de la guerre de 1914, *Documents Diplomatiques Français (1871–1914)*, 38 vols. (Paris: Imprimerie Nationale, 1929–1953), 2ème série, 6: 61-64 (hereafter cited as *DDF*).

6. Jusserand's memoirs are the most accessible account of the TR-Jusserand conversations. Jusserand also wrote about his conversations with the president in his dispatches to the French foreign ministry. See, for example, JJJ to TD, March 9, 1904, *DDF*, 4: 447. For the president's perspective, the best source is his correspondence. See,

for example, TR to JJJ, February 8, 1904, TR Papers, Library of Congress; and Morison, *Letters*, 4: 718.

7. See especially the following letters: TR to JJJ, February 8, 1904; TR to JJJ, July 11, 1905; JJJ to TR, August 9, 1905; JJJ to TR, December 23, 1905; TR to JJJ, January 15, 1906; TR to JJJ, June 27, 1906; TR to JJJ, August 16, 1906; JJJ to TR, January 15, 1907; JJJ to TR, June 25, 1907; JJJ to TR, September 17, 1907; TR to JJJ, August 3, 1908; TR to JJJ, February 25, 1909, TR Papers. These letters can also be found in Carton 24, "Correspondance Jusserand-Roosevelt," Papiers Jusserand.

8. For Jusserand's views on progress and politics, the best source is his own work. See, for example, *Befell*, pp. 243–44, 277, and 344. On Roosevelt and his era, see Frederick W. Marks III, *Velvet on Iron: The Diplomacy of Theodore Roosevelt* (Lincoln: University of Nebraska Press, 1979), pp. 1–36.

9. Jusserand, *Befell*, p. 230.

10. For Roosevelt's account of his tennis games with Jusserand, see his letters to Kermit on the following dates: November 19, 1905; April 12, 1906; April 18, 1906; May 15, 1907; January 20, 1908; February 2, 1908; June 13, 1908, in Will Irwin, ed., *Letters to Kermit from Theodore Roosevelt, 1902-1908* (New York: Charles Scribner's Sons, 1946).

At the time of its dispersal when Roosevelt left office, the "Tennis Cabinet" included Robert Bacon, James R. Garfield, George von Lengerke Meyer, Lawrence O. Murray, William Phillips, Gifford Pinchot, Herbert Knox Smith, Beekman Winthrop, and, of course, Jusserand.

11. For an example of such romantic overstatement, see the articles in Jusserand Memorial Committee, *Jean Jules Jusserand: Ambassador of the French Republic to the United States of America* (New York: Jusserand Memorial Committee, 1937).

12. Irwin, *Letters to Kermit From Theodore Roosevelt*. See especially Roosevelt's letters of January 21, 1906; May 27, 1906; December 8, 1907; and January 15, 1908. One can also read between the lines in Jusserand's own account to get a sense of the difficulty of his treks with Roosevelt. See his *Befell*, pp. 329-41.

13. Blake, "Ambassadors," and Esthus, *Theodore Roosevelt*, do not go this far; but both Zahniser, *Uncertain Friendship*, and Lewis, "Franco-American Diplomatic Relations, 1898–1907," minimize the role of individual diplomats, laying stress instead on the international balance of power as the only meaningful determinant of national policy.

14. Owing to Roosevelt's highly personal style of conducting affairs of state, the Department of State records compiled in the *Foreign Relations of the United States* series for these years are not as helpful as usual.

15. For further discussion of Sternburg, see Blake, "Ambassadors."

16. On the Franco-Russian alliance, see George Kennan, *The Fateful Alliance: France, Russia, and the Coming of the First World War* (New York: Pantheon, 1984). On the Entente Cordiale, see Dwight E. Lee, *Europe's Crucial Years: The Diplomatic Background of World War I,*

1902–1914 (Hanover, NH: University Press of New England, 1974), pp. 49–80. See also Keith Eubank, *Paul Cambon: Master Diplomatist* (Norman: University of Oklahoma Press, 1960); and Charles Porter, "The Career of Théophile Delcassé" (Ph.D. diss., University of Pennsylvania, 1936).

17. For Jusserand's analysis of his German counterpart's activities and President Roosevelt, see his dispatches to Foreign Minister Delcassé in *DDF*. See especially his reports dated March 9, 1903 (3: 161–64); February 16, 1904 (4: 364–66); March 9, 1904 (4: 443–46); October 18, 1904 (5: 456–57); January 25, 1905 (6: 61–64); and March 6, 1905 (6: 172–73). See also Jusserand's personal notes in Dossier no. 1, "Allemagne et États-Unis," Carton 58, "Dossiers relatifs à diverses puissances étrangères," Papiers Jusserand.

18. On the Russo-Japanese War, see Ian Nish, *The Origins of the Russo-Japanese War* (New York: Longman, 1985); and John A. White, *The Diplomacy of the Russo-Japanese War* (Princeton: Princeton University Press, 1964).

19. JJJ to TD, February 16, 1904, *DDF*, 4: 366–67; and JJJ to TD, October 18, 1904, *DDF*, 5: 456–57.

20. For the communication between Roosevelt, Jusserand, and Delcassé, see JJJ to TD, January 15, 1905, *DDF*, 6: 37–38; TD to JJJ, January 16, 1905, *DDF* 6: 43; JJJ to TD, January 18, 1905, *DDF*, 6: 47; JJJ to TD, February 18, 1905, *DDF*, 6: 140; and TD to JJJ, February 18, 1905, *DDF*, 6: 141.

21. On these conversations, see Jusserand's dispatches to Delcassé from January 15 through May 15, 1905, in *DDF*, vol. 6. Most helpful are Jusserand's reports of January 15, January 18, January 25, February 11, February 18, one without a date but received by the French Foreign Ministry on Feburary 21, April 1, and May 15.

22. JJJ to TD, May 16, 1905, *DDF*, 6: 511.

23. The Japanese request is quoted in Esthus, *Theodore Roosevelt*, p. 30.

24. JJJ to TD, June 6, 1905, *DDF*, 6: 595–96.

25. The regularity of Roosevelt's consultation with Jusserand is made clear in Jusserand's reports to Delcassé at this time. On the broader question of whether Roosevelt was cautious and thoughtful in his approach to diplomacy (as implied here), see Marks, *Velvet on Iron*, pp. 129–70.

26. TR to Whitelaw Reid, August 3, 1905, Morison, ed., *Letters*, 4: 1,298.

27. Jusserand to Maurice Rouvier, June 8, 1905, *DDF*, 7: 12--3.

28. On the Algeciras Conference, see Lewis, "Franco-American Relations During the First Moroccan Conference," *Mid-America* 55 (January 1973): 21-36; and Esthus, *Theodore Roosevelt*. On Venezuela, see Philip C. Jessup, *Elihu Root* (New York: Dodd, Mead, 1938), pp. 494–99. On the Treaty, see Jusserand, *Befell*, p. 262. This agreement was ratified by the Senate. On the tariff, see Lewis, "Franco-American Diplomatic Relations, 1898–1907," pp. 140–59. Franco-American friction over the tariff was endemic, the Senate being the source of much of the problem; but the amount of trade involved was slight,

and the problem was not unique to relations between the U.S. and France.

29. Zahniser, *Uncertain Friendship*, hardly mentions individual diplomats. Esthus and Lewis are both realists and give overwhelming priority to the role of interest in shaping foreign policy.

30. This interpretation is drawn principally from Manfred Jonas, *The United States and Germany: A Diplomatic History* (Ithaca, NY: Cornell University Press, 1986); and Holger Herwig, *Germany's Vision of Empire in Venezuela, 1871–1914* (Princeton: Princeton University Press, 1986), pp. 80–109 and 175–208.

31. Esthus, *Theodore Roosevelt*, p. 40. See also Beale, *Theodore Roosevelt*, pp. 81–171.

32. See Peter Larsen, "Sir Mortimer Durand in Washington: A Study in Anglo-American Relations in the Era of Theodore Roosevelt," *Mid-America* 66 (April-July 1984): 65–78.

33. Ibid. Perceptive observers at the time were aware of Durand's inability to get along with the president. See, for example, *Current Literature*, "The Diplomatic Game in Washington," January 1907, p. 20.

The leather diploma case for Theodore Roosevelt's Nobel Peace Prize citation. The diploma and case are on display at the Theodore Roosevelt Birthplace National Historic Site, 28 East 20th Street, New York City. Theodore Roosevelt was given the peace award for mediating an end to the Russo-Japanese War of 1904–1905. He was the first American to win a Nobel Prize in any field. TR gave the prize money to charity. The Theodore Roosevelt Association gave his gold Nobel Peace Prize Medal to the White House in 1982.

24

Theodore Roosevelt and the Naval Plans for the Occupation of Tangier, Morocco, 1904

George W. Collins

On June 16, 1904, from his flagship in Tangier harbor, Rear Admiral French E. Chadwick appointed a board of officers "to collect strategic information and prepare without delay a plan of military operations of a foreign force in Morocco, based upon the possible necessity of a punitive expedition directed against the bandit Raisuli and those allied with him."[1]

The plan was to be available for immediate execution. Two days later Chadwick demanded to know "without delay" what size force was at hand "for extended military duty on shore."[2] Thus the scene was set for another episode of gunboat diplomacy under President Theodore Roosevelt. The reason was the kidnapping on May 18 of an American, Ion Perdicaris, and his English stepson, Cromwell Oliver Varley, from Perdicaris's villa outside Tangier.[3] For a minor naval and diplomatic affair, it has received considerable scholarly attention,[4] and, in light of contemporary hostage crises, it continues to merit examination.

The kidnapping was the work of Mulai Ahmad Ben Raisuli, a dissident Berber chieftain who dominated the region around Tangier. Through the kidnapping Raisuli hoped to embarrass the government of Sultan Mulai Abdul Aziz IV and force concessions from it.[5]

Abdul Aziz was a young, vacillating, extravagant monarch with vague ideas of reform, but he lacked the resources or ability to accomplish them. Conditions in the country bordered on anarchy, and the government essentially controlled only the principal cities and the adjoining lands. Elsewhere, tribal chieftains, such as Raisuli, exercised almost independent authority.[6]

The responsible American and British officials in Tangier were Consul-General Samuel R. Gummeré and His Majesty's

Minister to Morocco, Sir Arthur Nicolson. They demanded that the Fez government instruct the Moroccan minister of foreign affairs at Tangier to follow their direction in securing the hostages' release. Despite his blustering intervention, Gummeré felt severely handicapped because he believed the Moroccans had "little or no regard for our country or its representatives." Therefore he quickly requested that an American warship be sent to support him.[7]

Contact was established with Raisuli, who held the hostages in the mountains about fifty miles from Tangier. His terms for their release were exorbitant: removal of the governor of Tangier, withdrawal of Moroccan troops from the area, imprisonment of several officials, release from prison of many of his followers, ransom of about $55,000, and a pardon.[8]

The terms stunned Gummeré and Nicolson who, although they initially had insisted that the sultan immediately comply with any demands, rejected these as unreasonable and offered counter-proposals, including a pardon, if the hostages were freed quickly. But Raisuli spurned their offers, increased his demands, and threatened to kill the hostages if his terms were not met by May 28. To save time while his terms were being considered, he would accept a guarantee from Nicolson and Gummeré that they would be met.[9]

President Roosevelt had responded almost immediately to Gummeré's request for naval support, ordering a warship to Tangier on May 19, the day he was notified of the incident, and later that day the order was extended to include Chadwick's entire South Atlantic Squadron.[10] Unfortunately, the squadron was in the mid-Atlantic and out of contact with Washington. Not until May 27, when the squadron steamed into the Canary Islands, did Chadwick receive the message. In addition, after Roosevelt learned of Raisuli's demands, which he considered "preposterous," Rear Admiral Theodore F. Jewell's European Squadron, then departing the Azores, also was diverted to Tangier.[11] Chadwick's warships reached the city on May 30, and Jewell's arrived two days later.[12]

On the scene, Admiral Chadwick was in command of the task force of five cruisers and two gunboats. He was an able officer with wide experience including sea command, as well as posts as the first U.S. naval attaché and as president of the Naval War College. He had known Gummeré and Nicolson for years.[13] After a briefing by Gummeré, he advised Washington that any military action would be foolhardy and would lead to the hostages' death. Instead, he thought it best to wait, meanwhile pressuring the sultan to concede.[14] Not wishing to exacerbate the situation, Chadwick landed only a few marines as guards; nevertheless, other marines and sailors were alerted for a possible landing and the collection of intelligence begun.[15]

After receiving word that Raisuli had threatened to kill the hostages, Roosevelt met with his cabinet and a cable was sent stating that "Raisuli's life will be demanded if Perdicaris is murdered."[16] Later, critical of Gummeré's readiness to negotiate a pardon, the consul general was ordered not to bind the United States to any guarantee.[17]

Admiral Chadwick was appreciative of the sultan's plight and he reported that Raisuli's "demands were undoubtedly unprecedented. They strike at the heart of government itself, and they are of course so felt by the Fez authorities." He continued with the warning that the United States should "look in vain to the [Moroccan] government should events unfortunately require a punitive expedition."[18]

On June 15, impatient with the failure to secure Perdicaris's release, Roosevelt directed Secretary of State John Hay to consider a joint military expedition with Britain and France.[19] The following day, the sudden arrival of 370 Moroccan soldiers in Tangier further complicated matters because it was feared that their presence would incite Raisuli as it was a violation of the agreement to remove the sultan's soldiers from the area.[20] It was in that setting that later that day Chadwick appointed the board of officers to prepare plans for a possible expedition on shore.

Negotiations continued and, with the sultan conceding to virtually all of Raisuli's demands, it appeared on June 19 that the hostages were about to be freed.[21] However, difficulties arose at the last minute, and, on June 21, Gummeré cabled in frustration that these were due to "the double dealing and treachery" of Moroccan officials in Tangier. If there was any further delay, he urged Washington to authorize a demand for a daily indemnity and the landing of the marines who would seize the customs house. He also stated that Chadwick agreed with him.[22]

That same day Chadwick summoned the warship commanders and read them a cable he was sending that expressed similar views. At least one officer, Lieutenant

Commander Edward J. Dorn, a member of the planning board who also was to command one of the landing parties, hurried ashore to reconnoiter the ground.[23] After further consideration, however, Chadwick changed his mind and wired Washington that although a daily indemnity would be appropriate, any active pressure would be dangerous to the hostages. Gummeré concurred, reluctant though he may have been.[24]

William J. Hourihan, in an article based upon his dissertation, wrote that "it appears the assault was to take place the next day," June 22. And Paolo E. Coletta, in his biography of Chadwick, declared that the admiral did order a landing but changed his mind.[25] However, whether or not a landing was ordered is a puzzling question. What most likely happened is that, exasperated as they were by the last minute holdup in the hostages' release, Gummeré and Chadwick momentarily were persuaded of the necessity for military intervention. If it was authorized by Washington, Chadwick wanted his task force to be ready. This is substantiated by Gummeré's cable in which he only requested authorization for a landing, and because shortly thereafter both he and Chadwick independently assured Secretary Hay that they never had contemplated a landing without specific instructions from Washington.[26]

If a landing was to take place on the twenty-second as some believe, Dorn spent a casual evening prior to it. He recorded in his diary that after he had a "very hard afternoon" scouting the ground, he and his wife dined aboard his ship to the serenade of the flagship's band. There Dorn was surprised to receive orders to take his ship to Gibraltar the next day.[27]

Also puzzling was Dorn's activity after his arrival in Tangier—and especially after June 16 when he was appointed to the planning board. As a board member, it is surprising that it was another five days before he personally reconnoitered. The most frequent entries in Dorn's diary refer to many walks in Tangier with his wife. In fact, on June 30 he recorded that "thus ends a very happy month, it being just four weeks . . . that my darling came to me at Tangier & we have had every day together since except Sat[urday] & Sunday last."[28] And several of Dorn's comments indicate that other officers were similarly engaged with their ladies.[29]

Despite Chadwick's cable advising against any active pressure, planning continued and on June 24 the board submitted a plan for landing two brigades totaling 1,228 marines and sailors. They would be supported ashore with five three-inch guns, ten machine guns, and three Gatling guns, besides the firepower of the seven ships in the harbor.[30]

The landing would begin with the South Atlantic brigade coming ashore at four points on approximately a 1,000-yard front. The lead element would be the marines on the right flank who were responsible for seizing the customs house. To their left would be the main contingent of sailors, next the artillery, and on the far left another company of sailors. In addition to taking the customs house, the brigade was to occupy the southeastern part of Tangier, block the roads to Fez, and establish a headquarters for the entire landing party.[31]

Following that first wave, the European brigade would land on the same beaches and take control of the roads leading southwest from Tangier. Guards would be posted at the U.S. Consulate, Gummeré's house, and at the Belgian Legation as that minister's wife was an American. Finally, the main units of both brigades were to camp on the Marchand Plateau southwest of the city.[32]

Several questions come to mind; first, Chadwick's directive appointing the planning board. Two copies are in the National Archives, both signed by the admiral and bearing the identical squadron file number, but differing in one important respect. While both order planning for a possible landing, one does not contain the clause: "based upon the possible necessity of a punitive expedition against the bandit Raisuli and those allied with him."[33] Whatever the reason for the two versions, it is obvious that the seizure of Tangier would not threaten Raisuli. Therefore, it must have been intended to coerce the local authorities to speedily capitulate. Second, both versions cite "operations of a foreign force." Did Chadwick mean that others beside Americans would be deployed? He and Gummeré had been instructed to collaborate with the British. However, there is no evidence that any landing plans were coordinated with or included them. Third, while the main camp would be on the Marchand Plateau, surprisingly no mention is made of the Moroccan soldiers already there. And fourth, it is astonishing that contingency plans were formulated so belatedly. Admittedly, from the beginning Chadwick had cautioned against military action, but he must have realized that it was a possibility and, if

Roosevelt so decided, he would be held responsible for its success. Although both squadrons had arrived by June 1 and he reported three days later that marines and sailors were prepared to land if necessary,[34] not until June 16 was the planning board appointed, and it was another two days before Chadwick sent to London for a topographic map of Morocco to assist in the planning.[35] Orders to prepare provisioning plans to sustain an expedition ashore were not given until June 22.[36]

Before any landing was carried out, however, there were two important developments. First, Washington's response to Gummeré's recommendation for a landing. The answer, decided upon at a presidential cabinet meeting, was the famous telegram of June 22: "We want Perdicaris alive or Raisuli dead. Further than this we desire [the] least possible complications with Morocco or other powers. You will not arrange for landing marines or seizing [the] custom house without specific instructions. . . ."[37] And, most important, the fundamental objective was achieved when Perdicaris and Varley were freed on June 24.[38]

Although the hostages were released, contingency planning continued the next day, with Chadwick's squadron preparing to leave Tangier, when Admiral Jewell ordered plans for a possible independent landing of his European Squadron's brigade. His objective, however, differed from Chadwick's and was "to protect the *European* residents of Tangier against attack by natives." Commander W. H. H. Southerland, the senior member of the previous board, was to prepare the plan using the earlier one as a guide. Jewell's directive also differed from Chadwick's in two other respects: there was no mention of seizing the customs house, and measures were to be taken to immobilize the Moroccan soldiers camped on the Marchand Plateau.[39]

Two days later, Southerland submitted a plan organizing the European Squadron's men into three battalions, one from each ship. The landing would take place on the same beaches as before with approximately 600 men and two each three-inch, Gatling, and machine guns committed. Deploying in similar fashion as in the earlier plan, the brigade would encircle the city.[40]

Upon leaving Tangier, Jewell forwarded a copy of the plan, together with maps and intelligence information, to the secretary of the Navy with the comment that he considered it "well devised and fully meeting the demands of the situation. The brigade of this squadron was prepared to land and act according to this plan."[41]

It is not known whether the landing plans were ordered by higher headquarters or if the decisions were made by Chadwick and Jewell themselves, nor is it apparent why Jewell was so concerned for the European residents of Tangier; certainly there were few Americans there. Like Chadwick's plan, nothing came of Jewell's either, and before the end of June both squadrons left Tangier.[42] Thus the Perdicaris affair came to an end. Among other things it demonstrated how communicative advances had enhanced control by Washington to the detriment of the field commander's prerogative. In 1842, for example, when Commodore Thomas Ap Catesby Jones seized Monterey, California from Mexico, that was a decision he had to make on the spot as timely communication with Washington was impossible.[43] By 1904, however, through telegraphic and cable connections, Chadwick and Gummeré were subject to almost immediate supervision.

President Roosevelt's handling of the affair was commendable and pertinent to contemporary hostage situations. Once Roosevelt heard of Raisuli's demands, he maintained a consistent position refusing to authorize any U.S. immunity or guarantee; instead, he insisted that Raisuli pay with his life if Perdicaris was murdered. The president had no qualms against soliciting assistance. Besides having his representatives work closely with the Moroccan government, he instructed them to collaborate with the British, and he requested the "good offices" of France. As Peter Larsen noted, Roosevelt delegated considerable authority to Secretary Hay, particularly in the first weeks.[44] Nevertheless, there is no question of the president's control of U.S. policy at the critical moments. He had no hesitancy about using gunboat diplomacy for, as Hourihan argued, it is inconceivable that the warships would have been sent without Roosevelt's approval.[45] The diversion of the two squadrons to Tangier was justified as evidence of how seriously the United States considered the kidnapping.

While Perdicaris was held captive his American citizenship was questioned. Because of the possibility of political repercussion if that uncertainty was made public, Roosevelt chose to act on the assumption that Perdicaris was an American, meanwhile quietly beginning an investigation. Ultimately, the

State Department determined that Perdicaris never had relinquished his American citizenship.[46]

Admittedly, having only the first part of the famous message, "we want Perdicaris alive or Raisuli dead," read at the Republican national convention then in session was a melodramatic, political gesture, but even that excerpt reiterated Roosevelt's position. Moreover, many scholars have missed an important point because they have slighted the closing passage: "we desire [the] least possible complications with Morocco or other powers. You will not arrange for landing marines or seizing [the] custom house without specific instructions." That clearly revealed Roosevelt's refusal to turn over policy decisions to his field representatives. Futhermore, it underscored his reluctance for military intervention in a hostage situation as he recognized that such action was not justified in the immediate circumstances.[47]

As contemporary events demonstrate, despite intense concern about the plight of hostages, efforts to free them can be very complicated and frustrating. The use of diplomacy is preferable to military intervention; nevertheless, a military presence can show determination and, at times, military force is justified as in the Entebbe raid or the interception of the *Achille Lauro* hijackers. In the Perdicaris affair, although President Roosevelt rejected a military expedition at the moment, he retained freedom of action in the event the situation should have changed adversely. Throughout the affair, it was the president who controlled American policy, as it should be.

NOTES

The author gratefully acknowledges the assistance of William J. Wooley and Kathleen Collins Beyer in the preparation of this paper.

1. Chadwick to Commanders W. H. H. Southerland, Henry Morrell, and E. J. Dorn, no. 364, June 16, 1904, *Correspondence of the South Atlantic Squadron*, p. 450, Records of Naval Operating Forces, Record Group 313, entry 85, National Archives (hereafter cited as *South Atlantic Squadron*).

2. Chadwick to CO, *Brooklyn*, no. 369, June 18, and to C-I-C, European Squadron, no. 370, June 18, 1904, ibid., pp. 462 and 467.

3. Samuel R. Gummeré to Francis B. Loomis, no. 586, May 20, 1904, *Despatches from U.S. Consuls in Tangier, 1904–1906*, National Archives, Microcopy T61, Roll 27 (hereafter cited as NA with microcopy and roll number).

4. Some of the issues raised are the political intent of Roosevelt's action (the Republican nominating convention met in June),

Perdicaris's citizenship, Roosevelt's naval policy, and credit for the hostages' release. See Luella J. Hall, *The United States and Morocco, 1776–1956* (Metuchen, NJ: Scarecrow Press, 1971), pp. 338–42; Barbara W. Tuchman, "Perdicaris Alive or Raisuli Dead," *American Heritage* 10 (August 1959): 18ff; Harold E. Davis, "The Citizenship of Ion Perdicaris," *Journal of Modern History* 13 (December 1941): 517-26; Thomas H. Etzold, "Protection or Politics? 'Perdicaris Alive or Raisuli Dead,'" *Historian* 37 (February 1975): 300–3; William J. Hourihan, "Marlinspike Diplomacy: The Navy in the Mediterranean, 1904," *U.S. Naval Institute Proceedings* 105 (January 1979): 42–51; and three dissertations, William J. Hourihan, "Roosevelt and the Sultans: The United States Navy in the Mediterranean, 1904," (University of Massachusetts, 1975), pp. 44–136; Peter Larsen, "Theodore Roosevelt and the Moroccan Crisis, 1904–1906," (Princeton University, 1984), pp. 1–73; and my "United States-Moroccan Relations, 1904–1912," (University of Colorado, 1965), pp. 6–36.

5. Walter B. Harris, "Raisuli," *Independent*, June 28, 1904, pp. 201–4; Ion Perdicaris, "In Raisuli's Hands," *Leslie's Monthly Magazine*, September 1904, p. 518; Rosita Forbes, *The Sultan of the Mountains: The Life Story of Raisuli* (New York: Henry Holt, 1924), pp. 62–65; E. Montet, "The Moroccan Question," *Outlook*, February 3, 1906, pp. 255–57; and Tuchman, "Perdicaris," p. 20.

6. Eugene N. Anderson, *The First Moroccan Crisis 1904–1906* (Chicago: University of Chicago, 1930; Hamden, CT.: Archon Books, 1966), pp. 3–4; and my "Mission to Morocco," *New Jersey History* 89 (Spring 1971): 41, 43, n.10.

7. Gummeré to secretary of state, tel., June 19, 1904, NA, T61, R27.

8. Nicolson to [Sir Thomas] Sanderson, May 22, 1904, Foreign Office 99/413, Public Record Office, Great Britain (hereafter cited as FO with number and PRO).

9. Nicolson to the Marquess of Lansdowne, no. 79, May 28, 1904, with enclosure no. 2, Muley Ali to Nicolson, May 26 and Raissuli [sic] to Muley Ali, [May 26 1904], FO 99/415, PRO.

10. Loomis to Gummeré, tel., May 19, 1904, and no. 356, May 24, 1904, NA, M17, R43.

11. Hourihan, "Marlinspike Diplomacy," p. 45.

12. Chadwick to secretary of the Navy, May 31 and June 4, 1904, Doris D. Maguire, French Ensor Chadwick: *Selected Letters and Papers* (Washington, DC: University Press of America, 1961), pp. 342, 347.

13. Cornelia J. Chadwick to John Hay, May 30, 1904, John Hay Papers, Library of Congress, Box 14 (hereafter cited as JH Papers); Louis A. Peake, "Rear Admiral French Ensor Chadwick: Sailor and Scholar," *West Virginia History* 42 (Fall 1980/Winter 1981): 75–87; Paolo E. Coletta, *French Ensor Chadwick: Scholarly Warrior* (Washington, DC: University Press of America, 1980), p. 128.

14. Chadwick to secretary of the Navy, June 31, 1904, Maguire, *Chadwick*, pp. 343–46.

15. Chadwick to secretary of the Navy, June 4, 1904, ibid., pp. 347–50; and "Report from South Atlantic Squadron," June 25, and "Military Features," June 6, 1904, Naval Attaché Reports, 1886–1939,

File L-3–01, Register 279, Tangier, RG 38, National Archives (hereafter cited as Attaché Reports with file and register numbers).

16. Hay diary, May 31, 1904, JH Papers; and Hay to Choate, May 31, 1904, U.S. Department of State, *Papers Relating to the Foreign Relations of the United States, 1904*, p. 338 (hereafter cited as *FR, 1904*).

17. Hay to Gummeré, tel., June 9, 1904, NA, M17, R43.

18. Chadwick to secretary of the Navy, June 12, 1904, Maguire, *Chadwick*, pp. 355-58.

19. Roosevelt to Hay, June 15, 1904, JH Papers.

20. Nicolson to Lansdowne, no. 91, June 16, 1904, FO 99/413, PRO.

21. Gummeré to secretary of state, tel., June 19, NA, T61, R27; and Nicolson to FO, tel., June 19, paraphrased in [Ambassador Joseph H.] Choate to secretary of state, tel., no. 145, June 20, 1904, NA, M30, R196.

22. Gummeré to Hay, tel., June 21, 1904, NA, T61, R27.

23. Edward J. Dorn diary, June 21, 1904, Edward J. Dorn MSS, Library of Congress (hereafter cited as Dorn diary). Hourihan interprets the diary to indicate that Dorn was to be the overall commander of the landing party, but Dorn only recorded that he would "have command of the battalion," an apparent reference to the unit from his own ship. Hourihan, "Marlinspike Diplomacy," p. 48.

24. Dorn diary, June 21, 1904; and Chadwick to secretary of the Navy, tel., June 22, 1904, RG 45, Area 4 File, Box 38, NA.

25. Hourihan, "Marlinspike Diplomacy," p. 48; and Coletta, *Chadwick*, p. 129.

26. Gummere to Hay, tel., June 23, 1904, *FR, 1904*, pp. 503–4; and Chadwick to Hay, June 24–25, 1904, Box 14, JH Papers.

27. Dorn diary, June 21, 1904.

28. Ibid., May 30 to June 30, 1904.

29. Ibid., May 31 and June 2, 5, 10 and 15, 1904.

30. Southerland, Morrell, and Dorn to Chadwick, June 24, 1904, in material collected in "A Suggested Plan for Landing Brigade of European Squadron at Tangier, Morocco." Included are two landing plans, reports on possible landing sites west of Tangier, an estimate of Morocco's navy, and two sketches of Tangier and the surrounding area. Attaché Reports, File L-3–a, Register no. 04–285.

31. Ibid.

32. Ibid.

33. Chadwick to Southerland, Morrell, and Dorn, no. 364, June 16, 1904, *South Atlantic Squadron*, pp. 445, 450. The first one, the one without the clause referring to Raisuli, has the handwritten notation "Nil See p. 450" but it is not known when that was added.

34. Chadwick to secretary of the Navy, June 4, 1904, Maguire, *Chadwick*, pp. 349–50.

35. Hourihan, "Roosevelt and the Sultans," p. 111.

36. W. V. H. Rose, *Cleveland* to (addressee not indicated but probably Southerland), June 22, 1904, Attaché Reports, File L-3–a, Register 04–285.

37. Hay to Gummeré, tel., June 22, 1904, NA, M17, R43.

38. Chadwick to Hay, June 24-25, 1904, Box 14, JH Papers.

39. Jewell to Southerland, no. 100–s, June 25, 1904, Attaché Reports, File L-3–a, Register 04–285 (emphasis added).

40. Southerland to Jewell, no. 158–C, 27 June 1904, ibid.

41. Jewell to secretary of the Navy, no. 19-D, June 29; and Lt. C. T. Jewell to C-I-C, European Squadron, July 1, 1904, ibid.

42. Chadwick to secretary of the Navy, July 6, 1904, Maguire, *Chadwick,* p. 364; and Jewell to secretary of the Navy, no. 24–D, July 7, 1904, RG 45, Area 4 File, NA.

43. George M. Brooke, Jr., "The Vest Pocket War of Commodore Jones," *Pacific Historical Review* 31 (August 1962): 217–33.

44. Larsen, "Roosevelt and the Moroccan Crisis," p. 9.

45. Hourihan, "Roosevelt and the Sultans," p. 68.

46. Davis, "Citizenship," pp. 517–26; and Etzold, "Protection or Politics," pp. 300–3.

47. During 1901–1902, Roosevelt exercised a policy of restraint in the kidnapping of Ellen M. Stone in European Turkey. See Randall B. Woods, "Terrorism in the Age of Roosevelt: The Miss Stone Affair, 1901–1902," *American Quarterly* 31 (Fall 1979): 478–95.

Courtesy of Theodore Roosevelt Collection,
Harvard College Library

In 1904 Theodore Roosevelt faced a crisis in Morocco when an American citizen was kidnapped. In 1906, TR resolved another crisis in Morocco through the Algeciras Conference when he mediated a dispute between France and Germany over the future of Morocco.

Courtesy of Theodore Roosevelt Collection, Harvard College Library

Alice Roosevelt, 1905

25

Theodore Roosevelt's Private Diplomat: Alice Roosevelt and the 1905 Far Eastern Junket

Stacy Rozek Cordery

The Russo-Japanese peace talks captured the world's attention during the late summer of 1905. As the foreign diplomats arrived in Portsmouth, New Hampshire, Secretary of War William Howard Taft left Washington with a large party of congressmen and their wives, newspaper reporters, and Alice Lee Roosevelt, eldest child of the president. The delegation was bound ostensibly for an inspection tour of the Philippines, but President Roosevelt sent Taft to Japan to confer informally with Tokyo.[1] He also directed Alice to China in the midst of the anti-American boycott to reassure Peking personally of his friendship. Accordingly, Alice stood in for the president as an unofficial representative, and foreign nations received "Princess Alice," as visiting royalty. She had an audience with the Dowager Empress of China and the Mikado, as befitting the president's private emissary. The lavish and celebrated gifts bestowed upon Alice by the heads of state were given to cement relations between countries, not simply to flatter an American citizen. Her status as an effective and popular goodwill ambassador reveals a new dimension to the conduct of Theodore Roosevelt's foreign policy.

The world remembers Alice Roosevelt today for her pungent wit and her prodigious talent with the caustic one-liner. As First Daughter, Alice played an important but little-studied role in America's international relations during TR's presidency. Her high profile made her America's most famous young woman and the first celebrity First Daughter. Dashing, beautiful, iconoclastic, and independent, she was the prototype of the "New Woman." Just seventeen years old in 1901 when her charismatic father assumed the presidency, Alice matured in a public crucible. She rebelled against family strictures under the ever-present eye of the fourth estate. Yet, Alice, like her famous father, enjoyed the media attention.[2] Her position was unique especially then, for American tradition bound the president to domestic trips. This did not pertain to her, for like the First Lady, the role of the First Daughter was ambiguous. Although the reasons for Alice's many trips away from Washington were also rooted in complex family alliances, there can be little doubt that President Roosevelt gained popular support because of her celebrity status.[3]

Prior to the Far Eastern junket, Alice had more than once proven her diplomatic talents. After her highly touted White House debut in 1902, the official visit of Prince Henry of Prussia tested Alice's ability to "fulfill the role as daughter of the President." In the glare of international flashbulbs, she gracefully christened Kaiser Wilhelm's American-made yacht. "It was a means by which to reduce the hostility in the public sentiment between the two countries," French ambassador Jules Cambon wrote of Alice's part in the delicate mission.[4] Sent away on a month-long trip to Cuba, Alice occupied herself with receptions of local dignitaries, charity entertainments, and sightseeing. Despite the attraction of the young men on the jai alai fields, Alice knew that, "As the daughter of the President, I was supposed to have an intelligent interest in such things as training schools, sugar plantations, and the experiments with yellow fever mosquitoes. . . ."[5] She returned to the tropics in 1903 as an unofficial emissary to Puerto Rico. There Alice entertained and was feted by Puerto Rican natives and visiting Americans alike. Her duties ranged from laying a cornerstone to reviewing the troops. President Roosevelt commended his daughter, writing, "You were of real service down there because you made those people feel that you liked them and took an interest in them and your presence was accepted as a great compliment."[6] Although Alice later in her life recalled that she did not often do "something in a public way," within the United States where her father usually controlled the political limelight, she conceded that "it was a little different when I was overseas. In places such as the Philippines and in Puerto Rico and Cuba I was called upon to fill a far greater number of public engagements."[7]

The 1905 trip stretched Alice's diplomatic skills to the utmost. She was twenty-one, away from home for four months, ready to see new lands, and in love. Publicly, she could never shed her role as First Daughter, and she faced an endless round of receptions, teas, balls, parties, and speeches that left her feeling on display.[8] Nevertheless, Alice left Washington, D. C., on July 1, in high spirits, accompanied by Secretary Taft, her two friends Mabel Boardman and Amy McMillian, her chaperone, Mrs. Newlands, and a few of the other seventy-five members of the party.

"There was a great curiosity to see Alice Roosevelt," noted Taft after their four-day stop in San Francisco. While the Secretary of War attended government meetings, Alice felt that "adventure seemed just around every corner and I was ready for it." Of Alice's conduct, the avuncular Mr. Taft wrote to his wife that "Alice conducts herself very well.... She is modest and girl-like."[9] Elsie Clews Parsons, wife of Representative Herbert Parsons, felt differently about the delegation's most famous member, and in her memoir emphasized Alice's vaunted position:

> The corridors of the Palace Hotel were filled with a "rubber-neck" heterogeneous crowd. The Secretary and Alice Roosevelt were dining there. We had a chance fully to appreciate for the first time what an attraction for the American public Alice, as everybody called her, was. To many, perhaps to most, Alice *was* the party. This was so outside as well as inside the country, before the trip, during the trip, and after the trip. Many times after our return, the only question that was asked me of experiences and impressions was "How did you like Alice?" "How did Alice behave?"[10]

After joining with the rest of the delegation, including Alice's future husband, Representative Nicholas Longworth, the party sailed on the Pacific Mail steamer *Manchuria* on July 8.[11] Five days later, they docked at Honolulu, and spent the day touring a sugar plantation and refinery, and learning to surf-boat and dance the hula. On board the *Manchuria* again, the delegation began the ten-day trip to Tokyo to pay their respects to the Japanese. On July 24, they docked in Yokohama, which was decorated in their honor and, Alice said, "*banzai, banzai, banzai'* all the way."[12]

The American minister to Tokyo, Lloyd Griscom, met the excited travelers. He tactfully intercepted the Japanese plan of having Alice stay at the Shiba Rikyu, one of the royal palaces, because "it might be embarrassing for the President of a democracy to have his daughter accorded the honors of a royal princess," and instead made sure that Alice stayed in his home.

Griscom believed that "The Japanese were firmly convinced that Alice was the Princess Royal of America" and so, he wrote, "our journey to Tokyo was a triumph." The Japanese lined the roads, waving American flags and cheering for Alice, "while the women bowed double again and again. Alice clutched my arm and exclaimed, 'Lloyd, I love it! I love it!'" A host of Japanese officials met them in Tokyo: Viscount Tanaka; Prince Tokugawa; Admiral Ito, the Vice-Minister of Foreign Affairs; Baron Hannabusa; Lieutenant-General Ishimoto, Vice-Minister of War; and a number of minor dignitaries.[13]

In her memoirs, Alice described the continuing cycle of diplomatic entertaining: lunch with Prince and Princess Fushimi, a reception for Count Matsukata and Count Inouye, a dinner given by the businessmen of Tokyo, lunch with the Minister of War and Mrs. Teraouchi, and standing in a reception line with Princess Nashimoto and Princess Higashi-Fushimi—where, to Alice's astonishment, the Japanese women filing past curtsied to her as well. Alice recognized that the enthusiasm of the officials sprang in part from the high expectations of the Portsmouth meeting:

> Not only the Government, but the man in the street as well was interested in and friendly to the Americans. Crowds followed us everywhere. . . . They cheered when the American Secretary of War went out on the balcony to wave good-by—they cheered the daughter of the American President when she appeared—and then they cheered us all over again.[14]

Alice Roosevelt and Secretary Taft received the highest honors from Japan because of President Roosevelt's role as mediator in the Russo-Japanese peace settlement. As negotiations continued in Portsmouth, Japan counted on American favor and expected to have their demands met, especially for an indemnity, for the control of Korea and railroad lines in Manchuria, and the cession of Sakhalin.

The delegation was introduced to the Mikado on July 26, the morning after they arrived in Tokyo. Presented to the Emperor in groups, they bowed three times and repeated the procedure in another room, where the Crown Princess received them in the place of the ailing Empress. The Emperor sought to influence President Roosevelt and the outcome of the peace treaty through royal treatment of his daughter. The desire for assistance helps to explain the uncommon honor shown the Americans by letting them see his private garden, "hitherto never exhibited to foreigners." It also explains why, according to Taft, "The Prime Minister said that he was very anxious to have an interview with me." The unplanned meeting resulted in "virtually a secret treaty whereby Roosevelt agreed that Japan was to absorb Korea."[15] Japan did achieve this objective in the Treaty of Portsmouth.

Leaving Tokyo for Kyoto, the delegation enjoyed more admiring Japanese crowds. Taft recounted the scene for his wife:

> I have never seen such a popular tumult and gathering. . . .
> Every member of the party was cheered to the echo,
> especially Alice . . . there were cheers and cheers and cheers
> . . . from Tokyo to Yokahama . . . whenever we stopped at a
> provincial capital they brought in presents for Alice Roosevelt
> and me and that continued until 1:00 the next morning when
> we reached Kioto.[16]

Griscom remembered the bouquets of flowers thrown to "the daughter of the Peacemaker," and he believed that "never had there been such a demonstration for foreigners."[17] The importance that the Japanese and the Chinese placed on family made Alice a particularly effective goodwill ambassador. After the conclusion of the Treaty of Portsmouth, a Japanese newspaper commented on the significance of the trip to Japan:

> Miss Alice Roosevelt, upon whose intelligence and resolute
> character the Americans pride themselves, frequently renders
> assistance to the President in delicate missions where tact and
> diplomacy are required. Some months ago Miss R. . . . was
> received in Tokio by the Emperor and Empress with the
> highest honors. This visit must be considered as one of the
> happy preliminaries of a peace so swiftly concluded.[18]

Amid more cheering crowds, the delegation left Japan for the Philippines, and Taft's real reason for making the trip abroad. His goal was an inspection tour of the Philippines, but he also hoped to encourage the legislators who accompanied him to lower the Philippine tariff and grant a greater measure of self-governance to the U.S. protectorate. To facilitate their education, Alice and the travelers listened to shipboard lectures on Philippine economy and history. Whereas Taft hoped to influence the legislators, President Roosevelt wanted to impress the Filipinos, as the secretary wrote to a friend: "The President would like to have his daughter Alice visit the [Philippine] islands, hoping on the way that he might show to the people of the islands his interest in them and his confidence in their hospitality and

cordial reception of his daughter."[19] The congressional
junketeers arrived on August 5 for what Taft described as "an
interesting and important visit." His primary concerns were tied
to the Chinese Exclusion Laws and their effect on Chinese,
Japanese, and Filipino labor problems, which had been an
important topic in Hawaii as well.[20]

Alice and Taft spent much of their ten days in Manila dealing
with this and other issues, on the by now familiar round of
receptions, banquets, speeches, balls, and information-gathering
sidetrips. Alice remembered a parade of 10,000 people passing by
the reviewing stand and a reception at Malacañan Palace where
she "stood for hours with the [Governor] Wrights and Mr. Taft,
all of us literally dripping, while we shook hands with the
hundreds of guests."[21] Alice also visited a Normal School and a
Manual Training School, and attended a meeting of the Women's
Club. Before they left Manila for a two-week tour of the other
islands, the Filipinos hosted a ball for Alice. "The eyes of the
whole world are upon her," according to the *Washington Post*,
"representing as she does not only the Chief Executive of our
nation, but the typical American girl." *Leslie's Weekly* noted that
twice in the Philippines Alice wore native clothes, because:

> These were occasions when it was thought that the natives
> would take offense if the daughter of the President would
> not honor them by so doing. At first she flatly refused, but
> was persuaded to wear the costumes when informed that
> these people, who held doubtful allegiance to the
> government, would not understand her refusal and might
> consider it an act of discourtesy.[22]

Rear Admiral Enquist of the Russian navy and his staff made
unusual guests at the glamorous ball. Between the treaty
negotiations and the First Daughter's triumphs, the *Washington
Post* slyly noted that "It is a little trying on the limelight artist to
keep a focus on Oyster Bay and Manila at the same time."[23]

Alice spent the next two weeks spreading American goodwill
around remote areas of the Philippine Islands. On Panay, the
delegation toured a sugar mill and listened to appeals from the
local populace to "Please take off the sugar Dingley tariff." They
dined in Iloilo, and left the next day for Bacolod. Sailing
southward, the party reached Sulu, where it was rumored that
the Sultan proposed to Alice, declaring "that his people wished
her to remain among them." As it meant joining his harem, Alice
politely declined. At Camp Keithly, the First Daughter stayed

with the officers' families in their bamboo houses before leaving at dawn the next morning to journey eighteen miles to Camp Overton in "mud to the horses' knees, ruts to the hubs of the wheels, and miles of bamboo corduroy that consisted mainly of holes." After more primitive island-hopping, the excursion returned to Manila, from there to sail for Hong Kong.[24]

Bishop Brent of the Philippines, who met with the Americans to argue for greater self-government, believed that Alice's visit helped to cement the ties between the two peoples:

> The very fact that our democratic system forbids the transmission of hereditary glory, or the reflection of official character even from parent to child, made the incident even more striking in the minds of a people who hold domestic ties in highest esteem, and who were ready to be influenced by the daughter of her father.[25]

Although the bishop acknowledged the earnestness of the visitors, the uplifting effect they had on the Filipinos, and their willingness to learn from and about the Filipinos, it was not enough to propel Congress into action on behalf of the Islands.

The delegation left Manila on August 31 and disembarked to the cheers of crowds in Hong Kong three days later.[26] While she visited the British colony, Alice decided that she wanted to see Canton, despite the Chinese boycott of American goods which threatened Sino-American relations. Because the boycott originated in that harbor city, and anti-American sentiment was violent at the time, according to Alice's memoirs, "only the men of the party would be allowed to land there, the women were not even to be permitted to go up the river."[27] The Chinese exclusionary laws, dating from the early 1880s, were intended mainly to keep the Chinese laboring classes out of the United States and U.S. protectorates like Hawaii and the Philippines. These laws and acts were motivated by racism and by fears that the Chinese would never assimilate as did other immigrants and their children. In response to the U.S. policies, the coastal Chinese organized a boycott of American goods, which damaged American trade and worried Washington. The U.S. Immigration Bureau officials' unequal enforcement of the anti-Chinese laws exacerbated the problem. President Roosevelt endeavored to mitigate the excesses of the visa-granting U.S. officials.[28] He also attempted to calm the diplomatic and economic waters by sending his daughter to visit Tsz-Hsi, Dowager Empress of China.

It is unclear whether Alice actually went to Canton. In her autobiography she maintained that she coaxed an American gun-boat captain to take them to the island of Shaneen, just across the narrow canal from Canton. From there, she wrote, "only an occasional coolie on the opposite bank shook his fist at us." Alice bore the brunt of the anti-American ire, and the boycott organizers placarded Hong Kong with "signs bearing the portrait of Miss Roosevelt in a sedan chair, being carried by four turtles in place of coolies."[29] The insulting poster was an attempt by the boycott organizers to threaten the rickshaw drivers, who were of the coolie, or laboring class, not to transport Alice. The turtles represented hen-pecked husbands, and were meant to shame the drivers into refusing to transport the Americans. Alice's visit had an important effect on the boycott, for it resulted in a split among the ranks of the organizing students, and it allowed American Foreign Minister W. W. Rockhill to win from Prince Ching an edict calling for an end to the boycott. The posters demonstrated the strength of Alice's symbolism, for there was no doubt that the Oriental-visaged woman in the poster was Alice Roosevelt.[30]

The delegation left Hong Kong safely. Taft and most of the party sailed for the United States, while Alice, her chaperone, Nick Longworth, and a few other congressmen, continued on to China accompanied by the ever-present reporters. In Peking, Alice stayed with the Rockhills for one night, then left the next afternoon for the audience with the Dowager Empress at her Summer Palace. Alice, her two friends, her chaperone, and the Rockhills spent the night in Prince Ching's palace, where Alice had a hall to herself. The audience with the Dowager Empress occurred at 8:00 a.m. Only the highest ranking members of the group could see the aging and powerful Tsz-Hsi.

Mrs. Rockhill presented Alice first. After she and the others had made their three curtsies (or bows) the women of the party dined with the Empress of the East and the Empress of the West. The Empress Dowager joined them after lunch to generously distribute expensive presents. She spoke through an interpreter, Dr. Wu Ting Fang, the international lawyer, scholar, and pro-Chinese spokesperson who served as foreign minister to the United States from 1897–1902 and 1907–1909.[31] Suddenly, Alice recalled, Wu "turned quite gray, and got down on all fours, his forehead touching the ground." He continued to interpret, lifting his head only to speak. Theodore Roosevelt, when questioned about it later by Alice, decided the Empress might have humiliated Wu "to show us that this man whom we accepted as an equal was to her no more than something to put her foot on."[32] As the party strolled through the Empress's gardens, Alice led the way in a royal sedan chair, held aloft on the shoulders of eight bearers.

The newspapers showered the First Daughter with exorbitant praise, despite this perilous proximity to "undemocratic" behavior. Nevertheless, the *New York Times* rhapsodized upon her return to America:

> It is all very well to preserve the majesty of the law, which knows no distinction of persons; of the social conventions, which leave no room for an American Princess. But even among us there are public and private persons of both sexes, and the President's daughter has an individual quality which the most rabid Americanism must recognize.[33]

The American Princess spent the rest of her time in China entertaining diplomats and high-ranking Chinese, such as the powerful Viceroy of Chili, Yuan Shih-kai, so that Alice's only complaint was the lack of time for sightseeing.[34]

From China, Alice and her party travelled to Korea on the battleship *Ohio*. The American minister, Edward Morgan, took them by special train to Seoul. Alice's memories were of a Korea "reluctant and helpless . . . [and] sliding into the grasp of Japan. The whole people looked sad and dejected, all strength seemed to have been drained from them."[35] Alice lunched with the Korean Emperor and the Crown Prince, received the Korean Cabinet, and was entertained "industriously" by Korean and Japanese officials. She stayed in the small country ten days, and by the time she left, was "more than fed up with official entertaining, with being treated, one might say, as a 'temporary royalty.'"[36]

Alice Roosevelt and her party returned to Japan on September 28, three weeks after the Treaty of Portsmouth had been signed. Regardless of President Roosevelt's pro-Japanese feelings, Japan considered the final outcome of the negotiations as a national disgrace. Japan's ally, Great Britain, expressed shock at the Japanese concessions, and according to historian Raymond Esthus, accused President Roosevelt for the paucity of the Japanese settlement.[37] Official entertaining decreased because the Japanese blamed President Roosevelt for the unsatisfactory conclusion of the peace treaty. Now, "there was not a *banzai* to be heard," as anti-American sentiment exploded in a series of riots. "I have never seen a more complete change,"Alice wrote. "We were told that if any one asked, it would be advisable to say that we were English."[38] Not all Japanese displayed public anger, however. Alice noted shrewdly that the anti-American feeling was strongest with the people, not the government officials. While Alice toured Japan, she received a reassuring letter from an upper-class girls' school:

> To our great regret, we have learned that during the recent riot in Tokyo some of your countrymen were insulted, and also some Christian churches were burned by the mob. But the fact is that they did not know what they were doing, and we sincerely hope that your countrymen will not misunderstand us on account of incidents of this nature. . . . What your distinguished father has done at this time will be remembered forever in Japan.[39]

On October 13, Alice and her delegation sailed for the United States from Yokohama and arrived in New York City a record-breaking thirteen days later.[40] Newspapers universally praised Alice's actions and behavior on the four-month trip except for a brief controversy about whether the magnificent presents given her by foreign leaders legally belonged to the federal government. In fact her gifts were gifts of state, and editors across the nation recognized that "Miss Roosevelt was placed in a position where she could not decline any of the presents without giving offense. The gifts came to her as the representative of the Government."[41]

President Roosevelt sent Alice as a personal and diplomatic emissary, and foreign nations admitted Alice as such. The First Daughter understood her position in the government, even though she had no job description and carried no explicit passport. "Doubtless," the *Paris Intransigeant* theorized on the occasion of Alice's wedding, "our gallantry toward Miss Roosevelt will serve to knit closer the ties of friendship which unite us to the great republic."[42] Japan, the Philippines, China, and Korea viewed Alice in this light as well. Theodore Roosevelt made the treatment of his daughter a test of each country's esteem toward the United States. Alice Roosevelt was twenty-one years old in 1905. She toured the Far East as an American goodwill ambassador. Never before had a president's child taken such an active part in world affairs. Never before had a woman Alice's age and with Alice's scant training been received by the most powerful rulers of the world. Today it is not unusual for presidents to entrust their children with semi-official diplomatic or political ventures, as Presidents Carter, Reagan, and Bush have done with their children. Accounts which focus only on the trivial and social aspects of Alice Roosevelt's life miss the important symbolic role that her father expected of her, and that she would continue to play even after her marriage. In 1905, Theodore and Alice Roosevelt forged new territory in diplomatic history, women's history, and the study of presidential families. It is time to look beyond the famous quips and the infamous acts to take Alice Roosevelt more seriously.

NOTES

The author wishes to thank Dr. Lewis L. Gould, Dr. John Gable, Dr. Henry Tsai, Paula C. Barnes, and Jin Jiang for their assistance in the preparation of this paper.

1. Henry F. Pringle, *The Life and Times of William Howard Taft* (New York: Farrar and Rinehart, 1939) 1: 297–98. For the Russo-Japanese War settlement, see Raymond Esthus, *Double Eagle and Rising Sun* (Durham: Duke University Press, 1988); Shumpei Okamoto, *The Japanese Oligarchy and the Russo-Japanese War* (New York: Columbia University Press, 1970); William H. Harbaugh, *The Life and Times of Theodore Roosevelt* (New York: Oxford University Press, 1975), chaps. 16 and 17; and Raymond A. Esthus, *Theodore Roosevelt and the International Rivalries* (Claremont, CA: Regina Books, 1982).

2. On Theodore Roosevelt as a celebrity, see Lewis L. Gould, "The Price of Fame: Theodore Roosevelt as a Celebrity, 1909–1919" *Lamar Journal of the Humanities* 10, 2 (Fall 1984): 7–18.

3. The best book on Alice Roosevelt Longworth is Michael Teague's series of talks with the grande dame, *Mrs. L.: Conversations With Alice Roosevelt Longworth* (Garden City, NY: Doubleday, 1981). Other biographies include Carol Felsenthal, *Alice Roosevelt Longworth* (New York: G. P. Putnam and Sons, 1988); Howard Teichmann, *Alice: The Life and Times of Alice Roosevelt Longworth* (Englewood Cliffs, NJ: Prentice-Hall, 1979); and James Brough, *Princess Alice: A Biography of Alice Roosevelt Longworth* (Boston: Little, Brown and Company, 1975). See also her autobiography, *Crowded Hours* (New York: Charles Scribner's Sons, 1933), as well as Sylvia Jukes Morris's helpful *Edith Kermit Roosevelt: Portrait of a First Lady* (New York: Coward, McCann and Geoghegan, 1980). On Alice as celebrity, see Stacy A. Rozek, "'The First Daughter of the Land': Alice Roosevelt Longworth as Presidential Celebrity, 1902–1906," *Presidential Studies Quarterly* 19, no. 1 (Winter 1989): 51–70.

4. Alfred Costes, ed., *Documents Diplomatiques Francais* 2 (Paris, 1931): 32–33.

5. Longworth, *Crowded Hours*, p. 52.

6. Theodore Roosevelt to Alice Roosevelt, May 27, 1903; Theodore Roosevelt Papers, Library of Congress, Manuscript Division, microfilm edition, reel 461 (hereafter cited as TRP).

7. Teague, *Mrs. L.,* p. 73.

8. For Alice's feelings about the trip, consult Longworth, *Crowded Hours,* pp. 71–107; Teague, *Mrs. L.,* pp. 84–108; and her cryptic diaries in the Alice Roosevelt Longworth Papers, the Library of Congress (hereafter cited as ARLP). The author wishes to thank Joanna Sturm for the privilege of consulting the Longworth diaries.

9. The Taft quotes are from his letter to his wife, Helen H. Taft, July 10, 1905; Wiliam Howard Taft Papers, Library of Congress, Manuscript Division, microfilm edition, ser. 2, reel 25 (hereafter cited as WHTP). Taft's fondness for Alice, and the pleasant reports of her which he forwarded on to his wife in Europe (who travelled with her sick children) could only have infuriated Helen Taft. For a number of reasons, Mrs. Taft did not like Alice. The only references to Alice Mrs. Taft makes to her husband in their Far Eastern correspondence are derogatory. See Helen H. Taft to William H. Taft, July 13, 1905 (WHTP, ser. 2, reel 25) for an especially virulent letter. Alice's reminiscences come from *Crowded Hours,* p. 72.

10. Elsie Clews Parsons, "Congressional Junket in Japan: The Taft Party of 1905 Meets the Mikado," *New York Historical Society Quarterly* 41, 4 (October 1957): 388.

11. According to Alice's diaries, she loved the wealthy Republican congressman from Ohio well before the trip began. Nick and Alice were married in an internationally publicized White House wedding on February 17, 1906. The only biography of Longworth is his sister's hagiographic *The Making of Nicholas Longworth,* by Clara Longworth DeChambrun (New York: F. Long and R. R. Smith, 1933). For information on his later career, see Arthur W. Dunn, "The Public Career of Nicholas Longworth," *Leslie's Weekly,* February 15, 1906, p. 154; Llewellyn Thayer, "The White House Bridegroom," *Leslie's Weekly,* March 1, 1906, p. 174; and the April 10, 1931 *New York Times,* which is full of many different accolades to Speaker of the House of Representatives Longworth on the occasion of his death.

12. On the day in Hawaii, see Longworth, *Crowded Hours,* pp. 75–78; Parsons, "Congressional Junket, pp. 394–96; and "Not Going to Australia," *New York Times,* July 14, 1905, p. 1. Alice's quote is from Teague, *Mrs. L.,* p. 84.

13. Lloyd C. Griscom, *Diplomatically Speaking* (Boston: Little, Brown and Company, 1940), pp. 257–58 and William H. Taft to Helen H. Taft, July 26, 1905, WHTP, ser. 2, reel 25. For the Japanese leg of the trip, see Longworth, *Crowded Hours,* pp. 7886; Parsons, "Congressional Junket," pp. 400–7; Teague, *Mrs. L.,* pp. 84, 87; "Enthusiasm for Taft," *New York Times,* July 27, 1905, p. 1; and "Taft Party Leaves Japan," *Washington Post,* August 2, 1905, p. 3.

14. Longworth, *Crowded Hours,* p. 85.

15. William H. Taft to Helen H. Taft, July 31, 1905, WHTP, ser. 2, reel 25; Parsons, "Congressional Junket," p. 402; Griscom, *Diplomatically Speaking,* p. 258 (Griscom was amazed that the

delegation would be allowed even to see the garden) and p. 298. The gist of the cablegram is printed in Griscom, pp. 298-99, and Taft described it to his wife in the above cited letter.

16. William H. Taft to Helen H. Taft, July 31, 1905, WHTP, ser. 2, reel 25.

17. Griscom, *Diplomatically Speaking*, p. 260. See also Longworth, *Crowded Hours*, p. 86; "Enthusiastic for Taft," *New York Times*, July 27, 1905, p. 1; "Great Crowds Cheer Taft," *New York Times*, July 31, 1905, p. 2, and "Taft Party Leaves Japan," *Washington Post*, August 2, 1905, p. 3.

18. ARLP, undated and unsigned letter file. This is a translation written by hand on paper which is stamped, "American Consulate, Lisbon." It is possible that this is translated from a Portugese newspaper.

19. William Howard Taft to Luke E. Wright, March 17, 1905. WHTP, ser. 8, reel 495. Taft never advocated the separation of the Philippines from the United States, as one of his delegates, Nicholas Longworth, did. See also Dunn, "Public Career," p. 154.

20. William H. Taft to Helen H. Taft, August 14, 1905, WHTP, ser. 2, reel 25. On America's Chinese exclusion policies, consult Henry Tsai, *China and the Overseas Chinese in the United States, 1868–1911* (Fayetteville: University of Arkansas Press, 1983). As ex-Governor General of the Philippines, Taft had a special interest in Congress's battle over the 1904 revision of the anti-Chinese Gresham-Yang Treaty of 1894, because he believed that development of the Philippine Islands could best be facilitated by the exclusion of Chinese laborers. See Pringle, *Life and Times of William H. Taft*, chap. 18.

21. Longworth, *Crowded Hours*, pp. 86–87.

22. Mabel T. Boardman, "A Woman's Impressions of the Philippines," *The Outlook* 82 (February 24, 1906): 435-46; "Miss Roosevelt's Reception in the Philippines," *Washington Post*, August 6, 1905, sec. 4, p. 6; Arthur W. Dunn, "The New Bride, Fortune's Favorite," *Leslie's Weekly* 102, 2633 (February 22, 1906): 172. I do not believe that Alice would ever hesitate to don native dress, nor would she have to be told that the Filipinos would consider her discourteous if she did not join in their customs. However, the *Leslie's Weekly* quote does illustrate again how the Philippine people looked upon Alice as a representative of her father—or if the magazine is incorrect, then it shows at least that the American media assumed that foreign peoples saw Alice as TR's emissary. Also see "Boosts Taft Boom," *Washington Post*, August 9, 1905, p. 2.

23. For the native dress, see "Miss Roosevelt's Ball Closes Manila Visit," *New York Times*, August 13, 1905, p. 4; and "Favor Freer Trade: Ball for Miss Roosevelt, *Washington Post*, August 13, 1905, p. 1. The *Post* article mentions Enquist, so does William H. Taft to Helen H. Taft, August 14, 1905, WHTP, ser. 2, reel 25. The Oyster Bay quote is from an untitled article in the *Washington Post*, August 6, 1905, sec. 2, p. 4.

24. The quotes in this paragraph can be found in Boardman, "A Woman's Impressions," p. 440. For the proposal, see "Sultan of Sulu

Offers to Wed Miss Roosevelt," *New York Times*, August 22, 1905, p. 7. See also, "Taft Party at Iloilo," *Washington Post*, August 15, 1905, p. 1.

25. Charles H. Brent, "The Visit to the Philippines of Secretary Taft and His Party," *The Outlook* 81 (October 14, 1905): 371. Brent and Boardman, "A Woman's Impressions," give the only thorough accounts of the actual travels of the delegation. Boardman is especially useful for the time spent away from Manila.

26. "Miss Roosevelt's Plans: Awaits Father's Answer to Invitation to Visit Peking," *Washington Post*, August 16, 1905, p. 2; "Taft Party at Hong Kong," *New York Times*, September 3, 1905, p. 1, and Longworth, *Crowded Hours*, p. 91.

27. Longworth, *Crowded Hours*, 91.

28. See Theodore Roosevelt to Victor H. Metcalf, June 16, 1905. Elting Morison, ed., *The Papers of Theodore Roosevelt* (Cambridge: Harvard University Press, 1951), 4: 1,235; Theodore Roosevelt to Herbert H. D. Peirce, June 24, 1905, ibid., p. 1,251. On the Chinese Boycott of 1905, see Tsai, *China and the Overseas Chinese in the United States*, especially chap. 6; Delber McKee, "The Chinese Boycott of 1905–1906 Reconsidered: The Role of Chinese Americans," *Pacific Historical Review* 55, 2 (May 1986): 165–91; Henry Tsai, "Reaction to Exclusion: The Boycott of 1905 and Chinese National Awakening," *The Historian* 34, 1 (November 1976): 95–110; Edward J. M. Rhoads, *China's Republican Revolution: The Case of Kwangtung, 1895–1913* (Cambridge: Harvard University Press, 1975); and Paul A. Varg, *Open Door Diplomat: The Life of W. W. Rockhill* (Urbana: The University of Illinois Press, 1952).

30. "Gunboat for Miss Roosevelt," *New York Times*, September 4, 1905, p. 1. Rhoads, *China's Republican Revolution*, pp. 86–87; Tsai, "Reaction to Exclusion," pp. 105–9. I am indebted to Dr. Tsai for his time and help in translating the poster. Any mistakes in interpretation are mine alone. Alice claims, in *Crowded Hours* (p. 92), that she interceded for the life of the poster artist and saved him from execution. I have not yet found corroborating evidence for her assertion.

31. Tsai, *China and the Overseas Chinese in the United States*, pp. 100-3.

32. Longworth, *Crowded Hours*, pp. 99–100; Teague, *Mrs. L.*, pp. 98-99; and Varg, *Open Door Diplomat*, pp. 59–60.

33. "The Young Lady of the White House," *New York Times*, October 19, 1905, p. 8.

34. For part of the extensive media coverage of Alice in China, see: "Miss Roosevelt at Peking," *New York Times*, September 13, 1905, p. 4; "Miss Roosevelt Visits Empress," *New York Tribune*, September 16, 1905, p. 2; "Chinese Empress Cordial," *New York Times*, September 16, 1905, p. 17; "Guests of Dowager Empress," *Washington Post*, September 16, 1905, TRP, reel 461; "Miss Roosevelt Will Get Imperial Honors," September 17, 1905, TRP, reel 461; "Rides on Royal Palanquin," *New York Times*, September 20, 1905, p. 1; "Empress Dowager and President's Daughter," *New York Herald*, September 24, 1905, magazine section, p. 1, TRP, reel 461.

35. Longworth, *Crowded Hours,* p. 103; Teague, *Mrs. L.,* p. 106.

36. Longworth, *Crowded Hours,* p. 104; From the *New York Tribune,* and all from TRP, reel 461: "Seoul Welcomes Her," September 20, 1905; "Emperor Toasts Miss Roosevelt," September 21, 1905; "Festivities in Corea [sic], September 23, 1905.

37. For the history of the Treaty of Portsmouth, see Esthus, *Double Eagle and Rising Sun;* pp. 171–72 document the British reaction.

38. Teague, *Mrs. L.,* pp. 84, 87; Longworth, *Crowded Hours,* p. 106. See also Griscom, *Diplomatically Speaking,* pp. 261–63 for a description of the public anger.

39. The Girls of the Kamibe Higher Elementary School [Koto Shogakko] to Alice Roosevelt, October 6, 1905, ARLP. I have used the translation already in the files, but the original Japanese is intact and with the letter. For Roosevelt's feelings about his part in the peace settlement, see Theodore Roosevelt to Alice Roosevelt, September 2, 1905, TRP, ser. 2, reel 339.

40. Longworth, *Crowded Hours,* pp. 106–7, "To Break All Records," *New York Tribune,* October 24, 1905, p. 1; "Miss Roosevelt Lands," *New York Times,* October 24, 1905, p. 1; "Harriman's Race Stopped," *New York Times,* October 25, 1905, p. 1; "Miss Roosevelt Here from Eastern Trip," *New York Times,* October 27, 1905, p. 1.

41. "Miss Roosevelt's Presents," *New York Times* editorial, October 21, 1905, p. 8, and "Miss Roosevelt Lands," *New York Times,* October 24, 1905, p. 1. The quote is from "Six Months in the Strenuous Life of Miss Roosevelt," *Indianapolis Sunday Star,* October 1, 1905, TRP, reel 461. See also Rozek, "'The First Daughter of the Land,'" pp. 63–64.

42. The *Paris Intransigeant* quoted in "A Princess of America," *The Literary Digest* 23, 11 (March 17, 1906): 413. Although Europe was not on the 1905 itinerary, Alice and Nicholas Longworth would honeymoon on the continent the following year, and much of their time would be spent in solidifying political and social connections not for Nick, but for President Roosevelt.

Alice Roosevelt

*Courtesy National Park Service,
Sagamore Hill National Historic Site*

Courtesy of Theodore Roosevelt Collection, Harvard College Library

On May 11, 1910, at Doeberitz, former President Theodore Roosevelt observed German army maneuvers at the invitation of Kaiser Wilhelm II. The Kaiser autographed this picture: "Wilhelm I. R." (Emperor King) and captioned it "The Colonel of the Rough Riders lecturing the Chief of the German Army."

26

A Misperception of Reality:
The Futile German Attempts at an Entente
With the United States, 1907–1908

Stefan H. Rinke

During the presidency of Theodore Roosevelt, diplomatic relations between the United States and Germany reached a high point of intensity prior to World War I. While the United States had not yet become a decisive power in the world system, its influence and importance had been growing continuously since the Spanish-American War.

Europe, especially Germany—itself a "newcomer" in the circle of great powers—was quick to recognize the effects of this development. Not that the Berlin government was more perceptive than its counterparts in Paris or London, but a series of diplomatic clashes like the Manila affair of 1898 and the Venezuela crisis of 1902-03 taught Germany not to underestimate U.S. imperialism. Simultaneously, the German desire to call upon American goodwill grew constantly and was expressed in the appointment of Roosevelt's friend Speck von Sternburg to the embassy in Washington in 1903. This desire was further intensified by changes in the European power constellation which seemed to threaten the aims of the German empire.[1]

Despite Berlin's wishful thinking, no reasonable German policy to achieve harmony with Washington was developed. On the contrary, the empire antagonized the United States more than once and never accepted the American claim to the Western Hemisphere as expressed in the Monroe Doctrine.

Nevertheless, the hope to influence U.S. foreign policy through Roosevelt's friend, Ambassador Sternburg, remained strong. This proved futile, since Roosevelt essentially sympathized with Great Britain. In many instances the president demonstrated his diplomatic capabilities by supporting

Germany's antagonists while at the same time soothing the kaiser with flatteries.

The spectacular events of the Roosevelt years regarding German-American relations such as the Venezuelan and the Moroccan crises have recently been thoroughly discussed by Edmund Morris and Peter Larsen.[2] However, German attempts to reach some kind of alliance or at least close cooperation with Washington in order to guarantee the integrity of China in 1907 and 1908 have been neglected by historians. This episode reveals rather clearly the basic problems of German-American cooperation during Roosevelt's presidency and allows a view behind the scenes of diplomacy prior to World War I.

In 1906, a conference of European powers and the United States in the Spanish town of Algeciras was supposed to settle Franco-German frictions over Morocco. The outcome of the conference amply demonstrated that German-American cooperation was a utopian dream. Roosevelt's diplomatic maneuvers had been, to a high degree, responsible for the defeat of the German claims. Nevertheless, Berlin's disillusionment did not last long. Already in May of the same year Chancellor Bernhard von Bülow outlined his conception of the future in a most revealing memorandum:

> The progress of the German Empire in world policy naturally arouses the jealousy of those European great powers who are fed up with the competition and the development of German power from political and commercial grounds. Therefore, more than ever, it is the duty of the German empire to rely on herself and to strengthen her own arms. This brings up the question whether it is not important for the security of Germany . . . to cultivate, beside her ally Austria, the friendship of the United States as well as of the neighboring . . . states of the Netherlands, Belgium, Denmark, and Switzerland.[3]

The perceived urgency of a rapprochement with the United States grew because of Germany's increasing isolation or—speaking in the contemporary terminology—encirclement. In 1907, the Far East was the region where Berlin's diplomatic failures seemed to lead to dangerous developments. A whole series of agreements among major powers like France and Japan (June 10), Russia and Japan (July 30), and finally even Great Britain and Russia, with regard to China in combination with the existing alliances, made Germany's containment seem complete.

Due to the imminent end of the Manchu dynasty, the partition of China seemed more likely than ever before. In Berlin, the Foreign Office and the kaiser feared exclusion from the Chinese market and sought the help of the United States, the only other power which had not yet concluded an agreement.[4]

Because of the diplomatic situation, German hopes were not completely unfounded. Economic rivalries in the aftermath of the Russo-Japanese War had revealed deep tensions between the United States and Japan. Late in 1906, discrimination against Japanese schoolchildren in San Francisco led to open protests by Tokyo. While Roosevelt was able to allay these tensions by an exchange of diplomatic notes—the so-called "Gentleman's Agreement"—the press continued to play on "yellow peril" notions.[5]

From the German point of view it was a natural consequence that Berlin should cooperate with Washington. Keeping up the open door for the trade of all countries had been the declared policy of the United States in China for several years. Now, in 1907, with its European competitors united against her, Germany sought to take cover from the United States in the Chinese question and announced that it worked for the same objective.[6]

One of the measures to win U.S. support was to try to arouse suspicion and fear against the other great powers. Thus, Kaiser Wilhelm II had already in September 1905 wanted to palm off on Roosevelt his favorite "yellow peril" picture, accompanied by a frank letter about the topic. Ambassador Sternburg, however, fervently opposed the wish of his imperial master having learned from experience that German propaganda which denigrated other powers usually backfired. Fortunately, the diplomat was able to convince his superiors and also advised them to wait for the United States to take the initiative for closer contacts. According to one contemporary, he had even gone so far as to threaten resignation in case the emperor's present should reach Roosevelt.[7]

By the end of 1906, when Sternburg and his colleague in Tokyo began to report the heightened possibility of a conflict between the United States and Japan, such an American initiative seemed likely.[8] On October 29, Sternburg could report that Roosevelt had brought up the topic of a probable war himself in a conversation between the two and had also asked for some information on the Japanese navy. The kaiser's marginal notes on the dispatch were exultant and in mid-January 1907, he spoke of an advantageous "reinsurance with Theodore Roosevelt."[9] Roosevelt's wish for data was fulfilled in early November and Sternburg received an order from Secretary of State Heinrich von Tschirschky, to encourage the President's mistrust in a careful manner.[10]

In February 1907, Sternburg reported growing anti-Japanese sentiments in the United States. On the other hand, he also stressed the fact that U.S. leaders supported the conciliatory policy of the president because of the inferiority of the U.S. Navy in the Pacific. The kaiser interpreted this as a confirmation of his point of view and commented:

> My forecasts have been amazingly sharply and quickly confirmed by this report. Three years ago [sic] in recognition of the Japanese thoughts I wanted to send a warning to the President to carefully observe the yellow peril and—with this aim in view—decided for my picture "peoples of Europe [Völker Europas]" as a gift for him. Specky [Sternburg], Foreign Office, and chancellor pretended to be despairing and outraged because of that. I was *forced* [sic] to intercept the letter and to take back the picture!! Now, the gentlemen will convince themselves that they did Teddy a bad turn. He remained unwarned and is now totally surprised and helpless because of the Japanese action. . . . Now my picture can be received?![11]

The kaiser took a deep interest in the matter. A few weeks earlier he had used the occasion of a visit by the ex-American ambassador to Russia, George von Lengerke Meyer, to warn against the "yellow peril" and to suggest a German-American alliance.[12]

Sternburg did not follow the example of his emperor but continued to act carefully. Hence, the next time that the ambassador raised the issue was when he transmitted a report of the German military attaché in Tokyo to Roosevelt on his own initiative. From this the president learned that Japan was not preparing for war and did not harbor aggressive intentions. Sternburg was right in assuming that this would interest Roosevelt "after the many strange stories which have been lately spread about."[13]

New racial conflicts in San Francisco in May, and the conclusion of the Franco-Japanese agreement in early June, made an alliance with the United States even more likely. Indeed, public opinion in the United States as well as in Europe became more and more convinced that a war against Japan was inevitable.[14] In addition, the German envoy in Peking, Rex, began to warn against the threat of Japanese expansion and suggested examining the possibility of cooperation with the United States, Russia, and China to prevent this.[15]

In July, Sternburg forwarded another message to Roosevelt. This time he had news from the German envoy in Mexico, who had reported that there was a substantial increase of Japanese immigration into the country. Since these men dressed in uniform-like clothes and were apparently led by officers, the envoy speculated that Japan was moving troops into Mexico in order to be able to wage an effective land war against the United States.[16]

Roosevelt conceded that this "Japanese business" was "very puzzling" but thought the idea of a Japanese invasion via Mexico absurd. Thus, he wrote: "It seems simply incredible that the Japanese should go to Mexico with any intention of organizing an armed force to attack us...."[17] This reaction caused Sternburg to move more cautiously. He replied that he had only sent the report because it came from an authority but that he personally believed the idea to be "quixotic." In order to keep the flame of suspicion alive, however, the ambassador enclosed a private letter from the retired Friedrich von Holstein—the leading thinker on foreign affairs in Berlin. In this message, the still influential ex-official of the Foreign Office warned against Great Britain which ". . . is using Japan as her bogey so as to appear as the saviour of the threatened powers."[18]

Apparently, Berlin succeeded in keeping Roosevelt's distrust alive since the president passed both letters on to U.S. Secretary of State Elihu Root and commented: "My own judgment is that the only thing which will prevent war is the Japanese feeling that we shall not be beaten."[19] Ambassador Sternburg continued his strategy of showing reserve while simultaneously demonstrating his goodwill towards the United States by passing on another report. In it the German military attaché in Tokyo judged that Japan did not intend to attack the United States in the near future. Its rearmament was rather a reflection of the Japanese fear of Russian revenge. In addition, the military attaché judged: "There is not a warlike feeling against the United States neither in the army of Japan or among the people."[20] Roosevelt agreed with Sternburg that this was a sound evaluation of the situation. In addition, Root reassured the president: "On the whole I am convinced that our European friends are overexcited. I think the tendency is towards war, not now but in a few years."[21] Even Berlin was informed by both Sternburg and the ambassador in Tokyo that a war seemed to be out of the question.[22]

A few weeks later, however, Sternburg again reported to the Foreign Office about his efforts. Now, he extensively quoted the president's thoughts about the course of a possible war and gave the impression that Roosevelt was actually planning for the contingency. In order to impress the emperor and his superiors in Berlin he quoted the president's comments on their talks: "I have discussed with you the deeply confidential sides of these great questions of vast importance because in the history of America no foreign representative has ever held the trust of her people as you do and in the future no foreign representative ever can hold this trust."

Roosevelt's comment did not fail to have the desired effect on Wilhelm II whose marginal note was: "Bravo! Sternburg! inform him of my telegraphic gratitude."[23] Indeed, the ambassador's report encouraged Berlin to seek to find out if the United States showed an interest in countering the Anglo-French-Japanese alliance in China.[24] A month later Bülow sent a new report from Rex in Peking which stated that China wanted to sound out Washington and Berlin about the possibility of an alliance due to the agreements of the other powers. The chancellor left it to Sternburg's evaluation of Roosevelt's interest in cooperation as to whether or not to mention German willingness to act in concert with the United States.[25]

Since the President was on a tour to the West, Sternburg had to wait, but he reported that a former conversation had shown Roosevelt's special interest in improving Chinese-American relations.[26] On November 2, then, Sternburg sent Bülow's message to Roosevelt in the form of a memorandum. As the chancellor had ordered, the diplomat stated that it was his personal opinion that Germany would be willing to cooperate with the United States.[27]

Indeed, the Germans had reason to believe in the success of their diplomatic maneuvers. At the end of 1907, preparations for the cruise of a U.S. battleship fleet around the world were in full swing. The cruise seemed to heighten the risk of war since the Japanese reaction was not easily predictable. Consequently,

Germany, which was still anxious to profit from further frictions in the form of an agreement with the United States, welcomed the plan.[28]

Nevertheless, Sternburg's next report of November 8 was not entirely satisfactory to Berlin. On the one hand, the president had voiced his conviction that Japan was now working in concert with Great Britain, Russia, and France to gradually carve up China. But, on the other hand, he did not think the time ripe for the Chinese alliance proposal. Even a public announcement in support of the integrity of China was still impossible since a sufficient cause was lacking, but according to the president this might come with the cruise of the fleet. In addition, Roosevelt stated that he was willing to cooperate further with the emperor "in the great Far Eastern questions" and that he would like to hear Wilhelm's opinion about the Chinese proposal.

Until this point, the ambassador's report read like a normal example of the president's polite but firm reserve toward the German offers. The second part of the dispatch, however, seems almost incredible. Sternburg went on that Roosevelt, in conversation, had discussed the possibility of a future naval cooperation between Germany and the United States against Japan. To this, the ambassador had proposed having German troops help the Americans to defend their country from an invasion. But Roosevelt had rejected this idea for the hair-raising reason that his country needed a devastating but sobering defeat in order to have its fighting spirit reawakened.[29]

Scholars have speculated about the authenticity of the president's words and have concluded that it was probably just random thought mentioned in the talk between the two friends.[30] The way Sternburg presented it was both careless and dangerous. Some comment about the nature of the president's remarks would have been highly appropriate, but the ambassador transmitted them without a word of explanation probably hoping that the report might be read by the kaiser, whose predilection for gossipy style he well knew.

Berlin reacted two weeks later and—apparently ignoring the second part—instructed Sternburg to report to Roosevelt that the emperor, like the president, preferred to wait for the Chinese initiative with regards to an agreement and that such a cooperation would be very desirable. The ambassador informed his government in return that Roosevelt had agreed with Wilhelm's point of view.[31]

On December 5, however, Sternburg modified the German ambitions. He reported that while an agreement might be possible, a formal alliance was out of the question.[32] But this was exactly what the emperor was fervently demanding when he commented on a new report from Rex that too much time had already been wasted and that he wanted to see results "immediately." At the end of the year the kaiser made his point of view clear in a letter to Chancellor Bülow in which he urged action and proposed, "We can work on Rooseveldt [sic] with high pressure through Sternburg so that, when he gets the proposal, he will accept it with goodwill."[33]

Bülow knew that a formal alliance was impossible. Nevertheless, he ordered Sternburg to work for the realization of a joint declaration about the integrity of China. The ambassador was instructed to be careful and to leave the initiative to the Chinese, since this was expected to happen soon, anyway.[34] Answering the dispatch a few days later, Sternburg agreed with the Foreign Office and suggested waiting for the reaction from the United States once the Chinese had moved.[35]

In late January, the Chinese foreign ministry eventually decided to send a special envoy to Washington in order to propose the agreement. This mission, however, was not to be realized until November. Meantime, the German emperor continued to urge the scheme and in February took matters into his own hands. He had the American ambassador, Charlemagne Tower, forward a new warning against the Japanese threat in Mexico. Roosevelt's reaction was to send the report by the German naval attaché, which Sternburg had supplied in July, to Root and to comment: "It helps to correct the imperial pipe dream forwarded thru Ambassador Tower."[36]

While Japanese-American tensions were by then gradually subsiding, Sternburg, who waited for the Chinese initiative, kept informing the president of the desirability of an agreement. But following his strategy of showing an attitude of restrained goodwill, he also passed on a report from Tokyo of June 1907 which stated that there were no war preparations against the United States. Roosevelt sent this to Root, calling it most interesting, and while he thought there would probably not be a war, he also commented that there was "a sufficient likelihood to make it inexcusable for us not to take measures as will surely prevent it."[37]

Shortly before he left the United States on his last trip to Germany in May 1908, Sternburg outlined his policy to the chancellor. The ambassador pointed out that during the last autumn and winter the idea of a "close combination" between the United States and Germany had been seriously disturbed by "ill advised remarks of certain persons." As an example, Sternburg mentioned a speech about the necessity of a German-American alliance by the Germanophile professor John W. Burgess. This speech had been interpreted as inspired by Berlin and had thus been rejected by the American press. According to the ambassador:

> The only means to foster the idea of such a cooperation was without doubt that Germany acted perfectly indifferent with regards to public opinion and the press. Because of this, I, too, pretended to be almost indifferent in all talks in which leading men and journalists touched upon the question to me because I had clearly understood that this would only strengthen the efforts of the United States to work hand in hand with us.[38]

By the time Sternburg left the United States in the summer of 1908, chances of reaching the desired agreement had almost vanished. Roosevelt never really wanted it and had politely expressed this more than once. Sternburg, however, had failed to emphasize this fact in his reports to Berlin. The ambassador was unable to completely dispel the president's distrust of Germany. Minor incidents like the problems arising out of the appointment of the new American ambassador to Berlin, David J. Hill, or the saber-rattling interview the kaiser gave the *New York Times* journalist William B. Hale strengthened the suspicions.[39]

A more decisive factor for Roosevelt's rejection of the scheme was his desire to keep peace with Japan and reach an agreement with that country. The president did not share the kaiser's racial fear of the "yellow peril"; on the contrary, he admired the Japanese. Thus, he was relieved when in late November, the Root-Takahira agreement between the United States and Japan was concluded. An exchange of notes guaranteed the maintenance of the status quo in the Pacific and the support of the open door as well as of the integrity of China.[40] Hence, the United States had basically concluded the same type of agreement with Japan as Russia and France had done earlier.

Instead of cooperating with Germany against the rest of the world, Roosevelt had joined the camp of the opponents, and the Chinese emissary who eventually arrived in Washington was faced with a *fait accompli*. Once again the plan of closer German-American cooperation had failed and, as after the Algeciras conference, Bülow, who saw his star waning, tried to save face by publicly stating in the Reichstag that he evaluated the agreement positively.[41]

Once again Berlin's trust in the use of the magic formula of the open door as a *sine qua non* of American foreign policy was unfounded. Every time when there was reason to fear the European rivals in some part of the world, the German Foreign Office claimed the open door. Berlin, oblivious to the fact that Roosevelt could see through the German schemes, clearly underestimated the president's capabilities as a diplomat.

The failure of the efforts at a German-American entente in 1907-08 was characteristic of the mutual relationship in the years of Roosevelt's presidency. Essentially, there had never existed the slightest chance for a German-American alliance. In the early years of the twentieth century, the United States was not yet willing to join any alliance at all. Moreover, American sympathies were becoming increasingly pro-British. The zigzag course of German foreign policy, the constant bullying of Berlin in times of diplomatic crises, and the kaiser's saber-rattling escapades in public were the reason for a growing mistrust and fear of Germany in the United States.

Berlin, however, was not able to grasp the basic facts of the relationship with Washington. Wishful thinking from the diplomats up to the kaiser and insufficient communication between the Foreign Office and the ambassador were responsible for the survival of unrealistic hopes for American support, or at least benevolent neutrality in times of crises.

NOTES

The author is heavily indebted to Dr. Lewis L. Gould and gratefully acknowledges the assistance of Dr. William R. Rock, Silke Schmidt, Catherine Elfe, Dr. John A. Gable, and the German Marshall Fund of the United States.

1. The most important studies of the subject in general are Ragnhild Fiebig-von Hase, *Lateinamerika als Konfliktherd der deutsch-amerikanischen Beziehungen, 1890–1903*, 2 vols. (Göttingen: Vandenhoek und Ruprecht, 1986); Holger H. Herwig, *Germany's Vision of Empire in Venezuela, 1870–1914* (Princeton: Princeton University Press, 1986); Manfred Jonas, *The United States and Germany: A Diplomatic History* (Ithaca-London: Cornell University Press, 1984); Reiner Pommerin, *Der Kaiser und Amerika: Die USA in der Politik der Reichsleitung, 1890–1917* (Cologne-Vienna: Böhlau, 1986); Alfred Vagts, *Deutschland und die Vereinigten Staaten in der Weltpolitik*, 2 vols. (London-New York: Macmillan, 1935). In addition, see Stefan H. Rinke "The German Ambassador Hermann Speck von Sternburg and Theodore Roosevelt, 1889–1908," *Theodore Roosevelt Association Journal*, 17 (Winter 1991): 2–12 and *Zwischen Weltpolitik und Monroe Doktrin: Botschafter Speck von Sternburg und die deutsch-amerikanischen Beziehungen, 1898–1908*, German American Studies, ed. Gale A. Mottox, et al., v. 11 (Stuttgart: Hans Dieter Heinz, 1991), which contains a fourteen-page summary in English.

2. Edmund Morris, "'A Few Pregnant Days': Theodore Roosevelt and the Venezuelan Crisis of 1902," *Theodore Roosevelt Association Journal* 15 (1989): 2–13; Peter Larsen, "Theodore Roosevelt and the Moroccan Crisis, 1904–06" (Ph.D. diss., Princeton University, 1984).

3. Bülow memorandum, May 30, 1906, quoted in Ivo N. Lambi, *The Navy and German Power Politics, 1862–1914* (Boston: Allen and Unwin, 1984), p. 291.

4. For the encirclement notion, see Bülow's Reichstag speech of Nov. 14, 1906, quoted in Imanuel Geiss, *German Foreign Policy, 1871–1914* (London: Routledge and Kegan, 1979), p. 121. For the English attitude toward Germany, see the important Crowe memorandum of Jan. 1, 1907, ibid., pp. 194–200. See also George W. Monger, *The End of Isolation: British Foreign Policy, 1900–1907* (London: Nelson, 1963), pp. 296–331. For the agreements, see Jonas, *The United States*, p. 87; Pommerin, *Der Kaiser*, pp. 180–81.

5. TR already sensed the Japanese danger during the Russo-Japanese War; see, for example, his letter to Henry Cabot Lodge, June 5, 1905, Henry C. Lodge, ed., *Selections from the Correspondence of Theodore Roosevelt and Henry Cabot Lodge, 1884–1918*, 2 vols. (New York: Charles Scribner's Sons, 1925), 2: 135; Raymond A. Esthus, *Theodore Roosevelt and Japan* (Seattle: University of Washington Press, 1966), pp. 3–4. For the segregation issue, see, especially, Akira Iriye, *Pacific Estrangement: Japanese and American Expansion, 1897–1911* (Cambridge: Harvard University Press, 1972), pp. 126–68; Jonas, *The United States*, p. 88; Werner Stingl, *Der Ferne Osten in der deutschen Politik vor dem ersten Weltkrieg, 1902–1914*, 2 vols. (Frankfurt: Haag und Herchen, 1978), 2: 574–99.

6. For the German efforts to reach an entente with the United States and China, see, especially Luella J. Hall, "The Abortive German-American-Chinese Entente of 1907–08," *Journal of Modern History* 1 (1929): 219–35. The policy of "taking cover" was initiated

already in 1902 (Stingl, *Der Ferne Osten*, 2: 444–49); for details about Sternburg's mission to Washington in 1902 see Rinke, *Zwischen Weltpolitik und Monroe Doktrin*, pp. 60–64.

7. Ursela Schottelius-Bock, "Das Amerikabild der deutschen Regierung in der Ära Bülow, 1897–1909" (Ph.D. diss., Hamburg University, 1956), p. 177; Bernhard von Bülow, *Memoirs of Prince Bülow*, ed. Franz von Stockhammern, 4 vols. (Boston: Little, Brown and Company, 1931), 1: 572; Jonas, *The United States*, p. 84. Ambassador Sternburg's impact on the incident apparently surprised those contemporaries who had categorized him as subservient (Rudolf Vierhaus, ed., *Das Tagebuch der Baronin Spitzemberg geb. Freiin von Varnbüler: Aufzeichnungen aus der Hofgesellschaft des Hohen-zollernreiches* [2d ed; Göttingen: Vandenhoek and Ruprecht, 1960] p. 464), diary entry of Sept. 18, 1906.

8. Schottelius-Bock, "Amerikabild," p. 180. See also John K. Kreider, "Diplomatic Relations between Germany and the United States, 1906–1913" (Ph.D. diss., Pennsylvania State University, 1969), pp. 344–45.

9. Wilhelm II to Bülow, Jan. 17, 1907, Johannes Lepsius et al., eds., *Die Grosse Politik der Europäischen Kabinette, 1871–1914*, 40 vols. (Berlin: Deutsche Verlagsgesellschaft für Politik und Geschichte, 1922–27), vol. 21, part 2, pp. 464–65. Sternburg to Foreign Office, Oct. 29, 1906, quoted in Ralph R. Menning, "The Collapse of 'Global Diplomacy': Germany's Descent into Isolation, 1906–09" (Ph.D. diss., Brown University, 1986), pp. 147–48.

10. Sternburg to TR, Nov. 6, 1906, *The Papers of Theodore Roosevelt on Microfilm*, 485 reels (Washington, DC: Library of Congress, 1967), reel 69 (hereafter cited as *TR Papers*); Tschirschky to Sternburg, Dec. 13, 1906, quoted in Menning, "Collapse," p. 149.

11. Sternburg to Foreign Office, Feb. 23, 1907, quoted in Schottelius-Bock, "Amerikabild," p. 183. The kaiser's marginal note quoted in ibid., p. 181, note 2.

12. Wayne A. Wiegand, "Ambassador in Absentia: George von Lengerke Meyer, Wilhelm II, and Theodore Roosevelt," *Mid America* 56 (1974): 12–13; Mark A. D. Howe, *George von Lengerke Meyer: His Life and Public Services* (New York: Dodd, Mead and Company, 1919), pp. 346, 366, and 383–85.

13. Sternburg to TR, April 1, 1907, *TR Papers*, reel 72.

14. Holstein to Maximilian Harden, June 27, 1907, Helmuth Rogge, ed., *Holstein und Harden: Politisch-publizistisches Zusammenspiel zweier Aussenseiter des Wilhelminischen Reichs* (Munich: Beck, 1959), pp. 173–74. Examples of German press opinion are listed in ibid. See also Eber M. Carroll, *Germany and the Great Powers: A Study in Public Opinion and Foreign Policy*, 2d ed. (Hamden, CT: Archon Books, 1966), p. 561; Stingl, *Der Ferne Osten*, 2: 588–89.

15. Envoy in Peking Rex to Bülow, July 4, 1907, *Grosse Politik*, vol. 25, part 1, pp. 67–69.

16. Sternburg to TR, July 14, 1907, *TR Papers*, reel 75. See also Friedrich Katz, *Deutschland, Diaz und die Mexikanische Revolution* (Berlin: VEB Verlag der Wissenschaften, 1964), pp. 161–64.

17. TR to Sternburg, July 16, 1907, Elting E. Morison and John M. Blum, eds., *The Letters of Theodore Roosevelt*, 8 vols., (Cambridge: Harvard University Press, 1951–54), 6: 720.

18. Sternburg to TR, July 19, 1907, *TR Papers*, reel 75.

19. TR to Secretary of State Root, July 23, 1907, Morison and Blum, *Letters*, 6: 725.

20. Sternburg to TR, July 29, 1907, *TR Papers*, reel 75.

21. Root to TR, Aug. 8, 1907, quoted in Pommerin, *Der Kaiser*, p. 184; TR to Sternburg, Aug. 3, 1907, *TR Papers*, reel 346; see also Esthus, *Japan*, pp. 193–94.

22. Bülow to Holstein, Aug. 18, 1907, quoted in Helmuth Rogge, ed., *Friedrich von Holstein: Lebensbekenntnis in Briefen an eine Frau* (Berlin: Ullstein, 1932), p. 286.

23. Sternburg to Foreign Office with Wilhelm's II marginal comment, Sept. 9, 1907, *Grosse Politik*, vol. 25. part 1: 72–74. See also Charles E. Neu, *An Uncertain Friendship: Theodore Roosevelt and Japan, 1906–1909* (Cambridge: Harvard University Press, 1967), p. 136.

24. Tschirschky to Sternburg, Sept. 15, 1907, *Grosse Politik*, vol. 25, part 1, p. 71.

25. Bülow to Sternburg, Oct. 17, 1907, ibid., pp. 74–75; Schottelius-Bock, "Amerikabild," p. 186.

26. Sternburg to Foreign Office, Oct. 18, 1907, Politisches Archiv des Auswärtigen Amtes [Political Archives of the Foreign Office], Bonn/FRG, Bestand Deutsche Botschaft Washington, 4 A 1c, vol. 501.

27. Sternburg to TR, Memorandum, Nov. 2, 1907, ibid.

28. The most important study on the cruise of the fleet is James R. Reckner, *Teddy Roosevelt's Great White Fleet*, (Annapolis: U.S. Naval Institute Press, 1988); Reckner supersedes Robert A. Hart, *The Great White Fleet: Its Voyage around the World, 1907–09* (Boston: Little, Brown and Company, 1965). For the German attitude see Pommerin, *Der Kaiser*, p. 183; William R. Braisted, *The United States Navy in the Pacific, 1897–1909* (Austin: University of Texas Press, 1958), p. 215; Vagts, *Deutschland*, 2: 1523; Neu, *Uncertain Tradition*, p. 216.

29. Sternburg to Foreign Office, Nov. 8, 1907, *Grosse Politik*, vol. 25, part 1, pp. 78-79.

30. Raymond A. Esthus, *Theodore Roosevelt and the International Rivalries* (Waltham, MA: Regina Books, 1970), p. 124; Esthus, *Japan*, pp. 204–5; Melvin Small, "The American Image of Germany, 1906–1914" (Ph.D. diss., University of Michigan, 1965), p. 198; Schottelius-Bock, "Amerikabild," pp. 187–88.

31. Foreign Office to Sternburg, Nov. 22, 1907, *Grosse Politik*, vol. 25, part 1, pp. 79–80; Sternburg to Foreign Office, Nov. 24, 1907, Politisches Archiv, Deutsche Botschaft Washington, vol. 501.

32. Sternburg to Foreign Office, Dec. 5, 1907, *Grosse Politik*, vol. 25, part 1, pp. 80. See also Pommerin, *Der Kaiser*, p. 185.

33. Wilhelm II to Bülow, Dec. 30, 1907, *Grosse Politik*, vol. 25, part 1, pp. 87–89; Rex to Foreign Office, with the marginal note of the emperor, Dec. 7, 1907, *Grosse Politik*, vol. 25, part 1, pp. 81–86.

34. Foreign Office to Sternburg, Jan. 6, 1908, *Grosse Politik*, vol. 25, part 1, pp. 90–92; Bülow to Rex, Jan. 3, 1908, *Grosse Politik*, vol. 25, part 1 pp. 89–90.

35. Sternburg to Foreign Office, Jan. 13, 1908, quoted in Menning, "Collapse," p. 151.

36. TR to Root, Feb. 17, 1908, Morison and Blum, *Letters*, 6: 946; TR to Ambassador Tower in Germany, Feb. 12, 1908, ibid., pp. 941–42. See also Foreign Office to Sternburg, Jan. 20 and March 21, 1908, *Grosse Politik*, vol. 25, part 1, pp. 92 and 92–93.

37. TR to Root, April 17, 1908, Morison and Blum, *Letters*, 6: 1010; Sternburg to Foreign Office, April 7, 1908, *Grosse Politik*, vol. 25, part 1, p. 94; Sternburg to TR, April 14, 1908, *TR Papers*, reel 82; Esthus, *Japan*, pp. 247–48.

38. Sternburg to Bülow, May 15, 1908, quoted in Stingl, *Der Ferne Osten*, 2: 606.

39. For the Hill affair see Pommerin, *Der Kaiser*, pp. 175–79; Wilhelm von Schoen, *Erlebtes: Beiträge zur politischen Geschichte der neuesten Zeit* (Stuttgart: DVA, 1921), pp. 90-93; Kreider, "Diplomatic Relations," pp. 135–48. For the Hale interview, see Oscar K. Davis, *Released for Publication: Some Inside Political History of Theodore Roosevelt and His Times* (Boston: Houghton Mifflin, 1925), pp. 81–92; Menning, "Collapse," pp. 152–59.

40. Esthus, *Rivalries*, 127; Schottelius-Bock, "Amerikabild," p. 192; Hall, "The Abortive Entente," p. 235.

41. Bülow speech of Dec. 7, 1908, Johannes Penzler and Otto Hoetzsch, eds., *Fürst Bülows Reden nebst urkundlichen Beiträgen zu seiner Politik*, 3 vols. (Berlin: Reimer, 1907–1909), 3: 160–61.

27

"I Had Great Confidence in the Fleet": Theodore Roosevelt and the Great White Fleet

James R. Reckner

Despite Theodore Roosevelt's expression of "great confidence" in the fleet, and the general—almost traditional—appreciation of the world cruise of the Atlantic battleship fleet (the Great White Fleet) as the apotheosis of his "Big Stick" diplomacy, a considerably more conservative interpretation of the motivation and impact of that cruise is warranted.

Throughout the Japanese-American "crisis" in the summer of 1907, President Roosevelt consistently held that the prospect of war was remote. But it would have been out of character for him to have failed to consider the military implications of the situation and to take steps to increase the preparedness of the armed forces.

Before he left Washington for a summer vacation at his home in Oyster Bay, Roosevelt had asked Assistant Secretary of War Robert Shaw Oliver to inform him regarding the Joint Board's plans "in case of trouble arising between the United States and Japan." For the navy, the problem was complex. Contingencies had been under study since the preceding year when strains in the traditional *entente cordiale* with Japan had caused planners to reconsider the American defense position in the Pacific.[1] The military's view of the Pacific strategic situation now was that owing to the "preponderance" of Japanese naval and military strength, the United States "would be compelled, whilst preparing for the offensive by the assembly of its fleet in the Atlantic, to take a defensive attitude" in the Pacific until reinforcements could be sent there.[2]

In response to the president's request the Joint Board outlined a number of preparatory naval and military measures intended for implementation when war seemed imminent.[3] The president in turn requested that army and navy representatives discuss the report with him at Oyster Bay. That meeting took place on June 27, 1907. Present were Secretary of the Navy Victor H. Metcalf, who was preparing to go on vacation to his home in Oakland, California, Postmaster General George von L. Meyer, Captain Richard Wainwright of the General Board, and Colonel W. W. Wotherspoon, acting president of the Army War College.

The president opened the discussion with the assertion that while he had "[n]o idea or belief that there would be war between the two countries," he concurred in the Joint Board's recommendations.[4] Concerning specific navy actions, he directed the secretary of the Navy: to immediately increase the coal stockpile at Subic Bay in the Philippines; to bolster the defenses of the base there; to order the four armored cruisers in Asiatic waters back to the United States Pacific Coast and the remaining naval vessels in the Philippines to concentrate at Subic Bay; and finally, to arrange for the transfer of the entire battleship fleet to the Pacific sometime in October.

As one might expect, the last directive, the genesis of the world cruise of the Great White Fleet, elicited further discussion. The president, in the first of many such assertions, stated that he wanted the fleet cruise "to partake of the character of a practice march," and he added that it would have a "strong tendency to maintain peace."[5] When asked specifically how many battleships were to be sent, Roosevelt responded that "if the Navy had fourteen ready, he wanted fourteen to go; if sixteen, eighteen, or twenty, he wanted them all to go."[6] The remainder of the discussion dealt with actions to be taken by the army.

The Oyster Bay decisions did not long remain secret. On July 1 the *New York Herald* reported that Roosevelt had decided upon an "important change of naval policy . . ." and with some accuracy disclosed the details of the meeting.[7] Responding to this and similar disclosures, presidential secretary William Loeb unequivocally—and untruthfully—stated that "such a movement had never been considered by the president."[8]

Any initial concern the administration might have felt over Japanese reaction to the announcement of the fleet's transfer to the Pacific was allayed when Japanese Ambassador Viscount Aoki stated publicly that Japan "would not regard" the transfer of the fleet as "an unfriendly act," nor would Japan "look upon it as a menace or regard it with regret."[9] Nevertheless, the president continued to equivocate. On July 4 he stated that there was "no intention of sending a fleet at once to the Pacific." He suggested that the upcoming fleet cruise might be to the Pacific, but might only be to the Mediterranean or South America. The whole business would be "determined as a matter of routine in the management and drill of the navy."[10] But just a few hours later, Navy Secretary Metcalf, who had now arrived in California, stated without reservation that "eighteen or twenty of the largest battleships would come around Cape Horn on a practice cruise, and would be seen in San Francisco Harbor."[11]

The reason for the administration's original denials of the early cruise reports remains somewhat obscure. They may have been made simply to permit Metcalf to make the official announcement in California. Concerning the apparently conflicting statements, a rationale might be found in the domestic political situation. The presidential statement was a masterpiece of obfuscation. It seemed to leave all options open and therefore tended to defuse potential opposition. Metcalf's announcement, however, promised in very definite terms that the Pacific Coast—the region that felt most threatened by the Japanese "crisis"—would soon receive the naval presence it craved. In effect, the administration had executed a skillful maneuver that permitted popular interest in the navy to coalesce into solid support for the government's plan. At the same time, those disposed to oppose the cruise were faced with the evasive presidential statement as the only "official" government position and therefore lacked a focal point upon which to base opposition.

The less-than-frank method of announcement gave rise to many efforts to fathom the "real" reason for the cruise. The fleet's transfer to the Pacific had been ordered as an exercise—one of the secret preparatory measures recommended by the Joint Board. But lacking knowledge of the Joint Board's recommendations or the president's decisions, the press and public were quick to discern a wide range of reasons why the cruise had been ordered at that specific time. Depending upon the individual viewpoint, the cruise promised either a wide range of beneficial results for the navy and the nation, or it threatened to plunge America into an easily avoidable war with Japan, or at the very least to stoke the insatiable fires of "naval aggrandizement." The popular reaction to the announcement, though, was expansive, almost euphoric: "It really is a great notion . . . this notion of having the pick and flower of the American navy perambulate the South American continent," the *New York Times* enthused.[12]

Americans in general seemed pleased to brandish the "Big Stick," and that is the image of the event that has persisted in the public mind to this day. But President Roosevelt took a much more conservative tack. In early July he advised Henry Cabot Lodge that, in the event of war, he knew the navy would have a "good deal" to learn about sending a fleet to the Pacific. Unwilling to risk failure at a time of crisis, he had ordered the fleet on what "would practically be a practice voyage. I want all failures, blunders, and shortcomings to be made apparent in time of peace and not in time of war," said Roosevelt.[13] Given Roosevelt's detailed knowledge of and interest in naval affairs, this statement, made at the time of the initial cruise planning, rings true. His 1911 assertion to British historian George Otto Trevelyan that "It was time for a show down [with Japan] . . . I had great confidence in the fleet," conveys an air of assurance not evident in 1907.[14]

Warships of the day lacked the mechanical reliability now taken for granted; Roosevelt well knew this. And the effect of a long voyage upon their battleworthiness was a question of considerable debate. The only previous modern fleet experience, the ill-fated voyage of the Russian Baltic fleet that had terminated disastrously in the Battle of Tsushima just two years earlier in 1905, was hardly encouraging. Further, important logistics and infrastructure limitations raised serious questions concerning the ability of the navy to support an extended fleet deployment to the Pacific.[15]

If, as has generally been assumed, the president had in mind an impressive display of battleship diplomacy, the ultimate brandishing of his cherished "Big Stick," surely it would be reasonable to anticipate that the State Department would play some role in formulating the fleet's itinerary. Yet there had been no State Department representation at the Oyster Bay meeting in June, or at subsequent planning sessions. Decisions concerning the fleet's route and ports of call on its voyage to the Pacific were based exclusively upon military considerations. The earliest State Department correspondence on the topic occurred more than two months after the Oyster Bay conference, when Secretary Metcalf announced the itinerary of the cruise and asked the State

Department to obtain diplomatic clearances for fleet visits to the ports the navy had selected.[16]

Secretary of State Elihu Root attested to the purely military nature of the circumnavigation of South America. Responding to an Argentine request to have one of its ports included in the navy itinerary, Root reported with some pique that "[t]he Navy Department declared . . . that this could not be done without practically destroying the whole plan and interfering with the . . . purpose of the practice cruise."[17] Battleship "diplomacy" clearly took a back seat to naval planning during this first phase of the world cruise—the essential test of the navy's ability to transfer a fleet to the Pacific and have it arrive there ready for battle. So uncertain were they of the condition the fleet would be in after sailing the 14,000 miles to the Pacific Coast that the administration prudently delayed announcement of the onward itinerary until they received an assessment of the fleet's readiness at the end of the first long leg of the voyage.

On March 13, 1908, Secretary Metcalf briefed the cabinet on the successful completion of the voyage as far as Magdelena Bay, Mexico, where the fleet had arrived in good repair and ready to conduct scheduled gunnery exercises. Roosevelt then, "with marked satisfaction," authorized the secretary to announce that the fleet would return to the United States via Australia, Manila, and the Suez Canal.[18] This itinerary announcement is important to understanding the nature of the second part of the cruise. At the time of the cabinet decision, the main point of discussion had been whether, if Australia's invitation for the fleet to visit was accepted,[19] it would be impossible to say "no" to any others. But, as no other invitations had arrived at the time of the cabinet discussion, it was accepted. At the same time the cabinet hoped to avoid the problem of future invitations by announcing a set itinerary for the remainder of the cruise.[20]

It subsequently proved diplomatically difficult to reject invitations tendered by the governments of Japan and China. That visits to those countries, replete with elaborate receptions and entertainment, were conducted, tends to obscure the fact that the original American intent had been to avoid the area entirely. And once committed to the Japan visit, the navy made no effort to further reinforce its strength in the western Pacific. Two battleships, the *Maine* and *Alabama*, which had been detached from the Atlantic fleet at San Francisco and ordered to proceed home independently, had already crossed the Pacific and Indian oceans and entered the Mediterranean.[21] Had increased naval strength been desired in the western Pacific at the time of the fleet visit, these units' departure from San Francisco might very easily and discreetly have been delayed to place them in the Philippines at the desired time. And the seven operational armored cruisers of the Pacific fleet, rather than lying in readiness in Honolulu or the Philippines, had been dispatched on a routine visit to American Samoa.[22] Even more distant from Japan, cut off from telegraphic connections to the outside world,[23] lacking coal stockpiles,[24] and deployed before the installation of their fire control systems had been completed,[25] the disposition of the main battle formation of the U.S. Pacific fleet during the Atlantic fleet visit to Japan was remarkably nonthreatening.[26]

These purely naval factors argue rather strongly that even after the military test of the first part of the cruise was successfully completed, President Roosevelt continued to pursue a prudent course and did not blatantly brandish America's new fleet in a crass display of strength designed specifically to intimidate Japan, his much later statement to the contrary notwithstanding.

And what of the diplomatic results of the world cruise? Of all the nations visited by the fleet, the Japanese connection was most important; therefore, it would be instructive to examine the fleet's impact on that relationship.

By the time the fleet reached the Pacific, deficits generated by greatly expanded post-war defense budgets had caused alarm in Japan, and a cabinet reshuffle in July 1908. As the new Japanese prime minister, Katsura Taro, struggled with the financial crisis, one significant aspect of Japan's foreign policy, entente with the United States, assumed increased importance. Several outstanding problems between the two nations, including the continuing problem of Japanese immigration, were resolved before the fleet reached Japan.[27] And two days after the fleet left Yokohama, Ambassador Baron Takahira Kogoro initiated negotiations that led to the Root-Takahira Agreement.[28] Although the fleet commander in chief, Rear Admiral Charles S. Sperry, felt the agreement was the "immediate fruit" of the fleet visit,[29] it seems most probable that such an agreement would have been negotiated with or without the fleet visit. The visit merely provided a suitable opening to initiate negotiations upon which the Japanese government, under pressure to reduce defense spending, had already decided to embark.

Although the world cruise of the Great White Fleet presented a colorful spectacle upon the international stage at the time, its impact on world events was minimal. The cruise touched on many U.S. foreign policy issues of the day, but the tendency to attribute diplomatic successes to the cruise, as in the case of the Root-Takahira Agreement, generally disregards the underlying reasons for those successes. The cruise might more validly be seen as a catalyst for certain developments in U.S. foreign relations, but not their cause.

The true significance of the battleship fleet cruise must be understood in terms of the developing capabilities of the U.S. Navy. The cruise was the first effective test of the "new navy's" sea legs, of its ability to respond to defense requirements in the Pacific. The experience gained led to a reappraisal of U.S. Pacific defense capabilities. By the time of the fleet's return in February 1909, all of the "failures, blunders, and shortcomings," to which Theodore Roosevelt had earlier referred, had become apparent, and the resultant improvements created a fleet in which he could justifiably have had "great confidence."

NOTES

1. Louis Morton, "Military and Naval Preparations for the Defense of the Philippines during the War Scare of 1907," *Military Affairs* 13, no. 2 (1949): 95; Richard D. Challener, *Admirals, Generals, and American Foreign Policy, 1898–1814* (Princeton: Princeton University Press, 1973), pp. 248–47; William Reynolds Braisted, *The United States Navy in the Pacific, 1897–1908* (Austin: University of Texas Press, 1958), p. 208.

2. Minutes of the Joint Board meeting of June 18, 1907, cited in Challener, *Admirals*, p. 235.

3. Challener, *Admirals*, p. 235.

4. No stenographic record of the meeting was kept. Fortunately Col. Wotherspoon prepared a detailed memorandum shortly afterward. Wotherspoon to Army Chief of Staff, June 29, 1907, AG 1280082, National Archives, quoted in Morton, "Military and Naval Preparations," pp. 96–97.

5. Ibid., p. 96.

6. Ibid.

7. *New York Herald,* July 2, 1907.

8. *New York Times,* July 2, 3, 1907.

9. Ibid., July 3, 1907.

10. Ibid., July 5, 1907.

11. Ibid.

12. Ibid., July 7, 1907.

13. Roosevelt to Lodge, July 10, 1907, Elting E. Morison, ed., *The Letters of Theodore Roosevelt*, 8 vols. (Cambridge: Harvard University Press, 1951–54), 5: 709. For similar sentiments see Roosevelt to Hermann Speck von Sternberg, July 18, 1907, and Roosevelt to Elihu Root, July 23, 1907, Morison, 5: 720–21, and 724–25.

14. Roosevelt to Trevelyan, Morison, *Letters*, 7: 393.

15. For a detailed examination of logistics and infrastructure problems, see James R. Reckner, *Teddy Roosevelt's Great White Fleet*, (Annapolis: Naval Institute Press, 1988), pp. 14–18.

16. Metcalf to Root, Aug. 28, 1907, National Archives, Record Group 59, File 8258, Case 1 (hereafter cited as NA, RG 59).

17. Root to Charge Wilson, Jan. 20, 1908, NA, RG 59: 8258/64.

18. *New York Times*, March 14, 1908.

19. Prime Minister Alfred Deakin to US Consul-General John P. Bray, Dec. 24, 1908, NA, RG 59: 8258/124.

20. *New York Times*, March 14, 1908.

21. For itinerary, Bureau of Navigation circular letter, May 29, 1908, NA, RG 59: 8258/494–95; for actual progress of the battleships, *New York Times*, Oct. 1908, pp. 1, 5, 11, 18–20 .

22. Rear Admiral Pillsbury (Chief of the Bureau of Navigation) to Acting Secretary of the Navy Truman Newberry, May 19, 1908. NA, RG 45: Area Files of the Naval Record Group, Area 4.

23. Rear Admiral Bradley A. Fiske, *From Midshipman to Rear Admiral* (London: T. Werner Laurie, 1919), p. 423.

24. Ibid; *New York Times*, Oct. 14, 1908.

25. E. T. Constein to William S. Sims, Aug. 20, 1908, Sims Papers, Library of Congress.

26. But despite these considerations, Fiske later recalled that the impression he had at the time was that the "real purpose of the trip was to get a considerable fighting force into the neighborhood of Japan." Fiske, *From Midshipman*, p. 423.

27. Secretary of Labor and Commerce Oscar Straus to Root, 51931/1, Oct. 3, 1908, NA, RG 59: 2540/744–49, and Oct. 12, 1908, NA, RG 59: 2540/756.

28. "Arrangement between the United States and Japan Concerning Their Relations in the Orient," NA, RG 59: 16533/1, with notation, "Handed to the President by the Japanese Ambassador on Oct. 26, 1908."

29. Sperry to C. S. Sperry, Jr., Jan. 9, 1909, Sperry Papers, Library of Congress.

28

Theodore Roosevelt, American Foreign Policy, and the Lessons of History

Frederick W. Marks III

Twenty years ago, as a young assistant professor of history at Purdue University, Woodrow Wilson was my beau ideal. The diplomatic slight of hand by which he kept the United States at peace through two and a half years of World War I and his incredibly gallant fight for American membership in the League of Nations, these were the high points of my lectures. I even vowed to one of my classes that I would write a book on Wilson!

Needless to say, such a book has yet to be written, and for a very simple reason. A colleague of mine, Walter Forster, took me aside on one occasion and asked me why I was so partial to Wilson. Did I not know about his notoriously high rate of military intervention? Did I realize how many Mexicans and Haitians had died at the hands of soldiers marching to Wilson's tune?[1] Was I conscious of how ill-prepared the United States had been for its role in World War I, how it took a full year to transport any sizable number of men to Europe and how Wilson had been obliged to equip this most unexpeditious of expeditionary forces with French and British artillery, British vessels, French aircraft, and French rifles (with a consequent diminution of America's voice in the peace settlement)? I must confess that at the time I knew as little about any of this as I did about the size and futility of Wilson's effort to intervene in the Russian Revolution on the side of the Whites. I have since caught up on my reading and learned incidentally that a junior troop trainer by the name of Dwight D. Eisenhower, stationed at Fort Colt in Gettysburg under orders to instruct his recruits in the art of tank warfare, could not obtain a single tank until three Renaults arrived from France complete with a team of British instructors.[2]

But to return to Professor Forster, he grilled me on other aspects of the diplomatic record and in due course popped what has proven to be the most important question of my academic life: had I ever taken a serious look at Theodore Roosevelt? Was I aware of his emphasis on preparedness, in particular the growth of the U.S. Navy under his leadership to a rank of number two in the world, second only to the Royal Navy? And had it ever occurred to me that this might have had something to do with TR's brilliant peace record? Forster proceeded to spell out in detail what he meant by "peace record": first, mediation to end the Russo-Japanese War; second, a significant part in averting the coming of war between Germany and France; third, the mediation of disputes between Nicaragua and Honduras as well as between Guatemala and El Salvador. TR had won the Nobel Peace Prize, he had negotiated scores of arbitration treaties, he had become the first leader in the world to go to arbitration over a dispute pitting his own countrymen against a foreign claimant. And unlike Wilson, who also won the Peace Prize but whose admirers were limited to select groups within a limited number of countries, TR had acquired a universal reputation for professionalism and practicality.

The result of this informal initiation ceremony at Purdue is that I put on a Sherlock Holmes cap and was soon caught up in the mystery of the Venezuela blockade crisis. Somewhat later, I donned my judicial robes to conduct hearings on the controversial affair of Panama, and I can assure you that my life has never been the same since!

They say that converts are known for their zeal and, to the degree that this may be true in my own case, I believe it is traceable to the persuasive power of comparison—to the fact that I came to Theodore Roosevelt from Woodrow Wilson. If one were to examine TR in isolation, treating him as if he were the first and last president of the United States, I suppose his record would be rather attractive. But when one places him alongside other chief executives who came before and after, particularly in the realm of foreign policy, it is then, I think, that he really begins to shine.

Take, for instance, his injunction to "speak softly and carry a big stick," indeed the whole issue of preparedness. If one could find presidents with superb peace records who did not prepare for war or, conversely, some who did prepare and yet failed to keep the peace, one might be tempted to write off TR's record as pure happenstance. But such is not the case. I have already alluded to Wilson's failure to keep up his military guard and to the embarrassments that followed. Early in the nineteenth century, Thomas Jefferson dry-docked or scrapped five out of seven capital ships before sustaining a series of insults to the American flag. Our citizens were held to ransom by the Barbary pirates and Jefferson found himself embroiled in a four-year war which he could not win despite his best efforts. Four hundred Americans had to die in combat before he realized he would have to pay annual tribute to guarantee the security of American shipping, and additional sums were needed to ransom hundreds of captives.

Let us pass over the War of 1812, which caught President Madison and the nation woefully unprepared, and recall Harry Truman's sweeping demobilization of U.S. armed forces after World War II. Against the advice of his military advisers, Truman chopped the defense budget to barest bones. He then went to war in Korea and to the brink of war over crises in Berlin, Trieste, Iran, and Greece.

What is interesting about the relationship between unilateral disarmament and war is that we begin to see a pattern that can be substantiated on positive, as well as negative, grounds. Invariably, preparedness on the part of the United States has led to peace. George Washington, after increasing the size of the army sevenfold and inaugurating a program of capital ship construction, dislodged the British from their bases on U.S. soil and brought peace to the American frontier. He also opened Spanish-occupied New Orleans to the American export trade, obtained the release of pirate-held hostages, and made the Mediterranean safe for American shipping.[3]

James Madison, after seeing the nation's capital in flames during the War of 1812, and without a single significant victory on the ground to show for it (until after the signing of the peace), was determined not to let this happen again. He therefore recommended a standing army of 13,000 men and, although Congress saw fit to fund a force of only 10,000, American strength was nevertheless maintained at unprecedented peace-time levels. Madison's successor, James Monroe, saw to it that our militia was reorganized, West Point expanded, and the navy bolstered. In 1816, Congress authorized the building of nine battleships. Legislators committed the nation to a peace-time fleet comparable to that of the leading European powers, and within three years Americans witnessed a succession of unparalleled diplomatic achievements. These included the establishment of our first claim to Pacific Ocean frontage, the acquisition of the Floridas (meaning the present-day state of Florida, along with the southern portion of the adjacent Gulf states), in addition, the fabulous Mesabi iron ore ranges of northern Michigan and Minnesota, not to mention some long-coveted fishing privileges off the coast of Newfoundland. The Great Lakes were demilitarized, and Great Britain, hitherto public enemy number one, extended a surprisingly cordial hand. Finally, Secretary of State John Quincy Adams, who framed what has since come to be known as the Monroe Doctrine, is on record as having said that "an efficient commerce and a growing navy, these are the pillars of my peace."[4] Few words could be more telling.

Vaulting from the early 1800s to the mid-1900s, we find President Eisenhower spending three times as much as his predecessor on peace-time defense after putting an end to hostilities in Korea. Ike also played a key role in pacifying French Indochina. Within two years of his accession to the presidency, the world was at peace for the first time in a generation, and historians were recording the first thaw in the Cold War. Liberal reform swept Eastern Europe, bibles poured into Russia, ambitious programs of Soviet-American cultural exchange were set in train, and Nikita Khrushchev sat with his opposite number around the fireplace at Camp David. One might add that Eisenhower, who thought of himself as a TR Republican, kept a Latin inscription on his desk, *suaviter in modo, fortiter in re* (gently in manner, mightily in deed), which comes about as close as one can come to TR's "speak softly and carry a big stick."[5] He also had a secretary of state, John Foster Dulles, who used to recommend, as a study in high-caliber statesmanship, TR's handling of the Venezuela blockade crisis coupled with the voyage of the Great White Fleet.[6]

Ronald Reagan was the last of the presidents to leave a significant mark in the area of peace-time defense spending. Congress, under strong executive prodding, voted funds for the MX missile, the B-1 bomber, the Strategic Defense Initiative, and a 600-ship navy. Along the way, it agreed to the extension of U.S. military power overseas through the sale of forty F-16s to Pakistan and the transfer of some highly sophisticated AWACS aircraft to Saudi Arabia. Thereafter, Reagan was instrumental in ending the war between Iran and Iraq while signing the first disarmament treaty in modern history. The Kremlin drew plans to evacuate Soviet troops from Afghanistan even as surrogate forces operating in Angola and Cambodia made similar plans. In the same vein, Soviet spokesmen announced unilateral cuts in the size of their army along with a pullback of twenty-five percent of their tank forces from Eastern Europe. Dissidents were permitted to leave the Soviet Union in record numbers and religious leaders began emerging from the underground.

It is interesting to note that TR achieved a similar détente when, on the aftermath of the world cruise of the Great White Fleet, a bellicose Tokyo slashed its defense budget and carried out its side of the celebrated Gentlemen's Agreement.[7] Under the first Roosevelt, Anglo-American relations were greatly eased as a result of understandings reached on Alaska and the Caribbean, and we are afforded one more example of peace through strength.

In sum, we can point to four presidents whose diplomatic style bears a striking resemblance to that of TR and who achieved strikingly similar results, while four other presidents operating in a conspicuously different manner wound up with conspicuously different results.

Which brings us finally to a discussion of Franklin Delano Roosevelt who, of all our chief executives, was at once the most closely and distantly related to TR—closely in terms of blood, distantly by virtue of diplomatic temperament and style. Unlike TR, FDR did not believe in military preparedness or the balance of power, nor was he sufficiently impartial to be regarded around the world as an "honest broker." And once again, the record demonstrates that ideas have consequences as one man's performance proves to be the direct antithesis of that of the other. FDR, who had all the same peace-keeping and peace-making opportunities as TR internationally, was unable to capitalize on any of them. In this respect, he and his cousin make perfect foils for one another, for where TR mediated a Far Eastern war and averted the coming of war in Western Europe, FDR attempted to do both and in both cases failed. He failed to reach a compromise agreement with Japan; he failed to bring the European antagonists to an early peace settlement; and unlike TR, who mediated two major disputes affecting Latin America, FDR mediated nothing. The Four Freedoms that he championed appear to have been no more prevalent five years after his death than they had been five years before. Worst of all, the United States clashed with two different antagonists on two separate fronts in two very distinct wars. Moreover, according to the facts as I read them, and as I shall attempt to elucidate them, it is highly unlikely that either of these wars would have occurred had TR occupied the Oval Office.

World War II was, of course, a disaster of untold magnitude, claiming as it did the lives of fifty million people, six million of them in a holocaust of bestial intensity. By utterly destroying the balance of world power in East as well as West, it forced Uncle Sam into the unwanted, unaccustomed, and financially debilitating position of world policeman. In a sense, the United States has never ceased fighting since December 7, 1941, a day that FDR said would "live in infamy." Hot war turned willy-nilly to Cold War and fifty years later we find ourselves reeling under a deficit of staggering proportions. To my knowledge, no one has ever stopped to calculate the cost of coping with the type of world bequeathed to us by Franklin Roosevelt: NATO, the Marshall Plan, presidential "doctrines" bearing the names of Truman, Eisenhower, Carter, and Reagan, foreign aid programs to woo neutrals, along with programs to retain allies, including erstwhile enemies. Nor does this include the cost of dozens of bilateral defense pacts, added to a network of overseas bases that makes the Roman Empire look puny by comparison. And do not think, for a moment, that FDR made a great power of the United States. We were great and powerful on the world stage as early as the time of TR without feeling any of the unpleasant side effects.

You will note that I have spoken thus far only of the cost to Americans. Is it not true, however, that the price paid by others for World War II was in some ways even greater? In this tipsy age of *perestroika* and *glasnost*, some are suggesting that Yalta is no longer a dirty word. Have they consulted the Eastern Europeans who, after parting with their freedom and self-determination, are only now, after forty-five years, beginning to see some light at the end of the tunnel? Have they consulted the Chinese, mainlanders as well as Taiwanese? If Mao Tse-tung and Chiang Kai-shek ever agreed on anything, it was the fact that the intrusion of Soviet influence in Manchuria, as sanctioned by FDR in violation of solemn pledges, was an international disgrace.

The tragedy of Yalta lies not so much in what FDR gave up as in the fact that he made absolutely no effort *not* to give it up.

Some have argued that he had no alternative in view of a widely perceived need to enlist Soviet aid in the war against Japan. This is pure speculation. Stalin, who was beholden to the United States for Lend-Lease aid, positively wanted to enter the lists against Tokyo. Furthermore, Roosevelt loaded Stalin with concessions that seem to have surprised even the Soviet dictator. When Stalin asked him, somewhat incredulously, if he did not think that some of the postwar agreements might not be a rather bitter pill for Chiang Kai-Shek to swallow, Roosevelt replied in effect: "Chiang will do what he is told, leave it to me."[8]

Franklin Roosevelt, the man who thought he could "charm" Stalin, wound up being the one charmed. "Uncle Joe," after dissolving the Comintern, posed as a champion of religious freedom and indicated that the Soviets would chart a postwar course between communism and capitalism. He even went so far as to say that he wanted to change the name of his country back to Russia (and the Soviet ambassador began going by that name).[9] FDR not only liked Stalin; he trusted him, believing implicitly that Russia would be exhausted and friendly once the fighting ended. Consequently, despite the lessons of history and Churchill's urgent warnings, he could never see the Russian bear as anything but tame, and, so far as we can tell, it is for this reason that he declined at Yalta to press for clauses that would have helped to ensure free elections in Eastern Europe.[10] This, essentially, is why he passed up an opportunity to liberate Berlin and Prague prior to the arrival of the Red Army. It is for this reason also that he failed to honor his promises to Chiang.

It all comes down to a failure to think as TR did, in terms of history and the balance of power. And such failure was evident before, as well as after, the outbreak of the Second World War. FDR could have advised London and Paris in 1938 and early 1939 to include Moscow in a triple entente with an eye to curbing the rising might of Berlin. Instead, he discouraged it![11]

He has been acclaimed as a successful commander in chief, yet the war in which he made his reputation dealt a stunning blow to many of the hopes and expectations reposed in him by his countrymen. To boot, it was a war in which the Allied cause came within a hair's breadth of defeat. Well may we wonder how the second Roosevelt would be regarded today if Stalin's armies had not worked miracles and clinched some of the more closely contested battles. Beyond this, is there any reason for believing that the United States owed its success in the war to Roosevelt rather than to such factors as geography, industrial capacity, size of population, and Allied fighting ability? I think not. Indeed, I shall argue that among the things for which FDR was personally responsible was an unpardonable lack of preparedness.

Franklin Roosevelt has been hailed as the father of the Good Neighbor policy even though he inherited the bulk of it from Hoover, but it is by no means clear that his lavish outlays of foreign aid, his self-denying pledges of nonintervention, and his tolerance of expropriation gained him anything in the way of authentic gratitude or respect. It is, after all, TR, not FDR, who was voted a special commendation by a congress of Latin American states.[12] Needless to say, TR tendered no foreign aid, made no self-denying pledges, and was not one to tolerate arbitrary expropriation.

FDR's best claim to cosmopolitan fame rests upon his role in establishing the United Nations. But here again, whatever one may think of Turtle Bay and its future as a force for world peace, one must record that the original impetus for international organization came not from Washington but rather from London. Roosevelt envisioned a world run by Four Policemen, something that Churchill and even "Uncle Joe" found rather far-fetched. Indeed, it was not until leaders of the opposition Republican party lit a fire under FDR that the president moved to appropriate the cause of internationalism and make it his own.[13]

One of the most powerful arguments in FDR's defense is that he was a victim of events and circumstances beyond his control. Again and again, historians have alleged that a combination of economic depression, isolationist sentiment, and the ravenous appetite of Hitler and Tojo tied his hands, thereby rendering him little more than a helpless spectator.

Theodore Roosevelt, were he alive today, would doubtless dismiss such an argument the way he did the rationale behind Wilson's League, as "floating to heaven on one wide sea of universal slush." It simply does not bear up under careful scrutiny. Were we compelled to go to war with Tokyo? American businessmen did not regard Japan's position in Manchuria as a serious threat to their commerce or an affront to the democratic ideal. Neither did the British. Neither did Joseph Grew, U.S. ambassador to Japan. Neither did John van Antwerp MacMurray or Nelson T. Johnson, heads of the American mission to China from 1925 to 1941 and men who spoke without an axe to grind. As for Manchukuo, the so-called "puppet state" created by Emperor Hirohito, there was a willingness to recognize it on the part of every major power in the world except the United States.[14]

And was the Tojo who confronted FDR really unique? Had TR not dealt with a proud, Samurai-led Japan, heady with victory over China and Russia and newly established in Korea on a protectorate basis. Did Tokyo not view U.S. acquisition of the Philippines in 1898 as an encroachment on its sphere of influence? Did it not have difficulty accepting the U.S. takeover of Hawaii? Overwhelmed by the apparent impossibility of curbing U.S. influence in Honolulu, the Japanese envoy stationed there in 1898 attempted suicide.[15] Japanese seal fishermen poached on American preserves; there were anti-Japanese riots on the West Coast, and Tokyo refused stubbornly to carry out its side of the Gentlemen's Agreement stipulating limits on Japanese emigration.[16] All of this under TR. If anyone is prepared to maintain that such a scenario was any less ominous than the one FDR faced thirty years later, I should like to see the evidence.

Similarly, in the case of Hitler's Germany, as compared with the land of von Hindenburg and von Tirpitz. Wilson's secretary of state, Robert Lansing, reflected a set of beliefs widespread during the era of TR when he asserted that Kaiser Wilhelm was out to conquer the world and that Wilhelm's defeat was absolutely imperative for the safety of the United States.[17] The English, obsessively fearful of Berlin, had to have their nerves calmed by Theodore Roosevelt. They were as concerned as we were that the German navy, powerful and growing more so by the year, had plans to acquire bases in the Caribbean athwart vital sea routes running to and from the isthmus—which is, of course, why TR went to the brink of war over Germany's blockade of Venezuela and why Wilson forced Denmark to sell us its Virgin Islands.[18]

Granted, German anti-Semitism was not as virulent in 1905 as it would be thirty years later, but then no one went to war in 1939 or 1941 over the fate of European Jewry. The holocaust did not commence as we know it until after the outbreak of hostilities in 1939, and during the war Jewish leaders became painfully aware of just how little FDR cared for them or for their cause. The fact is that the president himself showed signs of anti-Semitism as did a number of his more prominent appointees, including Breckinridge Long and Joseph Kennedy, U.S. envoys to Italy and Great Britain respectively.[19]

One can go further. Was there any more likelihood of war in 1939 than there was in 1905 given the degree of tension that existed during the earlier period between France and Germany, specifically over Morocco? Again, I think not. The difference between the two eras seems to lie less in the likelihood of war than in the peace-keeping and peace-making ability of a single individual, the president of the United States. TR was able to exercise twice the influence of FDR operating from a population base of little more than half the size. And he had to contend not only with the kaiser's navy which by World War II had ceased to exist for all practical purposes—Hitler's submarine warfare was strictly defensive in nature—but also with the Royal Navy, an agent that again had ceased to present a serious threat by the time FDR came to power. Recall that it was an Anglo-German combination that threatened Venezuela in 1902–1903, just as it was an Anglo-Japanese alliance that held sway in the Pacific. TR had to push the Brits hard over the Alaskan boundary dispute, as well as in Venezuela. I believe it may be fairly said that the Anglo-American rapprochement that TR did so much to foster deserves to be counted among the richest portions of the legacy left to cousin Franklin.

And what of isolationist sentiment? Was FDR any more hampered by it than TR had been at the turn of the century? So powerful was such feeling in the early 1900s that Congress refused to endorse either of the Hague peace declarations without protocols reaffirming the separation of the New World from the Old. We know, too, that TR's support of the Algeciras Peace Agreement failed to win Senate approval without an amendment denying American responsibility in any way, shape, or form for North Africa. As for the veto traditionally cast by Irish-American voters against cooperation with Great Britain, it would appear to have been a good deal stronger in 1905 than it was thirty years later.[20]

True it is that FDR, unlike TR, had to cope with widespread disillusionment stemming from Wilson's failure to steer the United States into the League, not to mention the failure of the League itself. On the other hand, FDR, for all the handicaps he faced, enjoyed a considerable advantage over TR in terms of the precedents and models upon which he could build. One such precedent was Portsmouth. Another was Algeciras. FDR did not enter the White House until after the United States had become a party to international naval limitation agreements signed in Washington, D.C. By 1933, Washington had assumed the role of co-sponsor with Paris of an international peace pact. In addition, it had denounced Japanese inroads on Chinese sovereignty. Highly advantageous, too, was the interventionist lobbying of a powerful and articulate Jewish minority, something unknown to TR. Those who recall the New Deal era can never forget the influence of the America First Committee, again something missing at the time of TR. The argument, however, is that TR, had he stood in FDR's shoes, would have headed off a European conflagration. And this, added to preparedness, would have eliminated the *need*, as well as the pretext for U.S. intervention. American ships would not have been sunk in the Atlantic, and Pearl Harbor would not have come under attack. As it was, Japan's decision to go to war with the United States was sharply contested by some of its foremost leaders.

Scholars have in fact confirmed that isolationism was not really formidable as a political force until the mid-1930s, by which time FDR had spoken and acted as a leader of such sentiment for several years.[21] One can only conclude that the isolationist movement that hampered him in the late 1930s owed its existence in large measure to things that he himself said and did during his first term. For example, reacting to the failure of the London Economic Conference in 1933, he suggested that the United States had no place in European affairs. In successive books published in 1933 and 1934, FDR came out against American entry into the League of Nations. He was equally isolationist in his public utterances, not to mention his support for the Nye Committee.[22]

But even if one is willing to assume, for the sake of argument, that FDR's hands were tied by a strong residue of isolationist sentiment not the result of his own making, assuming further that Germany and Japan were more of a threat in 1937 than they had been a generation and a half earlier (and I do not accept either one of these assumptions), it still does not excuse the president for failing to crank up his military establishment to the limits allowed by treaty and by Congress. TR would take a request for, say, four battleships, ask Congress for eight, and settle for three.

Courtesy of Theodore Roosevelt Collection, Harvard College Library

President Theodore Roosevelt reviews the departure of the American "Great White Fleet" on a good will cruise around the world, December 16, 1907.

FDR, on the other hand, would take a request for three battleships, ask for two, and accept one. Truth be told, he was less thwarted by public opinion than the one doing the thwarting. Newspaper czars Hearst and Howard came out for greater preparedness in 1933, the year of his inauguration, and for the next two years, while Gallup polls registered public sentiment as "overwhelmingly in favor" of building up American defenses, FDR let such defenses languish. In 1938, when Congress, in harmony with public opinion recommended additional fortification for U.S. bases in the Pacific, especially Guam, FDR turned a deaf ear.[23] He did all he could to do as little as he could. Two years later, with the president coming out against a two-ocean navy and requesting a mere billion dollars for defense, Congress voted five billion and mandated a two-ocean navy! FDR refused to get behind a draft bill until late 1940, by which time sixty-nine percent of the American people were on record as supporting it (a bill, incidentally, sponsored by a Republican and an anti-New Deal Democrat). The second Roosevelt was also frank about his position on arms. If you had them, you would use them; they were provocative.[24]

Scholars friendly to FDR have questioned whether a few extra planes and ships would have made much of a difference to jingoes like Hitler and Tojo.[25] The answer to this query is an emphatic yes. Decisions taken by Berlin and Tokyo were clearly rooted in perceptions of American weakness. German Foreign Minister von Ribbentrop viewed American threats to side with Britain and France as a "great big bluff." In Hitler's opinion, such intimations were "lies pure and simple." The führer assured his generals that it would take Washington until 1945, at the earliest, to project any significant force onto the continent of Europe. When Walter Schellenberg, Hitler's national security adviser, confided to Luftwaffe chief Hermann Goering that in spite of appearances Washington might not be as weak as it appeared, Goering told him to see a psychiatrist. And if the Germans were pleasantly surprised by what they saw, Russian, French, and Chinese observers, among others, were appalled that our army, as late as 1939, ranked only nineteenth in the world, behind Portugal. It stood at only seventy percent of the strength authorized by Congress and less than twenty-five percent measured in terms of combat readiness. Not until late 1938 and early 1939 did FDR begin to address the issue of preparedness, and then at such a snail's pace that American military standing, vis-a-vis other nations continued to decline. This "lamentable state" of affairs, to quote General Pershing, was not lost on overseas analysts.[26]

Still another argument advanced on behalf of FDR is that the severity of the Depression and the urgency of the legislation needed to deal with it distracted him and forced him to husband his political capital, thereby preventing him from sponsoring defense programs that might have alienated certain elements of Congress. In other words, TR did not have to deal with the crash of 1929 as FDR did. However plausible such a line may be, it runs counter to what we now know of the period. FDR channelled an enormous amount of energy into foreign affairs during the first Hundred Days; he was anything but pressed for time.[27] Second, his opposition to preparedness extended far beyond the years during which priority legislation was up for enactment (1933-35). Third, his foot-dragging confounded not only his military advisers but also his principal political and diplomatic advisers: Hull, Welles, Grew, Hornbeck, Davis, and Baruch. It cannot be overemphasized that the second Roosevelt, not content to stand in the way of American preparedness, urged the British and French to refrain from arming as well. At a time when Churchill, the proverbial voice crying in the wilderness, was calling for positive action, the man from Hyde Park was complaining about a "rearmament complex" on the part of Britain.[28] So much for the theory that FDR, as opposed to TR, was a victim of events beyond his control.

Turning to other points of comparison between the two Roosevelts, it is probably in their attitude toward foreigners and things foreign that one finds the greatest discrepancy. TR lectured his compatriots as they were never lectured before or since, on the evils of racial prejudice and on the rights of Oriental immigrants. It was perfectly in character for him to defend a Chinese boycott against American commerce on the basis, as he put it, that "we cannot receive equity unless we are willing to do equity." And when he insisted that "we have as much to learn from Japan as Japan has to learn from us" he meant it because he found something to admire in all the nations and ethnic groups with which he was familiar. He spoke with the people of India about cricket and Parsi as naturally as he chatted with Hungarians about the Arpad dynasty. After a trip to Latin

America, he informed his fellow citizens of various ways in which he felt they had been eclipsed by their neighbors to the south—in mitigating the effects of slavery for instance.[29]

The point is that with all of TR's insistence on 100 percent Americanism, he was anything but parochial. He read Oriental poetry. He studied *bushido*, Japan's ancient code of chivalry. He knew France's *Chanson de Roland* well enough to give points to the French ambassador. His second wedding took place in London with an Englishman as best man. He rode horseback with foreign envoys, hiked and played tennis with them, sought their advice on important issues. And he carried all of this off without the slightest hint of indiscretion.[30]

Franklin Roosevelt resembled his cousin in at least two respects. He was well travelled and familiar with several languages. But here the similarity ends. The second Roosevelt had no Jules Jusserand, no Speck von Sternberg, no Cecil Spring Rice as a part of his inner circle. When he journeyed to European health spas and encountered signs requesting guests to be as quiet as possible, he would deliberately slam the doors. He was proud to recount in a letter how one of his children had boasted to Mussolini that "the United States had three times the population and ten times the resources of Italy, and that the whole of Italy would fit comfortably into the state of Texas."[31]

Cousin Franklin liked to burlesque the accents of foreign envoys, to tell ethnic jokes, and to take sides in international disputes—so much so that it disqualified him for useful service as a mediator.[32] Where TR wanted to know the facts on every side of every issue, FDR was not, as a rule, interested.[33] His presidency began as it ended, with a heavy bias against Germany, Japan, and a number of other countries. When Breckinridge Long, his ambassador at Rome, tried to convey some of the background necessary for an understanding of Italian foreign policy, Long was suspected of being un-American, and he was twice investigated on this count.[34] As long as Germany remained weak, FDR brushed aside arguments for a revision of the Versailles Treaty; he would have none of Mussolini's Four Power Pact or Ramsay MacDonald's disarmament plan. However, as soon as the Axis began to flex a new set of muscles, he swung to the opposite extreme, attempting to outdo Chamberlain as an agent of appeasement. Regarding the Japanese, FDR believed that they suffered from underdeveloped skulls. More to the point, he was convinced that they were incapable of challenging the U.S. Navy. At no time does he seem to have given serious thought to their predicament. And there is no indication that he ever approached Tokyo in good faith despite repeated protestations of a willingness to negotiate. If Theodore Roosevelt believed that Japan had as much of a right as the United States to a sphere of influence, Franklin rejected this notion out of hand.[35]

The question of imperialism points up still another area of disagreement between the two Roosevelts. Whereas FDR condemned it as immoral across the board, TR saw it as sometimes good, sometimes bad, depending on the situation. For those incapable of self-rule, he felt it could be a blessing. Circumstances could change, however, and in his opinion the subjects of colonial rule were just as entitled to benefit from imperial arrangements as were their overlords. This is why TR fought so fiercely and over such a long haul for tariff concessions to bolster the Philippine and Cuban economies.[36]

Few are aware of the fact that Franklin Roosevelt was a confirmed imperialist until just a few years before he entered the White House. Thereafter, his rhetoric changed, but not, it would seem, his basic impulse, for while he set a timetable for Philippine independence (something TR had wanted to do thirty years earlier), he made no move to give up Guantanamo Naval Base. He was delighted to take control of Micronesia, and if he had his way, Washington would have acquired Chile's Easter Island, along with Ecuador's Galápagos Islands. Ironically, the United States grew far more under FDR than it did during the TR era when it actually dwindled in size.[37]

For TR, much of the moral law came down to a matter of keeping one's word. When he said he would do something, he did it. On one occasion, when an arbitral award involving U.S. access to Canadian fisheries went against Washington, and Congress proved reluctant to vote the requisite funds, TR took up the cudgels and worked "four gibbering years," as he termed it, to rouse the nation's sense of honor. By the same token, after promising to withdraw from Cuba (with the exception of Guantanamo), he proceeded to do so to the amazement of not a few. It is for this reason that Theodore Roosevelt enjoyed greater credibility with foreign statesmen and foreign observers than any other president in our history.[38]

With FDR, the story is entirely different. He was generally

regarded by overseas officials as amateurish, undependable, and slavishly beholden to public opinion. His record is positively strewn with broken promises. What is more, one is shocked at the number of falsehoods he uttered, many of them aimed directly at the American people.[39]

As a final basis for comparison between the two Roosevelts, there is the area of operational skill. Virtually everything on the diplomatic chessboard that TR touched turned to gold as compared with FDR's record which proves to be nearly the reverse. Of FDR's many offers of mediation, none succeeded and most were flatly rejected. I count over thirty protests and appeals on the international level from 1933 to 1945, all of them futile. Out of dozens of prewar diplomatic initiatives and schemes, all but a handful came to naught (and of this handful, most, I would submit, were of dubious value).[40] The Nobel Peace Prize that FDR sought and for which he yearned from the bottom of his heart, eluded him. He tried to obtain credit for bringing Hitler and Chamberlain together at the Munich Conference of 1938, and again he failed (fortunately for his reputation in subsequent months when the term Munich became synonymous with "sell-out").[41] Nothing, though, is quite as revealing in this respect as his performance during the first Hundred Days. His proposal for a world nonaggression pact was spurned at Geneva while, in his negotiations with Moscow (for diplomatic recognition), he ended up giving away more than he received. His tariff truces unravelled. The behavior of his delegation to the London Conference appeared farcical. His heavy-handed interference in the internal affairs of Cuba—part of an effort to democratize it—backfired. And when news of his secret effort to cancel foreign debts leaked, he was accused of conspiring to thwart the will of Congress and forced to retreat. After deciding to fight for discriminatory arms embargo legislation, something that would have strengthened his hand against a potential aggressor and which had been endorsed by the new House of Representatives by a vote of 285-19, as well as by the arch-isolationist William E. Borah in the Senate, he reversed himself no less than four times in four weeks. Where Hoover had pressed for such a bill in two separate messages to Congress, FDR had a similar message drafted but decided not to send it. Letters sent by Secretary Hull to committee chairmen were recalled after reaching their destination. Under Secretary of State William Phillips agreed to testify before a House committee, then cancelled. Hull himself refused to testify.[42] Notwithstanding the famed Destroyers for Bases agreement (which did not require a vote in Congress) and Lend-Lease (which came rather late in the game), the second Roosevelt had an uncanny way of getting hold of the wrong end of nearly every stick.

In conclusion, true greatness cannot be appreciated until one comes face to face with counterfeit greatness. And vice versa. Counterfeit cannot be seen for what it is until it is made to stand alongside the genuine article. I don't think I ever appreciated TR fully until I had the opportunity to study other chief executives, FDR in particular, nor did I ever realize how much FDR lacked in the way of diplomatic judgment and refinement until I observed TR at work—and not, mind you, the TR handed down to us by Henry Pringle and company. Not the TR of *Arsenic and Old Lace*, or *The Wind and the Lion*, or *Tintypes*. I mean the real TR! Any scholar willing to embark upon a systematic analysis of methods, ideas, and results across a broad spectrum of time will find that the first Roosevelt wears well. In one way or another, all of the things that I have written thus far are related to TR. *Wind over Sand* I regard as a companion volume to *Velvet on Iron*, and I suspect that my book on Woodrow Wilson, if and when it appears, will also be about Theodore Roosevelt, for the man from Oyster Bay is a magnet, a fixed point on the historical compass. As Louis Halle, distinguished scholar of international relations, once remarked of TR, he was "a statesman whose vision might have averted much of the grief that has come upon us in this century."[43] Future writers, I predict, will return to the first Roosevelt in ever larger numbers simply because they have nowhere else to go.

NOTES

1. Samuel Flagg Bemis, *The Latin American Policy of the United States* (New York: Norton, 1943), p. 178; Richard W. Leopold, *The Growth of American Foreign Policy* (New York: Knopf, 1966), p. 320. At Parral, Mexico, two Americans were killed along with forty Mexicans; at Carrizal, twelve more Americans were killed with two dozen captured. Nor does this include Pancho Villa's raids that resulted in the killing of sixteen Americans, then seventeen, and then four. Scores of Haitians were shot by U.S. Marines when the latter landed in 1915; and within six years, according to Richard Leopold, Haiti's death toll reached 3,000. See Bemis, *Latin American Policy*, p. 181, and Leopold, *Growth*, p. 318.

2. Stephen E. Ambrose, *Eisenhower: Soldier, General of the Army, President-Elect, 1890–1952* (New York: Simon and Schuster, 1983), pp. 64–65.

3. Frederick W. Marks III, *Independence on Trial: Foreign Affairs and the Making of the Constitution* (Baton Rouge: Louisiana State University Press, 1973), pp. 207–14.

4. John D. Hicks and George E. Mowry, *A Short History of American Democracy* (Boston: Houghton Mifflin, 1956), p. 182; Richard B. Morris, ed., *Encyclopedia of American History* (New York: Harper and Row, 1961), p. 153; Marie B. Hecht, *John Quincy Adams* (New York: Macmillan, 1972), p. 272 (JQA quote); Samuel Eliot Morison, *"Old Bruin" Commodore Matthew Galbraith Perry* (Boston: Little, Brown, 1967), p. 85.

5. Krock Memorandum, April 7, 1960, box 1, book 2, Arthur Krock Papers, Princeton University.

6. Andrew H. Berding, *Dulles on Diplomacy* (Princeton, NJ: Van Nostrand, 1965), p. 128.

7. Frederick W. Marks III, *Velvet on Iron: The Diplomacy of Theodore Roosevelt* (Lincoln: University of Nebraska Press, 1979), pp. 57–58, 179–80.

8. Frederick W. Marks III, *Wind over Sand: The Diplomacy of Franklin Roosevelt* (Athens: University of Georgia Press, 1988), pp. 181, 397n.

9. Ibid., p. 170.

10. Ibid., pp. 171–72.

11. Ibid., p. 151.

12. Marks, *Velvet on Iron*, pp. 171, 181–82 (see also 183–89).

13. Marks, *Wind over Sand*, pp. 179, 284–85.

14. Ibid., pp. 43, 45–46.

15. Marks, *Velvet on Iron*, pp. 4–5, 30n., 55–57.

16. Marks, *Wind over Sand*, pp. 55–58.

17. Robert Lansing, *The War Memoirs of Robert Lansing* (Westport, CT: Greenwood, 1970), pp. 19-20.

18. Marks, *Velvet on Iron*, pp. 5–10.

19. Marks, *Wind over Sand*, pp. 138–40, 142, 286, 391n.

20. Ibid., p. 19; Marks, *Velvet on Iron*, p. 3; William C. Widenor, *Henry Cabot Lodge and the Search for an American Foreign Policy* (Berkeley: University of California Press, 1980), p. 131; Alexander DeConde, *A History of American Foreign Policy* (New York: Scribner's, 1963), p. 395.

21. Marks, *Wind over Sand*, pp. 18–19.

22. Ibid., chapter 1, especially pp. 19–20, 26, 34–39.

23. Ibid., pp. 18, 113; Samuel P. Huntington, *The Common Defense* (New York: Columbia University Press, 1961), p. 249.

24. Marks, *Wind over Sand*, pp. 112–13, 279.

25. See, for example, *Diplomatic History* 13 (Spring 1989): 218.

26. Marks, *Wind over Sand*, pp. 112–13, 149–50.

27. Ibid., pp. 15–18.

28. Ibid., pp. 61, 278–79.

29. Marks, *Velvet on Iron*, pp. 93, 179, 184–85.

30. Ibid., pp. 196–97.
31. Marks, *Wind over Sand*, pp. 251–52.
32. Ibid., p. 253 (on burlesquing of accents).
33. For FDR's partisan disposition, see ibid., pp. 35–36.
34. Ibid., 255. See also, pp. 123–24.
35. Ibid., pp. 35–36, 42, 52–53, 117, 145–46 (132–37). On FDR's unwillingness to compromise, see chaps. 2–3.
36. Marks, *Velvet on Iron*, pp. 94, 191–92.
37. Marks, *Wind over Sand*, pp. 285–86. TR yielded Alaskan acreage equivalent to the size of Rhode Island and larger than the Panama Canal Zone.
38. Marks, *Velvet on Iron*, pp. 95–96.
39. For a detailed list of (a) broken promises and (b) lies and falsehoods, see Marks, *Wind over Sand*, pp. 304–6, 397–401. To cite one example, less than ten percent of the wartime aid promised to Chiang was ever delivered, ibid., p. 180.
40. For a detailed list of (a) mediation offers, (b) protests and appeals, and (c) diplomatic initiatives, see ibid., pp. 392–97.
41. Ibid., pp. 145–47.
42. Ibid., pp. 19–20, 22–26, 28, 35–39.
43. Louis J. Halle, *Dream and Reality* (New York: Harper, 1959), p. 260.

Courtesy of Theodore Roosevelt Collection, Harvard College Library

The "Great White Fleet," enters Chesapeake Bay, February 1909, returning from a cruise around the world.

The Bull Moose:

The Post-Presidential Years

In 1912 Theodore Roosevelt and his supporters founded the Progressive Party, which was nicknamed the "Bull Moose" Party because TR remarked that he felt "as fit as a bull moose." The Progressive Party adopted a far-reaching platform of political and social reform, and most of the planks in the Bull Moose platform eventually became law.

29

Theodore Roosevelt's African Safari

Tweed Roosevelt

This chapter will describe Theodore Roosevelt's African safari which he embarked upon shortly after leaving the White House at the completion of his second term in 1909.

First, some background. On September 6, 1901, at the Pan American Exposition in Buffalo, New York, a crazed anarchist shot President McKinley. Eight days later, having served only six months of his term, McKinley died and Theodore Roosevelt became the twenty-sixth president of the United States, much to the horror of certain Republican interests who thought they had buried him as vice president. "My God," said one, "now that damn cowboy is in the White House."

TR was elected in his own right in 1904 by a landslide. He had just turned forty-six, and on his birthday his friend, Elihu Root, sent him a congratulatory note: "You have made a very good start in life and your friends have great hopes for you when you grow up."[1]

TR had pledged on inauguration night that he would respect the two-term tradition and not seek another term in 1908. About two years before he was due to step down, he began to consider what he was going to do after the presidency. He would still be relatively young, only just fifty and a decorous retirement to oblivion on Long Island seemed clearly out of the question.

Much public discussion was generated. Some suggested that as Charles W. Eliot was ripe to retire as president of Harvard, TR could replace him. Others said he should run for Thomas Platt's senatorial seat. Henry Adams proposed that TR should follow J. Q. Adams's example and become a U.S. congressman. Philander Knox thought the solution was simple: "He," Knox proclaimed at a Washington party, "should be made a Bishop."[2]

TR had other ideas. First he needed to decide on his successor. Eventually he picked William Howard Taft. This choice may have been because Taft had faithfully served TR for many years and shown signs of following in his progressive footsteps. On the other hand, since Taft weighed more than 300 pounds, it might have been because TR had always loved the larger vertebrates.[3] He realized that, given his tremendous popularity, he would have difficulty convincing the American public he was not manipulating Taft from behind the scenes, and therefore knew he had to do something to get out of the way and give Taft a free hand.[4] He had always been interested in natural history and hunting was one of his great loves, especially big game. He had hunted extensively all over the United States, sometimes living in the wilderness for months at a time. Why not, he thought, go on an extended hunting expedition somewhere far from the political arena of Washington. Having settled on this solution he began to consider alternatives.

It happened that one night among the White House dinner guests was Carl Akeley, a famous taxidermist and African big game hunter. As the evening progressed, Akeley, with frequent verbal prodding from TR, told story after story about hunting in Africa. One of them was about sixteen lions he had seen emerging from a cave. TR was delighted and, turning to the man on his right, said: "Congressman, I wish I had those lions to turn loose on Congress." The congressman, a bit taken aback, managed to stammer: "Well, Mr. President, aren't you afraid they might make a mistake." With a snap of his prominent teeth, TR shot back: "Not if they stayed long enough."[5]

At the end of the evening TR had made up his mind, he would go to Africa and hunt big game. In typical fashion, he began at once to plan the trip. He wrote letters to everyone he thought might be able to help him, people in the United States, England, Europe, and British East Africa.[6] Before long he had determined his general itinerary. He would sail to Mombasa, proceed overland through British East Africa to Lake Victoria and then north to the Nile where he would take a steamer to Cairo. The trip, he calculated, would take about a year, surely long enough for the press and the American public to forget him and give Taft a chance.

Somewhere along the line, the basic purpose of the trip began to change. Originally conceived as a hunting expedition, it occurred to TR that it might be transformed into a collecting one. He wrote the secretary of the Smithsonian Institution proposing this idea. The response was enthusiastic. Now the planning became much more complex because a collecting expedition is far more elaborate than a hunting trip, involving more people and much paraphernalia.[7]

TR went about his preparations methodically and painstakingly, ignoring no detail, however small, even though they were frequently accomplished by transatlantic correspondence. What clothes to take, what food (jams yes, marmalade no), where would the money come from, who should accompany him, how many pairs of eyeglasses should he order (nine pairs, three less than he took to Cuba),[8] where exactly should they hunt, how could the press be kept away, what specimens were wanted, and so on.

He insisted that each box of provisions—containing a mix of the essential items of food so only one box need be opened at a time and each weighing sixty pounds, the amount a single porter could carry—include some cans of Boston baked beans. Furthermore, he ordered that virtually all the liquor, which it had been suggested he take, be replaced by canned tomatoes.[9]

Among the more important items was the arsenal.[10] Of course he would take an assortment of rifles and shotguns, both new and from his own collection. (One of his rifles bore the teeth marks of a mountain lion he had subdued in hand-to-paw combat after the rifle jammed.) One gun he ordered was an army Springfield .30-caliber rifle with a stock and sight mechanism which he himself designed.[11] When it arrived, he tested it in the White House basement, found it inadequate and sent it back with a stinging letter. Eventually he got what he wanted.

The most interesting weapon, however, was one given to him by a group of British notables.[12] It was a Holland and Holland .500/.450 nitro express elephant gun made especially for him. TR's comment: "Shoots very accurately but the recoil is tremendous." This was an understatement. The blast was so strong that on several occasions it gave bystanders nosebleeds. A single bullet could knock a charging elephant to it knees,[13] but its fearful kick caused one expedition member to suggest that anyone, except TR, would prefer to face the consequences of a charging elephant.[14] (Incidentally, the gun is currently owned by William E. Simon, former secretary of the Treasury, who keeps it in working order. It has frequently been ranked among the most historic and valuable firearms ever made.)[15]

Another important problem was the matter of reading

material. TR was a voracious reader. Not only were his powers of concentration such that he could read in the most distracting of circumstances, but he read with such speed that many who observed him thought he was merely leafing through a book he was actually reading. Furthermore, his retention was extraordinary. He once surprised a Czech visitor to the White House by quoting several dozen lines from a Czech poet little known to the rest of the world. When the suitably impressed visitor asked if TR had just read it, he replied: "I read it twenty years ago and haven't thought of it since."

It was hard to find something he hadn't read. Once a woman who was a frequent visitor to the White House came across a slim volume of Icelandic stories. She was convinced that TR would never have heard of it, and so the next time she sat next to him at dinner, she casually remarked: "I don't suppose you have any interest in Icelandic literature." "Have I not," he replied with enthusiasm and proceeded to tell her in detail not only about her author but about a dozen or so others of whom he obviously had considerable knowledge.[16]

TR was clearly addicted to reading, and he needed to take along enough to keep him occupied for a year. His solution was what has become known as the "pigskin library," sixty volumes, the smallest editions he could find of each work and all designed to fit into an aluminum case which would then weigh less than the sixty pounds a porter could carry.[17] TR wrote:

> Where possible I had them bound in pigskin. They were for use, not ornament. Often my reading would be done while resting under a tree at noon, perhaps beside the carcass of a beast I had killed or else waiting for camp to be pitched; and in either case it might be impossible to get water for washing. In consequence the books were stained with blood, sweat, gun oil, dust and ashes; ordinary binding either vanished or became loathsome whereas pigskin merely grew to look as a well used saddle looks.[18]

The titles were chosen not because they were the best but merely because they were what TR wanted to read at the moment. They covered a wide range, encompassing both classic and modern, fiction and nonfiction, but not one was about Africa, hunting, or animals. They included works in English, German, and French.[19]

His comments about some of them are interesting:

> [The poet] Lowell is represented here, but I think towards the

end of his life, he became too much a Bostonian. The best American is a Bostonian who has lived ten years west of the Mississippi.[20]

I took Morris's translation of various Norse Sagas, including the Heinskringla, and liked them so much, I incautiously took his translation of Beowolf, only to find that while it had undoubtedly been translated out of the Anglo-Saxon, it had not been translated into English, but merely into a language bearing a specious resemblance thereto.[21]

I took . . . Gogol's *Taras Bulba* because I wished to get the Cossack view of what was described by Sienkiewicz from the Polish side.[22]

In all, he brought with him eighty books (he added some along the way)[23] which meant he consumed about two per week while he was in Africa. Many he read several times.

TR took his role as the leader of a scientific expedition seriously. He certainly had the training for it. He had always been interested in animals, and in fact through his Harvard days was convinced he would become a professional naturalist. His first work was entitled *The Summer Birds of the Adirondacks* which, among other things, described a new species of bird for the area, and was published when he was eighteen.[24]

TR had studied taxidermy and was an expert on large American mammals. Once a mammal embryo arrived at the Smithsonian for dissection without its identifying label. Some scientists were having a debate as to whether it was animal A or B. The consensus was that it was an A, but they couldn't agree. Finally one of them suggested they send it to the White House and ask the president's opinion. So they did and it came back with a note identifying it as a B and when the lost label was found, the president's identification proved to be correct.[25]

TR had the basic training for the job, but he needed to know more about African animals. He wrote to Henry Fairfield Osborn, director of the American Museum of Natural History, asking for books. As they arrived at the White House, mostly technical and frequently multi-volumed, he consumed them at the rate of five per week.[26] (This in addition to his normal duties of running the country.) Osborn noted that at the end of several weeks, TR had ordered every book relating to the field, but what impressed him more was a luncheon held at Sagamore Hill a few weeks before TR embarked for Africa. He invited the leading American experts on African fauna for a kind of doctoral oral. Osborn recalls that by the end of the afternoon it was clear to everyone in the room that TR knew as much or more than any of them.[27]

As the date of departure grew nearer, public interest mounted. Gifts arrived from the public by the mail sack-full—rifles, cameras, walking sticks, hats, mosquito netting, and innumerable toy elephants and lions—more gifts than had ever inundated a president before.[28]

There was much concern about TR's safety in Africa. Some worried he might die of sleeping sickness, then raging in British East, but one of his former western hunting companions commented: "They don't know the Colonel. He may be in danger of wildebeests, rhinoceri, dik-diks, lions or snakes, but no one who ever saw him would believe that sleeping sickness would ever catch up with him. That man's immune from that disease."[29]

Most Americans wished him well, but the *Philadelphia Ledger* made the astonishingly tasteless suggestion that since TR had already enjoyed a picturesque career, it would be altogether fitting for him to meet his death in some striking manner in Africa. TR was immensely amused, but his wife Edith did not find it quite as humorous.[30]

Finally, two weeks after leaving the White House and after a tumultuous farewell, TR, his second son, eighteen-year-old Kermit, and three Smithsonian naturalists set sail from Hoboken, New Jersey bound for Mombasa. Thirty days later, after a more or less uneventful trip (nothing was ever uneventful when TR was around), they arrived in British East Africa.

It should be remembered that British East Africa was still very much a new country. It had been a British Protectorate for only fourteen years, slavery in Zanzibar had been abolished for eleven years, General H. H. Kitchener had put down the Mahdists ten years before, and the Uganda railroad had been operating for a year. In the whole country there were less than one thousand whites and perhaps only twenty-five to thirty Americans had ever visited it.[31] Yet it was an odd kind of frontier, with English clubs serving tea in the afternoons to parasolled ladies sitting next to bronzed ivory poachers who might have just returned from an expedition during which several of their porters and perhaps a white companion had been killed and sometimes eaten by natives.[32]

On the night TR and Kermit arrived, the merchants and

planters gave them a dinner at the Mombasa Club, which they enjoyed, but clearly they were anxious to be on their way.[33]

The itinerary was well planned. The first part of the trip would really be a series of excursions using the railroad or Nairobi as a base. Then on to Victoria and up to Uganda and down the Nile to Khartoum.

An idea of the distances involved can be conveyed by superimposing a map of the United Kingdom over a map of the area in which TR travelled. The United Kingdom only fills a small portion of the Sudan, the country in which TR ended his safari.

Early on the morning after the dinner at the Mombasa Club, the party went to the station to board Acting Governor Sir Frederick Jackson's special six-car train. They set out for the hinterland.

The Uganda railroad, often called the "lunatic express," had been conceived in Whitehall several years before when there were virtually no white settlers in the entire Protectorate, and therefore nothing for it to carry. The announced purpose of the railroad was to attract settlers, but the real purpose was to establish the British claim to the territory and keep out the Germans whose colony to the south represented a constant threat. In that purpose it had succeeded, but still in 1909 very little was shipped along the line.[34]

Between Mombasa and Nairobi, the British government had staked out a large game preserve which stretched far south of the railroad all the way to the German border and a mile north of the track As a result, there was an abundance of game along the way which could easily be observed from the train. On the cowcatcher was mounted a bench and on this TR sat for most of the trip.[35]

The first part of the trip was through desolate country. Soon, however, the plains opened up and game began to appear. In one sixteen-mile stretch, someone counted over six thousand animals.[36] Accidents frequently occurred. While TR was riding the line, some giraffes crossed the track and became entangled in the overhead telegraph wires thus disrupting communications.[37] As for rhinos, TR commented: "A rhinoceros is a large beast and its long suit is courage and its short suit is brains. And now and then one would start to charge the train. It was always bad for the rhinoceros, but it was sometimes bad for the train."[38]

At the river Tsavo, they crossed a bridge made famous during its construction when two man-eating lions developed a taste for the Indian workers who were trying to build it. In spite of the most extraordinary efforts on the part of many hunters, night after night workers were dragged from their bomas and often eaten noisily within yards of their former tentmates. Eventually, the workers went on strike, making the altogether reasonable point that they had been brought to Africa to build a railroad, not to provide food for the lions. It was several months before the lions were killed and work could begin again. The man who finally killed them was Colonel J. H. Patterson who wrote a book about the experience called *The Man-Eaters of Tsavo*. TR called it "the most thrilling book of true lion stories ever written,"[39] and made a point of meeting Patterson.

Man-eating animals were not uncommon in the region. One killed more than five hundred natives before it was finally dispatched.[40] Often the animal's cunning appeared almost demonically supernatural. One story concerns the superintendent of police of the Protectorate, an extremely experienced hunter, who, along with an Italian and a German set out after a man-eater which was operating along the railroad. They had their railroad car shunted off to the side, set out some bait and settled in for a long wait. It being hot, the door was left cracked open. The policeman had the first watch. As it got dark, the other two fell asleep, one on the floor and the other on a bunk. Suddenly, the man on the floor was awakened by a heavy jolt. To his horror, he discovered that he had been awakened by a lion standing on his chest and biting down on the policeman's neck. In an instant the lion was out the door dragging his unfortunate victim. The next day, as was the rule in such cases, all that was found was the policeman's head and the soles of his feet.[41]

On another occasion, a hunter was in his tent when suddenly a lion broke in and dragged him away. Fortunately, the lion did not go far and his porters were able to come to his rescue. He was alive but badly injured, so they bandaged him up and put him back to bed. A few hours later the lion took him again. The pieces were found in the morning.[42]

After the better part of two days, TR having stayed on the cowcatcher long after everyone else had escaped the elements for the more pleasant ride in the coaches, the train arrived at the tiny depot of Kapiti Plains, where the trip would really begin. Waiting for them, lined up in formation, was what appeared to be a small army but what was in fact their safari. Never before or since has a larger safari been organized. Four headmen, fifteen native soldiers to guard the group, a dozen or so tent boys, as well as assorted gun bearers, cooks, skinners, grooms, and two hundred-sixty porters.[43]

The expedition included seven whites. First was R. J. Cuninghame, safari manager and TR's "White Hunter." On his shoulders lay not only the task of managing an extraordinarily complex safari which at its peak had more than five hundred men, but also he felt the burden of being ultimately responsible for keeping TR alive. For, truth to tell, the leaders of British East were delighted to have TR because they believed that he would put them on the world map, but they were well aware that the kind of publicity they got depended to a large extent on Cuninghame's ability to deliver TR to his Nile steamer without having the portion of him between his head and the soles of his feet consumed by a lion. Cuninghame may have looked like a gold rush forty-niner, but actually he was a Cambridge man well-qualified for the job. He had lived in East Africa for years, much of the time making his living as a professional elephant hunter. Before that he had been a whaler in the Arctic, a naturalist in Lapland, a transport rider in South Africa, and a collector for the British Museum.[44] TR's assessment was: "A finer man for the task could not be found." Next was Leslie Tarlton, also an extremely experienced hunter. His job, viewed as only slightly less important than Cuninghame's, was to keep Kermit alive.[45]

Then there were the three naturalists. First was Major Edgar Mearns, U.S. Army, a physician as well as a zoologist and botanist. He had had extensive experience both in the Philippines and with the Mexican Boundary Commission. He was a most tenacious collector. For example, one night he told his fellow expedition members the following story, perhaps not fully aware of the interpretation his audience around the campfire might place on it. He was in the Philippines during the Moro wars, fighting with a small detachment of U.S. soldiers. All day their position was besieged by wave upon wave of Moros. Never, he said, had he seen such bravery, but the Yankees' guns were too much for them. By the end of the day, the bodies were piled high around their position. "I stepped out of the stockade that night," Mearns said, "and collected a most interesting series of skulls; they're in the Smithsonian today."[46] Next was Edmund Heller, mammalogist and field taxidermist. He was to be responsible for skinning and preserving all the animals collected by expedition members, no small task when you consider that even with a number of natives to help him it might take him several days to prepare a large pachyderm such as a rhinoceros.[47] Finally there was J. Alden Loring, an expert on small mammals. He was to collect anything and everything that was too small to shoot.

To complete the roster there was TR and his son Kermit. Kermit, of course, was along to keep his father company, but he also had an official role. He was the expedition's photographer and his efforts adorn TR's book, *African Game Trails*. Most of the pictures were shots of the various hunters standing over their slain victims. The rest were a series of distant shots of game, often blurred and indistinct. In fairness to Kermit it should be pointed out that photography in those days was in its infancy, such things as telescopic lenses were not yet invented. Given the available equipment, he did a credible job.

TR's outfit was notable. In those days the fad leaned toward the enveloping and the heavy. TR wore hobnailed boots, khaki pants which resembled jodhpurs, an army shirt, and a sun helmet. Even his socks, which had been knitted at his request by the wife of his old ranch manager from North Dakota, were of heavy wool. He felt wool was the best material for long tramps through the bush.[48]

The baggage needed to sustain this enormous army was substantial. First there were the essentials of life such as food and tents, fifty in all. Incidently, TR's was no different than the others except that it had a huge American flag always flying before it. Next there was the hunting paraphernalia, crates of guns, thousands of rounds of ammunition, cleaning equipment, and so on. By far the bulkiest luggage was the material necessary for the scientific part of the expedition. To preserve the skins they had to take salt, four tons of it. To catch the small animals they needed traps, four hundred of them. Two hundred of the two-hundred-sixty porters carried the scientific material.[49]

After two days getting organized at the Kapiti Plains station, they were ready to go. They certainly must have made an impressive picture as they marched along. First came the flag, proudly borne by one of the porters.[50] Next came TR, the whites and the elite of the natives, headboys, gunbearers, and so forth, and then the long line of porters.

Quite an expedition, but by no means the most bizarre ever

mounted. One of the most extraordinary was the balloon safari which had taken place a year or so earlier. The leader apparently wanted aerial pictures of animals, so he acquired a hot air balloon and hauled it from Nairobi over the Maru escarpment to the Rift Valley. He filled the balloon, hanging the camera from the bottom, and anchored it with a long rope to a mule. His idea was to maneuver the mule in such a way so the camera would be over the game. Everything worked except that when he got the balloon up, the wild animals took one look at this apparition and made off. For two days he repeated the charade with little success. Finally on the third day he had just managed to get the camera over some nearsighted beasts when there was a sudden updraft. Balloon, camera, and mule disappeared forever.[51]

TR's initial day of hunting wasn't particularly successful. The first to fall was a Thomson's gazelle, shot at 225 yards.[52] Several misses later, he shot a wildebeest. In fact, for most of the safari, the story was more or less the same. TR shot at a great many animals, and most of them survived the experience. Someone once asked him if he were a good shot. "No," he replied truthfully, "but I shoot often."[53]

Actually, he shot surprisingly well, considering that he was very nearsighted in one eye and totally blind in the other. The blind eye was the result of an injury sustained in a boxing match with a young Army officer in the basement of the White House.[54]

The first really exciting hunt came when they were after rhino. TR had just killed an eland for the table when a lookout informed him that a rhino was on the other side of the ridge. TR and his companion climbed the ridge and spotted the rhino standing in open country. They began their stalk downwind, using a small scrub bush as cover. The rhino was completely unaware of their approach and, when they were 100 yards off, lay down. When they reached the bush, TR released the safety on his big Holland and Holland double-barreled elephant rifle, and, stepping from behind the cover, took aim for what he thought was to be an easy shot. The rhinoceros leaped to its feet with amazing ease—"with the agility of a polo pony" was the way TR put it. As it rose, TR shot, the heavy .50-caliber bullet piercing the rhino's lungs. But the slug didn't stop it; it wheeled and began to charge the hunters, spouting blood through its nostrils. As it turned, TR shot again, the second slug striking the rhino between neck and shoulder and piercing the heart. His companion fired too and his bullet broke the animal's neck. Nonetheless, the animal continued its charge, dead on its feet, until it fell, plowing the ground with its horn to a spot just thirteen paces from where TR was standing.[55] Another second and the safari would have been over then and there.[56]

Incidentally, note that TR stepped into the open just before he fired, although he could easily have shot from behind cover. One of his friends once commented, "Nothing that I know of Roosevelt better illustrates his habit of coming out in the open and going straight to the point than the way in which he approached his [big game]."[57]

The next excitement occurred when Kermit was on one side of a thicket in which he thought there was a leopard. Beaters were placed on the other side, but they had not yet begun to beat, and Kermit had not begun to move when suddenly the leopard, without a growl or warning of any kind, launched itself out of the thicket straight for his throat. The nineteen-year-old Kermit fired at six yards, momentarily stopping the charge. The animal charged again, and Kermit fired, this time hitting it in the spine. The leopard dragged itself into the brush and hid. One of the beaters came too close in the excitement, and the leopard, dragging his wounded legs, emerged to chase the unfortunate native. In a second it caught him. Kermit's companion fired a third shot and a fourth forcing the leopard to let go and return to the bush. When Kermit approached, it charged again. The fifth bullet killed it.[58]

Many other stories could be told. For example, TR wrote afterwards about the elephant hunt, "The bull . . . was so near that he could have hit me with his trunk."[59] But the elephant suffered the fate of many of the other animals which were unfortunate enough to come within range of the expedition's arsenal. Its skin was removed for shipment to the Smithsonian.

A lion unexpectedly charges. J. Alden Loring commented with awe, "Contrary to general belief, a lion does not bound towards its enemy, it scoots or glide over the ground with a speed simply remarkable."[60]

What was thought to be a lone buffalo turns out to be a regiment. One false move and the *Philadelphia Ledger* would have had its way.[61]

A porter violates the rules and goes back to look for something he dropped. He is charged and tossed by a rhino.[62]

A hippo charges a canoe dumping TR into the water. A close call but in the end the hippo's salted skin was carried off.[63]

However, it wasn't all murder and mayhem. TR had much else to occupy him while he was on the trip. Not politics, however. The only newspaper he saw during the entire trip was a copy of the *Owego (NY) Gazette* which no doubt did not tell him much about what was happening in Washington.[64]

A major preoccupation was paying for the trip. TR had originally estimated that the expedition would cost $50,000, which in 1990 would be roughly equivalent to half a million dollars. His arrangement with the Smithsonian was that as there were five Americans on the safari, TR would pay two-fifths (for Kermit and himself) and the Smithsonian would pay three-fifths. TR was not a rich man and financed his part by contracting with Charles Scribner's Sons to produce a series of articles to be written while on the trip and published first in their magazine and later as a book to be called *African Game Trails*. The guarantee was for $50,000 plus twenty percent royalty on the book.[65] The Smithsonian raised $30,000 by private subscription.

However, about half way through the trip, TR realized the total cost was going to be closer to $100,000. He now became a fund-raiser, firing off letters to a number of possible sources. Eventually, Andrew Carnegie donated $27,000 and the expedition could go on.[66]

Incidentally, *African Game Trails* was extraordinary for a number of reasons. It is perhaps the only book of its kind written and published while the safari was in progress. Typically, TR would return from a day's hunt, take a bath and eat dinner, and then retire to his tent to write.[67] Few books have been produced under such adverse conditions, much of it being written on hot evenings in the dim light provided by an oil lamp, the author wearing gauntlets, a helmet and mosquito netting draped around his neck and face.

Night after night TR slaved away. By the time the trip was over, he had produced a 500-page book, almost every page of which was handwritten in triplicate. When he finished a chapter, he would keep one copy and dispatch native runners with the other two, one north along the long route to the Nile and Cairo and the other back along the way he had come from Mombasa. Incredibly, although somewhat battered, not a single page was lost.[68]

TR wrote frequent letters to his editors giving them carte blanche to make any changes they wanted.[69] Nonetheless, they published it almost exactly as he had written it.[70] (Perhaps, if one wants to free oneself from editorial meddling it helps to be an ex-president.)

TR also found time to write many letters on all kinds of subjects. For example, on September 10, 1909, he wrote two long letters, totalling about three thousand words. The first, to the English historian George Otto Trevelyan,[71] was, according to the recipient, "A wonderfully wise and eloquent comparison of Carlyle's and Macaulay's views on Frederick the Great."[72] The second, written to Henry Cabot Lodge, comments on Harvard President Charles W. Eliot's just announced list of the one hundred best books: "It is all right as *a* list of books which a cultivated man would like to read, but as *the* list it strikes me as slightly absurd."[73]

This was not all. He wrote a book review of the best seller, *A Certain Rich Man*, by William Allen White,[74] several book introductions, some articles for *Outlook Magazine*, and he kept extensive daily diaries in which he carefully recorded each shot.[75] His total literary output of approximately two hundred thousand words in eleven months would have been respectable even for a writer today sitting at home at his word processor.

Much of TR's time was taken up in less glamorous activities than hunting big game. After all, the main purpose of the safari was to collect for the Smithsonian and most specimens could not appropriately be collected with a Holland and Holland elephant gun—insects for example or various species of cane rat.

TR took the scientific part of the trip seriously and as a result was extremely popular with the naturalists. Early on in the trip they had quickly realized the caricature of TR as a dictatorial bully who was only interested in himself bore little relationship to what he was really like.[76] A truer picture is suggested by TR's comment, "When you are placed in the position that you have got to tell a man his feet aren't the same size, never tell him one foot is smaller than the other; save his self-respect by saying one foot is larger than the other."[77] Also, note that when he was president, he didn't have the bands play "Hail to the Chief" which had been a tradition since Tyler's time, but rather, "There'll Be a Hot Time in the Old Town Tonight."[78]

The expedition brought home specimens of many animals

that had never been seen before and not all of them were small. For example, in the deep forests lives an antelope called the bongo. This animal is so shy that it had rarely been seen and almost never shot by a European. Kermit shot not one, but two within a few days.[79] Another very shy animal is the situtunga which is almost aquatic, living in the reeds at the edge of the lakes.[80] The expedition brought back the first ever seen outside of Africa.

On December 19, 1909, the safari reached Kisumu on Lake Victoria where they boarded a steamer for the twenty-four hour trip to Entebbe in Uganda. They were now in sleeping sickness country. Two hundred thousand natives had died in the last few months. The scourge was so terrible that the British government had forcibly deported every human being from the infected areas along the banks of Lake Victoria.[81] Certainly tragedy on a cataclysmic scale is not new to Africa.

The expedition moved quickly on to Kampala. There they were greeted by the young king.[82] He was the grandson of King Metusa whom John Speke had met in 1862. Perhaps the most famous passage in Speke's book describes the meeting. They were in the king's tent. Speke had just given Metusa a gift of some guns. Speke writes:

> The king now loaded one of the carbines I had given him with his own hands, and giving it full-cock to a page, told him to go out and shoot a man in the outer court; which was no sooner accomplished than the little urchin returned to announce his success, with a look of glee such as one would see in the face of a boy who had robbed a bird's nest. . . . I never heard, and there appeared no curiosity to know, what individual human being the urchin had deprived of life.[83]

After meeting the king, TR visited a Church of England Mission where the school children, who of course didn't speak English, sang him the following song. *"O se ka nyu si bai di mo nseli laiti wati so pulauli wi eli adi twayi laiti silasi giremi."* (If read aloud, a knowledge of Ugandian is not required for translation. If baffled, try singing it to the tune of the U.S. national anthem.)[84]

From Kampala they went down the Nile to the Lado where they set up camp. It was a most unattractive spot. Mosquitoes, carnivorous ants, crocodiles all over the place, a prairie fire almost destroyed the camp and during the daytime the temperature often exceeded 112 degrees. TR's comment: "A very pleasant camp, and [I] thoroughly enjoyed it."[85] There they shot the white rhino. Next it was on to Nimule and an excursion into the Belgian Congo to shoot the giant eland.

Then, suddenly, it was over. They reached Khartoum on March 14, 1910, where TR's wife and younger daughter, Ethel, were waiting.[86] They spent two days in Khartoum being entertained by local dignitaries, both European and Arab, and sight-seeing, sometimes riding a camel at a ferocious pace. (Most people, following such a strenuous ten months, might have preferred to spend a few days lounging leisurely in bed.) Also during those two days at Khartoum, TR somehow managed to find time to write numerous letters, a three-thousand-word essay on the pigskin library, and the introduction to *African Game Trails*, which many believe is among his very best writings.

From Khartoum it was on to Egypt and then to Europe for a round of royalty visiting[87] and finally back to the United States. Far from being forgotten, public excitement had been building for months. A committee of 150 notables lead by Cornelius Vanderbilt prepared the reception. Cartoons appeared. One particularly popular one was of Uncle Sam perched on the top of the Statue of Liberty peering out to sea through a telescope. The caption read, "I can't see him, but I can hear him."[88]

Then he arrived. He transferred to a crowded tug filled with family and friends. Two of the passengers would become much better known some years later. They were TR's niece Eleanor and her husband Franklin Roosevelt.

Twenty-five hundred dignitaries waited at the ferry slip for a "private" meeting, one hundred thousand had waited since dawn at Battery Park to catch the first public glimpse of him, and well over one million people lined Fifth Avenue, held back by policemen spaced at sixteen foot intervals over the entire four miles of TR's parade route.[89]

Although TR certainly enjoyed the reception, he, no doubt, was delighted to get home to Sagamore Hill and he must have felt immense satisfaction with the trip for it was clear it had been a tremendous success. The Smithsonian had received over twenty-three thousand specimens for its collection, making it the most complete in the world. Even today there are still some crates which have not been fully examined.[90] The naturalists had established their reputations especially as TR, in defiance of custom, insisted on allowing them full credit for their work.[91]

TR had not only achieved the two primary aims of everyone

who goes on a hunting safari, that is, to shoot a lion and to live to tell about it, but also he had the satisfaction of watching *African Game Trails* become what the *New York Tribune* called "the book of the year."[92] It ultimately sold more than one million copies in the United States,[93] as well as in editions in England, France, Germany, and Sweden. He was also proud of his second work on the subject, a two-volume technical tome written in collaboration with Edmund Heller and entitled *Life Histories of African Game Animals.*

Finally, Kenya had been placed quite firmly and prominently on the world map.

Some time later, TR was asked by a reporter for a summary comment about his African safari. He replied: "It was bully while it lasted, but it lasted long enough."[94]

NOTES

1. Henry F. Pringle, *Theodore Roosevelt* (New York: Harcourt, Brace and Co., 1931), p. 490.
2. Joseph L. Gardner, *Departing Glory* (New York: Charles Scribner's Sons, 1973), pp. 107–8.
3. Dixon Wecter, *The Hero in America* (New York: Charles Scribner's Sons, 1941), p. 386.
4. Archie Butt, *Roosevelt and Taft: The Intimate Letters of Archie Butt,* 2 vols. (New York: Doubleday, Doran and Co., 1930), 1: 42.
5. Carl E. Akeley, *In Brightest Africa* (New York: Doubleday, 1923), p. 158; Frederick S. Wood, *Roosevelt as We Knew Him* (Philadelphia: John C. Winston Co., 1927), p. 224.
6. For some examples, see Theodore Roosevelt, *The Letters of Theodore Roosevelt,* ed. Elting E. Morison, 8 vols. (Cambridge: Harvard University Press, 1951–54); hereafter cited as *Letters* followed by the letter number and the recipient. In this case, see letter no. 4,645 to John Henry Patterson; no. 4,723 to Edward North Buxton; no. 4,825 to Edgar Mearnes; nos. 4,854 and 5,111 to Whitelaw Reid; no. 4,885 to A. H. Fox; and no. 5,112 to Winston Churchill.
7. Paul Russell Cutright, *Theodore Roosevelt: The Naturalist* (New York: Harper and Brothers, 1956), p. 188; *Letters,* no. 4,771 to Charles Walcott; Theodore Roosevelt, *African Game Trails* (New York: Charles Scribner's Sons, 1910), p. 293 (hereafter cited as *AGT).*
8. Cutright, *Naturalist,* p. 191, 193; and Pringle, *Roosevelt,* p. 184.
9. *AGT,* p. 22; Kate M. Stewart, "Theodore Roosevelt, Hunter-Naturalist on Safari," *The Quarterly Journal of the Library of Congress* 27, no. 3 (July 1970): 246; and *Letters,* no. 4,855 to Edgar Mearns.
10. For an excellent discussion of TR's guns, see R. L. Wilson, *Theodore Roosevelt, Outdoorsman* (New York: Winchester Press, 1971).
11. *AGT,* p.22.

12. For a list of donors see *AGT*, pp. 22–24.
13. *AGT*, pp. 258, 262, 263.
14. Kermit Roosevelt, *The Happy Hunting Grounds* (New York: Harcourt, Brace and Co., 1931), p. 18.
15. Private communication with R. L. Wilson; and Bartle Bull, *Safari, A Chronicle of Adventure* (New York: Viking, 1988), p. 164.
16. Kermit Roosevelt [Jr.], *A Sentimental Safari* (New York: Alfred A. Knopf, 1963), pp. 272–73.
17. *AGT*, appendix F, pp. 513–21, and Kermit Roosevelt, *Hunting*, pp. 29–30.
18. *AGT*, p. 515.
19. TR also spoke Spanish and Portuguese, but as his son Kermit commented, "Father was more fluent than exact in expressing himself in foreign languages. As he himself said of his French, he spoke it as if it were a non-Aryan tongue, having neither gender nor tense" (Kermit Roosevelt, *Hunting*, p. 43).
20. John T. McCutcheon, *In Africa* (Indianapolis: The Bobbs-Merrill Co., 1910), p. 161.
21. *AGT*, p. 516.
22. *AGT*, p. 517.
23. *AGT*, pp. 162, 368.
24. Henry Fairfield Osborn, *Impressions of Great Naturalists* (New York: Charles Scribner's Sons, 1925), p. 169.
25. Wood, *Roosevelt*, pp. 226–27.
26. *Letters*, no. 4,830 to Henry Fairfield Osborn. Cutright, *Naturalist*, p. 193.
27. Osborn, *Impressions*, p. 174.
28. Wecter, *Hero*, p. 386.
29. *Letters*, no. 4,904 to Cecil Spring Rice; and no. 4,899 to Kermit Roosevelt. Col. Cecil Lyon quoted in Cutright, *Naturalist*, pp. 196–97.
30. Certainly the trip was not without risk. Hunting lion, for example, was not totally a one-sided adventure, as is suggested by the fact that while in Nairobi, TR dined one evening with three men, each of whom had been mauled by a lion. See Bull, *Safari*, p. 175. *Letters*, no. 4,899 to Kermit Roosevelt.
31. John T. McCutcheon, "With Roosevelt in Africa," undated clippings from *Chicago Tribune*, 1910, in the Theodore Roosevelt Collection, Houghton Library, Harvard University, p. 1.
32. For an example, see *AGT*, p. 384.
33. *AGT*, p. 7.
34. An excellent history of the building of the railroad and of British Africa is contained in Charles Miller, *The Lunatic Express* (New York: Macmillan Co., 1971).
35. *AGT*, p. 13.
36. Noel Simon, *Beneath the Sunlight and the Thunder: The Wildlife of Kenya* (Boston: Houghton Mifflin Co., 1963), p. 206.
37. *AGT*, p. 14.
38. Theodore Roosevelt, *The Works of Theodore Roosevelt, The National Edition*, ed. Hermann Hagedorn, 20 vols., (New York: Charles Scribner's Sons, 1926), 5: 395. Also see Theodore Roosevelt, *A*

Zoological Trip Through Africa (Pasadena: Bulletin of Throop Polytechnic Institute 20, no. 51, July 1911).

39. *AGT*, p. 9.

40. J. T. Muirhead, *Ivory Poaching and Cannibals in Africa* (London: MacMillan and Co., 1933), p. 253.

41. J. H. Patterson, *The Man-Eaters of Tsavo* (London: MacMillan and Co., 1908), pp. 282–88.

42. *AGT*, p. 65.

43. Bull, *Safari*, p. 271. Gardner, *Departing*, p. 118; and *Letters*, footnote to no. 5,217 to Andrew Carnegie, 7: 13.

44. *AGT*, p. 3–4.

45. Kermit Roosevelt [Jr.], *Safari*, p. 97.

46. Kermit Roosevelt, *Hunting*, p. 25; and Kermit Roosevelt [Jr.], *Safari*, p. 100.

47. Francis Warrington Dawson, "Hunting with Roosevelt in Africa," *Hampton's Magazine*, November 1909, p. 100.

48. Archie Butt not only advised TR what to wear, but also purchased most of his outfit. Archie Butt, *The Letters of Archie Butt*, ed. Lawrence F. Abbott (New York: Doubleday, Page and Co., 1924), p. 102. *AGT*, p. 22. *Letters*, no. 5,079 to William Sewall.

49. Edwin P. Hoyt, *Teddy Roosevelt in Africa* (New York: Duell, Sloan and Pearce, 1966), p. 23.

50. *Letters*, no. 5,213 to Henry Cabot Lodge.

51. Miller, *Express*, pp. 514–15.

52. *AGT*, p. 26.

53. Wood, *Roosevelt*, p. 223.

54. Rudolph Marx, *The Health of Presidents* (New York: G. P. Putnam Sons, 1960), p. 290; and Kermit Roosevelt, *Hunting*, p. 20.

55. *AGT*, pp. 91–93.

56. Many other hunters were not so lucky. While in Nairobi, TR visited a churchyard where he saw the graves of eight men, seven killed by lion and one by a rhino (*AGT*, p. 64).

57. *Letters*, footnote to no. 5,014, to Kermit Roosevelt, 6: 1,375.

58. *AGT*, pp. 114–16.

59. Theodore Rosevelt, *Theodore Roosevelt: An Autobiography* (New York: Charles Scribner's Sons, 1921), p. 34; and *AGT*, pp. 249–53.

60. J. Alden Loring, *African Adventure Stories* (New York: Charles Scribner's Sons, 1914), p. 26.

61. *AGT*, pp. 140–42.

62. Hoyt, *Teddy in Africa*, pp. 115–16.

63. *AGT*, pp. 214-16; and Dawson, "Hunting," pp. 95–101.

64. *AGT*, p. 225.

65. *Letters*, no. 4,789 to Robert Bridges and footnote; and no. 4,799 to Robert Collier.

66. *Letters*, nos. 5,217, 5,226, and 5,237, all to Andrew Carnegie.

67. Kermit Roosevelt [Jr.], *Safari*, pp. 43–44.

68. Cutright, *Naturalist*, p. 217.

69. *Letters*, nos. 5,212, 5,218, 5,222, 5,234, and 5,246, all to Robert Bridges.

70. Hoyt, *Teddy in Africa*, p. 51.

71. *Letters*, no. 5,228 to George Otto Trevelyan.

72. Joseph Bucklin Bishop, *Theodore Roosevelt and His Times*, 2 vols. (New York: Charles Scribner's Sons, 1920), 2: 172–73.

73. Letters, no. 5,229 to Henry Cabot Lodge and Anna Cabot Mills Lodge.

74. *Letters*, no. 5,242 to William Allen White; and William Allen White, *A Certain Rich Man* (New York: The Macmillan Co., 1909).

75. The diaries are at the Theodore Roosevelt Collection at Houghton Library, Harvard University.

76. Wood, *Roosevelt*, p. 214.

77. Francis Warrington Dawson, *Opportunity and Theodore Roosevelt* (Chicago: Honest Truth Publishing Co., n.d.), p. 156.

78. Wecter, *Hero*, p. 382.

79. Dawson, *Opportunity*, p. 121; and J. Stevenson-Hamilton, *Animal Life in Africa* (London: Heinemann, 1912), p. 132; Frederick E. Drinker, *Theodore Roosevelt, His Life and Works* (Philadelphia: National Publishing Co., 1919), p. 256; Roosevelt, *A Zoological Trip*; and *AGT*, pp. 365–66.

80. *AGT*, p. 379; and Stevenson-Hamilton, *Animal Life*, pp. 140–41.

81. *AGT*, pp. 370–71.

82. *AGT*, p. 377.

83. John Hanning Speke, *Journal of the Discovery of the Source of the Nile* (Edinburgh and London: William Blackwood and Sons, 1863), p. 298.

84. *AGT*, p. 376.

85. *AGT*, p. 397.

86. *AGT*, p. 464.

87. TR could be extremely amusing on the subject. For a description of him telling of his experiences, see Butt, *Roosevelt and Taft*, 1: 421–30; and *Letter*, no. 5,521 to George Otto Trevelyan and no. 5,524 to David Gray.

88. Stefan Lorant, *The Life and Times of Theodore Roosevelt* (New York: Charles Scribner's Sons, 1914), p. 535.

89. Gardner, *Departing*, p. 171.

90. Cutright, *Naturalist*, p. 210; Bull, *Safari;* p. 173.

91. *Letters*, no. 5,260 to Charles Walcott; and Cutright, *Naturalist*, p. 208.

92. Cutright, *Naturalist*, p. 218.

93. Dawson, *Opportunity*, p. 20.

94. Charles Hanson Towne, ed., *Roosevelt as the Poets Saw Him* (New York: Charles Scribner's Sons, 1923), p. 96.

30

Teddy Roosevelt Creates a "Draft" in 1912

Fred Greenbaum

The election of 1912 was a landmark in American political history. Because Robert La Follette perceived that Theodore Roosevelt had undermined the Wisconsin senator's bid for the Republican presidential nomination, La Follette prevented unification of the progressive forces in the Republican convention, and ended Roosevelt's slim chance to be the nominee. Frustrated, both Roosevelt in 1912 and La Follette in 1924 led progressives out of the Republican party into third party efforts. For many progressives this was an avenue out of the party and contributed to the drift of the Republican party to the right until it reached the extremes of the Reagan years.

Contrary to contemporary historical wisdom, Theodore Roosevelt did not enter the 1912 presidential contest to save the Republican party from a Taft debacle, finally convinced of La Follette's weakness;[1] his decision followed growing awareness of unexpected progressive strength as reflected in the La Follette candidacy. Early in October 1911, with advisers, he devised a plan to arrest La Follette's momentum while reconsidering his earlier refusal to challenge Taft. Periodically, supporters floated rumors of a candidacy. Unable to court the public openly, James R. Garfield, after consultation at TR's home and club, maneuvered and spoke for him.

Long before 1912 it was clear to progressive Republicans that Taft was a hopeless candidate. Could he be denied re-nomination? Roosevelt and La Follette differed. Roosevelt expected Taft to be renominated and defeated. In August 1911, Roosevelt reported to Cecil Spring-Rice that the insurgent challenge was leaderless, foolish, and strengthened the president.[2] La Follette was confident that the nomination could be wrested from a sitting president. Most progressives began the campaign with a pessimistic outlook. In fact, La Follette's campaign manager, Walter Houser, fearing the interests, predicted failure in a worthy cause.[3] Yet, political experts had completely misjudged the situation, underestimating the strength of the progressive Republican movement. Five weeks after this letter, Roosevelt had to reconsider his role in the 1912 race, and by December 1, he had become a candidate.[4] To explain events, James R. Garfield's relationship with Roosevelt and their October 9 conference must be examined. Further, conflicting reports on the progress of the La Follette campaign must be evaluated and light must be shed on Roosevelt's behavior.

It is indisputable that Roosevelt was perceived to be a stronger candidate than La Follette. La Follette did not generate equal strength in all parts of the country, but that is true of many national candidates. It is arguable that La Follette would have been nominated with Roosevelt's support, though many thought so.[5] The party regulars seemed determined to nominate Taft.[6] But there is very strong evidence that by October, La Follette had become a formidable candidate, aided by some strong statewide progressive organizations. Progressives felt that the campaign had succeeded in blocking Taft's renomination even if La Follette fell short.[7] During the last three months of 1911, favorable state reports poured into La Follette headquarters.[8] Where Roosevelt was more popular almost all of the Roosevelt vote was expected to go to La Follette, but rumors of Roosevelt's candidacy restrained many from commitment.[9] In Colorado, La Follette was reported stronger than anyone but Roosevelt. An enthused Edward Costigan returned from the Chicago Progressive Republican convention predicting the collapse of the Taft candidacy. William Allen White confirmed La Follette's popularity there in a letter to Roosevelt.[10] Joseph Bristow reported La Follette had a good following in Kansas and their chances for victory depended on whether they could force a primary.[11] George Norris found La Follette strong in Nebraska farm districts and thought the Roosevelt strength in cities would go to La Follette.[12] George Loftus wrote of Minnesota, "The movement . . . is progressing far beyond our expectations. . . . La Follette sentiment prevails throughout the state."[13] Joseph Schafer reported that Oregon was favorable to La Follette.[14] Gifford Pinchot, who informed a correspondent of "the remarkable progress made by La Follette," was still optimistic in December while helping Garfield prepare the way for Roosevelt. Houser, initially so pessimistic, wrote in late September that La

Follette could control the convention and could be elected. At the same time, Gilson Gardner, delighted with La Follette's progress, perceptively commented that Roosevelt did not want him nominated.[15] Even in the East, Louis Brandeis reported progressive enthusiasm and was convinced that Taft could not carry Massachusetts.[16] Moses Clapp predicted either a La Follette majority in the convention or a stampede to Roosevelt.[17] Jonathan Bourne forecast a race between La Follette and Wilson.[18]

On the other hand, purported evidence of a stillborn La Follette candidacy is tainted. Albert J. Beveridge and Albert B. Cummins had presidential aspirations; Hiram Johnson, touted as Roosevelt's running mate, predicted difficulty in the East even for Roosevelt. Garfield was out of town all summer; Beveridge until October. Beveridge could not carry his state for any progressive. The regulars were determined to nominate Taft regardless of the consequences, Bristow reported gloomily. Roosevelt could save the party, but would be defeated by the Democrats. W. E. Chandler, though disturbed by La Follette's treatment of Senator Stephenson, wrote about the weakness of the Bourne organization in the East, not about La Follette. In fact, many of the doubtful states chose Taft over Roosevelt in 1912. In Colorado, progressives expected no more than a split delegation for La Follette, but produced *no* delegates for the popular Roosevelt.[19]

There can be no question that Roosevelt was aware of the growing strength of La Follette. Edwin Earl, a Roosevelt supporter, wrote to him that he was "glad to note the La Follette movement is growing throughout the country and the people are beginning to think he is the most available man."[20] And Ray Stannard Baker enthused: "I believe it to be a thorough-going sincere movement, based upon fundamental principles and with a very well-organized public opinion behind it. I have never seen such letters, nor such newspaper comment, as I have seen in connection with the spread of this progressive propaganda and La Follette's candidacy."[21] But, preceding these missives, he had digested similar tidings from Garfield, and they had already taken tentative steps toward his candidacy.

Garfield's biographer, Jack M. Thompson, concluded that he was more concerned with Roosevelt's fortunes than with political progressivism. Unlike Gifford Pinchot, he never criticized or deviated from any of Roosevelt's actions; and Roosevelt's every thought and deed became his own. Thompson considered him at best a cautious and conservative reformer who sought the backing of businessmen and others opposed to Taft. He never did endorse La Follette. Following Roosevelt, he refused to participate in the initiation of the Progressive Republican League; Gifford Pinchot thoughtfully added his name to the membership rolls.[22] Garfield wrote to Dan Casement in April, "We think that the National League is dead. . . ."[23] Away in Mexico and the Southwest most of the summer of 1911, lacking any negative correspondence about La Follette as a candidate, and admittedly "not well informed as to the present political condition," Garfield did not hesitate to insist that La Follette lacked strength in Ohio and the East—contrary to his own correspondence, to confident reports from Ohio progressives, and to worried letters by Taft's secretary.[24] On September 20 Garfield received a communication from Houser asserting, "I am now certain that we have more than an even chance to control the convention."[25] This was followed by an enthusiastic dispatch dated October 3 from his friend, Amos Pinchot: "Houser, Medill McCormick, and Rudolph Spreckles [sic] tell me that the La Follette boom has had a tremendous response throughout the West, and certainly I find that here in New York City there is increasingly favorable comment upon La Follette. . . . People are beginning to ask whether after all he is not a pretty safe kind of man. I believe that if we can raise money enough to finance a vigorous campaign we can defeat Taft."[26] On October 4 he conferred with Frederick C. Howe who confirmed Pinchot's optimism. "His reports show decided gains throughout the country," Garfield confided in his diary. By October 7, after speaking to John Fackler, La Follette's Ohio campaign manager, he decided that the time was ripe to speak out. First, he responded to Roosevelt's summons to discuss the political situation and left for New York.[27]

At this meeting Roosevelt decided to take his first tentative steps toward an avowed candidacy. Despite receiving a few letters during August and September urging that only he could unify the party, Roosevelt thought a sitting president could not be denied renomination—until he was aware of La Follette's progress. If someone too radical to be within the mainstream of the party could create a viable candidacy in only four months, then the mood of the country was not Democratic, as he had supposed, but progressive. A former president with a broad base of support could ride the crest of the progressive wave to victory. But if he made no move and La Follette was nominated, or prepared the way for Cummins or Beveridge, Roosevelt's options for the future would be narrowed. White had informed him that he expected the country to be ready for La Follette in 1916, not 1912; but Taft might speed the timetable up to 1912.[28] Roosevelt, still cautious and not fully convinced, had to prevent La Follette from cornering all the progressive delegates while sustaining a progressive challenge. Their ingenious solution was a novel entry in Garfield's diary on October 10. Roosevelt, he wrote, "agrees that the time has come when I should speak plainly about what we think should be done. . . . I shall go to Chicago and urge the progress of constructive measures and a real progressive candidate—leaving to each state to select progressive delegates. It would be useless to urge La Follette everywhere."[29] The wording, and subsequent events, confirm Roosevelt's role. If accepted, it would leave Roosevelt's options open without dividing the progressive challenge to Taft.

Why, then, did Roosevelt continue to write of his unwillingness to be considered a candidate? He could not change his standard response without premature commitment; any leak by a correspondent would create the negative public perception of the Rough Rider trying to steal a surging progressive movement from La Follette. There was also the concern of an historian with his historical image. Frank Knox, alerted by newspaper rumors and aware of Roosevelt's sensibilities, wrote: "I am wondering whether anything has transpired to change your opinion. Of course, I readily understand the reluctance you feel to discussing such views by letter." He suggested a meeting with Roosevelt on December 1, when he returned to New York.[30] In mid-November, buoyed by the reaction to his trust editorial, and inclined to take the plunge, Roosevelt, still repeating his unwillingness to run, invited many key correspondents to evaluation conferences and reserved a meeting room in the Union League Club for Tuesday, November 28, and Friday, December 1; thereafter, he permitted his supporters to begin working for his nomination.[31] On January 12, 1912—the day he decided officially to begin his candidacy—TR even wrote to his *sister* his standard statement that the nomination would be a misfortune.[32] Roosevelt's letters, then, were written not to inform his correspondents but to conceal his real intentions. As he confided to White, any appearance that he had instigated a movement in his own direction would weaken the value of the nomination.[33] After all, he had refused to be considered in 1908 out of respect for tradition and had repulsed earlier progressive feelers about 1912. Only a draft could justify his candidacy. Once again, we must observe Roosevelt by returning to Garfield.

Roosevelt had called the strategy conference because of the imminence of the Progressive Republican conference in Chicago. Garfield's assignment in Chicago was to implement the strategy of sending uncommitted progressive delegations to the national convention, without tipping Roosevelt's hand. Failing to deflect the overwhelming sentiment for the endorsement of La Follette, he insisted that a clear endorsement was not a pledge and he would continue to advocate unpledged progressive delegates; Roosevelt's organ, *Outlook*, echoed Garfield's position.[34] Moses Clapp more accurately described to La Follette the atmosphere at the conference, "words are inadequate to express the enthusiastic endorsement of yourself."[35] Cal O'Laughlin of the *Chicago Tribune* informed Roosevelt, "Among the Republicans I find a growing belief that it will be difficult to nominate Taft."[36]

Garfield now returned to Ohio to forestall affirmation of La Follette at the state Progressive Republican conference. To this end he floated rumors of a Roosevelt candidacy within the friendly press and planted carefully timed draft calls, hoping to discourage commitment to La Follette, and to increase the longing for the tested Roosevelt. Ohio, Taft's home, where the "old guard" Warren G. Harding had triumphed two years earlier, was a key state. A victory for La Follette would be a tremendous boost for his presidential aspirations. Aided by Gifford Pinchot, Garfield pressed the Roosevelt strategy with such single-minded devotion that he repeatedly wrote that he had convinced the key La Follette supporters, only to complain later that they were still resistant.[37]

Roosevelt's well-timed article about the trusts appeared just before a ten-county progressive meeting in Cleveland, stirred rumors about his intentions, and sidetracked an endorsement of La Follette. Garfield immediately reported to Roosevelt.[38] At the Garfield Club banquet in Youngstown, Roosevelt was called the next presidential nominee. The *Cleveland Leader* continued the planned boomlet with a front-page article printing favorable comments on the speech. La Follette supporters should not think he was responsible for the endorsements and become alienated, Roosevelt wrote; nevertheless, he reiterated that anti-Taft feeling would not lead to sufficient support for La Follette, a constant refrain necessary to an orchestrated draft. The majority of delegates at the January 1 inaugural meeting of the Ohio Progressive Republican League, according to a private poll, clearly favored endorsing the Wisconsin senator. Badgered by Garfield and his allies, concerned that issues, not individuals, be emphasized, they accepted Garfield's formula to preserve unity. Immediately, the Roosevelt press trumpeted that the resolution reflected the weakness of La Follette's support and the colonel's strength. Roosevelt expressed his pleasure to Garfield; the La Follette candidacy had been arrested.[39]

With Garfield protecting his options, Roosevelt was moving rapidly toward an active candidacy. In late October his letter to White declining to run was careful to leave the door open while skillfully discrediting La Follette without offending. He expressed willingness to be sacrificed if it would aid the cause, but it would hurt the cause—a transparent loophole. Responding to White's expressed willingness to support La Follette, Roosevelt characterized the badger as a provincial politician, successful on a state, but not a national level; after all, he had not attacked labor unions and socialists as fearlessly as he had attacked corporations.[40] Shortly thereafter, Taft's move to prosecute the steel trust provided both a catalyst and an opportunity. Now he could break with Taft openly and make Taft the villain. His position on trusts would reassure businessmen, who had the greatest reservations about La Follette, but who feared Taft would lose.[41] His editorial would signal a possible change in his plans, would undercut La Follette at a crucial moment in Ohio (the ten-county Cleveland meeting), and the national reaction would indicate to him whether his latent candidacy should be activated or dropped. The response was strongly favorable. Still, different correspondents called upon him to run and congratulated him on his trust policy; supporters had recognized an indication of his willingness to run.[42] His readiness for an active candidacy was confirmed by the November and December conferences.

Within a period of only three months Roosevelt's perception of the campaign had shifted dramatically. In August he had thought progressive attacks were strengthening Taft's position. By early October, aware of La Follette's surprising progressive strength, they developed a plan, implemented by Garfield, to prevent La Follette from assembling the entire progressive base essential to any challenge to Taft, without premature commitment and without appearing to seek support. By mid-November, convinced that he could win the presidential nomination, he prepared to be "drafted." La Follette had demonstrated that a progressive challenge was viable and concluded, correctly, that Garfield and Roosevelt had undermined his best opportunity for the nomination he so coveted. In return, La Follette thwarted Roosevelt's strategy to stampede the convention by winning the vote for permanent chairman. Long submerged political ambitions and philosophical differences had disrupted the unity without which success was clearly unattainable.

NOTES

1. Cf., George Mowry, *Theodore Roosevelt and the Progressive Movement* (New York: Hill and Wang, 1946), pp. 188–98; Arthur Link and William Catton, *American Epoch, A History of the United States since the 1890s,* 3rd ed. (New York: Alfred A. Knopf, 1967), p. 120.

2. Theodore Roosevelt (hereafter cited as TR) to Cecil Spring Rice, August 22, 1911, Theodore Roosevelt Collection, Library of Congress, Washington, DC (hereafter cited as TR MSS).

3. W. H. Houser to Robert Marion La Follette (hereafter cited as RML), June 17, 1911, Robert Marion La Follette Collection, Library of Congress (RML MSS; cf., Fred Greenbaum, *Robert Marion La Follette* (Boston: Twayne, 1975), pp. 98–120.

4. Cf., Mowry, *TR and the Progressive Movement,* pp. 183–219.

5. H. E. Thomason to TR, August 24, 1911; H. T. Talbert to TR, September 5, 1911; W. F. Schilling to TR, October 11, 1911, TR MSS.

6. Joseph Bristow to RML, October 16. 1911, RML MSS; T. E. Leupp argued that Taft could obtain the nomination unless he decided to withdraw voluntarily. T. E. Leupp to James Rudolph Garfield (hereafter cited as JRG), November 29, 1911, James Rudolph Garfield Collection, Library of Congress (hereafter cited as JRG MSS).

7. Cf., Martin L. Fausold, *Gifford Pinchot, Bull Moose Progressive* (Syracuse: Syracuse University Press, 1961), pp. 55–70.

8. Ibid., pp. 55–72; Louis Brandeis to RML, Dec. 19, 1911; Brandeis to Charles Henry Davis, Dec. 21, 1911, in Melvin Urofsky and David Levy, eds., *Letters of Louis Brandeis* (Albany: State University of New York Press, 1972), p. 523; Hoyt L. Warner, *Progressivism in Ohio, 1897–1917,* (Columbus: Ohio State University Press, 1964), pp. 356–84; Richard Lowitt, *George W. Norris, The Making of a Progressive, 1861–1912* (Syracuse: Syracuse University Press, 1963),

pp. 235–40; Bruce Larson, *Lindbergh of Minnesota* (New York: Harcourt, Brace, Jovanovich, 1971), pp. 133–37; Edward P. Costigan to Walter Houser, Edward Prentiss Costigan Collection, University of Colorado; George Record to RML, Oct. 4, 1911; Hugh Halbert to RML, July 13, 1911; Joseph Schafer to RML, Oct. 17, 1911, RML MSS; Coe Crawford to John Hannan, telegram, Sept. 3, 1911; Hannan to W. Houser, Sept. 5, 1911; Moses Clapp to Hannan, Sept. 15, 1911; Medill McCormick to Houser, Oct. 31, 1911; Miles Poindexter to Hannan, Nov. 8, 1911; Houser to Hannan, Dec. 1, 1911; R.H. Smith to Irvine Lenroot, Dec. 1, 1911; Walter Fahy to Hannan, Dec. 12, 1911; Louis Spencer to Hannan, Dec. 18, 1911, National Progressive Republican League Collection (hereafter cited as NPRL MSS), Library of Congress; James Garfield Diaries, entry Nov. 2, 1911, JRG MSS.

9. Cf., Houser to Hannan, Dec. 2, 1911, NPRL MSS; Lowitt, *George W. Norris*, pp. 235–40.

10. Unsigned to Duncan Carpenter, Dec. 7, 1911, Costigan MSS; *Rocky Mountain News*, Oct, 20, 1911; Fred Greenbaum, *Fighting Progressive, A Biography of Edward P. Costigan* (Washington: Public Affairs Press, 1971), pp. 25–55.

11. A Bowser Sageser, *Joseph L. Bristow, Kansas Progressive* (Lawrence: University of Kansas Press, 1968), pp. 122–23; Bristow to RML, Sept. 29, 1911, RML MSS.

12. Lowitt, *George W. Norris*, pp. 235–40.

13. Larson, *Lindbergh of Minnesota*, pp. 133–37.

14. Schafer to RML, Oct. 17, 1911, RML MSS.

15. Fausold, *Gifford Pinchot*, pp. 55-72; Houser to JRG, Sept. 20, 1911, JRG MSS.

16. Brandeis to RML, Dec. 19, 1911, in Urofsky and Levy, *Letters of Louis Brandeis*, p. 523.

17. T. M. Leupp to JRG, Nov. 29, 1911, JRG MSS.

18. John Braeman, *Albert J. Beveridge* (Chicago: University of Chicago Press, 1971) pp. 213–19.

19. Spencer C. Olin, Jr., *California's Prodigal Sons* (Berkeley: University of California Press, 1968), p. 60; Hiram Johnson to TR, Oct. 20, 1911; Charles C. Bull to TR, Nov. 12, 1911; Joseph Bishop to TR, Oct. 30, 1911, TR MSS; W. E. Chandler to RML, July 31, 1911, Nov. 8, 1911; Chandler to Houser, Aug. 12, 1911, William E. Chandler Collection, Library of Congress; Mowry, *TR and the Progressive Movement*, pp. 220–36; Greenbaum, *Costigan*, pp. 25–55.

20. Edwin T. Earl to TR, Oct. 23, 1911, TR MSS.

21. Ray Stannard Baker to TR, Nov. 21, 1911, Ray Stannard Baker Collection, Library of Congress.

22. Jack M. Thompson, "James R. Garfield: The Career of a Rooseveltian Progressive," (Ph.D. diss., University of South Carolina, 1958), pp. 203–34.

23. JRG to Dan Casement, April 25, 1911, JRG MSS.

24. Walter Pollock to JRG, Sept. 26, 1911; Henry Mergler to JRG, Oct. 18, 1911; JRG to Houser, Sept. 29, 1911; JRG to Amos Pinchot, Sept. 28, 1911; and JRG MSS, Aug. 1–Oct, 30, 1911; Charles D. Hilles (hereafter cited as CDH) to Charles P. Taft, Nov. 27, 1911; CDH to A. I.

Vorys, Nov. 27, 1911; CDH to George Hamilton, Nov. 27, 1911, Charles D. Hilles Collection, Yale University Library, New Haven, CT; Hannan thought it was the interests who floated Roosevelt's name to stop La Follette when he "addressed great crowds in cold weather." He was unaware of the role of Garfield. Hannan to Herman Walker, Feb. 7, 1912; Houser to Hannan, Dec. 2, 1911, NPRL MSS.

25. Houser to Garfield, Sept. 20, 1911, JRG MSS.

26. Amos Pinchot to JRG, Oct. 3, 1911, JRG MSS.

27. Garfield Diary, Oct. 4, 7, 9, 1911, JRG MSS.

28. W. A. White to TR, Oct. 18, 1911, Nov. 16, 1911, TR MSS; Bristow thought White supported Roosevelt for office and access to the president, Sageser, *Joseph L. Bristow*, pp. 122-23.

29. Garfield Diary, October 10, 1911, JRG MSS.

30. Frank Knox to TR, Oct. 18, 1911, TR MSS.

31. Cf., TR to George Ellis, Nov. 24, 1911; TR to Lawrence Embree, Nov. 24, 1911; TR's secretary to J. C. O'Laughlin Nov. 24, 1911; TR's secretary to the secretary of the Union League Club, Nov. 24, 1911, TR MSS.

32. TR to Anna Roosevelt Cowles, Jan. 12, 1912, *The Letters of Theodore Roosevelt*, ed. Elting Morison (Cambridge: Harvard University Press, 1954), 7: 476–77; Mowry, *TR and the Progressive Movement*, p. 210.

33. TR to White, Oct. 24, 1911, TR MSS.

34. JRG Diary, Oct. 15, 17, 1911, JRG MSS; JRG to RML, Oct. 17, 1911, RML MSS. Contemporaries suspected that Garfield spoke for Roosevelt; cf., Samuel K. Harvey to TR, Oct. 19, 1911, TR MSS.

35. Telegram, Moses Clapp to RML, Oct. 17, 1911, RML MSS.

36. Colonel J. C. O'Laughlin to TR, Oct. 17, 1911, TR MSS.

37. Thompson, "James R. Garfield," pp. 203–34; Fausold, *Gifford Pinchot*, pp. 55-72; Martin McGeary, *Gifford Pinchot* (Princeton: Princeton University Press, 1960), pp. 217–40; Warner, *Progressivism in Ohio*, pp. 356-84; Garfield Diary: Oct. 21, Nov. 11, 20, 29, 1911; Dec. 7, 27, 1911 and Jan. 1, 1912, JRG MSS; Garfield to Gifford Pinchot, Mar. 7, Nov. 16, and Dec. 2, 1911, Gifford Pinchot Collection, Library of Congress.

38. Garfield Diary, Oct. 21, 1911, Nov. 17, 10, 1911, JRG MSS; Belle and Fola La Follette, *Robert Marion La Follette* (New York: Macmillan, 1954), pp. 350-75.

39. Warner, *Progressivism in Ohio*, pp. 356–84; Thompson, "James R. Garfield," pp. 225-34; TR to JRG, Nov. 24, 1911, in Morison, *Letters of TR*, pp. 441-42; TR to JRG, Jan. 14, 1912, JRG MSS.

40. White to TR, Oct. 18, 1911; TR to White, Oct 24, 1911; cf., TR to Charles Bull, Oct. 28, 1911; TR to Alvord Cooley, Nov. 14, 1911, TR MSS.

41. Cf., Dan Hanna to TR, Oct. 26, 1911, TR MSS.

42. Cf., R. M. Easly to TR, Nov. 16, 1911; Joseph Houdlue to TR, Nov. 16, 1911; Frederick Lang to TR, Nov, 17, 1911; Clark Grier to TR, Nov. 23, 1911; J. E. Phelan to TR, Nov. 23, 1911, TR MSS.

31

Anti-Machine Politics and the Bull Moose Victory in Pennsylvania in 1912

Richard J. Donagher

Pennsylvania provided thirty-eight of the eighty-eight electoral votes that Theodore Roosevelt received in his 1912 Progressive party bid for the presidency. This was the largest single bloc he received in that election. Why did a large eastern industrial state, long controlled by one of the nation's most conservative Republican machines, support a third party reform candidate for president? The national causes Roosevelt espoused in 1912 undoubtedly appealed to some Pennsylvanians. However, the strength of the Bull Moose in that state probably had as much to do with the fact that it offered a vehicle for groups long restive under Republican machine control to challenge boss domination in Pennsylvania.

By the turn of the twentieth century Pennsylvania had effectively become a one party state. The Democrats elected a governor in 1890 but not again until 1934. No Democrat held a U.S. Senate seat from Pennsylvania between 1881 and 1935.[1] In Philadelphia the Democratic party remained a "kept party" given some crumbs of patronage to offer token opposition to the Republican machine.[2]

The secret of Republican success was traceable to several causes. After the Civil War the party had been adept at "waving the bloody shirt" and when this issue's effectiveness waned it increasingly argued that the maintenance of a high protective tariff, deemed essential to the continued prosperity of highly industrialized Pennsylvania, rested on the success of the national Republican party, which in turn demanded loyalty to the local and state GOP.[3] The decline of the Democratic party in Pennsylvania also came at a time that allowed a highly developed and efficient Republican organization, largely controlled by WASP politicians, to successfully secure the loyalty of the bulk of the newer immigrants, particularly in the state's two largest cities, Philadelphia and Pittsburgh.[4]

U.S. Senator Boies Penrose became Republican boss of Pennsylvania after the death of his Senate colleague Matthew Quay in 1904.[5] Both had had to contend with opposition within the party. In fact, as the Democratic party shriveled, the internal opponents posed a more serious threat.[6] Those opponents included restive local bosses but also other groups touched by the currents of progressive reform in the early twentieth century.

To thwart reform revolts, the state machine continued the argument that the maintenance of a protective tariff demanded Pennsylvania's loyalty to the Republican party. As in other parts of the country, there were attempts to circumvent this contention by separating local contests and arguing that reform at the local level could be bipartisan without challenging national loyalties.[7] The great Philadelphia reform revolt of 1905 was one attempt to put this hope into practice.

Philadelphia was an important component in the state Republican machine, but in 1905 the local bosses overreached themselves. City Council's vote to renew the lease of the privately owned United Gas Improvement Company on terms exceedingly generous to that firm created an uproar of public indignation and political revolt. Even Mayor John Weaver, originally elected with machine backing, jumped on the reform bandwagon.[8] The City party, created earlier in 1905, provided the vehicle to challenge the machine.

Theodore Roosevelt's election to the presidency in 1904 helped to convince many local Republicans that it was safe to speak out against bossism, even if it was Republican bossism. Franklin S. Edmonds, chairman of the City party, noted the change:

> Especially strong was the element which had hitherto been deterred from political action by the fear that in so doing they would unsettle the system of protective tariffs, which has been a potent factor in the development of Pennsylvania's industrial resources. The reelection of Mr. Roosevelt, however, convinced many honest Republicans that an attack could be in order upon the local machine without in any way disturbing the economic policies of the nation.[9]

Philadelphia's reformers even believed that they had received Roosevelt's support when his new secretary of state,

Elihu Root, spoke approvingly of Mayor Weaver's recent reform moves:

> I have acquired absolute confidence in the sincerity of your purpose [said Root] and in your pluck and persistency, and I have a strong desire that the city of Philadelphia, whose history and good name are so dear to every American shall be relieved from the strain which a corrupt and criminal combination masquerading under the name of Republicans have put upon her. [10]

The City party entered the November local elections for county commissioners, sheriff, and coroner.[11] Receiving the support of a temporarily chastened and opportunistic Democratic party, the City party carried these elections and the streets filled with jubilant Philadelphians singing "Onward Christian Soldiers."[12]

The momentum of the great Philadelphia reform revolt carried into state politics. The Democrats had nominated an attractive candidate for state treasurer, William Berry, former mayor of Chester. Reformers, apparently willing to apply the nonpartisan principle to clean up state politics, met in Philadelphia, organized the Lincoln party, and endorsed Berry.[13] With 350,696 Democratic votes and 127,512 votes on the Lincoln party ticket, Berry defeated his Republican opponent by 88,199 votes.[14]

The reform enthusiasm, engendered by the 1905 City party and Lincoln party victories, soon lost steam. To forestall further revolt, Penrose engineered the nomination of Edwin S. Stuart, a respected former mayor of Philadelphia, as 1906 Republican gubernatorial nominee.[15] The old fears were raised that local and state revolts might threaten the security of the national Republican party. Joseph Cannon, Speaker of the U.S. House of Representatives, and Senator Philander Knox, urged Philadelphians to vote again for the "full Republican ticket."[16] President Roosevelt himself expressed fears that the growth of reform sentiment would cut into the Republican strength in Pennsylvania. He spoke of "... a movement of genuine altho [sic] I think misguided reformers whose justifiable indignities at the antics of the Republican machine in the past has led them into taking what I regard as unwise action in the present."[17]

An ambitious Mayor Weaver, feeling cheated by the reform movement, deserted the cause.[18] Stuart's candidacy, Weaver's defection, and the pressure to return to party regularity led to a

Republican victory in the 1906 gubernatorial race.[19] The reformers also lost the 1907 Philadelphia mayoralty election.[20]

The fortunes of reform faced even more complications in Pennsylvania's second largest city, Pittsburgh. Here, while there were those loyal to the state machine, there also were maverick Republican politicians interested in autonomy from the Quay-Penrose organization. Pittsburgh also contained reform-minded individuals and groups who often found themselves caught between brawling state and local machines.

From the 1880s to 1902, Pittsburgh politics was dominated by a local machine headed by Christopher Magee and contractor William Flinn. The Magee-Flinn organization fought vigorously to maintain its independence from the Quay state machine and at times joined movements challenging Quay's position as state boss. Chris Magee died in 1901 and local reformers, aided for pragmatic reasons by the Quay machine, forced William Flinn's political retirement in 1902.[21] Buoyed by the success of the City party in Philadelphia, Pittsburgh reformers in 1906 rallied behind the successful mayorality candidacy of George Guthrie, a Democrat. Guthrie's administration, however, was hampered by large Republican majorities in the city council.[22] Limited by charter to one term, Guthrie was succeeded as mayor in 1909 by William Magee, the nephew of the late Chris Magee. The new mayor was a political independent but hardly a reformer. Magee, in fact, had defeated a bipartisan backed reform candidate.[23]

Many Pennsylvanians were incensed at what was argued to be a particularly arrogant display of political power by Penrose in the 1910 gubernatorial race. Not only did he arrange the Republican nomination for an obscure one-term Congressman, John Tener, a former major league baseball player, but it was alleged that he somehow rigged the Democratic convention into nominating the nondescript Webster Grim of Doylestown as its gubernatorial candidate in order to provide Tener with a pushover opponent.[24] In late July 1910, a coalition of reform-minded Democrats and Republicans organized the statewide Keystone party, and picked ex-state treasurer William Berry, whose reputation had been enhanced by his exposure of corruption in the building of the state capitol in Harrisburg, as its gubernatorial nominee.[25] Although Tener won, his plurality over the second-place Berry was a scant 33,487, with Grim a poor third.[26]

The Keystone party name was used successfully to elect a reform mayor in Philadelphia in 1911. Rudolph Blankenburg, a German-born businessman who had long been active in Philadelphia reform politics, was nominated by the local Keystoners and also received the backing of the Democratic organization.[27] Blankenburg, who considered his national loyalty to be Republican, very narrowly defeated the Penrose, candidate, George Earle, but only because of a serious rupture in Republican ranks. William Vare and his brothers were rising powers in South Philadelphia politics, an area heavily populated with blacks and newer immigrants. William Vare thought he deserved the 1911 Republican mayoralty nomination, but Penrose, fearful of a possible rival in Philadelphia, secured businessman Earle's selection. The result was a less than enthusiastic effort by the Vares, which enabled Blankenburg to win.[28] Significantly, Blankenburg promised a nonpartisan City Hall administration and was scrupulous in keeping his administration out of national politics.[29]

In Pittsburgh, Mayor Magee continued his efforts to remain friendly, but independent of the Penrose machine. This was cold comfort for Pittsburgh reformers since the Magee years were plagued by numerous convictions for corruption in city administration.[30] The Pittsburgh Voters' League, a reform organization, did successfully spearhead the passage in 1911 of legislation that ended Pittsburgh's old bicameral legislature, elected by wards, and replaced it with a new nine-seat city council elected at large.[31]

The emergence and success of the Roosevelt movement in Pennsylvania in 1912 should be examined against the backdrop of years of effort by some Pennsylvanians to break the dominance of the boss-ridden Republican state machine. Before 1912 their efforts had been only partially and temporarily successful. When Theodore Roosevelt decided to challenge incumbent William Howard Taft for the 1912 Republican presidential nomination, he provided an opportunity for elements within the Pennsylvania Republican party to come out in opposition to the Penrose machine, which supported Taft, and yet to argue that they were loyal Republicans simply attempting to revive and reform the GOP on both state and national levels.

Gifford Pinchot, a Pennsylvanian and the cause célèbre in the conservation quarrel that had helped alienate Progressives from

Taft, was a founding member of the National Progressive Republican League, an organization created to advance progressivism in the party but widely assumed to have a "dump Taft" purpose. Pinchot came out in support of Robert La Follette when the latter announced his candidacy in 1911.[32] However, Pinchot was ready to abandon La Follette if Theodore Roosevelt could be persuaded to challenge Taft. Millionaire Pittsburgh contractor William Flinn, once Chris Magee's partner as boss of Pittsburgh, came out of political retirement to support La Follette against Taft. Flinn's sudden conversion to Republican progressivism raised eyebrows but his financial backing would be quite valuable in Pennsylvania. Flinn, too, was willing to dump La Follette if Roosevelt would come forward.[33] Alexander P. Moore, owner-publisher of the *Pittsburgh Leader*, made no secret of his loyalty. The *Leader* in 1911 carried a headline over its editorial page, "For President in 1912, Theodore Roosevelt." It was reluctantly removed at the request of the still undecided ex-president.[34]

In February 1912, a Roosevelt city committee was formed in Philadelphia with John J. Crout, a local real estate expert, as chairman. Roosevelt's cause in the Quaker City was boosted by the support of the *Philadelphia North American*, edited by Edwin Van Valkenburg. The very active support of Dean William Draper Lewis of the University of Pennsylvania Law School gave Roosevelt considerable academic respectability.[35]

The Roosevelt Republican League of Western Pennsylvania, with Bill Flinn as chairman, was formally organized on February 19 with headquarters in Pittsburgh. Mayor Magee, rejecting Penrose's efforts to coax him into supporting Taft, joined the Roosevelt organization. H. D. W. English, distinguished leader in efforts to reform Pittsburgh and a member of the executive committee of the Voters' League, was also on the executive committee of the Roosevelt League along with David B. Johns, a Magee ally and Republican chairman of Allegheny County, and Richard Quay, son of the late boss Matt Quay.[36] In Philadelphia, Roosevelt supporters, faced with a Republican organization loyal to Taft and the Blankenburg administration committed to the philosophy of nonpartisan urban reform, had to construct an insurgent Republican organization to challenge the regulars—but in Allegheny County the Roosevelt cause could count on both reformers and many local Republican officeholders.

Bill Flinn's support was most controversial. Dean William Draper Lewis later acknowledged that Flinn's ability and experience were decisive in securing a victory for Roosevelt in Pennsylvania.[37] Flinn testified before a U.S. Senate committee that he personally provided ninety percent of the funds used in the Roosevelt forces in the Pennsylvania primary.[38] The presence of Mayor Magee and other Pittsburgh and Allegheny County Republican officeholders in the Roosevelt camp was curious but less widely commented on than Flinn's "conversion" to reform.

The primary results in Pennsylvania were a real boost to the Roosevelt campaign. Statewide, the ex-president obtained 282,853 votes to Taft's 191,179. While Taft carried Philadelphia by about 15,000 votes, Roosevelt, with local organizational support, badly defeated Taft in Allegheny County with a majority of over 35,000 votes.[39] Van Valkenburg's *North American,* while disclaiming the notion that the Roosevelt victory was simply a revolt against bossism, did argue that Roosevelt had been successful in convincing voters that "the power of special privilege does and must come through its alliance with political bosses. . . ."[40] The *Philadelphia Public Ledger,* strongly anti-Roosevelt, claimed that the election was not a defeat for Taft as much as a voter rebellion against Penrose.[41]

Roosevelt's victory in the Pennsylvania primary not only insured him an overwhelming majority of delegates from that state to the Republican national convention, it also enabled his supporters to pick the statewide party candidates for auditor general, state treasurer, congressmen-at-large, and many local candidates, as well as take charge of the upcoming state party convention where a state Republican platform would be drafted and the party's state structure reorganized. Indeed, when the Pennsylvania Republican convention opened in Harrisburg on May 1, newspapers commented that it was odd to witness Boies Penrose not even bothering to appear at the convention site.[42] The Roosevelt forces adopted a platform calling for a rather advanced program of progressive reform. Some midwestern states may have adopted more advanced progressive reforms, but considering how recently Pennsylvania had been considered a bastion of stalwart old guard Republicanism, the new platform represented a dramatic shift.[43]

Equally remarkable was the fact that the Roosevelt primary victory temporarily ended the Penrose domination over the Pennsylvania Republican organization. Pittsburgh lawyer Henry Wasson, a confidant of Bill Flinn, was selected to be the new Republican state chairman.[44] Later Flinn was chosen to succeed Penrose as Republican national committeeman from the Keystone State.[45] *The Literary Digest* helped focus attention on the changes in the Pennsylvania Republican party in an article entitled, "Pennsylvania's New Boss," which speculated that Bill Flinn's ultimate goal was to replace Penrose in the U.S. Senate.[46]

Although Roosevelt in 1912 won a heavy majority of those delegates elected to the Republican National Convention by direct primary, Taft, thanks to federal patronage, controlled the bulk of those picked in states where delegates were selected by convention. When it became clear that Taft thus controlled the national convention, Roosevelt decided to bolt the Republican party and accept a third party nomination for the presidency. Roosevelt's decision presented his Pennsylvania followers with a traumatic choice. Some who had supported him in the primary were unwilling to emulate his apostacy from the GOP. Allegheny County Republican Chairman David B. Johns voted for Roosevelt in the national convention, but refused to bolt when Roosevelt did.[47] Johns and later Mayor Magee decided to accept Taft's renomination and, along with some other Allegheny County and Pittsburgh officeholders, remained Republican.

Bill Flinn, on the other hand, loyally followed Roosevelt and helped to organize the Pennsylvania branch of the emerging Progressive party. Because Pennsylvania electoral laws permitted five voters to preempt a party name in any district, and several labels, such as Progressive and Roosevelt party had already been preempted by unauthorized individuals, Flinn arranged in great secrecy to have the title "Washington party" adopted across the state as the official label of the Pennsylvania branch of the national Progressive party.[48] Although Mayor Magee decided to remain in the Republican party, it was reported that he would do nothing to humiliate Flinn or help Penrose regain control of the Pennsylvania Republican organization.[49]

The situation in Philadelphia was different. Backers of Roosevelt had failed to carry the city in the primary and the regular Republican organization remained firmly committed to Taft. It was thus easier for Philadelphia Roosevelt loyalists to follow him out of the Republican party. Going that route lost them nothing in terms of control over a local party organization they had not captured and, although cutting their ties with the Republicans may have caused some psychological stress, the path was probably smoothed by the pro-Roosevelt and anti-boss enthusiasm worked up in the primary campaign.

The formal organization of the state Washington party took place at a caucus of the Pennsylvania delegates and alternates to the national Progressive party convention in Chicago in August 1912. Thomas J. Hicks, the recently resigned chairman of the Keystone party, was elected Washington party state chairman. Since it was agreed that the almost 200 delegates and alternates attending the national convention would constitute a state committee, real authority was vested in a fifteen-member executive committee chaired by Bill Flinn.[50]

There remained certain suspicions about the permanence of the Washington party. The Chicago caucus had extended Washington party endorsements to the Republican candidates for state treasurer, auditor general, and congressman-at-large. These candidates, of course, had been chosen by the Roosevelt-dominated Republican state convention. The caucus also made possible the extension of Washington party endorsements to other congressional candidates and to candidates for the state legislature who met certain conditions.[51] These decisions precluded the establishment of a completely Washington party ticket.

Bill Flinn proposed a plan that the presidential electors chosen in the April Republican primary remain on the Republican ticket and also be listed under the Washington party label. They would be pledged to vote for Taft or Roosevelt depending on which party received the highest vote.[52] The *Philadelphia North American* suggested that the plan was designed to prevent a Democratic victory and its threat to the protective tariff.[53] The plan, however, was dropped when Roosevelt strongly objected to it on the grounds that it would compromise the independent identity of the new party and deter progressive Democrats from crossing over to him.[54] Nevertheless, Flinn dragged his feet in removing Roosevelt delegates from the Republican ticket and placing them on the Washington party slate. It was not until October 10, after Penrose had threatened the creation of yet another party label to get Taft electors on the ballot, that the transfer took place.[55]

While Flinn left the GOP, resigning his position as Republican national committeeman, Henry Wasson, a Flinn protégé, remained as Republican state chairman. Although Wasson announced that he had accepted the president's renomination and would work for Taft's reelection, his Flinn connection made him suspect among regular Republicans. The Republican national chairman, C. D. Hilles, asked Philadelphia Congressman J. Hampton Moore to head a congressional campaign committee for Taft in Pennsylvania. This would bypass Wasson and also help to deflect attention away from the issue of bossism, since, as Hilles suggested, "this was not considered a good year to have Penrose too conspicuous in the campaign."[56]

In Philadelphia, the Washington party created a separate organization down to the ward and precinct levels. While some local Republican candidates received Washington party endorsements and even some Democrats and Keystoners got that backing, in many Philadelphia races the Washington party fielded separate tickets.[57] On the other hand, every Republican legislative candidate in Allegheny County received Washington party endorsement.[58] No less an authority than Bill Flinn contended that in-depth organization represented the old repudiated methods and tactics of politics.[59]

There is evidence to show that the lines between the Republican and Washington party in Pittsburgh were blurred. Paul S. Ache, chairman of the Bull Moose organization in Allegheny County, continued as chairman of Pittsburgh's eleventh ward Republican committee, Bill Flinn's home ward.[60] Stephen G. Porter, a friend of Flinn's and up for reelection to Congress with both Republican and Washington party endorsements, retained the chairmanship of the Republican city committee. In fact, only in three wards, where known Taft supporters were in control, was it deemed necessary to establish separate Washington party ward committees.[61] Many Republican candidates probably agreed with A. W. Powell, a Pittsburger and nominee for auditor general, who contended that his endorsement by the Washington party had been unsolicited but he would not, "put myself in the position of fighting men who are on the same ticket with me."[62] Taft supporters, apparently conscious of the unreliability of the

Republican city committee, organized the president's campaign through an executive committee of the Allegheny County Republican committee chaired by David B. Jones.[63]

Woodrow Wilson's biographer, Arthur Link, argues that the Democratic nominee entered the presidential races in 1912 assuming that the tariff would be the main issue but soon discovered that it was a "worn out issue" superseded by Roosevelt's New Nationalism.[64] That may have been true in other parts of the country, but in protectionist-minded Pennsylvania the tariff was still quite important. During the primary campaign, the Taft Club of Pittsburgh, an organization of financial and industrial leaders, ran ads in Pittsburgh newspapers warning that the Roosevelt movement threatened to divide the Republican party and lead to the election of a national Democratic administration favorable to free trade and that, "free trade spells industrial, commercial and agricultural disaster."[65] In the general election, the *Pittsburgh Gazette-Times*, owned by George Oliver, Penrose's Senate colleague and ally, labelled Flinn a threat to protection.[66] Taft, himself, urged that Pennsylvanians be made aware of the implications of the tariff.[67]

In a pre-primary speech in Pittsburgh, Roosevelt stressed his support for the tariff but argued that its purpose was not to help industrialists. Said TR, "The true meaning of a protective tariff is living wages for the man who toils."[68] After its creation, the Washington party worked to steal the tariff issue from the Republicans. Convinced that Wilson was TR's chief opponent, Roosevelt's Pennsylvania supporters argued that only a Roosevelt victory could forestall the triumph of Democratic free trade ideas. Bill Flinn arranged the mailing of thousands of postcards to Pennsylvanians warning that "a vote for Wilson is a vote for pauper wages and empty dinner pails."[69] Washington party state chairman Hicks acknowledged that some Republicans preferred Taft to Roosevelt but argued that only Roosevelt had a chance of defeating "an out and out free trader like Mr. Wilson."[70] Philadelphia Bull Moosers made much of prominent local industrialists who had long been advocates of a protective tariff and now supported Roosevelt.[71]

The Washington party achieved in Pennsylvania what previous third party movements have achieved only briefly on the local level. When Pennsylvanians went to the polls on November 5, 1912, they gave Roosevelt a plurality of their votes with Wilson second and Taft a poor third. Although Taft secured a comfortable but not overwhelming victory in Philadelphia, he was third behind Roosevelt and Wilson in Pittsburgh. Roosevelt was also victorious in Reading, Johnstown, Harrisburg, Scranton, and Wilkes-Barre. Wilson carried Allentown and Williamsport where Roosevelt was third. Taft carried Chester, with Roosevelt second, and Lancaster, where Roosevelt finished third.[72]

In Philadelphia, where the regulars retained control of the Republican organization, Roosevelt's vote in 1912 was apparently drawn from the same constituencies that voted for third party reform candidates in several elections before and after 1912. His greatest support came from the city's native white or northern European ethnic voters who lived largely in the ring wards of the city. Their ethnicity and their higher socioeconomic status were apparently the factors explaining their vote for Roosevelt. Taft's vote, on the other hand, came from voters of southern or eastern European ethnic extraction and blacks who inhabited the core wards in the city. They constituted the strongest element for machine candidates in several elections before and after 1912. However, there is evidence that low socioeconomic status rather than ethnicity explains their vote.[73]

The Pittsburgh vote for Roosevelt in 1912 followed the Philadelphia pattern but with some interesting variations. Generally his support in Pittsburgh was similar to that given to third party reform candidates in other elections but not as strongly as the pattern in Philadelphia. He drew from Pittsburgh's native white or northern European ethnic voters of higher socioeconomic status. However, in Pittsburgh as compared to Philadelphia, Roosevelt did not do as well with native-white northern European ethnic voters and he did better with southern and eastern European-black voters.[74]

The probable explanation is that in Pittsburgh in 1912 some local machine politicians supported or were at least neutral to Roosevelt's presidential bid and this muddied the kind of reform-versus-machine dichotomy that apparently affected Philadelphia voters.

The issues that Roosevelt raised in 1912 and his personal charisma partially explained his appeal to Pennsylvanians. However, the fact that his campaign began as a bid for the Republican presidential nomination allowed some to see the Roosevelt movement as a vehicle to challenge the Republican machine without being disloyal to the Republican party. He received support from anti-machine minded Pennsylvanians and from some Republican politicians simply interested in challenging Penrose's control of the party. They succeeded dramatically in the April primary, but faced a dilemma after Roosevelt bolted from the Republican national convention. Some stayed loyal to the GOP; some followed TR and organized the Washington party. Evidence suggests that some converts to the Washington party, such as Bill Flinn, were nervous about the permanence of the new party and reluctant to sever all ties with the recently won Republican organization. The Washington party, like its counterpart the national Progressive party, was dead by 1916 and, in the meantime, Penrose was able to reassert his control over the Pennsylvania Republican organization. The Bull Moose movement and Roosevelt's candidacy, however, had been the instrument for at least a temporary overturning of the machine in the Keystone State.

NOTES

This paper was partially funded by a grant from the Pew Memorial Trust.

1. Philip S. Klein and Ari Hoogenboom, *A History of Pennsylvania* (2nd and enlarged ed.; University Park, PA: The Pennsylvania State University Press, 1980), p. 368.

2. Joseph F. Guffey, *Seventy Years on the Red Fire Wagon; From Tilden to Truman Through New Freedom and the New Deal* (n.p.: privately printed, 1952), p. 18.

3. Sylvester K. Stevens, *Pennsylvania, Birthplace of a Nation* (New York: Random House, 1964), p. 266.

4. Klein and Hoogenboom, *History of Pennsylvania,,* p. 361.

5. Stevens, *Pennsylvania,* p. 272.

6. Klein and Hoogenboom, *History of Pennsylvania,* p. 361.

7. Clinton Rogers Woodruff, "The Municipal League of Philadelphia," *The American Journal of Sociology* 11 (November 1905): 336–37.

8. Issac F. Marcossan, "The Awakening of Philadelphia," *The World's Work,* 10 (September 1905): 6,649.

9. Franklin S. Edmonds, "The Significance of the Recent Reform Movement in Philadelphia," *The Annals of the American Academy of Political and Social Science* 28 (1906): 183–84.

10. Quoted in Wayne MacVeagh, "A Great Victory for Honest politics," *North American Review* 182 (January 1906): 15.

11. "Philadelphia's Battle for Civic Emancipation," *The Arena* 34 (November 1905): 528–29.

12. Lloyd Abernethy, "Insurgency in Philadelphia, 1905," *The Pennsylvania Magazine of History and Biography* 87 (January 1963): 16, 19; George Woodward, "A Triumph of the People," *The Outlook* 81 (December 2, 1905): 815.

13. Abernethy, "Insurgency," pp. 17–18.

14. *Smull's Legislative Handbook and Manual of Pennsylvania, 1906* (Harrisburg, PA: Printer to the State of Pennsylvania, 1906), p. 362.

15. William S. Vare, *My Forty Years in Politics* (Philadelphia: Ronald Swain, 1922), pp. 99–100.

16. T. Everett Harry, "The Backsliding of Philadelphia," *Harper's Weekly* 60 (May 4, 1905): 640.

17. Roosevelt to Henry Cabot Lodge, October 16, 1906, *The Letters of Theodore Roosevelt*, ed. Elting Morison (Cambridge: Harvard University Press, 1954), 5: 459.

18. Harry, "Backsliding of Philadelphia," p. 641.

19. *Smull's 1907*, p. 359.

20. "The Philadelphia Election," *The Outlook* 85 (March 7, 1907): 489.

21. Eugene Kaufman, "A Pittsburgh Political Battle of a Half Century Ago," *The Western Pennsylvania Historical Magazine* 25 (June 1952): 84.

22. Gerald W. Johnson, "The Muckraking Era," *Pittsburgh, the Story of an American City*, ed. Stefan Lorant (Garden City, NY: Doubleday and Co., 1964), p. 264.

23. Allen Humphrey Kerr, *The Mayors and Recorders of Pittsburgh, 1816–1951, Their Lives and Somewhat of Their Times* (Pittsburgh, PA: privately printed, 1952), pp. 251–52; Pittsburgh Voters' League, *Bulletin Members, 1909* (Pittsburgh, PA: Voter's League, 1909), p. 2.

24. Sylvester K. Stevens, *Pennsylvania: The Heritage of a Commonwealth* (West Palm Beach, FL: The American Historical Book Co., 1968), 2: 813, 814; William L. Quay, "Philadelphia Democrats: 1880–1990," (Ph.D. diss., Department of History, Lehigh University, 1969), p. 192.

25. *The North American* (Philadelphia), July 29, 1910.

26. *Smull's 1913*, p. 577.

27. *The Public Ledger* (Philadelphia), October 2, 1911.

28. *The Public Ledger*, November 29, 1911; Vare, *My Forty Years*, pp. 118-19.

29. Donald W. Disbrow, "The Progressive Movement in Philadelphia, 1910–1916," (Ph.D. diss., Department of History, University of Rochester, 1956), pp. 131–32.

30. "Municipal Corruption in Pittsburgh," *The Independent* 68 (March 31, 1910): 668–69.

31. Kerr, *The Mayors*, pp. 253–54; Samuel P. Hays, "The Politics of Reform in Municipal Government in the Progressive Era," *Pacific Northwest Quarterly* 55 (October 1964): 163–65.

32. *Public Ledger*, December 17, 1911.

33. George Mowry, *Theodore Roosevelt and the Progressive Movement* (New York: Hill and Wang, 1960), p. 206.

34. *The Leader* (Pittsburgh), January 20, 1912.

35. *The North American*, February 17 and March 19, 1912; Mowry, *Theodore Roosevelt and The Progressive Movement*, p. 186.

36. *The Leader*, February 20, 1912.

37. William Draper Lewis, *The Life of Theodore Roosevelt* (n.p.: United Publishers, 1919), pp. 348–49.

38. *Post* (Pittsburgh), October 2, 1912, in William Flinn Scrapbooks, Hillman Library, University of Pittsburgh, Pittsburgh, Pa., vol. 159.

39. *The Public Ledger*, June 5, 1912.

40. *The North American*, April 16, 1912.

41. *The Public Ledger*, April 15, 1912.

42. *The North American*, May 2, 1912.

43. *The Evening Bulletin* (Philadelphia), May 1, 1912; Disbrow, "Progressive Movement," p. 187.

44. *The North American*, May 2, 1912.

45. Ibid., June 18, 1912.

46. "Pennsylvania's New Boss," *The Literary Digest* 46 (May 25, 1912): 1,124.

47. *The North American*, June 23, 1912.

48. *The Public Ledger*, August 2, 1912.

49. *The Dispatch* (Pittsburgh), July 28, 1912, in Flinn Scrapbooks, vol. 152.

50. *The North American*, August 7, 1912.

51. Ibid., August 8, 1912.

52. *The Public Ledger*, July 14, 1912.

53. *The North American*, July 15, 1912.

54. Ibid., July 16, l912.

55. *The Chronicle-Telegraph* (Pittsburgh), October 10, 1912, in Flinn Scrapbooks, vol. 160.

56. *The Gazette-Times* (Pittsburgh), October 12, 1912; Moore quoted in Lloyd M. Abernethy, "The Progressive Campaign in Pennsylvania, 1912," *Pennsylvania History* 29 (April 1962): 188.

57. *The Public Ledger*, August 29 and September 29, 1912.

58. *The Post*, November 5, 1912, in Flinn Scrapbooks, vol. 164.

59. *The Dispatch*, September 23, 1912, in Flinn Scrapbooks, vol. 158.

60. Ibid., September 10, 1912, in Flinn Scrapbooks, vol. 157.

61. *The Gazette-Times*, November 4, 1912, in Flinn Scrapbooks, vol. 164.

62. *The Chronicle-Telegraph*, September 24, 1912, in Flinn Scrapbooks, vol. 158.

63. *The Gazette-Times Almanac*, 1913 (Pittsburgh, PA: Gazette-Times, 1913), p. 257.

64. Arthur Link, *Woodrow Wilson and the Progressive Era, 1910–1912* (New York: Harper and Row, 1954), p. 20.

65. *Spectator* (Pittsburgh), April 5, 1912, in Flinn Scrapbooks, vol. 142.

66. *The Gazette-Times*, October 13, 1912.

67. *The Press* (Pittsburgh), October 20, 1912, in Flinn Scrapbooks, vol. 162.

68. *The Leader*, April 10, 1912.

69. *The Post*, November 1, 1912, in Flinn Scrapbooks, vol. 164.

70. *The North American*, November 3, 1912.

71. Ibid., November 1–5, 1912.

72. *Smull's 1913*, pp. 599, 610, 619, 632, 633, 637, 650, 651, 656, 663, 664, 697, 716; historian John Allen Gable, in line with what he sees as a national trend, presents evidence that in Pennsylvania in 1912 Roosevelt did well in counties with high population. See Gable, *The Bull Moose Movement: Theodore Roosevelt and the Progressive Movement* (Port Washington, NY: Kennikat Press, 1978), pp. 133–34.

73. Computer analyses involved six Philadelphia elections between 1905 and 1916; the race for state treasurer in 1905, the 1910 gubernatorial election, the 1911 mayoralty contest, the 1912 presidential race, the 1914 gubernatorial race, and the 1914 U.S. Senate election. Machine and reform candidates were identified and ward level vote statistics were drawn from *Smull's Legislative Hand Book, 1906, 1911, 1913,* and *1915* for the elections of 1905, 1910, 1912, and 1914. Ward level returns for the 1911 mayoralty election were drawn from the *Public Ledger*, November 29, 1911. Ethnic and socioeconomic data on the ward level were drawn from U.S. Bureau of the Census, *Thirteenth Census, 1910* 3: 647-650. The system of computer programming used in this analysis was the Statistical Package for the Social Sciences (S.P.S.S.). See Norman H. Nie et al., *Statistical Package for the Social Sciences,* 2d ed. (New York: McGraw-Hill, 1975).

74. Computer analyses involved six Pittsburgh elections between 1909 and 1914: the 1909 mayoralty contest, the 1910 gubernatorial election, the 1912 presidential race, the 1913 mayoralty election, and the 1914 gubernatorial and U.S. Senate elections. Machine and reform candidates were identified and ward level election returns were drawn from *Smull's Legislative Hand Book, 1911, 1913,* and *1915* for the 1910, 1912, and 1914 elections. Ward level returns for the 1909 mayoralty election were drawn from *The Leader*, February 17, 1909, and for the 1913 mayoralty election from *The Leader*, November 6, 1913. Ethnic and socioeconomic data were drawn from U.S. Bureau of the Census, *Thirteenth Census, 1910,* 3: 651. The system of computer programming used was again S.P.S.S.

32

TR and the Pinchots: Conservation and Feminism in Modern America

John W. Furlow, Jr.

Ten miles southwest of Sagamore Hill on the Long Island shore, which was separated from Connecticut by the glaciers,[1] stands a substantial Georgian-style English country manor house. Surrounding it are 200 wooded acres and a deliberately natural formal garden. This estate overlooking the town of Roslyn and the Long Island Sound, was built by writer and publisher Lloyd Bryce with "old money" about 1895. Here he raised his daughter Cornelia in the privileged society that included Theodore Roosevelt.[2] One hundred miles southwest of the Bryce home on the other side of the urban sprawl of New York City, in 1886, James Pinchot used his hard-earned mercantile fortune to build a French castlelike home, Grey Towers, in Milford, Pennsylvania. Set in 3,600 acres in the heavily timbered Pocono Mountains and built with Pennsylvania blue fieldstones, this home provided a summer "retreat in nature" for James's son Gifford.[3]

On the morning of August 15, 1914, in a piazza extension of the Bryce mansion, Cornelia Bryce, thirty-three, and Gifford Pinchot, forty-nine, were married. Because of the illness of Gifford's mother, to whom he was very close, the wedding was small and quickly arranged. In traditional style, Cornelia's father gave her away and Gifford's brother Amos attended him. Among the guests beyond family members were Colonel and Mrs. Theodore Roosevelt.[4]

The former president's presence was the culmination of his role as matchmaker for the seemingly confirmed bachelor who had served him so tirelessly and for his energetic, red haired, socially active neighbor. This union brought about by Theodore Roosevelt had long-term effects in two particular areas of national development as legacies of his presidency to Modern America: feminism and conservation.

Both Gifford Pinchot and Cornelia Bryce had full lives before their marriage. As with many prominent women, Cornelia Bryce Pinchot's husband's name and achievements were and remain, far better known. Instead of bemoaning this certain injustice, which extended even to her *New York Times* obituary which headlined her as "Widow of Former Governor (Pinchot),"[5] Cornelia Pinchot saw her association with the energetic progressive politician and conservationist, Gifford Pinchot, as an opportunity and a challenge. She told an audience ten years after her wedding, "Pinchot happened to be lying around loose—so the women just made use of him."[6] She emphasized to a Pennsylvania meeting in 1925, "You must remember that I was a politician and have fought many times before I ever met Mr. Pinchot. . . ."[7] This process of self-identity, in contrast to a strong male personality, is part of the historical significance of Cornelia Bryce Pinchot in the post-suffrage period.

Her great-grandfather on her mother Edith's side was Peter Cooper, among whose noteworthy accomplishments was the founding of Cooper Union of New York City for needy students. Her grandfather, Edward Cooper, was an anti-Tammany mayor of New York City, who advocated improved tenement housing and was offered the nomination for governor which ultimately went to Grover Cleveland. Her father, Lloyd Bryce, was a Democratic congressman and political acquaintance of Teddy Roosevelt. Cornelia Bryce's earliest memory in recognition of this heritage was handing out political literature in her father's campaign at the age of six. Though she had a brother, Peter Cooper Bryce, and a sister, the political activism and social concern of the family appeared to be transmitted to her.[8]

As part of her heritage, also, Cornelia Bryce Pinchot had a Quaker pacifist religious imprint—an experience similar to that of many of the leaders of the fight for women's rights. She disagreed with her "Rough Rider"-like husband on this issue, stating, "Two minds don't think as one—it would be dreary if true."[9]

Cornelia Pinchot did obligate herself to reform. Before her marriage she worked actively for an end to child labor, an end to low pay and poor working conditions for women workers, an end to war, and an end to disenfranchisement. After 1919, she pursued reform armed with the vote.

On the subject of her social position, she declared before a meeting of the American Federation of Labor: "My idea of a lady is one who is not afraid to meet any challenge as it comes—but one who will never be standing on the side of oppression or injustice—one who will be the first to show the way and lead the fight for righteousness."[10] Thus, with position came a special responsibility. Rather than permitting one to be relieved of concern, wealth conferred a sense of *noblesse oblige*.

Through the influence of his father, to whom he gave full credit, Gifford Pinchot became America's first professional forester. In 1892, he applied his scientific management techniques learned in Europe to the estate of the Vanderbilts in North Carolina. From there he was drawn into government service through the Division of Forestry in the Department of Agriculture under President McKinley. When Theodore Roosevelt became president, Gifford Pinchot developed a close personal relationship with him based on the love of the outdoors and the active life, and on a social program that became known as "conservation."

According to Henry Clepper, historian of the forestry movement,[11] the concept of "conservation" had been developing for thirty years before Gifford Pinchot and Theodore Roosevelt focused public attention and concern on it at the beginning of the twentieth century. Several individuals are said to have actually used the word first in its modern connotation or suggested it to Pinchot.[12]

In 1910 Gifford Pinchot proclaimed that the basic principles behind conservation were development of and use of natural resources for the benefit of the many, and not merely for the profit of the few. He insisted on the scientific management of renewable resources to prevent waste and to guarantee their availability for future use.[13] Thirty-five years later in his autobiography, *Breaking New Ground*, published the year after his death, he wrote: "Conservation is the foresighted utilization, preservation, and/or renewal of forests, waters, and lands and minerals for the greatest good of the greatest number for the longest time ... it means everywhere and always that the public good comes first."[14]

Although his background was as a forester, Gifford Pinchot did not confine his original definition of conservation in 1900 to the protection of trees but broadened the resources to be wisely managed to soil, water, minerals, and grazing areas. In 1908 he was involved in the renaming of the journal of the American Forestry Association from *Forestry and Irrigation* to *Conservation* to denote these broader concerns. Pinchot also founded the Conservation League of America—which in 1909 became the National Conservation Association—to pressure for government action to realize the broad objectives of the conservation movement as defined by Pinchot.

Beyond expanding the natural resources to be managed for future use and exploring the wise utilization of public reserves, Gifford Pinchot participated in formally nationalizing and internationalizing the conservation movement. The White House Governor's Conference of 1908 on Conservation, for which Pinchot served as chairman, was so successful in terms of encouraging commitment to the cause by the leadership of the country that he called for a conference of the leaders of the United States, Canada, and Mexico. The positive results of that meeting resulted in invitations being sent by TR to the world to join in a gathering to promote cooperation in conservation. When William Howard Taft became president and rescinded the invitations, Pinchot was not able to carry the idea of internationalizing conservation any further at that time.[15]

Many historians have concluded that the progressive political reform movement was overwhelmed and ended by the "war to end all wars" and by the loss of leadership of Theodore Roosevelt and Woodrow Wilson by the early 1920s. Historians also lose sight of Gifford Pinchot after the Ballinger-Pinchot controversy forced him to leave federal government employment in 1910. Others see the Hetch-Hetchy battle with John Muir in the same period as the critical turning point of popular support away from Pinchot "conservation" and toward the Muir position of aesthetic conservation or "preservationism."[16]

In fact, after their marriage in 1914 the Pinchots entered a new phase of political activity, building on their progressive experience. They also carried on the concept of "conservation," helping it to evolve and expand. It is clear that through their efforts Roosevelt's progressive influence and programs were neither overwhelmed nor lost.

Gifford Pinchot credited TR with encouraging him to be involved with elective politics and with introducing him to the "stump."[17] The Pinchots' extended honeymoon in fact was a Progressive Party campaign by Gifford for the U.S. Senate from Pennsylvania. This unsuccessful 1914 effort was based on his residence established at the family estate in Milford.

Subsequently from that base Gifford was twice elected governor of Pennsylvania (1923-27; 1931-34). To general acclaim by historians of his administrative ability in this position, his progressive experience carried him through the Roaring Twenties and the Great Depression. By the time of his death in 1946, Gifford Pinchot had seen the Second World War concluded, had run for the U.S. Senate three times unsuccessfully while seeking to return to national political prominence, had lost the nomination for governor in the late 1930s, and had been a serious candidate for president in the early 1930s. This is hardly the record of someone who had become lost at the end of the progressive period. Perhaps of even more lasting impact was his political relationship with Cornelia Bryce. A long time supporter of suffrage for women, Gifford determined that, "You [women] haven't been part and parcel of the Party for as long a time and aren't as set and determined in the old ways as men. You're more realistic, more receptive to facts, more receptive to new ideas."[18]

Cornelia Pinchot responded by declaring, "I have fought many times before I ever met Mr. Pinchot for the things he represents so that I was already committed as it was—and even if he'd not been my husband, I'd have been for him—in common with most of the other women of the state, I may say."[19] On the issue of women in politics, Mrs. Pinchot also supported her husband's view of positive good. As she told an audience of college graduates, she believed that through the contact provided by political equality, men and women would become more realistic in their relations. In male-female relationships, men would not have to resort to flattery, to condescension—which she despised—or to threats. Women for their part, would not have to nag, to scold, or to stand in silent awe.[20]

Cornelia Bryce Pinchot's feminist political commitment came not only from the activism of her family but also from her association with Theodore Roosevelt. Invited into his Oyster Bay library during political discussions, she constantly referred to Theodore Roosevelt's complimentary statement that she had the best political mind among all the women of his acquaintance. She corresponded with him, contributing critical comments on his speeches, and joined in her first national campaign for the "Bull Moose" in 1912.[21]

Part of any commitment to the Roosevelt inner circle was to accept the physically energetic life. Cornelia Bryce fulfilled that role admirably. She was an "outdoors woman"—riding horseback, playing polo, and hunting. She told a meeting of Girl Scouts, "When I was your age . . . I did all my stunts alone. Older folks were always against me as a 'Tom Boy.' My own idea was to beat the little boys at their own games—to prove I was a "better sport . . . more enduring—and above all more reckless than any of them could be."[22] This competitive derring-do carried on through her life, even to her taking the controls of an airplane in the 1920s—something no "self-respecting female would do,"[23] she proudly telegraphed her husband.

The suffrage battle was finally won in the immediate postwar period, and Cornelia Pinchot contributed to the final push for ratification of the Nineteenth Amendment. As secretary in 1918 and 1919 of the Pennsylvania Woman's Suffrage Association, she gave money and worked on the telephone and telegraph to insure ratification by the Pennsylvania state legislature of the Nineteenth Amendment.[24]

"A grand and glorious victory,"[25] she proclaimed as she reflected on the achievement of suffrage. However, she commented, somewhat prophetically, on "the simplicity of the struggle."[26] This observation, five years after the vote was hers, may indicate that the struggle for the vote was in retrospect simple compared to the difficulties and combinations possible as an answer to the question of what was to happen to women after the vote, and of what women should do with that vote. Despite the apparent complexities of strategy, and of argumentation over the years, perhaps the struggle had been a relatively simple one with a single goal and purpose uniting the feminists.

In the immediate post-suffrage period, Cornelia Pinchot reflected also seriously on the responsibilities of the vote. Further, she concerned herself about the role women should play in politics.

As an individual, Cornelia Pinchot considered her right to vote so important that the choice of party registration was not automatic. After the difficulties encountered in achieving the franchise, Cornelia Pinchot was not about to thoughtlessly bargain away the power of choice that vote had given her. On July 26, 1919, the Allentown, Pennsylvania, *Chronicle and News* carried the story that "Cornelia Pinchot chooses the Republican Party."[27]

The choice had not been easy. Because of her concern for working women and children, if organized labor supported the Democratic party as the best alternative, then she was tempted to join with them.[28] However, Teddy Roosevelt's progressive Republican "Square Deal," proposing "equal opportunity" for all, was what in the end, as she told a group of university women, ". . . made common sense."[29] Despite the choice having been made, Cornelia declared, "I'm a Republican but I'm not one of those who are always for the party right or wrong."[30] By her example, women were not to trade away their hard-won vote thoughtlessly in a manner determined by any political organization.

The vote was not all suffrage meant to this activist. She could now participate in "politics"—of the kind she had seen practiced by TR and by Gifford Pinchot. One of her favorite stories involved two men: "One man says—'see what happens if the women get the vote.' 'No Sam,' says the other man, 'the vote's alright. Just don't let them get into politics.'"[31] Cornelia Pinchot explained patiently that since it was through the political process that decisions were being made daily that affected women, they must become involved. By participating effectively in the political decision-making process, one could gain control over one's destiny. Beyond that, she wrote, "I love my life. The political life is good—the excitement, the ups and downs, friends and enemies—best because one is fighting and working for and interested in aims outside of one's self." She concluded, "Politics is the best of all indoor sports."[32] Cornelia Pinchot did not like to use the term "women in politics" because that phrase made a separatist distinction that she hoped would be eliminated.[33] However, political power could be useful to improve or to protect women's position.

The political activism of Cornelia Pinchot resulted in several unsuccessful campaigns for a seat in the U.S. Congress and

John W. Furlow, Jr.

serious consideration by her of a run for governor of Pennsylvania. While contributing energy and wealth to her husband's and her own campaigns, perhaps her greatest impact was to sensitize Gifford Pinchot to the concerns of working women and children. As governor, Gifford stated, "I think you'll agree with me that she's this administration's best contribution to the cause of workers on farm or factory, mill or mine."[34] When the Great Depression struck its devastating blows on

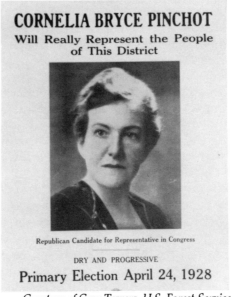

CORNELIA BRYCE PINCHOT

Will Really Represent the People of This District

Republican Candidate for Representative in Congress

DRY AND PROGRESSIVE

Primary Election April 24, 1928

Courtesy of Grey Towers, U.S. Forest Service
Cornelia Bryce Pinchot's campaign poster

Pennsylvania, the Pinchots were ready to respond actively using the resources of government. As Gifford noted, that the government could be a positive force for public good was learned by them under the tutelage of Theodore Roosevelt.[35]

The political relationship between Cornelia and Gifford which had its firm roots in the Roosevelt era lasted far beyond the so-designated Progressive Era. As Cornelia Pinchot developed her social feminism, the concept of "conservation" also evolved and lasted.

In Gifford Pinchot's *Breaking New Ground*, he had added the following phrase to his definition of conservation: "It is obvious, therefore, that the principles of conservation must apply to human beings as well as to natural resources."[36] During their service in the governor's mansion in Pennsylvania, the Pinchots moved strongly toward conservation not only of natural but also of human resources. In the 1920s they advocated Prohibition as a way of saving precious human resources. In the 1930s their effort—including milk stations for children, jobs for the unemployed, and laws to curb sweatshops—grew as more of their fellow humans were subjected to life-threatening deprivations.

The culmination of their efforts to broaden the definition of conservation as formulated in the Theodore Roosevelt era and to make it an international movement came after Gifford had died at the age of eighty-one.

It is fitting that Cornelia Bryce Pinchot would be the one to attend the postwar world conference in 1949, supported by FDR's successor, Harry Truman. Sponsored by the United Nations on the subject of conservation and utilization of resources, scientists from around the world and numerous interested observers were invited to share their collective wisdom with no thought to policy making.[37]

Trygve Lie, Secretary-General of the United Nations, set the tone for this first interdisciplinary, international, scientific meeting. In his opening remarks, he called upon the delegates to

> mobilize technical knowledge in support of one of the high purposes of the Charter—to raise the standards of living. This is one of the keys to peace. For behind most wars stand the specters of hunger and want—effective warmongers of the past. . . . Floods, crop failures, and droughts know no frontiers. Their effect cuts across national boundary lines. No country has a monopoly of the techniques in the sound use and conservation of natural resources, and both industrial and non-industrial countries can profit from the techniques developed in different parts of the world. . . . If we could really put science and technology to fuller use in peace as we did in war, I believe that no one could predict the world population our resources could support or the rise in the average standard of living that would be possible.[38]

Instead of a sense of triumph at the vindication of forty years of effort, the results of the conference disappointed Cornelia Pinchot. The grounds for her disappointment show clearly the course of progressive thought by conservationist Gifford Pinchot since the late nineteenth century. Speaking for herself and for her late husband, her main criticism was that the participants spent too much time discussing the narrowest technological grounds in relation to conservation. She called upon the conferees to regain her late husband's broader vision, "the conservation ideal," by saying,

> Every true conservationist knows that man himself is a natural resource, *the* basic resource; that without man's energy, the energy of coal, of electricity, of oil, or atomic fission itself, is inert and meaningless. To side-step the human and political implications of conservation, to deal with it exclusively in terms of materials, matter and technical processes, is to take a long step backward from where we stood a generation ago.[39]

In the period before the concept of ecology became as current as conservation, before Pennsylvanian Rachel Carson's books carried understanding of the interrelationships within the environment a giant step further, and before the serious discussion of the "quality of life" took place, Gifford and Cornelia Pinchot fought to raise the consciousness of mankind about its place in the world, and its responsibilities.

The connections that brought together the Bull Moose Progressive of Sagamore Hill, the feminist reformer of Roslyn, and the forester-politician of Grey Towers during the Roosevelt era laid the foundation for an enormous impact on modern America. Ideas on feminism and conservation fostered in the Progressive Era survived and evolved far beyond World War I and are still shaping today's society.

It is fitting that the Pinchot estate, Grey Towers, is now the Pinchot Institute for Conservation Studies, dedicated by President Kennedy and administered by the U.S. Department of Agriculture. The Bryce home was purchased by Henry Clay Frick for his son and daughter-in-law. It is now the Nassau County Museum of Art. Their individual homes, like their lives, became dedicated to the "public good."

NOTES

1. Bernie Bookbinder, *Long Island: People and Places; Past and Present* (New York: Harry N. Abrams, 1983), pp. 11–18.

2. Pauline Metcalf and Valencia Libby, *The House and Garden* (Roslyn, NY: Nassau County Museum of Art, 1986), pp. 7–29.

3. Forest Service, *Grey Towers: National Historic Landmark* (Washington, DC: U.S. Government Printing Office, 1985).

4. *New York Times*, Aug. 16, 1914, p. 8.

5. *New York Times*, Sept. 10, 1960, p. 5.

6. Cornelia Bryce Pinchot Papers (Library of Congress, Box 449) Speech to Louisville, Ky., Anti-saloon League, March 31, 1925. Hereafter cited as CBP Papers.

7. CBP Papers, Box 449, Statement, Kittanning, PA, Jan. 8, 1925.

8. CBP Papers, Box 495, February 26, 1931. See also, *New York Times*, Jan. 3, 1932, Section 9, p. 2; CBP Papers, Box 442, Memo from P. S. Stahlnecker; "Mrs. Pinchot, Candidate," *Women's Journal* 13 (April 1928): 28.

9. CBP Papers, Box 450, Oct. 22, 1923, Philadelphia Forum speech. See also, CBP Papers, Box 451, Speech to Pennsylvania Council of Republican Women, Nov. 10, 1925; CBP Papers, Box 451, Speech to St. Louis League of Women Voters, March 11, 1924; CBP Papers, Box 5, CBP to TR, Feb., 1917; CBP Papers, Box 232, CBS Radio speech, May 4, 1940; Gifford Pinchot Papers (hereafter cited as GP Papers), Library of Congress, Box 442, Memo to Stahlnecker.

10. CBP Papers, Box 454, Speech to AFL, Pen Argyl, Sept. 1, 1924.

11. Henry Clepper, *Crusade for Conservation: The Centennial History of the American Forestry Association* (Washington, DC: American Forestry Association, 1975), p. 29.

12. Clepper, *Professional Forestry*, p. 16.

13. Gifford Pinchot, *The Fight for Conservation* (New York: Doubleday, Page, 1910), pp. 44–46.

14. Gifford Pinchot, *Breaking New Ground* (New York: Harcourt, Brace, and Co., 1947), pp. 504–10.

15. Nelson McGeary, *Gifford Pinchot: Forester-Politician* (Princeton: Princeton University Press, 1960), p. 108.

16. Stephen Fox, *The American Conservation Movement: John Muir and His Legacy* (Madison: University of Wisconsin Press, 1985).

17. McGeary, *Gifford Pinchot*, pp. 67–68.

18. Commonwealth of Pennsylvania, *Legislative Journal*, 129th Session of the General Assembly, January 7, 1931, 12:10.

19. CBP Papers, Box 449, Kittanning, PA, Jan. 8, 1925.

20. CBP Papers, Box 456, Goucher College speech, Baltimore, MD, April 6, 1923.

21. Gifford-Pinchot Papers (Library of Congress, Box 442), Memo to Stahlnecker. See also, GP Papers, Box 642, Statement, Feb. 11, 1937; CBP Papers, Box 451, St. Louis Speech, March 11, 1924.

22. CBP Papers, Box 449, Speech to Girl Scouts, Philadelphia, PA, May 10, 1924. See also, CBP Papers, Box 449, Speech to National League of Women Voters, Richmond, VA, April 18, 1925.

23. GP Papers, Box 26, Telegram from Cornelia Pinchot to Gifford Pinchot, June 2, 1925.

24. Ida Husted Harper, ed., *The History of Woman Suffrage* (New York: Arno Press and the *New York Times*, 1969), 5: 516. See also, CBP Papers, Box 5, Oct. 10, 1918.

25. CBP Papers, Box 449, Speech to Pennsylvania League of Women Voters, Nov. 18, 1925.

26 Ibid.

27. CBP Papers, Box 642, July 26, 1919.

28. CBP Papers, Box 449, Dec. 28, 1919.

29. CBP Papers, Box 448, Speech to American Association of University Women, Harrisburg, PA, Dec. 8, 1926.

30. CBP Papers, Box 450, Sept. 19, 1924.

31. CBP Papers, Box 448, Stahlnecker Memo, July 30, 1923.

32. CBP Papers, Box 448, Speech, Chicago, Nov. 20, 1924.

33. CBP Papers, Box 495, *New York Sun*, Jan. 3, 1932.

34. GP Papers (Library of Congress, Box 2297), Speech by Gifford Pinchot, Oct. 11, 1934. Also, *New York Times*, July 16, 1933, p. 10.

35. The best summarizations by Gifford Pinchot of his relationship with TR are to be found in GP Papers (Library of Congress, Box 2,296), speech by Gifford Pinchot at Memorial Day Exercises conducted by the Quentin Roosevelt Post No. 4 of the American Legion at Oyster Bay, NY, May 30, 1931; Pinchot Papers (Library of Congress, Box 2,296), speech by Gifford Pinchot at Roosevelt Memorial at Maria Pass, MT, Oct. 25, 1931; Pinchot Papers Library of Congress, Box 790), in a letter to Colonel Ahern, Oct. 25, 1931; and Pinchot Papers (Library of Congress, Box 2,298), address by Gifford Pinchot before meeting of Roosevelt Commemoration Association of Western Pennsylvania at Pittsburgh, PA, Oct. 17, 1934.

36. Pinchot, *Breaking New Ground*, p. 506.

37. U.S. Department of Economic Affairs, *Proceedings of the U.N. Scientific Conference on the Conservation and Utilization for Resources*, August 17–September 16, 1949, Lake Success, NY, 7 vols. (New York, United Nations, 1950), 1: 319.

38. *Proceedings of the U.N.*, 1: 2.

39. *Proceedings of the U.N.: Plenary Meetings*, 1: 319.

Courtesy of Grey Towers, U.S. Forest Service

Cornelia Bryce Pinchot, 1922.

33

An Easy Alliance: Theodore Roosevelt and Emmett Jay Scott, 1900-1919

Maceo Crenshaw Dailey, Jr.

If Theodore Roosevelt, as his son observed, coveted adulation so much that at funerals he desired to be the corpse and at weddings he wanted to be the bride, at least one significant African-American of the twentieth century truly lamented the fact that the "Rough Rider" got his wish in 1919 in regard to one of the choices. Roosevelt, in his political ambition, had not always been kind to that African-American, Emmett Jay Scott, but the black man who had served as Booker T. Washington's private secretary from 1897 to 1912 and official secretary of Tuskegee Institute from 1912 to 1919 was a forgiving individual. He, in fact, had remained more loyal to Roosevelt than any African-American of the twentieth century. The nature of the relationship between Emmett Jay Scott and Theodore Roosevelt, which began in 1897 and continued through to 1919, was filled with promises and paradoxes. It was an easy, almost natural, alliance between two men radically different in demeanor. It was also a relationship couched in mutual respect and admiration, as much as race etiquettes of the time would permit. The illumination of that relationship tells us much about the intersection of education and politics, where racial considerations were fundamental preoccupations affecting choices, and what things were possible in the modern America of the twentieth century. The relationship is also another example of the means by which the twenty-sixth president made an indelible mark on modern America insofar as political choices had to be made in the realm of race relations.[1]

Theodore Roosevelt, a man of inordinate verve, had many things to ponder as he boarded the train for Booker T. Washington's Tuskegee Institute in Alabama the second week in December 1915. Paramount, of course, was Roosevelt's intended bid for the Republican party's presidential nomination in 1916. In travelling to Tuskegee as one of the most influential trustees of the school, Roosevelt had a chance to strengthen his political hand among African-Americans whom he had alienated earlier in the Brownsville decision to punish black soldiers for the sortie on that Texas town in 1906, and in 1912 when he booted black Republicans out of the Bull Moose convention. In order for Roosevelt to win the good will of the black community for another presidential bid in 1916, it was decided that TR would install in the Tuskegee principalship an African-American leader capable of the political wizardry of Booker T. Washington, the recently deceased black leader who had done so much to tie black Republicans to the chief executive and the Grand Old Party from 1901 to 1909.[2]

Roosevelt had decided that to accomplish his political aim, the vacuum in black leadership and the Tuskegee principalship had to be filled in the wake of Booker T. Washington's death by his alter ego and former private secretary, Emmett Jay Scott. Roosevelt's decision, regarding this matter, was based on a meeting with Washington's ranking New York political lieutenant, Charles W. Anderson, himself a close friend and ally of Scott. Even without Anderson's prodding, Roosevelt probably would have supported Scott for the position. Still lingering in Roosevelt's memory were the frequent and successful meetings with Scott, who was dispatched often to the White House to do Washington's bidding or to provide information on Republican party politics in the South in the years between 1901 and 1909. It appears that the first meeting between Roosevelt and Scott may have occurred, however, as early as 1897 when Roosevelt was undersecretary of the Navy and Scott was then busy adjusting to his new job at Tuskegee. The president developed an abiding respect for Scott's ability, his *savoir faire* and astute political judgment. Their meetings crossed racial and class boundaries—owing to the president's appreciation for intelligence, shrewdness, and style. And why not? Scott, as the black historian Carter G. Woodson once observed, was the "only man who could walk on snow without leaving footprints." A quick recounting of the careers of the two men provides some clues about the easy alliance between them and the importance of this relationship with respect to politics and education in the coming of age of modern America.[3]

Wealth and sickness through the formative years had given Theodore Roosevelt a keen patrician sense of the uses to which power could be put, as well as an appreciation for the underdog. Born in Houston, Texas in 1873, Emmett Jay Scott was the proverbial underdog in the American society. Racial restrictions and violence in the South made the life of most African-Americans extremely precarious. Whereas Roosevelt had the privileges of money and Harvard to see him through the formative years, Scott faced deprivation. An exceptionally bright young lad, Scott did well in the all-black school system of Houston. He attended Wiley College for a few years, but was forced to withdraw ultimately to help sustain his parents in the rearing of their eight children. While Roosevelt was making his initial intrusions into the realm of politics in New York City, Scott was struggling for means to support himself and assist his family.

He resolved the employment matter temporarily by working for the *Houston Post* in the early 1890s, and gained the confidence and courage there to embark upon the task of founding, along with two other individuals in his hometown in 1893, an African-American newspaper titled the *Texas Freeman*. While Roosevelt was realizing his political ambitions on the state level, Scott was hitching his political fortunes to local black Republicans in Texas. Through his newspaper articles and editorials urging blacks to "get together," Scott was invited to become private secretary to the state's most powerful black Republican party boss, Norris Wright Cuney. While Roosevelt moved through the Navy Department with his profound appreciation for the theories of Alfred T. Mahan and then headed for the Spanish-American Civil War to don his Brooks Brothers military suit before the charge up San Juan Hill, Scott was searching for other outlets for his talent, which he resolved by accepting the job as private secretary to Booker T. Washington.

The first meeting of Roosevelt and Scott, if indeed it did come in 1897, found both men in the ascendancy of their careers. Scott, as Washington's private secretary, had been dispatched to the District of Columbia to talk with government officials about preventing the encroachment of European powers on the tiny West African Republic of Liberia, the country the United States had helped to establish in the 1830s as a place for the repatriation of former slaves from the United States. Scott, it appears, ended up in a meeting with Theodore Roosevelt, who promised that he would try to seek some assistance for the West African country. The Spanish-American War, however, proved to be the little skirmish that, in part, diverted Roosevelt's attention from the woes of Liberia.[4]

The fame Roosevelt garnered in the Spanish-American War and his placement as the vice presidential candidate on the Republican party ticket in 1900 led to a necessary, but distant familiarity, with black politicians. The vice president, however, soon came to take a particularly keen interest in black politics as practiced by Booker T. Washington. Roosevelt's ambition, and his belief that he could win the presidency in his own right post-1900, led to attempts to strengthen his ties with Washington and Tuskegee even before the assassination of William McKinley. The assassination, in fact, prevented Roosevelt from keeping a date with Booker T. Washington in which the two had planned to discuss Republican party politics in the South. There can be no doubt that Roosevelt intended to make a strong political ally of Washington, and thereby strengthen his hand in the bid for the presidential office when the time came. It was an alliance to which both Washington and his private secretary Emmett Jay Scott looked forward, anticipating the consolidation of their influence and greater control of patronage positions to be allocated to blacks.[5]

All of this eventually came to pass when Roosevelt assumed the presidency in 1901. During his tenure in office, there developed the Tuskegee political machine which Washington and Scott directed in boss-like fashion from the small Alabama black school. Scott himself made numerous trips to the White House to discuss with Roosevelt the political climate in the South, African-American patronage jobs, and black problems Washington thought wise for the president to discuss from time to time. Washington and Scott, owing to this contact with the president, promptly lined up behind his choice of Taft for the presidential nomination in 1908 and supported the next chief executive during his four-year stint in office. In 1912, however, despite Scott's anxiousness to support Roosevelt for the nomination, Booker T. Washington decided to back discreetly the incumbent Taft prior to the nomination contest itself and openly after the matter was settled. As for Roosevelt during that time of frustration, he blamed blacks, in part, for his loss of the regular

Republican party nomination and, therefore, barred them from the Bull Moose convention.

To mend political fences all around in the quest for the presidential nomination four years later in 1916, in both the black and white political communities, was a tall order. Roosevelt, however, sought such an opportunity to make amends with African-Americans in the events following the death of Booker T. Washington. His trip to Tuskegee in late 1915 was motivated by this desire. To draw on the Tuskegee political alliance that had served him so well in 1904 and 1908, Roosevelt turned to Scott, not only Washington's main political lieutenant, but a person whose knowledge of Southern politics was unsurpassed. To some individuals, Scott, indeed, was the brains of the Tuskegee political machine, and this is no doubt what Charles W. Anderson, the black political boss in New York, had assured Roosevelt would be the case in the years after Washington's death. Boarding the New York train for Alabama and Tuskegee, Roosevelt planned consequently to use his power and influence as a trustee of the school to make Scott the principal and heir-apparent to the deceased black leader Washington. Roosevelt was convinced that Scott was the man to galvanize black Republicans and revitalize the Tuskegee political machine, and the former president had hoped to rely on this to win votes and support of African-Americans in his bid for the White House in 1916.[6]

Tuskegee would be no easy place for Roosevelt to work his serious brand of political magic in getting Scott installed as the next principal of the school. Factionalism had already developed at the institution as individuals discussed and sometimes openly stated their preference for the next principal. On the campus, the names of three Tuskegee employees emerged as favorites: Emmett Jay Scott, Booker T. Washington's brother John, and Warren Logan, the school treasurer. Robert R. Moton, employed in Booker T. Washington's alma mater, Hampton Institute in Virginia, was also receiving support for the post. Moton's claim to the post was strengthened considerably by the belief that Booker T. Washington, prior to his death, had endorsed Moton for the principalship. Yet, Booker T. Washington's wife, Margaret Murray, voiced her support for Scott for the position during the initial days of the discussion over a successor. She subsequently changed her mind, however, informing trustee William G.

Willcox that the appointment of either of the two men who then appeared to be the primary candidates, Scott, the school's secretary, or Logan, the Tuskegee treasurer, as principal, "would split the campus wide open."

As the decision became more crucial, there emerged unusual timidity and a foreboding mood on the campus over the succession question for two significant reasons: no one wanted to commit openly and thereby run the risk of becoming expendable for supporting the wrong candidate, and most recognized that the decision rested in the hands of the prominent and powerful white board of trustees. Among the most vocal and determined board members was Theodore Roosevelt, who proclaimed that the "President of Tuskegee should be . . . the leader of his race in this country"; Sears-Roebuck magnate Julius Rosenwald, who argued that the next head of the institute should be "looked upon as a leader by the Southern white and black people"; and William G. Willcox, who held that the next principal had to "carry sufficient weight . . . at the school and throughout the country."[7]

To make the decision regarding the successor, board of trustee members arriving on campus were afforded both social and educational opportunities to get to know better some of the candidates. Particular exercises of this nature were the scheduled ceremonial speeches in memory of the deceased Booker T. Washington. These were the so-called "maiden speeches," to see if the potential candidates had the savvy and political ability to satisfy blacks in the audience with a commitment to racial reform, while not alienating whites with brashness. The scheduling of Warren Logan to speak during the visit of the trustees was such an occasion. Unfortunately, Logan's wife committed suicide during this period, leaping from the academic building in rather dramatic fashion as student cadets were marching past the structure. The grief-stricken Logan was excused from the memorial exercises for Washington, and Emmett Jay Scott became the substitute speaker.[8]

Scott was basically a backroom political operator and smooth negotiator. On the public podium, his style was formal and stiff, and justly perceived at times as pedantic and pretentious to the hostile critic. He seldom erred in political judgment, but made a serious mistake in his commemorative speech on Booker T. Washington by characterizing him as the man who had laid the economic and political foundation for black uplift and suggesting that the time was ripe to move past 1915 more steadfastly and boldly in the acquisition of all citizenship rights. Addressing the audience and standing with board of trustee members seated behind him on the stage, Scott, in the process of speaking, did not realize the extent to which he had alienated one of his major supporters, Theodore Roosevelt. The former president, perturbed and disgruntled by Scott's presentation, turned to Julius Rosenwald to proclaim that "we can never make this man president because he will not be able to get along with the white folks."[9]

Theodore Roosevelt promptly reversed himself on the Scott appointment for principal of the school. In the first board of trustee session on December 13 (when the group was deadlocked on the choice of Scott or Robert Russa Moton from Hampton), Roosevelt led the movement for establishing a subcommittee of five to determine who should be the next head of Tuskegee Institute. Neither Roosevelt nor Rosenwald, still a firm Scott supporter, served on the committee, but there was no doubt that it was established to represent the two varying views of the two men. Rosenwald remained committed to Scott as the "one man [who] has sat at the feet of the master and imbibed his spirit, and in addition has the necessary intellectual qualities which the other [Moton] lacks." Roosevelt, however, was prone to reject this argument. On the return trip to New York, Roosevelt convinced several of the board members on his train to invite Moton to join their party on the segment of the journey from Richmond to Washington, D. C. Moton did so, and impressed all in the group, especially Roosevelt. Once in New York, Roosevelt telegrammed Rosenwald that Moton was the man for the job, that he lacked the "bumptiousness or self-assertiveness which would at once ensure failure in his position." Roosevelt concluded his statement with the observation that he felt "so strongly that in case the committee of Five do not agree [sic] on Major Moton," he would "advise their extending their enquire and looking throughout the Union to find the best man for the position."[10]

A prerequisite qualification for the best man had to be political admiration for Roosevelt. The former president wanted an African-American political ally in the South to marshall votes and support for him. In a Jim Crow society, Moton seemed docile and discrete enough, and able within the African-American community to mobilize black Republicans for the Roosevelt campaign for president. With respect to Scott, it is possible that Roosevelt may have promised him some coveted patronage job in the event the former president succeeded in a third bid for the White House. Rather than harboring disappointment, Scott enthusiastically prepared to galvanize black Republicans for Roosevelt. Scott's cooperation also assured Roosevelt the support of the wealthy Julius Rosenwald whose money and influence would be useful in the Midwest. Thus in that one trip to Tuskegee, Roosevelt had succeeded in many of his political objectives with respect to the African-American community.[11]

Roosevelt, consequently, had much to his political liking within the circle of black Republicans of the South in the initial campaign for the party's nomination in 1916. Scott coordinated the activities of Southern black Republicans in beating the bush for Roosevelt votes. The legendary political supporters of Booker T. Washington and those the Tuskegee principal had been able to deliver to Roosevelt so effectively in the past were all in the field again under Scott's direction, diligently backing the Rough Rider: P. B. S. Pinchback (Louisiana); Charles W. Anderson (New York); Henry M. Minton (Philadelphia); Robert R. Church (Tennessee); Charles Banks (Mississippi); Perry Howard (Mississippi); Ralph Tyler (Ohio); and Walter L. Cohen (Louisiana). Scott came to believe, along with Charles Anderson, that Roosevelt's primary competitor for the presidential nomination was former New York Governor and Supreme Court Justice Charles E. Hughes who, in good conscience, could neither "authorize the use of his name as a candidate with propriety, nor . . . (that) the convention can afford to nominate him in the absence of such authorization." Scott, however, would see such logic fall prey quickly to the vicissitudes of party wisdom and some unusual political chicanery within his own circle of allies. One of his closest political allies and lieutenants, James A. Cobb of Washington, D. C., had been duped by long-time Republican politico Frank H. Hitchcock and New York broker Eugene Meyer into accepting money to travel south to uncover as well as build support for Roosevelt. The two white New Yorkers, in reality, were Hughes supporters and wanted to find the extent of Roosevelt's popularity in the South. The duplicity of the two white New Yorkers and the stupidity of his own man Cobb caused some minor annoyance for Scott, but did nothing to deter his thinking that Roosevelt was still a certainty in the nomination contest. All the Tuskegee men further assured Scott that they would follow his lead in the convention and that Roosevelt was their first choice.[12]

The convention proved to be an exciting but disappointing one for Scott. At the conclusion of the convention, Scott felt that he had exhausted himself "putting in some hard licks in behalf of Roosevelt . . . hustl[ing] from sun up to midnight." He had indeed worked diligently. At the quadrennial meeting of black Republicans in the famous African-American Episcopal Church of Quinn Chapel in Chicago, Scott coordinated the activities for Roosevelt. African-American Republicans also held several other related activities, in particular a smoker at the Jones Place Restaurant presided over by the notable Chicago black politician Oscar DePriest, all as a part of the numerous social and political events to whip black Republicans into a feverish pitch for Roosevelt. Scott also held some renegade African-American politicians in check. The demands upon the Republican party emanating from this kind of African-American staging and political effort were fairly innocuous, limited primarily to the general but vague political requests of bland planks calling for "Negro Rights" and opposition to any legislation undermining the Fourteenth and Fifteenth Amendments.[13]

Roosevelt's resulting loss of the Republican nomination was, however, a bitter disappointment for Scott, who came to see the convention as nothing more than a "political carnival pulled off" for Hughes. Some of Scott's other political allies at the convention bemoaned similar complaints to him and the fact that Roosevelt's supporters had been caught waiting too late and were therefore outmaneuvered. Walter L. Cohen of New Orleans, long active in Republican party politics, groaned to Scott that it would have been "foolish" to have given delegate votes to Roosevelt on the sixth ballot when it was obvious that the struggle had been lost by that time. Something, however, could be salvaged out of the defeat of Roosevelt. Cohen wrote to Scott that Roosevelt would be wise to give "half-hearted" support to Hughes, anticipate his defeat, and vie for the nomination himself some four years later. Cohen perceptively predicted Roosevelt's tactical approach in the early stages of the presidential race of 1916.[14]

While Scott worked closely with his political ally Charles W. Anderson to get on the inside of the Hughes campaign and

control the African-American bureaucracy to elect the
Republican presidential nominee, Roosevelt remained aloof of
party politics, preferring to retire to Oyster Bay and let the
political pundits ponder his next move. Scott enjoyed a modicum
of success in establishing himself as a machine-style political boss
during the campaign and assisted in swaying African-Americans
to support Hughes. He, however, took more than a passing
interest in Roosevelt's curious silencing and cloistering of himself
in Oyster Bay. Under what probably was Scott's prodding,
Charles Anderson visited Roosevelt to discuss the campaign. The
black politician left the meeting with Roosevelt convinced, as he
later confided to Scott, that Hughes's approach was wrong and
that it seemed he was going to lose. Scott was also informed by
Anderson of his wish that Roosevelt would rally, stepping in to
give Hughes the necessary lift and eventual lead in the race.[15]

With Roosevelt continuing to nurse his bruised ego and the
new Republican leaders slow to draw on help from the black
community, Hughes's campaign sputtered. In general, the
Republican party machinery was lethargic, uninspired, and
unorganized. African-American Republicans, under Scott's
guidance, were particularly disgruntled; and all seemed rather
hopeless for Hughes the candidate—owing to the internecine
conflict in the party in both white and black camps alike. The
newspapers predicted that Woodrow Wilson's "commanding
lead" was too much to overcome. That fall of 1916, however,
witnessed a remarkable political blitzkrieg by the Republican
party, one that narrowly missed winning the presidential office
for Hughes. At the center of this effort were two important
individuals: Roosevelt and Scott.[16]

The black Republicans led by Scott launched the "Big Drive."
Scott turned to the institutional black community that he knew
so well, employing the churches, newspapers, black storeowners,
and especially the barbers and beauticians. The black community
became even more caught up in the political fervor as Scott
persuaded Hughes to give a speech on the "fundamental rights"
of the Negro. Black ministers received a copy of Hughes's
"Doctrine of Human Rights," and Charles W. Anderson, Scott's
ally, exhorted the preachers to get the black vote out by
pontificating on the Sunday prior to the election "that the
promise of St. John may be fulfilled that 'ye shall know the truth,
and the truth shall make you free.'" Added to all of this was the

fact that Roosevelt came out of his exile in Oyster Bay to give a series of forceful speeches for Hughes. The final days of the election campaign led to a significant erosion of Wilson's support among voters, and on November 7, the day of the election, Hughes actually went to sleep believing that he had eked out a narrow victory. Scott thought so too, mailing congratulatory telegrams to that effect to Hughes, Roosevelt, and Charles Anderson. There was, of course, shock for Scott when he realized the following day that Hughes had been defeated, but the black politician did not lament the loss for very long. Travelling to New York City a few days after the election, Scott met with John McGrath, a Roosevelt admirer and backer, to discuss the campaign of the Rough Rider for the presidential nomination and election in 1920.[17]

Scott redoubled his efforts to ensure that he would be in position in 1920 for a strong Roosevelt bid for the presidency by maintaining political ties to blacks and whites to be relied upon at that time. The war years, however, prompted Scott to turn to the more immediate question of the role of African-Americans in the U.S. Army in 1917 and what citizenship gains might be made by blacks owing to their gallant and heroic contributions to the military campaign. As in the past, African-Americans interpreted the war as a chance to demonstrate their patriotism and earn respect that translated into opportunity within the United States. As one African-American wit put it, blacks had to break into each war like burglars, and it was no different during the conflict of 1917.[18]

In the weeks prior to the U.S. declaration of war on Germany in April 1917, Scott drafted a set of resolutions calling for the utilization of African-American manpower and submitted it to Julius Rosenwald, then a member of the National Defense Board. While waiting for the War Department's decision regarding the utilization of black soldiers, Scott travelled to Oyster Bay on April 21, 1917, where he and Roosevelt discussed the formation of an African-American military regiment and appointment of officers the former president planned to take to Europe in the quest for glory. Details of the plan were not found in the papers of Roosevelt or Scott, so it is impossible to uncover the precise thinking of both men with regard to the venture. It is evident, however, that the political capital to be acquired by such an endeavor was the uppermost matter in the minds of both men, and the popularity garnered by such a move would have augured well for Roosevelt in the presidential contest of 1920.

Roosevelt had to bide his time without military recognition, however, and unfortunately, his death some two years later brought an end to one of the most extraordinary political careers in the United States. Scott, during the war, held the highest position accorded an African-American with his appointment as Special Assistant on Negro Affairs to Newton D. Baker, the secretary of the Army. He later moved to Washington in 1919 to serve as secretary-treasurer and business manager at Howard University. Many years later, during World War II, Scott headed yard number four of the Pew family-owned Sun Shipbuilding Company in Chester, Pennsylvania. Scott remained a lifelong Republican and lived until 1957, the eve of the Civil Rights Movement of the 1960s.

The relationship between Theodore Roosevelt and Emmett Jay Scott had a significant impact on historical development of modern America in the twentieth century. Scott's loss of the Tuskegee principalship propelled him to consider and capitalize on other career opportunities. Tuskegee Institute under Robert Russa Moton stayed within the orbit of the Republican party, with the principal of the school (Roosevelt's choice) remaining all too docile for many African-Americans. Roosevelt's calling of Scott to Oyster Bay for the discussion of the role of black troops in World War I was all part of the movement and thinking that military recognition and engagement of African-Americans could be made to serve political ends. White Republicans who began to dominate the party after 1916—with the purge of older politicians such as Roosevelt (who were keener and more sophisticated about relying on blacks and indeed exploiting the black vote)—demonstrated decreasing ability and interest in ways to hold African-Americans in the party of Lincoln. In many ways, it was Roosevelt's patrician sense, ambition, and appreciation for the underdog that allowed him to structure a relationship with an African-American, Scott, that crossed social and racial boundaries. This afforded both men the opportunity to be players, rather than mere passive objects, in the political game of chance and the art of the possible in politics and race relations. Scott, of course, learned what many black politicians of today all too often forget: that ambition and strength among the powerful can be turned to advantages for the powerless with the proper alliances, though individuals are not always guaranteed that personal ambition will be fulfilled.[19]

NOTES

1. John Milton Cooper, Jr., *The Warrior and the Priest: Woodrow Wilson and Theodore Roosevelt* (Cambridge: Belknap Press of Harvard University Press, 1983), p. 69; Maceo Crenshaw Dailey, Jr., "Emmett Jay Scott: The Career of a Secondary Black Leader," (Ph.D. diss., Howard University, 1983), pp. 236–318.

2. Dailey, "Emmett Jay Scott," p. 189.

3. Ibid., p. 189; John Blum, *The Republican Roosevelt*, (Cambridge: Harvard University Press, 1954), p. 127.

4. Dailey, "Emmett Jay Scott," pp. 1–34; this interpretation is also drawn from David McCullough, *Mornings on Horseback*, (New York: Simon and Schuster, 1981).

5. Dailey, "Emmett Jay Scott," pp. 72–73; Theodore Roosevelt to Booker T. Washington, September 14, 1901, Booker T. Washington Papers, Library of Congress, Washington, DC.

6. Dailey, "Emmett Jay Scott," pp. 66–197.

7. Ibid., pp. 187–89.

8. Jessie Thomas, *My Story in Black and White*, (New York: Exposition Press, 1967), pp. 53–58.

9. Ibid., pp. 53–58.

10. Ibid., pp. 53–58; "Tuskegee Institute Board of Trustees' Minutes," December 13, 1915, Tuskegee Paper Files, Hollis B. Frissell Library, Tuskegee, AL; *Tuskegee Student*, p. 1, n.d., College Files, Frissell Library, Tuskegee, Ala.; Ernest T. Attwell to Julius Rosenwald, December 15, 1915; Rosenwald to Seth Low, December 16, 1915; Rosenwald to Low, December 16, 1915; Roosevelt to Rosenwald, December 15, 1915, Julius Rosenwald Papers, University of Chicago Library, Chicago, Ill.; Scott to James A. Cobb, December 22, 1915, microfilm reel 203, Theodore Roosevelt Papers, Library of Congress, Washington, DC.

11. Thomas, *My Story In Black and White*, pp. 55–56; William G. Willcox to Rosenwald, December 23, 1915, Rosenwald Papers.

12. Dailey, "Emmett Jay Scott," pp. 236–41; Charles W. Anderson to Scott, May 4, 1916, cont. 2; Scott to Anderson, May 2, 1916, cont. 2, Emmett Jay Scott Papers, Morgan State University Library, Baltimore, MD.

13. Scott to Robert Russa Moton, June 4, 1916, cont. 11; Scott to Moton, June 16, 1916, cont. 11, Robert Russa Moton Papers, Hollis B. Frissell Library, Tuskegee, AL.

14. Dailey, "Emmett Jay Scott," pp. 244–45; Hanes Walton, Jr., *Black Republicans: The Politics of The Black and Tans* (Metuchen, NJ: The Scarecrow Press, 1975), pp. 156–57.

15. Dailey, "Emmett Jay Scott," pp. 245–53.

16. Ibid., pp. 257–58.

17. Ibid., pp. 258–62; Anderson to Scott, October 23, 1916, cont. 1; Scott to Parsons, October 17, 1916, cont. 10; Anderson to Scott, July 15,

1916, cont. 1; Anderson to Parsons, September 8, 1916, cont. 1, Scott Papers; George H. Mayer, *The Republican Party, 1854–1964*, (New York: Oxford University Press, 1964), pp. 344–47.

    18. Dailey, "Emmett Jay Scott," pp. 259–60, 263–65.

    19. Ibid., pp. 265–525.

Courtesy of Hofstra University Archives

Theodore Roosevelt in 1918 by Princess Vilma Lwoff-Parlaghy. From a copy hanging in Theodore Roosevelt Hall, Hofstra University, Hempstead, New York.

34

What Might Have Been: Theodore Roosevelt's Platform for 1920

Matthew J. Glover

The task of statesmanship is to attempt to shape events according to a vision of the future, with the moral fortitude to act boldly even when consensus and certainty are often unattainable.

Henry Kissinger[1]

Theodore Roosevelt, even during the turbulent years of World War I, had a vision for America's future. He had already rallied the United States to join the Allied cause, and as the war raged he sought to prepare America for life in the postwar world. During 1918, Roosevelt proposed reforms needed at home and outlined a postwar U.S. foreign policy. By 1918, TR was considered by most political observers as the most probable Republican nominee in 1920.[2] He died suddenly in January 1919 at 60. But in his speeches and articles he left behind are the outlines of what would have been the Roosevelt platform for 1920.

Roosevelt's path back to Republican leadership, accomplished by 1919, had been long and tortuous. TR had fought the old guard for mastery of the GOP during his years as president, 1901–1909, and was successful enough to name his successor, William Howard Taft. But once in office, Taft sided with the conservatives, and in 1912, TR, giving in to urgent pleadings by progressive Republicans, opposed Taft's renomination. TR swept the Republican primaries in 1912, but was "counted out" by Taft supporters at the GOP convention. Roosevelt and his followers then bolted and created the Progressive party, nicknamed the "Bull Moose" party. Roosevelt was the Progressive presidential candidate in 1912, and was defeated by Democrat Woodrow Wilson when he and Taft split the Republican vote.[3]

"Sooner or later," wrote TR after the Bull Moose campaign, "the national principles championed by the Progressives of 1912 must in their general effect be embodied in the structure of our national existence. . . . I shall continue to work for these ideals."[4] Roosevelt proved true to his word; these ideals were on his mind to his final hours.[5]

Very few Progressive candidates were elected in 1912 and 1914. Thus, with the demise of the Bull Moose movement imminent, Roosevelt carefully backed away from the Progressive party. TR, determined to avoid the "spoiler" label that critics gave him during his Bull Moose campaign, declined the 1916 Progressive party nomination and backed GOP nominee Charles Evans Hughes, who later lost to Wilson.[6]

During the 1916 campaign, Roosevelt proclaimed, "Our [the Progressives'] loyalty is to the fact, to the principle, to the ideal, and not merely to the name, and least of all to the party name."[7] TR did not desert the progressive ideals, but less than two years later Roosevelt repeatedly used a party name and it was Republican: "I wish to do everything in my power to make the Republican Party the party of sane, constructive radicalism, just as it was under Lincoln. If it is not that then I have no place in it."[8] Roosevelt continued to advance progressive ideas for the country's future, deciding that the Republican party was the best vehicle with which to achieve those ideas. "I am satisfied that many Republicans who did not believe these things [progressive ideas] three and six years ago, are going to believe them now."[9]

During 1917 and 1918, Roosevelt loomed larger and larger as a presidential candidate for 1920. United States entry into World War I seemed to vindicate his earlier calls for military preparedness. Roosevelt contributed scores of editorials on current affairs to the *Kansas City Star* newspaper and *Metropolitan* magazine, keeping his views in front of the voters.[10] His speaking tours on behalf of the war effort seemed to put him above party politics. GOP Senator James Watson of Indiana later noted that "the pre-eminently patriotic service of Colonel Roosevelt before and during the War, and the conspicuous part taken by all members of his noble family, beat down all opposition to him and made him easily the commanding figure of the Republican Party."[11] After the 1918 elections TR noted the change in his popularity among Republicans, saying "whereas four years ago . . . my attitude was not popular, I was now the one man whom they insisted upon following and whose statements were taken as the platform."[12]

Roosevelt's thoughts about his potential candidacy, spoken only to close friends, reveal his receptiveness towards running. While refusing to consider nomination for the New York governorship, in the summer of 1918, TR told his sister, "I think I should reserve my strength in case I am needed in 1920."[13] Later he confided to a newspaper reporter, "If . . . the Republican Party wants me . . . I will be a candidate."[14] In late 1918, TR was told that General Leonard Wood might enter the GOP race. "Well," TR replied, "probably I shall have to get into this thing in June."[15] Writing days before his death, TR told a friend, "Probably there will be insistence that I am a candidate in 1920."[16]

Meanwhile, those Republicans concerned with winning elections wanted Roosevelt in the 1920 race. New York boss William Barnes was asked if TR might be nominated by acclamation in 1920. "Hell!" Barnes shot back, "We'll nominate him by assault!"[17]

If the GOP bosses believed they had a winner in TR, the GOP rank-and-file was no less enthusiastic. A Republican from Oregon wrote, "I'm with you clear down the line for I'm getting to believe that you are the only man who can save the Republican Party in 1920."[18] Judging by TR's mail from this period, the public seemed eager to see Roosevelt reelected. A Pennsylvania editor in 1917 wrote, "I want to see you go to France and come back in time to enter the fight for president. . . . The Republicans, Democrats and the devil combined could not whip you."[19]

TR said he would probably be a candidate in 1920, but what of his chances for actually securing the nomination? Of the three main presidential contenders at the 1920 Republican Convention, two, Leonard Wood and Hiram W. Johnson, were TR's longtime friends and supporters. The two together had a large number of first-ballot votes, many of which would have been Roosevelt's had he lived.[20]

Roosevelt had proven operators to propel his planned presidential bid. Mining magnate William Boyce Thompson concluded that Roosevelt's ability and vision were America's need in 1920. Thompson financed John T. King's early search for Roosevelt delegates and eventually became the chief GOP fund-raiser for 1920, being fairly sure that Roosevelt would be the candidate. When TR died, Thompson became the first president of the Roosevelt Memorial Association.[21]

John T. King, a Republican national committeeman from Connecticut, was by 1918 TR's personal emissary and campaign manager for 1920. Writing to Will H. Hays, then a prospective GOP national chairman, Roosevelt outlined King's credentials as his main political operative:

> John King is very close to me. He will do everything he can for you . . . to elect you [chairman] . . . Will you treat him as my particular and confidential friend, and consult and advise with him? . . . You and I and John King . . . wish the [the Republican] Party to be the farsighted and efficient servant.[22]

While King never carried the formal title of campaign manager at the early date of 1918, his duties gave him the job de facto.[23]

Hays's 1918 race for GOP chief was successful and thereafter he and TR became close associates, working together to strengthen the party.[24]

Roosevelt died at his home on January 6, 1919. The last note he wrote read: "Hays see him; he must go to Washington for 10 days; see Senate & House; prevent split on domestic policies." The note referred to the chairman and the 1920 Republican platform. Roosevelt's early platform concern reflected Hays's ideas, which included a long-range study and preparation of the platform. Hays later wrote that he wanted to avoid the jam of work that usually results in a "haphazard, hastily conceived program." The new platform preparation represents further collaboration between the party chief and the man who might have been the GOP standard-bearer in 1920.[25]

Eight months before his death, Roosevelt highlighted progressive ideas at the Maine Republican state convention. Foremost he urged that America "speed up the War," and "take thought for after the War." The speech was a success and the Republican party had tens of thousands of copies distributed. Roosevelt said, "The Maine Progressives felt that my speech and its reception amounted to the acceptance, by the Republicans of Maine, of the Progressive platform of 1912 developed and brought up to date."[26]

TR's speeches of 1917 and 1918 updated the 1912 "Bull Moose" platform; they also contained ideas that may very well have been his 1920 platform. Of domestic issues, service by youth was near the top of TR's list. In a September 1918 Baltimore speech promoting war bonds, Roosevelt expounded on his bold idea of "universal obligatory military training."

Characteristically, Roosevelt was decades ahead of his time: "Let us demand service from women as we do from men, and in return give the suffrage to all men and women who in peace and war perform the service."[27]

Universal service was a natural outgrowth of TR's admonition that "people do [their] best to work in a spirit of brotherhood for the common good of man." Roosevelt had been a "universal service" advocate for many years, applauded the draft during war, and urged it be made permanent. Further, he pioneered a plank for woman's suffrage in his 1912 platform. His call for women's service came from his belief in women's rights.

Roosevelt wrote that he regarded "technical education as the prime need for the great multitude."[28] At Baltimore Roosevelt said he would provide all men and women with "certain forms of industrial training . . . in the ordinary work of the ordinary man and woman in their business occupations and in and around their home. . . . I think we should educate . . . [them] toward . . . their life work, toward the home, toward the farm, toward the shop. . . . I would use the introduction of a system of universal training and service as a means for securing this education."

Extolling men's training, Roosevelt was more specific when he cited the U.S. Army camps as his model. He said, "I believe that for every young man . . . to have six months in such a camp . . . [with] some field service, would be of incalculable benefit to him, and . . . to the nation."

TR pictured the benefits as being self-reliance, "mutuality of respect between himself and others, the power to command and the power to obey, . . . it would make him a soldier immediately fit for defense."[29] Roosevelt felt that "making these camps permanent would be the greatest boon this nation could receive."[30]

Defense, TR believed, was the training's prime benefit to the country. He told his audience, "we now have to do all this training during the war. . . . If four years ago we had had universal military training, so that service would have been immediately efficient when called for, the war would have been over [quickly] . . . bloodshed would have been spared."

Roosevelt argued against "a selective draft for a favored class" and the "privileges" of college training which provided students an advantage in becoming officers. He stressed "fair play for the workingman's son who has not had the chance to learn at college but who has the natural ability to command and lead men."[31]

Speaking at Billings, Montana, TR exempted one group from his proposed service: "mother[s] of small children.... But outside of her every man and woman ought to be spending his strength to the limit [for] the men at the front."[32]

TR's idea of universal service resembles the Civilian Conservation Corps (CCC) initiated during the presidency of his cousin, Franklin D. Roosevelt. Interestingly, the CCC had only young men; TR's earlier call included young women and men.

Roosevelt's universal service idea was later attacked by historian John Morton Blum, who said TR's "ardent advocacy of compulsory peacetime industrial service ... [was] an amalgam of conceptions which in another form the world later learned to dread." Blum maintains TR disgraced his own and his nation's reputation.[33] However, Blum's suggestion of fascism fails to take into account Roosevelt's Christianity, his dedication to democratic processes, and fails to understand TR's inclusion of women. Why does Blum compare the universal service to fascism instead of to the CCC?

In addition to the draft, widespread profiteering and governmental price fixing made business and labor a prime topic during the war. Roosevelt advocated the "brokered approach" that would subject both business and labor to more and different kinds of regulation than were presently enforced. Regulation of this type was not a new TR idea; it had been a Bull Moose platform plank.

Roosevelt was among a few leaders who were prepared to take radical measures "toward resolving the great inequities of the capitalist system."[34] Writing Hays, TR stated, "The new issues which will require a strongly centralized government are going to revolve about: transportation; price fixing; rigid public control if not ownership of mines, forests and waterways."[35] These were bold ideas. Suggestion of public ownership of mines in the press would have sparked an outcry from mine owners and businessmen as loud as the one heard during Roosevelt's presidency when he signed a bill setting aside many millions of acres as national forest.

Speaking in public, TR was less bold because he did not want to arouse the ire of the old guard, with whom he had begun a dialogue on major issues and to whom business was a sacred cow.

TR had provided William Howard Taft with an advance text of his Maine address, to which the former president had kindly and blandly replied. In Maine Roosevelt proposed that "all big corporations should, by a system of license . . . come under national control . . . subject to some national board at Washington." TR also suggested congressional action to establish regulations for these proposed boards. "Big business," TR said, "should not be left unregulated, uncontrolled," and noted it deserved "fair treatment."[36]

Taft responded positively that "corporations likely to abuse the power of large capital" should be subject to "close regulation," and that the GOP "might well pledge itself to such a provision."[37]

Speaking at Maine, TR also called for "labor's full right to cooperate and combine and [the] full right to collective bargaining and collective action." Pre-dating the New Deal, he proposed eight-hour work day legislation.[38]

, "Workers who are efficient should become in a real sense partners in industry," TR said. In 1914, he had "proposed that unions be given a share in industrial management, perhaps by allowing them to elect some of the directors in a company," this being a "fair division of the rewards of efficiency."[39]

"There can be no doubt," wrote TR to Hays, but "that labor must have a new voice in the management of industrial affairs." Further, he stressed that the "right of labor . . . to know exactly how the books stand in every industrial concern" is going to be a vital political question and the Republican party should take a constructive stand."[40] TR's call for corporate financial disclosure to labor, if made public, would have provoked more fierce outcry from the old guard.

Addressing those old guard complaints, Roosevelt might have repeated an idea from his Maine speech, that it made no sense to "try to dam the moving current of the times."[41]

In his Maine speech, TR gave attention to the problems of agriculture as well as labor. Roosevelt proved to be a prophet of the agricultural calamity that struck the United States after the war, and proposed reforms during the war that might have helped to head it off.

"The farmer is emphatically the producer. He has not had a square deal. More than half the people live on farms and [are] . . . the steadying influence on this country," explained TR as he pressed urgently for reforms.[42]

At Baltimore Roosevelt proposed experimental land grants to eligible veterans who would develop and farm the parcel, with eventual pay back to the government by the recipient. TR believed this to be a "stepping stone to further study of and action concerning ... farm production"; the end result being promotion of independent farmer prosperity. Further, TR stated that tenants of farms had rights "to compensation for all improvements or indeed on certain property rights to the land itself."[43]

At Maine he called for the individual ownership of farms versus the farmer who "holds his land as a tenant for an absentee owner." To achieve this, TR proposed special loans "be so shaped as to secure" money for the farmer "at not too high a price, for the actual work of production." He thought private loans best, but held government responsible for funding. TR also called for the building of better roads to help the farmer.

TR had faith in the strength and success of farmers and proposed cooperatives to make farmers stronger:

> Cooperative organizations of farmers . . . can hold their own with any of the great business concerns with which they have to deal, can eliminate such middlemen as are unnecessary and can use the services of those middlemen who fill a . . . useful function . . . to be a benefit to both, and . . . the public at large.

A farmer at his own Sagamore Hill, TR said repeatedly that "nothing must be allowed to interfere with ample production. . . . There must be no attempt by the government at price fixing . . . [this] has worked nothing but mischief."[44]

Had Roosevelt's reforms been enacted there may have been more individual ownership of farms, farmers cooperatives, and more efficient means of production which may have helped solve some of the problems of farmers in the 1920s and 1930s.

Other domestic issues TR discussed were the need for better housing, and for systems of unemployment and old age insurance, which would become part of the Social Security Act during the New Deal. Conspicuously absent were earlier Bull Moose planks relating to "direct democracy," with reforms such as the recall of judicial decisions.[45]

Of foreign issues facing the country at war's end, none were larger than the proposed League of Nations. Accepting the Nobel Peace Prize in 1910, TR expressed his belief that all "really civilized communities should have effective arbitration treaties among them."[46] However, he did not wholeheartedly support

Wilson's means of arbitration, the League. Roosevelt gave higher priority to U.S. defenses and, had he lived, would have sought to revise the League's charter with Republican leaders when U.S. League membership was debated in the Senate.

As to the history of such a league, TR noted the idea's similarity to the early nineteenth-century alliance of European nations "which worked such mischief" that the Monroe Doctrine was established to combat it.[47]

"My advice," said TR, "is that we accept internationalism . . . as an addition to, but not as a substitute for, our own military preparedness, and [that we] cultivate a spirit of intense American nationalism."[48] He conceded that "if [the League] is devised in sane fashion . . . for our own defense, it may do a small amount of good." As it turned out, Wilson accepted no changes and the League died.

Wilson's non-Allied membership clause received Roosevelt criticism for TR would in no way have the United States accept or "enter into a league in which we make believe that our deadly enemies, stained with every kind of brutality and treachery, are as worthy of friendship as the Allies who have fought our battles for four years." Instead of a new roster, TR wrote that "probably the best first step would be to make the existing League of Allies a going concern." He trusted the Allies and felt U.S. friendship with them should be first consideration, differing from Wilson's plan. "Let us at the peace tables," wrote Roosevelt in the *Kansas City Star*, "see that real justice is done . . . , and that sternest reparation is demanded from our foes." Roosevelt wrote that outlaw nations might, in time, be allowed to join, and that "conduct [should be] the test of admission."

Roosevelt was cautious about future U.S. activism in the League, stating "the American people do not wish to go into an overseas war unless for a very great cause. . . . We do not wish . . . [to send] our gallant young men to die in obscure fights in the Balkans or in Central Europe or in a war we don't approve of. Moreover, the Americans do not intend to give up the Monroe Doctrine."[49]

Advocating self-determination for ethnic groups, TR said there should be a new nation for the Armenians and a homeland for the Jews in Palestine.[50] His plan for self-determination was more thorough than that of Wilson's and the one adopted at Versailles.

Would TR's plan have kept the peace? That is impossible to determine. Historian George Mowry thought that had TR been president "something might have been salvaged from the peace that was no peace."[51]

Limited U.S. membership in the League of Nations was a major item of TR's foreign policy platform; domestically, he called for a "square deal" of reforms for farmers, new service and opportunity for American youth, more rigid regulation of corporations, and collective bargaining for labor. These were his ideas that might have been his platform as he sought support for his candidacy of 1920.

But even had he lived and been elected, could Roosevelt have been able to carry out his progressive ideals? TR biographer William Harbaugh writes that events "surely would have been different" if Roosevelt had won the presidency. But Harbaugh notes that the GOP's social and economic bias—a conservative one—had come to show its colors in TR's

> own turbulent administration and under Taft's . . . [and] in its opposition to the progressive legislation of the first Wilson administration. . . . It is hard to believe that Roosevelt . . . could have done in the 1920s what he had failed so dramatically to do from 1901 to 1912—change the Republican party's social and economic bias.[52]

A letter to TR from the secretary of the Oregon Republican State Central Committee, Edward D. Baldwin, reinforces Harbaugh's thesis:

> I'm a conservative in political thought, . . . I have a deep seated aversion to a third term; am a believer in local self government wherever possible and distrust centralization of power in the federal government—yet I'm willing to go down the line with you even if we can't agree on many things.[53]

There would have been many things not agreed on, for most of TR's proposals involved the exercise of power by the federal government, the anathema of conservatives. Of course, many conservatives envisioned Roosevelt as a winner in 1920 and therefore supported his unofficial election efforts. Roosevelt dreamed of a progressive Republican future and predicted astutely that "if the Republican party takes the ground that the world must be the same old world, the Republican party is lost."[54]

NOTES

1. Henry Kissinger, *For the Record* (Boston: Little, Brown and Company, 1982), pp. xi-xii.

2. Many Roosevelt contemporaries and historians have written that TR was the leading Republican candidate for president and would have sought the White House in 1920. Some have also written that TR would have been elected in 1920.

William Allen White wrote in his *Autobiography:* "I am sure that he [TR] wished to lead the Republican Party in 1920, either to be nominated himself or to control and direct the nomination." He also wrote, "I am satisfied that, if the Colonel had lived, he would have been the Republican nominee" (*Autobiography* [New York: Macmillan, 1946], pp. 540, 549).

In his biography of Calvin Coolidge, White wrote that at the time of TR's death, "most of the Republican leaders who had opposed him so bitterly in 1912 had become reconciled to his leadership. He [TR] felt and told his friends that he would be nominated by the Republican convention the next year" (*Puritan in Babylon* [New York: Macmillan, 1938], p. 180).

George E. Mowry noted that TR probably would have made the race, stating, "Roosevelt would have given his eyeteeth to have been elected president in 1920. Of this there can be little doubt" (*Theodore Roosevelt and the Progressive Movement* [Madison: University of Wisconsin Press, 1947], p. 375).

Lewis Einstein wrote, "Undoubtedly he would have been the Republican candidate in 1920. Undoubtedly, too, he would have been elected by at least the same overwhelming majority that put Harding into office. He would have thrown himself into the race with the same zest as before and was already giving thought to the men he wanted to surround him. He would have found once more that the country needed him in shaping its new destinies. . . . The people acclaimed him as the next leader" (*Roosevelt: His Mind in Action* [Boston: Houghton Mifflin Co., 1930], p. 242).

Richard Collin, author of *Theodore Roosevelt, Culture, Diplomacy, and Expansion,* did not take as positive a view in a 1966 thesis: "In spite of the fact that his health was broken—he was half-blind and half-deaf—and that he acquired enough political enemies to insure for anyone else an involuntary political obscurity, there seems to be little doubt that Roosevelt would have been a strong contender for the Republican presidential nomination in 1920 ("The Image of Theodore Roosevelt in American History and Thought" [Ph.D. diss., New York University, 1966], p. 254).

TR's earliest debunking critic Henry F. Pringle offered the opinion that had TR lived "he might have been elected president in 1920" (*Theodore Roosevelt: A Biography* [New York: Harcourt, Brace and Co., 1931], pp. 603-4).

William Harbaugh believes that "he was the Republican party's foremost candidate for the presidency in 1920" (*Power and*

Responsibility: The Life and Times of Theodore Roosevelt [New York: Farrar, Straus and Cudahy, 1961], p. 509).

John Milton Cooper agrees that Roosevelt was the "party's leading contender" for 1920 (*The Warrior and the Priest* [Cambridge: Belknap Press of Harvard University Press 1983], p. 333).

In a biography of Warren Harding, Francis Russell wrote that "even on his sickbed he [TR] was recognized as the undisputed postwar leader of his party, the only possible presidential choice of the 1920 Republican convention" (*The Shadow of Blooming Grove: Warren G. Harding in His Times* [New York: McGraw–Hill, 1968], p. 311).

3. John Allen Gable, *The Bull Moose Years: Theodore Roosevelt and the Progressive Party* (Port Washington, NY: Kennikat Press, 1978), chaps. 1 and 6.

4. The Progressive Party: Its Record from January to July 1916 (New York: Press of the Mail, 1916), p. 97.

5. Will H. Hays, *The Memoirs of Will H. Hays* (Garden City, NY: Doubleday and Co., 1955), p. 238.

6. Gable, *Bull Moose Years*, pp. 246–49.

7. *Progressive Party*, p. 97.

8. Theodore Roosevelt to William Allen White, April 4, 1918. Elting E. Morison, ed., *The Letters of Theodore Roosevelt* (Cambridge: Harvard University Press, 1951–54), 8: 1,306.

9. Joseph Bucklin Bishop, *Theodore Roosevelt and His Time*, 2 vols. (New York: Charles Scribner's Sons, 1920), 2: 446.

10. Ralph Stout, ed., *Theodore Roosevelt in the Kansas City Star* (Boston: Houghton Mifflin Co., 1921). See also, Cooper, *Warrior And The Priest*, pp. 329–30.

11. Frederick Wood, ed., *Roosevelt as We Knew Him* (Philadelphia: John Winston Co., 1927), pp. 447.

12. TR to Rudyard Kipling, November 23, 1918, *Letters*, 8: 1,405.

13. Corinne Robinson, *My Brother Theodore Roosevelt* (New York: Charles Scribner's Sons, 1926), p. 346.

14. John J. Leary, *Talks With TR* (Boston: Houghton Mifflin Co., 1920), p. 1.

15. William Allen White, *Autobiography* (New York: Macmillan, 1946), p. 548.

16. TR to Fred Muller, January 3, 1919, Theodore Roosevelt Papers, Library of Congress (hereafter cited as TRLC). See also, Edward B. Parsons, "Some International Implications of the 1918 Roosevelt-Lodge Campaign Against Wilson and a Democratic Congress," *Presidential Studies Quarterly* 19 (Winter 1989): 141–57.

17. Hermann Hagedorn, *The Magnate* (New York: Reynal and Hitchcock, 1935), p. 280.

18. Edward Baldwin to TR, May 4, 1917, TRLC.

19. C. C. Kaufman to TR, May 4, 1917, TRLC.

20. Congressional Quarterly, *National Party Conventions, 1831–1972* (Washington: Congressional Quarterly, 1976), p. 135.

21. GOP Chairman Will H. Hays initially approached Thompson in 1918 to contribute money to mid-term congressional campaigns, an

effort in which TR was the main attraction. Thompson's subsequent hefty contributions helped elect GOP majorities in both houses of Congress. Hagedorn, *Magnate,* pp. 279–81.

22. TR to Will Hays, February 6, 1918, TRLC.

23. Roosevelt's letters to King ask him to combat Wilson's Democratic propaganda machine, to see influential Republicans, and to keep in touch with journalists. Their close, working relationship is evidenced by TR's having borrowed money from King, perhaps for party work (TR to John King, February 28, 1918; January 18, 1917; February 6, 1918; December 27, 1918, TRLC). See also, Mark Sullivan, *Our Times: The United States, 1900–1925* (New York: Charles Scribner's Sons, 1935), 6: 351 and Russell, *The Shadow of Blooming Grove,* p. 327.

24. TR also made suggestions to Hays as to helpful contacts the chairman might make on his travels, along with methods that might be best to use. TR to Hays, March 26, 1918, *Letters,* 8: 1,305.

25. Hays, *Memoirs,* p. 238.

26. TR to William Allen White, April 4, 1918, *Letters,* 8: 1,307.

27. William Griffith, ed., *Theodore Roosevelt: His Life Meaning and Messages* (New York: Current Literature Publishing Co., 1919), vol. 3, "Americans Must Stand Together Or Hang Together," p. 1,305.

28. TR to Andrew Fleming West, December 28, 1918, *Letters,* 8: 1,418.

29. Griffith, *Messages,* "Americans Must Stand," 3: 987–89.

30. Stout, *TR in the KC Star,* "Performance of a Great Public Duty," pp. 172–74.

31. Griffith, *Messages,* "Americans Must Stand," 3:986–88.

32. James F. Vivian, *The Romance of My Life: Theodore Roosevelt's Speeches in North Dakota* (Fargo, ND: Prairie House, 1989), pp. 121–22.

33. John Morton Blum, *The Republican Roosevelt,* 2d ed. (Cambridge: Harvard University Press, 1977), p. 154.

34. Edmund Morris, *The Rise of Theodore Roosevelt* (New York: Coward McCann and Geohagan, 1979), p. 703.

35. Bishop, *TR and His Time,* 2: 446.

36. Griffith, *Messages,* "Speed Up the War and Take Thought for After the War," p. 928.

37. William Howard Taft to TR, March 11, 1918, TRLC.

38. Harbaugh, *Power And Responsibility,* p. 510.

39. Stout, *TR in the KC Star,* "Performance," p. 174, and John Allen Gable, "Bull Moose Years: Theodore Roosevelt and the Progressive Party, 1912–16" (Ph.D. diss., Brown University, 1972), p. 585.

40. Bishop, *TR and His Time,* 2: 446.

41. Griffith, *Messages,* "Americans Must Stand," 3: 990.

42. Wood, *As We Knew Him,* p. 450.

43. Draft of a TR speech, May 1917, TRLC.

44. Griffith, *Messages,* "Speed Up the War," 3: 922–26.

45. Harbaugh, *Power and Responsibility,* pp. 509–10.

46. Theodore Roosevelt, "An Address Before the Nobel Prize Committee," *Theodore Roosevelt Association Journal* 9 (Winter 1983): 34.

47. Stout, *TR in the KC Star,* "Further Consideration of The Fourteen Points," October 30, 1918, p. 246.

48. Claude Bowers, *Beveridge and the Progressive Era* (Boston: Houghton Mifflin Co., 1932), p. 498.

49. Stout, *TR in the KC Star*, "Further Consideration," pp. 246–48, and "The League of Nations," pp. 293–94.

50. Griffith, *Messages*, "Americans Must Stand," 3: 979.

51. Mowry, *Theodore Roosevelt and the Progressive Movement*, p. 377.

52. Harbaugh, *Power and Responsibility*, pp. 509–10.

53. Edward Baldwin to TR, May 4, 1917, TRLC.

54. Bishop, *TR and His Time*, 2: 446.

"He's Good Enough for All!"

35

If TR Had Gone Down with the Titanic: A Look at His Last Decade

John Milton Cooper, Jr.

Theodore Roosevelt did not merely break the normal rules of American politics, he reversed them. In a country that for the better part of two centuries has exalted the self-made man and woman, this child of privilege, this unabashed aristocrat made himself not just the most popular but the most beloved leader of his time. In a culture that has disdained intellect and refinement in favor of practicality and material reward, this creature of refined taste, this author and patron of the arts, this contemner of money grubbing and materialism struck deeper, stronger chords of sentiment and thought than any other public spokesman of his era. Such reversals of political norms lay at the heart of Roosevelt's career and are well known. What is not so well known is that his enduring impact on public life and his historical reputation likewise reversed an otherwise unbroken pattern in American history. Theodore Roosevelt is the only president who made a more significant impact on the nation and on the world after he left the White House than while he sat in the seat of power. He was and he remains America's greatest ex-president.

Roosevelt achieved that stature despite manifest failures and frustrations and despite the display of some of the least attractive and most disturbing aspects of his political personality. It should be noted that he was not the most successful ex-president. That honor belongs to Grover Cleveland, who has been the only former chief executive to win either a major party nomination or reelection after a period out of the White House. Both goals eluded Roosevelt in 1912, even though he came close to wresting the Republican nomination away from William Howard Taft, and even though as the candidate of a brand new third party he finished second, ahead of Taft. Roosevelt might have changed that if he had lived longer and won the Republican nomination and election in 1920, as he was almost universally expected to do at the time of his death in January 1919. That is the most haunting might-have-been which will always shadow the last years of Roosevelt's life and career.

Roosevelt does not stand as the most constructively employed former chief executive in public life, either. That honor belongs to one of two other men. The best-used former president was either John Quincy Adams or William Howard Taft. Adams served twenty years in the House of Representatives and championed the anti-slavery cause. Roosevelt's successor and erstwhile friend and foe, Taft, served for nearly a decade as Chief Justice, an office in which he found the personal fulfillment and made the enduring accomplishments that had eluded him in the presidency. Other ex-presidents have enjoyed longer lives and careers after leaving the White House and have made great contributions to American life and world affairs. Three such notable examples are Thomas Jefferson, Herbert Hoover, and, most likely, Jimmy Carter.

Still, with all those reservations noted, no one else has matched Roosevelt in importance as an ex-president. The reason is simple. He played an incomparably bigger role in politics than any other former occupant of the White House. Others before and since have attempted, with varying degrees of success, to keep their hands in the great game or to influence the development of policies. Two other former presidents, Roosevelt's fellow New Yorkers, Martin van Buren and Millard Fillmore, preceded him in running again as nominees of newly formed and short-lived third parties. But no one else has come close to altering the course of American politics the way Roosevelt did. No one else has overshadowed one and sometimes both of his successors, as Roosevelt did during his lifetime. Most important, no one else has had an ex-presidency that was more politically revealing and significant than his own presidency. Theodore Roosevelt is the only U.S. president whose place in history must be judged even more by the years after he left the White House than by his actual presidential wielding of power.

That may sound like a doubtful assertion. But consider what Roosevelt's historical reputation might be if, say, he had fallen victim to a determined lion or water buffalo on his African safari in 1909, or if he had perished in the sinking of an ocean liner on his way home from Europe in 1910, as his former military aide Archie Butt did two years later on the *Titanic*. If any of these eventualities had come to pass, Roosevelt's reputation would be dramatically different from what it has become.

In some respects, his reputation might be a better one. In some areas, it would almost certainly be a kinder, gentler reputation. In domestic affairs, if he were to be judged by his presidency alone, he would have left an exceedingly ambiguous legacy. For example, would black Americans regard him as a friend or foe, based upon his actions in the White House? Which of his deeds was more significant: the dinner invitation to Booker T. Washington, the partial tilt away from black political appointments in the South, or the swift, harsh, unjust punishment meted out to the black soldiers in the Brownsville affair? Unfortunately, for attempts to make Roosevelt an early hero of the civil rights struggle, his lily white strategy with the Progressives in 1912 leaves little doubt about which side of his presidential attitude lay closer to his heart. Conversely, if his stands on women's issues were to be gauged solely by his avoidance of the suffrage issue and lukewarm private statements as president, he would not look so good as he later did. It was his forthright, though admittedly opportunistic, endorsement of nationwide woman suffrage in 1912 that made him the first major male politician to embrace the cause publicly.

Similarly, in Roosevelt's two main theaters of thought and action—domestic reform and foreign policy—he would look quite different if his historical reputation rested only on his pre-presidential years and his presidency. It seems indisputable that, without the record of the last ten years of his life, Roosevelt would not enjoy nearly so great a regard as a progressive. In fact, there may be some question as to whether he would rank as much of a progressive at all. His legislative accomplishments in railroad regulation and pure food and drug enforcement are undeniable. So are his sweeping executive actions on behalf of conservation, as well as his thunderous preachments from the "bully pulpit" against the dangers of "materialism" and "malefactors of great wealth." But equally undeniable are his denunciations of radicals and anarchists, his distaste for "the man with the muckrake," and his disapproval of both antitrust policies and tariff reform. If Roosevelt's domestic reform legacy had to be judged solely on his record before 1910, it might resemble Abraham Lincoln's plan of reconstruction—a complex, tentative, incomplete set of words and deeds that later politicians and historians would have wrangled over in seeking to appropriate his aegis for conflicting policies and factions.

Likewise, in foreign affairs, Roosevelt would have cast a different shadow on subsequent events if he had ceased to be active after 1909 or 1910. His presidential legacy in foreign policy might be even more ambiguous and controversial than in domestic politics. Naturally, his build-up and modernization of the armed forces, his interventions in the Caribbean and Central America, and his ceaseless preachments about national strength and great power activism lend credence to the familiar hawkish Rooseveltian image. But his mediation of the Russo-Japanese War, his winning of the Nobel Prize for peace, his cautious, even appeasing policies in the Far East—including his conviction that the United States should get out of the Philippines—plausibly reinforce notions that he may have been some sort of closet dove. Moreover, his call for creation of a league of nations in his Nobel Prize address of 1910 further buttresses the impression of his pacific tendencies. If Roosevelt's foreign policy legacy were to be judged solely by his words and deeds up to 1910, it would be Janus-faced—a divided, conflicting set of influences that could have been invoked by both champions of bigger armaments and military intervention and by advocates of international peace-keeping organizations, such as his two presidential successors.

Any attempt to conjure up Roosevelt's place in history without his last decade serves to highlight how important that decade really was. But it takes a good bit more to argue that his ex-presidency made a greater historical mark than his presidency. This requires reexamination of the significance of his role after 1910 in those main theaters of thought and action—domestic reform and foreign policy. It is also tempting to examine his stands on issues that have become much more salient since his time, most notably questions involving race and gender, but that is a largely profitless enterprise. Rightly or wrongly, such questions did not loom uppermost in his mind. Racial segregation and discrimination, denial of the vote to black Americans, woman suffrage, and proper gender relations—all of these were minor matters to Roosevelt. He treated them according to how they affected what were to him larger considerations, which from 1912 onward mainly involved the creation of a new political party and reform coalition. Whether later he looks like a hero, as in the case of woman suffrage, or like a bum, as in the case of black political participation, is just a side effect. Roosevelt's last decade has to be judged by his involvement in domestic reform and foreign policy.

What emerged in both of these spheres during those years was a much fuller development of his political personality than either his early career or his presidency had allowed. What flowered during that decade was a Roosevelt freed from the constraints that had previously bound him. This new freedom had its ugly as well as its glorious aspects. As John Blum observed three and a half decades ago, the exercise of power had a salutary effect on Roosevelt. The restraints and responsibilities of office had tempered his imperiousness with caution and his unabashed love of power with circumspection. The loss of those disciplinary advantages brought sad consequences, especially in the misjudgments that he made when he ran again in 1912 and in the ferocity of his attacks on Woodrow Wilson after 1914. The "egotism" that he allegedly displayed in attempting to unseat his chosen successor and the often unbridled fury of his denunciations of Wilson have left the biggest warts on his historical reputation. They constitute the main reason why, if his last decade could be blotted out, the memories would be of a kinder, gentler Roosevelt.[1]

The fundamental truth of the view that he suffered from loss of restraint in those years cannot be denied. But that view can also be overworked. An equally fundamental truth about Roosevelt is that he was capable of regarding power from only one end—the operating end. Even at his most progressive or self-proclaimedly "radical," he never identified with people on the receiving end of power. This divergence in identification separated him not only from William Jennings Bryan, Woodrow Wilson, and the Democrats but also from Robert M. La Follette, the midwestern and western Republican insurgents, and, as he clearly recognized, the great bulk of the men and women who followed him into the Progressive party. Another basic fact about the last decade of Roosevelt's life is that he spent most of it, in one way or another, running for president. Like King Arthur, who was *rex quondam, rex futurus,* the once and future king, Roosevelt spent those years as *praeses quondam, praeses futurus,* the once and future president. The change in political personality between the presidential and the post-presidential years was one of degree, and it varied with time and circumstance. Both the change and the variability have to be kept constantly in mind in assessing his ex-presidency.

In the arena of domestic reform, Roosevelt's biggest contribution after 1910 was first his fathering and then his smothering of the Progressive party. No single series of acts by any former president has exerted so tremendous an effect on the course of American politics as what he did with his third party from 1912 to 1916. The shock waves and upheavals of Roosevelt's actions extended much further and delved far deeper than apparently insuring Wilson's victory in 1912, swelling the Democratic majorities in Congress, clearing the path for the New Freedom programs, and permanently disaffecting a number of liberals and intellectuals, such as Herbert Croly and Walter Lippmann, from the Republican party. The best way to gauge the impact that he made is by imagining alternative historical scenarios. This involves rushing in where historians always say they fear to tread and where they implicitly tread all the time—into what is pretentiously styled "counter-factualism," but is better dubbed "iffy history."

Three possible alternatives are most worthy of consideration. First, what might have happened if Roosevelt had wrested the Republican nomination from Taft in 1912? Second, what might have happened if Roosevelt had not contested with Taft in 1912, either by not challenging him for the nomination or by acquiescing in the results of the convention? Third, what might have happened if Roosevelt had died in 1914, as he nearly did, on his expedition up the Amazon and thereby had been removed from the political scene in 1916?

The first alternative—Roosevelt running as the Republican nominee in 1912—is the least plausible but most richly suggestive of the three. Conservatives' dominance in key states and the presidential nominating "steamroller" that he himself had fashioned made it unlikely that he could have received the nomination even if Taft and the old guard had behaved with greater finesse. But suppose Roosevelt had pulled off this near miracle. Then what would have happened? Obviously, he would have won or lost in the general election. Which result was more probable? It is not an open and shut proposition that he would have won. Although Roosevelt was the best known, most popular politician in the country in 1912, he was no shoo-in. Rather, his chances would have depended greatly upon whom the Democrats nominated. If they had chosen Champ Clark or Oscar Underwood, Roosevelt's far greater name recognition and experience, together with widespread public suspicions of machine politicians and Southerners, would probably have permitted him to win. But he would still have had to struggle against an undertow of conservative defections that would almost certainly have robbed him of anything approaching a landslide.[2]

But if Roosevelt had received the Republican nomination in 1912, the Democrats would almost certainly have nominated Wilson, whose public image and popular appeal most closely resembled and competed best with the ex-president's. It is by no means a foregone conclusion that Roosevelt would have beaten Wilson in a two-man race. The former president of Princeton and much publicized reform governor would have exacerbated conservative defections from Roosevelt because of his social and educational background. At the same time Wilson would have minimized potential Democratic defections to Roosevelt because of his own progressive credentials.

Here is one place where the speculation about what might have happened can gain some grounding in fact. There was one state in 1912 where Taft was not on the ballot and the other two nominees went head-to-head. That was California. Roosevelt did win there, but by 174 votes out of over half a million cast. If Roosevelt could do no better than that in a state that had given the last Republican nominee, Taft in 1908, nearly 63 percent of the vote, his chances nationwide did not look good. In short, the prevailing notion that Roosevelt made Wilson president in 1912 by splitting the normally Republican vote is no more than a notion, and a highly dubious one. Rather, Wilson was the likely winner in 1912, even in a two-man race, easily over Taft and probably more narrowly over Roosevelt.[3]

Without getting too fanciful, consider a few further ramifications of this scenario. Running in 1912 against any Democrat, Roosevelt would have had to run a much less progressive campaign than he did at the head of his new party. The need to woo back disaffected conservatives would have required him to soft-pedal his New Nationalist program, instead

of articulating his vision of reform as fully as he did in his de facto
debate with Wilson's New Freedom. If he had lost, that would
have sealed his fate against any possibility of a future presidency.
If, as is less likely, he had won, he would have had to take up
where he had left off in 1909, trying to bridge the chasm between
old guard and conservative Republicans, trimming sail, tacking
back and forth—in other words, a presidency as usual. The only
real chance to let Roosevelt be Roosevelt in 1912, to give him a
shot at the heroic, less tightly bridled kind of leadership he craved
was the chance he took with his new party in 1912. When he stood
at Armageddon and battled for the Lord, Theodore Roosevelt
fulfilled a destiny that was nearly as foreordained as the fate of
any tragic hero of Sophocles or Shakespeare.

The second alternative—his not leading the insurgent forces
either before or after the Republican convention in 1912—has
greater plausibility. Roosevelt's cannier political cohorts,
especially Elihu Root, advised him to stand aside and let the
nomination fall in his lap in 1916. That might have happened if
he had bowed to such counsels or at least given "lip loyalty" to
Taft's renomination. But if Roosevelt had done that, certain
things might well have happened anyway. First of all, a third
party might still have formed, led by La Follette. Failing that, a
separate ticket, like the one La Follette ran on in 1924, might well
have been mounted. The rifts in the Republican party ran so deep
in 1912 that it is hard to imagine some kind of insurgent defection
not occurring. Moreover, in view of the rise of the Non-Partisan
League on the Great Plains in 1915 and the founding of the
Farmer-Labor party in Minnesota three years later, it is easy to
envision a coalition of regionally based, left-leaning factions and
splinter parties coalescing earlier under the umbrella of
midwestern and western Republican insurgency. That such
developments took place later, rather than sooner, owed
something to Roosevelt's forming his Progressive party. In that
way, he did accomplish one of his principal aims in 1912: he was
able to temper, channel, and dampen what he regarded as
unsound, potentially dangerous radicalism within the insurgent
Republican ranks.[4]

Another way to assess the impact that Roosevelt made with
his third party is to consider the third alternative scenario—his
removal from the political scene before or during 1914. What
would have happened if he had not continued to lead the

Progressives down to their disbandment in 1916? Almost certainly, the party would have fallen apart without him, and that might have made political life easier for both the Wilson administration and the Republicans. Wilson would not have had to endure Roosevelt's attacks on his domestic and foreign policies, and the Republicans would not have had to worry so much about appeasing former Progressives. From Wilson's standpoint, this view is indisputably correct. He would have had an easier time of it if Roosevelt had not been around after mid-1914. But not so the Republicans, no matter how much they thought otherwise. Roosevelt's presence and the persistence of the Progressives as an intact, albeit shrunken, party down to the 1916 conventions helped the Republicans inestimably. Wooing back Progressives was their main motive behind their nominating Charles Evans Hughes, who was their ablest candidate, rather than some genial hack from a big electoral state, such as they did nominate four years later.

Likewise, Roosevelt's infanticide toward the Progressives and his prompt, energetic support of Hughes proved to be the critical element in the Republican nominee's coming as close as he did to defeating Wilson in 1916. Writing under the influence of realignment theory and seduced by the geographical similarities among electoral results since 1896, most recent historians have held that the lingering wounds of the Progressive bolt were the main reason why Hughes lost an election that he or any Republican should have won. The critical part that California played in 1916 has reinforced that view. It is true, moreover, that Roosevelt was not able to deliver the Progressives to Hughes *en bloc*. Also, activists and intellectuals such as Croly and Lippmann backed Wilson, and many thousands of Roosevelt's 1912 voters refused to follow their leader in 1916.[5]

But those defections did not supply Wilson's critical margin of victory. The president owed his reelection mostly to his near total sweep of the West and to cracking the normally Republican Midwest by winning Ohio. In both areas, the role of erstwhile Progressives really lay in depriving Wilson of a bigger margin of victory. In the West, ex-Progressives played a critical role only on the West Coast, where Wilson carried California and Washington, but not Oregon, one of only three western states he lost. Given the microscopic margin by which Roosevelt had bested Wilson in California in 1912, Hughes's coming as close as he did to winning the state owed mostly to support from former Progressives, led by Hiram Johnson's superb state organization. The Ohio result in 1916 was less of an anomaly than it appeared, because Wilson did far better than any Democrat had done since 1892 throughout the Northeast and Midwest. Without the support that Roosevelt gave Hughes in 1916, more states in those regions would almost certainly have gone to the president, and he would have won a more impressive reelection victory.[6]

The real value in examining such alternative scenarios lies in illuminating the true significance of what did happen. Roosevelt's role in American politics from 1912 to 1916 overshadowed everyone else's except Wilson's. Furthermore, great as his political achievements in the White House had been, neither individually nor in sum did those presidential actions equal the impact of what he did during these four years. In one sense, the image of the less restrained Roosevelt is appropriate, because he did resemble a force of nature, like a hurricane or an earthquake, that altered the political landscape. In another sense, however, that image is singularly inappropriate, because Roosevelt made his greatest impact in a constructive way. By building and holding together a political party, he channeled discontent into disciplined actions, and he thereby helped enable his original party, the Republicans, to regain their majority status and take out a new lease on national dominance. For Roosevelt himself, the final tragedy came when death deprived him of the chance to be the leaseholder who reestablished that Republican hegemony.

Long before the last curtain fell, the other main theater of his thought and action had overshadowed almost everything else. A nice symmetry governs the place of foreign affairs in Roosevelt's career. He first achieved national prominence through his advocacy of expansionism and a great power role for the United States, and his well-publicized heroism in the Spanish-American War furnished the magic springboard that catapulted him into the White House. Similarly, he occupied the second half of the last decade of his life increasingly, sometimes almost exclusively, with questions of foreign policy. Two matters loomed above all others in this sphere for Roosevelt. One was World War I and what part the United States should play in that titanic conflict. The other was a league of nations and what part the United States should play in such an international peace-keeping organization.

It is on these two matters that the significance of Roosevelt's ex-presidency in foreign affairs must be judged.

World War I cast a shadow of death over Theodore Roosevelt, just as it did over millions of people around the world. It broke out just after he returned from his brush with death in the South American jungles. It absorbed his energy and attention far more than anything else in the world from the time of its outbreak. It furnished the greatest disappointment of his life when, after the United States entered the conflict, President Wilson refused to let him raise a volunteer division to fight on the Western Front. It offered him the greatest pride of his life when his four sons all saw combat service. It brought him the greatest sorrow of his life when the youngest of them, Quentin, was killed in action as an aviator in France. It ended less than two months before his own death as he pondered the shape of the postwar world and the place of himself and his country in that world.

Like the Progressive party crusade, the World War brought out the best and worst in Roosevelt. In the fall of 1914, he published a series of articles in the *New York Times Magazine* in which he spelled out his grand design for U.S. foreign policy. Besides warning that the nation would be vitally affected by the outcome of the war, especially regarding the balance of power in Europe and on the seas, Roosevelt went public with some of his most sophisticated and restrained foreign policy views. He drew a most circumscribed defense perimeter of vital interests for the United States. Surprisingly to some observers, he narrowed the Roosevelt Corollary to the Monroe Doctrine by exempting the southern part of South America from the need for suzerainty and protection by the United States. Astonishingly to many people, he bared his decade-old private conviction that the United States should withdraw from the Philippines. Most important, Roosevelt renewed the proposal that he had first made in 1910 for the creation of a league of nations. In all, it was a foreign policy blueprint that anticipated and strongly resembled the most important elements of the course that Wilson began to follow within a few months.[7]

Yet this similarity in aims between the two men soon fell into eclipse in the blinding light and white heat of Roosevelt's denunciations of the neutrality policies of the Wilson administration. Nothing has played a larger role in sullying his historical reputation than the sometimes intemperate tone and content of those attacks. One student of his foreign policy later speculated that Roosevelt may have become emotionally unbalanced at times. His manner disgusted many people in those days. Edmund Wilson, who was then a college student, years afterward recalled "the red-faced and beefy ex-president whom one saw pounding his left palm with his right fist and bombarding his hearers with dogmatic opinions." There is no blinking away the unattractive, disturbing characteristics that Roosevelt displayed for thousands to see and hear and for more thousands to read and read about.[8]

Yet it would have been untrue to some of the deepest and greatest traits of his character if he had failed to unleash himself as he did. Roosevelt was speaking and acting as an idealist in two senses. First, as William Widenor has demonstrated so well, strategic realism and calculations of international security did not lie at the heart of the matter for Roosevelt. Instead, America's conduct toward the war was for him fundamentally a test of national character. Would Americans display the courage and self-sacrifice that were demanded in the face of German aggression on land and sea? That was the real point, not any fear that the Central Powers might defeat the Allies and undermine U.S. security. Would his countrymen live up to their highest ideals of honor and righteousness, or would they sink into craven selfishness and small-minded passivity? Roosevelt's denunciations of Wilson may have become intemperate, but they did literally spring from the bottom of his mind and heart.[9]

He was behaving idealistically also in eschewing all calculations of political advantage. Roosevelt's quasi-interventionism from 1915 to 1917 represented the most unpopular stand he ever took in his political career. He had nothing to gain from it, and much to lose. Lose he did, as nearly all of the leading Progressives publicly disavowed his stands toward the war and blasted whatever slim chance there might have been for him to head a combined Republican-Progressive ticket in 1916. Furthermore, Roosevelt compounded his sins against practicality by grasping the hottest political potato of all in 1916—the draft. No other prominent politician, not even the few who joined him in advocating vastly strengthened armed forces and a tougher foreign policy, dared endorse military conscription. As a thinly veiled interventionist and as an outspoken proponent of the draft, Roosevelt made himself the loneliest voice crying in the political wilderness in 1915 and 1916. Not profit but principle alone called the tune to which he danced before the United States entered the World War.

Yet this was indisputably a case of those who would lose their lives shall save them. Roosevelt's forthright belligerency before 1917 played the biggest role in his political resurrection after 1917. The part that he had played in supporting Hughes in 1916 went a long way toward reconciling his conservative foes within the Republican party to his renewed leadership. But the war was what restored his popularity and made him an increasingly attractive prospect as a presidential candidate. Almost as soon as the United States entered the war, Roosevelt's political stock skyrocketed. Despite the Wilson administration's attempt to mount a low-key, restrained war effort, public fervor, even hysteria, quickly erupted. No one better epitomized and spoke to popular yearning for an all-out crusading war than Roosevelt. A Democratic senator grasped the situation when, shaking his head over Wilson's refusal to allow the Roosevelt division, he sighed, "It doesn't seem like a war without Roosevelt." It was not. Roosevelt's career had come full circle. Even without fighting himself, he was the country's greatest hero, and his heroism was about to propel him toward the presidency one more time.[10]

The league of nations question also displayed Roosevelt in conflicting lights. His original advocacy of the idea had stemmed from the same mindset as his subsequent reactions to the World War. "We must ever bear in mind that the great end in view is righteousness," he had declared in 1910 in his Nobel Prize address. "Peace is generally good in itself, but it is never the highest good unless it comes as the handmaid of righteousness." At that time, he had called on "those great powers honestly bent on peace" to establish "a League of Peace, not only to keep the peace among themselves, but to prevent by force if necessary, its being broken by others." He had looked forward to the "establishment of some form of international police force, competent and willing to prevent violence among nations."[11]

In 1914, Roosevelt reiterated those arguments and again called for the "great civilized nations" to establish "a great World League for the Peace of Righteousness." These ideas clearly grew out of Roosevelt's imperialism. He was calling for the worldwide application of the Roosevelt Corollary, under which the United States as the only "great civilized power" exercised "an international police power" in the Western Hemisphere. Interestingly, Wilson later justified his own advocacy of a league of nations as the global application of the Monroe Doctrine.[12]

Yet well before Roosevelt's great rival embraced the league idea, the ex-president had excoriated efforts by others to advance such schemes. The ink had scarcely dried on the suggestions of the newly founded League to Enforce Peace, which Taft headed, before Roosevelt blasted those proposals. "A movement right in itself may be all wrong if made at the wrong time," he declared in the summer of 1915. "Even the proposal for a World League for the Peace of Righteousness, based on force being put back of righteousness, is inopportune at this time." That remained Roosevelt's stance toward proposals for a league of nations until near the end of his life. He denounced Wilson's endorsement of the idea in 1916 and early 1917 even more fervently than he had earlier denounced Taft's, and he applauded senatorial attacks on the president's proposals not only by his sophisticated foreign policy soulmate, Henry Cabot Lodge, but also by the isolationist William E. Borah.[13]

On its face, Roosevelt's position made some sense. He argued for putting first things first, namely that Americans must do their duty under existing international conditions by punishing aggressors with their own nation's armed might. Afterward, and only afterward, would come the proper time to think about reforming or replacing the present system of totally sovereign nation-states.

But such theoretical, tactical differences miss the heat and passion that surrounded the league issue for Roosevelt. Who advocated the idea weighed as heavily in his rejection of these proposals as anything else. Personal bitterness against Taft from 1912 mingled with Roosevelt's suspicions that his immediate successor was soft on questions of national honor, which he had aired in 1911 in his criticisms of Taft's proposed arbitration treaty with Britain. Those sentiments created a presumption of guilt-by-association toward the League to Enforce Peace. The inclusion of a number of veteran international arbitration advocates in the league's ranks deepened that presumption on Roosevelt's part, because he had long scorned such folk as "pacifists." Then when the hated Wilson endorsed the league and linked it to his spineless neutrality, that made the scheme seem irredeemable to Roosevelt.[14]

All this was most unfortunate, and it showed Roosevelt at nearly his worst. Not much of substance really separated his ideas for a league of nations from those of Taft and Wilson. A spirit of bipartisan cooperation on all sides might have yielded far different results in 1919 and might possibly have changed the course of twentieth-century history for the better. Interestingly, Roosevelt may have begun to recognize this possibility toward the end of his life. In 1918, he and Taft repaired their personal relations and resumed at least a guarded friendship. In December 1918, Roosevelt praised some of Taft's proposals for a league, and in one of his last public pronouncements, which was published after his death, he proposed to use the Allies as the basis of a league that would encompass "some kind of police system" in different regions, modeled after and embracing the U.S. role under the Roosevelt Corollary.[15]

The change involved not only personalities but also political prospects. Together with Lodge, who was about to become the Senate's majority leader and chairman of the Foreign Relations Committee, Roosevelt was assuming leadership of the Republican party in foreign policy, and the two men were already communicating with British and French leaders about the peace settlement. Most important, Roosevelt had become the odds-on favorite for the 1920 Republican presidential nomination and a likely future return to the White House. No matter what those prospects might have meant for Wilson's peace-making in 1919, Roosevelt's status as *praeses futurus* almost certainly portended a much better outcome than what eventually transpired for American membership in the League of Nations and participation in the Versailles settlement. In that way, the personal and political tragedy of Roosevelt's lost presidential restoration may have been the world's tragedy as well.

If that was so, then in foreign affairs, too, his ex-presidency made an even greater historical impact than his presidency. All the flaws and shortcomings of his role in foreign policy do not detract from the momentousness of his words and deeds. Just as even without fighting Roosevelt became the greatest American war hero, so without holding office or wielding power he began to shape the future international order. These were remarkable achievements. No other ex-president has ever matched them. Few presidents have either, not even Roosevelt himself.

NOTES

1. See John M. Blum, *The Republican Roosevelt* (Cambridge: Harvard University Press, 1954), especially pp. 147–50, 160–61.

2. On his chances of winning the nomination, see Norman M. Wilansky, *Conservatives in the Progressive Era: The Taft Republicans of 1912* (Gainesville: University of Florida Press, 1965).

3. On both California and TR's chances in a national two-man contest in 1912, see David Sarasohn, *The Party of Reform: Democrats in the Progressive Era* (Oxford: University of Mississippi Press, 1989), pp. 149–54.

4. For Root's advice, see Root to Roosevelt, Feb. 12, 1912, in Philip C. Jessup, *Elihu Root* (New York: Dodd, Mead and Co., 1938), 2: 173–76.

5. For raising searching questions about realignment theory, I am indebted to the work of my graduate student, Glen Gendzel, especially his seminar paper, "Up from Realignment: Time to Put the Politics Back In" (University of Wisconsin, May 1989). For an example of a mistaken interpretation, see John Milton Cooper, Jr., *The Warrior and the Priest: Woodrow Wilson and Theodore Roosevelt* (Cambridge: Harvard University Press, 1983), pp. 256–57.

6. On the 1916 results, see Sarasohn, *Party of Reform*, pp. 192–238.

7. The articles are reprinted in *America and the World War* (New York, 1915) which is also volume 18 of Hermann Hagedorn, ed., *The Works of Theodore Roosevelt* (New York: Charles Scribner's Sons, 1925).

8. Edmund Wilson, "The Pre-Presidential T. R.," in *The Bit Between My Teeth: A Literary Chronicle, 1950–1965* (New York: Farrar, Straus and Giroux, 1965), p. 76. The student of TR's foreign policy who made the statement about his mental state frequently orally, but not in print, was Howard K. Beale.

9. See William C. Widenor, *Henry Cabot Lodge and the Search for an American Foreign Policy* (Berkeley: University of California Press, 1980), especially pp. 165–67, 274–77.

10. The senator was, reportedly, John Sharp Williams of Mississippi.

11. TR Nobel Prize Address, May 5, 1910, *Works*, 17: 305–9.

12. Ibid., 18: 29–30.

13. See TR to Borah, January 15, 1917, Theodore Roosevelt Papers, Library of Congress, Letterbook 101.

14. See John P. Campbell, "Taft, Roosevelt, and the Arbitration Treaties of 1911," *Journal of American History* 52 (Sept. 1966): 279–98.

15. "The League of Nations," *Kansas City Star*, Jan. 13, 1919, *Works*, 19: 406–8.

TR: The Image and the Memory

516

"Roosevelt House," now known as the Theodore Roosevelt Birthplace National Historic Site, at 28 East Twentieth Street, New York City, was dedicated on October 27, 1923. The house was donated together with Sagamore Hill and an endowment to the National Park Service, U.S. Department of the Interior, by the Theodore Roosevelt Association in 1963. At this location Theodore Roosevelt was born on October 27, 1858.

36

Theodore Roosevelt Birthplace: Study in Americanism

John R. Lancos

Our nation's leaders have traditionally come from a wide variety of social strata. Theodore Roosevelt, twenty-sixth president of the United States, arose from one of the loftier levels of American society, being born into a wealthy family of Dutch merchants and southern landed gentry on October 27, 1858. He was born in a brownstone townhouse, given to his parents as a wedding gift by his paternal grandfather, at 28 East Twentieth Street on New York's Manhattan Island. One of his uncles, lawyer Robert B. Roosevelt, lived next door at 26 East Twentieth Street in an identical house, also given as a wedding gift by millionaire Cornelius Van Schaack Roosevelt.

By 1872, the Theodore Roosevelt family had vacated the Twentieth Street home for more spacious and elegant accommodations uptown. The Twentieth Street house, although owned by his sister Anna until 1899, was converted before the turn of the century into commercial space. The same fate befell Robert's house at 26 East Twentieth Street around the same time. The building at 28 East Twentieth Street was totally demolished in 1916.

Theodore Roosevelt died in his sleep at his beloved Sagamore Hill in Oyster Bay, Long Island on January 6, 1919, leaving a loving nation in mourning. On the morning following Roosevelt's death, Mrs. Henry A. Wise Wood and Mrs. William Curtis Demorest met to discuss the possibility of a memorial to the late president from the women of America. They interested a number of other influential New York women in the idea, and held their first formal meeting on January 19, 1919, at the home of Mrs. John Henry Hammond, who would later become their president for some twenty-five years.[1] Others invited included

Mrs. Cornelius Vanderbilt, Mrs. Andrew Carnegie, and Mrs. Jacob Riis.

A committee was formed to suggest possible forms for the memorial. Some ideas put forward included a chair at a university, a community center, a "historian in every city," and even a baseball/athletic stadium.[2] However, it was a suggestion by the president's widow Edith, made recently over lunch to Mrs. Robert Bacon, which received the most attention. Mrs. Roosevelt had expressed her "great desire to have her husband's birthplace restored as a memorial."[3] After three meetings this idea was adopted unanimously, and the new group, calling themselves the Woman's Roosevelt Memorial Association (WRMA) was formalized. The new organization was incorporated in the State of New York on January 29, 1919,[4] although nationwide activities were planned. By February, the women had accepted free office and meeting space at the New York Trust Company, One East Fifty-seventh Street in Manhattan, where they would reside for over four years. The group then elected officers and formed a variety of committees.

Although aware of Roosevelt's "antipathy to movements,"[5] the ladies were either unaware of or chose to ignore his strong opposition to the very project they were engaged in. In the fall of 1905, while Roosevelt was still in the White House, a small group of admirers formed the Roosevelt Home Club. These men purchased the old house on Twentieth Street with the intent of maintaining it as a national landmark. Working behind the scenes, Roosevelt attempted to dissuade the group, writing, "I have felt very uncomfortable about the effort to purchase and preserve the house at all. It does not seem to me worth while, and most emphatically it is something with which I should in no way be connected."[6] When gentle persuasion failed, Roosevelt ordered the club disbanded in August 1906, about the time they lost the house for failure to pay their mortgage.

As most of the WRMA members didn't even know where Roosevelt's birthplace was, the first order of business was to locate and inspect the site. To their dismay the women found a two-story commercial structure on the lot, the original building having been demolished just three years earlier. Robert Roosevelt's no. 26 house next door was still standing, although it was by now the home of the Cafe Thomas and other businesses.

Obviously, this would be a larger project than the women had first imagined.

A $5,000 option to buy the no. 28 building was quickly taken, raised from among a group of the WRMA's principal members. By June 1919, both buildings had been purchased, at a cost of $86,177.53,[7] again mostly raised from within the ranks of the original WRMA membership.

From its formation, the WRMA had as its main purpose the spreading of Rooseveltian ideals to the people, especially schoolchildren, as well as to new immigrants to America and others. Roosevelt House, as the restored site would be called, was not to be a static museum of relics and furniture (exhibit halls were not even planned), but rather a living memorial to Roosevelt and a "Center of Americanism." Toward this goal education became the prime focus of the group. "Junior members" were recruited (for twenty-five cents each), and soon Roosevelt Clubs were formed in over one hundred schools throughout the New York City school system. Activities in the schools included essay contests and by 1925 an annual Public Speaking Contest, still held at the Birthplace today, the oldest such program in the New York City public schools.

Soon after the WRMA formed, a Men's Committee also sprang up. Also based in New York City, but with national programs, the group included John Burroughs, General Leonard Wood, Elihu Root, Will H. Hays, James R. Garfield, and many other old friends and admirers. This organization was incorporated by act of Congress on May 31, 1920, as the Roosevelt Memorial Association (RMA).[8] The three initial goals of the RMA were to create a park in Oyster Bay, New York in TR's memory, to erect a memorial in Washington, D.C., and to assemble a comprehensive scholarly collection on the life and times of Theodore Roosevelt.[9] This included compiling and publishing Roosevelt's extensive writings, as well as collecting physical artifacts and mementos of his life and career. This collection would soon become one of the nation's finest.

Although on the surface the dealings between the WRMA and RMA seem to have been most cordial, a rivalry did exist from the beginning. Duplication of efforts, the close similarity between the groups' names and the much greater success of the men in both publicity and fund-raising caused considerable hard feelings among the women. Added to this were political differences between the groups' leaders as perceived by the women. Mrs. Wood stated that the two groups could never "pool interests," as Colonel William Boyce Thompson and social worker Raymond Robbins of the Men's Committee "so leaned toward socialism."[10] The men's group made an overture to the women to unite as early as April 1919,[11] but were rebuffed, as would be the case for many years to come. Probably, however, the most important reason for this reluctance by the women was their desire to maintain the identity and integrity of their own organization.

Now that the buildings had been acquired, the main fund-raising effort began. The goal set by the women was $1,000,000, of which $250,000 was expected to be needed for construction of Roosevelt House. The rest would be an endowment which would, they hoped, fund operation of the house on a permanent basis. The women looked into the use of professional fund-raisers to run the drive, but that idea was dropped as both too costly and too much of a gamble, as rather stiff fees would be due to the company regardless of the success of the drive.

Thus the ladies began their drive to fund and build Roosevelt House. Much of the needed funds, it was hoped, would come from the state committees, under the direction of Mrs. Henry A. Wise Wood. Eventually some thirty-three states as well as nine foreign countries would organize. For a time the District of Columbia had Mrs. Franklin D. Roosevelt, TR's niece, as its secretary. Eleanor Roosevelt also served as a board member of the WRMA. The campaign included a "Brick Drive," as well as a series of teas, garden parties, and other "entertainments." The money began to come in, but not at the rate hoped for. By October 1920, only $81,000 could be devoted to demolition and the initiation of the building project,[12] and delays were already occurring. These were due both to the lack of adequate funds and to problems in getting some of the building tenants to vacate.

A main part of the WRMA drive was a "mass rally" at New York's Carnegie Hall to be held on Roosevelt's sixty-first birthday, October 27, 1919. This coincided with a week-long drive by the Men's Committee. The two organizations discussed joining their efforts (for that week only), but a variety of differences and legal problems prevented any meaningful cooperation. Whereas the Carnegie Hall event brought in $33,000 for the WRMA,[13] the men's campaign, culminating in "Roosevelt Week," netted the men some $1,753,000.[14]

Several reasons can be postulated for the difficulties the WRMA had in those early years and even after Roosevelt House opened. Although the public was in a receptive mood for patriotic causes, following the recent victory over the kaiser and for democracy and "Americanism," not to mention the great public affection for Roosevelt, the women of the WRMA could never effectively capitalize on these assets. Telephone calls to friends, teas, and schoolchildren's pennies could not produce the results of a professionally organized and well-publicized national campaign. One of the most telling examples of the WRMA's approach to fund-raising occurred in late 1920, when an apple dealer was allowed use of part of the no. 28 building in return for a percentage on each barrel of apples sold.[15] An intense dedication to a laudable project would not be enough to bring success. The women had to get their message to the people.

There was, however, more than a question of scale and organization. A fundamental problem of the group was the gender of the principals involved. Regardless of how affluent the women were, they simply did not have the political and economic connections or the media "clout" that the men possessed. This was a fact of life in a male-dominated post-World War I world, women's suffrage not withstanding, and cannot be overlooked. This also explains much of the tension between the men's and women's groups. It actually speaks well of the WRMA that given these circumstances and the methods they employed that they did as well as they did.

Finally, demolition of the old buildings began, and the cornerstone of Roosevelt House was laid on January 6, 1921, the second anniversary of Roosevelt's death. Theodate Pope Riddle, a pioneer woman architect and friend and neighbor of Roosevelt's older sister Anna Roosevelt Cowles, had already drawn up plans for the house. The Tide Water Construction Company was selected as the primary building contractor.

Money wasn't the only need of Roosevelt House. A search began for original furnishings and other artifacts from the old house, or similar period pieces from the late 1860s. Much of this would eventually come from Roosevelt's sisters Corinne Roosevelt Robinson and Anna Roosevelt Cowles, as well as Edith Roosevelt, so that some forty percent of the pieces in the five "period rooms" would be from the original house. Reportedly, the only pieces of the original building to survive and be returned were several fireplace mantels donated by a private citizen.

Construction began in mid-1921, but was soon nearly halted due to lack of funds, the first of a number of construction delays for various reasons. The cost of demolition and building had risen appreciably, the house was now to cost some $450,000. Drastic measures were needed, so the ladies took out a mortgage on the land of Roosevelt House, as well as a $100,000 loan.[16] However, this would still not complete the project and added further debt in the WRMA's future.

Enter the Roosevelt Memorial Association. Roosevelt's father had said to the asthmatic future president when he was a boy, "Teedie, you have the mind, but have not the body." Likewise, the women had the place, but they had not the money to complete it; the men had the money and the extensive collection and library, but they had not the place to put them. Also, with the memorial project in Washington, D.C., delayed, they had no real objectives. A plan to satisfy both needs was proposed by the RMA and was supported by Corinne Roosevelt Robinson and other family members. The RMA would give the WRMA $150,000 toward completion of Roosevelt House. In return, the men would get a 999–year lease on the no. 26 half of Roosevelt House for their museum and library. The men would also contribute $15,000 for installation of exhibit and library cases, which had not been in the original plans.

Although there was stiff initial opposition to this plan from several of the principal women of the WRMA Board, as well as Elihu Root of the RMA, neither group, particularly the women, had much choice in the matter, as their project might fail otherwise. Although the women had planned to use much of the no. 26 side of the house as "activity rooms" and other space for their educational work, and so forth, they realized that a museum could also add to the appeal and educational value of the house.

Besides the donations from the RMA already mentioned, the men also agreed to pay half of the operating costs of Roosevelt House when it opened, which also later would turn out to be fortuitous for the ladies. A joint committee was formed between the groups to deal with all matters of mutual interest and to coordinate their activities. And so both groups clearly came away winners, and the money from the RMA went a long way toward solving the women's money woes, although when the house opened it would still not be completely paid for. Through the next few years, the women would still need another mortgage and additional loans.

Amid great fanfare and (finally) much media attention, Roosevelt House opened on Roosevelt's sixty-fifth birthday, October 27, 1923. As hundreds jammed East Twentieth Street outside, the ceremonies, open only to invited guests due to space limitations, were broadcast to the crowds outside via a public address system which in those days was housed in a truck! The new medium of radio was also used to publicize the event and the new attraction.

Roosevelt House would see 125,000 visitors, many of them schoolchildren, in its first five years of operation.[17] For a twenty-five cent admission fee one could see the five restored period rooms, as well as two exhibit halls. These are still the site's main visitor facilities today, along with its spacious auditorium for films and other programs

Now the women faced new realizations: running a museum, supervising and supporting a paid staff, and maintaining a complex structure. Building security, fire prevention, insurance, building repairs, book sales, and a host of other subjects now kept their attention. Roosevelt House, as well as being a Center of Americanism, was also a business and had to be treated as such.

By the tenth Annual Meeting of the WRMA in January 1929, the women were able ceremonially to burn the house mortgage, leaving no standing debt.[18] But meeting monthly operating expenses was often a problem, solved in many cases by a generous "bail out" by one of the group's board members. Another attempt at raising an endowment for the house, targeted at $250,000 had begun in February 1924. This time they used professional fund-raisers, but by the following spring the group had only raised some $62,000. [19] With state committee activity waning and neither memberships nor house revenues as high as expected, the women continually struggled with finances. The ladies would, however, weather the Depression better than most non-profit groups, having made wise (or lucky) investments of their assets.

In 1946, the WRMA changed their corporate name to the Women's *Theodore* Roosevelt Memorial Association (changes italicized),[20] something they had discussed for years but never could seem to agree on. This, it was hoped, would alleviate much of the confusion with the RMA, as well as prevent confusion with the late Franklin D. Roosevelt.

In 1953, the RMA opened Sagamore Hill, Roosevelt's home in Oyster Bay, Long Island, and summer White House, to the public. The RMA had restored the house after Edith Roosevelt's death in 1948. Also in 1953, another act of Congress changed the RMA's name to the Theodore Roosevelt Association, which it retains today.[21]

In 1955, still struggling to run and financially maintain Roosevelt House, the WRMA finally merged with the men, being absorbed (as they had always feared) into the larger Theodore Roosevelt Association (TRA).[22] After thirty-six years, the organization which accomplished one of the most unique projects in historic preservation history by creating the only Victorian "reconstruction" in America, would be no more.

In the late 1950s, the TRA approached the National Park Service to discuss the donation of both Sagamore Hill and the Birthplace to the American people to be administered by the National Park Service. Signed by President Kennedy, the act establishing Sagamore Hill and Theodore Roosevelt Birthplace as national historic sites was finalized on July 25, 1962.[23] The Park Service took over operations the next year. With the house came a $500,000 endowment to assist in funding preservation and artifact conservation at the two sites.

Today, the National Park Service carries on the work of a group of very impassioned, dedicated, and patriotic Americans. The Birthplace is as much a memorial to them as it is to one of our most charismatic and beloved national leaders.

NOTES

The author gratefully acknowledges the assistance of Dr. John A. Gable, Executive Director of the Theodore Roosevelt Association and long-time friend of the Birthplace and Verna Retzlaff, volunteer for the National Park Service who ably assisted with library and deed research on original house history.

1. "The Early History of the Theodore Roosevelt House," *The Roosevelt House Annual, 1950,* p. 7. Also see Charles B. Hosmer, Jr., *Presence of the Past,* (New York: G. P. Putnam's Sons, 1965), pp. 147–52.

2. Minutes, Woman's Roosevelt Memorial Association, January 19, 1919, handwritten or typed mss. (hereafter cited as Minutes).

3. *The Roosevelt House Annual, 1950,* p. 7.

4. Certificate of Incorporation filed with the New York Secretary of State, January 29, 1919.

5. Minutes, January 19, 1919.

6. Confidential letter to Mr. William D. Murphy, in *The Letters of Theodore Roosevelt*, 8 vols., ed. Elting Morison et al. (Cambridge: Harvard University Press, 1951-54), 5: 60, letter no. 3,708.

7. *Woman's Roosevelt Memorial Bulletin*, February 1920, p. 4, "Progress Told at Annual Meeting."

8. Act of Congress (41 Stat. 691, 1920).

9. The Roosevelt Memorial Association: A Report of its Activities, 1919–1921 (New York: Roosevelt Memorial Association, 1921), p. 10.

10. Minutes, Executive Committee, May 23, 1919.

11. Ibid., Board Meeting, April 11, 1919

12. Ibid., Board Meeting, October 22, 1920.

13. Ibid., November 14, 1919.

14. John Allen Gable, "The Theodore Roosevelt Association, A Brief History," *Theodore Roosevelt Association Newsletter*, August 1974, pp. 5–8.

15. Minutes, Executive Committee, November 4, 1920.

16. Minutes, Executive Committee, January 12, 1922.

17. "President's Report," *Roosevelt House Bulletin* 3, no. 5 (Spring 1929): 2.

18. Ibid.

19. "President's Report," *Roosevelt House Bulletin* 2, no. 5 (Spring 1925): 1.

20. Amendment to Articles of Incorporation, filed with the New York Secretary of State on January 22, 1946.

21. Amendment to Charter, approved by Act of Congress on May 21, 1953 (67 Stat. 27–28, 1953).

22. Consolidation Agreement between WRMA and TRA signed January 6, 1955. Approved by Act of Congress March 29, 1956 (70 Stat. 60, 1956), and by New York State Supreme Court on May 3, 1956.

23. 76 Stat. 217.

Sagamore Hill, Theodore Roosevelt's home on Cove Neck, near the village of Oyster Bay, Long Island, New York was built in 1884–1885. This photograph dates from c. 1907. The site was opened as a museum on June 14, 1953 by President Dwight D. Eisenhower. The Theodore Roosevelt Association gave Sagamore Hill with an endowment to the National Park Service in 1963.

37

Sagamore Hill: An Interior History

David H. Wallace

For the past six years, it has been my privilege as a reemployed annuitant of the National Park Service to start over again as a research historian. That is how I started my professional life, but in the course of time I became a supervisor of other people and thereafter had little time for hands-on research. Four years after taking an early retirement, I had the chance to come back, as a staff curator in the Service's Division of Historic Furnishings, and I am loving it. One reason I am enjoying it is because I have had the opportunity during these past six years to study several buildings operated by the National Park Service, including Carl Sandburg's home in North Carolina, Martin Luther King, Jr.'s Atlanta birthplace, the Faraway Ranch in Arizona, the Kettle Falls Hotel in northern Minnesota, a life-saving station on the Outer Banks, and lighthouse keepers' quarters at Cape Hatteras and on one of the Apostle Islands of Wisconsin, and to study the interaction between these buildings and the people who occupied them. Some of them are public buildings, where we are dealing mainly with specific events; some are private dwellings, and there we are usually interpreting the lives of the occupants. I have found it a most fascinating field of study.

Among the projects I have been working on are two directly related to Theodore Roosevelt. One is the Theodore Roosevelt Inaugural National Historic Site in Buffalo, New York, and the second is Sagamore Hill National Historic Site at Oyster Bay, Long Island. They have been especially interesting to me because of the contrast between them. At the Ansley Wilcox mansion in Buffalo, there is one event that the furnishings are intended to illustrate—the day in September 1901, when Vice President Theodore Roosevelt became President Theodore Roosevelt. That study has focused on what the house looked like at the time this dramatic event took place. The lives of the family are summarized in the report, but the furnishings themselves speak to the single event. It is very different with Sagamore Hill. Here, we are dealing with the house that was home to Theodore Roosevelt for almost thirty-two years and was intimately associated with his life before, during, and after his presidency. This greatly complicates the job of research and of interpretation.

The purpose of the historic furnishings reports which I prepare is to provide the people who operate the structure—the house, in this case—with information on who was there during the period to be interpreted, how they used the house, how they used each of the rooms, and how those rooms were furnished. It is partly a resource document which provides information for the interpreters' use; they can draw from it all kinds of factual and anecdotal material about each of the rooms they show to visitors. It is also an action document which provides a plan for acquiring and placing furnishings and a sort of template for putting the room back together after it has been taken apart for cleaning, repainting, repapering, or whatever.

The research on Sagamore Hill is probably about as fascinating a job as any person in my field could hope to find. For one thing, the house is already furnished, and a large percentage of the furnishings were there when the Roosevelts lived there. They are among the best of the primary resources. We are fortunate, also, in having many interviews that were taped—mainly in the 1960s and 1970s, but a few in the 1980s. These were with family members (particularly Ethel Roosevelt Derby, Alice Roosevelt Longworth, and Archibald Roosevelt), a few former employees, and friends who knew the Roosevelts either during TR's lifetime or during Mrs. Roosevelt's widowhood. But because it provided new information, the richest source was Mrs. Roosevelt's correspondence with her sister Emily Carow. Edith Roosevelt wrote to Emily almost weekly throughout the 1890s and into the early 1900s. I think Sylvia Morris and I are probably the only people who have read all of Mrs. Roosevelt's letters to her sister. For me, they were particularly helpful because Mrs. Roosevelt wrote to Emily mostly about the family and the house. Almost every letter is filled with details about what the children were doing, what illnesses they had, and the changes she might be making in the house. This was, by and large, new material, because Mrs. Roosevelt's letters were not available for research during the initial restoration period. TR's own letters are often full of insights into family matters. I have used only the published ones, particularly those to his children and to his sisters. There also is a great wealth of early photographs for the downstairs public rooms, but for the second floor there are only a few later ones—some snapshots taken when Ethel Derby and her children were living at Sagamore during the First World War—that were not available to guide the 1950s restoration. Of course, there are many memoirs and biographies, particularly Sylvia Morris's biography of Mrs. Roosevelt, that have been extremely helpful and full of insights for me.

It has been, as it always is in these projects, fascinating to delve into the inner workings of a house and the private environment of a family. As a result, I tend to see Theodore Roosevelt through the eyes of his children and his wife, who is reported to have described him once as the oldest of her children.[1] That side of Theodore Roosevelt comes through again and again as one studies the house, room by room. The purpose of this essay is to share a few of the impressions from my research, using the words of the people who lived in or visited the house.[2]

Theodore Roosevelt, Jr. (Ted), wrote in the mid-1920s:

To understand a family it is necessary to know what their house is like, for the home where a family grows up is always a part of the background of life for every child. The beauty of the house makes surprisingly little difference to the children. It is what happens there that counts.

It was a distinct shock to me one day not long ago when someone called our old home, Sagamore, ugly. On sober thoughts I suppose it is. [This was, of course, from the viewpoint of the twenties.] I do not know what you would call the architecture—perhaps a bastard Queen Anne. What if it is? It is still Sagamore.[3]

Ted's father, for whom architects Lamb and Rich designed the house in 1884, was himself rather ambivalent about its exterior, but not about the interior. Thirty years later he wrote:

I did not know enough to be sure what I wished in outside matters. But I had perfectly definite views what I wished in inside matters, what I desired to live in and with; I arranged all this, so as to get what I desired in so far as my money permitted; and then Rich put on the outside cover with but little help from me. I wished a big piazza, very broad at the n.w. corner where we could sit in rocking chairs and look at the sunset; a library with a shallow bay window opening south; the parlor or drawing room occupying all the western end of the lower floor; as broad a hall as our space would permit; big fireplaces for logs; on the top floor the gun room occupying the western end so that north and west it looks over the sound and bay. I had to live inside and not outside the house; and while I should have liked to "express" myself in both, as I had to choose I chose the former.[4]

Over the thirty-two years that this was Theodore Roosevelt's home, relatively few changes were made in the building. The biggest one, in 1905, was the construction of what they called the North Room, but which many people later referred to as the Trophy Room. This large, baronial hall served as a sitting room or living room for the family, making the original hall into no more than an entrance and passageway. A few years later, they added a couple of bathrooms and a little shower room onto the second floor, none of them seen by today's visitors. The shower room Mrs. Roosevelt referred to once as "the splash closet," apparently because the president did a great deal of splashing while taking his early morning cold shower.[5]

The house was lighted by gas, coal oil, and candles until 1918. Six months after the switch to electric power early that year, Mrs. Roosevelt reported to Kermit: "The electric light has been a convenience, and as yet we are not burned to the ground."[6]

For almost thirty years after Theodore Roosevelt's death in 1919, Mrs. Roosevelt continued to live at Sagamore, maintaining it as a home to which her children and grandchildren could return from time to time, but she did very little in the way of change or even maintenance. As her oldest son pointed out in the 1920s, there was always something broken.[7] Consequently, when she died in 1948, the house looked very much as it had thirty years earlier.

Shortly after Mrs. Roosevelt's death, the Roosevelt Memorial Association (now the Theodore Roosevelt Association) bought the property, intending to open it to visitors as a public shrine, and undertook an ambitious restoration. As part of that restoration, a committee headed by Mrs. Bertha Benkard Rose, undertook the refurnishing of the principal rooms in the house. At that time they were thinking mainly of the presidential period and the rooms that were of most public significance. With the generous cooperation of the family, the restoration committee did an excellent job of rehabilitating the structure and adapting it for public visitation. During the restoration, the furnishings were taken out; after it was completed, they were brought back and family members went through the rooms with Mrs. Rose and indicated which pieces they were interested in. As Mrs. Derby recalled years later, if Mrs. Rose said, "Oh, we need that for the refurnishing of the house," they would generally say, "That's fine, we'll just leave it there."[8] The consequence is that most of the furnishings in the main rooms downstairs and the second-floor bedrooms are those actually used by the Roosevelts before 1919.

The restored house was dedicated in 1953, with President Eisenhower as the principal speaker. A few years later, the Congress of the United States and President Kennedy agreed to have the National Park Service take responsibility for maintaining and interpreting Sagamore Hill as a national historic site.

In the words of Jacob Riis, an old friend of Theodore Roosevelt, Sagamore Hill was "the family sanctuary, whither they come back in June with one long sigh of relief that their holiday is in sight." It was, Riis continued "a very modest home for the President of the United States. . . . The house is comfortable, filled with reminders of the stirring life its owner has led in camp and on the hunting trail . . . but it is homelike rather than imposing. It is the people themselves who put the stamp on it—the life they live there together."[9]

It is important to remember that, from 1889 until 1909, Sagamore Hill was almost exclusively the Roosevelts' summer place. During those twenty years, the family spent most of the year in Washington or, for two years, in Albany. In 1898, because of Colonel Roosevelt's involvement in the Spanish-American War and the New York gubernatorial campaign, the family stayed on at Sagamore until January, when he became governor of New York, and they were also there much of the time during the six months he served as vice president. Normally, they moved back to Sagamore in May and stayed until September. It became a permanent, year-round residence in March 1909, when the Roosevelts moved out of the White House. The retired president wrote at that time:

> We could not have had a pleasanter homecoming. I wanted to be here in late Winter; and it *is* late Winter, and at night under the full moon the snow-covered landscape is beautiful beyond description. Good Ethel had the house as comfortable

as possible for us, and really it is a lovely house. I am dictating this in the North Room, with the big logs blazing on the hearth. So lovely is it that I am utterly unable to miss the White House, and though I miss very much the friends that I used to see at the White House, I am very glad to be home. Edith is already rested.[10]

Edith Roosevelt loved Sagamore Hill quite as much as Theodore, I'm sure, but since she was responsible for running it, she took a rather more practical view of its idiosyncracies, of which draftiness was only one of many. "Sagamore is just as warm as it ever was in cold weather," she wryly commented in 1918. "We have plenty of coal, but a bird cage is hard to heat."[11]

By 1910, the house full of children was a thing of the past. Alice and Ted were already married, and the other four children were soon to leave home. The arrival of grandchildren, the first of whom was Ted's Gracie, born in 1911, helped fill the vacuum, but it was still a wrench when Quentin left for college in 1915. "I am a little sad," his mother wrote to Kermit, "to think that the last of the boys has taken the first step of entrance to the great world." She thought of taking Father away somewhere as a distraction, but decided against it because, she wrote, "he does like his own Sagamore Hill, poor lamb."[12]

Even without small children, the house was seldom quiet, however, thanks to the many visitors: family, friends, and occasional groups, such as the Boy Scouts who came to pay their respects to the ex-president in 1916 and were greeted by him from the pulpit-like piazza. Mrs. Roosevelt and her staff were sometimes hard put to it to cope with the ebb and flow of visitors, especially because her husband had a tendency to invite people to stay for lunch or dinner without warning. In 1914, Mrs. Roosevelt told Kermit of one such instance:

Today he told me we should be thirteen at lunch, then twelve, then we came home and found we should be but eight. I was still doubtful, and had but two seats removed from the table, making ten. Before lunch was half over, four people arrived, so the two seats had to be put back. You can believe that I need servants of a placid temperament to deal with such contingencies.[13]

Mrs. Roosevelt was very lucky with her servants. In fact, she must have been a good mistress, because she tended to keep them for a long time, and they certainly did have to be very resilient. The one best remembered, perhaps, was Mame Ledwith, who had been nurse to Edith and Emily Carow in New York in the 1860s. She came to help Edith in 1887 when Ted was born, and stayed until she was pensioned off in 1908. As she aged, Mame got a little cranky, however. In one letter to her sister Emily, Edith wrote that Mame was "exhausted with much church going & as cross as two sticks," adding, "I shall be thankful when Easter is over."[14]

There were other servants, of course, and their presence is reflected in the furnishings of the house on the third floor. Mary Sweeney, for instance, was Mrs. Roosevelt's personal maid from 1910 to 1948. Then there were several cooks— Annie and Bridget and "good old Meta."[15] There were also a few black servants, most notably James Amos, who served as messenger, butler, and ultimately as valet to the ailing ex-president.[16]

Now I will take you on a brief tour of the house. For the most part, I will provide little vignettes of the various rooms, illustrating particular events that occurred within them—not necessarily the most significant, but indicative of how the Roosevelts made Sagamore a home.

We begin our tour in the entrance hall. I am reminded here of an episode in the 1890s, when TR climbed up the windmill outside to fix it—it was stuck for some reason—and as he did so, it suddenly started to turn, clipping him on the scalp. As Hermann Hagedorn tells the story in *The Roosevelt Family of Sagamore Hill:*

> He had a way of bleeding profusely when he bled, and could scarcely see as he entered the house. At that moment, Mrs. Roosevelt came down the stairs. Another woman, seeing her husband in that gory state, might have fainted or gone into hysterics. Not she. "Theodore," she remarked, in what Mr. Roosevelt subsequently described as a distinctly bored tone of voice, "I wish you would do your bleeding in the bathroom. You'll ruin every rug in the house."[17]

Next, we look into the library. In 1905, Baron Kentaro Kaneko, a Japanese diplomat, visited Sagamore Hill to discuss, among other things, the approaching Portsmouth Peace Conference. They spent the evening in this room, as he later recalled:

> After dinner . . . the President, Mrs. Roosevelt and I sat in the library surrounded by the Colonel's books and trophies. We discussed the forthcoming Russo-Japanese conference . . . with frequent references to Harvard days.

The household servants had all retired. At nine-thirty, the First Lady of the land folded up her knitting, turned down the lamp, and bade us good night, with injunction not to retire until we straightened out the affairs of the world. Her final act was to produce two tin candlesticks. Each contained a tallow dip and a box of matches. "Light yourselves to bed, gentlemen, and good night," she said, vanishing from the room. About eleven o'clock, as if ordered by the sandman, we traded yawns and got out of our easy chairs. "Just a moment, Baron," said the Colonel, "until I close up." While he was moving about the room adjusting the windows, snuffing the lamps, and putting a dog outside, I lighted the candles that Mrs. Roosevelt had left for beacons on the way to bed. Where else in the world could a similar situation have occurred; a President leading his foreign visitor upstairs by the light of a tallow dip.[18]

Courtesy of National Park Service, Sagamore Hill National Historic Site

The Library at Sagamore Hill

Across the hall from the library is the drawing room. This was originally known as the parlor, but when Mrs. Roosevelt redecorated it in 1901, she started calling it the drawing room. I suspect that her husband twitted her about this over the years, because in his autobiography, written several years later, he

The Drawing Room at Sagamore Hill in the late 1970s,
showing Philip de Laszlo's portrait of Edith Roosevelt on wall.

inserted parenthetically, "is drawing room a more appropriate
name than parlor?"[19] This was the most formal room in the house,
but it was also the scene of Easter egg hunts and the opening of
Christmas presents. My favorite drawing room incident occurred
about 1900, when young Ted brought a line of eighty-five
snapping mackerel into the drawing room to show his mother,
"when the string broke and they fell in a shining silver shower
on the carpet."[20]

When ex-President Roosevelt came home from the White
House in 1909, he placed Philip de Laszlo's portrait of Mrs.
Roosevelt on the west wall of the library, where he could see it
from his desk. In that location visitors could not see it, so when
the house was restored in the 1950s, it was decided that the
portrait should hang in Mrs. Roosevelt's drawing room "to show
that this was her room and reflected her taste."[21] The most
effective way to display Mrs. Roosevelt's portrait has recently
been the subject of discussions with the Theodore Roosevelt
Association and we have negotiated what we feel is a mutually
acceptable solution. It will not go back in the library where it

belongs historically, because it is quite true that nobody could see it there. And it is not going back in the drawing room, because we have the landscape that actually hung there and because of our strong feeling that her own portrait was the last thing Mrs. Roosevelt would have placed in her drawing room. So we have found a prominent position for it at the head of the main staircase, where visitors will have a very good view of it and where it will hang beside de Laszlo's portrait of President Roosevelt. Since the upstairs hall was originally lined with family portraits, some of which are no longer in the house, this location seems particularly appropriate.

We move on to the end of the hall and into the North Room, of which Theodore Roosevelt, Jr. wrote, "The North Room to me always means evening, a great fire blazing on the hearth, its flickering light dancing on the flags in the gloom of the ceiling, Father, a book under one arm, poking it with a long iron trident, Mother sitting sewing in a corner of the sofa by a lamp."[22]

This was the room in which, after President Wilson had denied Colonel Roosevelt's request to form a volunteer regiment to go to France in 1917, TR met with the friends who had offered to serve in that regiment with him, to console each other. As a rather romantic observer of the scene reported:

> Through the open window came the haunting chorus of the robins, the liquid calls of the little birds whose names the Colonel might have called offhand, the bright chatter of children. But these evidences of nature, awake and gay, fell blunted against the gloomy company. Only the Colonel spoke—rapid, emphatic sentences that beat hard upon every ear and still held silent every tongue.[23]

The next day, however, we have a very different scene in the North Room. Daughter Ethel and her husband Dick Derby were at Sagamore with their son, little Richard:

> Late this afternoon [the ex-president wrote], I found them in the North Room; the victrola was playing "Garry Owen," while Ethel, Richard and Dick, hand in hand, executed a dance-step march to the tune; where-upon I joined in and executed pigeon-wings in time, opposite them, while the enthralled Richard gazed at my feet.[24]

For the dining room, more quotations from Ted, whose book, *All in the Family*, is a great source of stories about these years:

> Father hated large centerpieces. He used to maintain that he had married Mother because he liked to look at her, and did

Courtesy of Theodore Roosevelt Association

The North Room at Sagamore Hill

not see why at table she should be concealed behind a mass of foliage. Once he confided to my wife, "Eleanor, these large table decorations are ridiculous. If we go on a picnic we do not select a bush and then sit around it in a circle to have lunch!"[25]

The children are grouped on each side. We always have had the two youngest by their mother. The eldest sit by their father. As the family increases, those by the mother are normally displaced by later arrivals. This, of course, places a premium on that seat. Father said, however, that it was carrying this too far when he heard Mother remark, "No, Archie, you have been bad. You cannot sit by me. You are to be punished. You must sit by your Father."[26]

Between the dining room and kitchen is the pantry, used mainly for storage of tableware and certain foods. Ted, again, is our best source for pantry memories:

The pantry at Sagamore, of course, had to be kept locked, or we would have gorged there continually. Archie, then aged six, was asked by his nurse, who had been calling him repeatedly without getting a response, where he was and what he had been doing. He replied, "In the pantry, watching Sissy-Wissy (Alice) eating."[27]

Katy O'Rourke Meany, who had been a kitchen maid during the presidential years, came back to Sagamore Hill in the 1960s and shared some of her memories with the site staff. She is recorded as remembering the kitchen stove "with both fondness and admiration." This coal-burning stove, incidentally, used to be pointed out with pride as one of the original pieces that had been in the house since it was built. Actually, Mrs. Roosevelt replaced the original stove in 1924, and even at that late date, she was able to buy a stove that looked very much like an 1884 stove. Katy recalled that she and Quentin rose every morning at a quarter to six or six o'clock, and came down to the kitchen. While she fired the stove and put the bread in to bake, Quentin would fetch the pans of milk from the walk-in icebox on the back porch and skim off the cream, then help himself to chocolate, buttered bread, fruit, and a "huge highball glass" of milk before returning to his room.[28]

Going up the back stairs, we come first to Alice's room. The restored room reflects the period before Alice married Nicholas Longworth and left home in 1906. Most of its furnishings she had inherited from her mother, who died shortly after Alice's birth. When she was persuaded to return this furniture in the 1950s, Mrs. Longworth drew up a detailed floor plan of her own room, but her memories of the house otherwise were rather sketchy. As she told a former curator at Sagamore Hill in the 1960s:

I was not there very much. From about 1902 I was never there
... not if I could help it.... Certainly I didn't want to be there
all that dreary time. . . . The family did have a good time
together; I suppose they did; we were expected to have a
good time and so we did. Only, gracious, it was a pleasure to
get away from it. I wasn't very enthusiastic about it, frankly.[29]

One of Mrs. Longworth's few room-specific memories
concerned the family bathroom, which she said had a bathtub
that resembled a "sarcophagus."[30]

The room next to Alice's we call the "boy's room." We don't
assign it to any individual boy because all four of them occupied
this room at some time during their boyhood years. There was a
lot of moving children around from room to room at Sagamore,
which makes refurnishing the second floor rather complicated.
When Ted was about six or seven, he recalled:

I crept to the room where we slept with our Irish nurse
Mame. Hitching a chair over, I climbed to the edge of the
washstand. I managed to fill the basin with water. There in
front of me, "all gloriously ranged in view," was a battalion of
bottles of varied colors. I poured them all into the basin, one
after another, stirring the concoction, meanwhile, with a
toothbrush, and chanting like a witch in *Macbeth*. I was just
topping off with Mame's holy water when a whirl of skirts
descended on me like a hurricane, and my soup-making
game was finished.[31]

Behind this room is a large closet, and next to that, what they
called "the little room" or "Quentin's hideaway." Again I quote
Ted, from a letter he wrote to his father when he was about ten
years old. The spelling and punctuation (or lack of it) are Ted's:

Yesterday morning Kermit and I roled stones down the shed
of Kermits window the object was to make them ketch in the
gutter nobody decovered it so we will play it again after that
we made a mus in the closet on Kermits plates with water
cabage jinger snaps bred muffins and prune and sugar first
we thought it would be nice to eat, but it turned out to be
nasty.[32]

At the east end of the third floor were the five servants' rooms:
the cook's room, three maids' rooms, and a sewing room. In 1953,
during the restoration, much of the third floor, including the
maids' rooms, was converted into exhibit spaces. In the process,
several partitions were removed. By the 1960s, when it was
decided that the servants' quarters should be restored and
refurnished, it had been forgotten that one of the two original

maids' rooms had been partitioned during the Roosevelt years, to accommodate a third maidservant. The only evidence remaining today is a 1950 blueprint, prepared before the partition was taken out, and a former maid's recollection of walking through another maid's room to get to her own.[33] We hope to restore the partition as part of our effort to make Sagamore look as it did before 1919.

A little farther down the third floor hall is a spare bedroom that served briefly as a school room between 1898 and 1901. Although the size and shape of this room were drastically altered to accommodate a new staircase to the second floor in 1953, since 1966 it has been furnished as a school room.

The adjoining room was Ted's during the years that his father was president; after Ted's marriage in 1910, it became Archie's. Archie remembered particularly a big wooden bench with animal skins on it, "in the window and rather high, so we could look out." Ethel described it a little more graphically as "a queer stand thing," which was built up to the level of the window, so that the room's occupant could use it as a sofa, "so that he could look at the bay, with all the books in the world on it, and it probably had a bear rug or something."[34]

Down at the end of the hall is the "gun room," called the "den or billiard room" on the original plan but renamed by young Ted in the mid-1890s because his father kept his guns there. In the early years Roosevelt used this as his study, and it was there that he wrote *The Rough Riders* in 1898. In a sort of scrapbook Edith Roosevelt called "The Babies' Journal," she recorded the following gun room story:

> The children were watching their Papa fussing with his guns upstairs when Ted who had climbed in a chair, leveled a gun case at Kermit & said, "There's a little wriggling scamp. Bang! Now he's dead-y." When Kermit . . . said instantly and decidedly in a very deep voice, "No, Teddy, not dead-y."[35]

Ted remembered the gun room as a fascinating place to play:

> There were two closets—one for some unknown reason containing Mother's dresses, and as such was of small interest to us. The other was very different. It faced the gun case and ran back under the eaves like a robber's cave. Like a robber's cave, it was fraught for us with every possibility. There were cartridge boxes, leather cases, ramrods, old pistols, and all the paraphernalia that collects around a sportsman. . . . We children spent many hours in it—though it was stiflingly

hot—for we never knew what treasures we might unearth while rooting among its contents.[36]

Descending the modern stairs to the second floor, we come first to a small room they called "Father's dressing room." Of it, Ted wrote:

The first rifle given us was a Flaubert. Father brought it out with him from town one day. I was off somewhere about the place on "affairs of Egypt," and did not get back until he was dressing for dinner. At once I made for his room, where I found him just preparing for his bath. The rifle was standing in a corner. Of course I fell on it with delight. He was as much excited as I was. I wanted to see it fired to make sure it was a real rifle. That presented a difficulty. It would be too dark to shoot after supper and Father was not dressed to go out at the moment. He took it, slipped a cartridge into the chamber, and making me promise not to tell Mother, fired it into the ceiling. The report was slight, the smoke hardly noticeable, and the hole made in the ceiling so small that our sin was not detected.[37]

Next door is the master bedroom shared by Edith and Theodore Roosevelt, although it was generally referred to in the family as "Mother's room." In the daytime, it served as her sanctuary, to which she could, after lunch, get away briefly from the cares of the household or, as the following incident reveals, from unwanted guests. As her husband explained to a daughter-in-law in 1917, one of the Italian royal princes accepted his invitation to make a courtesy call at Sagamore Hill and had an aide telephone ahead, "so that she would not miss His Highness."

Being fairly familiar with Mother [Roosevelt continued], I grinned to myself, knowing that the warning would enable her to make a getaway. Sure enough, when we reached the house, Mother was technically out having hastily run upstairs and gone to bed with her boots on, so to speak.[38]

On another occasion, Edith Roosevelt took care to be really "out" when an unwelcome visitor appeared, the Grand Duke Boris of Russia, who had scandalized American society by travelling with a mistress. When Mrs. Roosevelt learned that her husband was bringing the Grand Duke to lunch at Sagamore, Mrs. Roosevelt took off with Kermit, as she reported to her sister, and "lunched with Aunt Lizzie to avoid meeting the Grd Duke Boris. In Washington it would have been another matter," she explained indignantly, "but I could not receive him in my own private house."[39] Twelve-year-old Kermit recorded the same incident laconically in his diary: "Father had Prince Boris to lunch. We had lunch at Aunt Laura's. Played under the piazza in the afternoon."[40]

When her husband was away, Mrs. Roosevelt often shared her bed with one of the younger children. On one such night in 1909, she wrote: "[Archie] slept in Father's dressing room where he could talk to me after he had gone to bed and as Q[uentin] sleeps with me, we were very cozy. Scamp started the night with Archie but returned to his bed on my sofa."[41]

Adjoining the master bedroom is the "gate room," as the family called it. Starting with Alice and Ted in the late 1880s, this was the baby nursery, presided over by the nursemaid who took care of the smallest children, but with mother close at hand. In a 1911 letter to his daughter-in-law Eleanor, TR wrote: "How well I remember when we were fitting up our nursery for Ted . . . . I can see him now hanging on the little nursery gate and begging to be taken off to extra-nursery excitement."[42]

Another early picture of that room is recorded in an 1893 letter of Mrs. Roosevelt to Emily Carow, referring to her two-year-old daughter: "Ethel is crawling all over the nursery floor with her amber beads hanging from her mouth like a little poodle dog, banging at everything she can reach."[43] Fifteen years later, this had become the same Ethel's bedroom. Now a teenager, she wrote to Kermit in 1909:

> Josephine has been staying out here with me and I wish you could see our precautions at night. My stiletto that Klinke gave me is beside me and a Mexican dagger Father gave me beside her. A large dinner bell near us (as if anyone that it woke up could help us!) and all our cold cream bottles in front of the door so that the burglar will knock them over and wake us up when he comes in![44]

It was to this sunny room that Theodore Roosevelt was brought in his last illness, and it was here that he died early in the morning of January 6, 1919. As Mrs. Roosevelt wrote to Ted, "Father spent his last evening in your old nursery & loved the view of which he spoke, & as it got dark he watched the dancing flames & spoke of the happiness of being home, and made little plans for me."[45]

Next door is the room now called simply "the nursery," although historically it seems to have been a day nursery between two night nurseries. Based on a 1919 inventory and some snapshots taken in 1917-18, when Ethel's two children were at Sagamore, we plan to set it up as a working nursery, with a little folding canvas bathtub and an ingenious contraption called a "Kiddie Koop," a combination crib and playpen on wheels, with wire screening around the sides and a screened top that folds down over it, useful for keeping flies and mosquitoes off.

This room held an enormous wardrobe, now in the master bedroom. It was decided by the refurnishing committee in the 1950s that this wardrobe and the matching bed, sofa, chairs, and dressing table in the master bedroom belonged together, because they were a set inherited by Theodore Roosevelt from his mother. It now appears almost certain that Mrs. Roosevelt did not have it that way. In order to make room in her bedroom for some of her own furniture, including an Empire dresser and washstand, the bulky wardrobe was apparently banished to the nursery. Edith Roosevelt was not a slave to fashion, and she evidently felt no qualms about mixing furniture styles when it suited her needs. So we are planning to move the wardrobe back to its historic location in the nursery and restore the bedroom to its historic configuration.

Adjoining the "nursery" is the "south bedroom," which was for quite a number of years what Mrs. Roosevelt once called the "gregarious nursery." This was where the older children—the two children next in age to the baby in the "gate room"—would sleep and play under the tutelage of Mame. It was to this room presumably that TR was referring when he wrote to Ted in 1901:

> Recently I have gone in to play with Archie and Quentin after they have gone to bed, and they have grown to expect me, jumping up, very soft and warm in their tommies, expecting me to roll them over on the bed and tickle and "grabble" in them. However, it has proved rather too exciting, and an edict has gone forth that hereafter I must play bear with them before supper, and give up the play when they have gone to bed.[46]

That brings us to the end of our informal tour of Sagamore Hill, but not quite the end of the story. Research goes on to fine-tune the good work that the original restorers of the house did in the early 1950s. At a time when this sort of enterprise was, more often than not, carried out with scant attention to historical detail, the restoration and furnishing committees of the Roosevelt Memorial Association did an excellent job, with the help of the family, of putting the house back together in such a way that it fully exhibits the spirit of the Roosevelt era. Since there is no way to pinpoint any particular moment in time throughout that house, we are not attempting to do so. In fact, the relatively minimal changes that will soon be implemented will rather broaden than constrict the time period for interpretation, embracing the full span of thirty-two years Theodore and Edith Roosevelt lived here together, along with their children and visiting grandchildren, right up until the time of his death.

"I sometimes wonder," Bertha Rose wrote to Mrs. Derby in 1953, "how your father would feel if he knew I was wandering through his home, rearranging and changing. Perhaps he does and approves," she concluded.[47] For my own part, I too wonder how Theodore Roosevelt, as well as Edith Roosevelt and Bertha Rose, would feel about this latest effort to recapture the evanescent look and feel of the house that was home to the Roosevelts of Sagamore Hill. It is a humbling thought, believe me.

And now, as we set off ourselves for Oyster Bay, I can't resist one final quotation, from a letter on White House stationery from President Roosevelt to Kermit:

> Yesterday, Mother leaned out of her windows and heard Archie, swinging under a magnolia tree, singing away to himself, "I'm going to Sagamore, to Sagamore, to Sagamore. I'm going to Sagamore, oh, to Sagamore."[48]

NOTES

1. Hermann Hagedorn, quoted in U.S. Department of the Interior, National Park Service, "Sagamore Hill and the Roosevelt Family, Historic Resource Study" (Denver: Denver Service Center, 1972).

2. At the conference, this presentation was illustrated by slides from historic photographs of Sagamore Hill and its occupants and was followed by a visit to Sagamore Hill. Most of the known interior views of the house are reproduced in the author's *Historic Furnishing Report, Sagamore Hill*, 2 vols., (National Park Service, 1989, 1991), copies of which are in the Long Island Studies Institute at Hofstra University and at Sagamore Hill National Historic Site.

3. Theodore Roosevelt, Jr., *All in the Family* (New York: G. P. Putnam and Sons, 1929), p. 5.

4. Theodore Roosevelt to the editor of *Country Life in America*, October 3, 1915.

5. Edith K. Roosevelt to Kermit, September 8, 1912 (Papers of Kermit Roosevelt, Library of Congress); Charles Somerville, "How Roosevelt Rests," in *Broadway Magazine*, September 1907, p. 667.

6. Edith K. Roosevelt to Kermit, June 16, 1918 (Papers of Kermit Roosevelt, Library of Congress).

7. Roosevelt, *All in the Family*, p. 6.

8. Ethel Roosevelt Derby, taped interview by Gary G. Roth, February 6, 1975.

9. Jacob Riis, *Theodore Roosevelt, the Citizen* (Washington, DC: Johnson, Wynne Company, 1904), p. 313.

10. Theodore Roosevelt to Anna Roosevelt Cowles, March 9, 1909, quoted in Anna R. Cowles, ed., *Letters from Theodore Roosevelt to Anna Roosevelt Cowles, 1870–1918* (New York and London: Charles Scribner's Sons, 1924), p. 275.

11. Edith K. Roosevelt to Anna R. Cowles, February 1918, quoted in Hermann Hagedorn, *The Roosevelt Family of Sagamore Hill* (New York: The Macmillan Company, 1954), p. 392.

12. Edith K. Roosevelt to Kermit, September 26, 1915 (Papers of Kermit Roosevelt, Library of Congress).

13. Edith K. Roosevelt to Kermit, May 24, 1914 (Papers of Kermit Roosevelt, Library of Congress).

14. Edith K. Roosevelt to Emily Carow, April 16, 1893 (Theodore Roosevelt Collection, Harvard University).

15. Edith K. Roosevelt to Kermit, November 28, 1910 (Papers of Kermit Roosevelt, Library of Congress). Meta Bat was listed in the 1910 Census as a 48–year-old with one child, who had emigrated from Germany in 1890.

16. See James Amos, *Theodore Roosevelt: Hero to His Valet* (New York: John Day Co., 1927).

17. Hagedorn, *The Roosevelt Family of Sagamore Hill*, p. 50. Edith's diary (Theodore Roosevelt Collection, Harvard University) dates this incident to July 31, 1892, when she noted, "Theodore badly cut on windmill."

18. Quoted in "Bob Davis Reveals; Two Harvard Graduates in Session at Sagamore Hill," *Roosevelt House Bulletin*, 6, no. 4, (Fall 1945): 5.

19. Theodore Roosevelt, "Autobiography," *The Works of Theodore Roosevelt*, National Edition (New York: Charles Scribner's Sons, 1926), 20: 332.

20. Roosevelt, *All in the Family*, p. 131.

21. Bertha B. Rose, "The Sagamore Story," *Long Island Courant* 1 (October 1965): 30.

22. Roosevelt, *All in the Family*, p. 9.

23. Correspondent of the New York *Sun*, quoted in Hagedorn, *The Roosevelt Family of Sagamore Hill*, p. 365.

24. Theodore Roosevelt to Belle W. Roosevelt, quoted in Hagedorn, ibid., p. 366.

25. Roosevelt, *All in the Family*, p. 36.

26. Ibid., p. 33.

27. Ibid., p. 23.

28. Catherine O'Rourke Meany, interviewed at Sagamore Hill, 1968.

29. Alice Roosevelt Longworth, taped interview with Peter Steele, February 1, 1974 (Sagamore Hill National Historic Site files).

30. Alice Roosevelt Longworth, *Crowded Hours* (New York: Charles Scribner's Sons, 1933), p. 108.

31. Roosevelt, *All in the Family*, p. 52.

32. Theodore Roosevelt, Jr., to his father, probably during the summer of 1898 when TR was away on military service (Papers of Theodore Roosevelt, Jr., Library of Congress).

33. Chapman, Evans & Delahanty, preliminary plan, dated March 20, 1950, of "Electric Outlets and Hot Air Heating System, Attic Plan" (Sagamore Hill National Historic Site plan files); also, Catherine O'Rourke Meany, interview, March 31, 1969 (Sagamore Hill files).

34. Archibald B. Roosevelt and Ethel Roosevelt Derby, as quoted in an unpublished "Furnishings Plan, Third Floor, Sagamore Hill," prepared for the National Park Service in 1966 by Robert Rheinish (copy at Sagamore Hill).

35. Edith K. Roosevelt, "The Babies' Journal," July 21, 1891 (Papers of Theodore Roosevelt, Jr., Library of Congress).

36. Roosevelt, *All in the Family*, p. 118.

37. Ibid., pp. 118–19.

38. Theodore Roosevelt to Eleanor B. Roosevelt, June 27, 1917 (Papers of Theodore Roosevelt, Jr., Library of Congress).

39. Edith K. Roosevelt to Emily Carow, September 10, 1902 (Theodore Roosevelt Collection, Harvard University).

40. Kermit Roosevelt, diary, June 11, 1902 (Papers of Kermit Roosevelt, Library of Congress).

41. Edith K. Roosevelt to Kermit, June 16, 1909 (Papers of Kermit Roosevelt, Library of Congress).

42. Theodore Roosevelt to Eleanor B. Roosevelt, July 30, 1911 (Papers of Theodore Roosevelt, Jr., Library of Congress).

43. Edith K. Roosevelt to Emily Carow, September 30, 1893 (Theodore Roosevelt Collection, Harvard University).

44. Ethel Roosevelt to Theodore Roosevelt, Jr., January 12, 1909 (Papers of Theodore Roosevelt, Jr., Library of Congress).

45. Edith K. Roosevelt to Theodore Roosevelt, Jr., January 12, 1919 (Papers of Theodore Roosevelt, Jr., Library of Congress).

46. Theodore Roosevelt to Theodore Roosevelt, Jr., Sagamore Hill, April 9, 1901, quoted in Joseph B. Bishop, ed., *Theodore Roosevelt's Letters to His Children* (New York: Charles Scribner's Sons, 1947), p. 29.

47. Bertha B. Rose to Ethel R. Derby, June 1, 1953, quoted in Gary G. Roth, "The Roosevelt Memorial Association and the Preservation of Sagamore Hill, 1919–1953" (Master's thesis, Wake Forest University, May 1980), p. 141.

48. Theodore Roosevelt to Kermit, May 28, 1904, quoted in Bishop, ed., *Theodore Roosevelt's Letters to His Children*, p. 97.

38

Theodore Roosevelt: The Man and the Image in Popular Culture

Monica T. Albala

The image of Theodore Roosevelt is ageless in American popular culture, changing as it reflects the continuing evolution of the United States. Modern America carried the "Roosevelt mark" in various media in his own day and also throughout the twentieth century. He has remained visible in the language, literature, cartoons, photographs, films, plays, toys, and memorabilia. Aspects of the changing Theodore Roosevelt image relate to the Progressive, Imperialist, Nationalist, and Conservation movements. These themes can be explored in the many examples of the visible impact of his multifaceted life.

The Ceremonial Court, a new section at the Smithsonian's Museum of American History, contains a replica of the front corridor of the White House, Cross Hall, as it appeared when Theodore Roosevelt was president of the United States. This exhibit refers to his influence as one of the prominent presidents to focus national attention on family life in the White House as newspapers documented the activities of his children. One section of the exhibit is a tompe l'oeil painting of Kermit and Archie playing at the staircase.[1]

Roosevelt was rated fifth best president of the United States in a 1989 survey.[2] Existing signs of his influence persist in many different media and reinforce his status as an important president. TR's national prominence was recognized by his inclusion as one of the four presidents depicted on Mount Rushmore by sculptor Gutzon Borglum. Theodore Roosevelt clearly is a role model for Richard Nixon who referred to him in his farewell talk to his staff after resigning as president: "as ex-President he served his country always in the arena, tempestuous, strong, sometimes wrong, sometimes right, but he was a man." Nixon entitled his recent book of memoirs *In the*

Arena, quoting TR's 1910 speech, "The Man in the Arena."[3]

The Written Word

The American language is enriched by the words of Theodore Roosevelt. The maxim "speak softly and carry a big stick," was popularized when Roosevelt quoted the phrase as president. Richard H. Collin observes, "Roosevelt . . . did not always speak softly—he often bellowed."[4] However, this diplomatic ideal of force kept in check in a civil manner popularized TR beyond his own expectations. It was embraced by journalists, political cartoonists, and the world at large. "Gunboat diplomacy" is a term associated with TR's expansion of the navy during his presidency. He presented a "square deal" to the American public and became known as a "trust buster," a breaker of private monopolies. Theodore Roosevelt was the "first president to be widely known by his initials," a practice journalists have used for some of his successors.[5]

The "strenuous life" of being active and adventurous was the philosophy he adopted to build up his own strength to combat the asthma and other illnesses of his childhood. Roosevelt declared during his reelection attempt against Taft and Wilson that he was fit as a "bull moose." This became the popular name for the Progressive party, the third political party in the election of 1912. "My hat is in the ring" was another phrase coined during the campaign. Roosevelt's exuberant expression "Bully!" typifies his energetic, positive personality. The cry of "Charge!" was popularized during his famous stint in the Rough Riders, a volunteer regiment during the Spanish-American War. His phraseology is apparent in popular culture, such as the Maxwell House Coffee slogan he coined, "Good to the last drop." The term "Alice Blue" is part of popular fashion language. It refers to the pale blue color favored by TR's daughter Alice in dresses and mentioned in the popular song "In My Sweet Little Alice-Blue Gown."[6]

There are many books about Theodore Roosevelt. He himself wrote a total of thirty-eight books which include an autobiography, biographies of Thomas Hart Benton, Gouverneur Morris, and Oliver Cromwell, the history of the naval war of 1812, as well as works about the American West, natural history, and politics. In addition to the books he wrote, TR's letters, essays, speeches, and his public papers as governor and president have been published. Scholars have written many additional books about TR which are beyond the scope of this chapter. One could read a different work about Theodore Roosevelt every day for years.

The Roosevelt image has appeared in many forms in books and literature. Biographies, both adult and juvenile, historical novels mentioning or using TR as a primary or secondary character, detective novels, poetry, and nature books have been written. Some unusual examples of prose about TR were produced both during his life and even in our day. The image of Roosevelt seems to be larger than life, in that it serves as a magnet for writers, and this has lasted far longer than the sixty years he lived.

Many books reflect Roosevelt's personality. One example is Julian Street's description of the man behind the image in *The Most Interesting American:* "It is my belief that his indescribably vigorous manner of speaking has at times been confused in people's minds with what he has actually said." *The White House Gang* by Earle Looker is a book of the adventures of Theodore Roosevelt's youngest son, Quentin, and his friends in the White House; Looker was one of the gang. Eloise Cronin Murphy's local history pamphlet, *Theodore Roosevelt's Night Ride to the Presidency,* retells the details of TR's trip by buckboard to North Creek, New York where he boarded a train to go to Buffalo where President McKinley had died. *Masterson and Roosevelt,* by Jack DeMattos, contains the correspondence between TR and Bat Masterson, the Western frontier lawman whom he appointed Deputy U.S. Marshal of New York (1905–1907), in keeping with TR's cowboy image of being a man who could communicate and compete with cowboys.[7]

William M. Gibson's *Theodore Roosevelt Among the Humorists: W. D. Howells, Mark Twain, and Mr. Dooley,* contains the commentaries of Howells, Twain, and Dooley on Roosevelt. Mr. Dooley was Finley Peter Dunne's fictional Irish alter ego who privately liked TR, while faulting his imperialism and hunting of wild game. Gibson also discusses the opinions of other writers who knew Roosevelt, such as Stephen Crane, Henry James, E. A. Robinson, and Edith Wharton, who was a distant cousin of Edith Kermit Roosevelt, TR's wife. Gibson states that Roosevelt "probably entertained more writers at the White House than any President before or after him."[8]

Many juvenile books deal directly with Roosevelt. *Bully For You, Teddy Roosevelt!*, by award-winning author Jean Fritz, is the most recent biography for younger readers. *The One Bad Thing About Father*, by F. N. Monjo, is a whimsical view of TR's relationship with his children during his tenure at the White House, using Quentin as a first-person narrator. Some titles name themes in Roosevelt's life: Clara Ingram Judson's *Theodore Roosevelt: Fighting Patriot*; James C. Beach's *Theodore Roosevelt: Man of Action*; Edd Winfield Parks's *Teddy Roosevelt: All-Round Boy*; Ira Mothner's *Man of Action: The Life of Teddy Roosevelt*; Edwin P. Hoyt's *Teddy Roosevelt in Africa*; Lois Markham's *Theodore Roosevelt*; Louis Sabin's *Theodore Roosevelt: Rough Rider*; Eden Force's *Theodore Roosevelt*; and Rebecca Steoff's *Theodore Roosevelt: 26th President of the United States*. Classics Illustrated published *The Rough Rider*, a full biography in comic-book form.[9]

Theodore Roosevelt is also well represented in poetry and in biographical novels. Russell J. Wilbur wrote *Theodore Roosevelt: A Verse Sequence in Sonnets and Quatorzains* in 1919. The majority of the thirty-eight poems were completed before TR's death. Wilbur describes him in the first of these,"Proem,"

> . . . there looms one who doth bind
> Ulysses' tireless craft with Hector's rage.
> Look! sons and daughters of Columbia, find
> An epic hero on her living page!"[10]

His poems display a portrait of Roosevelt as a major American figure. Wendell Phillips Stafford, in his 1919 poem, "Theodore Roosevelt," declares that TR "ran to every task as to a sport/who leaped, a lion with lions, at Agincourt. . . ."[11] This is a view of Roosevelt as the active idealist. The theme is carried over in the 1912 satire by Simeon Strunsky, called "Through the Outlooking Glass, Being the Curious Adventures of Theodore the Red Knight in his quest of the Third cup, of his faithful companion Alice, of the old Lady who lived in a shoe behind a high tariff wall, and divers quaint and lively persons, all comprising a veritable Theodyssey of incidents, set down in simple third terms."[12] Obviously this is a parody of Lewis Carroll's *Alice Through the Looking Glass*, featuring Theodore Roosevelt as the Red Knight seeking a third term as U.S. president, and his daughter Alice.

Some recent books highlighting TR include a biographical novel, *TR* by Noel B. Gerson, and three murder mysteries: *The Big Stick* by Lawrence Alexander, set early in his police commissioner role in New York City; *Bully!* by Mark Schorr, set at the White House, told by a former Rough Rider; and *The Adventure of the Stalwart Companions* by H. Paul Jeffers, set just after TR's Harvard graduation. He also is visible in John Jakes's, *The Americans*, and Gore Vidal's *Empire*. These two books, whose titles immediately conjure visions of nationalism and imperialism, reflect his relation to these ideologies today, more than seventy years after his death. Incidentally, the biographical novel, *Alice and Edith*, by Dorothy Clarke Wilson, details the lives of TR's two wives, Alice Lee and Edith Kermit Carow.[13]

Visual Images

Roosevelt's appearance, personality, and independent nature provided a virtual heyday for political cartoonists throughout his public life. They drew him as policeman, naval secretary, Rough Rider, civil service commissioner, governor, president, statesman, sportsman, orator, and citizen. The basic features which illustrators portrayed in countless cartoons were introduced during the time he served as police commissioner of New York City: his wire frame or pince-nez glasses, his tendency to bare his teeth and open his mouth in laughter or amazement, his mustache, and his strong build. His night inspections without warning were a source of anxiety to police, but a delight to the public. Newspaper cartoonists as well as policemen watched for him. These distinguishing marks began to appear in local political cartoons. Later they were joined by his cowboy hat, lasso, guns, pith helmet, Rough Rider uniform, and "big stick," added by cartoonists as he changed careers. The well-known cartoonists of his age who sketched him included Thomas Nast, Clifford Berryman, Otho Cushing, Charles Bush, Homer Davenport, L. C. Gregg, John McCutcheon, J. N. ("Ding") Darling, Charles Dana Gibson, James Montgomery Flagg, Edward Penfield, Frederick Opper, and Joseph Keppler. Roosevelt became a national and international figure through the tremendous exposure he received in newspapers and journals throughout his lifetime. His activities and his policies of standing up to trusts, advocating imperialism, and promoting a "strenuous life" offered inspiration for countless artistic and satiric opportunities. He was truly a cartoonist's dream come true; drawing the president became a national pastime.

There are several especially well-known political cartoons

associated with Theodore Roosevelt. "Teddy Doodle," by
Keppler, was a parody of *The Spirit of 1776*, depicting the
all-American TR as all three marchers, the two drummers and the
fife player decked out in colonial garb with spectacles and big
toothy grins. "Drawing the Line in Mississippi," by Clifford
Berryman, highlighted a famous November 14, 1902 incident, in
which Roosevelt refused to kill a mauled bear which had been
tied to a tree by hunters and offered to him while on a hunt near
Smedes, Mississippi. He is pictured in the cartoon wearing his
Rough Rider uniform and hat with half-turned-up brim. The
original cartoon, in the November 16, 1902 *Washington Post*,
portrayed the bear as a hostile, angry adult. A second version of
the incident, showing the bear as a cowering cub, focused public
attention on Roosevelt's sportsmanship. Clearly the cartoon
showing the cub was the one which has persisted in popular
culture, despite the discrepancy with reality, and demonstrates
the power of the cartoonist to create a lasting myth.[14] This event
encouraged commercial production of stuffed bears, originally
known as "Teddy's bears" and led to a number of books,

Courtesy of Theodore Roosevelt Collection, Harvard College Library

Clifford Berryman's original cartoon as published in the *Washington
Post*, November 16, 1902, showing large, adult bear.

including the Teddy B and Teddy G series by Seymour Eaton (Peter Piper). These titles about Teddy Brown and Teddy Grey include: *The Roosevelt Bears, Their Travels and Adventures; More About the Roosevelt Bears; The Roosevelt Bears Abroad;* and *The Bear Detectives.*[15] Although TR disliked being called "Teddy," preferring "Theodore," he reluctantly accepted America's nickname in public and in print.

The cub bear myth enhanced his positive public image as a compassionate human being as well as an impassioned hunter of big game. This theme joined the militaristic and diplomatic aspects of TR's character often portrayed by cartoonists, showing him with a spiked club or "big stick." Otho Cushing's pictorial satire, *The Teddyssey,* a political spoof of Homer's *Oddyssey,* offered TR "Pallas Columbia" (from Pallas Athena, the goddess) and "Ze U.S." (Zeus, the god) as guides in his journey through

Courtesy of Theodore Roosevelt Collection, Harvard College Library

Berryman's later, more publicized version of "Drawing the Line in Mississippi" with the cub bear.

life against foes such as the "sirens" (caricatures of John D. Rockefeller, J. P. Morgan, and Andrew Carnegie).[16] This is another interesting example of how Roosevelt captured the imagination of America's premier cartoonists.

Roosevelt was widely photographed and lives on film in countless photographs and movies. TR was both charismatic and photogenic. His big toothy grin and twinkling eyes behind pince-nez glasses were riveting. In his lifetime, TR was photographed in suits, shirtsleeves, buckskin cowboy garb, Rough Rider uniform, and safari outfits. His appearance always reflected his strenuous lifestyle and versatility as a person whose aristocratic, monied background did not undermine his ability to fraternize with common Americans. In 1907, a famous composite picture made up of hundreds of varying sized Roosevelt photographs was produced by Henry Strohmeyer for Underwood and Underwood of New York. TR and his family were depicted in stereoscopic views as well as postcards. One postcard of him seated is captioned, "Keep your seat Teddy!" and is obviously from the 1904 election campaign.[17]

Even though Roosevelt died quite early in the history of film, a considerable number of newsreels and documentary films depicting him survive. Roosevelt has also been portrayed by actors in films. One of the earliest was the 1901 Edison satire called *Terrible Teddy, the Grizzly King*, which showed TR shooting into a tree and hitting an ordinary cat, while being followed by two men wearing signs that say "My Press Agent" and "My Photographer," perhaps berating him for too much media coverage.[18] Today, press agents and photographers are taken for granted, but in TR's time, they were viewed as questionable innovations. The noted film historian, Kevin Brownlow, attributes the development of the western, African expedition, and documentary movies to TR because of public attention focused on his career as a Rough Rider and safari hunter. An early cartoon parody series called *Colonel Heeza Liar* was popular for five years.[19] Some feature films depicting TR were *The Fighting Roosevelts* (1919), *The Rough Riders* (1927), *Yankee Doodle Dandy* (1942), *Buffalo Bill* (1944), *Fancy Pants* (1950), *The Wind and the Lion* (1975), and *Ragtime* (1981).

There have been a number of plays, musicals, and television programs paying homage to Theodore Roosevelt in varying degrees. The comedy *Arsenic and Old Lace* (1941), taken from the

Joseph Kesselring's play, is a film classic which has been performed on stage, in film, and television. It is about two elderly aunts who poison lonely old men and have the bodies buried in their house cellar by a crazy nephew who thinks he is Teddy Roosevelt. The play is often revived by amateur theatrical groups.

Fictional plays and films tend merely to glorify Roosevelt's exuberant personality, while documentaries have most accurately portrayed him. *Bully: An Adventure with Theodore Roosevelt* (1977) by Jerome Alden, has been both a successful as well as historically accurate one-man show and movie for James Whitmore. *The Indomitable Teddy Roosevelt* (1986) combines both historical footage, reenactments, and historical authenticity in a documentary. Other good documentaries are *Teddy Roosevelt: The Right Man at the Right Time* (1973), a brief dramatization of TR's first term as president and *My Father the President* (1981), a personal portrait based on a narration originally recorded for acoustaguide tours at Sagamore Hill by TR's younger daughter, Ethel Roosevelt Derby. *TR and His Times* (1984) was a part of Bill Moyers's "Walk Through the 20th Century" PBS series. "Bordertown," a western series on cable television Family Channel, aired the episode "Four Eyes," in 1990, featuring the actor Wayne Yorke as a young TR, in a barroom incident loosely based on fact, during his sojourn in the West.

Musicals about Theodore Roosevelt have had uneven success. In 1980, *1600 Pennsylvania Avenue*, a musical revue, played on Broadway for three months. *Teddy and Alice* (1987), about TR and his daughter, closed after a run of two months. None of the shows was able to fully develop Roosevelt as a balanced character since unfortunately the emphasis is still to present a singing and dancing character who shouts "Bully!" as much as possible without showing more of the real man.

Music and Memorabilia

Roosevelt is represented also in music, art, toys, and memorabilia. Famous songs associated with TR and his campaigns are "We Are With TR," "We're Ready for Teddy Again," "We Want Teddy For Four Years More," "You're All Right Teddy," "Teddy, Come Back," "The Song of the Bull Moose," "Roosevelt," and "Has Anyone Seen Teddy?"[20]

There are paintings, prints, statues, busts, medals, stamps, mechanical banks (for example, depicting him shooting at a bear in a tree), teddy bears, dolls, safari figures, game and puzzle sets, as well as campaign and inauguration buttons and posters. A c. 1910 Dentzel tiger carousel figure last used in Michigan, depicts a decorative carving of Teddy Roosevelt in pith helmet and safari uniform. Another unusual piece was a tin whistle, designed to look like Teddy Roosevelt's wide-mouthed toothy grin which fitted over the wearer's mouth and was sold during his time as police commissioner in New York City (1895–1897).[21]

Theodore Roosevelt's image in popular culture remains strong more than eighty years after his presidency. It continues to capture popular imagination in many forms, from the written word to visual manifestations, in children's books and toys to plays and documentaries. TR is a familiar image and therefore one that continues to affect and influence Americans. Roosevelt can still capture Americans' imagination, and his words and life provide a guide. "Keep your eyes on the stars, but remember to keep your feet on the ground" provides a challenge for Americans and modern America.[22]

Courtesy of Laura J. Labenberg

NOTES

1. Barbara Gamarekian, "A Bully New White House," *The New York Times*, April 27, 1989, p. C12.
2. Jack E. Holmes and Robert E. Elder, Jr., "Our Best and Worst Presidents: Some Possible Reasons for Perceived Performance," *Presidential Studies Quarterly* 19 (Summer 1989): 534.
3. Nixon quoted by Bob Woodward and Carl Bernstein, in *The*

Final Days (New York: Simon and Shuster, 1976), p. 455; Richard M. Nixon, *In the Arena: A Memoir of Victory, Defeat, and Renewal* (New York: Simon and Schuster, 1990); and John A. Gable, ed., *The Man in the Arena: Speeches and Essays by Theodore Roosevelt* (New York: Theodore Roosevelt Association, 1987), p. 54.

4. Richard H. Collin, *Theodore Roosevelt, Culture, Diplomacy, and Expansion: A New View of American Imperialism* (Baton Rouge: Louisiana State University Press, 1985), p. 2.

5. Noel F. Busch, *T.R,: The Story of Theodore Roosevelt and His Influence On Our Times* (New York: Reynal and Company, 1963), p. 2.

6. Roland Marchand, *Advertising the American Dream* (Berkeley: University of California Press, 1985), p. 57; John Ciardi, *A Browser's Dictionary: A Compendium of Curious Expressions & Intriguing Facts* (New York: Harper and Row, 1980), p. 5.

7. Julian Street, *The Most Interesting American* (New York: Century Company, 1916), pp. 10-11; Earle Looker, *The White House Gang* (New York: Fleming H. Revell Company, 1929); Eloise Cronin Murphy, *Theodore Roosevelt's Night Ride to the Presidency* (Blue Mountain Lake, NY: Adirondack Museum), 1977; and Jack DeMattos, *Masterson and Roosevelt* (College Station, TX: Creative Publishing Company, 1984).

8. William M. Gibson, *Theodore Roosevelt Among the Humorists: W. D. Howells, Mark Twain, and Mr. Dooley* (Knoxville: University of Tennessee Press, 1980), pp. viii, 2.

9. Jean Fritz *Bully For You, Teddy Roosevelt!* (New York: G. P. Putnam's Sons, 1991); F. N. Monjo, *The One Bad Thing About Father* (New York: Harper and Row, 1970); Clara Ingram Judson, *Theodore Roosevelt: Fighting Patriot* (Chicago: Follett Co., 1953); James C. Beach, *Theodore Roosevelt: Man of Action* (Champaign, IL: Garrard Press, 1960); Edd Winfield Parks, *Teddy Roosevelt: All-Round Boy* (Indianapolis: The Bobbs-Merrill Company, 1953, 1961); Ira Mothner, *Man of Action: The Life of Teddy Roosevelt* (New York: Platt and Munk Publishers, 1966); Edwin P. Hoyt, *Teddy Roosevelt in Africa* (New York: Duell, Sloan, and Pearce, 1966); Lois Markham *Theodore Roosevelt* (New York: Chelsea House Publishers, 1985); Louis Sabin, *Theodore Roosevelt: Rough Rider* (Mahwah, NJ: Troll Associates, 1986); Eden Force, *Theodore Roosevelt* (New York: Franklin Watts, 1987); Rebecca Steoff *Theodore Roosevelt: 26th President of the United States* (Ada, OK: Garrett Educational Corp., 1988); *The Rough Rider* (New York: Gilberton Company, December 1957), no. 141A.

10. Russell J. Wilbur, *Theodore Roosevelt: A Verse Sequence in Sonnets and Quatorzains* (Boston: Houghton Mifflin Company, 1919), pp. vii, 3.

11. Wendell Phillips Stafford, "Theodore Roosevelt," *Art and Archaeology* 8 (March-April 1919): 114.

12. Simon Srunsky, "Through the Looking Glass," reprinted *New York Evening Post*, c. 1912.

13. Noel B. Gerson, *TR* (Garden City, NY: Doubleday, 1970); Lawrence Alexander, *The Big Stick* (Garden City, NY: Doubleday, 1986); Mark Schorr, *Bully!* (New York: St. Martin Press, 1985); H. Paul

Jeffers, *The Adventure of the Stalwart Companions: Heretofore unpublished letters and papers concerning a singular collaboration between Theodore Roosevelt and Sherlock Holmes* (New York: Harper and Row, 1978), John Jakes, *The Americans* (New York: Jove Publications, 1980); Gore Vidal, *Empire* (New York: Random House, 1987); and Dorothy Clarke Wilson, *Alice and Edith* (New York: Doubleday, 1989).

14. The "Teddy Doodle" cartoon is reproduced on the cover of A. E. Campbell, *America Comes of Age: The Era of Theodore Roosevelt* (New York: American Heritage Press, 1971); information on the 1902 bear incident and the Berryman cartoons from John A. Gable, Director of the Theodore Roosevelt Association, September 1990; Peggy and Alan Bialosky, *The Teddy Bear Catalog* (New York: Workman Publishing, 1980), pp. 12–17; Linda Mullins, *The Teddy Bear Men: Theodore Roosevelt and Clifford Berryman.* (Cumberland, MD: Hobby House Press, Inc., 1987), pp. 31–40.

15. Teddy B and Teddy G books cited in Linda Mullins, *Teddy Bears Past & Present: A Collector's Identification Guide* (Cumberland, MD: Hobby House Press, 1986), p. 256.

16. Otho Cushing, *The Teddyssey* (New York: Life Publishing Company, 1907); and Ann Gould, ed., *Masters of Caricature from Hogarth and Gillray to Scarfe and Levine* (New York: Alfred A. Knopf, 1981).

17. See "The Great American Theodore Roosevelt Puzzle," *American Heritage*, October/November 1981, p. 112; the postcard is in the Nassau County Museum collection, Long Island Studies Institute, Hofstra University, Hempstead, NY.

18. Kemp K. Niver, *Early Motion Pictures: The Paper Print Collection in the Library of Congress*, (Washington, DC: Library of Congress, 1985), p. 322.

19. Kevin Brownlow, *The War, The West, and The Wilderness* (New York: Alfred A. Knopf, 1979), pp. xv, vi.

20. Some of these songs are included in "Teddy, You're a Bear," an audiocassette recording by the Oyster Bay Historical Band and Bay Singers, recorded at Oyster Bay (NY) High School, 1988 (copy in Long Island Studies Institute, Hofstra University).

21. Dentzel was the carousel manufacturer; a picture of the TR carousel figure is in Tobin Fraley, *The Carousel Animal* (Berkeley, CA: Zephr Press, 1984), pp. 84, 85; the tin whistle is in the Nassau County Museum collections at Sands Point Preserve, Port Washington, NY.

22. The quotation, which is also on a stone at Theodore Roosevelt's gravesite in Oyster Bay, was originally in a talk Roosevelt delivered at the Groton School in 1904 which is reprinted in Gable, *The Man in the Arena*, p. 48.

39

The Bully Prophet: Theodore Roosevelt and American Memory

Kathleen M. Dalton

When the news flashed by cable around the world that ex-president Theodore Roosevelt had died in his sleep on the morning of January 6, 1919, the story of TR and his relationship with America entered a new realm. He was dead, but his words and the allegory of his life would live again. TR would have a second career as a figment of the American cultural imagination. Like a cat TR had expended his first life, yet he still had many more lives to go. In his first life, however, he had exercised a measure of personal control over the shaping of his image.[1] In his successive afterlives, TR obviously had no say in how he was used. He could not sue for slander nor stifle idolatrous excess. Later generations would resurrect him as a symbol, a reminder, and a precedent to justify their own actions. Most of all, Roosevelt would serve as a means for Americans to use their past to instruct their present.[2] In death TR became public property—a cultural artifact coopted to serve a modern mass culture in all its exalted and popular forms.

In his new incarnation TR turned into what anthropologists call a "multivocal" cultural vehicle, a cultural symbol carrying many meanings.[3] Widely divergent cultural impulses found in the symbolic TR a unifying expression. TR's multivocal presence can be found in erudite studies and in carnival amusements, pervasive in literary dialogues and present in material culture, too. He has proven elastic enough to symbolize perpetual youth as a cartoon figure one day, while standing as a solemn repository of tradition in monument form the next. The TR symbol has travelled far and wide across the American horizon. America has found in him a nearly all-purpose expression, suitable for a great many occasions.

The story of America's memory and uses of TR is full of conflict. Of course, competing factions would fight over TR's memory after 1919 just as they fought over his worth while he was living. Not long after his death, parts of TR's legacy would be variously claimed by ambitious public figures of every political stripe, even by some of his worst enemies from the 1912 campaign. His mantle of leadership would be sought by the Republican party and by the most important American liberal of the twentieth century, his Democratic cousin Franklin.[4] Similarly, in the 1988 presidential campaign both Republican George Bush and Democratic Senator John Kerry of Massachusetts invoked Theodore Roosevelt's spirit in nationally televised speeches. Laying claim to the memory of TR is politically advantageous because he still appeals to the American people, and he is a symbol who works well to bring forth the authority of the past to legitimate concerns of the present. Shared memories of past heroes help any society view itself as keeping faith with its historical ideals.

Laying claim to the memory of TR can also be economically advantageous—a fact which those influential shapers of American culture, advertisers, discovered long ago. Because they have "invested more time, energy, and money than any other mass communicators" to discover what basic American needs and values are, they are often aware of which symbols of the past work best to enhance a product in the public's mind.[5] In their search to portray their products as enabling consumers to "live in a more exciting world," advertisers have been quick to recognize TR as a saleable, energizing, yet comforting cultural symbol to "wrap" around a product and make it more appealing.[6]

Advertisers have found that like the magic ingredients in Coca Cola, TR "adds life" to otherwise mundane products. Thus the TR symbol has been used to promote the effervescent qualities of baking powder, toilet bowl cleaners, and malt liquor, as well as the more quietly sparkling features of hotels, investment firms, and photography. Products also sell better when endorsed by Rooseveltian catch phrases, for example, "good to the last drop" Maxwell House coffee. Since the 1970s, TR's power to evoke our nostalgia for Victorian times has been brought into play by TR theme restaurants across the country; TR's sayings when placed on menus apparently encourage people to buy food and drink. His persistent cultural appeal enables the TR symbol to increase a product's sales potential; not long ago a major corporation even considered using TR in a national advertising campaign to sell hamburgers.[7]

While some manifestations of TR's recent mass media appeal are merely faddish, his appeal does not rest upon a cultural whim. TR's ability to stand for values and feelings larger than himself has had a truly enduring quality. TR's gift for resilience has been evident across the decades from pre-World War I days when *American Magazine* public opinion polls designated TR as the "greatest man in the United States" to the post-Vietnam era when he was featured as a great American hero on the cover of *Newsweek*.[8] In his own day and in ours TR speaks to many people as a symbolic "voice of America."[9]

The symbolic TR has proven its durability as well as its gift for changing with the times. Over the years much of the meaning of TR's memory has been adapted to the historical predicaments and preoccupations of later generations because, as one scholar wrote, "the past is being continually re-made, constructed in the interests of the present."[10] Accordingly, the symbolic TR has been molded to the needs of different historical eras. The symbolic TR has also passed through phases of reduced cultural salience. For instance, popular culture and novelistic uses of TR declined during the Great Depression when other types of symbolic expressions appeared more timely. Nevertheless, TR has never disappeared altogether as a cultural symbol. What TR meant in American culture from 1919 on usually coalesced with classically American themes which the needs of particular historical moments evoked.

As a result, each generation has projected its needs on the TR symbol. For example, during the Red Scare TR was invoked as the personification of 100 percent Americanism. Although Warren G. Harding had called TR a Benedict Arnold in 1912, he would ride TR's coattails into the White House by associating himself as much as possible with his own boosterish version of TR's memory.[11] During the Great Depression TR was resurrected again, but this time as a precursor to New Deal reform in a movie called *Theodore Roosevelt: Fighter for Social Justice*.[12] By the 1950s, as Cold War America faced threats abroad and threats at home such as juvenile delinquency, TR was refashioned as the defender of democracy and ideal American family life. In the 1960s, TR was again restyled—on one side as the liberal forefather of reform and on the other side as a racial reactionary and defender of law and order.[13] Such examples tell us little about TR's real opinions but a great deal about the flexibility of the symbolic TR over the past eight decades. TR has been used as a sacred precedent to justify many contradictory causes. While shifts in the use of the symbolic TR can provide many new insights about changes in modern American culture, we should look beyond the predictable shifts to see if any unchanging features can be found in the history of America's memory of TR. Are there, in fact, any elements of continuity in the way that America has remembered him?

There are several persistent themes we could explore which have carried across the decades, yet one paradoxical theme that deserves specific attention. This is the spiritual and religious impulse in modern American culture linked with the public memory of TR. At first glance, that presents a paradox—a political leader whose memory carries a spiritual meaning. As president, party leader, vice president, governor, assistant secretary of the Navy, police and civil service commissioner, and state assemblyman, Roosevelt always worked in political roles. Yet TR transcended his secular roles. He struck a deeper chord in the culture than most presidents have, for he carried a broader message to the public. The evidence of spiritual longings in America's memory of TR is visible. He has been remembered as an inspirational figure, to be honored in markedly sacred language. As later generations searched for ways to memorialize TR, they repeatedly turned toward religious expressions.

Religious undertones were evident in America's initial response to TR's death. When TR died, people's reactions transcended the usual grief felt at the loss of an ex-president. On the day of national mourning adults cried openly, and local communities organized services to assist in the shared grieving process. Religious services were held all over the country, with an estimate of over a million people in attendance. The national mourning process grew larger rather than smaller in the months after his death. To commemorate his birthday on October 27, 1919, community organizations, colleges, public schools, and government agencies held a memorial week as "an occasion of a great reconsecration of America to the patriotism and unselfish love of country which inspired Colonel Roosevelt."[14] Using a religious format to honor the dead hero, public schools held required memorial services which included the singing of "Onward Christian Soldiers" and having students recite TR's sayings.[15] An estimated 110 million people joined in the liturgical celebration of the TR memorial week ceremonies.[16]

In the months and years after his death, TR's followers also expressed their personal sense of loss in religious terms. One man recalled in TR a "deep fund of simple spiritual energy."[17] The naturalist John Burroughs, remembering TR's thundering moralism, said: "In his presence one felt that the day of judgment might come at any moment."[18] Echoing the same language of spiritual homage, William Allen White likened TR to an "Old Testament prophet... expounding the will of God and imploring his countrymen to obey it."[19] TR was honored in death as a Christ-like figure, a martyred "leader in a great moral revival."[20]

The loss of their revered hero was sometimes lessened because some followers believed TR would live on. Herbert Knox Smith wrote that TR "always will be, living or dead, my chief leader and spiritual commander."[21] Many felt the same disbelief voiced by Burroughs when he confessed he had trouble accepting the fact of TR's death because he "must have unconsciously felt that his power to live was unconquerable."[22] Because so many believed that his "conception of service to the State was a religion," TR's disciples drew comfort from the belief that even in death TR would still be "a steadying, cleansing, stimulating influence."[23] By summoning images of the prophets, the day of judgment, spiritual rebirth, and immortality, Roosevelt's followers showed that their conception of him was built upon a religious foundation.

Other uses of language later in the history of America's remembrance of TR also carry out the same spiritual theme. In the 1950s, TR's home Sagamore Hill was opened to provide "a beacon, sending across the spiritual confusion of our time the clear beam of Theodore Roosevelt's gospel of faith, character, courage, moral standards and civic righteousness."[24] When in 1958 the nation celebrated the hundredth anniversary of TR's birth, President Eisenhowever called TR a "prophet," and a centennial commission spearheaded a nationwide celebration to rekindle "TR's influence as a spiritual force." As part of the celebration the American Bible Society sent a filmstrip about TR as a "Doer of the Word" to 50,000 churches in order to spread TR's ideas to believers throughout the nation.[25]

Courtesy of Theodore Roosevelt Birthplace National Historic Site

A group called the "Gloria Trumpeters" played at the dedication of the Theodore Roosevelt Birthplace in New York City on October 27, 1923.

The frequent use of a religious language of remembrance also suggests that in actively promoting TR's memory his disciples were trying to achieve religious ends. When TR's birthplace and his Sagamore Hill home eventually were turned into national shrines, they were intended to serve the same inspirational purposes that more explicitly religious shrines do. Memorial groups went to great trouble and expense to purchase TR's birthplace. They worked throughout the 1920s to turn the birthplace into a museum ("a national shrine to Roosevelt Americanism") and a public education center because they believed their efforts would elevate American life spiritually. The birthplace was expected to serve America as "a shrine to which many visitors will go to have their ideals of Patriotism and Liberty, of personal honor, renewed and strengthened."[26] But one shrine was not enough. In addition to his birthplace, Sagamore Hill, and his gravesite, plans for other shrines were launched, some unsuccessfully. The current site of the Jefferson Memorial in Washington, D.C., was originally intended as a TR memorial, and friends of TR tried without success to get Herald Square in Manhattan renamed Roosevelt Square. Despite the fact that some memorial crusades failed, TR achieved enshrinement in many sacred spots—in the Mt. Rushmore monument, in a seventeen-foot statue on Theodore Roosevelt Island outside of Washington, D.C., in the Theodore Roosevelt National Park in North Dakota, and in a formidable equestrian statue in front of New York's American Museum of Natural History.[27]

Just as shrines have been central to America's memory of TR, the language of spiritual healing provided the rationale for memorializing TR. Each generation hoped that monuments and historic places would serve as meccas of the Roosevelt ideals to refresh and improve the public. As early as March 1919 such spiritual aims were announced by TR memorializers who hoped to build monuments, museums, and a journal to spread "the truth about Roosevelt" in order to "make his life an example to posterity, in a manner to lead men to better and cleaner lives, and for the education and uplift of humanity."[28] Later generations of believers would view the perpetuation of TR's memory as a cure for the ills of their own times, too. During the Cold War when "the American home" was "being subjected to unprecedented strains," some Americans looked to TR's home and the example of his family life at Sagamore Hill to serve as a "national shrine that shall dramatize the highest traditions of American family life."[29]

Books of his quotations would be sold at TR shrines as inspiration to young people to uphold his beliefs, and missionaries for TR would uplift the public by bringing them in contact with his message of hope, duty, democracy, patriotism, and familial renewal from the hallowed walks of Sagamore Hill. Sagamore Hill was preserved to become "a shrine in the deepest sense of the word, where Americans of all ages and conditions may, in a time of fear and violence, find inspiration to renew allegiance to those principles of government, those standards of individual and national conduct, which are the foundations of western civilization."[30] While the specific prescription for religious renewal changed with each generation, the recurring pattern never altered—homage to TR and a quest for inspiration and cure through his powers.

Sacred language, the building of shrines, and the quest for religious healing point toward a religious meaning in the TR symbol, as does the fact that TR's followers acted the part of faithful disciples. TR's closest followers responded to his death as disciples would respond to the death of any great religious leader. They met during the mourning period to assess the eternal meaning of their lost leader. They reaffirmed his beliefs and vowed to carry on his work by creating a new organization, the Roosevelt Memorial Association. Then the disciples used that organization to seek new converts and to spread his beliefs. Those familiar with the history of the Roosevelt Memorial Association (RMA) will recognize that to characterize its founders as disciples is accurate. The leaders of the RMA set as their purpose the perpetuation of "the memory of Theodore Roosevelt for the benefit of the people of the United States of America and the world."[31] Disciples like Hermann Hagedorn would devote much of their professional careers and talents to keeping alive TR's memory. Magnates like William Boyce Thompson would donate large chunks of their fortune to support such memorializing efforts. Loyalists who had been referred to as TR's "incense swingers" during his presidency readily joined this new crusade.

TR's disciples soon created rituals that structured in sacred forms the process of remembering TR. From 1921 to the 1940s the band of faithful made an annual pilgrimage on the anniversary of his death to TR's grave and then held a meeting to recall his words and teachings. Edwin Van Valkenberg, the editor of the Philadelphia *North American*, proposed the ritual of the pilgrimage to other disciples because Roosevelt's

> principles of universal righteousness and virile progressive Americanism are a sacred creed to which they give devout adherence. With a fitting sense of reverence we assert that the teachings of Theodore Roosevelt are as essential to the normal, moral life of a nation as the laws of Mount Sinai are to the normal, moral life of man.[32]

Believing that TR had been given to America by the "same Providential guardianship which ever has guided our national destiny," the Roosevelt pilgrims believed that TR was linked to America's exceptionalism and divine purpose. In their judgment the nation had been charged with the mission of uplifting all humanity, and as the champion of that sacred errand TR defended "the same democracy taught by the Carpenter of Nazareth nineteen centuries ago."[33]

Leaderless they were still devout. TR's widow Edith Kermit Roosevelt joined them in the ritual pilgrimage to TR's grave until she became too frail to make the trip in 1942. Often after the visit to TR's burying place, she would invite the faithful back to Sagamore Hill to revel in the past and in memories of her husband.[34] For Roosevelt loyalists the pilgrimages were a trip to the holy land, an occasion to "draw from this hallowed spot renewed faith" and a "solemn reaffirmation of devotion" to TR.[35]

The pilgrimages made by these devoted followers were not the only such rituals of remembrance. Organized spiritual pilgrimages by groups to TR's grave have continued into the late twentieth century. Although the Bull Moosers are gone, the Masons, war veterans, the Navy's Fleet Reserve, and the local public schools still combine reverence for God, country, and TR in their regular pilgrimages.[36] The ritual practice of visits to TR's grave as a sacred place for spiritual renewal was first widely publicized during TR's birthday week commemoration in 1919. A "Roosevelt flag" without stars became the central symbol in this complex statewide ritual. Beginning at the Wilcox mansion in Buffalo where TR had been sworn in as president, relay runners, mostly Boy Scouts, carried the "Roosevelt flag" to forty-eight historic places across the state where patriotic parades awaited them. At each historic site five young girls who were "descended from heroes of the nation's wars" sewed a star on the flag. Almost two months after the zig-zagging thousand mile trip began, the runners joined in a solemn ceremony at which the completed flag was laid to rest on TR's grave in Oyster Bay on his birthday.[37]

Reverence for TR as a spiritual symbol in American culture has rarely been confined to his disciples. At one time a million Americans belonged to the Roosevelt Memorial Association, evidence that outside Roosevelt's personal following many Americans saw the value in organized homage to TR.[38] When the RMA raised a memorial fund for TR, it chose to aim for modest donations in order to include admirers from all walks of life. The public outpouring of support for the RMA call for funds was overwhelming: $1,753,696 in $1 and $5 contributions poured in.[39] Each year since his death thousands to tens of thousands have journeyed to TR's shrines, an informal pilgrimage which further signifies lasting mass veneration for Roosevelt.

Even during periods of lessened popularity for TR, his usefulness as a spiritual symbol persisted. In the 1930s the National Re-Dedication movement, the brain-child of the RMA, brought together the American Federation of Labor, the National Grange, the Boy and Girl Scouts, the Camp Fire Girls, the National Council of Christians and Jews, and the Federal Council of Churches to create a mass "moral rearmament" movement. TR was used as a central symbol to "take the leadership of a national effort to revitalize the nation's faith in democracy and to rebuild the moral and spiritual values."[40] Even today TR is remembered for his spiritual leadership outside the circle of active memorializers. The original RMA has been renamed the Theodore Roosevelt Association, and the new organization, more pluralistic and scholarly, attests through its publications and growing membership to the fact that public reverence for TR as a moral and spiritual symbol lives on.

By tracing the religious undercurrents running through America's memory of TR, we have found evidence that religious customs and language structured that memory, and religious motives undergirded efforts to preserve TR shrines and to build mass movements in his name. When these religious undercurrents in America's memory of TR are assessed in the larger context of American cultural history, they do not stand out as oddities. Rather they flow from the main currents of U.S. history—from the utopian and messianic roots and from the long-standing links between religious and political issues in the American mind. America has been called "the nation with the soul of a church" because these religious currents have overflowed with such regularity into other areas of national life.[41] America's memory of TR provides historians with a classic case study in the interpenetration of religion and politics throughout U.S. history.

Just as America has a long history of blending religion and politics, the preservation of political icons of the past has often been justified in sacred terms. Even before TR, Americans were building memorials and promulgating the teachings of presidents and other political leaders in hopes of revitalizing democracy and teaching current generations virtues cherished in the past. This utopian goal of moral and patriotic uplift gave the historic preservation movement its start. This movement began before the Civil War with the preservation of George Washington's home Mount Vernon and his Revolutionary headquarters at Newburgh, New York. Washington's memorializers used the same religious language employed by the RMA to claim that their shrine would exert "moral influence" on the public and rekindle its flagging patriotism. Thus, in words similar to the ones used later by TR memorializers, Washington was honored as a "Christlike liberator" and Mount Vernon as "a patriotic mecca."[42] As the political and the holy blur together, religious patterns of remembrance have shaped America's memories of many of its presidents.

Preservationists who honored past heroes often believed that their generation had suffered a declension or loss of fundamental belief in political or moral values. This loss created a need for instruction and reform. In the eyes of preservationists, the sacred visit to the source of high political ideals would have a refreshing effect on the pilgrim and would spread eventual renewal throughout the society. Icons of the past displayed in a museum would purify and cure the present. Roosevelt memorializers who wanted to preserve TR's birthplace and Sagamore Hill shared with many other American preservationists "an almost mystical belief in the transforming power of the house museum."[43] This utopian-preservationist impulse, of which the restorers of TR's birthplace are early representatives, had many precedents. Preservationists inherited the same faith that had inspired the rural cemetery movement and public parks movement—a faith that citizens could be educated and uplifted by visiting sacred public preserves. While nature would be the teacher in some cases and the homes of heroes in others, reviving democracy and promoting spiritual revival were the aims of all the early movements for the creation of sacred public preserves.[44] Yet the movements diverged in emphasis. Parks and the preservation of open expanses of untouched nature appealed to the romantics, while those who preserved presidents' homes sought patriotic renewal through communion with the past.

When TR's memorializers defined his memory as the highest repository of spirituality and Americanism, they were partaking of a long American tradition observed by Alexis de Tocqueville in the early nineteenth century when he wrote that "religious zeal is perpetually warmed in the United States by the fires of patriotism."[45] However, the religious and patriotic fires of America's memories of presidents have burned much brighter since the 1890s. Patriotism itself became almost a religious cause in the hands of veterans' groups and organized hereditary societies such as the Sons and Daughters of the American Revolution. By promoting the belief that American institutions were in danger of neglect or corruption due to the influx of the new immigrants, the patriotism lobby added to many Americans' sense of emergency about preserving and protecting their sacred past.[46] By the time of TR's death, therefore, presidential memorializing in many patriots' eyes needed to serve the added function of promoting Americanization and moral instruction.[47]

No doubt some of TR's early memorializers, as a result, felt a great sense of urgency because of their belief in the precarious status of American institutions and because TR's initial memorials were started just as aroused wartime nationalism was being channeled into the Red Scare of 1919-20. When the Woman's Roosevelt Memorial Association began restoration of TR's birthplace, they received a letter from a recovering World War I veteran which said that "I believe that in restoring his birthplace and in attempting to teach American ideals to our young Americans of foreign parentage, the women of America are doing a great national service in nipping Bolshevism in the bud."[48] Patriotic urgency coupled with the perception of foreign and domestic threats to democratic institutions have increased America's tendency toward sacred forms of presidential memorialization in the twentieth century. Of course, patriotic urgency also brought with it critics. Recent presidents like TR have been more affected by an atmosphere of conflict over the uses of their memories because a climate of heightened religious and patriotic sentiment has provoked partisan conflict and competition between memorializers.

While it is crucial to recognize what TR and his memorializers have in common with other presidents and their memorial movements, it would be a mistake to overemphasize the similarities. TR should not be dismissed as a cultural symbol who is identical to other presidents. He is not. America's memory of TR is unique because he was an important precedent-shattering president. He also played a more active role as a cultural reformer than most presidents do. His presidential behavior invited eventual religious memorialization because he used the White

House as a "bully pulpit" so often. As president he stepped outside of the political arena often—preaching a full baby carriage, duty to country, the remasculinization of American culture, both cultural and political nationalism, and a host of other causes. In his books, articles, and speeches, he sermonized about the need to uphold Victorian morality and to resist ominous modernist social trends like divorce and childlessness. In short, he became a cultural spokesman for resurgent Victorian morality and a religiously inspired sense of public service and reform. In 1912 he played the role of religious savior as he stood at Armageddon and battled for the Lord in the Bull Moose campaign. As president and cultural spokesman, TR stood near the center of a diffuse reform movement we know as progressivism—which in retrospect we see was a highly religiously charged movement. Progressivism has in recent years been reinterpreted as the Third Great Awakening, a time when a revival of religious spirit spilled over into the political arena just as it did with antebellum reform.[49] Believers in the "progressive ethos" cherished "a religious or quasi-religious vision of democracy."[50] If religion dwells at the core of progressivism, we know who its high priest was—Theodore Roosevelt. Therefore, because TR has a deeper religious and cultural significance than most presidents, he is a better candidate for inspiring religious memorialization than most other presidents.

As TR's meaning in American cultural history comes into focus, the strong religious hues should not be allowed to dominate the whole spectrum of TR's meanings. Religious uses of TR are primarily found in formal memorializations and in expressions in the realm of political culture. Since America's memory of TR is much larger than that, in many other areas of the culture the TR symbol stands for other things. At the outset, TR was defined as a multivocal cultural symbol, and as such he gives voice to many divergent cultural impulses. Within contemporary popular culture—in cartoons, ads, and movies, for example—TR appears most often in secular guise.

In popular culture TR has often embodied the enthusiasm in his old campaign song "There'll be a Hot Time in the Old Town Tonight." It is not TR's spiritual meaning, but his flamboyance and effusiveness that crop up caricatured in movies such as *Arsenic and Old Lace* and *The Wind and the Lion*. The most pervasive example of the TR symbol's diffusion into American culture has no religious content at all. America's deeply affectionate cultural attachment to the TR symbol can also be found in millions of American homes: teddy bears are everywhere. They have been popular since they became famous during his presidency. Ever since the original hunting incident which gave stuffed bears TR's name, teddy bears have merged the Winnie-the-Pooh toy bear with the personal warmth of TR. Theodore Roosevelt is the only president remembered as being sufficiently playful and huggable to become the basis of a best-selling child's toy. In general, TR's symbolic appearance in popular culture has taken on affectionate and humorous forms, while political culture has used him more reverentially and instrumentally as a tool for later political agendas.

America's memory of TR is a fascinating hodge-podge, a mixture of religious and secular, reverent and irreverent uses. Today TR reverberates so well with current American culture that he simultaneously appears in a sacred place in the Cabinet room of George Bush's White House and as the source of popular entertainment in a Broadway play.[51] TR's widow wrote that her husband in death had turned into "a conglomerate of Santa Claus and a tribal deity."[52] Certainly ample evidence points to TR functioning as a "deity" in American culture, as well as a flexible all-purpose "Santa Claus" figure in popular culture. TR still earns high ratings both for his entertainment value and his religious meaning.

NOTES

The author gratefully acknowledges the assistance of John A. Gable and Wallace F. Dailey for their help in the research stage and E. Anthony Rotundo in the writing stage of this work.

1. It should be noted at the outset that there is a major difference in America's response to TR while he was living and its response since his death. I discussed some of the ways TR consciously appealed to the "charisma-hunger" of the public in Kathleen Dalton, "Why America Loved Teddy Roosevelt: Or, Charisma is in the Eyes of the Beholders," in *Our Selves/Our Past: Psychological Approaches to American History*, ed. Robert J. Brugger (Baltimore, MD: Johns Hopkins University Press, 1981), pp. 269–91. See also Lewis L. Gould, "The Price of Fame: Theodore Roosevelt as a Celebrity, 1909–1919," *Lamar Journal of the Humanities* 10 (Fall 1984): 7–18.

2. Collective memories help a society see itself as continuous with the past and worthwhile because of such ties with the past. Memories change according to changed historical circumstances.

According to David Thelen, "If we change the way we think about the world, we automatically update memories to reflect our new understanding." David Thelen, "Memory and American History," *Journal of American History* 75 (March 1989): 1,120.

3. Victor Turner, "Encounter with Freud: The Making of a Comparative Symbolist," in *The Making of Psychological Anthropology,* ed. George D. Spindler (Berkeley: University of California Press, 1978), p. 573.

4. Speech by David Reed, Middlesex Club, *Roosevelt Night,* Hotel Somerset Boston, October 27, 1923, Theodore Roosevelt Collection, Houghton Library, Harvard University (hereafter cited as TRC-HU); Calvin Coolidge, *The Price of Freedom: Speeches and Addresses* (New York: Charles Scribners' Sons, 1924); Geoffrey C. Ward, *A First-Class Temperament: The Emergence of Franklin Roosevelt* (New York: Harper and Row, 1989); Alan R. Havig, "Theodore and Franklin: F. D. R.'s Use of the Theodore Roosevelt Image, 1920–1936," *Theodore Roosevelt Association Journal* 5, no. 2 (Spring 1979): 6–10.

5. Roland Marchand, *Advertising the American Dream: Making Way for Modernity, 1920–1940* (Berkeley: University of California Press, 1985), p. xix.

6. Marchand, *Advertising,* p. xvii.

7. Interview, John A. Gable, Oyster Bay, NY, April 28, 1987.

8. Dalton, "Why America Loved," p. 270.

9. James B. Diggs, "Theodore Roosevelt: The Voice of America," *An Address Delivered January 12, 1919, at Roosevelt Memorial Exercises,* Tulsa, OK.

10. Frederick C. Bartlett, *Remembering: A Study in Experimental and Social Psychology* (Cambridge, England: Cambridge University Press, 1932) quoted in Fred Davis, *Yearning for Yesterday: A Sociology of Nostalgia* (New York: The Free Press, 1979), p. 122.

11. Warren G. Harding, *Theodore Roosevelt: The Most Courageous American,* pamphlet, An Address delivered before the Ohio Legislature, January 29, 1919, Theodore Roosevelt Papers, Manuscript Division, George Arents Research Library at Syracuse University.

12. Americanization Day in the Indiana Public Schools on October 24, 1919, (Indiana State Board of Education, 1919), TRC-HU; Dr. Henry Waldo Coe, "Roosevelt and Patriotism," *Medical Sentinel,* November 1919, TRC-HU; *Theodore Roosevelt: Fighter for Social Justice,* Roosevelt Memorial Association film, 1934, Theodore Roosevelt Association Film Collection, Library of Congress, Washington, DC.

13. Archibald B. Roosevelt, compiler, *Theodore Roosevelt on Race, Riots, Reds, Crime* (Metairie, LA: Sons of Liberty, 1968); John A. Gable, "The Historiography of Theodore Roosevelt," at an Exhibition/Conference at the Lyndon B. Johnson Library, Austin, Texas, October 1984.

14. "Americanization Day in the Schools of New Mexico in Memory of Theodore Roosevelt," October 24, 1919, in the *Bulletin of the State Board of Education of New Mexico* 5, no. 111 (September 1919): 7.

15. "Americanization Day in the Indiana Public Schools"; *Roosevelt Day*, October 27, 1919, Roosevelt Memorial Week (Charleston, WV: Roosevelt Memorial Associaton, 1919); Roosevelt Memorial Association, "Annual Report," 1926, typescript, TRC-HU; *Standard Plan of Campaign Organization For Use of the Campaign Committee in the Local Community*, TRC-HU.

16. Hermann Hagedorn, "Was Roosevelt Week a Success?" *The American Review of Reviews*, 1919, pp. 483–84.

17. Royal Cortissoz, "The Heart of TR," *New York Herald*, August 10, 1924, clipping enclosed in letter to Edith Kermit Roosevelt, August 12, 1924, Derby Papers, TRC-HU.

18. Letter from John Burroughs to Major G. H. Putnam in *Theodore Roosevelt*, Memorial Addresses Delivered Before the Century Association, February 9, 1919, Resolutions adopted February 9, 1919 (New York: Printed for the Century Association, 1919), p. 59.

19. William Allen White, "Foreword," *Theodore Roosevelt Cyclopedia* (New York: Roosevelt Memorial Association, 1940), p. vii; Dalton, "Why America Loved"; Cover, "Where Have All the Heroes Gone?" *Newsweek*, August 6, 1979.

20. *Theodore Roosevelt*, Delivered by Herbert S. Hadley at a Memorial Meeting of the Churches of Boulder, Colo., January 12, 1919, p. 2.

21. Herbert Knox Smith to Anna Roosevelt Cowles, January 14, 1919, TRC-HU.

22. Dalton, "Why America Loved," p. 290, n. 85.

23. Joseph S. Auerbach, *Theodore Roosevelt*, A Memorial Meeting of the Republican Club, p. 23; Guy Emerson to Edith Kermit Roosevelt, January 6, 1919, Derby Papers, TRC-HU.

24. Roosevelt Memorial Associaton, "Statement of Purpose," appeared in the *Oyster Bay Enterprise-Pilot*, March 29, 1951, reprinted in Gary G. Roth, "The Roosevelt Memorial Association and the Preservation of Sagamore Hill, 1919–1953," M. A. thesis, May 1980, Wake Forest University, pp. 180 (hereafter cited as "RMA"); John A. Gable, "The Theodore Roosevelt Association: A History of a Historical Society," (unpublished paper).

25. *Final Report of the Theodore Roosevelt Centennial Commission*, Relating to a Celebration of the Hundredth Anniversary of the Birth of Theodore Roosevelt 1858–1958, Senate Document #36, 86th Cong. (Washington, DC: Government Printing Office, 1959), pp. 4, 167, 11.

26. William Roscoe Thayer to Corinne Roosevelt Robinson, January 5, 1921, in *The Letters of William Roscoe Thayer*, ed. Charles Downer Hazen (Boston: Houghton Mifflin Co., 1926), p. 402.

27. Memo from Hermann Hagedorn to Members of the Executive Committee of the Roosevelt Memorial Association, February 19, 1925, James R. Garfield, Jr., Papers, Library of Congress; Hermann Hagedorn and Gary R. Roth, *Sagamore Hill: An Historical Guide* (Oyster Bay, NY: Theodore Roosevelt Association, 1977).

28. Russell J. Coles speech, *Theodore Roosevelt*, Memorial Meeting at the Explorers' Club, March 1, 1919 (privately printed), p. 12.

29. Memorandum, Prepared by the Trustees of the Roosevelt Memorial Association in Connection with the Proposal to Purchase Sagamore Hill and to Establish it as a National Shrine, reprinted in Roth, "RMA," pp. 153–55.

30. Roosevelt Memorial Association, Statement of Purpose, appeared in the *Oyster Bay Enterprise-Pilot*, March 29, 1951, reprinted in Roth, "RMA," p. 180.

31. Minutes, Roosevelt Memorial Association, 1919–1921, in Theodore Roosevelt Association offices, Oyster Bay, NY; John A. Gable, "The Theodore Roosevelt Association: A Brief History," *Theodore Roosevelt Association Newsletter*, August 1974, pp. 5–8.

32. *The Roosevelt Pilgrimage of 1922*, Being a Record of the Pilgrimage of Certain Friends of Theodore Roosevelt to his Grave and to his Home, on the Third Anniversary of His Death (privately printed, 1922), p. xiv.

33. Ibid., p. xv.

34. Sylvia Jukes Morris, *Edith Kermit Roosevelt: Portrait of a First Lady* (New York: Coward, McCann, and Geoghegan, 1980), p. 452.

35. Van Valkenberg clipping from *North American*, December 28, 1921, in Garfield Papers, Library of Congress; Alan R. Havig, "Presidential Images, History and Homage: Memorializing Theodore Roosevelt, 1919–1967," *American Quarterly* 30 (Fall 1978): 514–32.

36. "TR Masonic Pilgrimages," *Theodore Roosevelt Association Journal*, 4, no. 3 (Summer 1978), p. 6.

37. *Whole Nation Honors Memory of Roosevelt*, Roosevelt Memorial Association film, Theodore Roosevelt Association Film Collection, Library of Congress; Hagedorn, "Was Roosevelt Week a Success?" pp. 483–84.

38. Hagedorn, ibid., pp. 483–84.

39. Roosevelt Memorial Association, "Annual Report," 1926, typescript, TRC-HU.

40. Roosevelt Memorial Association, "Annual Reports," 1937–1940, typescript; plans in 1937 report and results in 1940, TRC-HU; and RMA pamphlet, "The Torch of Theodore Roosevelt," in TRC-HU.

41. G. K. Chesterton quoted on p. 22 in Joseph Gordon Stapleton, "Theodore Roosevelt: Theologian of America's New Israel Concept" (Ph.D. diss., Temple University, 1973). See Cushing Strout, *The New Heavens and New Earth: Political Religion in America* (New York: Harper and Row, 1974); Sidney Mead, "The Nation with the Soul of a Church," *Church History* 36, no. 3 (September 1967): 262–83; Robert N. Bellah, "Civil Religion in America," *Daedalus* 96 (Winter 1967): 1–21; Gerald M. Platt and Rhys H. Williams, "Religion, Ideology and Electoral Politics," *Society* 25, no. 5 (July/August 1988): 38–45; Martin E. Marty, *The Irony of It All 1893–1919*, vol. 1 of *Modern American Religion* (Chicago: University of Chicago Press, 1986).

42. Charles B. Hosmer, Jr., *Presence of the Past: A History of the Preservation Movement in the United States Before Williamsburg* (New York: G. P. Putnam's Sons, 1965), pp. 9, 41. See also Karal Ann Marling, *George Washington Slept Here: Colonial Revivals and American Culture 1876–1986* (Cambridge: Harvard University Press, 1988).

43. Roth, "RMA," p. 144.

44. Barbara Rotundo, "A Cheerful Light: A History of Mount Auburn Cemetery," mss., Mount Auburn Cemetery; see also the chapter on "Crusades for Beauty," in Neil Harris, *The Artist in American Society: The Formative Years 1790–1860* (Chicago: University of Chicago Press, 1982). For other examples of American culture's hope that monuments, parks, gardens, and even rural cemeteries would provide spiritual and democratic uplift, see David Schuyler, *The New Urban Landscape: The Redefinition of City Form in Nineteenth-Century America* (Baltimore: Johns Hopkins University Press, 1986).

45. Tocqueville quoted in Strout, *New Heavens*, p. 249.

46. Wallace Evan Davies, *Patriotism On Parade: The Story of Veterans' and Hereditary Organizations in America 1783–1900* (Cambridge: Harvard University Press, 1955); Merle Curti, *The Roots of American Loyalty* (New York: Columbia University Press, 1946); Norman Hapgood, ed., *Professional Patriots* (New York: Albert and Charles Boni, 1927).

47. Ray H. Abrams, *Preachers Present Arms* (Scottsdale, PA: Herald Press, 1933), pp. 223–26; Robert K. Murray, *Red Scare: A Study in National Hysteria, 1919–1920* (New York: McGraw Hill, 1955), pp. 174–75.

48. "America Without Roosevelt Seems Different to Doughboy," *Woman's Roosevelt Memorial Bulletin*, no. 1 (December 1919): 4.

49. Ann Douglas has coined the term "remasculinization." William G. McLoughlin, *Revivals, Awakenings, and Reform: An Essay on Religion and Social Change in America, 1607–1977* (Chicago: University of Chicago Press, 1978); Robert M. Crunden, *Ministers of Reform: The Progressives' Achievement in American Civilization, 1889–1920* (New York: Basic Books, 1982); John D. Buenker, John C. Burnham, and Robert M. Crunden, *Progressivism* (Cambridge, MA: Schenkman Publishing Co., 1977).

50. Buenker, Burnham, and Crunden, *Progressivism*, p. 5.

51. R. W. Apple, Jr., "In the Capitol," *New York Times*, March 29, 1989, quoted in *Theodore Roosevelt Association Journal* 15, no. 2 (Spring 1989): 15–16.

52. Quoted in S. Morris, *Edith Kermit Roosevelt*, p. 487.

40

FDR's Use of the Symbol of TR in the Formation of his Political Persona and Philosophy

James L. Golden

Much has been written about Franklin D. Roosevelt in the past seven decades. Through these writings and assessments we have gained an understanding of the enormous fascination FDR has generated in the minds of historians, political scientists, and communication theorists. Their contributions to the literature of FDR, frequently cited by researchers in a wide variety of fields, are so well known they do not need to be recounted here. But notwithstanding the significant body of materials devoted to the study of Roosevelt's role as political leader, there are numerous aspects of his life yet to be analyzed if we are to develop a full appreciation of his leadership style. Among these challenges is the need to show in greater detail the nature of the specific forces which molded him and his ideas.

Unquestionably, Theodore Roosevelt—Franklin's fifth cousin and Eleanor's beloved uncle—had a persuasive influence, at least partially in the formation of FDR's political persona and philosophy. That TR's influence on FDR was perhaps the greatest single force in shaping his career and vision of America seems evident. From the time that young Franklin entered Groton and visited cousin Theodore's home at Oyster Bay, until he began his fourth term as president forty-eight years later, he repeatedly expressed an admiration bordering on adulation for his distant relative of the opposite political party. Indeed, on numerous occasions he noted: "He [TR] was the greatest man I ever knew."[1] In the face of these data, it is surprising that two Roosevelt scholars recently found it necessary to say: "A serious work on the impact of TR upon the personality and politics of his younger cousin has yet to be written."[2]

In tracing TR's influence on FDR, three important stages in the latter's career must be considered: (1) the early years, covering his period as a student at Groton, Harvard, and Columbia which extended from 1896 through most of the first decade of the 1900s; (2) the middle years, 1910-1920, in which he served as a New York State senator, as assistant secretary of the Navy, and as the Democratic party's candidate as vice president; and (3) his terms as governor of New York and as president, 1929-1945. These stages, chronologically considered, provide an insight into how FDR's emulation for TR evolved, and how it affected FDR's own persona and philosophy of leadership.

The Early Years, 1896–1909

What impressed FDR most in his early formative years as a student was a TR persona characterized by the cardinal virtue of courage, an appealing physical prowess and vitality, and an aura of excitement and success. Moreover, he saw in TR a man who was willing to apply his talent, energy, and cultural and social standing to a world view based on service-of-the-state. He was, in short, a brave and glamorous public servant who championed the cause of justice against the forces of evil.

With considerable pleasure Franklin wrote letters to his parents from Groton describing speeches "Cousin Theodore" delivered at the school on such compelling subjects as his experiences on the New York City Police Board and on the need for virtuous men to enter the field of politics.[3] Even though he was the only Democrat among a total of 150 students at Groton, he enthusiastically informed his parents in November 1898, "We were all wild with delight when we heard of Teddy's election" as governor of New York.[4] Two years later he wrote that "the whole school cheered when Teddy's picture was thrown on the screen."[5]

By the time Franklin graduated from Groton he was able to take with him the firmly held image of a famous cousin who had served with distinction in the state legislature, on the New York City Police Board, in the governor's mansion, in the federal government as assistant secretary of the Navy, in a cavalry brigade during the Spanish-American War as a colonel leading a charge up San Juan Hill, and in the nation's capital as vice president of the United States. These were images that would be enlarged as Franklin followed his predecessor to Harvard University.

From the outset of his undergraduate years, FDR took advantage of every opportunity to strengthen his association with TR. In the spring of 1901, for example, while serving as a reporter for the *Harvard Crimson*, he heard that the vice president would be on the campus of his alma mater. Immediately Franklin called his cousin to arrange for an interview, and was told to meet him, following a lecture he was scheduled to give the next day. Out of this telephone conversation came the following banner headline: "Vice President Roosevelt to Lecture in Government 1 this Morning at 9 in Sanders Theatre."[6] This journalistic scoop, which led to an over-capacity crowd, enhanced FDR's reputation as a reporter who had a celebated name and significant political connections.

When FDR was elected secretary of the *Crimson* during the following year, local newspapers began to emphasize his close relationship to the vice president. In some instances, he was falsely depicted as TR's nephew—a type of error often repeated in later years.[7] By the time Franklin was a junior, TR had become president. This fact contributed in part to FDR's developing interest in genealogy. The name Roosevelt gave him a feeling of pride, prompting him to associate it with the phrase: "true democratic spirit." His family, as personified by his father and by Theodore Roosevelt, was committed to the notion that they were obligated "to do voluntarily what others had to do of necessity—work—and to direct those energies outward to the community, and not into mere money making."[8] This family philosophy, discovered by FDR's genealogical search, was to have a profound influence on his subsequent political career.

FDR's Harvard years did not always meet his intellectual expectations. Often he was not stimulated by his courses, his readings, and his professors. But he enjoyed immensely his extracurricular activities, especially his six-hour days working for the *Crimson*.[9] More importantly, as a Harvard student he spent hours engaging in self reflection, and "habitually measured himself and his progress against the personality and career of his famous cousin."[10]

Shortly after leaving Harvard, FDR enrolled in the Columbia University Law School and made plans to marry his cousin (fifth cousin once removed) Eleanor whose appeal was enhanced because she also held title to the name Roosevelt. When the wedding took place in the spring of 1905, Theodore Roosevelt, then president, gave the bride away. A few months later while the couple travelled in Europe, they were treated as honored guests by world leaders because of their family connection with the president. On September 7, 1905, Franklin wrote to his mother from England: "Everyone is talking about Cousin Theodore saying that he is the most prominent figure of present day history. . . ."[11]

As FDR began his practice of law in New York City in 1907, he reflected on his future goals and aspirations. His admiration of TR had approached the level of idolatry. With the revered model of his cousin before him, he envisioned a comparable career that would parallel every stage that marked the path which Teddy had followed to the White House. It was his purpose, he told his colleagues in the law firm, to enter politics by being elected to the New York state legislature. This would be followed, he added, by being appointed assistant secretary of the Navy and by winning the governorship of New York and then the presidency.[12] Not even the smile and the half-joking manner he used in making this bold prediction could conceal FDR's strongly held belief that it was his special mission to perpetuate the Roosevelt tradition in American politics.

By the year 1909 the preparatory phase of FDR's career had ended. Now he was ready to put into practice a series of carefully calculated steps patterned after the political stages successfully employed by TR. It was during this middle period that FDR adopted a persona that bore a remarkable resemblance to the man he most earnestly wished to emulate. At times, in fact, he went too far in his efforts to imitate his illustrious cousin.

The Middle Years, 1910-1920

As the 1910 state election campaign drew near, the political climate in New York was changing. The Progressives, under the leadership of Theodore Roosevelt, had split the old-line Republican party, thereby giving the Democrats renewed hope in the state contests. It was against this background that FDR emerged as a candidate for a state senate seat from the normally Republican twenty-sixth district. There was little doubt that his selection was primarily due to a "magic name" that promised to attract supporters from both parties.[13]

Courtesy of Geoffrey C. Ward, Franklin and Eleanor Roosevelt Institute,
and Franklin D. Roosevelt Library

Newspaper photograph of fifth cousins Theodore Roosevelt and
Franklin D. Roosevelt, in Syracuse, New York, May 4, 1915, published
in the *Syracuse Journal*, May 5, 1915. The photograph was recently
discovered by Geoffrey D. Ward. Franklin D. Roosevelt was in Syracuse
to testify on TR's behalf in the Barnes libel trial. Republican boss William
Barnes, Jr. unsuccessfully sued TR for libel when the former president
charged that Barens worked in collusion with the Tammany Hall
Democrats. FDR testified as a Democrat confirming TR's assertions. TR
was at this time the leader of the Progressive Party, and FDR was
assistant secretary of the Navy in Woodrow Wilson's administration.

For a period of several months in 1910, FDR could be seen in his red Maxwell automobile touring the large district he hoped to represent. In small towns and wayside places he stopped up to six times a day to deliver speeches to appreciative audiences.[14] His rhetorical strategy adhered to a consistent pattern. Often he began his remarks with the familiar phrase "My friends," and then proceeded to say: "I am not Teddy." Amidst laughter he would then tell one of his favorite campaign anecdotes: "A little shaver said to me the other day that he knew I wasn't Teddy—I asked him why and he replied, 'Because you don't show your teeth.'"[15] The fact of the matter was, however, that he frequently did bare his teeth in a manner reminiscent of TR;[16] and, moreover, he was inclined to use a term then closely identified with his cousin—the word "bully."[17]

The content of FDR's speeches stressed such issues as farm problems, the preservation of natural resources, and civic virtue. But the subject which commanded his greatest attention was the need to eliminate or curtail political corruption and "bossism." In emphasizing these topics, the candidate made it easy for many Republicans to strike "a blow for Teddy" even while voting for FDR.[18] When the campaign was over, he "won by a margin of 1,140 votes of 32,000 cast, running ahead of the ticket."[19]

Almost immediately following his installation as a member of the senate, FDR sought to carry out the promises he had made throughout the campaign regarding the debilitating practice of "bossism." Assuming the role of leader of an insurgent movement, comprised of twenty-one Democratic lawmakers who wished to assert their independence, he set for himself the task of blocking the nomination of William Sheehan, Tammany Hall's hand-picked candidate for the U.S. Senate.[20] Not only was he successful in his courageous endeavor in the New York senate but he and his collaborators helped to rivet "the attention of the entire country on Capitol Hill."[21] One of the Tammany regulars noted that FDR had caused trouble faster in the legislature than had TR when he was a member of the assembly.[22]

With his newly developed celebrity status, reinforced by his TR connection, FDR became a favorite theme for newspaper copy. On January 22, 1911, he was interviewed by a *New York Times* correspondent who wanted to probe the TR relationship. The reporter asked, "Have you heard from your uncle-in-law? "No," observed FDR. "But I will hear from him some time when this is over. I have no doubt. I am sure that any fight for principle would have his blessing and approval."[23] FDR proved to be correct in his prediction. A short while later a letter arrived from TR saying: "We are all proud of the way you handled yourself. Good luck to you!"[24]

During his brief tenure in the New York senate, FDR never wavered in his devotion to his famous relative. When asked, for example, whether or not he was an admirer of TR, he confidently noted, "Why, who can help but admire him? I differ with him on a great many questions, but they are the differences between men who both are seeking to do their best for the public good. . . ."[25]

These types of praise so often articulated by FDR sometimes made an indelible imprint on the minds of those who heard him speak. The following example is typical. More than three decades after her introduction to her future boss, who then was a state senator, Frances Perkins recalled hearing FDR give "a spirited defense" of TR to a group of critics who had scorned his "progressive" ideas.[26]

The foregoing description suggests that as a state senator FDR had developed a persona largely derived from the example of TR. From his predecessor he had learned with telling force the value of independence, the risks and rewards resulting from courageous acts based on perceived justice, the persuasive power of image politics, and the importance of a particular position and timing. It was for these reasons that he challenged the Tammany leaders who followed a policy of "bossism," came down hard on the side of the farmers, expressed his belief in protecting the environment, and nurtured his family ties with TR as well as the vocabulary associated with his name.

The second significant event of the middle years began in 1912. In FDR's victorious reelection campaign for the state senate, he supported Woodrow Wilson's candidacy for the presidency. This fact, along with the national fame he had achieved as an insurgent leader with a glamorous name, caught the fancy of Josephus Daniels, Wilson's newly appointed secretary of the Navy. When Daniels asked FDR to serve as assistant secretary, the response was couched in the language of TR, "I'd like it bully well."[27]

When FDR accepted this position in the Wilson administration, he took comfort in knowing that he would be able to continue his quest to pursue the role of

servant-to-the-state. He was similarly pleased to know that this
new assignment met with the approval of TR who wrote:

> Dear Franklin: I was very much pleased that you were
> appointed as Assistant Secretary of the Navy. It is interesting
> to see that you are in another place which I myself once held.
> I am sure you will enjoy yourself to the full . . . and that you
> will do capital work.[28]

On a more mundane level, FDR was proud to learn that he
would be assigned the desk once held by his cousin. One day as
he sat at his desk during Daniels's absence, he told reporters with
an attitude of mock seriousness: "There's a Roosevelt on the job
today.... You remember what happened the last time a Roosevelt
occupied a similar position."[29]

As the seven years FDR spent in Washington unfolded, the
pervasive influence of the image he had of TR was a consuming
reality. It was the principal driving force, for instance, that led to
the assistant secretary's flamboyant decision to introduce a
rigorous physical fitness program for all new navy personnel,
and to place himself in dangerous combat situations that went
beyond the boundary of reasonableness. Moreover, it stimulated
him to hold clandestine meetings with his chauvinistic cousin for
the purpose of providing him with damaging information on our
country's lagging state of preparedness and to testify on TR's
behalf during the Barnes Libel Trial in 1915.[30]

Finally, at TR's urging, FDR sought without success on
several occasions to resign from his administrative office in order
to volunteer to be an enlisted man. Such bravado was in keeping
with TR's own attempts in 1917 to gain permission to lead an
expeditionary force in Europe, but it did little to persuade Wilson
who wanted to bring the war to an end as rapidly as possible.[31]

FDR's term as assistant secretary, it would appear, reflected
TR's preoccupation with patriotism, military victories brought
about by physical prowess and courage, and bold
decision-making relying on contingency plans. On many of the
issues relating to World War I, observes one authority, FDR "was
a Rooseveltian in the Wilson camp."[32]

But this experience in the Navy Department had an
additional meaning for FDR. It represented to him the important
fact that he had successfully completed stage two in his purpose
to reach his ultimate goal by traversing the road travelled by his
cousin. His next venture, as we shall now observe, was to seek

the office of the vice presidency—a position which had launched TR into the White House.

Following FDR's selection in July as vice presidential candidate to run on the Democratic ticket with Governor James M. Cox in 1920, commentators were quick to observe that his primary appeal was his "attractive personality, his relationship to the other Roosevelt, his opposition to Tammany, his Progressivism," and his tendency to display "the courage of his convictions."[33] All of these traits now used to describe the Democratic nominee were virtues that FDR had attributed to TR during the previous two decades. It was difficult to resist the practice of drawing comparisions between the careers of the two Roosevelts. A *New York Times* reporter, for example, after pointing out the remarkable parallel in the careers of the two Roosevelts, noted that FDR "is a candidate for vice president four years younger than Theodore Roosevelt when he was chosen to run with McKinley."[34]

Because of this striking parallel and the enduring appeal of TR in the western portion of the nation,[35] FDR was asked to tour that region in August for the specific end of persuading Republican progressives and independents, many of whom had supported the Bull Moose campaign in 1912. Accepting this challenge with enthusiasm, he opened the western campaign with a speech in Chicago on August 11 before an estimated crowd of 3,000 people. In this address he invoked the name of TR, calling him a "great American leader" who "marched with the times." He then moved to the central thrust of his message: "Make possible in the future a restoration of the Republicanism of Lincoln and Roosevelt. . . ."[36] This linking of TR with America's foremost president became a trademark of some of Roosevelt's speeches and letters as president.

FDR's pointed attempt to win Republican votes by both overtly and covertly identifying himself with his cousin created a strong negative response on the part of Colonel Robert McCormick, the conservative owner of the *Chicago Daily Tribune.* In an editorial entitled "The One Half of One Per Cent Roosevelt," the Colonel ridiculed the notion that the vice presidential candidate was "another Teddy." "If he is," he said tauntingly, "then Billy Sunday is a Mormon . . . Elihu Root is Gene Debs, and [William Jennings] Bryan is a brewer."[37]

Nor did Republican enthusiasts limit their efforts to disassociate the two Roosevelts to newspaper attacks. They persuaded Lt. Colonel Theodore Roosevelt, Jr., to follow FDR on his speaking tour in the West to counteract the possible notion that the latter would be perceived to be the son and legitimate heir to his political mantle.[38]

This confusion concerning FDR's relationship to TR was a persistent source of resentment for the Oyster Bay Roosevelts. Not only were they disturbed with the tendency on the part of many members of the electorate to regard FDR as TR's son, but with the voters' occasional view that FDR was TR himself. Commenting on this point, the editors of *Time* magazine observed that "many a backcountryman was said to have voted in 1932 under the impression that he was again voting for Teddy Roosevelt...."[39]

Despite these efforts to brand FDR as a Roosevelt in name only, he persevered in his determination to refer in glowing terms to TR, and to identify his own ideas, personality traits, and language with the philosophy and image exemplified by his cousin. He called for a "square deal" for labor in Helena, Montana,[40] and grouped TR with other memorable presidents including Washington, Lincoln, and Wilson, in a speech in Manchester, New Hampshire.[41] In late October in Cumberland, West Virginia, he gave his warmest tribute to the man who still remained his idol.

> Today is the anniversary of the birthday of Theodore Roosevelt.... I wish he were alive today. He ... had definite convictions. He was not afraid to take a position and to maintain it. He never wobbled. He never sought to evade even when members of his own party disagreed with him. To me his memory will always stand for one characteristic more than another—fair fighting.[42]

Throughout the presidential campaign FDR remained optimistic about the eventual outcome even though there were telltale signs of an impending Republican landslide. The Democratic party commitment to supporting the League of Nations ran counter to the growing isolationist sentiment resulting from America's involvement in the war. When the voters on election day cast a large majority of their ballots for Warren G. Harding, FDR, surprisingly, was not visibly disappointed. He viewed the experience as a positive one and as an important step in fulfilling TR's belief that a political leader should travel to every section of the country so that he could earn the right to be a representative of all the people rather than a spokesman for local or regional interests.

Governor and President, 1928-1945

It is clear that in the early and middle years, FDR openly sought to develop a political persona and philosophy consistent with that associated with TR. Consequently, he tried to project an image of one who was courageous, independent, patriotic, masculine, and self-confident. Moreover, like his idol, he had mapped out a strategy, as noted earlier, that would enable him to follow a series of steps leading to the White House. At times, as in the case of losing the 1920 campaign, his technique of identifying with his cousin seemed contrived and overly solicitous.[43] In the ensuing years, his approach became more mature and subtle, but his tendency to adhere to the TR model of leadership remained unusually strong.

With FDR's election as governor of New York in 1928, he had reached the third step in paralleling the career of TR. In his two terms in this office, he was a persuasive spokesman for one of his cousin's major causes—the need for conservation. So effective was he in his advocacy of this theme that President Kennedy often told his western audiences that the two Roosevelts, both from an eastern state, were our country's foremost champions of the preservation of our natural resources and the beautification of our land.[44]

It was FDR's good fortune, as Frank Freidel correctly observed, that "at the beginning of the '30s the Theodore Roosevelt legend was still in full bloom."[45] Now that a second Roosevelt had become governor of the most powerful state in the union, newspapers throughout the world began to hail him as the next Democratic presidential candidate. One foreign newspaper, anxious to show the close connection between the two men with the magic name, described the governor as TR's son.[46]

In the third year of his governorship, FDR saw the culmination of his vigorous fight to raise funds for the creation of a Theodore Roosevelt Memorial Hall at the Museum of Natural History in New York City. At the cornerstone laying, which occurred on the anniversary of TR's birth in 1931, he asserted that this was the most satisfying and exciting achievement of his gubernatorial career.[47]

In the months preceding and during the 1932 presidential campaign, FDR again held up his kinsman as a national leader to be admired and emulated. Observe, for instance, how he linked him with two of the founding fathers in a Jefferson Day Dinner speech at St. Paul, Minnesota, on April 18:

> We have had in our history three men who chiefly stand out for the universality of their interest and their knowledge—Benjamin Franklin, Thomas Jefferson and Theodore Roosevelt. All three knew at first hand every cross-current of national and international life. All three were possessed of a profound culture in the best sense of the word, and yet all three understood the yearnings and lack of opportunity, the hopes and fears of millions of their fellow beings.[48]

This bold inclusion of TR in a highly select group of culturally minded political leaders was based on his academic achievements and on his productive work as a publishing scholar.

Later in the same address, FDR quoted from the works of Jefferson, Jackson, and Lincoln. But he devoted the most space to TR by citing three extended paragraphs from one of his speeches. It would appear, therefore, that it was not always enough for FDR to link his cousin with the greatest presidents: in some cases, he singled him out as one who had a special relevance and significance for meeting the demands of the 1930s.

It is further instructive to observe another speech delivered by FDR in the 1932 contest—the famous Commonwealth Club Address presented in San Francisco in September. This presentation, regarded by many as being the foundation for the New Deal program, also contained a tribute to TR. To set the stage for his eulogy, FDR reminded his listeners to recall the unhappy period of the disappearing frontier at the end of the nineteenth century and the accompanying rise of giant industrial corporations that were concerned with financial profits more than with the economic plight of the typical citizen and the welfare of the country at large. It was at this juncture, noted FDR, that "Theodore Roosevelt, the first great Republican Progressive, fought a Presidential campaign on the issue of 'trust busting' and talked freely about malefactors of great wealth."[49]

Meanwhile on the eve of the election and during the interim period in which he was waiting to be inaugurated, FDR wrote letters defending the purity of TR's character and acknowledging the support he had given to his Republican relative when he was running for office. To Cousin Leontine he said on November 2, 1932, "My first Presidential vote, though I was a Democrat, went to Cousin Theodore in 1904."[50] This confession regarding his 1904 vote was repeated often in subsequent years for the purpose of demonstrating the importance of political independence and the need to place the national interest above party loyalty.

The New York State Theodore Roosevelt Memorial Hall of the American Museum of Natural History, located on Central Park West, New York City, was dedicated by President Franklin D. Roosevelt on January 19, 1936. In his speech at the dedication, FDR declared: "Everything about him was big and vital, and above all national. He was able to see great problems in their true perspective, because he looked at the nation as a whole. There was nothing narrow or local or sectional about that man. . . . We know and the nation knows and yes, the world knows, that Theodore Roosevelt was a great patriot and a great soul."

One of the most significant features of the twelve years FDR occupied the White House was his constant reliance on the TR model of leadership.[51] This model upheld the notion that a president must be a "transcendent national leader" whose task it is to use his office as a "bully pulpit" for the moral good of all the people. One who cannot see beyond a regional boundary may be elected to a state office or to Congress, but he can never fully serve the national purpose. During his campaign for a second term in 1936, FDR told an audience in Dallas, Texas that he got the idea "to know the people" when he and Eleanor visited the White House shortly after their wedding in 1905. Following dinner, FDR noted in one of his favorite stories, TR paced a floor in the Oval Room expressing disgust with congressional leaders for their failure to pass legislation for the creation of a number of new recreational parks. "Sometimes," he said, "I wish I could be president and Congress, too." If that could happen, he added, he would make it obligatory for all high public officials to certify that "they had visited every state of the union."[52] In presenting this anecdote, FDR observed that he also endorsed the principle upon which it was based.

To be a national leader, FDR further believed, a president must, when the challenge requires it, place the interests of the country on a higher plane than the wishes of a political party. This is the mark, he said, of a transcendent leader. To illustrate this point, he asserted in a Jackson Day Dinner speech in 1938: "In these recent years the average American seldom thinks of Jefferson and Jackson as Democrats or of Lincoln and Theodore Roosevelt as Republicans; he labels each one of them according to his attitude toward the problems that confront him as President, where he was active in the affairs of government . . . ."[53] It was this Theodore Rooseveltian philosophy of leadership that gave FDR his inspiration and justification for seeking to enlarge the Supreme Court in 1937 on the grounds that the justices had ignored the national popular will; for using the "analogue of war" for combatting the Depression; and for establishing a national consensus in order to cope effectively with international crises.[54]

The TR model of governance also persuaded FDR to incorporate novelty and experimentation into his decision-making processes,[55] and to be able to stir the people not only on "profound moral issues" that are abstract and comprehensive in nature but on "specific individual events" as well.[56]

Finally as president, FDR had a compelling desire to quote from the speeches of TR for the goal of buttressing his own arguments. He also used citations, which took the form of aphorisms, to demonstrate the personality traits and leadership style of the former president. It was only reasonable, therefore, for him to urge his audience in an "Address at the Dedication of the Theodore Roosevelt Memorial" in 1936 to remember the quotations that have become an essential part of his legacy. Not the least of these phrases and statements, he observed, are the following which have worked their way into our language: "square deal," "malefactors of great wealth," "the wealthy criminal class," "the lunatic fringe," "muckraker," and "speak softly and carry a big stick."[57] These insightful descriptive words represented more to FDR than a communicator's talent for using trenchant and graphic prose. They also demonstrated something about his personality traits and his moral political philosophy.

It seems clear that Franklin D. Roosevelt, one of the most distinguished names in the history of the Democratic party, developed a persona and philosophy that reflected the overriding influence of his famous Republican predecessor who is affectionately referred to as TR. This influence, first of all, helped FDR strive to exemplify the cardinal virtues of courage, wisdom, and justice. It also imprinted upon his mind the value of civic pride and patriotism which, in turn, motivated him to put aside any desire to enhance his wealth and follow a course of action that would make it possible for him to be a servant-of-the-state. The image that was to be portrayed, therefore, was that of a bold, informed, and morally earnest leader whose altruistic spirit would be the principal guiding force for his personal life.

Another aspect of TR's model of leadership contributed significantly to the style of governance of FDR. It was the influential nature of the political philosophy and rhetorical vision that became a part of the progressive movement. In carrying out his perceived role as the guardian of TR's legacy, FDR centered his attention almost exclusively on what he regarded to be the liberal tendencies in TR's philosophy and practice.[58] He was particularly impressed with the Progressive platform adopted by the Bull Moose party in 1912, even though he himself felt constrained to support Wilson. Not to be overlooked in this connection was his appointment of former Bull Moosers to important positions in his administration.[59] With the vivid example of this type of progressivism before him, FDR implemented the Theodore Rooseveltian ideas that governmental policies must be geared to the needs of all the people; a battle plan utilizing the metaphor of war must be instituted to solve domestic problems such as the Depression and the conservation of natural resources; a national consensus, based on preparedness and anti-isolationism, must be forged to come to grips with international crises; and pragmatism should take precedence over ideology in the modern world. Under such circumstances, experimentation should be the order of the day because it alone has the flexibility to adjust to a changing society. These progressive policies and practices, according to Tugwell, led both TR and FDR to think of themselves "as saving the capitalist system by making capitalists behave. . . ."[60]

When we look back at FDR, we see a man who took pride in his heritage, who believed in the power of symbols, and who demonstrated that knowledge moves on an evolutionary plane. But, as noted throughout this study, we also see a man who sought mightily to pattern his personality and political philosophy on a distant relative he had come to admire and most earnestly wished to emulate. The fact that the two Roosevelts achieved distinction as members of opposing political parties mades FDR's heavy reliance on TR a remarkable historical phenomenon that invites further study.

NOTES

1. Otis L. Graham, Jr., and Meghan R. Wander, eds., *Franklin D. Roosevelt: His Life and Times, an Encyclopedic View* (Boston: G. K. Hall, 1985), p. 375. This point was reaffirmed in a letter from John Gable to the author, May 3, 1989.

2. Ibid., p. 375.

3. James David Barber, *Presidential Character* (Englewood Cliffs, NJ: Prentice-Hall, 1972), pp. 218–19.

4. Elliott Roosevelt, ed., *F.D.R.: His Personal Letters*, 4 vols. (New York: Duell, Sloan and Pearce, 1947), 1: 230 (hereafter cited as *Letters*).

5. Ibid., p. 379.

6. Ibid., p. 457n.

7. See ibid., p. 478.

8. Barber, *Presidential Character*, p. 221.

9. *Letters*, 1: 456.

10. Kenneth Davis, *FDR: The Beckoning of Destiny, 1882–1928* (New York: Putnam, 1972) p. 164. Also see Alan Nevins's essay, *New York Times Magazine,* October 22, 1933, p. 4.

11. *Letters,* 2: 84.

12. Graham and Wander, *Franklin D. Roosevelt,* p. 374.

13. Ibid., pp. 113 and 175.

14. W. A. Warn, "Senator Franklin D. Roosevelt, Chief Insurgent at Albany," *New York Times,* January 22, 1911, p. 11.

15. *Poughkeepsie News Press,* October 27, 1910. Cited in Frank Freidel, *Franklin D. Roosevelt: The Apprenticeship* (Boston: Little, Brown, 1952), p. 93.

16. Graham and Wander, *Franklin D. Roosevelt,* p. 375.

17. Nathan Miller, *FDR: An Intimate History* (New York: Doubleday, 1983), p. 66

18. Freidel, *The Apprenticeship,* p. 93.

19. Barber, *Presidential Character,* p. 224.

20. Warn, "Senator Franklin D. Roosevelt," p. 11.

21. Ibid.

22. Ibid.

23. Ibid.

24. Barber, *Presidential Character,* p. 225.

25. Warn, "Senator Franklin D. Roosevelt," p. 11.

26. Frances Perkins, *The Roosevelt I Knew* (New York: Viking Press, 1946), p. 47.

27. Graham and Wander, *Franklin D. Roosevelt,* p. 375.

28. Oyster Bay, March 18, 1913. Elting E. Morison, ed., *Letters of Theodore Roosevelt* (Cambridge: Harvard University Press, 1951), 8: 714.

29. *New York Sun,* cited in Freidel, *The Apprenticeship,* p. 158.

30. In commenting on the first of these two points, John Gable has noted that according to Franklin D. Roosevelt, Jr., his father was like a "mole" for TR in the Wilson administration. Letter to the author, May 3, 1989.

31. Freidel, *The Apprenticeship,* p. 301.

32. John Milton Cooper, Jr., *The Warrior and the Priest* (Cambridge: Harvard University Press, 1983), p. 348.

33. *New York Times,* July 7, 1920, p. 10.

34. Ibid.

35. Early in his career, TR had been a cowboy in North Dakota.

36. The speech was printed in the *Chicago Daily Tribune,* August 12, 1920, p. 3.

37. August 13, 1920, p. 6. Also see the *New York Times* summary of a *Helena Independent* column, August 17, 1920, p. 10.

38. *New York Times,* August 14, 1920, p. 3.

39. *Time,* January 27, 1936, p. 15.

40. "Extracts from Speech of F.D.R. at Helena, Montana," August 18, 1920, in Franklin D. Roosevelt Library, Hyde Park, NY.

41. *The Manchester Union,* September 13, 1920, pp. 1, 3, 12.

42. "Extracts from Speech of Honorable Franklin D. Roosevelt," Cumberland, West Virginia, October 27, 1920, in Franklin D. Roosevelt Library. For additional valuable information describing

FDR's 1920 campaign, see Frank Freidel, *Franklin D. Roosevelt: The Ordeal* (Boston: Little, Brown, 1954); and Ted Morgan, *FDR: A Biography* (New York: Simon and Schuster, 1985).

43. Freidel, *Franklin D. Roosevelt: The Ordeal*, pp. 80–85.

44. On at least twelve different occasions during his presidency, Kennedy praised the two Roosevelts for their significant contribution to conservation. See the *Public Papers of the Presidents of the United States: John F. Kennedy* (Washington, DC: Government Printing Office, 1961–63).

45. Frank Freidel, *Franklin D. Roosevelt: The Triumph* (Boston: Little, Brown, 1956), p. 200.

46. *Calcutta Statesman*, November 6, 1930, cited in Freidel, *Triumph*, p. 167.

47. Freidel, *Franklin D. Roosevelt: The Triumph*, p. 100.

48. Samuel I. Rosenman, ed., *The Public Papers and Addresses of Franklin D. Roosevelt*, 13 vols. (New York: Random House, 1938), 1: 628.

49. Ibid., p. 749.

50. *Letters*, 3: 304.

51. See Cooper, *The Warrior and the Priest*, p. 351.

52. *The Public Papers and Addresses of Franklin D. Roosevelt*, 5: 215. The story was repeated in modified form in a "Graduation Address at the United States Naval Academy," June 2, 1938, 7: 367.

53. Ibid., 7: 38.

54. Cooper, *The Warrior and the Priest*, pp. 349–61.

55. Ibid.

56. *Letters*, 3: 467.

57. *The Public Papers and Addresses of Franklin D. Roosevelt*, 5: 61–64.

58. FDR's inclination to ignore the conservative emphasis that was also a major part of TR's legacy was another factor responsible for a lengthy feud that often existed between the Oyster Bay Roosevelts and the Hyde Park Roosevelts. See Alan R. Havig, "Theodore and Franklin: FDR's Use of the Theodore Roosevelt Image, 1920–1936," *Theodore Roosevelt Association Journal*, 5 (Spring 1979): 8; and the speech delivered by Theodore Roosevelt, Jr., at the New York State Theodore Roosevelt Memorial Ceremony on January 19, 1936. The latter, along with other members of the family, resented FDR's belief that TR would have supported many of his New Deal policies.

59. Otis Graham, *An Encore for Reform: The Old Progressives and the New Deal* (New York: Oxford University Press, 1967), p. 7.

60. R. G. Tugwell, "The Two Great Roosevelts," *The Western Political Quarterly* 5 (March 1952): 91.

41

The Men in the Arena: Presidential Co-option of the Image of Theodore Roosevelt, 1916-1989

John Robert Greene

Each new President has the prerogative of exiling or resurrecting his predecessors—in portraiture, at least. . . . President Bush has moved out a grim Calvin Coolidge and a portly William Taft, and has installed a favorite, Theodore Roosevelt. There is already a bust of Teddy Roosevelt in the Oval Office. But Mr. Bush wanted two images of the man he admires as "a take charge kind of person."[1]

Ever since Theodore Roosevelt left the White House, many of his successors have chosen to co-opt his image in some way. All have quoted him in at least one speech. Each one of them who has left behind a set of memoirs has referred to Roosevelt, with all references favorable. One even viewed his own personality as alike to Roosevelt's, and justified several key decisions of his presidency by quoting Roosevelt on that subject.

This is by no means an insignificant set of coincidences. Only the images of Washington, Lincoln, and Franklin Roosevelt have been used more by occupants of the White House as they strive to position their own image in the minds of the public.[2] There is no other president whose words have been utilized as often when the sitting president wants to position himself as strong, self-possessed, or internationalist. This is all the more striking as several of his successors were quite violent TR haters.

It is a worthy exercise, then, to explore the extraordinary amount of exploitation of the image of Theodore Roosevelt in modern presidential politics. Through an analysis of the types of instances and situations in which this image has been co-opted, an attempt will be made to assess the use of the Roosevelt image by his successors, and analyze what this phenomenon means to a study of the modern presidency.

One must begin with an analysis of the image that many have felt was worth co-opting. However, this exercise is somewhat frustrating. The literature on presidential imagery tends to concentrate on how a public figure manipulates the popular perception of himself in the mass media.[3] Roosevelt is mentioned in virtually all of this literature, but he presents a particular problem for students of image making. While there is little question that Roosevelt understood both the intricacies and the value of modern public relations, few observers accuse him of deliberately remaking his image in order to look better in the media. Indeed, most admit the opposite—his natural personality was tailor-made for the newly emerging mass media. One must be clear, then, when speaking of a Roosevelt "image": with Roosevelt, perception was quite close to reality.

The present Roosevelt image is comprised of four component parts. The first two—his charisma and his power—are the traits most often mentioned by the general public. Roosevelt was—and for many, even after FDR, remains—the typification of positive presidential charisma. Arthur Schlesinger, in his analysis of cousin Franklin, described this view: "Theodore Roosevelt transfixed the imagination of the American middle class as did no other figure of his time. With his squeaky voice, his gleaming teeth, his overpowering grin, and his incurable delight in self-dramatization, he brought everything he touched to life . . . ."[4] Closely tied to this is the view of TR as a powerful individual. This is not meant to refer to the use of political power, a point on which all scholars agree that Roosevelt was a master, but rather the view that Roosevelt's sheer force of personality remains unmatched by his predecessors. One of John F. Kennedy's favorite catchwords to describe his presidency was "vigor"; Roosevelt lived the word, and stories abound to illustrate the point. Like so much of Roosevelt's image, it can be best illustrated by borrowing the words of biographer Edmund Morris, who noted that Roosevelt was "not unlike a piece of engineering himself. Many observers are reminded of a high-speed locomotive."[5]

To a greater or lesser extent, scholars tend to agree that these two components make up the heart of the Roosevelt image. They furthermore add two political ones. The first is the view of Roosevelt as being progressive. Whether or not Roosevelt was, in the socio-political parlance, *a* progressive is a matter open to some scholarly debate. However, with few revisionist exceptions, Roosevelt is treated in the literature as being reformative in nature, to the point of his often being inaccurately (certainly from his own point of view) described as a "liberal." The point was not lost on future presidents who wanted to be viewed in the same light. Scholars tend to put these three points together, along with others which arise from their own observations, and come to the conclusion that Theodore Roosevelt was the First Modern President. In *The Imperial Presidency*, Arthur Schlesinger, Jr., summarizes this view, as he labels the two Roosevelts and Wilson as "model presidents."[6]

This image is strong, essentially favorable and, from the point of view of his fifteen successors in office, immensely useful. In the minds of the public, who have consistently kept TR as one of their favorite presidents, all of his successors suffered in some way by comparison. Unlike TR, most of his heirs saw the need—some of them, rightfully so—to recast their image in the mass media, so as to be seen more favorably by the public. Only Franklin Roosevelt, Kennedy, and perhaps Ronald Reagan have approached TR in charisma. For sheer power of personality, none of the Colonel's successors comes close. At some point in their tenure, all would feel the need to posture themselves as a strong, charismatic leader. The value, then, of co-opting parts of TR's image was not lost on any of the men who followed him in office.

Not surprisingly, neither William Howard Taft nor Woodrow Wilson found any use for either TR or his image while in the White House. The debilitating relationship between Taft the protege, and TR the mentor, has been well documented.[7] For his part, Wilson distanced himself from TR as far as possible, assuming that he would make another run for the White House in either 1916 or 1920. Yet it was surprisingly tricky for the Republican presidents of the Roaring Twenties to use the spirit of the recently deceased (1919) TR in their favor. With his memory still fresh in the minds of the American people, neither Warren Harding nor Calvin Coolidge could have avoided praising the TR image, even if they had wanted to. Yet the newly invigorated relationship between the White House and big business made a direct parallel to "TR the Trust Buster" politically inappropriate. In a sense, then, Harding and Coolidge were caught in the middle. While as Republican presidents, they both were obligated to praise the memory of TR, the boom mentality of the period made it difficult to tie themselves too closely to his method of dealing with business.

Harding, quite typically, tried to sit on both sides of the fence at once. In deference to TR's powerful legacy, he chose Theodore Roosevelt, Jr., as his assistant secretary of the Navy.[8] Yet, in a message released on the sixty-third anniversary of Roosevelt's birth in 1921, Harding, never a TR supporter, employed Roosevelt's legacy to support the new drift toward a government-business coalition, while trying not to scare off business with the Rough Rider's radicalism: "In his zest, he was the radical, as all crusaders are, but when he saw the business conscience of America awakened, he gladly welcomed the conservative supersedure. He was really less the radical than he ofttimes appeared, and sometimes spoke radically against his own judgement."[9]

From the beginning of his administration, Herbert Hoover suffered from the most direct comparison to TR since Taft and, as William Allen White put it, it was expected that Hoover would measure up as president along with "the big ones": Washington, Lincoln, Roosevelt, and Wilson.[10] In what was, perhaps, an attempt to co-opt some of the TR luster for his own administration, Hoover did as did Harding, and chose a close TR associate for a cabinet position. Secretary of State Henry Stimson was a protege of both TR and Elihu Root, and a man who Roosevelt once called "my kind of man." Both Hoover and Stimson continually invoked the spirit of TR to support their attempts to form a foreign policy that would steer the United States back to its pre-World War I role.

Hoover was, however, most haunted by the legacy of TR as conservationist. This was a field in which engineer and Secretary of Commerce Hoover was remarkably well versed. As a young man, Hoover had greatly admired TR, primarily, as two of the most thoughtful analysts of his administration have pointed out, because "of the vision with which [TR] related national power to the continuing existence of the great natural resources of the United States. . . ." Yet as president, Hoover led the fight, begun by Coolidge, to turn both the care of the nation's natural resources and the production of power from those resources, over to the private sector. A large segment of the Republican party was opposed to Hoover's stance and, citing the example of TR as their bulwark, argued for government protection of natural resources. The issue came to a head over the Muscle Shoals Dam project, and was a large factor in the split in the Republican party which predated the Depression, and helped spell the early doom of the Hoover administration.[11]

More so than any other president, with the exception of Washington and Lincoln, the ghosts of the two Roosevelts have been resurrected in the midst of political campaigns. Far from being the special property of the Republican party, every presidential candidate in the post-TR period has quoted from the Colonel in at least one campaign speech. This comes as no great shock: TR is eminently quotable, particularly if the candidate is attempting to show himself as more macho than his opponent.

Yet few used TR's political ghost with the vigor of his cousin Franklin. In his campaign to separate his 1932 candidacy from what he argued was Hooverian stagnancy, FDR consistently invoked TR's name, particularly his penchant for action and the use of the presidency as a "bully pulpit" (which FDR modified to mean a presidency that was "preeminently a place of moral leadership").[12] There are those who argue that the memory of TR continued to run strong in the blither of reform legislation in FDR's first hundred days, and in what philosophical commitment he had to the more liberal tenets of the New Deal.[13]

During the 1936 campaign, FDR once again used his cousin's ghost with a vengeance. He began his campaign for a second term on January 20, 1936, when he dedicated the Roosevelt Memorial in New York, reciting TR's Square Deal pledge, and praising TR's "creed for social justice." As the campaign wore on, the family of TR tried to end FDR's attempts at comparison. On October 25, 1936, Democratic Senator Vic Doinahey of Ohio made a speech in which he said that FDR championed the same progressive ideals as TR. Infuriated TR's Secretary of the Interior James Garfield made public a letter which he had sent to TR's widow: "I was one of those who believed most strongly in your husband and served under him in the Progressive Party in 1912, and I bitterly resent any such comparisons." Mrs. Roosevelt replied: "I feel as you do . . . [The Progressive Party's] liberalism was in accord with our theories of democracy and personal liberty, and in no way resembled the policies of the present administration in Washington."[14] Such criticism, however, did not deter the president, who continued to petition the ghost for the rest of the 1936 campaign—even quoting from the Man in the Arena speech on the night before the election—and in each of his two final campaigns.[15]

In the 1960s, the hands-on executive style of Harry Truman was favorably compared by some historians to that of TR. Many agreed with Clinton Rossiter who observed that "I am ready to hazard an opinion, to which I came, I confess manfully, with dragging feet, that Harry S Truman will eventually win a place as president alongside Jefferson and Theodore Roosevelt [as] the president who grows in office."[16] Truman would, publicly at least, encourage the comparison by making glowing remarks of the Rough Rider. In speeches and memoirs, Truman described Roosevelt as an "Outstanding Republican President" who "contributed to the perpetuation of progressivism in American life."[17]

Yet the aforementioned statement from his memoirs was a far sight from how he really felt about the Rough Rider. In a diary entry written during the 1948 campaign, Truman sputtered that "I don't believe the USA wants any more fakirs—Teddy and Franklin are enough. So I am going to make a common sense, intellectually honest campaign. It will be a novelty—and it will win."[18] In a memorandum cited by Truman's daughter Margaret in her biography of her father, Truman shows even more bile: "Professional liberals aren't familiar with the Ten Commandments or the Sermon on the Mount. Most Roosevelts aren't either!"[19] In a 1964 interview given as part of a plan for an unpublished textbook on American history, Truman paid TR the ultimate insult: "I have always thought that the greatest thing [TR] ever did was when he split the Republican party and caused the election of Woodrow Wilson who was one of the greatest of the great presidents."[20] It is possible that Truman's feelings toward TR may have surfaced as a result of his inability to distance himself from what William Leuchtenburg called the "shadow of FDR,"[21] but it is just as possible that Truman's zealous partisanship would not allow him to admit that *any* Republican, except for Lincoln, had any redeeming qualities.

These same historians who later lauded Truman's activism would criticize the seemingly passive attitude of his successor. During his eight years in office, Dwight Eisenhower's references to TR (aside from the usual Republican campaign rhetoric) were largely aimed at adjusting his growing image as a hands-off president. This was something that Eisenhower, who received a constant nagging from the press on this point, did frequently. For example, when dedicating Sagamore Hill as a national shrine in 1953, Eisenhower used the occasion to note that it was a misconception that Roosevelt was a "bull in a china shop," and that instead of threats, he used cajolery to deal with his opponents, even inviting them "to many breakfasts." The reference to Eisenhower's own way of dealing with his congressional opponents brought laughter from the audience.[22] On the whole, however, Eisenhower's image was deliberately cast in the opposite direction as was TR's; the need to borrow from the Rough Rider was slight.

Unlike Truman and Eisenhower, John F. Kennedy needed, and profited from, comparisons between himself and TR. A few weeks before the 1960 Democratic convention, former president Truman, who was supporting fellow Missourian Stuart Symington, publicly charged that Kennedy was too young to be president. Kennedy responded in a July 4 news conference by listing names of statesmen who had assumed national prominence at the age of 43 or younger. TR topped a list which included Alexander the Great, William Pitt, and Napoleon.[23]

The issue of youth and inexperience loomed large for Kennedy in 1960, and he compared himself to TR to help dull this criticism. Once elected, his youth was quickly perceived to be an asset to his administration, the analogy was picked up by an approving press. A *New York Times* editorial printed a week before Kennedy was sworn in gushed that "if the parallel is to continue, we can look forward to vigor in the White House just as our grandfathers half a century ago saw vigor in the happy antics of that intrepid warrior, Theodore Roosevelt."[24]

Kennedy himself enjoyed the parallel. He certainly encouraged vigor, not only in the nation, but in his rather slovenly staff. After reading a letter that TR wrote in 1908 to the commander of the Marine Corps, suggesting that all Marines hike fifty miles at regular intervals to improve their stamina, Kennedy suggested to his staff that they might do the same thing. Portly Press Secretary Pierre Salinger refused, noting to newsmen that while he "might be plucky, he was not stupid."[25]

Although quotes from TR in Kennedy speeches were not a regular occurrence, it bears a historical footnote that TR was prominently featured in a speech that Kennedy never delivered. The 1964 campaign had begun before he went to Dallas in

November 1963; the trip was meant to bring the feuding wings of the Texas Democratic party into line, and stop a defection of conservative Democrats to the most likely Republican challenger, Arizona Senator Barry Goldwater. In an attempt to woo these conservative Democrats, Kennedy planned to quote extensively from TR in a speech at the Dallas Trade Mart, scheduled for delivery on November 22. His assassination ended the president's plans to note that TR's maxim to "speak softly and carry and big stick" was the smart way to deal with the post-Test Ban Treaty Soviets, and "a good standard for all."[26]

It was FDR, not Theodore Roosevelt, who was Lyndon Johnson's role model, both in life and in politics.[27] Yet in one instance, Johnson utilized the TR image to attempt to put a favorable public relations spin on a major foreign policy crisis. From January to April 1964, Johnson capitulated to the demands of Panamanian nationalists, after a confrontation brought about by students raising the American flag in front of a Panamanian high school. With what seems to have been misguided logic, Johnson invoked TR's ghost to defend his Panamanian policy. The parallel immediately fell flat, as the press was quick to note that TR would have unquestionably disagreed with the constant use of his name to defend Johnson's Panamanian policies. In hindsight, it is arguable that a careful use of TR's reputation for strength in foreign affairs might have helped Johnson weather the early storm of Vietnam; certainly Johnson could only have profited from any type of image that would have helped him to be seen as a strong, decisive leader in foreign affairs.[28]

It is in this area—crisis management—that the spirit of TR has been most often, most blatantly, and most strongly co-opted by his successors. From "The Buck Stops Here" to "Read my Lips," each of TR's successors—indeed, each chief executive since Washington—has spent considerable time positioning his image as one of a strong, decisive leader. A key component of this positioning is the use by all of TR's successors of his Man in the Arena speech. Even the most ardent Roosevelt-haters have been drawn to this statement of personal strength:

> It is not the critic who counts; not the man who points out how the strong man stumbles, or where the doer of deeds could have done them better. The credit belongs to the man who is actually in the arena, whose face is marred by dust and sweat and blood; who strives valiantly; who errs, and comes short again and again, because there is no effort without error and shortcoming;

but who does actually strive to do the deeds; who knows the great enthusiasms, the great devotions; who spends himself in a worthy cause; who, at the best knows in the end the triumph of high achievement, and who at the worst if he fails, at least fails while daring greatly, so that his place shall never be with those cold and timid souls who know neither victory nor defeat.[29]

No one quoted from this statement more often than Richard Nixon. Indeed, Nixon co-opted the image of Theodore Roosevelt with an intensity that surpassed any of TR's successors. This was not a worship of TR, as some have concluded (Nixon would tell Garry Wills that it was Wilson, not TR, who was his hero).[30] This was more a way of identifying with an American politician who typified how Nixon felt about himself: at his best in a crisis, a man in the arena, a Republican progressive, able to make what he often called the "big play." During an interview in 1960, Wills asked Nixon about this closeness with TR. Nixon replied, "Not much in his ideas, I guess. I'm like him in one way only: I like to be in the arena."[31] Unquestionably, Nixon liked TR for his style, rather than for his substance.

It was this perceived kinship with TR's style that helped Nixon through his explanations of his most bitter political setbacks. When doing so, he invariably quoted the Man in the Arena speech. In his memoirs, Nixon says that the Fund Crisis of 1952 led him to "quickly . . . feel a kinship with Teddy Roosevelt's description of the man in the arena," and on the morning after he was defeated by Kennedy in 1960, Nixon sent a copy of the speech to his supporters. Nixon's use of TR's Arena speech during his August 8, 1974 resignation speech fit this pattern,[32] but his invoking of the spirit of TR during his farewell speech to the White House staff the next day was at the same time more poignant and more telling. After a stiff, almost dazed beginning, son-in-law Ed Cox passed a book to Nixon—the biography of TR by Noel Busch.[33] Nixon put on his eyeglasses, which he had never done in public before, and read a quote from Roosevelt's diary about the death of his first wife: "And when my heart's dearest died, the light went from my heart forever." The weeping in the room was audible to even the television audience. Nixon went on: "That was TR in his twenties. He thought the light had gone from his life forever—but he went on. And he not only became president, but as ex-president he served his country always in the arena, tempestuous, strong, sometimes wrong, sometimes right, but he was a man."[34]

This identification of himself as being in the "arena" with TR has not left Nixon, even after the presidency. Nixon entitled the final chapter of his 1982 book, *Leaders*, "In the Arena."[35] After attending the October 8, 1981 funeral of Anwar Sadat, Nixon travelled on to Saudi Arabia where, in a state dinner at Jidda, he pulled out the draft manuscript of *Leaders* and quoted the Man in the Arena speech during his toast.[36] The identification has remained so strong that Nixon's most recent book, a memoir of the years following his resignation, is entitled *In The Arena*.[37] As William Safire, former Nixon speechwriter and then a columnist for the *New York Times*, observes: "Mr. Nixon viewed the lines in 1960, and does today, 'straight'—without irony—as vividly expressive of his own attitude toward life in general, and to the political life in particular. . . ."[38]

In the post-Watergate era, one would expect that the image of TR would be utilized a great deal. As the predominant goal of the image makers of both Gerald Ford and Jimmy Carter was to position their man as being the antithesis to Nixon, and as the goal of the public relations staff of Ronald Reagan was to portray him as a pro-business, family values Republican of the 1920s stock, it would seem logical that the image of TR might have been helpful in those ventures. For the most part, however, it was not. Ford, Carter, and Reagan largely ignored the image of TR during their presidencies, and Ford and Reagan only invoked it, to no one's surprise, during their electoral campaigns. One can only speculate as to the reason for this, but it is possible that their image makers did not want to risk an unfavorable comparison between the dynamic Roosevelt and these more low-key leaders.

Indeed, any public comparison made between TR and these leaders was usually unflattering. Richard Reeves acerbically observed when castigating Ford's Whip Inflation Now (WIN) campaign that "if Theodore Roosevelt saw the president as being the man in the arena, Gerald Ford was going to be the man in the bleachers, the cheerleader urging the nation to win this one for the big dollar."[39] In the 1976 campaign, as he tried to rid himself of the label of a nice incompetent, Ford often observed that "there was a great, great president a few years ago named Teddy Roosevelt who once said, 'Speak softly and carry a big stick.' Jimmy Carter wants to speak softly and carry a fly swatter."[40]

As Carter negotiated a 1977 treaty which would eventually phase out absolute U.S. control of the Panama Canal, as well as acknowledge Panamanian sovereignty, his critics savaged him with unfavorable comparisons to TR.[41] While many observers compared Reagan's use of television to TR's concept of the "bully pulpit," there was little overt use of TR's image by Reagan.[42] Indeed, Reagan found himself slightly beaten up with the TR image during the controversy over Secretary of the Interior James Watt.[43] However, there was an interesting parallel to TR that Reagan doubtless knew nothing about. In the fall of 1986, Oliver North sent an electronic mail report to his boss, National Security Council head John Poindexter: "Sincerely believe that RR can be instrumental in bringing about an end to Iran/Iraq war—a la Roosevelt w/Russo/Japanese War in 1904. Anybody for RR getting the same prize?"[44]

George Bush feels the strongest kinship with Theodore Roosevelt since the days of Bush's mentor, Richard Nixon. In view of his background as an athlete and an outdoorsman, the gravitation is a natural one. Yet there is much pragmatic usefulness to the attachment as well, as Bush the presidential candidate was immediately faced with the issue of what would be dubbed the "wimp factor." Throughout the campaigns of both 1980 and 1988, Bush tried to erase this image by constantly linking himself to the Rough Rider. His speeches often included TR's line that "true toughness is mental toughness . . . [and this is why] I'm going to win the nomination and the presidency next year. . . ."[45]

As soon as he took office, Bush proclaimed, "I'm an Oyster Bay kind of guy," and proceeded to make the comparison as obvious as possible.[46] Since then, Bush has utilized TR's image at almost every turn, from the domestic "drug war" to the December 1989 invasion of Panama. The TR image has been used more effectively in Bush's campaign to amend the Clean Air Act, as the president has, to date, made a consistent effort to tie his legislation to the memory of TR's successes in the field of natural resource conservation.[47] Bush also borrowed a page from TR's textbook on how to be an executive when he called a meeting of the nation's governors to discuss the problems of the educational system. In his speech to the National Governor's Association, during which he announced the summit, Bush noted that only two other presidents have called the governors together to help make policy—TR, who convened a meeting on conservation, and FDR, who had a meeting to discuss possible remedies for the Depression.[48] There can be little question, as one journalist has observed, that " . . . Bush, in search of a role model, may have found one in the Oyster Bay Roosevelt. . . ."[49]

Theodore Roosevelt's ghost has been at the side of each of his successors. A few have tried to avoid it; fewer still have embraced it openly but criticized him privately. Most have utilized it to strike a chord with the voters, fill a void in their own personality or executive style, or, depending on the issue, either call attention to or deflect attention away from a major issue. Next to FDR (who ignored the party and philosophical differences between him and his cousin, and co-opted the image during elections as if it was family property), Kennedy, Nixon, and Bush used it the most, all co-opting TR's perceived strengths to improve perceived weaknesses in their own images. One of the key legacies of TR, then, may well have been to add an unwritten codicil to Article II, which might read: "The president shall be a strong, vibrant, charismatic man," or one might say, a man who lives through the arena. Or, as put by TR with characteristic bluntness, "While President, I have *been* President."[50]

Those who have *been* president have been more successful presidents. This view is voiced by no less an expert than Clinton Rossiter: After Roosevelt, "To be a great president a man must think like a great president; he must follow Theodore Roosevelt and choose to be a 'Jackson-Lincoln,' a man of strength and independence, rather than a 'Buchanan,' a deferential Whig."[51] Certainly, each of his successors has had to live up to this ideal. Until a president of equal vitality hits the American scene, living up to the image of Theodore Roosevelt will be a political necessity.

NOTES

The author gratefully acknowledges the assistance of Stacy McIntosh, Myra Shiminski, and Elizabeth Harwick for their research assistance, as well as Dr. John Allen Gable.

1. *New York Times*, March 22, 1989, p. A25.

2. See theme developed in William E. Leuchtenburg, *In the Shadow of FDR* (Ithaca: Cornell University Press, 1983).

3. Students should consult Daniel Boorstin, *The Image: Or What Happened to the American Dream* (New York: Atheneum, 1962); George C. Edwards, *The Public Presidency: The Pursuit of Popular Support* (New York: St. Martin's Press, 1983), particularly, pp. 70–82; Michael Baruch Grossman and Martha Joynt Kumar, *Portraying the President: The White House and the News Media* (Baltimore: Johns Hopkins University Press,

1981); Kathleen Hall Jamieson, *Packaging the Presidency* (New York: Oxford University Press, 1984); George Reedy, *The Twilight of the Presidency* (New York: World Publishing Company, 1970); and Larry J. Sabato, *The Rise of Political Consultants* (New York: Basic Books, 1981). The most recent popular discussion of presidential imagery is found in Hedrick Smith, *The Power Game* (New York: Random House, 1988).

4. Arthur M. Schlesinger, Jr., *The Crisis of the Old Order*, vol. 1 of *The Age of Roosevelt* (New York: Houghton-Mifflin Co., 1957), pp. 18-19.

5. Edmund Morris, *The Rise of Theodore Roosevelt* (New York: Coward, McCann and Geoghegan, 1979), p. 18.

6. Arthur M. Schlesinger, Jr., *The Imperial Presidency* (Boston: Houghton-Mifflin Co., 1973), p. 210.

7. See William Manners, *TR and Will: A Friendship That Split the Republican Party* (New York: Harcourt, Brace, 1969); and Archie Butt, *Taft and Roosevelt: The Intimate Letters of Archie Butt, Military Aide* (New York: Doubleday, 1930).

8. Francis Russell, *The Shadow of Blooming Grove: Warren G. Harding and His Times* (New York: McGraw-Hill, 1968), pp. 501, 547.

9. *New York Times*, October 24, 1921, p. 10.

10. Quoted in Edgar Eugene Robinson and Vaughn Davis Bornet, *Herbert Hoover: President of the United States* (Stanford: Hoover Institution Press, 1975), p. 24.

11. Ibid., pp. 53–67; Kendrick A. Clements, "Herbert Hoover and Conservation, 1921–1933," *American Historical Review* 89 (February 1984): 67–89.

12. James MacGregor Burns, *Roosevelt: The Lion and the Fox* (New York: Harcourt, Brace, Jovanovich, 1956), p. 476.

13. Ibid., pp. 43, 179, 476; William E. Leuchtenburg, *Franklin D. Roosevelt and the New Deal* (New York: Harper and Row, 1963), p. 34; Arthur M. Schlesinger, Jr., *The Coming of the New Deal*, vol. 2 of *The Age of Roosevelt* (Boston: Houghton-Mifflin Co., 1959), p. 92; and Alan R. Havig, "Theodore and Franklin: FDR's Use of the Theodore Roosevelt Image, 1920–1936," *Theodore Roosevelt Association Journal* 5 (Spring 1979): 6-9.

14. *New York Times*, October 26, 1936, p. 5.

15. *New York Times*, November 3, 1936, p. 3.

16. Clinton Rossiter, *The American Presidency*, 3d ed. (Baltimore: Johns Hopkins, 1987), p. 145.

17. Harry S Truman, *Years of Trial and Hope*, vol. 2 of *Memoirs* (Garden City: Doubleday and Co., 1956), p. 173.

18. Diary entry, July 16, 1948, in Robert H. Ferrell, ed., *Off the Record: The Private Papers of Harry S Truman* (New York: Harper and Row, 1980), p. 144.

19. Margaret Truman, *Harry S Truman* (London: Hamish Hamilton, 1973), p. 8.

20. Transcript of Recording for Proposed History of the American Presidency, January 7, 1961, Harry S Truman Papers, Post-Presidential Files, Harry S Truman Library, Box 3 (Recording no. 1178, Tape no. 4).

21. Leuchtenburg, *In the Shadow of FDR*, chap. 1, passim.

22. *New York Times,* June 15, 1953, p. 10.

23. Theodore Sorensen, *Kennedy* (New York: Bantam Books, 1965), p. 152.

24. *New York Times,* January 12, 1961, p. 28.

25. Jim F. Heath, *Decade of Disillusionment: The Kennedy-Johnson Years* (Bloomington: Indiana University Press, 1975), p. 95.

26. Sorensen, *Kennedy,* pp. 579–80.

27. See Leuchtenburg, *In the Shadow of FDR,* chap. 4, passim.

28. Lyndon B. Johnson, *The Vantage Point: Perspectives on the Presidency, 1963–1969* (New York: Holt, Rinehart and Winston, 1971), chap. 8, passim.

29. John Allen Gable, ed., *The Man In The Arena: Speeches and Essays by Theodore Roosevelt* (Oyster Bay, NY: Theodore Roosevelt Association, 1987), p. 54.

30. Garry Wills, *Nixon Agonistes: The Crisis of the Self-Made Man* (New York: New American Library, 1969), pp. 30–31.

31. Ibid., p. 28.

32. Richard M. Nixon, *Memoirs* (New York: Grosset and Dunlap, 1978), pp. 109, 1,076. According to Nixon, it was Press Secretary Ronald Ziegler who reminded him of the passage on the night before the speech was to be delivered.

33. Noel Busch, *TR: The Story of Theodore Roosevelt and His Influence on Our Times* (New York: Reyal and Co., 1963).

34. Bob Woodward and Carl Bernstein, *The Final Days* (New York: Simon and Schuster, 1976), p. 455; Nixon, *Memoirs,* pp. 1,086–88.

35. Richard Nixon, *Leaders* (New York: Warner Books, 1982), p. 363.

36. Robert Sam Anson, *Exile: The Unquiet Oblivion of Richard M. Nixon* (New York: Simon and Schuster, 1984), pp. 259–61.

37. Richard Nixon, *In the Arena: A Memoir of Victory, Defeat, and Renewal* (New York: Simon and Schuster, 1990).

38. William Safire, "Man in the Arena," *New York Times,* June 7, 1973, p. 45.

39. Richard Reeves, *A Ford, Not a Lincoln* (New York: Harcourt, Brace, Jovanovich, 1975), p. 160.

40. Gerald R. Ford, *A Time to Heal* (New York: Harper and Row, 1979), p. 428; John Robert Greene, "'A Nice Person Who Worked at the Job': The Dilemma of the Ford Image," delivered at the Conference on the Presidency of Gerald R. Ford, Hofstra University, April 1989.

41. Jimmy Carter, *Keeping Faith: Memoirs of a President* (Toronto: Bantam Books, 1982), pp. 152–85.

42. See Hedrick Smith, *The Power Game: How Washington Works* (New York: Random House, 1988), pp. 703–4.

43. See Lou Cannon, *Reagan* (New York: Perigee Books, 1982), pp. 359-70.

44. Quoted in Bob Woodward, *Veil: The Secret Wars of the CIA, 1981–1987* (New York: Pocket Books, 1987), p. 556.

45. Elizabeth Drew, *Portrait of an Election: The 1980 Presidential Campaign* (New York: Simon and Schuster, 1981), p. 25.

46. *New York Times*, March 29, 1989, p. A16, reprinted in *Theodore Roosevelt Association Journal* 15 (Spring 1989): 15–16.

47. John Whitaker, interview with author, November 19, 1987; Margaret Kriz, "Politics in the Air" [on Bush's recommendation for a New Clean Air Act], *National Journal*, May 6, 1989, pp. 1,098–1,102; Maureen Dowd, "Bush, in the Driver's Seat, Sets Clean Air Course," *New York Times*, June 14, 1989, p. A24.

48. *New York Times*, August 1, 1989, p. A14.

49. *New York Times*, March 29, 1989, p. A16.

50. Quoted in John Morton Blum, *The Progressive Presidents* (New York: W. W. Norton and Co., 1980), p. 58.

51. Rossiter, *The American Presidency*, pp. 129–30.

Courtesy of Theodore Roosevelt Association

John T. McCutcheon's cartoon drawing of Theodore Roosevelt's nomination at the Progressive Party National Convention of 1912.

610

Theodore Roosevelt chopping wood at Sagamore Hill

Epilogue

A composite 1924 drawing of many images of the many-sided Theodore Roosevelt by Hubbell Reed McBride.

During this Heroic Period, scores of Roosevelt books appeared. The Roosevelt Memorial Association and Charles Scribner's Sons published the *Memorial* (24 volumes) and *National* (20 volumes) editions of *The Works of Theodore Roosevelt* in 1923-1926, which stand as the most complete collections of Roosevelt's books, essays, speeches, and papers. Joseph Bucklin Bishop's "official" biography, *Theodore Roosevelt and His Time, Shown in His Letters*, came out in 1920, and although much maligned by later historians, still remains of some value because Bishop made extensive use of TR's letters in a work authorized by Roosevelt, who approved part of the first draft before his death. Some useful monographs, essays, studies, and recollections of Roosevelt were published in these years, such as Hermann Hagedorn's *Roosevelt in the Bad Lands* (1921) and Tyler Dennett's *Roosevelt and the Russo-Japanese War* (1925). But most of the many biographies of the Heroic Period, including those by William Roscoe Thayer, Eugene Thwing, William Draper Lewis, Harold Howland, and Lord Charnwood, are of little value to posterity. Of the first generation of biographies, only Lewis Einstein's wins praise from later generations.[5]

William Roscoe Thayer had written a respected biography of Cavour, and Lord Charnwood was the author of an important biography of Lincoln. But their works on Roosevelt are superficial and disappointing. Thayer had been a friend of Roosevelt's since their days together at Harvard, while Lord Charnwood candidly confessed to a case of "boyish hero-worship" for TR. And this hero worship was the central problem with most of the writings about Roosevelt in the decade after his death. The early biographies lacked depth, objectivity, and perspective. John Chamberlain sarcastically said of the early biographers that they "were blinded by the remembered brilliance of the sun itself."[6]

Moreover, during the "Normalcy" of the 1920s, in a period of isolationism and political reaction when most Americans seemed to reject or turn away from much that TR had stood for in public life, it was difficult or perhaps impossible to appreciate Roosevelt's career. TR the politician and statesman was gone in more ways than one. What remained was the hero who overcame childhood illness, became a cowboy and Rough Rider, and preached flag-waving Americanism. These were real facets of the many-sided TR, but this did not add up to the whole man or his entire career. TR had been turned into a giant Boy Scout by his admirers.[7]

The Debunking Period

In the 1930s the inevitable reaction set in, and the Debunking Period began with the publication of Henry F. Pringle's *Theodore Roosevelt: A Biography* (1931), winner of the Pulitzer Prize, in print for over six decades, and probably the most widely read biography of TR. Pringle's biography was brilliantly written, a masterpiece of literary construction, entertaining, and witty. To Pringle, Roosevelt's career was colorful and amusing, but seldom marked by solid accomplishment. Pringle's thesis, stated at the outset, was that Theodore Roosevelt "was the most adolescent of men." Pringle's underlying assumption, not explicitly stated, was that politics and politicians were essentially ridiculous and quixotic. Further, as Richard H. Collin notes, Pringle subscribed to a kind of materialistic and psychological determinism that ruled out idealism as a motivating force, "without which Theodore Roosevelt would of necessity appear half charlatan and half neurotic."[8]

Pringle made his case by carefully selecting and manipulating evidence, emphasizing the humorous aspects of the old Rough Rider's colorful political battles, and pointing out that Roosevelt's achievements usually fell short of his goals. Typical of his technique, Pringle devoted less than two pages to conservation in a book of over 600 pages, while a relatively trivial though embarrassing incident involving Vatican politics and two of TR's close friends, Bellamy and Maria Storer, was given four pages. There is no mention in Pringle of the national parks, wildlife refuges, and national monuments established by the Roosevelt administration. In the 1931 first edition of the biography, Pringle says that the first conference of governors ever held, called by TR in 1908, was a failure. This in spite of the facts that the governors' conference of 1908 led to the first inventory of national resources, further conferences on conservation, extensive legislation on conservation in the states, and the tradition of the annual governors' conferences, none of which are mentioned by Pringle. All reference to the 1908 conference is deleted in Pringle's 1956 revised edition of the biography. Pringle gives the same amount of space in his book to TR's futile attempt to reform spelling that he does to the Pure Food and Drug and Meat Inspection Acts. A master of innuendo and the artfully used adjective, Pringle, in the first edition of the book, described Roosevelt at the Battle of San Juan Hill leading "his men against a hail of inaccurately aimed bullets," in spite of the fact that 89 of the 490 Rough Riders in the battle were casualties. Pringle sought at every turn to reduce Roosevelt from a hero to a Falstaffian buffoon.[9]

In discussing the history of the Progressive or Bull Moose party, 1912-1916, Pringle portrays TR as fickle, unstable, and mercurial. As proof Pringle utilized a telling quotation that sticks in the minds of many readers:

> War was to crowd new interests into his consciousness. . . . In all probability, Roosevelt would have turned his back on the Progressive Party even had these changes not come. Soon after 1912 a friend called at Sagamore Hill and talked of victory in 1916.
>
> "I thought you were a better politician," Roosevelt answered. "The fight is over. We are beaten. There is only one thing to do and that is to go back to the Republican Party. You can't hold a party like the Progressive Party together . . . there are no loaves and fishes."[10]

Pringle ignored the fact that Roosevelt labored long and hard to perpetuate the Progressive party in 1912, 1913, and 1914, and that the party was badly beaten in the state and congressional elections of 1914, leading to the return of many Bull Moosers to the Republican party. With the decline in popular support, and the exodus of many leaders, by 1915 there was little left of the Progressive party except TR and some diehard followers. As for the famous "loaves and fishes" quotation (used again to make the same points by Richard Hofstadter in 1948), Pringle cut TR's alleged remarks to alter the meaning of what Roosevelt had been reported as saying. In Pringle's notes, now in the Theodore Roosevelt Collection at Harvard, the full quotation, which appears to come from the recollections of the steel manufacturer Horace S. Wilkinson, reads:

> "Horace," said the Colonel, "I thought you were a better politician. The fight is over. We are beaten. There is only one thing for us to do and that is to go back to the Republican Party. You can't hold a party like the Progressive Party together. If there were loaves and fishes to distribute it would be different. But there are no loaves and fishes. The Republicans have the loaves and fishes and before long you will see the Progressives drifting back to them. One after another you'll find them on one pretext or another going

back to the Party that can give them jobs. You must go back, and I must go back too. But I as the captain will be the last to leave the ship."[11]

Pringle's view of TR was dominant in the historical community from the 1930s to the 1950s, and his biography remains influential long after much of it has been discredited by later historians. Following Pringle's lead, historians and writers during the Debunking Period attacked TR from all sides. John Chamberlain, in *Farewell to Reform* (1932), called TR a "careerist," "showman," and "surface swimmer" who had no real understanding of government or economics. The diplomatic historian Dexter Perkins said that TR's own account of the Venezuelan Crisis of 1902 was "false," a "product of Rooseveltian imagination," and Alfred Vagts and others also questioned TR's veracity on the episode. In short, TR was a liar. Daniel Aaron, in *Men of Good Hope: A Story of the American Progressives* (1951), dismissed TR as a "pseudo-progressive."[12]

Richard Hofstadter, one of the most influential historians of his generation, in his classic work *The American Political Tradition and the Men Who Made It* (1948), delivered a summary of the debunkers' view in his chapter "Theodore Roosevelt: The Conservative as Progressive." Hofstadter claimed that TR was a conservative who pretended to be a reformer, "the master therapist of the middle class," with "the intellectual fiber of a muscular and combative Polonius." TR quieted the people's fears by "scolding" social evils rather than by taking effective action. "In retrospect," Hofstadter wrote, "it is hard to understand how Roosevelt managed to keep his reputation as a strenuous reformer." Hofstadter also saw TR as a warmonger.[13]

Hofstadter made his case by denigrating the legislative record of the Roosevelt administration, ignoring the subject of conservation as Pringle had, and, on the subject of war and peace, discussing the Spanish-American War at length while relegating TR's settlements of the Russo-Japanese War and the Moroccan Crisis to a footnote, and not mentioning the fact that TR won the Nobel Peace Prize. Like Pringle, Hofstadter was a brilliant writer whose prose dazzled both the general public and professional historians.[14]

During this time, the long presidency of Franklin Delano Roosevelt, 1933-1945, and the popular Broadway play *Arsenic and Old Lace* (1941) both had in different ways profound effects on TR's reputation, and helped prolong the Debunking Period.

The administration of President Franklin D. Roosevelt contributed to the decline of Theodore Roosevelt's reputation and historical importance. (FDR was TR's fifth cousin and married to TR's niece Eleanor. TR was FDR's hero, and FDR consciously modeled his career after TR's.) The historian Richard H. Collin writes: "It is impossible to overstate the effect Franklin D. Roosevelt's election had upon the image of Theodore Roosevelt. Franklin D. Roosevelt didn't merely downgrade the Republican Roosevelt, he totally eclipsed him." TR's legislative record now could be made to seem paltry and even conservative in comparison with New Deal reforms. TR's progressivism had largely been rejected by the Republican party—in other words, TR was something of a failure—whereas FDR remade the Democratic party in the image of New Deal liberalism. And while Theodore Roosevelt loomed large in comparison to all of his presidential predecessors stretching back to Lincoln, and all of his successors except Wilson up to 1932, Franklin D. Roosevelt, as he was elected to a third and fourth term and led the Allies in World War II, was clearly a president to rival all previous presidents in importance. The Roosevelt Memorial Association was forced to change its name to the Theodore Roosevelt Association.[15]

By 1941, when Joseph Kesselring's hit play *Arsenic and Old Lace* opened at the Fulton Theater in New York City, for a great many Americans the funny and crazy character Teddy Brewster was the mirror image, only slightly distorted, of Teddy Roosevelt. It is hard to overestimate the influence of *Arsenic and Old Lace*, which became a major motion picture and was frequently produced by high schools and amateur theatrical groups. The play has perhaps been more formative of Roosevelt's image on the popular level than any book written about Roosevelt. David McCullough, a biographer of TR, speaks of seeing *Arsenic and Old Lace* as a boy as his "first encounter with Theodore Roosevelt." McCullough reports: "I came away . . . with pretty much the impression of our twenty-sixth President that so many of us have grown up with. . . ."[16]

The Era of *Realpolitik*

By the 1950s several factors led to a major reevaluation of Theodore Roosevelt, and the Debunking Period faded away in what may be called the Era of *Realpolitik*, the third period or cycle in Roosevelt historiography. After World War II, and with the advent of the Cold War and global American commitments, TR's activist foreign policy and involvement in world affairs, his use of *realpolitik* in foreign policy, and his many diplomatic successes, such as his mediation of the Russo-Japanese War and the Algeciras Conference, were widely appreciated. Robert E. Osgood, Howard K. Beale, and other scholars of the "realist school" of foreign policy praised TR's rejection of isolationism and his understanding of power politics. Osgood, in his influential study *Ideals and Self-Interest in America's Foreign Relations* (1953), wrote of Roosevelt that "no president since George Washington had been more sensitive to the factor of power in international relations or more concerned with the impact of the international environment upon the national interest." Howard K. Beale said: "Long before most Americans he saw that America was inextricably involved in the world and he set about trying to order that world."[17]

Liberals and conservatives alike in the 1950s began to see that TR's model of a strong presidency, his "stewardship theory" of government, and his skillful brokerage of the problems of industrial and urban society were important, durable, and useful contributions to the American polity. TR was viewed as the first "modern president," and as in most respects a fit role model for his successors in the White House. After years of what James McGregor Burns called a "deadlock of democracy," with relatively few new major bills passed by Congress, TR's legislative record now appeared more impressive than it had in the dynamic days of the early New Deal, and TR's conservation policies received universal attention and praise. Historians in the 1950s and later seemed to have difficulty in deciding whether TR had been a conservative or a liberal. John M. Blum classified Roosevelt as a conservative, while Arthur M. Schlesinger, Jr. and Eric F. Goldman saw TR and his Square Deal and New Nationalism as a major source of twentieth-century liberalism. Schlesinger saw a direct line of continuity from the Square Deal and New Nationalism to the New Deal and Fair Deal. But historians agreed that TR was an important subject for further study.[18]

The publication in 1951-1954 by the Theodore Roosevelt Association and Harvard University Press of eight volumes of *The Letters of Theodore Roosevelt*, superbly edited and annotated by Elting E. Morison, John M. Blum, Alfred D. Chandler, Jr., and others, was vitally important to the reevaluation of Roosevelt. Now historians and other intellectuals could see TR in all his sophistication, skill, and charm. And as I. E. Cadenhead points out, "the mere fact that the letters were easily available to more historians provided the opportunity for further reinterpretation." At last, in the *Letters*, TR was allowed to speak for himself, and as in life he was more than able to hold his own. Arthur S. Link, the biographer of Woodrow Wilson, wrote of the *Letters* that "the man that emerges from among these pages is a sort far different from the caricature of Henry F. Pringle's." And Howard K. Beale said:

> These letters have revealed a man of unusual training and intelligence and catholicity of taste and interest that gave him a breadth of knowledge equaled by few public men. He understood the history he was helping make as few men do; he showed prophetic qualities in both domestic and foreign matters that are at times uncanny. He exhibited capacity to grow with changing times.[19]

John M. Blum, one of the editors of the *Letters*, in 1954 published *The Republican Roosevelt*, one of the most important studies of TR ever written. Blum saw Roosevelt as a skillful *realpolitiker* in foreign and domestic affairs. Unlike Pringle, and also unlike many of TR's most ardent admirers, Blum had a mature appreciation and understanding of politics and politicians. Blum wrote:

> Theodore Roosevelt was a professional Republican politician from New York. He made a career out of seeking and holding public office. His professional concern was with politics and government, with parties, elections, legislation, and rule. These simple, central facts in Roosevelt's life have been ignored. . . . The builders and destroyers of a Roosevelt legend have demonstrated to their own satisfaction that he was either a great man or a perpetual adolescent. . . . Too little, however, has Roosevelt been examined against the background of the institutions in which he deliberately chose to excel. Harvey Cushing without a scalpel, John Marshall without a robe, Stonewall Jackson without an army make no more sense than Theodore Roosevelt without public office in hand or on order.[20]

A sophisticated comprehension of the problems of power and politics in domestic and foreign affairs characterized the works that were part of the favorable reassessment of Theodore Roosevelt that took place after 1950. And this third period of

Roosevelt historiography saw the publication of many books of enduring value, including works by Howard K. Beale, Paul Russell Cutright, Carleton Putnam, Edward Wagenknecht, George E. Mowry, G. Wallace Chessman, and William Henry Harbaugh. Howard K. Beale's *Theodore Roosevelt and the Rise of America to World Power* (1956), though by no means exhaustive of the subject, and lacking in some crucial respects, remains the most comprehensive study of TR and foreign policy. Beale upheld TR's account of the Venezuelan Crisis of 1902, showing that the president had firmly but discreetly forced Germany to accept arbitration, and refuting earlier attacks on TR's veracity by Dexter Perkins and others. (Beale's view and TR's account have subsequently been sustained by Frederick W. Marks III and Edmund Morris.) Paul Russell Cutright's *Theodore Roosevelt the Naturalist* (1956) was a much needed study of TR's work in natural history and conservation. Carleton Putnam's *Theodore Roosevelt: The Formative Years, 1858-1886* (1958) has been widely praised. Roosevelt biographer Edmund Morris says that Edward Wagenknecht's *The Seven Worlds of Theodore Roosevelt* (1958) "succeeds more than any other work in capturing the size and complexity of TR." George E. Mowry's *The Era of Theodore Roosevelt and the Birth of Modern America, 1900-1912* (1958), a volume in the New American Nation Series, places the Roosevelt and Taft administrations in the context of the times with concise yet rich detail, informed analysis, and balanced judgements. G. Wallace Chessman, *Governor Theodore Roosevelt: The Albany Apprenticeship, 1898-1900* (1965) provided an in-depth study of an important phase of TR's career. In 1961 the first full-length scholarly biography of TR since Pringle was published, *Power and Responsibility: The Life and Times of Theodore Roosevelt* by William Henry Harbaugh, which has endured as the best complete biography of Roosevelt. Summing up the findings and opinions of the Era of *Realpolitik*, Harbaugh wrote:

> Whatever the Colonel's ultimate place in the hearts of his countrymen—and it yearly grows larger and warmer—there is no discounting those incisive perceptions and momentous actions that made him such a dynamic historical force from his civil service years to the day of his death. . . . Long after the rationalizations, the compromises, the infights, the intolerance and the rest have been forgotten, Theodore Roosevelt will be remembered as the first great President-reformer of the modern industrial era.[21]

Reviewing Harbaugh's biography Senator Hubert H. Humphrey of Minnesota wrote: "It will no longer be possible to pretend that TR didn't matter or to judge him superficially as historians once did." Indicative of the historical climate, Richard Hofstadter's major studies *The Age of Reform* (1955) and *Anti-Intellectualism in American Life* (1962) presented far more favorable views of TR than Hofstadter's earlier debunking essay of 1948.[22]

In the 1950s, TR was once again back in the news and public consciousness. Sagamore Hill, TR's Oyster Bay, Long Island home, was opened to the public in 1953. *The Roosevelt Family of Sagamore Hill* (1954) by Hermann Hagedorn made the best-seller list. The centennial of TR's birth in 1958 was widely observed: *Life* ran an editorial, *Time* did a cover story, and public events ranging from civic meetings and banquets to college seminars were held across the nation. Befitting TR's new status, Congress in 1960 appropriated funds to build a seventeen-foot statue of the twenty-sixth president and memorial area on Theodore Roosevelt Island in Washington, D. C., something which the Theodore Roosevelt Association had been pushing since the 1920s. In 1967 the new TR memorial in Washington was dedicated by President Lyndon B. Johnson and Chief Justice Earl Warren.[23]

The New Left Attack

No sooner did Theodore Roosevelt's historical stature seem secure than new attacks on the old Rough Rider were mounted in the 1960s and 1970s, most notably by historians and writers from the political left. In the midst of the civil rights movement, the Vietnam War, the rise of the New Left, and the crises of the "Imperial Presidency," TR's reputation declined in what may be called the New Left Period of Roosevelt historiography, the fourth cycle or phase in the "history of the history" of Theodore Roosevelt. As early as 1961, the historian Dewey W. Grantham, in an important essay on the historiography of TR since World War II, insisted that "historians and biographers have swung too far away from the skeptical approach of the prewar scholars." Within a decade, the scholarly community was caught up in a period of questioning, upheaval, and radical change, a time when most assumptions about American society and the past were assaulted. While some favorable studies in the *realpolitik* tradition continued to appear, such as Wallace Chessman's *Theodore Roosevelt and the Politics of Power* (1969) and Raymond Esthus's *Theodore Roosevelt and the International Rivalries* (1970), the dominant mood and concerns of the era seemed to many to be at odds with TR's image and legacies. And the New Left historians had no use for TR, who was attacked as an imperialist, racist, militarist, and warmonger.[24]

Civil rights for blacks had never been a priority for TR, and thus it was natural and to be expected that Roosevelt's stature would decline at a time when civil rights became a burning issue. Back in 1901, TR had been widely attacked for inviting the black leader Booker T. Washington to dinner at the White House, but in the 1960s and 1970s historians were critical of TR's civil rights record and his positions on the question of racism as it related to many issues at home and abroad. One historian wrote in 1972:

> Presidential heroes lose their luster very slowly, but it's high time we reviewed the evidence on Theodore Roosevelt. One only needs to escape from the shackles of patriotic myth, and keep an open mind while investigating the complete record in order to realize that Theodore Roosevelt was an overt racist.[25]

TR was, as Thomas G. Dyer shows in *Theodore Roosevelt and the Idea of Race* (1980), a neo-Lamarckian who believed in the equipotentiality of all races. In other words, TR, well-read in science, did not believe in the biological or inherent superiority or inferiority of any race. TR favored civil rights for blacks. Yet in his time the courts had severely restricted the powers of the federal government on the race question, as was shown in the great difficulties TR had in ending school segregation for Oriental children in San Francisco. But in general Roosevelt did not push the cause of civil rights. And his actions in the Brownsville Affair of 1906, when he summarily dismissed an entire battalion of blacks after an incident in Texas, and in 1912, when he advocated a "lily white" Bull Moose party in the South, provided ample ammunition for TR's critics.[26]

The tragedy of Vietnam called into question all the assumptions upon which American foreign and defense policy had been based since World War II, and with this new debate came condemnation of TR as the early prophet of military preparedness and world involvement. Lloyd C. Gardner, Walter F. LaFeber, and Thomas J. McCormick, respected historians of the New Left, as well as others, saw TR's foreign policy as basically directed to the creation of a global American capitalist empire. TR was particularly criticized for issuing the Roosevelt Corollary to the Monroe Doctrine, and for his actions in securing rights to build the Panama Canal. TR became a kind of "whipping boy" for the supposed sins of the United States in Latin America and the Caribbean from the early nineteenth to the late twentieth centuries. The veteran diplomatic historian Thomas A. Bailey joined the chorus of critics, and wrote that Theodore Roosevelt, the "disciple of Mars" and "perpetual adult-adolescent," had sought "to pervert the Monroe Doctrine, use it as a tool of American imperialism, and intensify the Bad-Neighbor policy."[27]

Most historians since the 1930s, both those with essentially favorable and those with unfavorable views of TR's diplomacy, have been critical of Roosevelt's dealings with Colombia and Panama. Much the same can be said of the Roosevelt Corollary, which defined the role of the United States as a policeman for Latin America. It is hard to fault TR's handling of the debt crises in Venezuela and Santo Domingo, except from a Marxist perspective, but the Roosevelt Corollary, issued at the time of the Dominican crisis, most historians agree "converted a triumph of action into a near tragedy of words," as William Henry Harbaugh puts it.[28]

Yet negative assessments during the New Left Period and later of TR's foreign policies were curiously incomplete in covering the record of the Roosevelt administration. In discussions of TR's views on war and peace, it was seldom noted that Theodore Roosevelt was the first world leader to submit a foreign dispute to the Court of Arbitration at The Hague, that he had been the first world leader to call for holding the Second Hague Peace Conference, which met in 1907, and that TR worked hard though unsuccessfully to bring about international agreements to curb the naval arms race. In discussions of TR's Latin American policies, Roosevelt's critics seldom mentioned the successful efforts of the United States to include representatives of the Latin American nations in the Second Hague Peace Conference, and to have the Drago Doctrine adopted by the conference. The Drago Doctrine, which outlawed the use of force in the collection of foreign debts, and addressed problems raised by the Venezuelan and Dominican debt crises, "represented one definite advance in international law," says Barbara W. Tuchman in her analysis of the Second Hague Peace Conference. Also often left out in accounts of TR's Latin American policies is the Roosevelt administration's peaceful resolution of disputes among Central American nations, and the establishment in 1907 of the Central American Court of Justice for the adjudication of international problems. Contrary to widespread myths about TR's "Big Stick" policies, TR often "spoke softly"—which accounts for the absence of records on the Venezuela dispute of 1902—and the United States under TR did not invade any nation in Latin America or elsewhere.[29]

The Watergate Crisis, as well as widespread opposition to Presidents Lyndon B. Johnson and Richard M. Nixon, tarnished what was now called the Imperial Presidency, and with it TR's image as the father of the modern presidency. At the same time, calls for major changes in government policies from both the left and the right made TR's progressivism (as well as the New Deal liberal tradition) seemed dated and irrelevant. Gabriel Kolko, one of the leading New Left historians, delivered a powerful and much-cited attack on Theodore Roosevelt's administration and the entire progressive movement in his book *The Triumph of Conservatism: A Reinterpretation of American History, 1900-1916* (1963). Kolko stated: "It is business control over politics (and by 'business' I mean the major economic interests) rather than political regulation of the economy that is the significant phenomenon of the Progressive Era." In short, the Republican, Democratic, and Bull Moose progressives were, in socialist terms, counter-revolutionaries, in league with big business, who sought to subvert public demands for substantive reform.[30]

Kolko supported his thesis by examining in some detail the major legislative achievements of the Roosevelt and Wilson administrations, and showing how again and again big business had worked its will against genuine reform. For instance, in discussing the meat inspection law, introduced by TR's ally Senator Albert J. Beveridge as an amendment to the Agricultural Appropriations Act of 1906, and passed in the wake of the furor created by Upton Sinclair's novel *The Jungle*, Kolko insists that the big packers favored the legislation, which, Kolko notes, was shepherded through Congress by Representative James W. Wadsworth, chairman of the House Committee on Agriculture and ardent champion of the packers. Kolko makes much of the fact that the packers won two of their pet points in the legislative process: the paying of inspectors by the government rather than by the packers, and the omission of dates on cans of meat.[31]

While it is true these concessions were won by the packers in the final compromise passed by Congress, Kolko fails to mention that Roosevelt, after struggling with Wadsworth, obtained four key points opposed by Wadsworth and the packers: that inspectors were to be under the civil service system; that inspection would be stopped in plants failing to comply with government recommendations; that uninspected meat was to be barred from interstate commerce; and that the law would be promptly enforced without judicial review. An amendment for judicial review, inserted by Wadsworth but eliminated by the president, would have made enforcement of the law difficult at best. Kolko also "omits mention of packer approaches to one of the president's commissioners and to Roosevelt himself, promising self-reform if given enough time, without the need for new legislation," notes the historian James Harvey Young. As the historian John Braeman states, "the legislation was not passed without a bitter fight—and it was only T. R.'s masterful handling of the political situation that carried the day." Braeman concludes: "In the light of the evidence . . . , I believe Mr. Kolko's interpretation is untenable."[32]

In case after case, Kolko made his points by selective use of the facts. And in general, the extreme criticisms of TR in the 1960s and 1970s could only be sustained by twisting the historical record or overlooking parts of it. Consequently, by the 1980s many of the attacks from the New Left Period had been washed away, and the *realpolitik* interpretations for the most part remained.[33]

The Roosevelt Renaissance

By the late 1970s, the "Rise of Theodore Roosevelt" or a Roosevelt Renaissance was under way, the fifth period in Roosevelt historiography, and popular and scholarly interest in Theodore Roosevelt reached levels comparable to the attention the former president had received in the 1950s and 1920s. Roosevelt's reputation seemed to have weathered the attacks of critics from Henry F. Pringle to the New Left, and the Roosevelt Renaissance saw a new emphasis on TR as hero and presidential giant.

Edmund Morris's biography *The Rise of Theodore Roosevelt* (1979), a best-seller, played a major role in the Roosevelt Renaissance. Morris's biography, which took TR up to 1901, and David McCullough's *Mornings on Horseback* (1981), another important study of TR's youth, both convincingly showed TR as an extraordinary and heroic figure. At the same time, other writers and historians, such as Frederick W. Marks III, portrayed the Roosevelt administration as a success story. In 1976 TR was on the cover of a *Time* magazine "special report" on the American presidents. And in 1976 the Rough Rider was shown on the cover of *Newsweek*, "leading the charge up San Juan Hill," under a headline that asked, "Where Have All the Heroes Gone?" In this August 6, 1979, issue of *Newsweek*, Edmund Morris wrote:

> Clearly the magic of the great Teddy still lurks in our collective consciousness. Recently, indeed, there have been signs that Old Four Eyes is making a comeback in popular esteem.... Why this sudden flood of nostalgia for a man who died 60 years ago? It is not just that TR was, as Walter Lippmann observed, our only lovable President. . . . We are wistful for the "essentially moral and essentially manly" qualities that the 26th President had in such abundance. Wistfulness traditionally impels a declining civilization to gild and elevate its virile great. Often as not, the gilt and the stature are artificial accretions, yet the more one analyzes Theodore Roosevelt in the harsh light of historical research, the more authentic a hero he becomes.[34]

TR's star was rising in the scholarly community as well as in the nation at large. Arthur M. Schlesinger, Sr. in 1948 and 1962 had conducted two famous polls of scholars to rate the presidents. TR ranked seventh in both Schlesinger polls. TR moved up to fifth place in a poll of scholars by David L. Porter in 1981, and was rated fourth in polls of experts by the United States Historical Society in 1977 and the Chicago *Tribune* in 1982. Scholarly conferences devoted to TR were held at Canisius College, Buffalo, New York in 1985 and at Hofstra University, Hempstead, Long Island, New York in 1990; the quarterly *Theodore Roosevelt Association Journal* began publication in 1975; and the Roosevelt Study Center, dedicated to Theodore Roosevelt, Franklin D. Roosevelt, and Eleanor Roosevelt, was opened in Middelburg, the Netherlands, in 1986. New articles and books on TR were published in a steady stream.[35]

Edmund Morris's *The Rise of Theodore Roosevelt* (1979) won the Pulitzer Prize, as Pringle's biography had decades before, and

David McCullough's *Mornings on Horseback* (1981) received the National Book Award. The sparkling prose and thorough research of Morris and McCullough more than matched that of Pringle's book, and the two new works joined Pringle's biography as historical classics. Frederick W. Marks's *Velvet on Iron: The Diplomacy of Theodore Roosevelt* (1979) gave a spirited and detailed defense of TR's foreign policies, as did two books by Richard H. Collin, *Theodore Roosevelt, Culture, Diplomacy, and Expansion* (1985) and *Theodore Roosevelt's Caribbean* (1990). *The Bull Moose Years: Theodore Roosevelt and the Progressive Party* (1978) by John Allen Gable provided a detailed history of the Bull Moose party; Jay Stuart Berman published the first scholarly monograph on TR's years as New York City Police Commissioner, *Police Administration and Progressive Reform* (1987); *Theodore Roosevelt: The Making of a Conservationist* (1985) by Paul Russell Cutright was a sequel to Cutright's 1956 study on TR as a naturalist; Thomas G. Dyer's *Theodore Roosevelt and the Idea of Race* (1980) was a much-needed monograph; A. A. Norton published a study of TR as a writer, *Theodore Roosevelt* (1980); and James R. Reckner's *Teddy Roosevelt's Great White Fleet* (1988) examined the technology of TR's Navy. Lewis L. Gould's important volume on *The Presidency of Theodore Roosevelt* (1991) was part of the American Presidency Series. John Milton Cooper's *The Warrior and the Priest: Woodrow Wilson and Theodore Roosevelt* (1983) was a fascinating dual biographical study, and William C. Widenor's *Henry Cabot Lodge and the Search for an American Foreign Policy* (1980) studied what Widenor called the "Rooseveltian solution" of Lodge and TR to the challenges of international affairs. There were other valuable studies as well, and new collections and editions of Roosevelt's writings were published. While in some ways the Roosevelt Renaissance resembled the Heroic Period of the 1920s, particularly on the popular level, the new studies published in the 1970s and into the 1990s were well-documented and professional in perspective and judgement, unlike most of the books of the 1920s, and like the works of the Era of *Realpolitik*.[36]

The historians of the Roosevelt Renaissance had the perspectives of time and the benefits of decades of research and scholarly debate which the writers of the 1920s had lacked, but it was striking that the dominant views of the 1980s were not dissimilar to those of the Heroic Period in seeing TR as one of the most impressive leaders in American history. To be sure, there were differences between the Roosevelt Renaissance and the Heroic Period. Historians of the later era were quite aware that, as Edmund Morris said of TR, "just as his virtues loom large, so do his faults." The new popular interest in TR was in part a nostalgia for simpler times, as Edmund Morris noted, and also an aspect of the "new patriotism" sparked by the Bicentennial of the American Revolution in the 1970s and evident throughout the 1980s. The search for role models and heroes by the general public was of course a different quest than the pursuits followed by historians. But the popular concern was not less socially useful or morally justifiable than the work of scholars. And there were certain parallels between the public and the professional interests, as shown by the Schlesinger, Porter, and other polls on the presidents within the scholarly community. Both the public and scholars were involved in the search for values, and both were affected in many and varied ways by the past and the present.[37]

The Roosevelt Renaissance was still in full swing into the 1990s, and though much had been published over the decades since TR's death, much still remained to be done in the field of Roosevelt scholarship. No study of TR's presidency ranks with James G. Randall's four-volume work on the Lincoln administration. There are many excellent monographs and studies of aspects and periods of TR's life and career, such as Wallace Chessman's on TR's governorship and Thomas G. Dyer's on race, but many subjects still need scholarly attention. William Henry Harbaugh's one-volume biography endures as a valuable and useful work, and Edmund Morris's *The Rise of Theodore Roosevelt* was the first installment of a multi-volume biography. But as of 1992, there is still no multi-volume biography of Roosevelt to rank with those of Thomas Jefferson by Dumas Malone, Andrew Jackson by Robert V. Remini, or James Madison by Irving Brant.

As the Roosevelt Renaissance or the "Rise of Theodore Roosevelt" continued, the question remained to be answered whether there would be further up-and-down cycles or phases in the "history of the history" of Theodore Roosevelt, repeating the pattern of the past, or whether perhaps Roosevelt's reputation had reached a kind of permanent and high plateau, as is the case with Washington and Lincoln. The question hangs in the air, nor can we be certain of the answer for some decades to come. But it does seem clear that TR will always be counted as among the most important figures in American history.

Continuing Traditions

A survey of the history of what has been written about Theodore Roosevelt and of TR's image over the years shows distinct periods, cycles, or phases in which definite and differing viewpoints have been dominant, though in every era there have been significant minority opinions. The periodization of Roosevelt historiography displays a kind of repetitive or cyclical pattern with Roosevelt's reputation successively rising and falling. This cyclical seesaw pattern of Roosevelt historiography is entirely natural in that received and dominant interpretations are subjected to the process of revisionism by succeeding generations of scholars and writers. A particular interpretation usually has limitations, and when these intellectual borders are reached a new direction is taken. Theodore Roosevelt, through this process, has been subjected to extreme fluctuations of opinion as much as any figure in American history, probably because his career involved much that is important to modern American history. It may be, however, that the cyclical pattern in Roosevelt historiography has reached its limits, and that new patterns or dynamics will be operative in the future.

In addition to the cyclical pattern, there have been at least two constant major traditions in Roosevelt historiography, forming continuing themes through all the different periods: the debunking tradition and the tradition of reverence for Roosevelt. Each major tradition may be broken down into sub-categories, but there is a coherent and definite duality in Roosevelt historiography. The debunking tradition actually predates Henry F. Pringle's 1931 biography, and may be traced back to the iconoclastic writings of the literary figures Stuart Sherman, George Sylvester Viereck, and H. L. Mencken in the years immediately following Roosevelt's death, when theirs was a minority viewpoint. And the debunking tradition continued beyond the Debunking Period of the 1930s and 1940s. The counter tradition of reverence for Roosevelt, carried on in both prosperous and lean times since 1919 by successive generations of admirers and what is now the Theodore Roosevelt Association, was responsible for a steady flow of publications, and for establishing and supporting Roosevelt memorials.[38]

The debunking tradition has included voices from the right like George Sylvester Viereck and from the left like the New Left historians, but the continuing and uniting theme has been that Theodore Roosevelt was something other than what he said he was—a sordid careerist rather than a practical idealist, a reactionary rather than a reformer, a berserker rather than a statesman, a warmonger rather than a servant of the "peace of righteousness." The tradition of reverence for Roosevelt has included respected scholars like Albert Bushnell Hart as well as those mainly interested in promoting patriotism; and the history of the Theodore Roosevelt Association shows a remarkable variety of activities, ranging from the commemorative and patriotic to work in historic preservation and scholarship. Such projects as the reconstruction of the Theodore Roosevelt Birthplace and saving Sagamore Hill, assembling the Theodore Roosevelt Association Film Collection now at the Library of Congress and the Theodore Roosevelt Collection now at Harvard, and sponsoring the publication of collections of Roosevelt's works and letters have won universal praise. And in spite of numerous counterattacks by historians, the writings of debunkers like H. L. Mencken, Henry F. Pringle, and Gabriel Kolko endure and are still read. The two traditions have preserved a measure of pluralism in Roosevelt historiography throughout successive periods. And while some might assume that truth must reside somewhere in the middle ground between these two extremes, adherents of both traditions would hotly deny that this is the case.[39]

What is thought and written about history helps a nation define itself in each generation and era, and therefore the study of historiography can reveal much about the concerns, beliefs, problems, and values of a nation. The historiography of Theodore Roosevelt, stretching back over many decades, can teach a great deal about the United States in the twentieth century, particularly in regard to the place of heroes in American culture, the role of the presidency, and views on foreign policy, the military, regulation of the marketplace, and political ideology. Thus the subject of the history of the history of Theodore Roosevelt presents a promising area for future research and study. Historiography is also, of course, a productive approach to any subject in history, and the historiography of Theodore Roosevelt shows that there is still much work to do on TR, especially with regard to the major phase of his career after 1901. Roosevelt's youth and the years up to 1901 have been thoroughly examined by Carleton Putnam, David McCullough, Edmund Morris, and others, but TR's presidency and his final years have yet to receive the same detailed analysis, though much has been written about foreign policy, the regulation of business, and the Bull Moose campaign. No historian would claim that TR's career after 1901 has been exhaustively studied. Many of the important chapters in the history of the history of Theodore Roosevelt have yet to be written.

NOTES

1. On the historiography of Theodore Roosevelt, see I. E. Cadenhead, Jr., *Theodore Roosevelt and the Paradox of Progressivism* (Woodbury, NY: Barron's Educational Series, 1974), pp. 242–76; Richard H. Collin, "Henry Pringle's Theodore Roosevelt: A Study in Historical Revisionism," *New York History* 52, no. 2 (April 1971): 151–68; Richard H. Collin, "The Image of Theodore Roosevelt in American History and Thought, 1885–1965" (Ph.D. diss., New York University, 1966); John Allen Gable, "The Two TRs—Mythic and Real," *Theodore Roosevelt Association Journal* (hereafter cited as *TRA Journal*) 9, no. 4 (Fall 1985): 4-7; Dewey W. Gratham, Jr., ed., *Theodore Roosevelt* (Englewood Cliffs, NJ: Prentice Hall, 1971); Dewey W. Grantham, "Theodore Roosevelt in American Historical Writing, 1945–1960," *Mid-America* 43, no. 1 (January 1961): 3–35; Morton Keller, *Theodore Roosevelt: A Profile* (New York: Hill and Wang, 1967); Frederick W. Marks III, "Theodore Roosevelt and the Righting of History," *TRA Journal* 12, no. 1 (Winter 1986): 8–12; Serge Ricard, "The French Historiography of Theodore Roosevelt," *TRA Journal* 15, no. 2 (Summer 1984): 21–23; William Tilchin, "The Rising Star of Theodore Roosevelt's Diplomacy: Major Studies from Beale to the Present," *TRA Journal* 15, no. 3 (Summer 1989): 2–24. The most complete bibliography on Theodore Roosevelt, including writings about and by TR, are the catalogues of the Theodore Roosevelt Collection at Harvard: Gregory C. Wilson, ed., *Theodore Roosevelt Collection: Dictionary Catalogue and Shelflist*, 5 vols. (Cambridge: Harvard University Press, 1970); Wallace Finley Dailey, ed., *Theodore Roosevelt Collection: Dictionary Catalogue and Shelflist Supplement* (Cambridge: Harvard College Library, 1986).

2. Rudyard Kipling, "Great Heart," in *Roosevelt as the Poets Saw Him*, ed. Charles Hanson Towne (New York: Charles Scribner's Sons, 1923), pp. 113–14.

3. Hermann Hagedorn, *The Boys' Life of Theodore Roosevelt* (New York: Harper and Brothers Publishers, 1918), p. 2.

4. Towne, *Roosevelt as the Poets Saw Him*; Hilah Paulmier and Robert Haven Schauffler, eds., *Roosevelt Day* (New York: Dodd, Mead

and Company, 1932); on the reconstruction of what is now Theodore Roosevelt Birthplace National Historic Site, 28 East Twentieth Street, New York City, see Charles B. Hosmer, Jr., *Presence of the Past: A History of the Preservation Movement in the United States Before Williamsburg* (New York: G. P. Putnam's Sons, 1965), pp. 147–52, and David H. Kahn, "The Theodore Roosevelt Birthplace in New York City," *The Magazine Antiques* 116, no. 1 (July 1979): 176–81; on Mount Rushmore, see Rex Alan Smith, *The Carving of Mount Rushmore* (New York: Abbeville Press, 1985); on Roosevelt memorials, also see Alan R. Havig, "Presidential Images, History, and Homage: Memorializing Theodore Roosevelt, 1919–1967," *American Quarterly* 30, no. 4 (Fall 1978): 513–32. The Roosevelt Memorial Association was founded in January 1919, and chartered by Congress, May 31, 1920, "to perpetuate the memory of Theodore Roosevelt for the benefit of the people of the United States of America and the world." The Woman's Roosevelt Memorial Association was chartered by New York State, January 29, 1919, to build a memorial to TR in New York City. Both organizations joined in reconstructing Theodore Roosevelt Birthplace, and made their headquarters at the site. The organizations merged in 1956 to form the present Theodore Roosevelt Association. See John Allen Gable, "Theodore Roosevelt Association," in *Theodore Roosevelt Cyclopedia*, rev. 2d ed., ed. Albert Bushnell Hart, Herbert Ronald Ferleger, and John Allen Gable (Oyster Bay, NY: Theodore Roosevelt Association and Meckler, 1989), pp. 677–79.

   5. Hermann Hagedorn, ed., *Memorial Edition: The Works of Theodore Roosevelt*, 24 vols. (New York: Charles Scribner's Sons, 1923–1926); Hermann Hagedorn, ed., *National Edition: The Works of Theodore Roosevelt*, 20 vols. (New York: Charles Scribner's Sons, 1926); Joseph Bucklin Bishop, *Theodore Roosevelt and His Time, Shown in His Letters*, 2 vols. (New York: Charles Scribner's Sons, 1920); Hermann Hagedorn, *Roosevelt in the Bad Lands* (Boston: Houghton Mifflin Company, 1921); Tyler Dennett, *Roosevelt and the Russo-Japanese War* (Garden City, NY: Doubleday, Page and Company, 1925); William Roscoe Thayer, *Theodore Roosevelt: An Intimate Biography* (Cambridge: Houghton Mifflin Company, 1919); Eugene Thwing, *The Life and Meaning of Theodore Roosevelt* (New York: Current Literature Publishing Company, 1919); William Draper Lewis, *The Life of Theodore Roosevelt* (Philadelphia: The John C. Winston Company, 1919); Harold Howland, *Theodore Roosevelt and His Times: A Chronicle of the Progressive Movement* (New Haven: Yale University Press, 1921); Lord Charnwood, *Theodore Roosevelt* (Boston: The Atlantic Monthly Press, 1923); Lewis Einstein, *Roosevelt: His Mind in Action* (Boston: Houghton Mifflin Company, 1930). In addition to Joseph Bucklin Bishop's biography, and the books cited above by Hagedorn and Dennett, other useful memoirs and studies from the early period of Roosevelt historiography include Lawrence F. Abbot, *Impressions of Theodore Roosevelt* (Garden City, NY: Doubleday, Page and Company, 1924); Archibald W. Butt, *Taft and Roosevelt: The Intimate Letters of Archie Butt, Military Aide*, 2 vols. (Garden City, NY: Doubleday, Doran and Company, 1930); Anna Roosevelt Cowles, *Letters from Theodore*

Roosevelt to Anna Roosevelt Cowles, 1870–1918, 2 vols. (New York: Charles Scribner's Sons, 1925); Oscar King Davis, *Released for Publication: Some Inside Political History of Theodore Roosevelt and His Times, 1898–1918* (Boston: Houghton Mifflin Company, 1925); Howard C. Hill, *Roosevelt and the Caribbean* (Chicago: University of Chicago Press, 1927); John J. Leary, Jr., *Talks with T. R.* (Boston: Houghton Mifflin Company, 1920); Henry Cabot Lodge, *Selections from the Correspondence of Theodore Roosevelt and Henry Cabot Lodge, 1884–1918*, 2 vols. (New York: Charles Scribner's Sons, 1925); Corinne Roosevelt Robinson, *My Brother Theodore Roosevelt* (New York: Charles Scribner's Sons, 1921); Owen Wister, *Roosevelt: The Story of a Friendship, 1880–1919* (New York: Macmillan Company, 1930); Frederick S. Wood, ed., *Roosevelt as We Knew Him: The Personal Recollections of One Hundred and Fifty of His Friends and Associates* (Philadelphia: The John C. Winston Company, 1927).

6. See Thayer, *Theodore Roosevelt*, pp. vii, 19–24; Lord Charnwood, *Theodore Roosevelt*, p. 3; John Chamberlain, *Farewell to Reform: The Rise, Life and Decay of the Progressive Mind*, 2d ed. (New York: The John Day Company, 1933), p. 262.

7. For one of Roosevelt's contemporaries and friends who saw that the ethos of the 1920s was at odds with TR, see William Allen White, *Masks in a Pageant* (New York: Macmillan Company, 1928); for a discussion of the interplay of TR's legacy with the events and trends in the United States since 1919, and also of Woodrow Wilson's legacy, see John Milton Cooper, Jr., *The Warrior and the Priest: Woodrow Wilson and Theodore Roosevelt* (Cambridge: The Belknap Press of Harvard University Press, 1983), pp. 346–61.

8. Henry F. Pringle, *Theodore Roosevelt: A Biography* (New York: Harcourt, Brace and Company, 1931), "adolescent," p. 4; Collin, "The Image of Theodore Roosevelt in American History and Thought," p. 322, also see pp. 304–22, and Collin, "Henry Pringle's Theodore Roosevelt." Pringle published a condensed and revised version of the biography without footnotes in 1956 (New York: Harcourt, Brace, Harvest Book, 1956). The original edition is cited here. Besides its readability, one of the main reasons for Pringle's durability, as Collin notes, is that Pringle's biography was the only full-length, scholarly biography of TR based on primary sources until William Henry Harbaugh's TR biography was published in 1961.

9. See Pringle, *Theodore Roosevelt*, on conservation, pp. 430–31; the Storers, pp. 454–58; governors' conference, p. 485; spelling reform, pp. 465–67; Pure Food and Drug and Meat Inspection Acts, pp. 428–29; "inaccurately aimed bullets," p. 4. On the casualties of the Rough Riders, see Theodore Roosevelt, *The Rough Riders* (New York: Charles Scribner's Sons, 1899), pp. 155–59. On the governors' conference, see Paul Russell Cutright, *Theodore Roosevelt: The Naturalist* (New York: Harper and Brothers, 1956), pp. 179–83.

10. Pringle, *Theodore Roosevelt*, pp. 570–71.

11. Pringle cited in his footnote for the quotation "Roosevelt House Papers," the collection that became the Theodore Roosevelt Collection at Harvard in 1943. The quotation appears in Pringle's

notes, now part of the Theodore Roosevelt Collection at Harvard, with the identification "H. W. to H. H. en route Chicago to New York after Republican National Convention 1920." "H. W." is identified as Horace Wilkinson in Pringle's notes, and "H. H." is probably Hermann Hagedorn. This is the only evidence that has ever been found suggesting that TR intended to leave the Progressive party prior to the defeats of 1914, and of course the quotation in the original form does not have the meaning of Pringle's published version. For Richard Hofstadter's use of the Pringle version of the quotation, see Hofstadter, *The American Political Tradition and the Men Who Made It* (New York: Alfred A. Knopf, 1948), p. 232. On the history of the Progressive party, see John Allen Gable, *The Bull Moose Years: Theodore Roosevelt and the Progressive Party* (Port Washington, NY: Kennikat Press, 1978).

12. Chamberlain, *Farewell to Reform*, pp. 234–35, 268; Dexter Perkins, *The Monroe Doctrine, 1867–1907* (Baltimore: The Johns Hopkins Press, 1937), pp. 379, 385, 387; Alfred Vagts and other doubters of TR's account are cited and discussed in Edmund Morris, "'A Few Pregnant Days': Theodore Roosevelt and the Venezuelan Crisis of 1902," *TRA Journal* 15, no. 1 (Winter 1989): 2–13; Daniel Aaron, *Men of Good Hope: A Story of American Progressives* (New York: Oxford University Press, 1951; Galaxy edition, 1961), pp. 245–80. TR said that he had privately given the Germans an ultimatum to accept arbitration in a dispute with Venezuela in 1902.

13. Hofstadter, *The American Political Tradition*, pp. 203–33.

14. Ibid., discussion of TR and war, pp. 206–12; footnote on Russo-Japanese War and Moroccan Crisis, p. 212.

15. Collin, "The Image of Theodore Roosevelt," p. 333, and see, pp. 333–42; on TR's influence on Franklin D. Roosevelt, particularly Geoffrey C. Ward, *A First-Class Temperament: The Emergence of Franklin D. Roosevelt* (New York: Harper and Row, 1989).

16. David McCullough, *Mornings on Horseback* (New York: Simon and Schuster, 1981), p. 9. Other important books dating from the Debunking Period, include Howard L. Hurwitz, *Theodore Roosevelt and Labor in New York State, 1880–1900* (New York: Columbia University Press, 1943), which is critical of TR's attitudes on labor; and George E. Mowry, *Theodore Roosevelt and the Progressive Movement* (Madison: University of Wisconsin Press, 1946), which says that TR's Progressive party destroyed the liberal movement within the Republican party.

17. Robert E. Osgood, *Ideals and Self-Interest in America's Foreign Relations: The Great Transformation of the Twentieth Century* (Chicago: University of Chicago Press, 1953), quotation, p. 67, and see pp. 66–70, 135–53; Howard K. Beale, in a review of *The Letters of Theodore Roosevelt*, quoted by Collin, "The Image of Theodore Roosevelt," p. 364; on views of TR's foreign policy by historians in this period, see Cadenhead, *Theodore Roosevelt*, pp. 256–62, Grantham, "Theodore Roosevelt in American Historical Writing," and Tilchin, "The Rising Star of Theodore Roosevelt's Diplomacy"; on American foreign policy and TR's legacies, also see William Tilchin, "Theodore Roosevelt, Harry Truman, and the Uneven Course of American Foreign Policy in

the First Half of the Twentieth Century," *TRA Journal* 10, no. 4 (Winter 1984): 2–10.

18. On TR and the modern presidency, see the widely accepted views expressed in Edward S. Corwin, *The President: Office and Powers*, 4th ed. (New York: New York University Press, 1957), and James MacGregor Burns, *Presidential Government: the Crucible of Leadership* (Boston: Houghton Mifflin Company, 1966). Also see James MacGregor Burns, *The Deadlock of Democracy: Four-Party Politics in America* (Englewood Cliffs, NJ: Prentice-Hall, 1963). On views of Roosevelt as a conservative or liberal, see John M. Blum, *The Republican Roosevelt* (New York: Antheneum, 1962), pp. ix-xi, 56, 23, 71, 121–22; Eric F. Goldman, *Rendezvous with Destiny* (New York: Alfred A. Knopf, 1953), pp. 161–65; Arthur M. Schlesinger, Jr., *The Age of Roosevelt: The Crisis of the Old Order, 1919–1933* (Boston: Houghton Mifflin Company, 1957), pp. 18–26, 35–36.

19. Elting E. Morison, John M. Blum, Alfred D. Chandler, Jr., et al., eds., *The Letters of Theodore Roosevelt*, 8 vols. (Cambridge: Harvard University Press, 1951–1954); Cadenhead, *Theodore Roosevelt*, Cadenhead quotation, p. 257, Beale quoted, pp. 257–58; Link quoted by Collin, "The Image of Theodore Roosevelt," p. 343; on the influence of the *Letters*, see Collin, "The Image of Theodore Roosevelt," pp. 343–72.

20. Blum, *The Republican Roosevelt*, p. 7. The original edition of John M. Blum's *The Republican Roosevelt* was published by Harvard University Press, 1954. The Antheneum edition of 1962 included the "Preface to the Second Edition," pp. ix-xi, which discussed criticisms of Blum's assertion that TR was a conservative. Harvard University Press published a Second Edition in 1977 which omitted the Antheneum preface and included a new "Preface and Prologue to the Second Edition," pp. vi-xix.

21. Quotations: William Henry Harbaugh, *Power and Responsibility: The Life and Times of Theodore Roosevelt* (New York: Farrar, Straus and Cudahy, 1961), pp. 521–22; Edmund Morris, *The Rise of Theodore Roosevelt* (New York: Coward, McCann and Geoghegan, 1979), p. 750. Works cited: Howard K. Beale, *Theodore Roosevelt and the Rise of America to World Power* (Baltimore: The Johns Hopkins Press, 1956), on Venezuelan Crisis of 1902, see pp. 395–422; Paul Russell Cutright, *Theodore Roosevelt: The Formative Years, 1858–1886* (New York: Charles Scribner's Sons, 1958), the first and only volume of what was intended to be a multi-volume biography; Edward Wagenknecht, *The Seven Worlds of Theodore Roosevelt* (New York: Longmans, Green and Company, 1958), the "seven worlds" being those of action, thought, human relations, the family, spiritual values, public affairs, and war and peace; George E. Mowry, *The Era of Theodore Roosevelt and the Birth of Modern America, 1900–1912* (New York: Harper and Row, 1958); G. Wallace Chessman, *Governor Theodore Roosevelt: The Albany Apprenticeship, 1898–1900* (Cambridge: Harvard University Press, 1965). Harbaugh's biography was subsequently issued in paperback editions by Collier, 1963, and by Oxford University Press, 1975, under the title *The Life and Times of*

Theodore Roosevelt. The 1975 edition has an updated annotated bibliography. Quotations from Harbaugh in this essay are from the first edition. Other noteworthy books and articles from the Era of *Realpolitik* in Roosevelt historiography, not previously cited, include Nelson M. Blake, "Ambassadors at the Court of Theodore Roosevelt," *Mississippi Valley Historical Review* 92, no. 2 (September 1955): 179–206; Noel F. Busch, *T. R.: The Story of Theodore Roosevelt and His Influence on Our Times* (New York: Reynal, 1963); Arthur M. Johnson, "Theodore Roosevelt and the Bureau of Corporations," *Mississippi Valley Historical Review* 95, no. 4 (March 1959): 571–90; Arthur M. Johnson, "Theodore Roosevelt and the Navy," *United States Naval Institute Proceedings* 48, no. 10 (October 1958): 76–82; William Davison Johnston, *T. R.: Champion of the Strenuous Life* (New York: Farrar, Straus and Cudahy, 1958); Stefan Lorant, *The Life and Times of Theodore Roosevelt* (Garden City, NY: Doubleday and Company, 1959); Richard Lowitt, "Theodore Roosevelt," in *America's Ten Greatest Presidents*, ed. Morton Borden (Chicago: Rand McNally and Company, 1961), pp. 185–206; Robert W. Sellen, "Theodore Roosevelt: Historian with a Moral," *Mid-America* 41, no. 4 (October 1959): 223–40; Robert H. Wiebe, "The House of Morgan and the Executive, 1905–13," *American Historical Review* 115, no. 1 (October 1959): 49–60. Also see Grantham, "Theodore Roosevelt in American Historical Writing, 1945–1960," for a discussion of the historiography of this period; and for further bibliographical reference, see Wallace Finley Dailey, "Theodore Roosevelt in Periodical Literature, 1950–1981," *TRA Journal* 8 no. 4 (Fall 1982): 4–15.

22. Humphrey quoted from cover of Collier paperback edition of Harbaugh, *Life and Times of Theodore Roosevelt*; Richard Hofstadter, *The Age of Reform from Bryan to F. D. R.* (New York: Alfred A. Knopf, 1955); Richard Hofstadter, *Anti-Intellectualism in American Life* (New York: Alfred A. Knopf, 1962).

23. See Hermann Hagedorn and Gary G. Roth, *Sagamore Hill: An Historical Guide* (Oyster Bay, NY: Theodore Roosevelt Association, 1977), revised edition of booklet first published in 1953; Hermann Hagedorn, *The Roosevelt Family of Sagamore Hill* (New York: Macmillan Company, 1954); *Life* editorial, December 2, 1957; *Time* cover story, March 3, 1958; *Final Report of the Theodore Roosevelt Centennial Commission*, 86th Cong., 1st sess., Senate Document No. 36 (Washington, DC: United States Government Printing Office, 1959); John Allen Gable, "Theodore Roosevelt Island," *TRA Journal* 9, no. 3 (Summer 1983): 2–4. Hermann Hagedorn, after serving as secretary and director of the Theodore Roosevelt Association, 1919–1957, was the director of the federal Theodore Roosevelt Centennial Commission, a fitting climax to his long career. In the Commission's *Final Report* (1959), Hagedorn wrote with satisfaction of the new books on TR: "These books were significant not only for their number and for the publicity they aroused, but for the new attitude toward Mr. Roosevelt on the part of historians which they revealed. In none of them is there a trace of the patronizing, even sneering skepticism of the appraisals that had been adopted by too many of the historical

writers of the last 30 years as the proper attitude to take toward Mr. Roosevelt; an attitude that in too many high schools, colleges, and universities had achieved the dignity of a canon. The books . . . are critical—as they should be—but they are all respectful, and all dare to admit the quality of greatness in Mr. Roosevelt which a decade ago would have drawn on the writer blasts from the groves of Academe."

24. Grantham, "Theodore Roosevelt in American Historical Writing, 1945–1960," pp. 33–35; on the New Left historians, see the essays by Jonathan M. Wiener, Staughton Lynd, Jesse Lemisch, and others in the *Journal of American History* 76, no. 2 (September 1989): 393–488. Works from this period in the *realpolitik* tradition include David H. Burton, *Theodore Roosevelt: Confident Imperialist* (Philadelphia: University of Pennsylvania Press, 1969); G. Wallace Chessman, *Theodore Roosevelt and the Politics of Power* (Boston: Little, Brown, 1969); Raymond A. Esthus, *Theodore Roosevelt and Japan* (Seattle: University of Washington Press, 1966); Raymond A. Esthus, *Theodore Roosevelt and the International Rivalries* (Waltham, MA: Ginn-Blaisdell, 1970); Charles E. Neu, *An Uncertain Friendship: Theodore Roosevelt and Japan, 1906–1909* (Cambridge: Harvard University Press, 1967); Nicholas Roosevelt, *Theodore Roosevelt: The Man As I Knew Him* (New York: Dodd, Mead and Company, 1967); Eugene P. Trani, *The Treaty of Portsmouth: An Adventure in American Diplomacy* (Lexington: University of Kentucky Press, 1969).

25. Quotation: Melvin Steinfield, *Our Racist Presidents From Washington to Nixon* (San Ramon, CA: Consensus Publishers, 1972), p. 202; on the Booker T. Washington dinner, see Willard B. Gatewood, Jr., *Theodore Roosevelt and the Art of Controversy: Episodes of the White House Years* (Baton Rouge: Louisiana State University Press, 1970), pp. 32–61, and Dewey W. Grantham, "Dinner at the White House: Theodore Roosevelt, Booker T. Washington, and the South," *Tennessee Historical Quarterly* 17, no. 2 (June 1958): 112–30; on TR and the blacks, see particularly, Seth M. Scheiner, "President Theodore Roosevelt and the Negro, 1901–1908," *Journal of Negro History* 47, no. 3 (July 1962): 169–82, and John Hope Franklin, *From Slavery to Freedom: A History of Negro Americans*, 4th ed. (New York: Alfred A. Knopf, 1974), pp. 316–19, 324–25; also see Gatewood, *Art of Controversy*, on the Indianola Post Office Affair, pp. 62–89, on the appointment of William D. Crum, pp. 90–134; and Michael Kelly, "Tablescraps: Mementos of the Washington-Roosevelt Dinner," *TRA Journal* 14, no. 4 (Fall 1988): 7–11.

26. Thomas G. Dyer, *Theodore Roosevelt and the Idea of Race* (Baton Rouge: Louisiana State University Press, 1980), pp. 33–44; on Brownsville, see Stephen R. Fox, *The Guardian of Boston: William Monroe Trotter* (New York: Antheneum, 1970), pp. 150–54, Emma Lou Thornbrough, "The Brownsville Episode and the Negro Vote," *Mississippi Valley Historical Review* 44, no. 3 (December 1957): 469–93, and James A. Tinsley, "Roosevelt, Foraker, and the Brownsville Affray," *Journal of Negro History* 41, no. 1 (January 1956): 43–65; on TR and the blacks in 1912, see Gable, *The Bull Moose Years*, pp. 60–74, and

George E. Mowry, "The South and The Progressive Lily White Party of 1912," *Journal of Southern History* 6, no. 2 (May 1940): 237–47.

27. Thomas A. Bailey, *Presidential Greatness: The Image and the Man from Washington to the Present* (New York: Appleton-Century-Crofts, 1966), pp. 307–8; Lloyd C. Gardner, Walter F. LaFeber, Thomas J. McCormick, *Creation of the American Empire: United States Diplomatic History* (Chicago: Rand McNally and Company, 1973), pp. 262–78, passim; on the Panama Canal, see Walter F. LaFeber, *The Panama Canal* (New York: Oxford University Press, 1977); on the Roosevelt Corollary, see Thomas A. Bailey, *A Diplomatic History of the American People* (Englewood Cliffs, NJ: Prentice-Hall, 1974), p. 505, Harbaugh, *Power and Responsibility*, pp. 193–97.

28. Harbaugh, *Power and Responsibility*, p. 197. Frederick W. Marks III says that TR's acquisition of the Panama Canal Zone is "one of the most heavily criticized moves in the annals of American diplomacy," and that the Roosevelt Corollary has been seen "as a cover for imperial designs on Latin America." See Frederick W. Marks III *Velvet on Iron: The Diplomacy of Theodore Roosevelt* (Lincoln: University of Nebraska Press, 1979), pp. 96–97, 146. One of the few defenses of TR's actions in Panama is Robert A. Friedlander, "A Reassessment of Roosevelt's Role in the Panamanian Revolution of 1903," *Western Political Quarterly* 14 (June 1961): 535-43.

29. Barbara W. Tuchman, *The Proud Tower: A Portrait of the World Before the War, 1890–1914* (New York: Macmillan Company, 1966), quoted, p. 286, on the Second Hague Peace Conference, pp. 274–88; all the matters mentioned in this paragraph are discussed in Marks, *Velvet on Iron*, passim, also see Marks, "The Righting of History."

30. Gabriel Kolko, *The Triumph of Conservatism: A Reinterpretation of American History, 1900–1916* (New York: The Free Press, 1963), p. 3; on the problems of the presidency in this period, see Arthur M. Schlesinger, Jr., *The Imperial Presidency* (Boston: Houghton Mifflin, 1973).

31. Kolko, *Triumph of Conservatism*, pp. 98–108.

32. Quotations: James Harvey Young, *Pure Food: Securing the Federal Food and Drugs Act of 1906* (Princeton: Princeton University Press, 1989), p. 281; John Braeman, "The Square Deal in Action: A Case Study in the Growth of the National Police Power," in *Change and Continuity in Twentieth Century America*, ed. John Braeman, Robert H. Bremner, Everett Walters (Ohio State University Press, 1964; New York: Harper and Row, 1966), p. 74; On the Meat Inspection Act, see Braeman, "The Square Deal in Action," pp. 35–80; Mark Sullivan, *Our Times*, 6 vols. (New York: Charles Scribner's Sons, 1926–1935), 2: 471–552; Young, *Pure Food*, pp. 221–95.

33. Compare Kolko, *Triumph of Conservatism*, on the Pure Food and Drug Act, pp. 108-10, with the accounts in Sullivan, *Our Times*, 2: 471–552, and Young, *Pure Food*, pp. 221–95. For a solid account of the role of business in reform legislation, see Robert H. Wiebe, *Businessmen and Reform: A Study of the Progressive Movement* (Cambridge: Harvard University Press, 1962). Three well-written popular works from this period, not connected with the New Left, are

Joseph L. Gardner, *Departing Glory: Theodore Roosevelt as Ex-President* (New York: Charles Scribner's Sons, 1973); Virgil Carrington Jones, *Roosevelt's Rough Riders* (Garden City, NY: Doubleday, 1969); and William Manners, *TR and Will: A Friendship That Split the Republican Party* (New York: Harcourt, Brace and World, 1969).

34. Edmund Morris, "The Saga of Teddy," *Newsweek* 44, no. 6 (August 6, 1979): 46–47; and see Morris, *The Rise of Theodore Roosevelt*; McCullough, *Mornings on Horseback*; Marks, *Velvet on Iron*; *Time: Special Report, The American Presidents* (Chicago: Time, Inc., 1976), the special issue with TR on the cover; also see Edmund Morris, "The Many Words and Works of Theodore Roosevelt," *Smithsonian* 14, no. 8 (November 1983): 86–90, 92, 94–95; Edmund Morris, "Theodore Roosevelt, President," *American Heritage* 32, no. 4 (June-July 1981): 415.

35. On the presidential polls, see Morris, "The Saga of Teddy," p. 46; David L. Porter, "American Historians Rate Our Presidents," in *The Rating Game in American Politics: An Interdisciplinary Approach*, ed. William Pederson and Ann McLaurin (New York: Irvington Publishers, 1987), pp. 13–37. Porter gives charts of the Schlesinger, Porter, and Chicago *Tribune* polls. In the U.S. Historical Society poll the ranking was Lincoln, Washington, FDR, TR, Jefferson; the Porter poll listed Lincoln, Washington, FDR, Jefferson, TR. See *TRA Journal* 12, no. 1 (Winter 1986): on the Canisius College TR conference, pp. 78; on the Roosevelt Study Center, Middelburg, the Netherlands, p. 13.

36. Titles mentioned not previously cited are Richard H. Collin, *Theodore Roosevelt, Culture, Diplomacy, and Expansion: A New View of American Imperialism* (Baton Rouge: Louisiana State University Press, 1985); Richard H. Collin, *Theodore Roosevelt's Caribbean: The Panama Canal, the Monroe Doctrine, and the Latin American Context* (Baton Rouge: Louisiana State University Press, 1990); Jay Stuart Berman, *Police Administration and Progressive Reform: Theodore Roosevelt As Police Commissioner of New York* (Westport, CT: Greenwood Press, 1987); Paul Russell Cutright, *Theodore Roosevelt: The Making of a Conservationist* (Urbana: University of Illinois Press, 1985); Lewis L. Gould, *The Presidency of Theodore Roosevelt* (Lawrence: University of Kansas Press, 1991); Aloysius A. Norton, *Theodore Roosevelt* (Boston: Twayne Publishers, 1980); James R. Reckner, *Teddy Roosevelt's Great White Fleet* (Annapolis, MD.: Naval Institute Press, 1988); William C. Widenor, *Henry Cabot Lodge and the Search for an American Foreign Policy* (Berkeley: University of California Press, 1980); new collections of Roosevelt's writings and speeches included John Allen Gable, ed., *The Man in the Arena: Speeches and Essays by Theodore Roosevelt* (Oyster Bay, NY: Theodore Roosevelt Association, 1987); Paul Schullery, ed., *American Bears: Selections from the Writings of Theodore Roosevelt* (Boulder: Colorado Associated University Press, 1983); Paul Schullery, ed., *Theodore Roosevelt: Wilderness Writings* (Salt Lake City, UT: Gibbs M. Smith, 1986); James F. Vivian, *The Romance of My Life: Theodore Roosevelt's Speeches in North Dakota* (Fargo, ND: Theodore Roosevelt Medora Foundation, 1989). Other studies from the Roosevelt Renaissance period include Kathleen Dalton, "The Early Life of Theodore Roosevelt," (Ph.D. diss., Johns Hopkins University, 1979);

Kathleen Dalton, "Theodore Roosevelt and the Idea of War," *TRA Journal* 7, no. 4 (Fall 1981): 6-12; Kathleen Dalton, "Why America Loved Teddy Roosevelt, Or, Charisma Is in the Eyes of the Beholder," in *Our Selves/Our Past: Psychological Approaches to American History*, ed. R. J. Brugger (Baltimore: The Johns Hopkins University Press, 1981); John L. Eliot, "T. R.'s Wilderness Legacy," *National Geographic* 162, no. 3 (September 1982): 340–63; John Allen Gable, *Adventure in Reform: Gifford Pinchot, Amos Pinchot, Theodore Roosevelt and the Progressive Party* (Milford, PA: Grey Towers Press, 1986); John Allen Gable, *The Many-Sided Theodore Roosevelt: American Renaissance Man* (Middelberg, the Netherlands: Roosevelt Study Center, 1986); John Allen Gable, "Theodore Roosevelt: The Renaissance Man as President," in *The Rating Game in American Politics*, Pederson, McLaurin, eds., pp. 336–53; Lewis L. Gould, "The Price of Fame: Theodore Roosevelt as Celebrity, 1909–1919," *Lamar Journal of the Humanities* 10, no. 2 (Fall 1984): 7–18; Peter Larsen, "Theodore Roosevelt and the Moroccan Crisis, 1904–1906" (Ph.D. diss., Princeton University, 1984); Sylvia Jukes Morris, *Edith Kermit Roosevelt: Portrait of a First Lady* (New York: Coward, McCann and Geoghegan, 1980); Richard W. Turk, *The Ambiguous Relationship: Theodore Roosevelt and Alfred Thayer Mahan* (Westport, CT: Greenwood Press, 1987). Negative assessments of Roosevelt continued to be published in this period: see, as examples, Serge Ricard, "Theodore Roosevelt and the Diplomacy of Righteousness," *TRA Journal* 12, no. 1 (Winter 1986): 14–17; John Edward Wilz, "Did the United States Betray Korea in 1905?" *Pacific Historical Review* 54, no. 3 (August 1985): 243–70.

37. Morris, "The Saga of Teddy," p. 46.

38. On the early debunkers, see H. L. Mencken, "Roosevelt and Others," *Smart Set* 61, no. 3 (March 1920): 138–44; H. L. Mencken, "Roosevelt: An Autopsy," from *Prejudices: Second Series* (1920), reprinted in *Theodore Roosevelt*, Keller, ed., pp. 52–65; Stuart P. Sherman, "Roosevelt and the National Psychology," in his *Americans* (New York: Charles Scribner's Sons, 1922), pp. 256–87; George Sylvester Viereck, *Roosevelt: A Study in Ambivalence* (New York: Jackson Press, 1919). See criticisms of the work and publications of the Roosevelt Memorial Association and Woman's Roosevelt Memorial Association, predecessor organizations of the present Theodore Roosevelt Association, and of activities of the Theodore Roosevelt Centennial, in Collin, "The Image of Theodore Roosevelt," pp. 265–67, 272–79, 341–42, 399–403.

39. For examples of the continuing debunking tradition after 1950, see William M. Gibson, *Theodore Roosevelt Among the Humorists: W. D. Howells, Mark Twain, and Mr. Dooley* (Knoxville: University of Tennessee Press, 1980); Ray Ginger, *Age of Excess* (New York: Macmillan Company, 1965); Gore Vidal, "An American Sissy," *New York Review of Books* 28, no. 13 (August 13, 1981): 19–23. On the Theodore Roosevelt Association, see Gable, "Theodore Roosevelt Association"; Wendy-White Henson, Veronica M. Gillespie, *Theodore Roosevelt Association Film Collection: A Catalog* (Washington, DC: Library of Congress, 1986); Gary G. Roth, "The Roosevelt Memorial

Association and the Preservation of Sagamore Hill, 1919–1953" (M. A. thesis, Wake Forest University, 1980).

From "The Bull Moose Years" by John Allen Gable
John T. McCutcheon's drawing shows the Progressive ticket of 1912, Theodore Roosevelt of New York shaking hands with his vice-presidential running mate, Governor Hiram W. Johnson of California.

IN HIS FAVORITE
CHAIR ON THE
PIAZZA.

43

Theodore Roosevelt:
A Selected Annotated Bibliography

John Allen Gable

This bibliography is divided into four sections. Following "Bibliographical Aids," the section on the "Works, Letters, and Papers of Theodore Roosevelt" is subdivided into a chronological listing of books by TR and published collections. The third section is "Biographies and Biographical Profiles" and the final section is devoted to "Monographs and Other Works on Theodore Roosevelt."

I. Bibliographical Aids

Black, Gilbert J., ed. *Theodore Roosevelt, 1858–1919: Chronology, Documents, Bibliographical Aids.* Dobbs Ferry, NY: Oceana Publications, 1969.

Collin, Richard H. "The Image of Theodore Roosevelt in American History and Thought, 1885–1965." Ph.D. dissertation, New York University, 1966. Available from University Microfilms, Ann Arbor, MI. Discusses virtually every book and major article on TR in period 1885–1965, and includes extensive bibliography.

Grantham, Dewey W., Jr. "Theodore Roosevelt in American Historical Writing, 1945–1960." *Mid-America* 43, no. 1 (January 1961): 3–35. Important bibliographical and historiographical article.

Theodore Roosevelt Collection: Dictionary Catalogue and Shelflist. 5 vols. Prepared for publication by Gregory C. Wilson. Cambridge: Harvard University Press, 1970. Reproduction of the over 52,000 cards in the catalogue of the Theodore Roosevelt Collection at Harvard, the most complete collection of printed materials on TR. This together with the 1986 *Supplement* (see below) is the most complete bibliography on TR.

Theodore Roosevelt Collection: Dictionary Catalogue and Shelflist Supplement. Prepared for publication by Wallace Finley

Dailey. Cambridge: Harvard College Library, 1986. Updating the original Harvard *Catalogue* (see above), the *Supplement* contains virtually all publications and dissertations on TR in the years 1951–1986.

Index to the Theodore Roosevelt Papers. 3 vols. Washington, DC: Library of Congress, 1969. In the Library of Congress's Presidential Papers Index Series, this guide describes the Theodore Roosevelt Papers at the Library of Congress, and lists letters sent and received by TR alphabetically and chronologically. The TR Papers include about 250,000 items, and are available on microfilm.

The Theodore Roosevelt Association Film Collection: A Catalog. Prepared by Wendy White-Hensen and Veronica M. Gillespie. Washington, DC: Library of Congress, 1986. Lists the contents of the Theodore Roosevelt Association Film Collection in the Motion Picture, Broadcasting, and Recorded Sound Division of the Library of Congress. The collection consists of over 140,000 feet of negative, duplicate negative, and positive stock on TR and his times.

Tilchin, William, "The Rising Star of Theodore Roosevelt's Diplomacy: Major Studies from Beale to the Present." *Theodore Roosevelt Association Journal* 15, no. 3 (Summer 1989): 2–24. Essay on historiography of TR and foreign policy in the years from the 1950s to the end of the 1980s.

II. The Works, Letters, and Papers of Theodore Roosevelt

1. Chronological listing of books by Theodore Roosevelt

1882	*The Naval War of 1812*
1885	*Hunting Trips of a Ranchman*
1887	*Thomas Hart Benton*
1888	*Essays on Practical Politics*
	Gouverneur Morris
	Ranch Life and the Hunting Trail
1889–1896	*The Winning of the West*, 4 vols. (vol. 1 and vol. 2, 1889; vol. 3, 1894; vol. 4, 1896)
1891	*New York*
1893	*The Wilderness Hunter*
1895	*Hero Tales from American History*, with Henry Cabot Lodge
1897	*American Ideals*
	Some American Game
1899	*The Rough Riders*
1900	*The Strenuous Life*
	Oliver Cromwell

1905	*Outdoor Pastimes of an American Hunter*
1907	*Good Hunting*
1909	*Outlook Editorials*
1910	*African and European Addresses*
	African Game Trails
	American Problems
	The New Nationalism
1912	*The Conservation of Womanhood and Childhood*
	Realizable Ideals
1913	*Autobiography*
	History as Literature and Other Essays
	Progressive Principles
	Through the Brazilian Wilderness
1914	*Life-Histories of African Game Animals*, 2 vols.,
	co-author with Edmund Heller
1915	*America and the World War*
1916	*Fear God and Take Your Own Part*
	A Book Lover's Holidays in the Open
1917	*The Foes of Our Own Household*
	National Strength and International Duty
1918	*The Great Adventure*

Note: Theodore Roosevelt was co-editor with George Bird Grinnell and contributed to three books published by the Boone and Crockett Club: *American Big-Game* (1893), *Hunting in Many Lands* (1895), and *Trail and Campfire* (1897). TR, T. S. Van Dyke, D. G. Elliot, and A. J. Stone were the contributors to *The Deer Family* (1902).

2. Published collections of Theodore Roosevelt's works, letters, papers, writings

Bishop, Joseph Bucklin, ed. *Theodore Roosevelt's Letters to His Children.* New York: Charles Scribner's Sons, 1919. Letters from 1898–1911.

Griffith, William, ed. *The Roosevelt Policy.* 3 vols. New York: The Current Literature Publishing Company, 1919. Collection of TR's speeches, state papers, and articles which includes some World War I speeches not available in other collections.

Hagedorn, Hermann, ed. *Memorial Edition: Works of Theodore Roosevelt.* 24 vols. New York: Charles Scribner's Sons, 1923–1926. Most complete edition of TR's books, essays, state papers, and other writings, supplants the Sagamore, Elkhorn, Allegheny, and other editions of Roosevelt's collected works published in his lifetime. Introductions and bibliographical notes with each volume.

————. *National Edition: Works of Theodore Roosevelt.* 20 vols. New York: Charles Scribner's Sons, 1926. Shorter version of *Memorial Edition* listed above.

Hart, Albert Bushnell, and Herbert Ronald Ferleger, eds. *Theodore Roosevelt Cyclopedia.* 1941. 2d ed., edited by John Allen Gable. Oyster Bay, NY: Theodore Roosevelt Association and Meckler, 1989. Quotations from TR listed topically; revised edition includes annotated bibliography, introduction, chronology of TR's life, history of Theodore Roosevelt Association.

Irwin, Will, ed. *Letters to Kermit from Theodore Roosevelt, 1902–1908.* New York: Charles Scribner's Sons, 1946. Letters from TR to his son Kermit Roosevelt.

Letters from Theodore Roosevelt to Anna Roosevelt Cowles, 1870–1918. New York: Charles Scribner's Sons, 1924. Letters from TR to his sister Mrs. William Sheffield Cowles.

Morison, Elting, John M. Blum, et al., eds. *The Letters of Theodore Roosevelt.* 8 vols. Cambridge: Harvard University Press, 1951–1954. The most complete published collection of letters by TR, includes approximately 6,500 letters; appendices with essays by John M. Blum, Alfred D. Chandler, Jr.; superb footnotes and indexes; chronology of TR's daily activities, 1898–1919, in vols. 2, 4, 6, 8.

Roosevelt, Theodore. *Presidential Addresses and State Papers and European Addresses.* 8 vols. Homeward Bound Edition. New York: The Review of Reviews Company, 1910. Includes almost every speech given by Roosevelt in 1901–1910, many not found in any other collection.

————. *Theodore Roosevelt's Diaries of Boyhood and Youth.* New York: Charles Scribner's Sons, 1928. Diaries from 1868 through 1877.

Selections from the Correspondence of Theodore Roosevelt and Henry Cabot Lodge, 1884–1918. 2 vols. New York: Charles Scribner's Sons, 1925. Letters between TR and his close friend Lodge with some passages deleted by Senator Lodge.

Stout, Ralph, ed. *Roosevelt in the Kansas City Star: War-Time Editorials by Theodore Roosevelt.* Boston: Houghton Mifflin Company, 1921. World War I newspaper articles written by TR for the *Kansas City Star* and syndicated.

III. Biographies and Biographical Profiles

Bishop, Joseph Bucklin. *Theodore Roosevelt and His Time, Shown in His Letters.* 2 vols. New York: Charles Scribner's Sons,

1920. This is an "official biography" of Roosevelt, authorized by TR, who approved part of the first draft before his death in 1919. Bishop stated that the work "supplements and completes" TR's *Autobiography* (1913). Extensive use made of TR's letters. The work, much maligned by critics, has real value since it expresses TR's own views on his career; but, of course, Bishop should be used with the caution needed in evaluating any autobiography.

Burton, David Henry. *Theodore Roosevelt.* New York: Twayne Publishers, 1972. A short biography in Twayne's Rulers and Statesmen of the World series by a perceptive scholar.

Cadenhead, I. E., Jr. *Theodore Roosevelt: The Paradox of Progressivism.* Woodbury, NY: Barron's Educational Series, 1974. A basic biography which includes a good discussion of the historiography of TR.

Chessman, G. Wallace. *Theodore Roosevelt and the Politics of Power.* Boston: Little, Brown and Company, 1969. From the Library of American Biography series, at 214 pages this is the best short biography of TR.

Einstein, Lewis. *Roosevelt: His Mind in Action.* Boston: Houghton Mifflin Company, 1930. Few of the early biographies of Roosevelt, including those by William Roscoe Thayer, Lord Charnwood, Harold Howland, and William Draper Lewis, have much utility, except for selected sections, for later scholars, but diplomat Einstein's interpretative biography still merits consideration.

Gardner, Joseph L. *Departing Glory: Theodore Roosevelt as Ex-President.* New York: Charles Scribner's Sons, 1973. Detailed and well-written account of TR's last years, 1909–1919.

Grantham, Dewey W., Jr., ed. *Theodore Roosevelt.* Englewood Cliffs, NJ: Prentice-Hall, 1971. A good collection of writings by TR's contemporaries and later historians in the Great Lives Observed series.

Harbaugh, William Henry. *Power and Responsibility: The Life and Times of Theodore Roosevelt.* New York: Farrar, Straus, and Cudahy, 1961. *The Life and Times of Theodore Roosevelt.* Rev. ed. New York: Oxford University Press, 1975. Dewey W. Grantham, Jr., states that Harbaugh has produced "the most comprehensive and reliable one-volume biography" of TR, "an authoritative and fair-minded study." This remains the best one-volume complete biography of TR. Excellent bibliography with update in 1975 edition.

Keller, Morton, ed. *Theodore Roosevelt: A Profile.* New York: Hill and Wang, 1967. This volume in the American Profiles series contains assessments of TR by contemporaries and historians, and includes important negative judgements on TR by H. L. Mencken, Stuart P. Sherman, John R. Chamberlain, and others.

McCullough, David. *Mornings on Horseback.* New York: Simon and Schuster, 1981. An analytical and narrative account, marked by psychological insight and attention to social history, of TR and his family circle in the years 1858–1886; winner of the National Book Award.

Morris, Edmund. *The Rise of Theodore Roosevelt.* New York: Coward, McCann and Geoghegan, 1979. Morris's brilliantly written book, which won the Pulitzer Prize, follows TR up to 1901, and is the first volume of a projected three-volume biography. Morris gives a detailed account of the first part of TR's career, with informative notes explaining the sources and reasons for interpretations. This is one of the most important and widely read books on TR.

Pringle, Henry F. *Theodore Roosevelt: A Biography.* New York: Harcourt, Brace and Company, 1931. The Harcourt, Brace paperback edition (1956) lacks footnotes and is condensed, and therefore the 1931 edition should be used by scholars. Pringle's biography won the Pulitzer Prize, and for many years was the most influential book on TR. A product of the "debunking" school of biography, Pringle's biography is useful as a negative assessment of TR, although Pringle's scholarship has long since been supplanted by the work of Harbaugh, Morris, George E. Mowry, and many other historians.

Putnam, Carleton. *Theodore Roosevelt: The Formative Years, 1858–1886.* New York: Charles Scribner's Sons, 1958. Putnam's work stands with Morris and McCullough as one of three great studies of Roosevelt's early life and career. Rich in detail, Morris says the Putnam biography is a "masterpiece." Putnam originally intended to write further volumes, but the project was abandoned.

Robinson, Corinne Roosevelt. *My Brother Theodore Roosevelt.* New York: Charles Scribner's Sons, 1921. This biography by TR's sister, the poet Mrs. Douglas Robinson, is an admiring tribute; "sentimental and inaccurate, but of prime importance nevertheless," Edmund Morris says.

Wister, Owen. *Roosevelt: The Story of a Friendship, 1880–1919.* New York: Macmillan Company, 1930. Wister, the author of *The Virginian,* a novel dedicated to TR, was a close friend of

Roosevelt's over the years, and this biographical study shows the views of Roosevelt partisans.

Wood, Frederick S., ed. *Roosevelt As We Knew Him: The Personal Recollections of One Hundred and Fifty of His Friends and Associates.* Philadelphia: John C. Winston Company, 1927. Arranged in biographical sequence, this is a useful collection of memories and anecdotes of many who knew TR.

IV. Monographs and Other Works on Theodore Roosevelt

Beale, Howard K. *Theodore Roosevelt and the Rise of America to World Power.* Baltimore: Johns Hopkins University Press, 1956. The best-known and most detailed study of TR and foreign policy, but not exhaustive of the subject.

Berman, Jay Stuart. *Police Administration and Progressive Reform: Theodore Roosevelt as Police Commissioner of New York.* Westport, CT: Greenwood Press, 1987. Monograph on TR's service as president of the Board of Police Commissioners of New York City, 1895–1897.

Blum, John Morton. *The Republican Roosevelt.* Cambridge: Harvard University Press, 1954. Major study of TR as a *realpolitiker* by a leading historian who was one of the editors of *The Letters of Theodore Roosevelt.*

Burton, David H. *Theodore Roosevelt: Confident Imperialist.* Philadelphia: University of Pennsylvania Press, 1969. Major interpretative study on TR's views on foreign policy.

Butt, Archibald W. *The Letters of Archie Butt, Personal Military Aide to President Roosevelt.* Edited by Lawrence F. Abbott. Garden City, NY: Doubleday, Page and Company, 1924. Butt's letters describing the last year of the Roosevelt administration.

———. *Taft and Roosevelt: The Intimate Letters of Archie Butt, Military Aide.* 2 vols. Garden City, NY: Doubleday, Doran and Company, 1930. Major Butt continued as military aide under Taft, and recorded in his personal letters the split between Taft and TR.

Chessman, G. Wallace. *Governor Theodore Roosevelt: The Albany Apprenticeship, 1898–1900.* Cambridge: Harvard University Press, 1965. Thorough and scholarly account of TR's term as governor of New York.

Collin, Richard H. *Theodore Roosevelt's Caribbean: The Panama Canal, The Monroe Doctrine, and the Latin American Context.* Baton Rouge: Louisiana State University Press, 1990. Detailed revisionist study sympathetic to TR's handling of the Venezuelan and Dominican crises, Cuba, Colombia, the Panama Canal, and the Monroe Doctrine.

———. *Theodore Roosevelt, Culture, Diplomacy, and Expansion: A New View of American Imperialism.* Baton Rouge: Louisiana State University Press, 1985. Revisionist study favorable to TR which puts foreign policy and expansion in a cultural context; includes detailed bibliographical essay.

Cooper, John Milton, Jr. *The Warrior and the Priest: Woodrow Wilson and Theodore Roosevelt.* Cambridge: Belknap Press of Harvard University Press, 1983. Fascinating dual biographical study of two antagonists.

Cutright, Paul Russell. *Theodore Roosevelt: The Making of a Conservationist.* Urbana: University of Illinois Press, 1985. One of two studies on TR and natural history and conservation written by Cutright, who was a biologist and historian in the field of natural history.

———. *Theodore Roosevelt the Naturalist.* New York: Harper and Brothers, 1956. Should be used in conjunction with Cutright's 1985 book on TR for a complete view of TR as naturalist and conservationist.

Davis, Oscar King. *Released for Publication: Some Inside Political History of Theodore Roosevelt and His Times, 1898-1918.* Boston: Houghton Mifflin Company, 1925. Recollections of newspaper reporter and aide to TR.

Dennett, Tyler. *Roosevelt and the Russo-Japanese War.* Garden City, NY: Doubleday, Page and Company, 1925. Early study of TR and diplomacy.

Dyer, Thomas G. *Theodore Roosevelt and the Idea of Race.* Baton Rouge: Louisiana State University Press, 1980. Informed study showing different meanings and uses of the concept of "race" in Roosevelt's times. TR is shown to be a racial moderate and a neo-Lamarkian who believed in the equipotentiality of all races.

Esthus, Raymond A. *Theodore Roosevelt and the International Rivalries.* Waltham, MA: Ginn-Blaisdell, 1970. Good brief study.

———. *Theodore Roosevelt and Japan.* Seattle: University of Washington Press, 1966. Useful work on important subject; good bibliography.

Gable, John Allen. *The Bull Moose Years: Theodore Roosevelt and the Progressive Party.* Port Washington, NY: Kennikat Press, 1978. History and analysis of the Progressive or "Bull Moose" party on both state and national levels, 1912–1916.

Gatewood, Willard B., Jr. *Theodore Roosevelt and the Art of Controversy: Episodes of the White House Years.* Baton Rouge:

Louisiana State University Press, 1970. Useful analysis of seven controversial episodes of the Roosevelt administration, including the Booker T. Washington dinner, the quarrel with Maria Storer, and the secret service controversy.

Gould, Lewis L. *The Presidency of Theodore Roosevelt*. Lawrence: University of Kansas Press, 1991. Important study of Roosevelt's administration, 1901–1909, in the American Presidency Series of the University of Kansas.

Hagedorn, Hermann. *Roosevelt in the Bad Lands*. Boston: Houghton Mifflin Company, 1921. Detailed account of TR's ranching days in the Dakota Territory.

———. *The Roosevelt Family of Sagamore Hill*. New York: Macmillan Company, 1954. The Roosevelt family seen through rose-colored glasses, but an important source on TR's personal life that captures the charm of the Sagamore Hill family.

Hill, Howard C. *Roosevelt and the Caribbean*. Chicago: University of Chicago Press, 1927. Study critical of TR.

Hurwitz, Howard L. *Theodore Roosevelt and Labor in New York State, 1880–1900*. New York: Columbia University Press, 1943. Detailed and essentially negative assessment of TR's pre-presidential dealings with labor.

Leary, John J., Jr. *Talks with T. R. from the Diaries of John J. Leary, Jr.* Boston: Houghton Mifflin Company, 1920. Private conversations with TR recorded by a newspaper reporter at Sagamore Hill; important source material on TR's post-presidential years.

Marks, Frederick W., III. *Velvet on Iron: The Diplomacy of Theodore Roosevelt*. Lincoln: University of Nebraska Press, 1979. Major and controversial revisionist study which defends TR's foreign policies as president. Marks must be taken into account in any study of the foreign policy of the Roosevelt administration. There is much that is new or neglected in this provocative and well-argued work. Includes a good bibliography on TR and foreign policy.

Mowry, George E. *The Era of Theodore Roosevelt and the Birth of Modern America, 1900–1912*. New York: Harper and Brothers, 1958. Volume in the New American Nation Series. Solid, informed, and balanced account of the Roosevelt and Taft administrations, and of the social and intellectual history of the period; perceptive analysis of the progressive movement; good bibliography for works up to 1958. All students of the period should begin with this book.

————. *Theodore Roosevelt and the Progressive Movement.* Madison: University of Wisconsin Press, 1946. Narrative and analysis of the split in the Republican party and the rise and fall of the Progressive party, with an emphasis on the years 1909–1912.

Neu, Charles E. *An Uncertain Friendship: Theodore Roosevelt and Japan, 1906–1909.* Cambridge: Harvard University Press, 1967. Analysis of TR's dealings and problems with Japan after the Russo-Japanese War.

Norton, Aloysius A. *Theodore Roosevelt.* Boston: Twayne Publishers, G. K. Hall and Company, 1980. Informative and useful book in Twayne's United States Authors Series.

O'Gara, Gordon C. *Theodore Roosevelt and the Rise of the Modern Navy.* Princeton: Princeton University Press, 1943. Account of TR's work in building the modern navy.

Gifford, Pinchot. *Breaking New Ground.* New York: Harcourt, Brace and Company, 1947. Autobiography of TR's chief forester; covers conservation policies up to the time of Pinchot's break with the Taft administration.

Reckner, James R. *Teddy Roosevelt's Great White Fleet.* Annapolis, MD: Naval Institute Press, 1988. Account of the voyage of the U.S. fleet around the world, 1907–1909; good analysis of naval technology.

Roosevelt, Nicholas. *Theodore Roosevelt: The Man As I Knew Him.* New York: Dodd, Mead and Company, 1967. Perceptive and admiring memoir by a cousin who was diplomat, newspaper writer, and conservationist.

Vivian, James F. *The Romance of My Life: Theodore Roosevelt's Speeches in Dakota.* Fargo, ND: Theodore Roosevelt Medora Foundation, 1989. Chapters devoted to each of TR's trips and stays in North Dakota, 1886–1918, giving the text of virtually every speech delivered in North Dakota and the historical background of the speeches.

Wagenknecht, Edward. *The Seven Worlds of Theodore Roosevelt.* New York: Longmans, Green and Company, 1958. Looking at the "worlds" of action, thought, human relations, family, spiritual values, public affairs, and war and peace, Wagenknecht brilliantly analyzes the many-sided Roosevelt. Excellent bibliography. Edmund Morris states: "Succeeds more than any other work in capturing the size and complexity of TR."

Theodore Roosevelt Sites, Collections, and Association

Public Sites and Memorials

Bulloch Hall, 180 Bulloch Avenue, Roswell, GA 30075. Family home of Theodore Roosevelt's mother, Martha Bulloch Roosevelt, owned by the city of Roswell and open as a house museum.

Mount Rushmore National Memorial, Rapid City, SD 57709. Located in the Black Hills of South Dakota, Gutzon Borglum's monumental sculptures of the heads of Washington, Jefferson, Lincoln, and Theodore Roosevelt, completed in 1939. Operated by the National Park Service.

Sagamore Hill National Historic Site, Cove Neck, Oyster Bay, NY 11771. Theodore Roosevelt's home, built in 1885, served as the "summer White House" in 1902–1908; operated by the National Park Service. Old Orchard, home of Theodore Roosevelt, Jr., has museum on TR and family.

Theodore Roosevelt Birthplace National Historic Site, 28 East 20th Street, New York, NY 10003. Reconstruction of brownstone townhouse where TR was born October 27, 1858; period rooms and extensive museum collection; operated by the National Park Service.

Theodore Roosevelt Inaugural National Historic Site, 641 Delaware Avenue, Buffalo, NY 14202. The Wilcox Mansion where TR took the oath of office on September 14, 1901, after the death of President William McKinley; period rooms, exhibits; operated by National Park Service.

Theodore Roosevelt Island, Potomac River, Washington, DC. Mailing address: Theodore Roosevelt Island, Turkey Run Park, George Washington Memorial Parkway, McLean, VA 22101; access and parking on Virginia shore on George Washington Memorial Parkway. An 88–acre nature preserve and memorial; 17–foot bronze statue of TR by Paul Manship in memorial area with fountains and carved tablets; operated by National Park Service.

Theodore Roosevelt Memorial Hall, American Museum of Natural History, Central Park West at 79th Street, New York, NY 10024. Entrance wing of the American Museum of Natural History; contains murals and exhibits on the life of TR.

Theodore Roosevelt National Park and *Town of Medora, North Dakota.* Theodore Roosevelt National Park, Medora, ND 58645; for Medora tourist information: Theodore Roosevelt Medora Foundation, Medora, ND 58645. The scene of Theodore Roosevelt's ranching days in the Bad Lands of Dakota Territory; park consists of three units and over 100 square miles, museum, and TR's ranch cabin; Medora retains flavor of the Old West; Burning Hills Amphitheater has nightly musical in summer season.

Youngs Memorial Cemetery and Theodore Roosevelt Bird Sanctuary, Cove Neck Road and Oyster Bay Cove Road, Oyster Bay, NY 11771. The graves of Theodore Roosevelt and First Lady Edith Kermit Roosevelt are in Youngs Memorial Cemetery. Theodore Roosevelt Bird Sanctuary, a bird and nature preserve, forms a protective green belt around the cemetery.

Theodore Roosevelt Collections

Roosevelt Study Center, Middelburg Abbey, Middelburg, Netherlands. Address: Roosevelt Study Center, P.O. Box 6001, 4330 LA Middelburg, The Netherlands. Dedicated to Theodore Roosevelt, Franklin D. Roosevelt, and Eleanor Roosevelt, three Americans with Dutch roots, and opened in 1986, the Roosevelt Study Center, located in the abbey complex which is the headquarters for the government of the Province of Zeeland, has the largest collection in Europe of materials on the Roosevelts and their times.

Theodore Roosevelt Association Film Collection, Motion Picture, Broadcasting, and Recorded Sound Division, Library of Congress, Washington, DC 20540. Collection of over 140,000 feet of film on TR and his times; originally assembled at Theodore Roosevelt Birthplace and donated to the Library of Congress in the 1960s.

Theodore Roosevelt Collection, Harvard College Library, Cambridge, MA 02138. Collection of over 12,000 printed items, 3,500 cartoons, 10,000 photographs, manuscripts, Roosevelt family papers; housed in the Houghton and Widener libraries at Harvard.

Theodore Roosevelt Papers, Manuscript Division, Library of Congress, Washington, DC 20540. Consists of Theodore Roosevelt's office files, letters received and copies of letters sent; collection available on microfilm.

The Theodore Roosevelt Association

Three organizations, the Roosevelt Memorial Association, the Woman's Roosevelt Memorial Association, and Roosevelt Memorial Association of Oyster Bay, were founded within months of Theodore Roosevelt's death. Eventually these merged to form the Theodore Roosevelt Roosevelt Association (TRA), a national nonprofit historical society with membership open to all. An Act of Congress incorporated the national Roosevelt Memorial Association on May 31, 1920, "to perpetuate the memory of Theodore Roosevelt for the benefit of the people of the United States of America and the world."

The TRA and its predecessor organizations reconstructed TR's Birthplace (1923), built a Memorial Park in Oyster Bay (1928), purchased Theodore Roosevelt Island in Washington, D.C. (1931), opened Sagamore Hill to the public (1953), assembled the TR Collection at Harvard and the TRA Film Collection at the Library of Congress, donated Theodore Roosevelt Island, the TR Birthplace, and Sagamore Hill to the National Park Service, published books and periodicals, and began a broad spectrum of programs.

The TRA continues to work with all public sites, research collections, and programs dedicated to Theodore Roosevelt. It maintains an office in Oyster Bay which regularly provides information and research assistance to the media, scholars, and the general public. Address: Theodore Roosevelt Association, P.O. Box 719, Oyster Bay, NY 11771. Phone: 516–922–1221. Fax: 516–922–0364.

Publications of the Theodore Roosevelt Association

Some of these titles were published under the TRA's former name, the Roosevelt Memorial Association, and some were published in cooperation with other publishers and presses.

Roosevelt in the Kansas City Star, ed. Ralph Stout (1921)

Roosevelt in the Bad Lands, by Hermann Hagedorn (1921); reprinted by Theodore Roosevelt Nature & History Association (Medora, ND)

*The Americanism of Theodore Roosevelt, ed. Hermann Hagedorn (1923)

*The Works of Theodore Roosevelt: Memorial Edition, ed. Hermann Hagedorn, 24 volumes (1923–1926)

*The Works of Theodore Roosevelt: National Edition, ed. Hermann Hagedorn, 20 volumes (1926)

Theodore Roosevelt Cyclopedia, ed. Albert Bushnell Hart and Herbert Ronald Ferleger (*1941); revised edition ed. John Allen Gable (1989; Meckler/Greenwood Press)

*The Letters of Theodore Roosevelt, ed. Elting E. Morison et al, 8 volumes (1951–1954)

*A Guide to Sagamore Hill, by Hermann Hagedorn (1953)

The Free Citizen, by Theodore Roosevelt, ed. Hermann Hagedorn (1956)

TR: Champion of the Strenuous Life, by William Davison Johnston (1958)

A Theodore Roosevelt Round-Up, ed. Sidney Wallach (1958)

*Gouverneur Morris, by Theodore Roosevelt, American Revolution Bicentennial Edition (1975)

Theodore Roosevelt Association Journal (1975-date)

Sagamore Hill: An Historical Guide, by Hermann Hagedorn and Gary G. Roth (1977)

The Man in the Arena: Speeches and Essays, by Theodore Roosevelt, ed. John Allen Gable (1987)

*Out of print, 1992

Contributors

Editors

NATALIE A. NAYLOR is Director of Hofstra University's Long Island Studies Institute and editor-in-chief of its publications. She teaches American history at Hofstra where she is Professor and Teaching Fellow in New College. Dr. Naylor has published on educational and local history, was on the editorial board of the *History of Education Quarterly*, and is co-editor of the *Nassau County Historical Society Journal*.

DOUGLAS BRINKLEY is Assistant Professor of History and Teaching Fellow in New College, Hofstra. He is the author of *Dean Acheson: The Cold War Years, 1953–1971*, co-author of *Driven Patriot: The Life and Times of James Forrestal*, and editor of *Dean Acheson and the Making of U.S. Foreign Policy* and *Jean Monnet: The Path to European Unity*. He is currently writing a biography of Jimmy Carter.

JOHN ALLEN GABLE is the Executive Director of the Theodore Roosevelt Association, an historical society and public service organization with headquarters in Oyster Bay, New York. He is the author of *The Bull Moose Years: Theodore Roosevelt and the Progressive Party* (1978), and the founder and editor of the quarterly *Theodore Roosevelt Association Journal*. Dr. Gable is a graduate of Kenyon College, received his Ph.D. at Brown University, and teaches as an adjunct at New College, Hofstra University.

Contributors

MONICA T. ALBALA is a curator for Nassau County Museum at the Long Island Studies Institute. She is also an archivist, holding an M.A. in history and a certificate in Archival Management, Historical Society Administration, and Historical Editing from New York University. In 1991, she presented a paper "More Singing! Less Talking!: The Operatic American Musical" at Hofstra University's "Opera in the Golden West" conference.

JAY S. BERMAN is Associate Professor of Criminal Justice at Jersey City State College. He is a former Visiting Fellow at the

Graduate School, Princeton University. He is the author of *Police Administration and Progressive Reform: Theodore Roosevelt as Police Commissioner of New York* (1987).

LAWRENCE H. BUDNER, a retired banker, is a student of history and a frequent lecturer on various historical and business subjects. He has taught courses in the Department of Continuing Education at Southern Methodist University in Dallas and lectured at the University of Wisconsin at Madison. He received an M.A. in American history from Southern Methodist University; his thesis dealt with Theodore Roosevelt and the effects of his western experiences. Mr. Budner is vice president of the Theodore Roosevelt Association.

ROBERT B. CHARLES is an attorney at Weil, Gotshal & Manges in New York City. He has published law journal articles in American and Indian legal history and computer law. He serves on the board of contributors of several newspapers and on the Board of Directors of The Forum for World Affairs. He is a member of three state bars and the Council on Foreign Relations.

RICHARD H. COLLIN is Professor of History at the University of New Orleans, a specialist in comparative cultural, political, and diplomatic history of the late nineteenth century and early twentieth century. His most recent books for Louisiana State University Press are *Theodore Roosevelt's Caribbean: The Panama Canal, The Monroe Doctrine, and the Latin American Context* (1990) and *Theodore Roosevelt, Culture, Diplomacy, and Expansion* (1985).

GEORGE W. COLLINS, Emeritus, Wichita State University, also taught history at the U.S. Air Force Academy and at Kabul University, Afghanistan, and military history and strategy at the U.S. Air War College. He has lectured and published articles on United States relations with Morocco.

JOHN MILTON COOPER, JR. is William Francis Allen Professor of History at the University of Wisconsin-Madison. He is the author of *The Warrior and the Priest: Woodrow Wilson and Theodore Roosevelt* (1983) and *Pivotal Decades: The United States, 1900–1920* (1990).

STACY ROZEK CORDERY is a Visiting Assistant Professor of History at East Carolina University (Greenville, North Carolina). She received her Ph.D. at the University of Texas at Austin. Her dissertation, "Alice Roosevelt Longworth: Life in a Public Crucible," is a political biography of Theodore Roosevelt's eldest daughter. Her previous publications include a study of Alice Roosevelt and the concept of celebrity in *Presidential Studies Quarterly* (Winter 1989) and a biographical sketch of Alice Roosevelt Longworth for a forthcoming biographical and genealogical directory of the Roosevelt family.

MACEO CRENSHAW DAILEY, JR., was born in Norfolk, Virginia. He obtained his Ph.D. from Howard University and has taught at Smith College, Boston College, Brown University, and Howard University. He has published essays and articles in several scholarly journals and books. He currently is Associate Professor of History at Spelman College, and now is working on a biography of Emmett Jay Scott.

KATHLEEN M. DALTON is the Cecil F. P. Bancroft Instructor of History at Phillips Academy in Andover, Massachusetts. Author of several articles on Theodore Roosevelt and *A Portrait of a School: Coeducation at Andover*, she is currently working on a cultural biography of TR, titled *The Manly Reformer: Theodore Roosevelt and American Culture*.

RICHARD J. DONAGHER is Associate Professor of History and is currently serving as acting Academic Dean at Rosemont College in Rosemont, Pennsylvania. His special teaching interests are the United States in the twentieth century and Pennsylvania history. He has lectured and written on local history and is working on a book on the history of Montgomery County, Pennsylvania.

DAVID M. ESPOSITO received his Ph.D. from Penn State University in 1988 and is an adjunct professor of History at Penn State. He has published articles in the field of international relations and politics; his current research is on the history of America's strategic vulnerability.

AARON P. FORSBERG is a graduate student in the Department of History at the University of Texas at Austin. His specialty is modern American foreign relations. He is currently completing a doctoral dissertation on "America and the Resurgence of Postwar Japan."

JOHN W. FURLOW, JR. is an Assistant Professor of History at

Penn State University. He teaches Pennsylvania history and is Director of Academic Affairs at Penn State's DuBois Campus. He has lectured and published widely on Pennsylvania history, focusing on women's history and on the Progressive Era.

MATTHEW J. GLOVER is a graduate student at the S. I. Newhouse School of Communications, Syracuse University. His B.A. is from Eastern Illinois University, where he was a member of the Board of Governors of State Universities. He is a former New York State Senate Fellow and has been a member of the Theodore Roosevelt Association since 1982.

JAMES L. GOLDEN is Professor Emeritus of Communication at Ohio State University, and a frequent Visiting Professor of Communication Studies at Emerson College. He is a member of the Advisory Board of the journal *Argumentation*, and has published numerous essays on rhetorical theory and political communication.

FRED GREENBAUM received his B.A. from Brooklyn College, his M.A. from the University of Wisconsin, and his Ph.D. from Columbia University. For more than three decades he has taught in the City University of New York, first at Brooklyn and Queens and then as founding member and first chair of the History Department at Queensborough. He has published biographies of Robert M. La Follette and Edward P. Costigan and co-edited a Western Civilization reader and numerous articles, most on twentieth-century political history.

JOHN ROBERT GREENE, an Associate Professor of History at Cazenovia College, Cazenovia, New York, also lectures at University College, Syracuse University, where he has been honored as that school's Outstanding Teacher. He is the author of *The Crusade: The Presidential Election of 1952* (1985) and *The Limits of Power: The Nixon and Ford Administrations* (1992). A member of the Theodore Roosevelt Association and the Center for the Study of the Presidency, he received his undergraduate degree from St. Bonaventure University, and his Ph.D. from Syracuse University.

RICHARD P. HARMOND is in the History Department at St. John's University, Jamaica, Queens. He is the co-author of *Long Island As America* (1977), and co-editor of *Technology in the Twentieth Century* (1983). He has published in a number of journals, including the *Journal of American History*.

JOHN R. LANCOS currently teaches Ranger Skills at the Gateway Job Corps Civilian Conservation Center. He served as Site Manager of Theodore Roosevelt Birthplace National Historic Site, New York City, 1983–1990, and has held numerous other positions around the country during his career in the National Park Service, U.S. Department of the Interior.

WILLIAM LEMKE is Associate Professor of History at Saint Joseph's College in Standish, Maine. He is the author of a history of Maine, *The Wild, Wild East* (1990), and a member of the Maine House of Representatives. He teaches courses in American history and has published articles on Maine history and politics.

EDWARD S. LEWIS is a graduate in political science from Westminster College in Missouri. He has been associated with the Aetna Life Insurance Company in Boston, Massachusetts for more than a decade.

RICHARD J. LOOSBROCK is Professor of History at Chadron State College, Chadron, Nebraska. He is currently working on a biography of Theodore Roosevelt, Jr., as well as a series of videotapes on historic western trails.

ROBERT WILLIAM LOVE, JR. is Professor of History at the U.S. Naval Academy. He is the editor of *Changing Interpretations and New Sources in Naval History*; editor and co-author of *The Chiefs of Naval Operations* and the forthcoming *The Chiefs of Staff of the U.S. Army*; and author of the two-volume *History of the U.S. Navy, 1775–1991*. Volume one of his *From Pearl Harbor to Tokyo Bay: The U.S. Navy in the Era of Fleet Admiral Ernest J. King* will appear in 1993.

ROBERT B. MACKAY is Director of the Society for the Preservation of Long Island Antiquities. He received his doctorate in American studies from Boston University in 1980.

FREDERICK W. MARKS III, a specialist in American diplomatic history, is the author of several books including *Velvet on Iron: The Diplomacy of Theodore Roosevelt* (1979) and *Wind Over Sand: The Diplomacy of Franklin Roosevelt* (1988), both of which are available in paperback.

CLARECE MARTIN is a certified archivist and historian, member of the Academy of Certified Archivists, and archivist for the Sea Island Company in Georgia. She established the City Archives and the Fire Museum in Roswell, Georgia, is author of four books, contributing author to five books, and has written numerous articles for state and national publications. On the board of several historical and professional organizations, she is a trustee of the Theodore Roosevelt Association, and listed in the *International Who's Who of Professional and Business Women*.

CHAR MILLER is a member of the History Department of Trinity University in San Antonio, Texas. He is the author of *Fathers and Sons: The Bingham Family and the American Mission* (1982), coeditor of *Urban Texas: Politics and Development* (1990), and is currently writing a biography of Gifford Pinchot.

EDMUND MORRIS is the author of *The Rise of Theodore Roosevelt*, which won the Pulitzer Prize for Biography in 1980. He is working on a sequel, *Theodore Rex*. In 1985 he was appointed the official biographer of President Ronald Reagan.

SYLVIA JUKES MORRIS is the author of *Edith Kermit Roosevelt, Portrait of a First Lady*. She is currently working on a biography of Clare Boothe Luce to be published by Random House.

WILLIAM D. PEDERSON is a political scientist at Louisiana State University in Shreveport. He is the editor of *The Rating Game in American Politics* (1987), *Grassroots Constitutionalism* (1988), *The "Barberian" Presidency* (1989), *Morality and Conviction in American Politics* (1990), and *Congressional-Presidential Relations* (1992). He has served as the president of the International Lincoln Association (1990–1992).

WILLIE PIGG is Assistant Professor of Political Science at California University of Pennsylvania. He has contributed to a number of scholarly journals and reference works. He is currently working on a study of the role played by selected justices of the U.S. Supreme Court as presidential advisers during the twentieth century.

JAMES R. RECKNER, a retired naval officer, teaches military and naval history at Texas Tech University in Lubbock, Texas. He won the annual Theodore and Franklin D. Roosevelt Naval History Prize for *Teddy Roosevelt's Great White Fleet* (1988). He held the Secretary of the Navy's Research Chair in Naval History, 1991–92, and is continuing research into the Navy during the era of Theodore Roosevelt.

STEFAN H. RINKE received an M.A. at Bowling Green State University in Ohio in 1989 and a diploma in history at Otto-Friedrich University, Bamberg, Germany, in 1990. His book *Zwischen Weltpolitik und Monroe Doktrin: Botschafter Speck von Sternburg und die deutsch-amerikanischen Beziehungen, 1898–1908* is in the German-American Studies Series edited by Gale A. Molton, et. al. He is now completing his dissertation on German-Latin American relations, 1918–1933.

TWEED ROOSEVELT, an investment advisor, works with Wingate Financial Corporation in Lexington, Massachusetts, and is a managing Director of Roosevelt & Cross, an investment advisory firm. He has lectured widely on his great-grandfather's African and western experiences, as well as other subjects including the early Dutch of New York and New Jersey. He has also taught at Columbia University's Graduate School of Business.

ARTHUR M. SCHAEFER served as Provost of the University of the South, Sewanee, Tennessee, from 1977 to 1988 and is currently Owen Distinguished Professor of Economics at the University of the South. He has published articles dealing with presidential intervention in labor disputes including one which was read at the Hofstra conference on President Harry S Truman, and is currently working on a book on the evolution of the modern market system.

EDWARD L. SCHAPSMEIER is University Distinguished Professor of History at Illinois State University. His twin brother, FREDERICK H. SCHAPSMEIER, is Rosebusch Professor at the University of Wisconsin-Oshkosh. They have co-authored biographies of *Walter Lippmann* (1969), *Henry A. Wallace* (1970), *Ezra Taft Benson* (1975), *Everett M. Dirksen* (1985), and *Gerald R. Ford* (1989).

PAUL SCHULLERY is the author, co-author, or editor of eighteen books on history, nature, and outdoor sport, including *Mountain Time, American Fly Fishing: A History, The Bears of Yellowstone*, and *Theodore Roosevelt: Wilderness Writings*. He has written for many publications, including *BioScience, Encyclopedia Britannica Yearbook of Science and the Future, National Parks*, the *New York*

Times, and *Outdoor Life.* He currently works as a research naturalist in Yellowstone Park for the National Park Service and is an adjunct Professor of History at Montana State University.

CHARLES W. SNYDER is a practicing attorney with the firm of Jones, Boykin & Associates, Savannah, Georgia, and was formerly an attorney with the Federal Election Commission in Washington. He is a member of the Theodore Roosevelt Association.

RICHARD TURK is Professor of History at Allegheny College. He is the author of *The Ambiguous Relationship: Theodore Roosevelt and Alfred Thayer Mahan,* and presently is working on a biography of Elliott Roosevelt.

JAMES F. VIVIAN is Professor of History at the University of North Dakota. He is the editor of *William Howard Taft: Collected Editorials, 1917–1921* (1990), and the author of *The Romance of My Life: Theodore Roosevelt's Visits and Speeches in Dakota* (1989), in addition to numerous scholarly and popular articles.

DAVID H. WALLACE is a staff curator in the Division of Historic Furnishings, Harpers Ferry Center, National Park Service, U.S. Department of the Interior. His paper draws on intensive research for his recently completed study of Sagamore Hill's furnishings. Dr. Wallace was chief curator, Independence National Historical Park, Philadelphia (1958-1968), is the author of *John Rogers, The People's Sculptor* (1967), and co-author of *The New York Historical Society's Dictionary of Artists in America, 1564–1860* (1957).

Index

Numbers in **bold** refer to illustrations

The Long Island Studies Institute

Hofstra University's Long Island Studies Institute encourages the study of Long Island's history and heritage through its publications, conferences, educational services, and reference collections. The Institute was established in 1985, when the Nassau County Museum Reference Library moved from the Museum in Eisenhower Park to Hofstra, to join the University's New York State History Collections as part of the Department of Special Collections, in the Axinn Library. The Institute also houses the historical research offices of the Nassau County Historian and Division of Museum Services. For information on Institute conferences, publications, and collections (including hours open to the public), contact the Long Island Studies Institute, Library Technical Services and Resource Center, West Campus, Hofstra University, Hempstead, NY 11550; 516-463-6411.

Long Island Studies Institute Publications

Heart of the Lakes Publishing:

> *Evoking a Sense of Place*, ed. Joann P. Krieg (1988)
> *Robert Moses: Single-Minded Genius*, ed. Joann P. Krieg (1989)
> *Long Island and Literature*, ed. Joann P. Krieg (1989)
> *The Aerospace Heritage of Long Island*, by Joshua Stoff (1989)
> *Long Island: The Suburban Experience*, ed. Barbara M. Kelly (1990)
> *Long Island Architecture*, ed. Joann P. Krieg (1991)
> *From Airship to Spaceship: Long Island in Aviation and Spaceflight*, by Joshua Stoff (1991)
> *The Blessed Isle: Hal B. Fullerton and His Image of Long Island, 1897–1927*, by Charles L. Sachs (1991)

Long Island Studies Institute:

> *To Know the Place: Teaching Local History*, ed. Joann P. Krieg (1986)
> *Nassau County Historical Society Journal, Cumulative Index, 1958–1988*, by Jeanne M. Burke (1989)

The Calderone Theatres on Long Island: An Introductory Essay and Description of the Calderone Theatre Collection at Hofstra University, by Miriam Tulin (1991)

Exploring African-American History, ed. Natalie A. Naylor (1991)

Greenwood Press:

Suburbia Re-examined, ed. Barbara M. Kelly (1989)

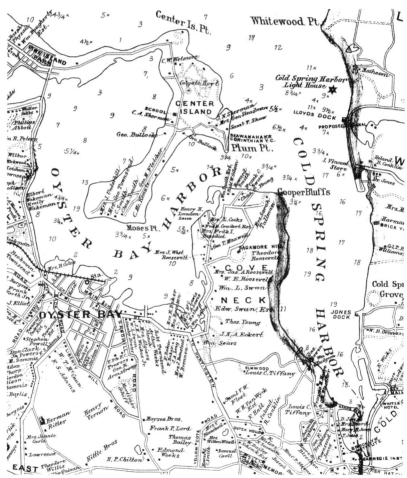

Courtesy of Long Island Studies Institute

Map of Oyster Bay showing Sagamore Hill,
from E. Belcher Hyde, *Map of Long Island*, 1906.

Roosevelt Genealogy

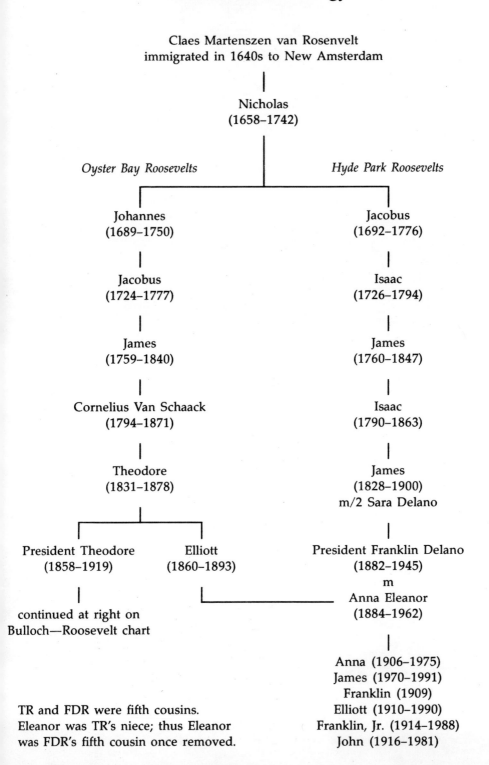

Claes Martenszen van Rosenvelt
immigrated in 1640s to New Amsterdam

Nicholas
(1658–1742)

Oyster Bay Roosevelts   *Hyde Park Roosevelts*

Johannes   Jacobus
(1689–1750)   (1692–1776)

Jacobus   Isaac
(1724–1777)   (1726–1794)

James   James
(1759–1840)   (1760–1847)

Cornelius Van Schaack   Isaac
(1794–1871)   (1790–1863)

Theodore   James
(1831–1878)   (1828–1900)
                                            m/2 Sara Delano

President Theodore   Elliott   President Franklin Delano
(1858–1919)   (1860–1893)   (1882–1945)
                                            m
                                            Anna Eleanor
continued at right on   (1884–1962)
Bulloch—Roosevelt chart

                                            Anna (1906–1975)
                                            James (1970–1991)
                                            Franklin (1909)
TR and FDR were fifth cousins.   Elliott (1910–1990)
Eleanor was TR's niece; thus Eleanor   Franklin, Jr. (1914–1988)
was FDR's fifth cousin once removed.   John (1916–1981)